THE FIRST 100 YEARS

THE FIRST 100 YEARS

A History of Virginia Polytechnic Institute and State University

By DUNCAN LYLE KINNEAR

Duncan Lyle Kinnear

CENTENNIAL

Published By
**VIRGINIA POLYTECHNIC INSTITUTE
EDUCATIONAL FOUNDATION, INC.**
Blacksburg, Virginia 24061
1972

PRINTED IN THE UNITED STATES OF AMERICA
BY THE WILLIAM BYRD PRESS, INC.
RICHMOND, VIRGINIA

Table of Contents

Dedicated to alumni, faculty, staff, students, friends and benefactors of Virginia Polytechnic Institute and State University.

Introductory Notes:

Duncan Lyle Kinnear

In the late afternoon of a sparkling summer day Lyle Kinnear relaxed on the broad veranda of his gracious old home at Price's Fork, nursed a cool drink, and peered back across the half a century that has made him as much a part of Virginia Tech as the tower of Lane Hall. He is a friendly man, quick to laughter smothered in quiet chuckles; the little ironies of life and living rarely escape his alert and searching mind. His thick grey hair and horn-rimmed glasses, his bemused expression and ever present hearing aid, lend almost a classic professional air to his appearance. Almost overly modest and self-effacing, Duncan Lyle Kinnear, professor of education and psychology, appeared for all the world exactly what he is, an extraordinarily able teacher.

For nearly 18 months Dr. Kinnear—invariably known by friends and colleagues as "the Deacon"—had been immersed in the records and archives of Virginia Polytechnic Institute and State University, methodically verifying, checking, rechecking, following the tangled skein of a thousand personal histories that collectively constitute the history of the institution that has been much of his life. In the paper-cluttered dining room of the big red brick home which the Prices built more than half a century ago, the results of Dr. Kinnear's labors methodically were committed to paper in the firm, clear longhand that is his trademark. In the late summer of 1971, only a few months after his scheduled retirement, Dr. Kinnear heaved a sigh of relief and delivered up the final draft of the manuscript which became the pages of this volume. It was a task begun under protest, and completed with the professor's characteristic modesty. But no man alive could have pulled together the record of a hundred years in so brief a time, and packaged it with such style and sensitivity, as has this self-effacing professor. Even Lyle Kinnear, in more candid moments, might confess to the predestinationism of his Presbyterian upbringing, for clearly he had spent a good part of a lifetime in preparation for the task.

Lyle Kinnear arrived on the campus of Virginia Agricultural and Mechanical College and Polytechnic Institute in the fall of 1923, fresh from Timber Ridge, in Rockbridge County, one of the seven sons and daughters of John Joseph Lyle Kinnear, a prominent Rockbridge County farmer who served for 20 years on the County Board of Supervisors. The younger Kinnear's intent, upon graduating from Mountain View School, was to study agricultural engineering at VPI. But the little school was not accredited, and the young Kinnear had not been admitted to VPI; apparently the local school superintendent had not been able to find the courage to inform Lyle's father. The details of Kinnear's subsequent adventures on the campus themselves would make a fascinating volume; they are intimately intertwined with VPI's history. But examinations were taken; Kinnear was admitted and enrolled. His initial introduction to college life terminated abruptly three years later at summer ROTC Camp at Fort Monroe as the result of a bad case of influenza. The young Kinnear went back to Rockbridge County to regain his health and strength. Looking back, half a century later, the professor insists that his "greatest contribution to engineering was to get out of the field."

Half a dozen years elapsed before Lyle Kinnear returned to VPI, years which he later came to believe were as valuable to his future teaching career as any he had experienced. He taught school, helped operate the family farm, was appointed deputy commissioner of revenue, served as a bank appraiser, became president of the local telephone company, and even found time to commute to Lexington to study at Washington and Lee University. His strength must have been more than renewed, for most of these activities were concurrent. Later, recalling his almost frenzied out-of-school years, he remembered the ultimate realization that for the kind of future he wanted he must complete his education. In 1932 he returned to Blacksburg and fell into the clutches of the fabled I. D. Wilson, now professor emeritus of biology, and Dr. Wilson's ambitions for an extensive science education program. "I had an idea I wanted to prepare for the teaching of science," Kinnear recalled, "and I. D. embraced me like a long lost brother. Before long I was studying everything listed in the college catalog."

Young Kinnear's initial VPI experience immersed him in the Corps of Cadets, but on his return he lived at the Chrisman House, a favorite boarding house near the campus for seniors and graduate students. Being the eldest and most restrained of the student residents of the house, occasionally at meal time Kinnear was compelled to call down his boisterous fellows. A visiting contractor named L. R. Stewart, (VPI '13), living at the Chrisman House while engaged in the construction of Davidson Hall, supplied the familiar nickname which Dr. Kinnear has cheerfully acknowledged ever since: "We are going to make you the deacon of the crowd," Stewart said; generations of students and colleagues have found it a most appropriate sobriquet.

Kinnear's renewed academic ambitions and Dr. Wilson's wide ranging curriculum combined to immerse the erstwhile Rockbridge County farmboy in an overwhelming academic load. He finished his undergraduate work and immediately plunged into the pursuit of what he believed would be a Master's degree in education, with a minor in biology. After completing more than twice the hours of course work necessary for the Master's degree, Kinnear thought it time to move on. Since VPI wasn't permitted to award degrees in education, President Burruss finally ruled that the M.S. degree would be awarded in biological science, with a minor in vocational education. It was a good many years later, when Kinnear was writing this volume, that VPI finally was authorized to award degrees in education, as such.

Aside from the three years in which Kinnear returned to Rockbridge County to teach science and serve as principal of Mountain View and later Natural Bridge High School, his teaching career focused on Virginia Tech. He returned to the campus in 1936 and except for brief summer incursions at Peabody, and later at Ohio State University (where Kinnear received his Ph.D.) he has been on the campus ever since. During World War II he accepted a joint appointment teaching both at VPI and Radford College (then the women's division of VPI). The scope of his teaching effort has ranged from vocational education, to mathematics, to psychology and applied psychology, and a good many other things, structured for many years as service courses for engineering and agriculture students.

With his teaching career established, Kinnear also acquired a wife, who naturally also turned out to be a teacher. In 1942 he married Miss Florence Price, who for many years taught Latin at Blacksburg High School. A graduate of Randolph Macon Women's College, she had taken her graduate work at the University of Virginia and Columbia University. With a historian's perspective, Kinnear noted that two centuries earlier her family had settled in the New River Valley at about the same time his antecedents had moved into the Shenandoah Valley.

Kinnear's Ph.D. dissertation at Ohio State was entitled "A History of Agricultural Education in Virginia," a subject which immersed him in historical research. In later years he liked to call himself an amateur historian, which he defined as one "who remembers events whether they happened or not." The remark is characteristic. During much of his adult life he had come to be fascinated by the principal families of early Virginia; he continually stumbled across their records in libraries and county courthouses. By the early fifties he had accumulated a mass of information about the early history of VPI, and perhaps more important, had developed a keen sensitivity as to original sources of VPI-related materials.

For a good many years prior to beginning work on a formal history, the searching out of VPI documents and data about the College's early history was a challenging hobby for Kinnear. "VPI has less recorded history, written down for posterity, than any institution I've ever looked into," he observed. "I think it reflects the kind of institution VPI was for so many years: practical, pragmatic, busy with getting the job done. Nobody worried about putting it down on paper." As for his own involvement in historical research "a fascination with history becomes a disease; you can't get it out of your blood," he said. Perhaps it is a fact for which readers of this volume may count themselves fortunate.

Thus it was that when the University faced up to the need for a history of its first century, as it prepared to commemorate its centennial, there was no more natural choice for an author than Duncan Lyle Kinnear, the Deacon. Kinnear had come to be much in demand by campus and alumni groups for after-dinner talks on the history of VPI; his cheerfully irreverent comments on the earlier years of the land grant college found ready and appreciative audiences. His growing treasury of VPI information, and wide ranging knowledge of VPI source materials, made it possible to do what otherwise would have been an impossible task in the time available.

In the bittersweet warmth of summer, looking back across the years, Kinnear relaxed and reminisced with mixed emotions. His good natured cheerfulness at times became subdued, immersed in a thousand memories. He was apprehensive, as authors tend to be, thinking of the detail and scope of a hundred years of history. But the results of his labors speak for themselves, in the pages which follow.

—WARREN STROTHER

Preface and Acknowledgments

Dr. WILSON BELL ('34), director of university development, retains the same fearless outlook on life that as a member of Tech's baseball team enabled him to earn an enviable batting average and establish a record for stolen bases. Late in the spring of 1969 he suggested that I write a "brief history of VPI, popular in nature, for the upcoming Centennial." I objected. He persuaded.

The next day I found myself in a conference attended by Bell; Stuart Cassell ('32), vice-president for administration; Dr. Leslie Malpass, vice-president for academic affairs; Dr. Richard V. Dietrich, associate dean, college of arts and sciences; and Dr. Rufus W. Beamer ('38), head of the department of education. Operating with smooth efficiency, this group of individuals quickly removed all barriers standing in the way of my undertaking the project. The assistance of the publications department was promised in securing illustrations and arranging for printing "anything you write." As I continued to hesitate, I was informed that Dr. G. Burke Johnston, former dean of the college of arts and sciences, and currently Miles Professor of English, had agreed to edit the manuscript if I wrote it. This information proved to be a decisive factor. If the scholarly Johnston was willing to tangle with my syntax, surely I ought to be willing to undertake producing that syntax. With this thought in mind I agreed to undertake the project.

The next day some misgivings set in. How much "persuasion" had Bell and his confederates exerted on Johnston? I've never had sufficient courage to ask. The discovery that VPI had more than thirty-five thousand living alumni and nearly one hundred emeriti faculty members did nothing to reduce my misgivings either. Each member of this group of alumni and retired faculty, to say nothing of the thousands of descendants of earlier staff and alumni, would have his version of VPI history. Obviously, differences of emphasis, omissions, inclusions, and interpretations would occur between these personal histories and anything I might write. A moment's reflection, however, quickly reminded me that such differences would exist no matter who wrote the history.

With this consoling thought in mind I have recorded what Dr. Burke Johnston says might be called "a partial history of VPI." Alumni and friends having additional information about any of the "parts" recorded, or having information about "parts" which have not been included, are invited to submit written accounts of such incidents to our VPI archivist for filing. Enough such written accounts will go a long way toward closing the "information gap" always existing between bare official records and alumni memories of the events.

Admittedly, the shortness of time between the beginning of this project and the date set for its completion influenced my plan of operation and presentation of events. My effort has been to present a chronology of the major and a few of the minor events in the first century of Virginia Polytechnic Institute and State University. No attempt has been made to present a definitive or an interpretative history of the institution or of any of its component parts, although the contributions of VPI to Virginia and the nation more than warrant both approaches.

Although I have departed from the comforting security of documenting each event related herein, all events included have been derived from written records or eyewitness accounts.

During the first half century VPI was buffeted by the social, political, and economic conditions of the state to a greater degree than at any subsequent period in its history. For this reason the events of the first half century have been presented with more attention to these conditions than have the events of the last half century.

Hitherto the ante-bellum efforts to establish a system of agricultural-technical education in Virginia, the disrupted conditions of the state following the Civil War, and the circumstances surrounding the Preston and Olin Institute have been largely overlooked as factors affecting the early history of VPI. This oversight is regrettable, since these factors influenced not only the legislative debates leading to the establishment of the institution but its subsequent development as well. Therefore, I have presented a brief summary of these pre-VPI events. As far as I can determine, this is the first time such a summary has been developed in its relationship to early VPI.

Some disappointment was encountered in the attempt to locate definitive material relating to the historical development of VPI and its component teaching, research, and extension services. Such material is surprisingly meager, considering the size of the institution and the contributions of its alumni to the state and the nation. Beyond a shadow of doubt VPI in its first century was more concerned with making history by rendering service on all fronts than it was with recording this history once it had been made. This condition is a noteworthy heritage in itself, but VPI is worthy of and deserves an in-depth study of the contributions of its programs, faculty, and alumni to the state and the nation.

In 1922 a bulletin entitled "A Brief History of the Virginia Agricultural and Mechanical College" was prepared by Professor E. A. Smyth and issued in connection with the semi-centennial being celebrated by the College. In 1961 J. P. Cochran, then a member of the department of history at VPI, wrote his Ph.D. dissertation on the topic "The Virginia Agricultural and Mechanical College: The Formative Half Century, 1872-1919, of Virginia Polytechnic Institute." This dissertation, submitted to the graduate school of the University of Alabama, examined the development of the institution against a national as well as a state background.

Smyth's bulletin, largely factual in nature, concentrated on the administrations of Presidents McBryde, Barringer, and Eggleston, although it also included a brief summary of developments prior to McBryde as well as a summary of developments for the first two years of Burruss' administration.

Undoubtedly, the most valuable source for documentary material relating to early VPI history is to be found in the typewritten material collected by former librarian Ralph M. Brown and housed in the VPI archives. Individuals desiring to quote from these documents would do well, however, to check the original documents for spelling, punctuation, and "dropped words" which sometimes occur even with the best of typists. In 1942 some of Brown's material was published in bulletin form as the "VPI Historical Index." In 1964 Jenkins M. Robertson, then information officer at Tech, completely revised and updated Brown's earlier work and published it in bulletin form as the "VPI Historical Data Book." Currently Robertson is revising and updating this valuable publication.

With the notable exception of works dealing with John L. Buchanan, William H. Ruffner, and Joseph D. Eggleston, biographies dealing with VPI's early leaders are sketchy or nonexistent. Even the biographies of these men devoted far more attention to their work as state superintendents of public instruction than to their efforts in connection with VPI. The situation with respect to alumni and former faculty members is but little better. Happily, more material relating to early leaders, alumni, and early days of the institution is accumulating as word spreads that such information is eagerly sought by our archivist.

Regrettably, most of the official correspondence, the minutes of the faculty, committee reports, and all the minutes of the Board of Visitors prior to 1900 were lost in the February, 1900, fire which destroyed the administration building. Tantalizing excerpts from the lost minutes and copies of letters from early officials have been sent to the University within the past few years by descendants of some of the earlier leaders. Undoubtedly, this source of information has rich potential worthy of further exploration. Currently, official records and correspondence subsequent to 1900 are being organized and stored in fireproof rooms in Burruss Hall and Newman Library. The collection is imposing in bulk, variety, and portrayal of the growth of the institution in physical size and service to the state and nation.

In collecting information for this history, I spent some time in the Alderman Library at the University of Virginia, the Jones Memorial Library in Lynchburg, the McCormick Library at Washington and Lee University, the Preston Library at the Virginia Military Institute, the Roanoke Public Library in Roanoke, and the Virginia State Library in Richmond. The friendly, efficient assistance given to me by members of the staff at these libraries is appreciated.

The friendly reception and assistance given to me by the director and the library staff at the Historical Foundation of the Presbyterian and Associate Reformed Presbyterian Church, Montreat, North Carolina, went beyond the call of duty in helping me examine pertinent information in the William H. Ruffner papers on deposit there.

The delightfully air-conditioned, comfortable working space assigned to me at the Louis Round Wilson Library at the University of North Carolina, where I examined the John M. McBryde manuscripts in the Southern Historical Collection, is more than appreciated.

But regardless of what was found away from the campus, local sources were richest in material for this particular history; therefore, substantial assistance was given to me by the staff of the Carol M. Newman Library. Special recognition is due Miss Lucy Lee Lancaster ('25), associate librarian, and to Mrs. Mary R. Larimer, head of the archives department, for their help. Miss Lancaster through her friend Mrs. R. B. Lancaster, at the time assistant librarian at Randolph-Macon College, also uncovered some hitherto unknown material relative to the Preston and Olin Institute and the Baltimore Conference of the Methodist Church. The enthusiastic cooperation and help I received from Mr. Douglas Martin, agency records administrator at Tech, saved me days of searching through the vast accumulation of records stored in Burruss Hall.

The time between the beginning of this history and the date set for its completion was entirely too brief for many interviews with persons concerning events of an earlier day, or for an extensive search for documents in the hands of descendants of earlier leaders. Appreciation, however, is extended to Miss Mary Apperson of Blacksburg, a granddaughter of Dr. Harvey Black, first Rector of the Board of Visitors, for permission to use the Black papers. The oldest known official document concerning the University was found among these papers. Appreciation also is extended to Dr. Ellison A. Smyth ('25) for his generous assistance in making available numerous records kept by his father, Professor E. A. Smyth. I am also indebted to Mrs. Julia Price Ivey, wife of W. M. Ivey ('22) of Lynchburg and one of the vocal soloists at the Golden Jubilee celebration in 1922, for a colorful description of this affair. Appreciation for the use of some secondary material is also expressed to Mrs. Robert W. Cutshall of Villamont, to Mrs. Winnie Jewell Shields of Christiansburg, and to Mrs. D. S. Phlegar of Blacksburg.

Appreciation for help given in placing some campus events in better perspective is extended to Professors Emeriti R. L. Humbert, J. B. Jones, A. B. Massey, R. H. McNeil, E. T. Swink, I. D. Wilson, and H. N. Young. Professor Humbert, who served as executive secretary to the president for much of the Burruss administration, also read and commented on the Burruss chapters in the history. Dr. and Mrs. F. L. Robeson not only helped place many campus events in perspective but also donated a collection of mementos dealing with many of the events as well. Mrs. Robeson, the daughter of D. O. Matthews long connected with the College, has a wealth of reminiscences worthy of a chapter in themselves.

For one year of reduced teaching responsibilities and one year of no teaching responsibilities while working on this project, gratitude is due administrative officials of the University.

Mrs. Sherilyn McConnell did a superb job of translating my longhand script into typed form. To Sheri and Mrs. Olene Hubbard thanks are due for the long hours they spent in typing and checking the manuscript.

The promised assistance from the publications department was forthcoming at all times. Warren Strother, director of the division of information services, was never too busy to discuss the expected and unexpected problems as they arose. In addition to reading the entire manuscript, he gave invaluable help in bringing the overwhelming mass of information relating to the Newman and the Hahn administrations into manageable shape. Jenkins M. Robertson, director of university publications, assumed responsibility for collecting and arranging illustrations to be included. H. D. Damant, director of the university press services in the division of information services, assumed major responsibility for the many details involved with the actual printing of the manuscript. H. E. Cameron, director of publications in the division of information services, read the manuscript and gave helpful advice. Mr. Kenneth W. Baker of the department of physical plant planning, helped me study old campus maps and locate old buildings and campus landmarks of an earlier day.

Mr. E. B. Evans, business manager, took time out from his busy schedule to confirm the accuracy of some of my statements relating to state personnel policy.

Professor George W. Litton, director of centennial programs, took over all responsibilities for maintaining the office, providing needed supplies, and securing extra help when needed. His ready wit and cheerful observations on life, delivered in his southwestern Virginia drawl, were priceless at all times in morale building.

Dr. Wilson Bell was a constant source of encouragement. I am especially indebted to him for his attention to all details connected with my release from teaching duties and for the comfortable working space he arranged for me to occupy. I am also indebted to him for the complete freedom he insisted I have in developing the history as I saw fit. Hopefully, readers will not hold him responsible for the results.

Appreciation is due the VPI Educational Foundation for its part in publishing this history.

I am grateful indeed to Dr. G. Burke Johnston for editing the entire manuscript and helping get it ready for the printer.

My wife Florence gave me unflagging encouragement and assistance at every stage in the preparation of the manuscript. Her cheerful acceptance of "deferred maintenance" of house, yard, and garden for the entire period of preparation also is appreciated.

Writing this brief history has been a delightfully rewarding experience to me personally. But in the end, while enumerating and thanking for their help those named above, I realize that the responsibility for the final product is mine. This realization leads me to share some of the sentiments expressed in the following letter pieced together from its fragments found in President McBryde's papers.

February—1901.

Dear Dr. McBryde,
    You asked if I can explain my son's behavior. No. After being so long at your college my son often makes mistakes. Doctor he is surprised at the thing he got into. So am I. Please bear with him if it turns out a mistake. He meant well.
Yours truly,

———————————————

    P.S. Some of his friends at college helped him do it. They meant well. Please bear with them too.

If any alumni and friends at VPI are surprised "at the thing I got into" by writing this history—so am I. If it "turns out a mistake," perhaps it is because I too have been "so long at your college"—and mine. Please bear with me. I meant well. Some of my "friends at college" helped me do it. They too meant well. Please bear with them.

D. Lyle Kinnear

Blacksburg, Virginia
July, 1971

Prologue

"Hurrah for Hurrah!"

Thus did the Christiansburg *Montgomery Messenger* in March, 1872, headline its announcement that the eagerly sought prize, a portion of the proceeds from the state's share of the Morrill Land-Grant Act scrip with which to establish a college of agriculture and mechanic arts, had been won by the Preston and Olin Institute in Blacksburg.

The arrival of the news of this victory relayed by Gabriel C. Wharton from Richmond to Christiansburg by telegraph, and from Christiansburg to Blacksburg by messenger arriving on horseback in the evening "as the lamps and candles were being lighted," called for a celebration. And celebrate is what the boys at Preston and Olin did, "not by study," it seems, but by burning lights late into the night and indulging in sporadic outbursts of yelling. The yelling greatly annoyed some and alarmed other residents of the village, who not knowing the reasons for such conduct, surmised that Principal Conrad of the Institute was having difficulty with his boys.

"Correspondent," however, writing from Christiansburg was neither jubilant over the victory nor sure that the prize was worth the effort. No doubt some kind of a celebration was in order, he observed, but just now it was too cold to get far enough away from the warm stove to work up any excitement one way or the other about the matter. In the warming glow of his stove, however, he did warm up enough to express the hope that more information about the agricultural and mechanical college would soon be available for the public.

Within the year "correspondent's" desire for more information about the agricultural and mechanical college spread throughout the state, and, according to William H. Ruffner, a member of the first Board of Visitors, grew to include not only a desire for information about the college but also a desire for information concerning the circumstances relating to its creation and location at Blacksburg. Ruffner, sometimes referred to as Virginia's greatest Reconstruction Statesman, felt that the early circumstances surrounding the creation and growth of the college could be understood only in the context and circumstances of the time. But understanding the circumstances of the time, he said, often depended on an understanding of earlier events and circumstances. The history of the Virginia Polytechnic Institute and State University more than supports Ruffner's view.

Virginia's land-grant institution at Blacksburg, especially in the nineteenth century, was heavily influenced by the social, political, economic, and industrial circumstances of the times. The focus and impact of these circumstances on the establishment and early development of the college was oftentimes sharpened

1

and at times dominated by a pervasive legacy inherited from Virginia's pre-Civil War efforts to establish a system of agricultural education suitable for a state dominated by a distinctive agricultural economy.

The creation and early development of the College on the site of the older Preston and Olin Institute also was influenced by some of the circumstances associated with the founding and subsequent development of this school. It is possible, of course, to record much of the early history of Virginia's land-grant University and at the same time ignore these ante-bellum developments. But it is impossible to understand the reasons for many developments in the College's early history if such a practice is followed. Consequently a brief review of (1) the ante-bellum efforts to establish a system of agricultural education, (2) the establishment of the Preston and Olin Institute, and (3) the chaotic conditions following the Civil War is essential before turning our attention to the specific events in the history of the College.

It is a well documented but often overlooked fact that efforts on behalf of agricultural education began at an early date in Virginia. Actually the first recorded agricultural education in the state, if not in the nation, took place at Jamestown in 1607 when Captain John Smith captured two Indians, Kemps and Tassore, and had them instruct the colonists on how to grow corn. No thread of historical continuity other than its significant contribution to the survival of the colonists is known—or claimed—to exist between this incident and the establishment of Virginia's land-grant institutions; but the same statement cannot be made with respect to many subsequent activities which got under way during the early nineteenth century as a result of significant developments in the state's agricultural economy.

By the beginning of the nineteenth century the section of the state east of the Blue Ridge Mountains, settled largely by a non-agricultural people, nonetheless had developed an agricultural life heavily dominated by the production and sale of tobacco. The early prosperity of the planter promoted a life of ease, independence, and leisure for many who early turned to government and worked to promote their values and way of life. Commercially, the numerous rivers stretching inland furnished easy outlets to the sea and enabled foreign vessels loaded with a variety of merchandise to navigate far inland and exchange their goods for tobacco. The huge profits from tobacco tended to discourage manufacturing enterprises other than those which could be carried on at home by surplus labor. Tobacco production required large land holdings and a continuous supply of fresh ground to be cleared annually. This requirement resulted in the development of the huge plantation which, with its retinue of slaves and servants, became a unit largely sufficient unto itself and fostered a tendency toward individualism and seclusion.

The method of producing tobacco by clearing, planting, and then abandoning the land soon led to a condition of soil depletion. To survive, the planters had to have yet more land; this need caused expansion to be looked upon as the only solution. The larger landowners tended to swallow up the smaller ones. Many of these smaller landowners, not content to remain and compete against slave labor, migrated west in great numbers. The result was the development in eastern Virginia of a preponderance of the wealthy aristocratic upper class and the "poor white" lower class, the "head and the tail," as one contemporary described it. The aristocratic upper class early took over control of the colony and later the state and enacted laws and promoted customs designed to protect and perpetuate the two-class social system. This aristocratic two-class system was clearly reflected in the provisions for education advocated by this section in that a system of private literary-type schools was promoted for the wealthier upper class, and a publicly supported system of the basic fundamentals consisting of the three R's and vocational education through apprenticeship was promoted for the poor and the unfortunate.

West of the Blue Ridge Mountains, the state was quite unlike the eastern part. It had been settled by many different nationalities but predominantly by middle class Germans and Scotch-Irish from the farming regions of Europe. These people, without ready access to markets and not finding one staple crop, early turned to a highly diversified type of farming. The hardships of frontier life and the common need of such things as markets and roads leading to the markets tended to bring the people together into small communities rather than disperse them over large plantations. In contrast to eastern Virginia, the type of farming practiced tended to conserve the already high natural fertility of the soil rather than to deplete it. Consequently when eastern Virginia, because of extreme soil depletion began to agitate for agricultural education as a basis of relief, the western part of the state, not feeling the need for such relief, not only did not support the movement but more frequently bitterly opposed it.

By the beginning of the nineteenth century, the lines along which the two sections of the state moved for the next half century had been rather clearly developed. The east continued its development as an older, aristocratic, conservative society in which the plantation system of agriculture was dominant. The west, on the other hand, continued to develop as a newer, more democratic society based on a more diversified agriculture and increasing dependence upon manufacturing and the development of natural resources. Prior to the outbreak of the Civil War, the great Valley of Virginia lying west of the Blue Ridge but east of the Alleghanies, for the most part had cast its lot with the west in those state affairs which affected education, agriculture, and agricultural education. By the outbreak of the Civil War, however, the valley's interests had become closely enough identified with those of the east to cause most of its leaders to cast their lot with the east when the war did erupt. Long before the outbreak of the Civil War, the interests, the needs, and the aspirations of the east and the west had developed along such divergent lines that in a sense the state was a state in name only, held together by a thin thread of political association. Under such conditions it became extremely difficult to generate united efforts for any internal program of improvement or development, especially with respect to education in the sciences and agriculture. Prior to the outbreak of the Civil War, numerous efforts were made, however, which had such significant effect in creating a climate of opinion on the value and nature of scientific and agricultural education as to deserve considerable attention.

As soil depletion in eastern Virginia became more acute, despair and inertia tended to spread over the country like a cloud. Many of Virginia's political leaders realized what was happening and began to seek remedies. One of the earliest and most influential agencies for improvement used by these early leaders was the local agricultural society. These societies, as they originated in Virginia, were a semiliterary, social type of organization made up of the gentlemen-farmers of the area. Thus, in the forefront of the movement for agricultural reform to be achieved in part by agricultural education, were such great Virginia names as Barbour, Cabell, Cocke, Garnett, Giles, Jefferson, Madison, Nicholas, Preston, Randolph, Ruffin, Taylor, Tyler and many others. These names are usually remembered more for their political activities in the state and nation than for their leadership in agricultural reform and education. If it is true, as some claim, that preoccupation of Virginia's leaders during the early national period with national politics contributed to the decline of agriculture in the state, it most certainly is true also that many of these early leaders were in the vanguard of those seeking to rectify the damage. In their advocacy of agricultural reform and education, they not only laid down the fundamental lines of endeavor which on the eve of the Civil War had greatly resuscitated ante-bellum agriculture in the state, but they also suggested the basic approach which today is embodied in the agricultural education programs of research, extension, and teaching, not only in Virginia but in the entire nation.

These leaders working through the societies and a friendly press soon developed the increasingly popular agricultural fairs, which became instrumental in helping disseminate the reform ideas to the general populace. These societies and their fairs kept up a veritable drumfire of agitation for agricultural education, with or without state aid. Much of this agitation reached seasonal peaks on the occasions of the annual fairs when the president or an invited guest, often selected for his already demonstrated oratorical powers, mounted the rostrum to address the assembly of gentlemen-farmers and their friends. Many of these gentlemen-farmer orators, as a result of study, correspondence, and extensive travel were familiar with the agricultural and manual labor schools established and being developed in Europe. It was only natural, therefore, for them to weave this knowledge into their own proposals for advancing the cause of agricultural education in Virginia. While many if not most of the early schemes advanced by these orators were interwoven with flights of emotional oratory filled with numerous Latin quotations having dubious relevancy for the cause of agricultural education, these speeches, if considered *in toto,* included most of the ideas and often the actual practices of every major approach later to be used and developed by VPI in promoting agricultural education.

These societies and their fairs spread throughout the state, including what is now the state of West Virginia, but they were much more popular and active east of the Blue Ridge Mountains. In all instances, the programs dealt with the problems of agriculture peculiar to the locality. Since the agriculture differed considerably in the great geographic divisions of the state, this practice of the societies and their fairs tended to promote the belief that agricultural education would have to be different for each major geographical division.

Since western Virginia was not suffering so greatly from soil depletion and the decline of one-crop agriculture as the east, the need for agricultural reform through education was not felt to be so great; therefore, the cause of agricultural education was never advocated so strongly in the west as in the east. These differing types of agriculture and differing needs for education plagued all ante-bellum efforts on behalf of agricultural education and continued to do so long after the formation of the state of West Virginia and the creation of the Virginia Agricultural and Mechanical College.

As one immediate result of the activities of the societies, a number of unusual proposals on behalf of state aid for agricultural education began reaching the legislature. The sectional interests slowly but surely splitting the state and paralyzing much internal progress are clearly evident in the legislative debates following the introduction of these proposals. In general, the western delegates lined up in bitter opposition to the proposals, while the little support afforded came from the eastern gentlemen-farmer delegates and the country lawyers. The westerners, painting an image of state aid to agricultural education as a wild-eyed scheme thought up to benefit the eastern aristocrats, heaped ridicule and scorn on most of the proposals. Such proposals, they claimed, were unnecessary, extravagant, book-farming attempts to help practical farmers who needed no science to teach them "how to handle the plow, the ax, the maul." One member of the legislature attacked all legislative aid for agriculture with a blistering attack on the state geologic survey, which, in spite of Edmund Ruffin's impassioned protest to the contrary, the member claimed was an illustration of the results of legislation supposed to aid the farmers. But the farmers, according to the complaining member, had waited year after year for valuable assistance from the survey; however, the "only fact that had been developed was that some oyster shells had been discovered on the Blue Ridge, a fact no doubt interesting to the philosopher but of no practical value to the farmer."

If the "kid-gloved" easterners really wanted to improve their agriculture, argued another member, let them visit the Valley of Virginia, where the best farmers were to be found. The best farmers, he argued, were "those who had been brought up to the plough handle, those who trod their own soil, the honest plain-spoken German who never saw the printed report of an agricultural board" and had no need for book-farming. These arguments, though poorly based, reflected the thinking of large segments of the public. Unfortunately, the ideas involved persisted and in one form or another greatly handicapped the founding and the development of the Virginia Agricultural and Mechanical College two decades later.

The legislative defense of the proposals was usually as weak, uncertain, and as groping as the opposition was dogmatic, specific, and unenlightened. In general, the legislators supporting the proposals seem to have been the country lawyers living in the small villages. Most of them confessed they were not sure just how such proposals would help agriculture, but they felt the people were concerned and that something should be done for an interest that paid such a large share of the taxes. One legislator in a speech that goaded the great agriculturist Edmund Ruffin to a point almost beyond endurance, argued: "Yearly laws were enacted to take care of the terrapins, oysters, fish, and wild fowl of Virginia. Should it be said that we could and would do nothing for the great cause of agriculture?" Having thus grouped the agriculturists, he proceeded to urge, "Let an effort be made, and even if no good should result we should have the consolation of knowing that we had made an effort for the cause."

Despite such ineffective legislative support, the societies and their leaders continued their agitation on behalf of agriculture. This agitation gradually began to crystalize around the idea of a school or schools to teach agriculture. Many of these proposals for schools, like others of the time, were impractical and utopian in nature, with the exception, perhaps, of Jefferson's proposal that instruction in agriculture be included in his beloved University of Virginia when it should open its doors. This proposal, probably the first one ever advanced to include agricultural education in a state university, was not realized at the time. Unhappily, the circumstances surrounding the debate, not only on this proposal but on the entire question of establishing a state university, left deep sectional bitterness which incredibly enough was remembered and erupted nearly half a century later in the prolonged debate over the location of Virginia's first land-grant college.

Nearly all the proposals for agricultural education singled out the University of Virginia as the institution to lead the way. As one result, the opponents of such education began to have a field day as they scoffed and ridiculed the idea of any practical benefits to the farmers to be derived from such a program. Efforts to refute the claims of impracticability only aroused greater opposition, especially from the far western delegates who disliked the University anyway. Regardless of the merits or the demerits of the arguments, the idea became strongly entrenched that if any agricultural education was to be established it must be practical in nature. In addition to this conviction, the belief began to develop that the University was either unwilling or unable to provide the practical education wanted. This conviction that agricultural education must be practical grew into a near obsession with the people of Virginia and exercised a dominating influence on its land-grant institutions for nearly three quarters of a century. The hostility toward establishing agricultural education at the University also grew. In fact, this hostility eventually developed into full-fledged opposition against the University and played a dominant role in preventing this institution from becoming the recipient of the land-grant funds.

By the mid-nineteenth century, thinking in Virginia as well as throughout the nation began to stabilize around more practical schemes. Threads of clarity began to penetrate the confusion of the proposals as leaders began to develop a better insight into the real nature of the problem. Thus Edmund Ruffin, one of Virginia's greatest pioneer leaders in agriculture, in his widely publicized essay prepared in 1853 and entitled "Agricultural Education" cut through much of the utopian nature of the earlier proposals. He presented in some detail a plan which Earle D. Ross, the noted historian of the land-grant college movement said "anticipated in essentials the land-grant agricultural college in state support, manual labor, experimentation, and military organization." Two decades later, as Virginia was attempting to organize a suitable curriculum for her own land-grant colleges, Ruffin had died, but his proposal was available. The circumstances were so radically different, however, that only portions of his plan could be adopted.

Contrary to the statements of many twentieth-century writers, the decade of the fifties seems to have been one of considerable growth, progressive change, and progress in ante-bellum Virginia. Unhappily, much of the spirit of progress and change and all of the prosperity were casualties of the Civil War, not to be regained until several generations later. Many of these ante-bellum changes, on the other hand, were of significance to the cause of agricultural education. The state, although overwhelmingly agricultural, was witnessing the development of manufacturing enterprises in several urban centers, such as Lynchburg, Petersburg, Portsmouth, Fredericksburg, Alexandria, and especially Richmond. In many instances, these manufacturers had started taking advantage of the premiums offered for farm machinery and other manufactured products at the annual fairs held by the agricultural societies. For instance, in Richmond the Tredgar Iron Works under the leadership of Joseph Reed Anderson, who later held a key position on the first Board of Visitors for the Virginia Agricultural and Mechanical College, was especially active in promoting cooperative relations between the Virginia State Agricultural Society, its annual fair, and his company. The Tredgar Company as early as 1845 had shown concern for the education and welfare of its employees and had organized a Mechanics Institute in 1854 which was chartered by the state in 1856.

This institute not only inaugurated a highly successful school for mechanics but also entered wholeheartedly into the preparation of mechanical exhibits for the state agricultural fair. Thus, in a sense these fairs helped bring the planter, the farmer, the manufacturer, and the politician together in a common vocational setting. As one result, it was not long before many agricultural societies began to be agricultural and mechanical societies and to bill their fairs as agricultural and mechanical fairs. With such a union of common interests, it was inevitable that agitation for agricultural education would be expanded to include mechanical education as well.

In 1854 the Virginia State Agricultural Society, finding itself in a relatively flourishing condition as to membership, finances, and progressive leadership, resumed its agitation for a professorship of agriculture at one of the state schools.

This time the more than three decades of agitation for agricultural education began to assume a more realistic direction and shape. Many leaders began to cut through or abandon entirely the extravagant laudations of agriculture and the frills and flights of oratorical fancy with which so many of the earlier appeals for agricultural education had been surrounded. Instead, they began well-reasoned discussions and proposals not only on the question of whether a professorship of agriculture should be established but also on whether it should be established in a state school, a private school, or in a school especially created to serve the cause of agricultural and mechanical education. These discussions provoked further discussions on such aspects as public versus private financing; the role of a school farm; manual labor; military versus nonmilitary organization; control by a board of trustees or more directly by the farmers themselves; theoretical versus practical training; and above all else the organization, the control, and the location of such a professorship to serve best the practical interests and needs of the farmers. Many persons later involved in the struggle to establish the Virginia Agricultural and Mechanical College developed much of their earliest philosophy and many of their life-long convictions concerning agricultural education in the public discussion of these and other questions. Thus, William Henry Ruffner, who later was the chief architect of the curriculum for the new college for its first decade, writing as editor of the *Valley Farmer* in Harrisonburg, warned that any type of agricultural education, whether established at the University or elsewhere, to be of value to the farmer had to be kept practical, whatever else it might be. *The Southern Planter,* probably because of changing editors rather than because of changing opinions, created more confusion than clarity by attacking and then defending the practical value of agricultural education at any school in general and at the University in particular. This periodical, in one vigorous editorial strikingly familiar in tone with some thinking of today, denounced in no uncertain terms the proposed military feature often assigned agricultural schools. Arguing that exercises in agriculture should be substituted for exercises in military, the editor convinced himself at least that "to know how to kill men is all very proper and sometimes very necessary but it is hardly less useful to teach the great art of feeding and clothing them . . . running a furrow is not more laborious or less useful than mounting guard over nothing . . . the boys should be taught to drill—corn; to plant, not standards but potatoes; to open, not trenches but ditches; to clean, not cavalry but work horses; in short to be creative rather than destructive."

With steadily mounting public discussion and pressure for agricultural education being stirred up by the State Agricultural Society, the politicians lost little time in joining the debate. Governor John Floyd, who was born in Montgomery County, at Smithfield, tried unsuccessfully to get professorships of agricultural chemistry established at Virginia Military Institute and the University of Virginia. In 1855, Henry A. Wise, an intrepid individualist, in his successful gubernatorial canvass of the state, included agricultural and mechanical education in the state-wide system of education he proposed for Virginia.

Wise, although a resident of eastern Virginia, fully recognized the sectional differences which were playing such havoc with the progress of the state and at the same time slowly but surely alienating the west from the east. As candidate for governor, he attempted to develop a progressive platform which would be acceptable to both sections. In this endeavor he was remarkably successful, particularly in his proposals on behalf of education. This individual, with a flair for the kind of oratory so dear to the Virginians of that day, elicited round after round of applause and sometimes standing ovations whenever he described certain conditions of the state which in his opinion could never be fully remedied without a system of complete education from the common school to the university. Scornfully rejecting as unworthy of Virginia "any little day school, night school, common school, a-b-c single rule of three, or Peter Parley Yankee system of instruction," Wise skillfully enlarged the original plan of state-wide education advanced by Thomas Jefferson, who, said Wise amidst resounding applause, "knew that if it was inhuman to starve the body of a child, it was much more inhuman to starve the mind of a child." Rejecting outright the growing sentiment for federal aid for any internal state improvement, Wise insisted that the time had come for Virginia to establish as a part of a state-wide system of schools at least one school of applied science. A school, said Wise, which would help the state marshall her resources and direct her energies to the development of her abundant natural resources and to the survival of agriculture, an agriculture, proclaimed Wise, brought to a deplorable condition largely because of ignorance on the part of the farmers and planters of the principles of applied science. Humorously chiding the people of Virginia for their inattention to industrial development and their failure to develop their natural resources because of too long reliance upon the single power of agriculture, he continued,". . . and such agriculture! Your ledge patches outshine the sun. Your inattention to your only source of wealth has scarred the very bosom of Mother Earth. Instead of having to feed cattle on a thousand hills, you have to chase the stump-tailed steer through the ledge patches to procure a tough beefsteak."

Wise's campaign for the governorship was successful. He was elected by a comfortable majority from all sections of the state. Upon assuming office in 1856, he continued his support of scientific education for agriculture; but, no doubt recognizing the opposition of the western part of the state both to the University and to agricultural education, he shifted his position a bit to advocate not one but two colleges for agriculture. One school was to be established at Blue Sulphur as a "Moeglin" institute to operate in the summer only and teach the applied sciences needed for the agriculture of the cold mountain climate. The other for eastern Virginia was to be established on the plan of "Father Von Thaer of Prussia." This school was to operate in the winter only and teach the agriculture of the warmer eastern part of the state. In both instances, Wise stressed the importance of organizing these schools in such a way they would not at any time be in competition with the already established "literary" schools. He did not push very hard for any legislative program designed to implement his proposals for agricultural and mechanical education, a tardiness attributed by some historians to his increasing desire to secure the nomination for the presidency of the United States. On the other hand, there is no doubt that his proposals, coming as they did amidst the growing debate over scientific, agricultural, and mechanical education, had a state-wide impact on these developing discussions. Partly as a result of Wise's influence but more specifically as a result of the activities of those wishing to promote the development of a state system of public education, educational conventions were held in Richmond in 1856 and 1857. These conventions for the first time in the long history of such educational meetings in Virginia gave special prominence to the consideration of scientific and industrial education especially as related to agriculture. Wise addressed both meetings and in his own inimitable oratorical manner once more advocated scientific schools to teach agriculture. It was at one of these conventions that he uttered the statement often quoted since then that "ignorance of agriculture had ruined more men in Virginia than any other cause . . . except brandy, foxhounds and horse racing." The convention itself approached the question of scientific industrial education very cautiously. After a consideration of the merits and the demerits of science it was concluded that science, although deficient in its promotion of moral values, did have sufficient merit to be given a place in the curriculum of the colleges in the state. A committee was appointed to investigate and report on the practicability of establishing within the state a school of "applied science combining agricultural chemistry, botany, geology, the mechanical arts, and such other studies as may be deemed expedient with a view primarily of educating agriculturists and mechanics for their calling." This committee, fully aware of the hostility existing in some of the colleges of the state toward "applied science" and equally aware of the increasing hostility against the University as the place for a school of agriculture, presented a cautiously worded report recommending that agriculture should be included in the scheme of education to be supported by the state. An answer to the vexing question of location of an agricultural school was neatly sidestepped in the report by the observation that whether agricultural education should be "connected closely or only remotely with our university is a question not submitted to our committee."

The report of the convention, actually the culmination of nearly three decades of effort to promote education by such means, was criticized by many as offering something for all. Indeed, its report in proposing state support for elementary schools, primary schools, secondary schools, colleges, a medical school, a military school, a university, and three new colleges or schools for instruction in applied sciences and agriculture may have been designed to do just that.

In the meantime a series of other events significant for the cause of agricultural and mechanical education in Virginia were taking place simultaneously. It has been noted that about 1854 the State Agricultural Society resumed its

activities on behalf of a professorship of agricultural education. This society during this period reached a peak enrollment of about ten thousand members scattered throughout the state. Largely as a result of the efforts of W. H. Richardson,
adjutant general of the state, as well as an agent of the society, this organization's membership now included not only Virginia gentlemen-farmers, manufacturers, and politicians, but also many of the rank and file farmers and mechanics. A proposal was well received that the society endow a professorship of
agriculture "at one of the state's institutions of learning." At once there broke
out an argument as to which institution was to be selected. After much consideration, the University of Virginia was chosen, but by this time the executive
committee of the society had decided that the state, not the society, should assume
financial responsibility for the professorship. Before this decision could be imple-
mented, Philip St. George Cocke, a wealthy planter of a distinguished Virginia
family and at the time president of the State Agricultural Society, offered to donate $20,000 toward the proposed professorship. Cocke, who in connection with
another venture had prepared an igenious, detailed, and comprehensive plan of
state agricultural education, shared with many the fear that a professorship at
the University might not be practical. His proposed remedy was simple: he would
reserve to himself the right to name the person selected to fill the professorship.
After his demise this right would pass to the State Agricultural Society forever.
This provision proved to be a major stumbling block. The Board of Visitors of
the University rejected this feature of the plan, correctly so, it would seem, on
the grounds that accepting it would tend to divide the authority for administering the University. Cocke, who seems to have entertained some doubts as to the
board's sincerity in its expressed willingness to establish a professorship of
agriculture, refused to modify his proposal. The Board of Visitors thereupon
rejected the proposed donation. This rejection started a chain reaction of far-
reaching consequences for the cause of agricultural and mechanical education
throughout the state. Angered by the action of the University Board, some of the
officials of the agricultural society determined to seek legislative support to
compel the University to accept the donation on the proposed terms. This action
precipitated controversy within the society and tended to dissipate the effort and
sap the energy of those advocating agricultural education. Letters, pro and con,
reasonable and unreasonable, appeared in the press. Many of them echoed the
sentiment voiced by one writer that "carriage horses don't draw well with plow
horses. If we want our agricultural school, we had better have our own team of
horses." Even many of the gentlemen-farmers turned against the University or
began to despair of it as the best place for their longed-for school of agriculture.
It is ironic that more than four decades of almost continuous agitation for a
professorship or chair of agriculture at the state university should terminate with
a series of incidents which lined up so many leading farmers against the University as the best place for establishing a school of agriculture. A decade later these
incidents were a factor in aligning the powerful State Agricultural Society against
the University as the recipient of the land-grant funds.

Thwarted in his efforts at the University, Cocke, who in the meantime had
become a member of the Board of Visitors of the Virginia Military Institute,
turned his attention to this institution. VMI, founded in 1839 at Lexington, was
at this time under the remarkably able leadership of General Francis H. Smith,
a graduate of West Point. Smith was seeking to develop and expand the applied

science aspect of VMI's curriculum. Cocke became greatly interested in this feature of the school and provided funds to enable Smith to visit Europe and make a detailed study of the outstanding scientific, military, and agricultural schools there. Upon his return, Smith formulated a well-organized plan which proposed that the Virginia Military Institute be reorganized into a technical and military institute with three divisions: agriculture, engineering, and the fine arts. His report was printed by order of the legislature and given wide circulation with quite favorable reception. His proposed reorganization of VMI was accepted by the Board of Visitors of that institution; whereupon Cocke immediately donated his $20,000 to VMI, and then William C. Rives directed to the Institute a fund of some $10,000 donated by W. N. Mercer. These gifts, quite munificent for the day, were followed almost immediately by a donation from Mrs. E. L. Claytor for the erection of a Hall of Natural History. With these funds at hand the Board of Visitors proceeded as far in the reorganization of the Institute as to establish two chairs of agriculture with William Gilham and M. B. Hardin as incumbents. With these chairs an accomplished fact, a full report was made to the legislature along with a request for funds to complete the reorganization and to erect additional buildings. The request was granted; but with war clouds plainly visible over the horizon, it is a debatable point whether the appropriation was prompted by enthusiasm for agricultural education or by a desire to strengthen the state's facilities for military training. Considerable evidence supports the latter view.

William Gilham seems to have taken the lead in the development of agricultural instruction in this newly established division, but hardly had he begun his work when it was terminated by the outbreak of the Civil War. He left the Institute to join the Confederacy; and the embryonic agricultural school, along with so many efforts of the day for agricultural education, became another war casualty. The story of the fruitless efforts to resuscitate this school of agriculture after the war properly belongs to the post-bellum struggle in the state to establish a land-grant college of agriculture and mechanics within the dictates of the federal Morrill Land-Grant Act.

All of the ante-bellum efforts to promote the cause of agricultural and mechanical education came to an abrupt stop with the outbreak of the Civil War. The heritage of these efforts survived the war, however, and continued to be an important factor not only in the birth but also in the early growth of the Virginia Agricultural and Mechanical College.

Another influence of an earlier day which affected the Virginia Agricultural and Mechanical College, especially its location at Blacksburg, grew from the conditions surrounding the establishment and the management of the Preston and Olin Institute by a group of Methodist leaders. The establishment of such an institution was not unusual in Virginia. The history of education in the state is filled with instances wherein religious denominations encouraged the establishment of schools "for the instruction of youth." About 1850 the fervor for establishing "seminaries of learning wherein youth might be instructed within a Christian atmosphere" possessed a group of Methodist leaders in Blacksburg. Thereupon, this group, most of whom were trustees in the Blacksburg Female Academy established around 1841, decided to establish a "seminary of learning" for the boys.

Following a prevalent custom of the Methodist Church of that day to name such schools after religious and business leaders, it was decided to call the school the Olin and Preston Institute after Stephen Olin and William Ballard Preston.

Stephen Olin, a beloved Methodist minister, had served for a time as president of Randolph-Macon College but had relinquished his duties because of ill health. Following his recovery, he had resumed active participation in the educational and religious activities of the Methodist Church. In this capacity, he had become well known and highly admired, not only among the Blacksburg leaders but throughout the entire Methodist realm as well. He died in 1851 while the Blacksburg group was in the midst of organizing its new school. This group, wishing to honor his memory, decided to use his name in connection with the institution.

William Ballard Preston, son of former Governor James P. Preston and resident of Smithfield in Montgomery County, was a well-known lawyer, politician, and business man. By the time of the establishment of the Olin and Preston Institute, he had served in both branches of the Virginia General Assembly and in the Congress of the United States and was completing a short term as Secretary of the Navy. His name, well known far beyond the borders of the state, was chosen as the second name to be used for the new school.

A tract of approximately five acres was bought from Jacob Keister and his wife Mary, and the new school with William R. White as "principal" opened sometime in 1851. A complete roster of the faculty and the students of this early school is not available; but evidently the school got off to a successful start, since the organizing group decided to erect a new building for it in 1854. In an effort to broaden the school's base of support, the organizing body also requested a charter from the state to be granted to a board of trustees to be named by the official governing body of the Methodist Conference serving Blacksburg. The state charter was granted in 1854 to a board of trustees made up largely of outstanding local leaders.

The new building, completed in the summer of 1855, was located on the hillside overlooking the present Main Street of downtown Blacksburg at a point southeast of the present entrance to the mall, a site through which U. S. Route 460 now passes.

Hardly had the school comfortably settled in its new quarters, however, before it ran into financial trouble, both unexpected and beyond the ability of the trustees to solve.

In 1854 Blacksburg was in the Baltimore Conference of the Northern Methodist Episcopal Church. By 1856 most of the influential Methodist Church papers had been taken over by the abolitionists who were mounting a steady attack on slavery. The southern branch of the church, resenting what it considered to be unfair aspects of this attack, retaliated by attempting to win over to its side all of the Methodist churches up to the Mason-Dixon Line. The Baltimore Conference, being a border one, was caught in the middle of the struggle. In 1860 at a meeting in Staunton, a portion of the Baltimore Conference withdrew from the northern branch and established itself as a separate branch. This organization maintained a separate and independent existence until 1866 when it affiliated with the Methodist Episcopal Church South. A minority of the old Baltimore Conference, however, had continued to adhere to the northern church and had continued to claim to be the legal Baltimore Conference.

Dr. Harvey Black, a trustee of the Olin and Preston Institute, had been the representative of the Blacksburg Church to the Staunton Convention. Largely through his efforts the Blacksburg Methodist Church was persuaded to go along with the group that withdrew from the northern branch and affiliated with the southern branch. These moves split not only the conference but the Board of Trustees for the Olin and Preston Institute as well. As one result of the several divisions, the expected financial support for the new school from the several charges making up the conference, whether the old or the new ones, had not been forthcoming. The trustees consequently found themselves unable to meet the payments on the new building they had just erected.

In 1859 John N. Lyle, one of the institution's largest creditors, brought suit against the Olin and Preston trustees for money owed him. The trustees, by this time quite demoralized, made no objection to the suit and accepted court judgment against the property for the debt owed Lyle.

It is not clear from available records whether the institution closed its doors at this time or not. Tradition in one branch of the Lyle family has it that it did not. According to this tradition, Lyle, a widower, was courting a lady in Blacksburg who refused to marry him if he refused to let the trustees continue to operate the school on the property against which Lyle now had judgment for debt. Whatever the real situation may have been, when the Civil War broke out, Lyle had married the lady and still held legal judgment against the Olin and Preston Institute, which did close during the war.

Following the war, the Blacksburg Methodist Church, under the leadership of their minister Peter Henry Whisner, determined to reopen the school. By this time, John Lyle had died, and his estate was in the hands of his son John N. Lyle, Jr., a practicing attorney in Christiansburg. The younger Lyle, planning to move to Texas, was eager to settle the estate promptly. Following the war, however, the legislature of Virginia had declared a moratorium on the legal collection of most debts; therefore, the school was temporarily protected against any foreclosure on the debt it owed the Lyle estate. Taking advantage of this reprieve, the Methodists appealed to both the Baltimore Conference and to the Virginia Conference for support similar to that afforded Randolph-Macon College by these conferences.

The records do not indicate how much financial support this appeal secured, but the debates and discussions in these conferences relative to the "Olin and Preston Institute in Blacksburg," plus the glowing reports of the prospects of this school presented at these discussions by the energetic Whisner, succeeded in familiarizing the name of the school throughout much of Virginia Methodism.

Just as the trustees seemed on the verge of winning additional financial support, concern developed as to which branch of the church, north or south, owned the school. Apparently, the Blacksburg Church in 1854, at the time the state charter was issued to the board of trustees under the northern branch of Methodism, was on the Christiansburg charge. Following the war, both northern and southern branches sent ministers to nearby Christiansburg and were waging a spirited contest for possession of the Methodist Church in that town.

This dilemma of ownership of the Olin and Preston property was resolved by an unusual series of actions which not only cleared the question of ownership but also placed the school under a new board of trustees completely in sympathy with the southern branch of Methodism. The trustees of the Olin and Preston Institute agreed to waive the moratorium on the debt they owed the Lyle estate and asked John Lyle, Jr., as administrator of the estate to execute his judgment against them. He did so, and after due legal process the property was sold to him. He took legal possession of the institute, thereby technically at least taking the property out of the control of both the northern and the southern branches of the church.

At the same time in response to a properly presented petition, Judge Robert M. Hudson, of the Circuit Court of Montgomery County, on January 2, 1869, issued a charter to trustees appointed by the Baltimore Conference, M. E. Church South, to establish a "seminary of learning" to be located at Blacksburg and to be "called and known by the name of Preston and Olin Institute." Having created a "new" institution by the simple expedient of reversing the name of the old one, Judge Hudson appointed six trustees for the new school, only one of whom, Dr. Harvey Black, was a carry-over from the board having been appointed for the original Olin and Preston Institute.

Following the creation of the "new" school under a "new" board, John Lyle, Jr. proceeded to sell to this new board the Olin and Preston Institute property. At the same time he kept a lien of nearly $3,000 as security for his debt.

The new board of trustees met at once and in an effort to secure wide support for the school named nine additional trustees. This enlarged board, which included Harvey Black and Robert T. Preston as the only members from the old Olin and Preston board, consisted of well-known business, social, political, and religious leaders, who with the exception of the latter group, lived within a hundred mile radius of Blacksburg.

This board, with Peter H. Whisner and Harvey Black playing the leading roles, set about developing the "new" school. Agents appointed to solicit funds from a number of the charges in the conference were well received as they collected pledges of financial support and carried the name of the Preston and Olin Institute through the conference.

The Reverend Peter H. Whisner was transferred to a charge in Maryland and was succeeded by Thomas N. Conrad as principal, or president, of the school. Conrad seems to have entered upon his task with great enthusiasm. Possessed as he was with a flair for writing and a "tongue for speaking," this ex-Confederate secret agent brought a new dimension of excitement to the school and to the town of Blacksburg. Prospects for the school seemed to be excellent in all respects except one—finances. The stringencies of the postwar period prevented a number of people from paying their financial pledges, and none of the conferences in the Methodist Church were in a position to extend financial aid. In spite of a promising enrollment, the school was facing financial difficulties.

At this stage, Whisner, who according to a tradition in the Black family was visiting in the home of Harvey Black, read about the deadlock in the Virginia Legislature concerning the disposition of the proceeds from the state's share of the Morrill Land-Grant Act. He discussed the matter with Dr. Black, and these two individuals wrote to State Senator John E. Penn, suggesting that the fund or a portion of it be donated to the Preston and Olin Institute.

Senator Penn, who had practiced law in Montgomery County, felt that the Preston and Olin Institute was too small to have much chance of getting the land-grant funds; nevertheless, he agreed to support the request. As it turned out, he pressed the claim in an astute manner at critical periods when the legislative debates concerning the disposition of the land-grant funds were deadlocked chiefly because of the heritage of the ante-bellum efforts for agricultural and mechanical education and the radically changed postwar conditions in the state.

The account of Penn's efforts and final success, achieved with the aid of a number of other individuals, rightfully belongs to the legislative struggle to use the funds from the land-grant act to establish an agricultural and mechanical college.

Ironically, Penn's success placed the state's agricultural and mechanical college at a school which in no way had been associated with the ante-bellum efforts for such a school. Furthermore, his success placed the school in a section of the state which during ante-bellum times had consistently, even bitterly opposed the idea of agricultural and mechanical education. As one result, the friends of the Preston and Olin Institute were shocked with what they got as an agricultural and mechanical college. The friends of the new college were shocked with the lack of enthusiasm in the community for agricultural and mechanical education. Both groups had to do a lot of adjusting as the new college was launched.

The conflicting philosophies concerning agricultural and mechanical schools generated during the ante-bellum period survived the Civil War. The shaping influences of the social, political, economic, and industrial conditions in postwar Virginia, however, were radically, even dramatically different from the ante-bellum circumstances. Certain aspects of these shaping conditions can best be told as a part of the postwar legislative struggle to establish an agricultural and mechanical college with the funds derived from the Morrill Land-Grant Act and will be included in succeeding chapters. Other features of the postwar conditions which affected the establishment and early development of Virginia's agricultural and mechanical college can be presented briefly as a separate summary.

The final struggle between the armies of Lee and Grant had left Virginia in such a state that desolation and despair continued to rule most of the agricultural sections for three decades after Appomattox. As Moger so well expressed it, "While joy and prosperity had spread through the North, sorrow and weeds were more common in the South, and Virginia was no exception. In physical destruction and material impoverishment for all classes, her people had suffered more from the war than any other southern state." The conditions in the agricultural areas of the older slave-holding sections whence most of the agitation and leadership for agricultural and mechanical education had come for so long were particularly tragic. The freedmen for the most part, through no fault of their own, were completely untrained and totally lacking in any knowledge of systematic agriculture. The poor whites were but little better. With the huge plantations being broken up and sold into smaller units and many of the owners moving into nearby towns and cities, an intelligent economic system was almost impossible.

The state's transportation system of canals was in utter ruin and either had to be rebuilt or replaced by railroads before agricultural produce could be moved readily to market. The railroads were not in much better shape than the canals.

The state of West Virginia had been carved from Virginia's territory, and the tax-paying capacity of the remaining territory had been drastically reduced. Neither local nor state capital was available for rebuilding the state and developing its natural resources at the same time. A mad scramble and questionable, if colorful, politics ensued, wherein out-of-state financial interests sought to gain possession or control of much of the state's natural resources, utilities, and property. In many instances, long range potentials for the development of the state's resources had to be sacrificed on the altar of survival. As one result, people in many sections of the state became increasingly embittered as they saw their interests in property and natural resources pass into control of Northern capital. Discouragement, bitterness, frustration, defeatism, and a paralyzing loss of pre-war vigor tended to creep in and delay attempts to adapt to new conditions. Excessive laudations of the "lost cause" and its heroes, along with nostalgic references to the glories of the past, became one of the politician's most effective campaign devices. The device proved to be quite effective in winning elections, but unfortunately, it also was effective in postponing constructive attention to urgent problems of internal improvement and growth.

The confusion and uncertainty of the period spread to the legislature, which suddenly found itself face to face with the necessity of dealing with such internal problems as railroad finances, race politics, education, and other social services vitally affecting the immediate and future welfare of the people. Since prewar legislatures in Virginia had developed vast skill in debating and dealing with national issues but very little in dealing with internal social problems, the legislature found little if any relevant legislative precedent to call upon as it grappled with the pressing social problems of the early postwar period. To add to the confusion, franchise privileges and requirements for holding both local and state offices changed and remained cloudy for nearly a decade after the close of the war. For a part of the postwar period state and local government by elected officials was suspended and the state was operated under federal military au-thority as Military District Number One. During this period the state and local affairs considered to be essential by the United States Congress were conducted by personnel approved by or appointed by and directly responsible to the occupy-ing military authorities. Some pessimists even predicted that the name of Virginia would be denied the state if and when it was readmitted to the Union.

Numberless disputes raged as how best to cope with the total post-bellum situation. Some welcomed the changed conditions as a new day in the making. Others with excessive nostalgic reminiscences of the past were unable to adjust. Some, while looking to the past with nostalgic longing, were pushed into the present and prepared for the future without knowing it. Others, in no way de-meaning the past, resolutely adjusted to the changes and planned for the future. Representatives of all these groups participated vigorously in the legislative debates beginning in 1865 and extending into 1872 concerning the establishment of an agricultural and mechanical college with the proceeds from the Morrill Land-Grant Act.

The postwar climate was not a favorable one within which to operate, yet it was amidst this postwar turmoil that legislation creating the Virginia Agricul-tural and Mechanical College was effected.

The Commonwealth of Virginia,

To All To Whom These Presents Shall Come—Greeting:

Know Ye, That our Governor, in pursuance of authority vested in the Executive by law, hath constituted and appointed

Harvey Black

A visitor to the Virginia Agricultural and Mechanical College.

to execute the duties of that office according to law.

IN TESTIMONY WHEREOF, These our Letters are sealed with the Less. Seal of the Commonwealth and made patent.

WITNESS, _Gilbert C. Walker_ **Esquire,** our said Governor, at Richmond, this _Nineteenth_ day of _March_ in the year 18_72_, and in the _96th_ year of the Commonwealth.

BY THE GOVERNOR:

Jas. McDonald
Secretary of the Commonwealth.

Oldest known document connected with the Virginia Agricultural and Mechanical College. Harvey Black was elected first Rector of the Board.

Chapter 1

The Legislative Struggle

1864-1872

ALL EFFORTS to establish agricultural and mechanical schools in Virginia came to an abrupt standstill at the outbreak of the Civil War. The conflicting philosophies concerning such schools generated during the ante-bellum period remained, however, and played a significant part in shaping the course of agricultural and mechanical education undertaken in Virginia for the remainder of the nineteenth century. This ante-bellum influence was particularly effective in shaping the debate concerning the use of Virginia's share of the proceeds from the Morrill Land-Grant Act to establish an agricultural and mechanical college.

This debate started quickly following the close of the war, not, as some historians have asserted, because of a burning desire on the part of the people of Virginia for an agricultural and mechanical college, but because federal financial assistance was available for the establishment of such a school. Any "burning desire" manifested at the time was generated by colleges struggling to get a share of the money.

The specific cause of the postwar resumption of debate on the question of an agricultural and mechanical college for Virginia was the Morrill Land-Grant Act passed by Congress in 1862. The subsequent success of the colleges through-

out the United States brought into existence largely as a result of this act has led
to a surprisingly extensive study and examination of the act itself. Some of the
conclusions reached in these studies are equally surprising, but no doubt would
be gratifying to Morrill, who before his death had showed considerable vacillation in his own attempts to interpret the meaning of the statute which bore
his name.

The act provided that 30,000 acres of land be given each state for every member of Congress from the state according to the representation based on the 1860
census. The land thus donated was to be sold and the proceeds invested in state,
federal, or other bonds considered safe, yielding not less than five per cent
interest. The income thus derived, none of which could be used for building
purposes and only ten per cent for the purchase of land, was to be used for the
"endowment, support and maintenance of at least one college where the leading
object shall be, without excluding other scientific and classical studies and including military tactics, to teach such branches of learning as are related to agricultural and mechanical arts in such a manner as the legislatures of the states may
respectively prescribe in order to promote the liberal and practical education
of the industrial class in the several pursuits and professions of life."

This language, upon a first reading, may seem to be quite clear. As a guide
for founding a college, however, it proved to be quite puzzling not only in Virginia but throughout the entire country. By the terms of the act, each state could
accept or reject the grant, decide upon the disposition of the resulting funds,
and within the terms of the act, decide upon the character of the college to be
established and the curriculum to be followed. At first glance it does not appear
that these should have been difficult decisions. It did not turn out to be so simple,
either in the country as a whole or in Virginia in particular, where, in addition
to the vagueness of the act the surviving legacy of ante-bellum efforts on behalf
of agricultural and mechanical education and the turbulent postwar conditions
influenced the legislative debates for years.

At the time of the passage of the Morrill Act, Virginia was involved in
the Civil War and therefore took no immediate action relating to it. On
February 5, 1864, the "Unionist" or loyal legislature meeting in regular session
at Alexandria, Virginia, passed an act accepting the donation. At the time the
war was still in progress; and this legislature was in control of only a small part
of the state, and that by virtue of federal bayonets. The act, therefore, merely
provided for Virginia's aceptance of the grant "under the conditions and provisions therein prescribed." It made no effort to secure the fund or donate it to
any college.

Following the war, this legislature by presidential proclamation was declared
to be the legal or provisional government of Virginia. Most, if not all, of its
legislative action, including its acceptance of the land grant, by this proclamation
became binding upon the state. This government was quickly moved from
Alexandria to Richmond, with Francis H. Pierpont, a native of West Virginia,
continuing as governor.

Upon establishing the seat of government in Richmond, Pierpont immediately
called a special session of the legislature to meet in June, 1865. This legislature—
made up of only three senators and nine delegates—nonetheless was able, largely
because of Pierpont's leadership, to restore the rights of suffrage to enough
citizens to enable the state to elect members for a general assembly. As it turned

out, this assembly was remarkably representative of the geographic sections, but under control of the conservative, mostly pro-Confederate element of the state. Convening in December, 1865, this legislature proved to be weak in leadership and understandably uncertain of its real authority and role. To add to the confusion, the legislature as a whole and many of its members as individuals immediately came under bitter partisan attack from the so-called radicals, who claimed the legislature was an illegal one, since many of its members, in the opinion of the radicals at least, were ineligible to serve because of their previous activities on behalf of the Confederacy. Pierpont, on the other hand, went ahead with what was apparently a sincere effort to get state governmental machinery operating once more.

In his message to the legislature on December 4, 1865, Pierpont reminded the members of the availability of the land-grant fund. At the same time, he briefly reviewed the purposes of the Morrill Act and outlined the steps the state would have to follow in order to secure the fund. He also spoke at some length on Virginia's need for a "polytechnic school for the education of her young men." After outlining the functions of the institution and stressing the importance of determining an excellent location for it, Pierpont made what turned out perhaps to be the greatest understatement of his career when he speculated before the legislature that "doubtless a number of institutions of learning in the state will be willing to add the agricultural and military feature required by this act to their institutions to procure the endowment thus offered." This thinly veiled invitation soon helped every male college, several academies, private schools, and numerous institutes in the state to discover their long-standing, burning desire and unique fitness to teach agriculture. Since the conflicting claims put forward by the several colleges could be resolved only by action of the legislature, this body soon found itself hopelessly involved in a struggle which newspapers humorously labeled the "War of the Colleges."

Having unwittingly set the stage for a six-year struggle, Pierpont proceeded to discuss his proposal at some length. Unfortunately his discussion did not reflect a sound grasp of the nature of agricultural and mechanical education which had been developing in Virginia in the decade of the fifties. On the contrary, it resembled more closely the fanciful orations so common at the agricultural fairs of the thirties. After reviewing his decidedly encyclopedic ideas as to curriculum content for the new school, Pierpont suggested it have a 300-acre farm on which to cultivate "all the crops of the state." Then as if fearing something might have been overlooked, he suggested a five-year school with no vacation at all. Rather, the students and the staff would spend the summer months in tents in the fields where he felt "the state with its agriculture, botany, mineralogy, geology, and geography would afford an ample field for investigation to the corps of teachers and pupils." Having presented his opinions on what the new school should do, he then pointedly observed that the "routine of the old collegiate course" had not qualified the young men of Virginia, "equal in intellect to those of any state or nation," for developing the true wealth of the great commonwealth. Surprisingly, in view of his earlier speculation that a number of institutions in the state probably would be interested in the fund, Pierpont closed his remarks by recommending to the legislature that the land-grant fund be given to the Virginia Military Institute, provided the Institute move from Lexington to Richmond. He felt that this institution already had "the elements of proper organization to take charge of this school and give it proper direction."

Pierpont's recommendations concerning the land-grant fund seem to have taken the legislature by surprise. Apparently many members had never heard of the fund and knew nothing about procedures for securing it and even less about creating an agricultural and mechanical college with it. As it turned out, there were a number of persons more than willing to solve this last problem for the legislature.

The day following Pierpont's message to the legislature, George Graham presented a memorial to the Virginia House of Delegates, seeking the land-grant fund for the Virginia Military Institute. This memorial, a very able one, had been prepared earlier in the fall of 1865 by Francis H. Smith, superintendent of VMI, at the suggestion of W. H. Richardson, who had taken such an active part in the ante-bellum efforts for agricultural education. In preparing his plan, Smith simply updated and reworked his proposal for a scientific school at VMI which he had presented to the legislature in 1859.

Graham's memorial on behalf of VMI came at a perplexing and novel time for the legislature. The national Congress had just refused to seat Virginia's elected representatives to that body, thereby raising the question of the state's relationship to Congress and indirectly its rights with respect to the land-grant fund. The right of many individual members of the state legislature to sit in that body also was being challenged. At the same time, the naive hope that West Virginia, if given an opportunity, would return to the mother state was held by many in and out of the legislature. Obviously, the resolution of all these factors would have bearing on the land-grant fund available to the state.

To add to the novelty and difficulty of the situation, Pierpont was governor of the state by presidential proclamation rather than by popular election. Regrettably for him, at this time he did not have the confidence of the majority of the conservatives, who disliked and distrusted him because of his role in carving the state of West Virginia out of Virginia. The radicals, on the other hand, who wanted control of state affairs wrested completely from ex-Confederates, were attacking him because of his conciliatory attitude toward this group of citizens. At the time, a number of these individuals were complaining to the federal authorities that the Negro and loyal or Union men were not safe in Virginia under Pierpont's government. One individual had even testified before a congressional committee that if left alone, the Virginia leaders "would entirely extirpate . . . from the face of the earth" the Union men and the Negro!

Surrounded by all these distractions and operating in an environment of uncertain but increasing hostility from the federal authorities, the legislature understandably hesitated to assign the fund at this time.

Graham's memorial was referred to the House Committee on Schools and Colleges, which, with some prudence, started action designed to secure the fund before donating it. The committee also secured the publication and distribution of 500 copies of the Morrill Act. The distribution of these copies throughout the state plus the press accounts of the act and of Pierpont's address touched off a veritable avalanche of conflicting requests and arguments for the money.

When the legislature reconvened after the Christmas recess, David S. G. Cabell presented a request from the Board of Trustees of Washington College for a portion of the land-grant fund. Four days later John Trout presented a similar request for Roanoke College. These last two petitions introduced a new factor into the developing discussion. Instead of asking for all the fund, these requests asked only for a donation from the fund. This wording introduced the possibility of donating the fund to more than one college. Since this idea was in harmony with the method by which a portion of the Virginia Literary Fund had been distributed during ante-bellum times, it was favorably received in the legislature and remained a major factor throughout the entire period of debate.

Understandably enough, considerable skepticism developed within the legislature itself as to whether Virginia actually would receive any of the fund. At the time, some mutterings and objections to the entire Morrill Act as an invasion of states' rights cropped up, but this objection never came into the open as it had done in Virginia during the Congressional debates of 1858-59 over an earlier Morrill Act, vetoed by President Buchanan. Under the circumstances, "states' rights" was not a politically healthy topic in Virginia. As the state's relationship with the national Congress continued to deteriorate, persons outside the legislature began to doubt openly that the state would ever receive the fund. Thus one individual, signing himself "Farmer," advised the legislature to quit wasting time and the taxpayers' money trying to donate the fund, since it did not have the fund and probably never would have it. Probably as a result of all the uncertainties of the time, the legislature of 1865-66 did not set in motion any action toward disposal of the fund. An abortive act designed to secure payment of the fund to the state was passed; but before federal officials would recognize the legality of the act, Virginia was plunged into the turmoil of congressional reconstruction, during which time the fund was purposely withheld by congressional action.

At the 1866-67 session of the Virginia General Assembly, Governor Pierpont once more brought up the subject of disposal of the land-grant scrip. This time he helped add even more confusion to the already confused situation by switching his support from the Virginia Military Institute to the College of William and Mary, which he felt should be moved to Richmond and made over into "the great polytechnic school contemplated by the munificence of Congress, and so much needed by the state." By this time, considerable publicity had been given to the existence of the fund, and numerous colleges lured by this potential bonanza had convinced themselves of their fitness for spending it. Thus, before the legislature could take any action on Pierpont's second proposal, petitions for the fund or a part of it were introduced into the legislature on behalf of William and Mary, Washington College, Richmond College, Hampden-Sydney College, and the University of Virginia.

At the same time, additional elements began to enter into the discussions. The Virginia State Agricultural Society was being reorganized following its period of inactivity during the war. The society had long been working for a school or professorship of agriculture. Of even more significance for the growing debate was the society's almost fanatic belief and determination that such a school must be practical in nature. Acting in keeping with this determination, the society in January, 1867, presented a memorial to the legislature, urging (some say demanding) that the legislature use the fund to establish one independent agricultural and mechanical college completely separate from any of the literary institutions. This proposal, apparently surprising to the legislature, was not entirely unwelcome; but as one harassed member complained, it raised more questions than it answered.

At the same time that the agricultural society was promoting the cause of a separate college, a number of individuals over the state began urging the disposition of the fund. William T. Sutherlin and William H. Ruffner may be mentioned as individuals typical of this group.

William T. Sutherlin, a wealthy and socially prominent business man of Danville, in a lengthy address delivered before the Mechanics Association of Danville, bemoaned the fact that adequate provisions for a complete system of public education had never been made in Virginia. The colleges, he felt, had been open only to the rich. Now, however, since Congress had made an appropriation for agricultural and mechanical education, he felt "some wise plan should be devised that would place in reach of all classes the opportunity of sound instruction in practical knowledge." It was his conviction that "to make the federal endowment most available it should be appropriated to a new educational enterprise designed to secure practical benefits to the masses." Sometime prior to this address, Sutherlin had expressed these same views to a committee of the legislature. Sutherlin's address and his appearance before the legislative committee were given wide publicity in the press. As one result, mechanics' associations, particularly in the eastern part of the state, began to add their voices to those of the agricultural interests demanding a separate school. Sutherlin's position at this time is particularly noteworthy. Before any disposition of the land-grant fund occurred, he became a member of the legislature, where he played a key role in the final disposition of the fund. With the creation of the agricultural college he was named to its governing board, where he exercised tremendous influence in charting the course of his "new educational enterprise."

William H. Ruffner, of Lexington, who later earned undying fame as Virginia's first superintendent of public instruction, had taken a strong stand as early as 1856 for a practical system of agricultural education. Because of his pioneering success in the field of public education, many of his activities on behalf of a separate college of agriculture and mechanics have gone relatively unnoted. As a towering figure, perhaps *the* towering figure, in shaping the early destiny of the Virginia Agricultural and Mechanical College, his earlier activities as well as others to be recounted later deserve attention.

In the fall of 1866, he appeared before a legislative committee and urged that the land-grant money not be given to any college already in existence. He followed up his appearance with a lengthy communication setting forth his arguments in some detail. Ruffner, quite correctly it would seem, did not believe there was any popular demand in Virginia for an agricultural and mechanical college. On the other hand, he did believe there was a greater need for one in the post-bellum period than had existed before the war. At the same time, he was firmly convinced that agricultural and mechanical education as a radically new departure for Virginia would be emasculated if made a part of an already established school with a successful tradition. He wanted such a school placed in the care of friends.

Ruffner's activities on behalf of a separate school were all the more remarkable because of his close association with Washington College (now Washington and Lee University), where his father had been president and of which he himself was a trustee. In addition to his close contact with Washington College, he had a wide circle of influential friends at the University of Virginia, where he had served for a time as chaplain; moreover, a number of his relatives and family

friends had close contact with the Virginia Military Institute. Upon his retirement from the Presbyterian ministry because of a throat ailment, this versatile
individual had assumed the operation of several farms and for a short period
of time the editorship of an agricultural journal. From time to time he had also
assisted with the family-owned salt works in Kanawha County, Virginia (now
West Virginia). These varied experiences, especially the ones derived from his
contact with the German farmers of the Valley of Virginia, thoroughly convinced
him, he wrote privately, that the working man, especially the farmer, would
totally reject any theoretical agricultural and mechanical education.

Following his appeal to the legislature for a separate agricultural school,
Ruffner contacted Superintendent Smith of VMI and proposed that the interests
of that school and Washington College be united against the University of
Virginia as the recipient of the fund in favor of a separate school. Smith, who
was vigorously promoting the interests of VMI, just as vigorously and somewhat
indignantly rejected this surprising proposal from his fellow townsman. The
Virginia Military Institute, argued Smith, from its very beginning had been
trying to supply the kind of education contemplated by the federal land-grant
act. Furthermore, the plan of organization for VMI submitted to the legislature
in 1859 and revised and resubmitted in 1865 was in perfect harmony with the
provisions of the land-grant act. Any other institution in the state, if it got the
fund, would, by nature of the act, have to institute radical changes in its system
of discipline and instruction before it could fulfill the objectives of the law.
The chances and claims of the University of Virginia for the fund, held Smith,
were slight, since it had been known from "time immemorial" that prejudices
had existed there against the type of instruction and organization that would
be necessary to carry out the provisions of the act. If anyone, concluded Smith,
could show that any college in the state could meet the demands of the act
better than VMI, then he would withdraw VMI from consideration.

It appears that the most immediate effect of Ruffner's proposal and this
exchange of opinion was a slight coolness not only between Ruffner and Smith
but also between Ruffner and certain friends of Washington College. Although
rebuffed in this instance, Ruffner kept up his agitation for a separate college
until he became an active and successful candidate for the office of state superintendent of public instruction. At this time he discontinued his activities in
connection with the disposal of the land-grant money, but following the creation
of the college had an even greater opportunity to work for the new school since
he was placed on its first Board of Visitors.

In the midst of all the developing debates over the best use of the land-grant
fund, Virginia, by the Federal Reconstruction Act of March 2, 1867, was made
Military District Number One and placed under the direct command of General
John M. Schofield. This action put a temporary end to the legislative debate
which had been warming up, an end which some of the press welcomed on the
grounds it would give the colleges that had begun to show mounting excitement
over the fund an opportunity to re-examine their conflicting claims and resolve
their conflicting views. As it turned out, the colleges did seize the opportunity
to re-examine their claims, not to resolve them, but to reinforce them when debate should be resumed.

When Virginia was readmitted to the Union on January 26, 1870, the socio-
political-economic scene had once more changed radically as a result of the events,

planned and unplanned, which had occurred during the so-called period of reconstruction. A new constitution had been adopted, providing among other measures for the creation of a public school system and for the granting of the voting franchise to the Negro. Political disputes had caused and were continuing to cause drastic crossing of party lines by individuals as political and philosophical aspirations gradually polarized into what would become the Democratic and the Republican political parties. The state debt had climbed alarmingly and had to be dealt with. Confusion, a lot of it fantastic and much of it resulting from the attempt to apply the "test-oath" to all office holders, had prevailed at all levels of civil government as individuals and parties strove for power and survival. A huge residue of this confusion remained when the state attempted to resume normal governmental functions after readmission to the Union.

Even the military personnel in charge of the occupying forces reflected the confusion of the time. General Schofield removed Pierpont as governor and replaced him with H. H. Wells. Schofield was in turn removed from command of the state forces and succeeded by General Stoneman. Stoneman removed Wells, who was immediately reinstated by higher federal authority in Washington. Stoneman was succeeded by General Canby, who at least remained in command of the district long enough to see the state restored to the Union. Faced with political defeat, Wells resigned as governor; whereupon General Canby appointed Gilbert C. Walker to succeed him. Walker had been elected to the governorship for the four-year term beginning in January, 1870, but because of Wells' resignation he had been inaugurated in September of 1869 instead of January, 1870. Instead of calming emotions, this switch from customary procedures drove a deeper wedge between the Wells faction and the Walker faction in the state.

The "test-oath" of loyalty to the Union, which barred so many ex-Confederates from holding civil office, had been particularly disruptive and corrosive throughout much of the state. In fact, because of the elasticity with which the party in power often used this oath, local government had been suspended in several sections of the state. In other instances, public offices had been filled by recent arrivals from the North and in a few cases by foreigners who had moved into the state following the end of the war. Many Virginians bitterly resented these newcomers, whom they contemptuously referred to as "carpetbaggers, invisible in war and invincible in peace." Even the make-up of the convention which prepared the new constitution required before the state could be readmitted to the Union aroused indignation. The conduct of the convention itself as it went about writing the constitution sowed seeds of bitterness and resentment which grew and flourished long after the convention adjourned and Virginia had been readmitted to the Union.

When the legislature of 1869-70 convened, so many of its members came under violent attack on the basis of the "test-oath" that concern was expressed as to whether this legislature legally could take the steps necessary to restore the state to the Union, even if all other steps had been completed. This emotionally explosive situation was met by a ruling of the United States Attorney General that members of the Virginia General Assembly might meet to facilitate the restoration of the state to the Union without taking the "test-oath" but could not enact any general legislation until after such a restoration had taken place.

When it became apparent that Virginia would be readmitted to the Union, several newspapers attempted to evaluate the implications that many of the events just enumerated carried for the future. While evaluations reflected the political bias of the editors, there was general agreement that the next few years would be politically difficult ones. *The Richmond Whig* in particular warned that the disturbed conditions would produce turmoil in the legislative sessions to follow. This prediction proved to be quite accurate, especially with respect to using the land-grant fund to establish a college of agriculture and mechanics in the state.

Before conditions had become stabilized enough to permit renewal of legislative debate on the disposition of the land-grant fund, certain other events having direct bearing on attempts to establish agricultural and mechanical colleges had developed in the state. Since these developments had such an impact not only on the legislative debates surrounding the land-grant fund but also on the Virginia Agricultural and Mechanical College for a number of years following its establishment, it seems well to outline these developments before resuming consideration of the legislative debate.

In 1869 the University of Virginia received a bequest of $100,000 from Samuel Miller, a native of Albemarle County, to be used for the establishment of a department of scientific and practical agriculture. By the time the legislature was able to resume consideration of the land-grant fund, the University by combining the proceeds of this fund with one similar in nature donated by Thomas Johnson, of Augusta County, had employed a professor of analytical and agricultural chemistry and a professor of mechanics and engineering as applied to agriculture. In addition, a farm to be operated in conjunction with the instruction in agriculture had been secured. Professor John W. Mallett had been appointed as professor of analytical and agricultural chemistry. In this capacity he had already spoken before a number of agricultural societies and had contributed a number of articles to the agricultural press. The University was now ready, it was commonly reported, to develop this new agricultural and mechanical feature in the manner contemplated by its great founder, Thomas Jefferson. To accomplish this objective, the University had prepared a memorial to the legislature requesting the land-grant money. This memorial, perhaps the most able one presented during the entire legislative debate, was both comprehensive and persuasive. It antedated much of the organizational structure of agricultural and engineering schools presently being used by many land-grant universities and at the same time embodied many of the principles which the agricultural societies had been advocating on the eve of the Civil War. Although this memorial when introduced into the legislature generated strong support, it also displayed facets which in the turbulent context of the times became elements of legislative disunity in the debates which followed.

In Lexington, Washington College, under the leadership of Robert E. Lee, had not been idle. One of the first men in the South to see the real need for a practical education, Lee in conjunction with his faculty had worked out a plan of reorganization for the College to include a school of agriculture with a farm for the demonstration of agricultural methods and for agricultural experiments. Cyrus McCormick, of reaper fame and a native of Rockbridge County, then residing in Chicago, had been approached by Lee himself on behalf of financial assistance for the proposed school of agricultural and mechanical arts. McCormick, although not donating so generously as hoped for, did contribute $10,000. At the same time, he indicated the possibility of additional contributions as the program matured. Following McCormick's response, the trustees of the College created "The McCormick Professorship of Experimental Philosophy and Practical Mechanics" and then appointed Robert S. McCulloch to the chair. Upon assumption of the position, McCulloch began a discreet but effective publicity campaign, which coupled with the proposed physical survey of the state to be conducted by the well-known Jed Hotchkiss, secured wide recognition, favorable and unfavorable. Lee died in 1870 before debate was resumed in the legislature on the land-grant fund; but when debate was resumed, his great name remained as a powerful influence on the small "Confederate clique" in the legislature.

In addition to instruction in agriculture, Washington College and neighboring VMI were planning physical surveys of the state, which were being billed by both institutions as having great potential value for the agricultural interests. Some rivalry, confusion, and misunderstanding developed not only between the two institutions but among their supporters in the state as well. It was inevitable that this confusion should become intermingled with the claims of these schools in the legislative debates to follow. One development, apparently brought about in an effort to reconcile the opposing claims, was a rather detailed plan proposing the establishment of a separate agricultural institute to be operated jointly by Washington College and the Virginia Military Institute. The plan called for a farm, a shop, a manual-labor feature, a complete and detailed agricultural and geological survey of the state, and a practical agricultural journal. The plan also presented ways of coordinating the work of the two colleges to prevent duplication but at the same time provide for joint faculty participation in operating the new institute. The proposed institute was to offer daytime instruction for youth and night classes in practical instruction to adults. In addition, all instruction was to be "open to all colors and both sexes," advanced proposals indeed, which would require nearly a century before complete achievement in Virginia.

In addition to the activities of the three larger colleges in the state, the smaller colleges also had been casting longing eyes at Morrill's bonanza. The straitened financial circumstances of these institutions following the war helped each one to discover not only a burning desire to teach agriculture or mechanics or both but also a unique fitness to do so if given the land-grant money. Not only did individual colleges discover their own unique fitness to teach these subjects, but they also discovered a multitude of reasons that other institutions were unfit to do so. Not being able to establish instruction in agriculture or mechanics with which to lure the money, these schools based their hopes on direct appeals in and through the legislature. Since these schools were scattered throughout the geographic sections of the state, it is easy to understand the divisive effect their separate petitions requesting the land-grant money had upon the legislature.

In addition to the collegiate developments concerning agricultural education, from time to time the agricultural journals of the state, slowly recuperating from the effects of the war, expressed definite opinions favoring practical agricultural schools, although they did not support any one proposal or any one school. Their major demand was that any school for the farmers and the mechanics be practical. Several editorials appeared emphasizing the necessity that the land-grant fund be used for a "digested scheme" of practical education. The editor of *The Southern Planter* frankly stated that under the circumstances he approached the subject of agricultural education with considerable trepidation. His honest confession seemed to be good for his editorial soul, for he immediately launched a vigorous attack on the idea that practical benefits resulting from agricultural instruction would materialize at the University of Virginia and at the Virginia Military Institute. Proceeding, he urged that steps be taken to set up a separate practical school combining manual labor with intellectual effort.

When Virginia's legislature resumed consideration of the land-grant fund, as it did shortly after being readmitted to the Union in late January, 1870, all these confusing, contradictory, and perplexing factors had to be dealt with in one way or another. On March 8, 1870, Governor Walker once more called attention to the fund and suggested dividing the money between two colleges, one of which would be a college or high school for the Negroes, since no institution for them comparable to the colleges for the whites existed in the state at the time. When Walker submitted his recommendation to the legislature, he seemed to be unaware of the developments in the state concerning the fund. Walker himself had come to Virginia as a result of the war and was looked upon by some as a "carpet-bag governor." He made no specific proposals for the actual disposition of the fund beyond this rather strong suggestion on behalf of the Negroes. He did observe in a rather casual manner that the University of Virginia had presented a very able memorial seeking the fund and that similar applications might be made by other colleges in the state. This time not only the "other colleges" but other agencies as well were ready to help the state dispose of "Morrill's Manna." As a result, petitions, claims, and proposals for utilization of the fund poured into the legislature in bewildering confusion.

Altogether, some twenty-four schools and colleges presented claims for a part or all of the fund. At the same time, while these schools were arguing their special advantages for teaching agriculture and mechanics, an increasing number of petitions from boards of trade, mechanical associations, agricultural societies, and interested groups of citizens began to pour in, urging that the money be used to create a separate school especially designed to teach the subjects proposed in the federal act.

As the flood of petitions and proposals continued, the legislature itself became confused, not only as to the disposition of the fund but as to the best disposition of the many proposals as well. This confusion seemed to encourage the advocates of the many different schemes for disposing of the fund and caused them to increase their pressure on the legislature. In the face of all this pressure, this body became divided and hesitated to act for fear of offending some segment of the population or section of the state. As a result, after authorizing the auditor of public accounts to secure the land scrip for Virginia, the legislature adjourned without appropriating the fund to any institution at all.

The legislative session of 1870-71 was scarcely under way before debate on the fund was resumed. A resolution was introduced proposing that the memorial presented requesting the fund for the University of Virginia be withdrawn from the file for consideration by the House of Delegates. This resolution was immediately followed by one requesting that all the memorials and petitions on file be withdrawn for consideration. Hardly had this action, which in effect activated all the petitions and memorials of the 1869-70 session, been completed when a bill was introduced proposing that two-thirds of the fund be given to the University of Virginia and the Virginia Military Institute, with the remaining one-third going to the Hampton Institute for the colored. This bill failed to pass. This failure was immediately seized upon by advocates of other plans as a good omen for their own special plans with the result that additional pressure and petitions poured in upon the legislature. To deal with the situation, this time the legislature set up a joint committee of the House and the Senate and invited patrons to appear before it to speak on behalf of their special proposals. This invitation was eagerly accepted by the colleges and schools of the state, with each college selecting its best orator to present its claim. This group of eloquent speakers, in a day when oratory was much admired in the state, soon attracted so much attention that night sessions were resorted to in an effort to accommodate the crowds. The hearings, which one writer delightedly described as far more entertaining than opera, produced an amazing parade of claims for the fund by the different institutions of the state. The parade of arguments against sister institutions as the recipients of the fund was no less amazing and no less entertaining to the audience.

Never before or since has the cause of agricultural and mechanical education received such rapt, prolonged, and impassioned attention in Virginia as it received during these sessions. Apparently the only effect of the hearings was to harden legislative lines previously formed. The press quickly joined the discussion, at first in almost complete support of the University of Virginia. As the advocates for a separate school became more and more articulate, however, this medium began a slow swing toward the same solution of the problem. When it became apparent that the legislature was either not inclined to move toward any solution or was unable to do so, the press became quite critical of both the legislature and the colleges. *The Richmond Dispatch* on one occasion headlined the debate as the "War of the Colleges" while the *Whig* charged that "the House is sadly deficient in steadiness and consistency. Its course on the Land Scrip bill has been so fluctuating, inconstant, and contradictory as to seem to indicate a total absence of conviction." Then as the hearings and debates dragged on and on, the *Whig* complained that jealousy of the competing institutions was not only hindering action on the land-grant bill but also exhausting the patience of the public, although the patience of the competing institutions was not at all affected.

Throughout the legislative session of 1870-71 and most of the one of 1871-72, proposal after proposal for disposing of the land-grant fund followed one another in bewildering succession. By some parliamentary maneuvering and vote switching, it was claimed that a proposal would be passed one day only to be reconsidered and defeated the next. The reverse fate awaited other proposals, which would be defeated on one occasion only to be reintroduced the next day for further consideration.

The discussions tended to become heated and at times acrimonious. Old sectional jealousies, which played such havoc with ante-bellum efforts at internal improvements, were aroused to full pitch. Sectarianism which was both affirmed and denied was projected into the discussions. Hampden-Sydney College was depicted as championing the Presbyterians, Richmond College (now the University of Richmond) the Baptists, Emory and Henry and Randolph-Macon (at Ashland) the Methodists, and Roanoke College the Lutherans. Even the Virginia Military Institute was accused of favoring the Episcopalians! The University of Virginia, on the other hand, was denounced as unfit because it was not affiliated with any religious denomination. Therefore, being a godless institution, it was unfit to teach the farmers and mechanics.

In the heat of the discussions, other charges and claims equally unrelated to agricultural and mechanical education were generated and aired. The advocates for the southside section of the state claimed the fund for Hampden-Sydney College on the grounds that the southside agriculture had suffered more as a result of the war than that of any other section in the state. Besides, argued one southside citizen with a long memory, in the legislative debates of 1816-19 the supporters of the bill to establish the University of Virginia had promised financial assistance to the southside in return for the southside's support of the University. The southside had extended such support; the University had been created; but the promised financial aid and support had never been forthcoming. It was now time, the writer argued, for the supporters of the University to keep this long-broken pledge by supporting Hampden-Sydney and abandoning their selfish claims to the land-grant fund. If they did not do so, he threatened, the southside would swear eternal hatred of the University and fight their appeals for financial help forever. There is no evidence that this threatening appeal changed any votes in the legislature.

Emory and Henry College claimed that giving her the fund would go a long way toward rectifying the long-standing practice of state discrimination against the great southwest. Richmond College advocates argued that this school located in Richmond, the largest manufacturing center in the state, could do more than any other institution for the "soot besmeared mechanic" if given the fund. Randolph-Macon supporters largely contented themselves with claiming that their school already was serving segments of the public intended to be reached by the federal land-grant act and therefore deserved the fund.

On the negative side, different proponents attacked each other's claims. Especially long, bitter attacks were leveled against the University of Virginia and the Virginia Military Institute as long as these institutions appeared to be in the forefront of the race for the fund. The University especially was held up as too aristocratic, too expensive, and too theoretical to help the great masses intended to be benefited by the act. The ante-bellum conduct of the University in rejecting the proposal for a professorship of agriculture advanced by the State Agricultural Society was recalled and given prominence not calculated to win friends to the University's cause. It was rumored abroad and whispered in the cloak rooms that the faculty of this school was still divided over whether it wanted or would accept the land scrip money even if offered to them. The supporters of the University strongly denied this claim and made an even greater effort to secure the fund.

The Virginia Military Institute, on the other hand, suffered from lack of support bordering on actual hostility from one faction in the legislature. In fact, in the recently adjourned constitutional convention, one representative of this faction had ventured to propose that a committee be appointed to "inquire into the expediency of obliterating the Virginia Military Institute."

As far as Washington College (now Washington and Lee University) was concerned, although its memorial to the legislature prepared under the direction of Robert E. Lee before his death showed broad understanding of the nature of the educational program envisioned by the act, no concerted effort beyond oratory was made for the fund after Lee's death. Even the strongest supporters of this school seemed to realize the futility at the time of seeking to share in a federal grant by a school recently headed by the Commander-in-Chief of the Confederate armies. An even greater barrier, perhaps, was recognized in the fact that the College was changing its name to Washington and Lee, while the movement in the legislature itself to authorize the hanging of Lee's portrait in the capitol was drawing bitter attack from some members of the legislature.

As the partisan supporters for the different schools and colleges continued to devote their energy to debate, parliamentary maneuvering, attacks on each other, diversionary and even stalling tactics, the advocates of a separate college became more and more articulate and insistent. The gradual evolution and growth of this claim can be traced through the maze of conflicting claims as it gradually picked up supporters. Ironically, some of the strongest points advanced by the supporters of the already established colleges were often lifted from context and presented as strong arguments for a separate college. Thus were B. Johnson Barbour's ideas lifted from his more than able presentation of the claims of the University of Virginia for "concentration, concentration, concentration" of the fund in one school as being absolutely necessary if Virginia was to realize maximum benefit from the fund and at the same time "avoid many beginnings but no endings." The advocates of the separate school immediately rejected the University as the recipient of the fund but accepted Barbour's "concentration" argument and used it with telling effect in arguing to concentrate the fund in a new school. The supporters of VMI, particularly Francis H. Smith, depreciated concentrating the fund at the University but dwelt at length on the necessity of setting up a proper organizational structure specifically designed to teach agriculture, mechanics, and the applied sciences. The advocates of a separate school then accepted Smith's arguments for a school specifically designed to teach agriculture and mechanics but went a step further and argued that such an organization could be obtained most successfully in a separate school especially created for the purpose. Colonel William Allen, speaking on behalf of Washington College, made yet another approach. By presenting a lengthy review of the disposition of the land-grant fund which other states had followed, he sought to prove the soundness of donating all or a portion of the fund to a private school, in this case Washington College. Following his able presentation, which heartened the supporters of the private schools, some of the advocates of a separate school began to think in terms of finding a private school which could be completely made over into an agricultural and mechanical college. With these three ideas being tossed back and forth, it was but a question of time until they would crystallize into the idea of concentrating the fund at a private institution willing to undergo complete reorganization into an agricultural and mechanical college.

In spite of, or perhaps because of, the conflicting claims for the money faced by the legislature, the session of 1870-71 came to a close without arriving at a disposition of the fund. At the same time, the debates had rather sharply polarized around two basic questions:

1. Should the fund be donated to a presently existing college or colleges?
2. Should it be used to establish a separate school specifically organized to promote agricultural and mechanical education?

As the session ended, the press felt this latter solution was gaining support.

The "War of the Colleges," as *The Richmond Dispatch* called the struggle for the land-grant money, was quickly resumed in the legislative session of 1871-72. This legislature, particularly on the House side, had a number of new members, many of whom were as inexperienced in legislative affairs as had been the members they succeeded. Some of these newcomers had made the disposition

of the land-grant fund an issue in their campaigns for election; therefore, they
came to the legislature with commitments already made or convictions already
reached. As a result, a new element of rigidity was added to the already confused
debates in a legislature woefully divided on the question. One additional development which tended to prolong or even disrupt the process of legislative decision
making must be kept in mind when considering the legislative action of 1871-72.
As a result of the turbulent postwar conditions and the changed voting privileges, not only had there been an increased rate of turnover in the legislature but
there also had been a decided increase in the diversity of backgrounds represented by the members. As one result, the legislature of 1872 included in its make-
up representatives from practically every spectrum of the social, political, economic, and racial life of the state. In this respect it truly was "the people's legislature"; but like other bodies of a similar nature, it experienced considerable
difficulty in speaking with one voice. It tended to use up vast amounts of energy
in debate and argument as it sought to bring its sometimes "vaulting visions" into
accord and translate them into coherent legislative proposals for action. Nowhere
is this tendency better illustrated than in the land-grant debates of the session.

Immediately upon the convening of the legislature in December, 1871, Governor Walker reminded it that the previous legislature, instead of selling the
land scrip and investing the money, had spent all of its time arguing over what to
do with it. As a result, Walker said, the state was losing about $25,000 a year in
interest. He urged the legislature to take the steps necessary to convert the scrip
into interest-bearing bonds and then, and only then, resume debate on the question of donating the fund to a school or schools. At the same time, he rather
forcefully renewed his suggestion that a portion of the fund be used to establish
a school for the Negroes. Beyond these two suggestions Walker made no further
effort to guide the legislature in the disposition of the fund.

By this time many members of the legislature were so thoroughly aroused and
apparently suspicious of each other's motives that some difficulty was experienced
even in reaching an agreement on the simple matter of selling the scrip and investing the proceeds. Eventually, however, a bill was passed on February 7, 1872,
which authorized the State Board of Education to sell the scrip and invest the
proceeds in "safe bonds or stocks not bearing less than five per cent interest."

When consideration of the disposition of the land-grant fund was resumed,
as it was almost immediately following the convening of the legislature, it was
evident that no immediate solution was in sight. As the debate developed, both
in the Senate and in the House, the trend of the debates to polarize around the
idea of donating the money to an existing college or colleges versus the idea of
using the fund to create a separate school accelerated rapidly. Along with this
accelerated polarization, however, the idea of a separate school became more and
more identified with the demands and needs of the industrial class. While the representatives of the established schools strongly objected to this identification, it
nonetheless became such a strong factor that many came to agree with W. H.
Ruffner's claim that the debates represented "the claims of the people as against
the claims of the colleges."

Perhaps the staunchest and most effective advocate of the idea of a separate
school throughout the entire debate was William T. Sutherlin, whose earlier
efforts have been mentioned. He never wavered from his earlier conviction that a
separate school could and would best meet the needs of the great mass of people

for a practical education. Considering the turbulent postwar passions of the time, Sutherlin was in the unique position of having the confidence and respect of most political factions in the legislature and the state. His activities during the war, particularly his relations with the ex-president of the Confederacy, Jefferson Davis, following the fall of Richmond, endeared him to the Confederate element inclined to nostalgic reminiscences of the past; his membership on the famous "Committee of Nine," which worked so hard to get Virginia to accept the facts of war and proceed with the steps necessary for restoration to the Union, tended to identify him with the progressive elements of all factions; while his outspoken espousal of the cause of public education suitable for the working classes made him welcome to this group. Early in the legislative session of 1870-71, speaking on behalf of the State Agricultural Society, he had strongly advocated the establishment of a new college which in his words should be "purely agricultural and mechanical and which should be a nucleus around which the accretions of time would gather a really great institution."

In the fall of 1871, Sutherlin was elected to the Virginia House of Delegates, where he immediately began to support the idea of a separate college. On January 24, 1872, he delivered a long, well-planned, and forceful speech which reviewed the entire problem as he saw it. Pointing out that the federal act was designed to achieve the specific objective of an agricultural and mechanical education, he proceeded to relate this type of education to the development of the agricultural and industrial needs peculiar to Virginia. He then asked bluntly if either the University of Virginia or the Virginia Military Institute could achieve the objectives of the act as related to Virginia without a radical reorganization of their present structure or without an even more radical departure from the high mission they presently were fulfilling so well. He thought not. Neither did he think those two schools should reorganize just to get the fund. At this point, Sutherlin reintroduced with telling effect many of the old ante-bellum attacks on the idea of immediate value of a theoretical education for the farmers and mechanics. While he praised the value of the "theoretical and elegant farming and mechanics" which the University of Virginia and the Virginia Military Institute would develop if given the fund, he argued that this was not the kind of education needed now. Sutherlin's viewpoint was presented as follows in the *Richmond Whig:* "The professors of the university were able men, and knew a great deal about the earth and everything on it, under it, and around it, but he doubted if any of them knew how to harness a horse, and he would make a trip any day to see one of them attempt to plow." The prevailing type of education in Virginia colleges, Sutherlin claimed, educated youth away from the farm and created prejudice against manual labor and the common pursuits of industry whether in the shop or field. He was no opponent of this type of school, he insisted, but it could not and would not meet the needs required and desired by the federal act. At this point, Sutherlin then reminded the legislators that even then the national Congress was investigating several states to see if they had violated the terms of the land-grant act. Virginia, he warned, risked forfeiture of the entire fund if it failed to comply with the federal requirements. What Virginia needed, he urged, was an independent school where practice would be united with theory and where instruction in agriculture and mechanics would be the chief feature. Only such a school, he felt, could meet the new age dawning in Virginia. Turning to the situation in the legislature he deplored the injection into the debate of sectional factional politics rather than the interests of education. Without mentioning names, Sutherlin nonetheless implied that too many legislators were following the path of one member whom he had heard admit saying he did not care anything about the disposition of the land-grant proceeds just so his constituents got a portion of it.

Sutherlin's speech made a significant impression both in the legislature and in the press. Probably because of it, a number of additional petitions from agricultural societies, mechanics associations, merchants, and other spokesmen for the industrial interests urging a separate college or one specifically charged to teach agriculture and mechanics poured into the legislature. The idea of a separate school began to pick up supporters. The Republicans in a legislative caucus agreed not to support the claims of the University of Virginia or of the Virginia Military Institute. No positive program was advocated by this group; but at the time it was generally conceded that the Republicans in the legislature would support an independent school located in any county or city offering the greatest aid to it. Additional newspapers in the state began to swing toward the idea of a separate school as a desirable disposition of the fund. More than one paper echoed the fear expressed by one member of the legislature that the fund would be insufficient to develop a good independent college which could be more than "a miserable, sickly, bantling of an agricultural college, which would, after dragging out a short existence, finally perish." As one remedy for this feared insufficiency of funds, a number of newspapers and speakers, including Sutherlin, openly urged communities to bid for the location of the college. The *Richmond Whig*, which consistently had favored a separate school, sided fully with Sutherlin's position, but warned that unless his proposal was reduced to a more tangible plan, it too would fail. Coincidentally, just such a plan was slowly but surely developing in the Senate, largely because of the activities of Senator John E. Penn of Patrick County.

John E. Penn, a successful and popular attorney, had an extensive law practice not only in his native Patrick County but also in Montgomery County as well, where he was connected by marriage with a prominent family. Descended from a Revolutionary War patriot, graduated from Randolph-Macon College while it was located at Mecklenburg, and further educated at the University of Virginia, he had served with distinction as colonel and for a short time as brigadier general in the Confederate forces. As a result of a serious wound received in battle he had lost a leg, a loss which by no means became a liability to his professional career in postwar Virginia. Described as rather quiet by nature, he nonetheless had the fortunate personality which seemed to draw to him people from all walks of life. An eloquent and persuasive speaker, he had been elected to the state Senate in 1867, where he served for two successive terms, thereby being in that body for most of the period covering the debates over the land-grant fund.

Penn felt that the fund should be used to establish an independent agricultural college rather than be given to an already established school, "the university for instance, and [thereby] make the agricultural and mechanical features subordinate." When the bill was introduced into the Senate proposing to donate one-third of the land-grant proceeds to Hampton Industrial and Normal Institute and two-thirds to the University of Virginia and the Virginia Military Institute, Penn had introduced a substitute to this bill. His substitute proposed donating one-third of the fund to Hampton Industrial and Normal Institute and two-thirds to a new school or to a school which would agree to give up its previous name and organization and become the Virginia Agricultural and Mechanical College. A blank space had been left in his proposal which had only to be filled in with the name of a college to complete it. Writing a year later, W. H. Ruffner claimed that Penn intended all along to try to get the name of the Preston and Olin Institute inserted into the blank space as the recipient of the fund. Whether this actually was Penn's intent at the time he first introduced his proposal is not entirely clear; if not, it quickly became his intent upon receiving a petition from the trustees of the Preston and Olin Institute requesting his support in seeking the fund for their institution. It will be recalled that this school, while experiencing an increasing enrollment and a widening geographic support, was experiencing severe financial difficulties. In late 1871, motivated by this financial pinch rather than by any particular commitment to the cause of mechanical and argicultural education, the trustees of this school, apparently at the suggestion of P. H. Whisner and Rector Harvey Black, had addressed petitions to Penn in the Senate and R. A. Miller in the House, requesting their support in securing the fund for their school. In addition to these petitions, the Preston and Olin cause received strong support from other prominent residents of Montgomery County, notably Judge Waller Staples of the Virginia Supreme Court, Attorney Charles A. Ronald, former member of the legislature and known in legal circles as "the Patrick Henry of Southwest Virginia," and members of the influential Preston family.

The receipt of the Preston and Olin Institute petition surprised both Penn and Miller. The latter had just received and presented to the proper committee of the House, a petition from "residents of Montgomery County" endorsing the claims of Hampden-Sydney College for the fund. Circumstances surrounding this petition are vague. Apparently it had been secured by Charles Martin, a former professor at Hampden-Sydney College who had moved to Christiansburg to teach in the Christiansburg Female Institute. The residents of Christiansburg not knowing that Black and Whisner were planning to press the claims of the Preston and Olin Institute for the fund had endorsed the claims of Hampden-Sydney College. Penn immediately notified Black of this conflicting position and the energetic Black seemingly went at once to Christiansburg and apprised the group there of his efforts on behalf of the Preston and Olin Institute. Unfortunately, the records for the Christiansburg group end here; but apparently this group, if it did not swing to Black's support, at least did not oppose him. With the matter of the conflicting petitions apparently settled to his satisfaction Penn, in a letter to Black dated January 6, 1871, agreed to support the Preston and Olin claim. A short time later in another letter to Black, dated February 14, Penn sent Black a copy of the proposal he had introduced into the Senate.

In his letter to Black, Penn set forth his belief that the money to be derived from the fund would be ample to support the proposed institution. At the same time, he reminded Black that the federal act prohibited the use of any of the money for erecting buildings. Penn felt this restriction explained the necessity of finding a college that would abandon its present organization and substitute the features of the Penn bill. Continuing, Penn had added the following significant comments and suggestions:

> In reference to your college, I fear the buildings would not be large enough, but would it not be a good investment for your *county* to erect additional build-

ings? The school would be on a permanent footing, and from its very character every county in the state would be interested. It would have a state reputation at the very outset and a large number of young men who did not desire a strictly *classical* education would attend it and in a few years . . . the money they would bring into your county would soon repay for the taxation expended in buildings. Show this to the President of your college and others interested and let me hear from you. I will not here enlarge on the plan. Enough has been said to indicate its features.

Of course, I cannot assure you that it can be carried in the legislature but there are many reasons why your county would be a desirable location and the fund is worth the effort.

Details concerning the immediate effect of Penn's letter or the roles played by individuals in Montgomery County upon its receipt are not available. The results are well-established, however. A promise, apparently oral, was made by the trustees of the Preston and Olin Institute to permit the reorganization of the school into an agricultural and mechanical college in return for the land-grant money; furthermore, a pledge of $20,000 to the new school, should it become a reality, was made by someone speaking for the people of Montgomery County.

With these assurances of support, Penn resumed his efforts in the Senate on behalf of his proposed substitute. His strategy at the time was to get his amendment, with the name of the college left blank, passed, and then with the legislature committed to the idea of a separate school or one willing to undergo radical reorganization, seek to get the name Preston and Olin Institute inserted into the blank. During the waning days of the session of 1870-71, the portion of Penn's amendment proposing that the land-grant fund be donated to a separate school or to one willing to be reorganized into an agricultural and mechanical college passed the Senate, but the legislature adjourned before the House could act on it. When Penn renewed the struggle for his amendment in the session of 1871-72, a practically new team, as indicated, had appeared.

Among the newcomers in the House of Delegates convening in the fall of 1871 was General Gabriel C. Wharton from Montgomery County, who succeeded Miller. Following the close of the war, Wharton, a graduate of VMI, had become closely identified with the interests seeking to promote the industrial development of the state, particularly of the southwestern part. In this capacity, he had developed a wide acquaintanceship with prominent industrial leaders throughout Virginia. After his election to the House, he immediately joined forces with Penn in the Senate on behalf of the Preston and Olin Institute. Wharton seems to have been one of the first individuals to point out that success of Penn's bill in the Senate and one quite similar to it which he, Wharton, had introduced in the House would actually meet all the demands for a separate, independent college. The advocates of a separate school, even Sutherlin, seemed quite reluctant to accept this point of view; but as the debates developed, more and more of this group swung to this position. This swing, when added to all the other factors involved in the debate, greatly alarmed the supporters of the established colleges and caused them to intensify greatly their efforts on behalf of their particular schools. As a result, the debate became deadlocked in both the House and the Senate as first one proposal and then another would be introduced, accepted, and then reconsidered and rejected. The newspapers which had followed the debates all along became quite critical of both the way the question was being handled and the conduct of certain factions within the legislature. In an editorial the

Richmond Whig complained: "The public are tired of the eternal talk expended upon it [the land-grant], and the dilly-dallying, and shilly-shallying which have so long been exhibited. They want action. It may suit the colleges but it does not suit the people to keep this subject bandied about between pillar and post for weeks, months, years. There is something almost scandalous in the rapacity which has been displayed. All the colleges cannot get it and those whose prospects are hopeless should abandon the field at once. The dog-in-the-manger policy is not to be commended."

Undaunted by this criticism, the legislature continued to set up a proposal, pass it, and then by voting to reconsider the vote by which it had been passed, knock it down; action which in the eyes of the *Whig,* at least, "looked like sheer nonsense and child's play . . . incomprehensible caprices of the House." At one stage in the debate the House became so excited and confused over its own parliamentary maneuvering that the speaker had to leave the chair and take the floor to explain that failure to accept an "amendment as amended"would put a permanent end in the House to all considerations of the land-grant fund for the remainder of the session. Needless to say, the amendment as amended was then accepted, although one member proposed killing the bill and telling Congress that Virginia did not want the money, since it was causing more trouble than it was worth. Another member with a greater sense of humor, after watching the legislature spend ten days debating one combination only to drop it, declared that the expense of keeping the legislature in session to settle the problem would dispose not only of Virginia's share of the scrip but that of some sister states as well. As the deadlock continued, emotions, particularly in the House, began to rise higher and higher, and elements in no way related to agriculture and mechanics slipped into debates. Commenting on this development, the *Whig* declared:

> We scarcely know how to comment upon the proceedings on the subject of the Land Scrip. It took nearly the whole of the session [of one day] to reach a vote upon Mr. Wharton's substitute and when reached proved to be a very decisive one against that substitute. It [Wharton's substitute] passed Tuesday by a vote of ayes 60, noes 52, and was rejected yesterday by a vote of ayes 44, noes 71. This doing and then undoing, this raising up only to pull down has characterized the whole action of the House on the Land Scrip bill.
>
> Acrimonious elements were introduced into the proceedings which had a very unpleasant effect. They acted as an irritant to race antagonisms and party passions. The House was left in a perturbed and unamiable condition . . . whether indeed any schemes can now pass are questions we shall not undertake to pass upon.

The *Whig* was of the opinion that much of the changed voting which constantly prolonged the debate in the house was caused by "certain influence" upon the Negro members which led this group to believe that by switching support they stood a better chance of getting, instead of one-third of the fund, the five-twelfths they were demanding for their school. It was further implied that it was the supporters of the University who were exercising this influence. This charge was vigorously denied by the leading supporters of the University, although some of them supported the five-twelfths claim for the Negroes.

In the Senate the debate although spirited and vigorous was never so turbulent as it was in the House. Finally, as the session drew toward a close in March, 1872, the Senate, in what appears to have been a determined effort to solve the land-grant problem, agreed to consider the problem once more. To permit some freedom of action, the Senate resolved itself into a committee of the whole. In committee it was decided to divide the fund, one-third to the Negroes and two-thirds to the whites. Following this action, each member was asked to submit his perference of the school or schools to receive the fund. When this list had been submitted, it was found that nine combinations of schools had been submitted, with Hampton Institute appearing on each combination. A system of competitive voting was agreed upon whereby the combination receiving the smallest number of votes would be dropped until one combination received a majority.

At this point word spread through the capitol as to what was happening in the Senate, and the galleries rapidly filled to overflowing as members from the House and interested spectators gathered to see if the disposition of the land-grant fund so long debated was about to be solved in at least one branch of the legislature. The combination of schools as arranged to be voted upon by the committee as a whole included:

1. Preston and Olin Institute and Hampton Normal Institute
2. Randolph-Macon, Richmond College, and Hampton Normal Institute
3. University of Virginia, Virginia Military Institute, and Hampton Normal Institute
4. Independent school at Fredericksburg and Hampton Normal Institute
5. Richmond College, Hampden-Sydney College, Roanoke College, and Hampton Normal Institute
6. Emory and Henry College and Hampton Normal Institute
7. New Market Polytechnic Institute and Hampton Normal Institute
8. New Market Polytechnic Institute, Richmond, Hampden-Sydney, Randolph-Macon, Emory and Henry, and Hampton Normal Institute
9. University of Virginia and Hampton Normal Institute

In the voting which followed the presentation of these combinations, the combination of Preston and Olin Institute and Hampton Normal Institute led in all the voting, receiving an overwhelming majority on the third ballot. With this voting accomplished, the committee of the whole then rose and resolved itself back into the Senate, which on March 13, 1872, voted to donate one-third of the land-grant money to Hampton Industrial Institute for the Negroes and two-thirds to the Preston and Olin Institute for the whites. Since the proposal as passed at this time embodied the additional features of Penn's amendment, which required the school for whites receiving the money to give up its previous organization and become the Virginia Agricultural and Mechanical College, Penn is usually given a lion's share of the credit for getting a separate college located at Blacksburg.

The proponents of a separate school were delighted with this victory in the Senate but realized the fight had yet to be won in the House. It is doubtful if anyone at the time realized just what a "fight" the struggle was to turn into in that body. Time for adjournment of the legislature was rapidly approaching. If the Senate bill was to pass the House, immediate consideration was necessary. Mr. Walker of Pulaski County, a supporter of Preston and Olin, therefore determined to introduce the Senate bill into the House the next day. In the meantime the House had sent a resolution to the Senate, asking its concurrence in a proposal to extend the legislative session beyond its regular adjournment date. The Senate in a blunt message back to the House rejected (although it later accepted) the proposal in language which members of the House interpreted as insulting and casting strong aspersions on their legislative ability. This message, which was received in the House on March 14, the very day Walker planned to introduce the Senate bill appropriating the money to Preston and Olin Institute, threw the entire House into a furious uproar. A temporary speaker was presiding at the time and apparently added to the confusion by his attempts to restore order. The actual sequence of events is not clear now, since the several newspapers reporting the session did not agree at the time. The *Richmond Whig* reported that the House was completely demoralized by the Senate message and "could not for a long time get into harness." All the papers agreed that the Senate's message had created a stormy outburst in the House. Finally, just as the House was slowly settling down, Walker presented the Senate bill appropriating the land-grant money to Preston and Olin Institute and the Hampton Industrial Institute. It was an unfortunate moment for Walker and an almost fatal one for the bill. Turmoil even more tumultuous erupted at once. Several delegates tried to get the bill rejected outright, not because of its merits or demerits, but because it was a Senate bill. The supporters of the remaining colleges and schools saw the prize slipping from their grasp and immediately resorted to the parliamentary tactics and combination of forces with which they had blocked final action thus far. The majority of the nineteen Negroes in the House were unhappy because the bill donated only one-third of the income to Hampton Institute. They were quite satisfied with the choice of Hampton, but they wanted five-twelfths of the fund instead of the offered one-third. Delegate P. J. Carter from Norfolk made an impassioned plea that the House reopen the question of proper distribution of the fund to the Negroes and the whites before acting on the Senate bill. No doubt aided by the fact that both the Democrats and the Republicans at the time were wooing the Negro vote, his plea was heeded, and this aspect of the question was taken up for further consideration.

According to most of the press of the day, the Negro delegation in the House had some very able orators in its group. These speakers, throwing syntax, parliamentary procedure, and protocol to the wind, were quite able to get their point of view before members of the House. As the debate proceeded, the Negro members, according to one report, became excited. The excitement and perhaps anger spread as motions were made and everyone tried to speak at once. The *Whig* reported that "great disorder prevailed, various motions were made and voted down or pronounced out of order." Charges of insincerity and intimation of political dishonesty began to boil to the surface. As the excitement grew, Mr. Deneale of Rockingham County and Mr. Riddleberger of Shenandoah County got into a heated argument during which Deneale, the older man, was accused of calling Riddleberger a "scoundrel and a puppy." The speaker, fearing a fight on the floor or a duel outside, ordered the sergeant-at-arms to arrest both men. For a few minutes following the arrest, it appeared that the members of the House would divide immediately in support of one or the other of the two men. Cooler heads prevailed, and the House after some debate supported the sergeant-at-arms. A small element of humor was injected into the proceedings at this point, when the sergeant-at-arms through the speaker plaintively reminded the House that he had acted under orders in arresting the two gentlemen and now awaited further instructions as to what to do with them. This posed another threatening problem, which was quickly solved by use of the procedure legislative bodies usually resort to in such cases: the appointment of a committee to decide on appropriate action. This committee subsequently recommended a conciliatory line of action which was immediately accepted and the matter was dropped, to the apparent relief of all concerned.

In the meantime, the House, having appointed the committee to deal with the arrested members, resumed consideration of the two-thirds versus the five-twelfths issue. The experiences of the morning, climaxed by the Deneale-Riddleberger altercation, seemed to have had a decidedly sobering influence on most of the members, both experienced and inexperienced in legislative affairs. Anyway, the ensuing debate, according to press reports, was much more restrained and dignified, although spirited. The decision to divide the fund on the basis of one-third to the Negroes and two-thirds to the whites was upheld; whereupon debate upon the Senate proposal donating the fund to the Preston and Olin Institute was resumed. Immediately the old familiar proposals to amend the bill by substituting names of favored schools in place of the one included in the bill, in this instance the Preston and Olin Institute, were forthcoming. It appeared that the House would go through the same old dreary process once more of considering all schools but agreeing on none as the recipient of the fund. At this point, Mr. Taliaferro of Orange County, got the floor and in a graceful speech observed that the friends of Hampden-Sydney College had made a fair, earnest, and gallant effort to get the fund for that school but had been beaten fairly in open debate. Since the friends of Hampden-Sydney did not wish to make a "factious fight," they were withdrawing Hampden-Sydney from consideration for the fund. Taliaferro was immediately followed by Mr. Poage of Rockbridge County, who not only withdrew Virginia Military Institute from consideration but at the same time announced his support of the Preston and Olin Institute. At this point Mr. Hill of Albemarle County, credited by some with being the leading architect of several proposals which had kept alive the hopes of the University of Virginia by preventing the donation of the fund to any of the smaller institutions, withdrew the University from consideration and simultaneously announced his support of the Preston and Olin Institute. From this point the action was something of an anticlimax. Upon the motion of Mr. Fitzgerald of Roanoke County the names of all institutions other than the Preston and Olin Institute and Hampton Industrial Institute were dropped from consideration, and the bill as passed in the Senate the day before was put to a vote and passed by a margin of 86 to 19. This bill provided that one-third of the land-grant fund be donated to the Hampton Normal and Industrial Institute and two-thirds to the Preston and Olin Institute, if the latter institute relinquished its charter, donated its property to the state, and was reorganized as the Virginia Agricultural and Mechanical College. Governor Walker signed the bill on March 19, 1872, making the bill official at last.[1]

Thus, the Virginia Agricultural and Mechanical College was born.

[1] Hampton Normal and Industrial Institute, founded as a private school in 1868, continued to derive a portion of its support from the land-grant fund until 1920. On this date the Virginia Normal and Industrial Institute, founded at Petersburg by the state in 1883 as the Virginia Normal and Collegiate Institute, was designated as the Virginia land-grant college for Negro youth and started receiving support from the land-grant fund. In 1946, by legislative action, the name of the institution was changed to Virginia State College. In effect, then, Virginia has supported two land-grant institutions for the past century.

Chapter 2

Launching the College

1872

A FTER THE LONG STRUGGLE in the legislature resulted in the legal creation of the Virginia Agricultural and Mechanical College and its location at Blacksburg, the governor proceeded to select the members of a board of visitors for the new institution. The choice of board members was of tremendous importance because of the great power and responsibilities invested in the board by the act creating the College. Included in these responsibilities were the appointment of a president and faculty, the setting up of a curriculum, the handling of all matters of student life and discipline, the determination of salaries to be paid, and the responsibility for all College property. Obviously, the early decisions the board would be forced to make would have a great effect on the College for years to come.

Governor Walker, who had carefully kept out of the legislative wrangle concerning the location of the College, evidently had been giving the matter of board membership considerable attention. Immediately after signing the bill creating the institution, he named the following persons to serve on the board: Joseph R. Anderson, one of the owner-operators of the well-known Tredgar Iron Works of Richmond; Robert Beverly, of Fauquier County, a nationally recognized leader in agricultural organizations; Harvey Black, M.D., of Mont-

gomery County, whose efforts in securing the location of the College at Blacksburg have been noted; Joseph Cloyd, of Pulaski County, a prominent farmer
and leader in the Southwest Virginia Agricultural Society; John T. Cowan, of
Montgomery County, a prominent farmer and vice-president in the Virginia
State Agricultural Society; D. C. DeJarnette, of Caroline County, an active member of the Virginia State Agricultural Society; John Goode, a native of Bedford
County, who had moved to Norfolk City, where he was practicing law and
serving in the state legislature; William A. Stuart, of Smyth and Wythe Counties,
a farmer, business man, and operator of the salt works at Saltville; and William
T. Sutherlin, of Danville, whose activities on behalf of the College have been
noted. In addition to the individuals appointed by the governor, the president
of the Virginia State Agricultural Society and the members of the State Board
of Education were to serve as ex-officio members. This latter provision brought
onto the board William H. Ruffner, of Lexington, state superintendent of public
instruction; James C. Taylor, of Christiansburg, attorney general of the state;
Gilbert C. Walker, governor of the state, who had recently moved into Virginia;
and Lewis E. Harvie, of Amelia County, president of the Virginia State Agricultural Society. Harvie completed his term as president of the agricultural society
in December, 1872, and was succeeded by General W. H. F. Lee, who immediately
entered upon his duties as a member of the board. In an effort to secure wider
geographic representation and at the same time secure some continuity of experience, early in 1873 the legislature provided staggered terms of office for board
members. As one result of this provision, Cowan and Cloyd were succeeded on
January 1, 1873, by John E. Penn, of Patrick County, whose activities as state
senator on behalf of the College have been noted; and by E. M. Tidball, of
Frederick County, who had worked vigorously for a separate college of agricul-
ure and mechanic arts while a member of the legislature.

All men appointed by Walker to the first board were prominent in the affairs
of the state. All had been active in ante-bellum agricultural and mechanical
societies and fairs at both local and state level, while one, Robert Beverly, was
even then a nationally known leader in agricultural organizations. All came from
well-established Virginia families, most of them with roots extending to the
American Revolution or earlier. All had participated in one way or another in
the Confederate cause; while in politics, all were supposed to be in sympathy
with the conservative camp, which had rallied behind Walker in his campaign
for governor. Since Walker, as a Republican, was not considered to be a bona
fide member of the conservative "establishment," his appointments to the board
caused some surprise and slight grumblings in his own party but not enough to
be particularly disruptive at the time.

Considering the excitement and hopes aroused and dashed during the legislative debates over the disposition of the fund, it was perhaps natural that there
should be some continuation of divergent opinions concerning the new College;
therefore, Walker's appointments to the board did come under some criticism.
One critic sourly felt he had appointed too many of his political friends from
the eastern part of the state who no doubt would try to make the College "an
eastern machine run in western territory." Others felt aggrieved that certain
geographical sections of the state had not secured representation on the board.
One disappointed applicant for the presidency of the new College publicly
charged that the board, because of its make-up, would apply to all prospective

faculty members such criteria as: Is he from Tidewater? Is he an Episcopalian? Is he an alumnus of the University of Virginia? Is he a descendant of George Washington, Justice Marshall, Bishop Meade, or Colonel Harvie? Since Colonel Harvie was a member of the board at the time, the implication intended by the disappointed applicant was clear. These charges and criticisms leveled against Governor Walker and the board do not seem to have been justified; but the tiny seeds of discontent had been sowed, and within less than a decade these seeds grew and multiplied into a full-scale attack on both the board and the faculty selected to run the College.

Upon its appointment by the governor, the board acted at once and held its first meeting in Richmond on March 25 and 26, 1872. At this time, Black was chosen Rector, and Ruffner was made clerk of the board. A committee consisting of Anderson, Sutherlin, and Ruffner, the latter serving as chairman, was appointed to draw up and present to the board a plan of organization and instruction for the College when next the board met. By agreement, this meeting was to be held at Montgomery White Sulphur Springs on July 18, 1872.

Perhaps it is an understatement to say that there was much to be done before the College could admit its first class in the fall. A president and a faculty had to be selected, a program of courses developed, the requirements for the transfer of the Preston and Olin property had to be met, while steps had to be taken to secure the $20,000 pledged on behalf of Montgomery County. Obviously, the execution of these last two activities would not and could not rest entirely with the board.

The circumstances surrounding the money pledged and collected from Montgomery County for the Virginia Agricultural and Mechanical College are intriguing even to this day. It is well known that the money was pledged, but by whom or by whose authority remains a mystery. On March 21, 1872, two days after the governor signed the bill creating the College, Senator Penn succeeded in winning approval of legislation which permitted the county court of Montgomery "or of any of the counties adjoining or near the said county" to order the polls to be opened to "take the sense of the legal voters of such county on the question" of whether the county should raise money for the new College. The act spelled out in considerable detail the procedures to be followed in conducting, reporting, and acting on the results of the referendum; but it was in no way mandatory on the county court to order the referendum to be held, and certainly the results of the referendum, if held, could not be known in advance. It would appear that someone had absolute confidence that the people of Montgomery County would support the new College with more than lip service. One can but speculate as to what the fate of the fledgling college would have been if this faith had been misplaced and the people had refused to raise the promised money. Happily, the faith was not misplaced.

But, to return to the circumstance surrounding the money—if a referendum was to be held, it had to be ordered by the judge of the county court, who at the time was John N. Lyle. Judge Lyle, as administrator of his father's estate, held an unsatisfied lien on the property of the Preston and Olin Institute. These two circumstances in effect gave him unprecedented and unexpected power over the immediate future of the agricultural and mechanical college. At the same time, these circumstances put him in a position which today would most probably be considered as involving conflict of interest. If he refused to order the referendum, the $20,000 pledged the College might be jeopardized; if he ordered the referendum, he might be accused of doing so in order to aid an institution in which he had a financial interest. If the trustees of the Preston and Olin Institute did not pay him his lien, or if he refused to accept accelerated payments on it, he could block transfer of title of the property to the state. In either instance, he had it in his power to erect or remove serious roadblocks in the way of meeting the two major requirements of the act appropriating the land-grant money to the Preston and Olin Institute.

To add to Lyle's difficulties, he was already under so much criticism and threatened litigation for the way he had been handling his father's estate that his bondsman had become alarmed and was pressing for clarifying action. As a student at Washington College and as an officer in the "Liberty Hall Volunteers" in the Confederate forces, the youthful Lyle had already demonstrated his willingness to lay his personal interests aside and act in line with what he considered to be the best interests of all concerned. Once while being considered for promotion from lieutenant to captain in the Confederate forces, he even withdrew his name from consideration for fear his inability to grow a full beard would embarrass some of his company or superior officers. In the instance concerning the referendum, as judge of the County Court, Lyle overlooked his personal involvement and proceeded at once to order a county-wide vote to be held on May 23, 1872, on the question of raising the promised money for the College.

Prior to this vote, a number of speakers toured the county in behalf of favorable support for the College. During this campaign one of the speakers, Charles Martin, of the Christiansburg Female Institute, expressed the fear to Ruffner that "we shall have hard work to carry the vote owing to the location of the college on one side of the county." However, he assured Ruffner that if the vote failed, the sum would be readily raised in donations.

One of the most active, persistent, and persuasive speakers on behalf of a vote favorable to the new College was Captain Thomas N. Conrad, president of the Preston and Olin Institute. This individual had a distinct aptitude for speaking and writing in the language of the people. As a Methodist minister, he had traveled over most of Montgomery County, where he had already demonstrated his skill as a speaker. When the referendum was decided upon, Conrad used his contacts throughout the county and mounted such a vigorous speaking campaign favoring raising the money that one admirer proclaimed the Captain's "tongue was loose at both ends" on behalf of the College. Conrad's speeches marked but the beginning of this colorful individual's influence on the new College for the next decade and a half, during which time some decidedly less complimentary and more specific descriptions of his tongue would be made.

It is quite likely that Conrad's speeches did influence the referendum, which when held, resulted in a vote of 1137 to 154 in favor of honoring the pledge of $20,000 to the new school. Following this favorable vote, the Montgomery County Board of Supervisors met at once and issued bonds for the money, most of which they had ready by the time the Board of Visitors met in July. It is thought by some that this bond issue represents the first of its kind ever issued by a county in Virginia on behalf of higher education, while others hold that it is the first of its kind ever issued by any county in the state for any level of education.

With the compliance on the part of Montgomery County in raising $20,000 for the agricultural and mechanical college, the remaining legislative stipulation to be met was the legal conveyance of the Preston and Olin Institute property to the state through the Board of Visitors. This rather simple procedure was accomplished, but not without some embarrassment and elements of comedy for the hapless Preston and Olin. The trustees of this institution met in the late spring of 1872 and officially agreed to transfer the property to the Board of Visitors. At the same time, the trustees authorized a committee to prepare the deed necessary to transfer the property to the state. In the process of preparing this deed, it was discovered that the lien held against the Preston and Olin property by John Lyle as administrator of his father's estate had not been satisfied. If the litigation threatening Lyle's administration of this estate materialized, it certainly would delay, if not entirely block, efforts to get a clear title to the property. To add to the urgency, it was known that Lyle was making tentative plans to relinquish administration of his father's estate to a substitute administrator to be appointed by the court and then to move to Texas. If these plans materialized, further delay in clearing the title was inevitable. Faced with this threatening situation, the committee arranged a hasty meeting with Lyle. Although later probed in court, the details of this meeting are not clear beyond the fact that Lyle, as administrator of his father's estate, executed a deed giving the trustees clear title to the Preston and Olin property. With a clear title to the property (actually for the first time in more than a decade) the trustees set about preparing a deed to convey the property to the Board of Visitors of the new agricultural and mechanical college. The confusion was not over. The Reverend P. H. Whisner, president of the Board of Trustees of the Preston and Olin Institute, had moved from Montgomery County, Virginia, to Montgomery County, Maryland. Official documents mailed to or from him, if bearing the designation of Montgomery County, had a way of being returned to the sender or of being delayed before delivery. Finally, this problem was overcome, and a deed thought to be suitable was prepared for delivery to the board at their meeting on July 18. Upon the presentation of this deed to the board, it was discovered that the seal of the Preston and Olin Institute had not been affixed to it in any way. Furthermore, the seal could not be found. Without the seal of the institution, would such a deed be legally acceptable? James C. Taylor, attorney general of the state, advised the Board of Visitors not to accept the deed until he checked "certain papers." As a resident of Christiansburg in Montgomery County, Taylor was familiar with the entire situation. Following his investigation, he advised the board to accept the deed to the property. The board did so, thereby bringing an official end to the hapless Preston and Olin Institute but at the same time receiving into its care the nucleus which ultimately became the Virginia Polytechnic Institute and State University.[1]

While the developments just mentioned were unfolding in Montgomery County, the Board of Visitors was being bombarded individually and collectively with applications for the presidency and for teaching positions in the new school. Most of these applicants had well-placed social and political connections which they did not hesitate to use freely in their personal behalf. Others, to borrow a

---

[1] *Epilogue.* A number of years later, an energetic young lawyer in Blacksburg in attempting to collect an old debt created by the Preston and Olin Institute before its demise, challenged the legality of this deed and the action of the board in accepting it. The court ruled that the property had been conveyed to the board in a legally acceptable manner and that the board's actions at the time were both proper and legal.

statement of Morris Bishop, were well-connected failures. Many had distinguished records of service in the Confederate cause. Perhaps the most prominent in this latter group was General L. L. Lomax, whose friends, in seeking to promote his cause for the presidency, sought the endorsement of his former comrades-in-arms. In this connection, a request for endorsement was sent to General Jubal A. Early. The testy "Old Jube" duly mailed the letter of endorsement from his home in Lynchburg. At the same time he wrote to a mutual friend, stating that he had sent the letter but did not expect it to carry much weight with certain members of the board, since they belonged "to the [Governor] Walker school of politicians with whom I have no influence." In this same letter, Early further unburdened himself and probably expressed the prevailing sentiment in certain circles of the state when he wrote, "I hardly think the position of professor in this new 'Agricultural and Mechanical College' would be of much advantage to Lomax. I think the school a humbug which will not last long. . . ."

While applicants for the presidency were numerous, friends of the cause of agricultural education were active in suggesting names and urging individuals to become applicants. John Lyle Campbell, a distinguished member of the faculty of Washington and Lee University, was one such individual. Campbell had already distinguished himself as a recognized authority in the field of agricultural education and in college administration. At the same time, he was one of the chief architects for Robert E. Lee's proposed school of agriculture, which has already been mentioned. Campbell declined to become a candidate but wrote to Ruffner, urging him to seek the office.

Campbell's letter took Ruffner by surprise. He immediately replied to Campbell, stating that the idea had not even occurred to him, although the possibility, now that it had been mentioned, did have strong appeal and "would accord with my tastes, and with my studies and experience." At the same time, Ruffner depreciated his chances, saying that he was a stranger personally to most of the members of the Board of Visitors, "who no doubt take me for a seedy parson without business experience—just the sort of man they don't want." At this particular time, Ruffner was near the end of his first term as state superintendent of public instruction in the newly created public school system. While he had more than successfully met the turbulent drumfire of bitter attacks on the public schools, he nonetheless was becoming discouraged; therefore, he did not completely withdraw his name for consideration for the presidency. But as he told Campbell, he would not "candidate" [sic] for the office, since he felt it "important for the interests of my public school work that I, the leader, should not even seem to falter."

When the rumor spread that Ruffner was being considered for the presidency of the new College, he was deluged with letters, part of which urged him to continue as superintendent of public instruction and part of which, after endorsing him for president, sought his endorsement in return for faculty positions in the College. Especially notable in the first group were letters from Barnas Sears and John B. Minor.

As agent for the Peabody Fund, which was pouring money into Virginia and other southern states to aid public schools, Barnas Sears was in an excellent position to judge Ruffner's work on behalf of public education. When he heard that Ruffner was being considered for the presidency of the College, he wrote a long letter to him urging, in fact practically begging, him to continue in the office of superintendent. No other man, wrote Sears, could do for Virginia what Ruffner was doing. If Ruffner gave up his post now, much of the progress toward public education, not only in Virginia but throughout the entire South, would be lost. Sears said Ruffner's reports on public education were having a favorable impact over the entire South and being read with approved interest throughout the entire nation. These reports, continued Sears in a prophetic vein which time would prove correct, would cause Ruffner to go down in history alongside Horace Mann.

Almost simultaneously with this letter, Ruffner received another one similar in nature from John B. Minor, distinguished professor of law at the University of Virginia. Minor, who had helped Ruffner draft the original plan largely adopted by the legislature when it launched Virginia's first public school system, confessed that in his opinion Ruffner would make an excellent president of the College. At the same time, he expressed his belief that Ruffner had the support of the people and urged him to continue in his present office. These two letters came at an opportune time for the cause of public education, since Ruffner, although offered the presidency on several occasions, chose each time to remain superintendent of public instruction.

Letters to Ruffner soliciting his support on behalf of applicants for faculty positions usually showed little if any concept of the work to be done by the new school. In fact, some did not pretend to do so, but based their appeal on entirely different and sometimes surprising ground. Thus, the wife of one front-running candidate, wishing to help her husband, wrote to Ruffner, soliciting his support on the somewhat dubious ground that her husband had *wished* for Ruffner's appointment and success as superintendent of public instruction. Continuing her line of feminine logic she added, "Somehow it seems to endorse your success for my husband to want anything [for you]." She confessed to some embarrassment and fear of being thought unladylike in writing to him under the circumstances but added that because it had been her lifelong habit to trust in Presbyterian ministers, she would ask him not to answer her note or tell anyone she had written, only help her husband get a position on the new college faculty if possible. This note is one of the very few that Ruffner apparently did not pass on to the full board, an action which, when coupled with the fact that the lady's husband was elected to the first faculty of the College, no doubt greatly strengthened her trust in Presbyterian ministers. It is worthy of mention here that with her husband on the faculty the lady in question, according to student reports, became a second mother to many of them.

The effect on the College of Ruffner's declination of its presidency is a matter of speculation. The work that he did as chairman of the committee to present a plan of organization and instruction for the school, however, is a matter both of speculation and of solid, recorded achievement, mostly the latter. While he showed some hesitancy and doubt about accepting the presidency, he did not hesitate in helping plan a course for the newly established College to follow. Indeed, he seems to have entered vigorously and enthusiastically into the task of drafting such a plan. In the preparation of the plan he embarked on a program of extensive reading and study of industrial education in the United States and abroad. In addition to his wide reading and study, he engaged in extensive correspondence with interested persons and visited schools in the eastern United States already embarked or just embarking on programs of agricultural and mechanical education.

At Cornell, as he happily wrote his wife, he was conducted on a tour of the campus by Ezra Cornell himself. Of this fledgling university he wrote, "Cornell is a young giant who is destined to amaze the world with a combination of erudition and handicraft as has nev•r been seen; but as he gets older he may grow less practical." Upon his return to Virginia, he prepared for the board a voluminous report dealing with the theoretical nature of industrial education and with the many types of educational organizations being utilized at home and abroad in promoting this particular kind of educational endeavor.

With this voluminous and carefully organized material as a background, Ruffner then turned to the consideration of a course of instruction and a plan of organization for the new agricultural and mechanical college which would be specifically adapted to the needs of the "industrial class" of Virginia. In pursuit of this objective, Ruffner soon found he had plentiful assistance, both solicited and unsolicited, with which to deal. In what proved to be a masterful stroke of good public relations, he had written to representatives of all the schools in Virginia which had sought the land-grant fund, asking them for their suggestions and advice on how the new College should be organized and conducted. Most, if not all, of the individuals so addressed responded with suggestions which Ruffner publicly acknowledged and turned over to the Board of Visitors. Since most of the suggestions submitted were rather general in nature, it was easy for a contributor, once the new College did open, to discover, or imagine he discovered, in the college program some element of his submitted proposal. Undoubtedly, this development was a factor in helping eradicate much of the bitterness of defeat felt by so many colleges over the loss of "Morrill's Manna."

In addition to the solicited help which Ruffner found to be so valuable, he also found an immediate appearance of unsolicited advice addressed to the board through letters and editorials in the press. Many of these press articles in strong contrast to the confusion of the legislative debates, indicated a surprisingly clear understanding of the nature of agricultural and mechanical education and of the problems to be faced by the Board of Visitors in charting a course for the new College. Almost all the writers agreed that the school must be designed for the sons of the farmers and mechanics, or as one expressed it, the "sons of the People." Its curriculum would have to be limited by the funds available; the expenses would have to be kept low; and the military feature should be subordinate to instruction in agriculture and mechanics. One writer expressed apprehension and doubt as to just what kind of school the legislature would support, since in its debates on the disposition of the land-grant fund it had rejected the University of Virginia with its "lofty science," the Virginia Military Institute with its "boasten [sic] practical theoretical instruction," and all of the other "colleges with little of either." Other writers were not beset by this individual's doubts; although after reviewing both the Morrill Act and the action of the legislature, several agreed that the school at the beginning should not be a university or a military institute and should not attempt the special work of either. Perhaps the thrust of opinions publicly expressed before the board had organized the College can be summed up by noting two articles, one carried in *The Lynchburg Daily Virginian* and the other in the *Richmond Whig*. The former paper, after expressing the hope that the location of the college would correct the feeling so prevalent in southwestern Virginia of being discriminated against by the east, warned: "The new college starts under critical conditions to say the least. Its Board of

Trustees—though eminent in their respective individual callings, and most of them engaged in pursuits germain to the objects of the college—are not known to have any particular experience in the management of educational institutions." The *Virginian* then predicted that the board itself, because of its varied geographic and professional background, would likely experience difficulty in reaching an agreement or holding to one if reached—a prediction, it may be added, which subsequent events in the life of the young College proved to be quite correct. Continuing, the *Virginian* further warned: "All the various theories of education from the most abstract and theoretical, to the most meagre and so called practical will be urged on the consideration of the new Board of Trustees." But, warned the *Virginian,* any action of the board which would try to rival the University or VMI would be contrary to the wish of the legislature which refused to grant the money to either of these schools. On the other hand, "To make it [the College] merely practical without a proper scientific basis of instruction is to disappoint the most hopeful and intelligent of agriculturists and mechanics. To attempt to excel the university or the institute in their respective fields of endeavor [i.e. in the pure and technical sciences] is impossible with the funds at the command of the Board, and the liberal provision made for free tuitions and other college expenses." What the board should do, concluded the *Virginian,* was to set up "a simple, practical system on a sound scientific and disciplinary basis." The *Whig* in a similar vein felt that "for the present at least it should be content to be a good practical school for farmers' and mechanics' sons." At the same time if the press of the day is to be relied upon, the *Whig* expressed the prevailing sentiment when it said of the College, "In a few words, it ought to touch our immediate wants, and grow into something larger as times demand and means afford." This latter admonition turned out to be quite significant in that it represented the actual course of action undertaken not only by the first board but by many subsequent ones as well.

When the Board of Visitors convened on July 18, 1872 at the Montgomery White Sulphur Springs for its second meeting, it found much activity under way. The Montgomery White Sulphur Springs, located about nine miles east of Blacksburg, was a flourishing summer resort which usually reached the height of its popularity, or "season," during July and early August. The summer of 1872 was no exception; therefore, when the members of the board arrived, they found a "host of visitors" already on the scene. Included among this group, it soon developed, were many who hoped to improve their condition of health by drinking the waters of the spring and the conditions of their pocketbooks by influencing the action of the board. At the same time, whether by chance or by design, a huge political rally on behalf of Horace Greeley for President of the United States had been scheduled to meet at the springs during the time the board would be there. Governor Walker, John Goode, and other members of the board with known ability as political orators were invited to address the rally and did so at some length. This action on the part of a few board members was immediately seized upon by some of the anti-Greeley press, and subsequently by disappointed office seekers, as unwarranted partisan political activity on the part of the entire board. Unhappily, the use of the charge of partisan politics as a means of expressing disapproval of board action became one of the favorite methods of attack on the board and persisted long after the Greeley campaign passed into history.

Following this diversionary but no doubt pleasant excursion into national politics on the part of a few of its members, the full board then settled down to the less exciting and more laborious task of developing a statement of purpose and a plan of curriculum content, organization, and administration for the new College. The report of the committee appointed at the March meeting to prepare such a plan was called for and "heard" at this point. There is no doubt that Ruffner was the chief if not the only architect of this report. Anderson and Sutherlin, the other members of the committee, were freely consulted throughout the entire period of preparation but finding themselves in full agreement with the major thrust of Ruffner's ideas soon contented themselves with approving rather than producing the report. In fact, Anderson liked Ruffner's approach so well he was reported as "playfully" threatening to make Ruffner president of the College. Since this report had such a profound effect on the College not only for its immediate future but for at least the first half a century of its existence, it is worthy of considerable attention.

In mechanical arrangement the report consisted of two parts. Part one, which was quite voluminous, set forth in considerable detail a description of polytechnic and agricultural institutions in Europe and America. This section drew heavily on the well-known report on "Education in Europe and the United States" made by John W. Hoyt. Throughout this entire section, Ruffner added penetrating comments which served to focus and relate the information and conclusions presented in Hoyt's report to the situation and needs existing in Virginia. With part one serving as a broad background, the report then came to a much sharper focus in the second part entitled, "What Sort of School Should Be Established at Blacksburg?" Since the conclusions set forth in the report as answers to this question were so dominated by Ruffner, a further understanding of this individual's background and educational philosophy will be quite helpful, not only in understanding the report but also in understanding the reasons for the direction taken by the College.

Ruffner, as superintendent of public instruction for Virginia, served on the Board of Visitors of the College for nearly a decade after its establishment, a longer period than any of the other earlier board members. He brought with him a broad experience in industry, agriculture, theology, and education. As editor of an agricultural journal in the late 1850's, he had closely followed the ante-bellum developments toward a system of agricultural education. In this movement, he had lined up solidly behind the idea that to be of any real value such an education would have to be practical, regardless of where the school should be located. A student of educational history by avocation, he was also familiar with the national debates being waged with respect to the place of vocational, technical, and scientific education as part of a system of higher education. He felt that much of the attack being made at the national level against the early land-grant institutions grew from the tendency of these institutions to encroach upon and imitate the liberal arts colleges rather than to develop a program designed for the masses of people. At the same time, he was firmly convinced that a practical, technical education once established was in constant, perpetual danger of being taken over and reorganized into a more theoretical or "liberal" program, which did not fit the student for anything. "It is true," he wrote, "that a liberal education improves a man's capacity for everything, but it does not fit him for anything." Ruffner felt that the tendency of the liberal arts to take over the practical, technical programs grew from several factors, the main one being the fact that public sentiment on the subject was largely controlled by scholarly men whose tastes revolted at the narrow, short, practical courses.

"Owing to the difficulty of getting men of literary habits to accept practical objectives," he wrote, most schools in the United States which professed to educate farmers and mechanics "did no such thing. By the time [these] schools were done with the students, a ball and chain would not have kept them in a shop or on the farm."

Ruffner's skepticism as to the value of a "literary education" for the farmers and mechanics is not to be taken as an attack on such education in the liberal arts colleges and universities. On the contrary, he was a strong supporter, even crusader, for a complete system of public education. He wanted the program to embrace elementary schools, high schools, a technical college, and a university, with each element closely coordinated and articulated into a unified statewide system. In a manner somewhat suggestive of some present-day thinking, he did entertain some apprehension lest the people of Virginia indulge in excessive multiplication of colleges.

Ruffner was firmly convinced of the abstract values of education but felt the conditions in postwar Virginia needed the immediate as well as ultimate benefits to be derived from a complete system of education. To get immediate results, which he also felt would help secure more widespread support for all education, he felt that the schools, especially the technical college, should be geared to the needs of the state at the time. This "Reconstruction Statesman" was in the forefront of the leaders who recognized that Virginia was moving and should be encouraged to move toward a new type of agricultural and industrial production. At the same time, he was aware of the problems faced in setting up a system of wages and labor which would replace the older system of slavery and also be satisfactory for the new conditions. He knew that because of the "changed circumstances" in postwar Virginia, many whites, totally unprepared by tradition, experience, and inclination, in increasing numbers would be, and even then were being, forced to enter the labor market as unskilled workmen. He believed sincerely that the right kind of education would go a long way toward reducing the prejudice so prevalent in ante-bellum Virginia and yet persisting in much of postwar Virginia against manual labor on the part of whites. Of equal, if not more importance, he felt that a practical education if properly applied would result in such immediate increased productiveness to industry and agriculture as to offset completely the cost to the state of such education.

Ruffner, in keeping with one school of thought of his day, held there should be a differentiation in the assignment of responsibilities to the institutions of higher education. He believed the University should devote its program to the highest level of literary and theoretical studies, with little if any concern for the utilitarian or practical. On the other hand, the technical college should emphasize the practical application of its program. The University by its very nature, he contended, could not and should not attempt to modify its program to meet the needs of the people. Such adaptation was not its mission. A technical college could and should adapt and change its program to meet the practical needs of the people. That was its mission. In accomplishing this mission, he recognized the ever present problem of establishing and maintaining a proper balance be-

tween the practical training and general scientific education upon which this practical training would have to be based. Because the limited funds available would
make it impossible to establish both practical and theoretical programs simultaneously, he felt that the new agricultural and mechanical college should concentrate on a program which prepared for the immediate entrance into gainful
employment. He believed the success of such a beginning would insure increasing support from the masses of the people and at the same time produce an "enlightened sentiment" which would in due time permit the college to expand its
program as the need arose. Until this need did arise, he believed the programs
already under way at the University of Virginia and at the Virginia Military Institute offered sufficient opportunity for those desiring an advanced theoretical
study of agriculture and technical science. Ruffner was fully aware of the strong
literary tradition which had dominated all aspects of the educational scene in the
state for more than a century. Therefore, he warned that pressure to conform to
this literary tradition would beset the new college from the very outset and if not
strongly resisted would turn it aside from its true mission. Ruffner readily admitted the absence of a body of organized information in the areas of agriculture
and mechanical education as he envisioned it. He felt this absence was more of
an asset than a liability, though, because he believed it would force the professor
to keep his instruction relevant to the practical interests and the needs of the
students and thereby prevent the classes from becoming mere mental exercises.
He warned, in a statement even today having a familiar ring, that the "mental
gymnastics" quite appropriate for a university level of theoretical study if introduced into technical schools of a practical cast would be utterly rejected as humbug by the students once they saw the lack of relevancy such "gymnastics" had for
their real interests in life.

It will be readily recognized that many of Ruffner's ideas were not original
with him. Yet, it was from a background of these and other ideas of a similar
nature that Ruffner attempted to answer the question, "What sort of school
should be established at Blacksburg?" The answers given to this question in the
report submitted to the board by the committee clearly reflected Ruffner's philosophy and interpretation of the contemporary scene in Virginia.

The plan, especially its aspects advocating the preparation of the students for
an immediate entrance into agricultural and mechanical pursuits, drew the warm
support of Anderson and Sutherlin, the other members of the committee. This
support is understandable. Both men had participated fully in the ante-bellum
activities of the Virginia State Agricultural Society. As operator of the Tredgar
Iron Works in Richmond, Anderson had been faced with both ante-bellum and
post-bellum difficulties in securing skilled artisans for his plant, although he did
have his own apprenticeship training program. On several occasions he had imported skilled technicians from outside the state, but often these transplanted
workmen after remaining a short time became dissatisfied and departed. One of
the leading industrialists in Virginia, Anderson is supposed to have been among
the first to recognize the potential value of an agricultural and mechanical college
to the nonagricultural industries of the state.

Sutherlin also supported the idea of a practical school as a start. It will be
recalled he had urged over and over that the legislature establish a practical
school of agriculture around which the "accretions of time" would build a truly
great institution. Sutherlin, as operator of a number of farms in Virginia and as

operator of a tobacco manufacturing plant in Danville, Virginia, also felt the new college, if properly directed, would help improve Virginia's artisan class.

As a first step in attempting to determine the nature of the college to be established, the committee report directed the board's attention to the wording of the Morrill Act. Upon a first reading, the language of this act may seem perfectly clear; but it should be remembered it proved puzzling to founders of colleges throughout the United States that attempted to use the wording as a guide in developing new schools. Two extreme positions were developing by opposing groups. One group argued for a broad, inclusive interpretation of the language, while the opposing group insisted on a narrow, strict limitation to the studies that were clearly related to agriculture and the mechanic arts. The "broad gauge" faction argued for the inclusion of English and ancient and foreign languages as well as mathematics and science which would enable the student to understand the principles of his business. The "narrow gauge" adherents took a practical and in some instances almost trade-school view, which included only the subjects directly, not remotely, related to agriculture and mechanic arts. Ruffner was thoroughly familiar with both positions but was firmly convinced that the situation in Virginia demanded some form of a "narrow gauge" technical school. To his surprise, he found that a majority of the board entertained a different opinion. Years later in reminiscing about this problem, Ruffner recalled that a majority of the board at first "were full of the idea simply of reproducing the University of Virginia for the benefit of the southwest." Others felt that the school should be patterned after VMI. Ruffner claimed the issue was only settled "after a fearful struggle" in which he was able to win over all but two of the board members to the idea of a technical school. These two members, according to Ruffner, in opposing the idea of a technical school "never were anything but marplots and nuisances!" Strong language indeed but perhaps indicative of the "fearful struggle" as well.

In defending his proposals for a technical school, Ruffner skillfully invoked a review both of the socio-economic conditions of the state and of the legislative debates concerning the disposal of the land-grant fund as well. Afterwards the board accepted the organization and plan of instruction proposed by the committee. It was agreed that the purpose of the institution was to further the education of the industrial classes. At this particular point, the board defined the industrial class as comprising those who handled tools or worked in the fields, mines, or workshops. This rather narrow definition of the group to be served may have been in harmony with the viewpoint of aristocratic ante-bellum Virginia, but in practice it was never observed by the general populace or the board. Records clearly indicate that "the people" of all walks of life without entering into any argument whatever as to the nature of the industrial class simply sent their sons to the College to be educated.

With the purpose agreed upon, the board then determined that the new school should be one of applied science, "a technical school with a liberal appendage if you choose, but still a technical school" which was to have as its ultimate object the immediate utilization of science for the development of the material resources of the country. Little did anyone at the time realize that almost exactly one century later this same institution would be involved in efforts to develop a program for the immediate utilization of science for the development of ways and means to remedy some of the side effects on the environment caused by the success in achieving this first "ultimate objective."

With a technical school agreed upon, the board concluded that "the new college ought to trench as little as possible upon ground well-occupied by institutions already existing in the state." Once again, while the official records do not show it, private sources clearly indicate that this conclusion was not a happy one with some of the board members, who felt the restriction might become too binding on the future development of the College.

The act appropriating the land-grant fund provided that a number of students equal to the number of members serving in the Virginia House of Delegates should be given free tuition. Ruffner wanted this free tuition privilege extended to all Virginia students, but in view of the prevailing financial circumstances readily altered his position to a demand that costs to students be kept as low as possible. Apparently the board did not engage in any "fearful struggle" over this feature. Fees and tuition were set at $40 per academic year; then after a report on living conditions in Blacksburg, board was set at $10 a month, while room, heat and light were set at $3 a month. A neat uniform costing $17.50, to be worn to classes, was also decided upon. Having explored the problem of cost, the board happily concluded that students could attend the College a full year at a cost of less than $200. Within a few years, the board found it necessary to increase the cost of the uniform from $17.50 to $18.00. Although the increase was a small one, letters from students with a decidedly familiar tone were immediately forthcoming, protesting the increase as unfair, unjustified, and profiteering.

Following the formulation of guiding principles for the College, the board turned its attention to the establishment of a suitable curriculum. At the very outset, it realized this would be a pioneering endeavor since no pattern of courses, especially in agriculture, existed anywhere in the country which could be used as a definitive guide. There was no one discerned path on which schools of agriculture were converging, while the others that were discernible often were obscured with conflicting claims. In addition to this lack of a guiding pattern, there was no body of agricultural or mechanical content available for pedagogical organization. This total situation was a stimulating, absorbing challenge to Ruffner, "the only member of the board who knew anything at all about technical education." Therefore, it is not surprising that he once more dominated the discussions of the board. It is even less surprising to find that the curriculum report adopted by the board at this time was largely an expression of his philosophy. Since this report (a combination of guiding principles, of subjects to be taught, of content to be included, and of explanations for decisions) played such a decisive role in shaping the College, especially in the eyes of the public, it deserves more attention than it would otherwise justify. The report itself has been ably analyzed and summarized by J. P. Cochran in his study of the Virginia Agricultural and Mechanical College, who concluded as follows:

> Although courses in engineering were offered in most of the colleges of the state, some engineering courses were to be a part of the curriculum of the Virginia Agricultural and Mechanical College. Disclaiming any intention of introducing a complete curriculum in all phases of engineering because of lack of money, the board concluded that course emphasis would be placed on the construction of roads, bridges, and drainage facilities and on the study of surveying, mining, mechanics, and engines. Similarly the group determined against graduating architects but endorsed the committee's recommendation that basic courses

be taught in building and building materials, the laws of proportion and ornamentation, and the different types of architecture. Likewise the board endorsed
the study of the rudiments of chemistry and its practical application, with no
attempt to graduate professional chemists.

It was the aim of the board that the farmer or mechanic should attend college chiefly to learn what there was in science, improved methods, and new
machinery to make him a better farmer or mechanic. They agreed there should
be no pointing toward theoretical study, which might educate students away
from their vocation with a distaste for manual labor, and with a desire for
more literary or less toilsome pursuits. The pragmatic goal of the new college
was to educate students into their vocations, to instill in them zest for their
work and a higher sense of its dignity and its challenge.

The board, officially at least, reiterated its determination not to compete with
other institutions. Rather, its aim was to fill what it considered to be an educa-
cational lacuna in the state's system of higher education. The board did lament
that lack of endowment prevented it from establishing a comprehensive, adequately equipped technical college such as Ruffner had seen getting under way
at Cornell. As for competing with other colleges of the state, all of which, with
the possible exception of VMI, were of the liberal arts type, the board stated:
"Even if it would not be a perversion of the fund to use it for the establishment
of an ordinary college, it certainly would be very bad economy to do so . . . sadly
have our people already erred in the undue multiplication of colleges." Even the
matter of inadequate endowment was accepted, or perhaps rationalized, by the
board as a situation "we need not regret," since it felt the facilities developing at
the University of Virginia soon would "afford the grand desideratum of a high
grade [i.e. theoretical] school of agriculture and mechanic arts." The "grand
desideratum" never materialized at the University, but the rationalization of the
board survived and plagued the College for the next three decades.

In further reference to the summary of the board action, Cochran says:

> Having thus set the aims and objectives of the institution, the committee
> then set entrance requirements and courses of instruction. Applicants for ad-
> mission were required to pass entrance examinations in spelling, reading, writ-
> ing, elementary grammar, intermediate geography, and simple arithmetic. The
> board planned to offer an initial three-year program of study; the first year was
> to be the same for all students, but in the second and third years the agricul-
> tural and mechanical students would have separate programs of study. The first-
> year curriculum specified instruction in commercial arithmetic, bookkeeping,
> algebra (through equations of the first degree), English, geography and map
> drawing, descriptive astronomy, penmanship and free hand drawing, physiology,
> hygiene, habits and manners, French or German, farm or shop practice, mili-
> tary tactics, and lectures on the sociological value of the agricultural and the
> mechanical arts.
>
> During the second year both agricultural and mechanical students wou!d
> study geometry, plane trigonometry and mensuration, history, literature, French
> or German, and the composition of essays. The agricultural students were to re-
> ceive instruction in surveying, agricultural engineering, agricultural physics and
> mechanics, and agricultural architecture and machines. The mechanical course
> for the second year students required the additional subjects of descriptive
> geometry, physics, and mechanics.
>
> In the third year, students of both curricula were required to attend classes
> in French or German, psychology or ethics, political economy, business economy,
> and government. The third year agricultural students were to study agricultural
> chemistry and geology, with special emphasis on soils and geological structures
> of Virginia, agricultural botany and zoology, systems of farming, planting, gard-

ening, dairying, fruit growing, and stock raising, with special emphasis being placed on climate and crops of Virginia, and farm economics, including labor, accounts, buying, selling, and renting. The mechanical students were to study analytical geometry, industrial chemistry, mineralogy, metallurgy, steam engines, mill wheels and gearing, planing and boring machines, and building and building materials. The students were also to attend lectures concerning water power, timber, metals, ores, and minerals of the state.

Cochran ends his summary with the conclusion that this curriculum closely parallels the one adopted by Michigan State College in 1857; however, in its somewhat encyclopedic listing of topics to be studied, it is even more closely related to the numerous ante-bellum curricula which had been proposed at different times by the agricultural societies in Virginia. This close resemblance is not surprising when it is recalled that at least nine of the twelve board members present when the curriculum was determined had been active participants in ante-bellum agricultural societies of the state.

After reviewing different practices being followed by technical schools with respect to the manual-labor feature, the board was unable to come up with a specific plan for this practice. In general, it went along with the great ante-bellum agricultural leader, Edmund Ruffin, and concluded that manual labor should be thought of as an instructional feature rather than as a means of defraying cost to students.

If the board was vague with respect to the manual-labor feature, it was even more so with respect to military tactics. In introducing the section of the report concerning this topic, the board concluded, "The military feature offers another embarrassing problem." An effort to determine the intent of Congress in passing the original Land-Grant Act proved fruitless, while an exploration of how other colleges were meeting this military requirement gave no help either. "In point of fact," reported the board, "the colleges which received the land grant have, with a few exceptions, given no prominence to this feature, and would be glad to omit it altogether. Still whilst the law exists, military tactics must be taught in some form." To satisfy the law, the board decided an opportunity should be given to the students for military drill. Then as if an afterthought, the board stated, "Some of the disciplinary regulations might be usefully adopted if it should be concluded to board all the students on the College grounds." The failure to determine a more specific policy with respect to the military feature at this time proved to be nearly fatal to the new College before it even completed its first decade of existence.

With a plan of organization and instruction agreed upon, although not fully understood by some members, the board decided to visit Blacksburg the next day to inspect the Preston and Olin property and to buy a college farm if at all possible. The trustees of Preston and Olin and the executive committee of the Virginia State Agricultural Society, having been invited to the meeting at White Sulphur Springs, happily decided to accompany the board on the mission. These groups had not been able to offer much help in the formulation of the plan for organization or instruction, but advice as to buildings and farm lands was an entirely different matter.

As it turned out, there were several tracts of land available and several immediate opinions as to which tract should be bought. After much discussion "and a lot of walking," the board bought the "Solitude" tract of approximately 250 acres, a part of the famous Smithfield plantation belonging to Robert T. Preston.

The substantial frame house standing on the farm at that time, although having undergone several renovations, is still standing today across the "Duck Pond" from the entrance to the campus golf course. Currently this house is serving as campus headquarters for the Hokie Club.

In purchasing this tract of land, the board had not been able to follow all of the advice given at the time by the non-board members. Unfortunately, this action left some ruffled feelings which erupted later on as an attack on the board itself when it appeared the farm might become a liability rather than an asset. There is also some faint evidence of this hostility in the abortive proposal of the president of the Virginia State Agricultural Society two years later to use a portion of the society's $150,000 assets to establish a college of agriculture near Richmond, thus by-passing the Virginia A and M College.

Ruffner was delighted with the farm but privately was disturbed by the fact that it lay about a quarter of a mile from the Preston and Olin campus. He quickly realized that students moving to and from the farm would have to cross private property or follow rather circuitous public roads. To remove this difficulty, Ruffner felt the board should purchase the intervening tract of land which, he discovered to his dismay, belonged to Edward and John Black, relatives of Harvey Black, rector of the Board of Visitors. Since some mutterings of favoritism had occurred immediately following the purchase of Preston's farm, Ruffner feared any immediate purchase of land from the Black family might agitate the situation. He therefore refrained from any public expression concerning this situation but after securing a right of way across the Black lands, he did start a very discreet, private effort which eventually led the board to purchase the intervening land, thereby uniting the campus and the farm.

It had been generally assumed that the board would start selecting a faculty at its July meeting. The candidates were numerous; the testimonials of their fitness were even more numerous and bore some of the most prominent names in the state; and sponsors or spokesmen were on the grounds, ready to speak in behalf of each leading applicant. The board did elect V. E. Shepherd, of Botetourt County, treasurer and secretary of the faculty, and then to the surprise and disappointment of many decided to adjourn, to meet again in August to complete its selection of a faculty. No public explanation was given for this delay, but one disappointed candidate and his supporters later claimed the decision resulted from a shrewd political maneuver on the part of the eastern board members to prevent the appointment to the faculty of any applicant from the western part of the state. It is difficult to evaluate the accuracy of this claim, but the charge of sectional bias it raised lived to plague both the faculty and the administration of the College for the next several decades.

After having advertised its proposed meeting in August to elect a faculty, the board met, this time at the Yellow Sulphur Springs in Montgomery County. The "host of visitors" was not so great as it had been at the White Sulphur Springs in July, but the pressure on the board was even greater, since most of the candidates for office had used the intervening time to renew their applications and strengthen their claims for appointment.

At the July meeting of the board, Ruffner had spent considerable time directing attention to the problem of staffing a new school such as an agricultural and mechanical college. The real problem, he felt, would be to find men competent to teach something they had not been taught. He believed a few men of talent possibly could accomplish this task by inventing new methods, organizing new materials, and devising new equipment related to agricultural and mechanical education. At the same time, he realized that slow progress toward the accomplishment of this type of teaching could have an adverse effect on the public's confidence in the school. As it turned out, the report adopted by the board reflected all of the foregoing ideas. With respect to the faculty, the board resolved to employ individuals "in sympathy with the objects of the institution, who have a natural versatility, and who have had some experience in the direction aimed at." The office of president was recognized "as of course the most important." The board felt that the president, in addition to directing the varied internal affairs of the institution "should give much thought and labor to its advancement in public estimation, and especially in securing an enlarged endowment, and donations for special purposes." Undoubtedly, this latter sentiment can be credited to Ruffner, who as trustee for Washington and Lee University was witnessing the success of this policy in enlarging the endowment for that school. He was also aware of the slowly developing interest on the part of a number of philanthropists in the cause of higher education in Virginia. Since so much oratory had been expended in the state extolling the virtues of agricultural education, Ruffner believed that the proper use of "a flattering unction" would channel much of this growing interest toward the Virginia Agricultural and Mechanical College.

The performance of the faculty was to be in the future, however. The immediate problem of the board meeting in August at the Yellow Sulphur Springs was to select a faculty to perform. Once more the records available do not tell the full story of the events which surrounded this election of a faculty. Ruffner nearly three decades later in reminiscing about the occasion yet remembered it with considerable emotion and perhaps bias. Regarding it he said:

> When the time came to elect a faculty, we had even more trouble in getting suitable men than we had in shaping a suitable scheme. They all had to be Virginians, Democrats, Confederates, whilst a previous technical education and practice was not deemed at all important.
>
> The college property having been given by the Methodists, they claimed the moral right to name the president. Their man was Thom Conrad, a hickory preacher and a knave who had been the principal of the Academy [Preston and Olin Institute]. The faculty chosen consisted of educated gentlemen not one of whom had the least idea of what a technical college ought to be. No two agreed in their views. They argued and they struggled and they wound up in a fist fight.

Subsequent events, letters, and editorials tend to confirm much of the aptness of Ruffner's description of this meeting, although his blunt description of Conrad certainly was not shared by all, then or later. The chief contenders for the presidency in addition to Conrad were Charles Martin, principal of the Christiansburg Female Academy; Charles L. C. Minor, a native Virginian on the faculty of Sewanee; and General L. L. Lomax, a graduate of West Point. It is perhaps indicative of the complex uncertainties of the day, as well as interesting to note, that three of these individuals eventually served as president of the College, while the fourth was intimately involved with the school during its formative years.

As Ruffner noted, Conrad had the strong support of the Methodists, especially those having been connected with the Preston and Olin Institute. The articulate Charles Ronald and the influential Robert Preston were particularly active in Conrad's behalf even to the extent of annoying some members of the board. These two individuals, according to one account, appeared before, dur-

ing, and after the board meeting and put forth "frantic efforts" on Conrad's behalf. The board, in spite of these "frantic efforts," declined to appoint not only
Conrad but all other ex-faculty members of the Preston and Olin Institute to the
faculty of the new College. This decision, whether or not it was politically inspired as charged, created a strong resentment throughout the interested Methodist community and soon led to sniping attacks on the administration of the College. Following his failure to secure the presidency, Conrad assumed the editorship of the weekly *Montgomery Messenger* in nearby Christiansburg, where he
proceeded to keep an eagle eye on all the activities of the College. Conrad would
be heard from again.

General L. L. Lomax does not appear to have been a very strong contender
for the office at this particular time. Apparently he entered the race a bit late
with most of his endorsements for the office coming from former wartime comrades-in-arms. Lomax's personal activities on behalf of his candidacy remain
somewhat obscure. Seemingly this scion of an aristocratic old Virginia family followed the rather customary practice of personally remaining in the background
while his family and friends pushed his candidacy. His approach was not successful on this occasion; but more than a decade and a half later under entirely
different circumstances, the prize was his.

The real race for the presidency developed between Martin and Minor, a surprising fact, since Martin at first had sought only a professorship. It appears that
Martin's entrance into the race for the presidency occurred when the local Methodists, realizing that Conrad would not be appointed, threw their support to
Martin. If they could not have a local Methodist, they would settle for a Christiansburg Presbyterian. Martin is reported to have lost the appointment by one
vote. Following his defeat as president, he was elected to a professorship, which
was probably more to his liking anyway. Certainly there is no indication whatever that he harbored any resentment for not receiving the presidency.

Charles Landon Carter Minor, the successful candidate elected by the board
as first president of the Virginia Agricultural and Mechanical College, was a native of Hanover County, Virginia, and a graduate of the University of Virginia
in 1858 with an M.A. degree. Descended from a long line of distinguished Virginia ancestry, he had mounted a comprehensive, thorough, aggressive, yet tactful
campaign for the presidency. Through well-placed connections, he secured endorsements from many outstanding lawyers, politicians, clergymen, farmers, businessmen, and college professors.

Especially notable in this latter group were the endorsements he received
from Charles S. Venable, John B. Minor, and William H. McGuffey (of *McGuffey's Reader* fame), all beloved and highly respected professors at the University
of Virginia.

In a delicately phrased letter to Ruffner in which he fully endorsed Minor,
Venable implied that if the board would select its faculty from distinguished
young graduates of the University of Virginia, it not only would get competent
men but it also would get the much needed approval of both the academic community and the people of the state as well. Subsequent events proved Venable's
accuracy of judgment of the academic community to be exceeded only by his
ignorance of the temper of the people of the state.

McGuffey, obviously writing at the solicitation of a third person, endorsed
Minor; then, apparently getting a bit mixed up, he concluded his endorsement

by commending Mr. Blackford as one having had experience with an agricultural school in Maryland. Evidently Blackford had sought McGuffey's endorsement of Minor.

John B. Minor's letter of endorsement addressed personally to Ruffner not only endorsed Minor's distant cousin, C. L. C. Minor, for the presidency, but also endorsed the proposed "narrow gauge" plan of instruction for the College. At the same time, this "molder of opinion," who was standing shoulder to shoulder with Ruffner in the struggle for a public school system in Virginia, felt that the area of instruction for the College could be and should be expanded in due time when "demanded by an educated public sentiment." Admitting to his original support of the claims of the University of Virginia for the land-grant money, Minor confessed some relief now that a new college had been established. Such a school, he believed, could accomplish objectives from the very beginning which would be impractical if not impossible at the University of Virginia. Disclaiming any and all jealousy toward the new school, this notable leader wrote, "I trust with all my heart that it may be soon the glory of the Commonwealth, blending its lustre with that of the other nurseries of education and affording powerful aid in resuscitating the dimmed, but not, I trust, the declining renown of the Old Dominion."

This latter sentiment was echoed with varying degrees of audibility by representatives from most of the institutions in the state, the one possible exception being VMI, whose superintendent, Ruffner privately felt, never forgave him for his opposition to VMI as the recipient of the land-grant fund.

Many individuals in endorsing Minor for the presidency of the Virginia Agricultural and Mechanical College stressed his experience gained as president of the Maryland Agricultural College. Strangely enough, the fact that his tenure in this office had lasted only about one year was never adequately explained. Minor himself felt this experience gave him "some advantage" over the other applicants since as president he had spent much time studying the organization of agricultural and mechanical colleges already established in other states. In addition to this study, he had made numerous visits to examine the exhibits and experiments of the Federal Bureau of Education, only nine miles from the Maryland school. These visits, he confidently wrote, had also given him "considerable advantage for learning what little is known about the very difficult question how to teach the science and art of agriculture."

There is no question whatever but that Minor with his broad base of support and experience came the closest of all the presidential candidates to meeting the criteria, official and unofficial, which the board had set up for the presidency of the new school. The fact that the name Minor had been so prominent in the affairs of the ante-bellum Virginia State Agricultural Society certainly did not hurt his candidacy either. Even so, his margin of victory was a close one over Charles Martin, who according to one editorial lost out because two of his known supporters were absent when the president was elected.

Following the election of Minor as president, the board turned to the appointment of a faculty. To Ruffner's surprised dismay, the board first rearranged the curriculum plan agreed upon in July, in the direction of the typical literary institution and then elected a faculty in conformity with this new plan. James H. Lane, a graduate of VMI, was appointed to the chair of natural philosophy and chemistry to which was attached the responsibility for military tactics; Charles

Martin, a graduate of Hampden-Sydney College and erstwhile candidate for the presidency, was appointed to the chair of English language and literature to which was attached the responsibility for ancient language; Gray Carroll, a graduate of the University of Virginia, was appointed to the chair of mathematics to which was attached the responsibility for modern language. Natural history was attached to the originally proposed chair of technical agriculture and mechanics, but such a behind-the-scene dispute developed concerning the responsibilities of this chair it was decided to postpone filling this position until the next meeting of the board to be held in the following January. Apparently Ruffner was the only member of the board who sensed any incongruity in opening an agricultural and mechanical college without first employing a teacher of agriculture and mechanics.

The action of the board in reorganizing the curriculum toward strengthening the "literary" feature and in failing to appoint a professor of agriculture or mechanics was subsequently pounced upon by Thomas Conrad, editor of the *Montgomery Messenger,* as political maneuvering by "eastern politicians," notably John Goode and Lewis E. Harvie, to prevent the appointment of any western man to the faculty. The western representatives on the board, claimed Conrad, wanted "Colonel Preston" (presumably Colonel Robert Preston) on the faculty if not as professor of agriculture at least as farm manager. The western members, Conrad contended, were the true farmers and businessmen of the board, ever ready to vote their honest convictions; but unfortunately, they were so "naive" in politics they had not even recognized Harvie's adroit and skillful tactics for what they were: namely, an effort to block Preston's appointment and secure the appointment of Harvie's son to the faculty.

Whatever factual basis Conrad's charges may have had, they added fuel to the smouldering fires of resentment slowly building up in the minds of many in Montgomery County formerly associated with the Preston and Olin Institute. This group had not anticipated the extent to which their institute, in Ruffner's words, would be "completely swept away" and pass completely from local control in the transition from a local to a state institution. Ruffner recognized the existence of this resentment and warned Minor to take it into consideration in his administering the new College. Even with this ample forewarning, Minor was never completely successful in coping with this problem. In fact, every administration from Minor's day to the present has had to deal with varying degrees of local approval and disapproval of the ways the college affairs have been run.

The board in the meantime, having at last adopted a plan of organization, formulated a course of study, bought a farm, set college fees, employed the nucleus of a faculty, and set October 1, 1872, as the date for opening the new College, adjourned to meet in January, 1873.

Two thousand copies of the report setting forth the plan of organization and the curriculum of the College were printed and given wide circulation throughout the state. At the same time Ruffner, at the request of the board, prepared a more popular condensation of the report. In addition to these releases, Ruffner, as superintendent of public instruction, sent an official notice of the nature of the new school to all the city and county superintendents of schools throughout the state. In this notice he not only outlined the nature of the new school but also called attention of the superintendents to their responsibilities in nominating students for state scholarships.

Ruffner's condensation of the report was given much wider publicity and editorial support in the press of the state than the more voluminous report itself. This condensation, once dubbed "Ruffner's plan to keep them down on the farm," plainly reflected Ruffner's conviction that the new school should be accepted as a partner and not a competitor in a state system of education. Through an approach reconciling much of the sentiment expressed in the petitions and the legislative debates concerning the disposition of the land-grant fund, Ruffner sought to secure widely based public support for the school. This endeavor was partly successful, especially with respect to the ideas included in the following extract: "The school will be *sui generis*—a truly technical school of secondary [practical] grade. Its whole cast will have special reference to the wants of the industrial classes, by which are meant those who are directly (not remotely) engaged in producing, developing, or shaping the material products of the state; and its ultimate object is not to educate them out of but in and for their vocations."

These ideas received hearty endorsement from most of the press and numerous letters to the editor signed "farmer" or "mechanic." The use of the term "secondary grade" to describe the school as practical rather than theoretical did prove to be unfortunate. Many people interpreted it to mean the school would be a technical high school rather than a college. It took President Minor and his faculty more than a year to undo the damage caused by this unfortunate choice of words.

After dwelling at great length on the practical features to be developed in the new school, Ruffner, almost as if pained to admit it, so great was his fear that the literary would swallow up the practical, did say, "The course of instruction though aiming at practical results will not as before intimated exclude the liberal studies . . . ." The entire report left no doubt whatever that such "liberal studies" were to be taught in an "eclectic style with special reference to the objects" of an agricultural and mechanical college. For those who might feel the beginning curriculum was too restricted, the cautious hope was held out that as financial means increased and further needs developed, the standards would be raised and offerings increased.

With respect to military tactics required by the federal act, Ruffner's report merely stated that "military tactics will receive a degree of attention not yet determined."

In retrospect, it appears that the entire report setting forth the plan of organization, the three-year course of study, the restriction to a practical technical school, and the assignment to the faculty of responsibility for preparing a working program to carry out the proposals, received widespread public approval in all respects with the exception of the "not yet determined" attention to be given military tactics. With respect to this feature, many individuals, no doubt influenced by military experiences of the Civil War, suddenly discovered their fitness and desire to advise the board on this problem. They advised. As a result, "the people" were choosing sides on the proper role of military training before the College even opened its doors.

One strongly pro-military advocate urged that all academic instruction of whatever nature be dropped in favor of a complete military organization in which the students under rigid military supervision would perform practical work in the shop and on the farm. The students, he felt, should be organized into military units and marched to and from the fields and shops. Once in the field or shop, the group should be broken up into smaller details, and still under military regulations carry out assigned tasks.

The anti-military advocates in no uncertain terms proclaimed the belief that would echo and re-echo throughout the first century of the College's existence: namely, that in order to become farmers and mechanics it should not be necessary first to become soldiers. One anti-military individual, protesting against any type of comprehensive military organization, warned of the demerit system such organization would have to set up. Any student not having an aptitude or bent for such training, he warned, could accumulate enough demerits because of behavior in no way related to skill in farming or mechanics sufficient to warrant his dismissal from school. Such a dismissal, he triumphantly concluded with unescapable logic, would prevent the student from getting the type of education intended and offered by the school in the first place.

In spite of, or perhaps because of, so much free advice, the board continued to temporize on the question of military instruction for nearly a decade, during which time the college administration tried out several approaches to the baffling problem.

The curriculum described by Ruffner in his report and widely accepted in the state, with the exception of proposing a three-year program instead of the usual one of four years, was not radically different from the courses offered in other land-grant institutions having been founded a bit earlier in other states. The conservative nature of the state, coupled with its limited financial resources, did work to cause the concept of a program restricted to practical scientific offerings to survive in Virginia's land-grant College at Blacksburg long after most major land-grant institutions in the country had moved to more comprehensive programs.

Chapter 3

The Early Years: President Minor

1872-1879

EVEN THOUGH PROFESSORS to teach agriculture and mechanics had not been secured, plans went ahead to open the College on October 1, 1872. President Minor had been detained at Sewanee until September 18, but he had written to Black and to Professor Martin, urging them to go ahead with all preparations necessary for the opening. These two individuals set to work with diligence. In addition to cleaning the building, repairing the classroom furniture, and cutting weeds and grass on the campus, they prepared and circulated a small folder describing and advertising the new College. No copy of this first circular supervised by a faculty member is known to exist today. In a private letter to Ruffner, Minor stated his approval of the zeal shown by Black and Martin but also expressed his disapproval of the results. The circular, he complained, was a very unattractive and "shabby one" which did not do justice to the college program. Within less than a month after Minor's arrival in Blacksburg, he sought permission to replace this circular with a "neat" attractive one worthy of the College and truly depicting the actual program being undertaken. Unfortunately, if this circular was ever produced, no known copy is available either.

67

On October 1, 1872, the Virginia Agricultural and Mechanical College officially opened its two doors to students. The faculty gathered early; President
Minor unlocked the front door, and he, Lane, Martin, Carroll, and Shepherd
filed into the building and somewhat nervously, it can be imagined, awaited the
arrival of the first student. The wait was much longer than had been anticipated,
but finally William A. Caldwell from Craig County "drifted" in. There is a completely unverified tradition that Caldwell's appearance at the College was motivated more by curiosity than by any intention to enroll as a student. Certainly
he had not been nominated for a state scholarship by his county superintendent
of schools, as it sometimes has been asserted. Whatever his real motive may have
been, immediately he was given a state scholarship by the faculty and enrolled
as the first student in Virginia Agricultural and Mechanical College.

The official opening of the College that, in time, became the largest in the
state, received no fanfare or ceremony of dedication beyond the critical appraisal
bestowed upon it by the village loafers gathered at the post office and on the
veranda of the nearby Luster's Hotel. The state press, while not so critical as the
local observers, was almost as casual in its announcement of the opening. *The
Richmond Dispatch* contented itself with declaring there would be as many
students present as facilities would accommodate. This was not a very revealing
statement, since very few people in the state knew anything about the facilities.
The Southern Planter, the leading agricultural journal in the state, after announcing the opening of the College, declared that the faculty members were fully
qualified for their positions. The editor of this journal then added a few extracts
from Ruffner's report describing the College and its program. Other papers in the
state in announcing the opening tended to follow similar approaches. In nearly
all instances, the extracts selected from Ruffner's report were designed to portray
the College as a practical one organized to train the "youth of the state for work,
not ornament."

The slow initial enrollment, which reached only twenty-nine by the end of the
first week, naturally enough worried the faculty. Officially, this small enrollment
was attributed to the shortness of time available to the board within which to
advertise the school before its opening. Privately, Minor was coming much
closer to the real reason. In a long letter to Ruffner he said a misunderstanding
had developed as to the meaning intended in the description of the school as a
"technical college of secondary grade." This idea of operating the College strictly
on a technical basis while leaving to other colleges all training in the literary or
liberal areas, he wrote, seemed to be "not only rejected by the people of the
vicinity but generally regarded as intolerable and not to be patiently entertained."

As a result of this attitude he was convinced that a number of prospective
students were holding back on registering while waiting to see if any changes
would be made which would enable them to get any of the same kind of instruction they had been accustomed "to receiving from the Preston and Olin Institute." In addition to the group holding back on registration, another group had
come demanding instruction in areas other than "the strictly technical training
enjoined by the organization committee report." This group, Minor wrote,
claimed that the action of the board in revising its curricular organization at its
August meeting justified the demand for more extensive offerings. As one result
of this interpretation of the board action, Minor complained, "Material very different from what I expected showed up at the College. Very few students want or

will have a course especially adapted for farmers or mechanics," he warned. Faced with this unexpected situation, the faculty, with some relief it is suspected, adjusted its program in the direction of these new demands. "As a result," Minor wrote, "the College is forced to make work much like that of other schools except it has more science and less ancient language."

It is fascinating to speculate as to what this faculty with a liberal arts background would have done if the first students to arrive had demanded training in agricultural or mechanical education.

The shift in direction of the program had been approved by the local board member, Minor explained to Ruffner; but since it was Anderson and Ruffner who had championed the cause of the strictly technical school, he, Minor, would appreciate approval of the shift and at the same time would be very glad to know if they "could approve of a circular which announced the actual state" of the work as a result of the shift. Anderson's and Ruffner's response to this request is not known, but perhaps its nature may be gleaned from the fact that no official report issued by Minor during his entire administration ever made any reference to this shift or the necessity for it. On the contrary, one gets the distinct impression from reading his reports that he went out of the way to promote the image of a technical school in agriculture and mechanics. The designation as a "technical school of secondary grade," however, was abruptly dropped from all official reports and never used again. While it appears that Minor gave a rather accurate appraisal of the pressure facing the College when it opened, it also appears that his designation of the pressure as being local in nature may have been too restricted, since a number of expressions, such as "the people's college," "our people's college," "the college for the people," "our college for the masses," and "our college at Blacksburg" had begun to appear in the papers of the state by the time the College opened. Indeed there is strong evidence to indicate a somewhat paradoxical situation in which the people accepted Ruffner's articulate description of the College as one to be developed to meet the needs of the great mass of people, but at the same time rejected or ignored his equally articulate conclusion that such needs could be met best by a program severely restricted to agriculture and mechanics. This conclusion is strengthened by the fact that many students entered the College and completed the first one or two years work and then, before concentration on agriculture or mechanics, transferred to other institutions to complete their education.

The discovery that the sons of the men who tilled the fields, fed the cattle, built the bridges, and manned the factories wanted more than a technical education in agriculture and mechanics was a perplexing one to both Ruffner and Minor. Ruffner had long foreseen this probability but felt it would be overcome as soon as an agricultural and mechanical college became available to the people. This minister-turned-educator wanted the agricultural and mechanical features protected and promoted, because he believed the industrial economy of the state desperately needed such an education. Minor agreed with this point of view but warned that the development of a technical school would be difficult, "since people do not see its real value or need"; therefore, he wanted some relaxation of the restricted agricultural and mechanical program toward one more in harmony with the demands of the people. Both points of view proved to be essential for the College, but it required much pioneering effort before they were woven together successfully in one program.

While Minor's explanation and defense of the adjustments which moved the College curriculum toward that of the traditional college seem to be valid, it must be remembered that the board had not appointed anyone to teach agriculture or mechanics or to manage the college farm. The cause of agriculture and mechanics had no advocate with "vested interests" on the faculty.

Before the board acted to fill these positions, the legislature had met and enacted certain changes in the procedures whereby individuals were appointed to the Board of Visitors for the College. These changes, while minor in nature, introduced certain elements of uncertainty as to tenure on the first board. Of much greater significance, as it turned out, these changes unintentionally demonstrated to the legislature and to the people the degree to which the course of the College could be controlled by enacting legislation affecting the board. The particular change of immediate concern directed the governor, with the consent of the Senate, to appoint a nine-member board, with three members to serve one year, three to serve two years, and three to serve three years. All terms were to begin on January 1, 1873. The three members of the State Board of Education and the president of the Virginia State Agricultural Society were to continue as ex-officio members. (By another legislative enactment in 1874, all ex-officio members except the state superintendent of public instruction were dropped from membership on the board.)

Probably because of the charges of sectionalism leveled at the make-up of the board first appointed by Governor Walker, the new enactment provided that the members to be appointed should be "distributed as nearly equally as practicable between the four grand divisions of the state." Even this feature, well-intended as it was, proved to be embarrassing during the early critical years of the College, for no governor was ever able to find nine persons from the four divisions of the state to serve staggered terms of office in such a combination as to win complete approval from all the sections at the same time.

These changes in method of appointment to the board, while not made final until February, 1873, had been under consideration from the time the legislature had convened in December, 1872. The board was fully aware of these legislative discussions and therefore felt an understandable hesitancy in attending to more than routine matters concerning the College until after some decisions had been reached.

Since Black, Cowan, Cloyd, and Stuart lived in southwestern Virginia, the first three within a short distance of the College itself, it was obvious that all four could not be reappointed to the board under the new conditions. In appointing the board under the new requirements, Governor Walker therefore replaced Cowan and Cloyd with John E. Penn, of Patrick County, and E. M. Tidball, of Frederick County, and reappointed all the remaining members of the first board. This action, surprisingly enough, drew the immediate ire of at least one editor, who claimed the replacement of Cowan and Cloyd was an act of discrimination against the "true farmers" of western Virginia.

Since the College catalog for the session of 1872-73 was prepared after this change in the board had taken place, the names of Cowan and Cloyd do not appear in this publication as members of the first Board of Visitors for the College. Unfortunately, this omission has tended to cause some confusion not only in College records but also in according proper recognition of the important contributions made by these two gentlemen in terms of time and financial support given the College during its critical infancy.

When the board met in January, 1873, for the purpose of appointing a farm manager and a professor of agriculture and mechanics, it had a large number of applicants for both positions. J. Seddon Harvie was appointed as farm manager, but it was decided to postpone the appointment of the professor of agriculture and mechanics until another meeting in February. This delay is a bit puzzling. It would seem such a professorship would be the first instead of the last to be filled in an agricultural and mechanical college. In fact, it seems the delay was caused by uncertainty as to the outcome of the pending legislative action concerning appointment to the board and, more significantly, by an inability on the part of the board to agree on the nature of agricultural and mechanical education to be undertaken at the new College, which seemed to be getting along rather well without such a professor anyway. Admitting it would not know what to do with a professor of agriculture and mechanics even if it had one, the board appointed a committee to define the duties of a professor of technical agriculture and then adjourned to meet in February.

This delay aroused much speculation and some criticism throughout the state. One critic bitterly denounced the delay as a combination of factional political maneuvering and abysmal ignorance on the part of the board of the true nature of agriculture. On the other hand, one Allen, writing in *The Lynchburg Daily Virginian,* defended the board and claimed that the delay was caused by uncertainties faced with respect to the income to be had from the state bonds which had been purchased with the proceeds of the sale of the land scrip.

The handling of these bonds during the College's infancy is an intriguing and at the same time revealing story of the almost casual manner in which the state went about financing the Virginia Agricultural and Mechanical College during its earliest years. The money derived from the sale of the land scrip had been invested in state bonds. Because of the discount sale price of the bonds on the date of purchase, the total value of the bonds acquired amounted to approximately $516,468. On January 1, 1873, no interest from the bonds had been paid to the Board of Visitors; in fact, these bonds were being caught up in the debates revolving around the entire question of state indebtedness, which instead of decreasing was increasing at a rate alarming to many. There was developing in the legislature a faction advocating an adjustment of all state indebtedness. The proposals for readjustment as far as the College was concerned ranged from an alarming complete repudiation of the bonds to a reduction of the interest rate. Happily none of these proposals, which would continue to plague the College for nearly a decade and a half, received legislative sanction at this particular time. On the contrary, the legislature, encouraged by the strenuous effort of the board members, did agree to pay one year's interest due on the bonds. This limitation to one year's payment proved to be an unexpected embarrassment because of other developments in connection with the bonds.

In investing the proceeds from the land scrip in state bonds as instructed by the legislature, the Board of Education had done so through a Richmond bank. When the bonds were ready for delivery, the bank, following the governor's instructions, delivered them to Ruffner's office, where they were checked by the Board of Education. Then, over Ruffner's strong protest, the remaining board members departed, leaving him with the responsibility for more than half a million dollars worth of coupon bonds. Ruffner, relating the incident several years later, said that he and his secretary thereupon tied the bonds into packages and hid them under a pile of papers in his office. Then locking his office door and leaving his secretary on guard in an outside office, Ruffner went to a nearby bank where he located a strong box in a "locked pigeon-hole." Thereupon he carried the box to his office, placed the bonds in it, locked the box, and carried it under his arm down the street back to the bank. Since most of the bonds were of the coupon type, Ruffner said in order to collect the interest due on them, it was necessary to clip the coupons, but there was no place suitable in the bank to do this; therefore, he had to carry the bonds to his office, clip the coupons, return the bonds to the "pigeon-hole," and deposit the coupons. Ruffner said he had to perform this act at least twice before he and President Minor succeeded in getting the bonds changed to a certificate which was placed in custody of the second auditor's office in Richmond. Other records available seem to confirm Ruffner's account of these financial transactions, although it is not clear whether all of the interest due on the bonds was first collected in this manner. In clipping the coupons for the first time Ruffner made one mistake. He clipped coupons for all interest due on January 1, 1873, which, as it turned out, added up to more than one year's interest. The excess was only $3,402; but since the legislature had authorized the payment of interest for one year only, the extra coupons could not be cashed. Ruffner thereupon sealed the coupons in an envelope and stored them with the bonds to await payment the next year. By next year, however, the entire question of state debt and state bonds had become so fantastically interwoven with politics that the legislature once more refused to pay more than one year's interest. Perhaps some small inkling of the swirling debates surrounding state finances, debts, and bonds during the College's infancy may be gained when it is realized that this modest sum was not paid until nine years later, under a legislature controlled by members elected to office on a platform pledged to "readjust" once and for all the state debt.

With the troublesome question of finance at least partly resolved and the date upon which the Board of Visitors was to appoint the professor of agriculture and mechanics rapidly approaching, speculation and advice began to appear in the press as to the probable appointee. The *Richmond Whig,* alluding to "mutterings of sectionalism" in connection with the make-up of the Board of Visitors and of the faculty, advised the appointment of a person from the Valley of Virginia. When the board, meeting a few days later, failed to do so, the *Whig* immediately wrote a strong editorial denouncing, not the appointee, but the board and demanded that the legislature, which was in session at the time, take the matter of appointment of the board in hand to prevent discrimination against any section of the state.

Perhaps the bitterest charge of sectionalism, politics, incompetence, and partisanship ever leveled at the board was the one launched by Thomas Conrad in an editorial almost immediately after he assumed the editorship of the *Montgomery Messenger* in nearby Christiansburg. This attack is noteworthy because it illustrates in a single editorial the nature of many of the attacks and charges with which the board and the College had to contend for nearly two decades of its earliest existence.

In his editorial, after assuring the public that he was attacking the board and not the College, which he said belonged to the people, Conrad belittled the achievements made by the board to date. Announcing that the board would meet on February 11 for the fifth time in ten months, he continued:

At the first meeting they organized, appointed one or two committees, shook hands and adjourned. At the second meeting (at White Sulphur Springs) they heard Mr. Ruffner read his *voluminous* essay, received the legal documents appertaining to the "County Bonds" and transfer of the "College" property, and then organized into a Greeley mass meeting with speeches from members of the *Board Only*. At the third meeting (at the Yellow Sulphur Springs) by the stimulating influence of cigars and mint juleps they elected four teachers and adjourned. At the fourth meeting, held in Richmond, they heard the President of the College, talked over the interest question, heard testimonials read, elected a "farm manager or foreman" and adjourned. The fifth meeting takes place on the 11th instant in Richmond at which time they are *expected* to elect another teacher.

Then Conrad attacked the board for spending so much of the taxpayers' money to conduct business which, in his opinion, any competent board should have been able to complete in one or at least two meetings. He further charged that the election of the professor of agriculture would be influenced by the sectional, political, and religious bias of the board members, who after all, he asserted, were not competent to determine the qualifications needed for a faculty. One member of the board, according to Conrad, was supporting for the professorship of agriculture a man "who can catch a hat full of water during every rain storm, analyze fertilizer (with the formula already given), tell blue grass from broom-sedge, and cure a horse with botts." Another member of the board, he charged, had heard of "Horticulture, Pomology, Veterinary Surgery, Entomology, Zoology, Geology, and Pisciculture" and wanted a man who could teach each one. What the board would do, he charged, was appoint a man of social prestige, without scientific attainment, but with high testimonials, who sought the position because of salary but detested "the mechanic and laboring man as he does a skunk." Since the board was dominated by the eastern politicians who always outmaneuvered the true farmers on the board from the west, charged Conrad, all the western applicants including Carson from Abingdon; Grabowski from Montgomery; Bradford, Mead, Hardy and others from the valley might just as well withdraw their applications for the professorship of agriculture. Individual board members were singled out for personal attack and ridicule: Anderson for the "big dinner" he usually gave the board and Goode for his ineffectual efforts on behalf of Horace Greeley. Ruffner was depicted as "the daddy of all the public schools, looking as learned as a stuffed owl and feeling as important as a strutting peacock." Continuing his attack he wrote:

Beverly of Fauquier who scents for the strongest trail and never barks until he finds it will be there [at the board meeting] . . . for Fauquier has four applicants, and their claims must be adequately considered. Attorney General Taylor will be there as he is still the hazy tail to the Gubernatorial Comet. Major Sutherlin, of Danville, who can see beyond the Dan River, over the James River, and over the steeples of Richmond, and the dome of the university, yea a man of enlarged views, liberal policy, and philanthropic aims . . . will be there. General W. H. F. Lee, [son of Robert E. Lee] will be there for there is a major general applying for the chair. The ex-member from Amelia [Lewis E. Harvie] will surely be there for there is another appointment to be made.

At this point Conrad hinted, and in another editorial charged, that Harvie resorted to delaying tactics in earlier meetings of the board just to secure the appointment of his personal choice to the faculty and of his son to the position of farm manager. Concluding his attack on the individual board members, he damned the western members with faint praise by observing, "As to the western members we cannot affirm, except for the business-like Stuart and the punctual Black."

Having concluded his attack on the individual members, Conrad resumed his charges of discrimination against the southwestern part of the state and warned that if the board continued such discrimination, the southwest would desert the board. In concluding his fulminations against what he considered to be the injustices of the board, Conrad claimed that the janitor was the only "relic of the Preston and Olin Institute which Mr. Ruffner did not sweep away." To remedy this and other discriminatory practices against the west, Conrad sarcastically advised the western members of the board to hold a caucus and try to unite to secure the appointment, if at all possible, of someone from the west, to act as groom for the thoroughbred Alderney bull which a board member had "generously given the college." "Cannot the bull-groom," he asked, "be a living witness that the western members rallied at last and secured a bull-y appointment?"

Conrad's attack drew immediate rebuttal from citizens of Montgomery County. One particularly indignant individual, after using the columns of the *Lynchburg Virginian* to give an almost point by point rebuttal, concluded his letter with a thinly veiled suggestion that Conrad, having been judged unfit for the College faculty, no doubt would prove equally unacceptable to the bull as its groom, if the bull were permitted a choice.

Another citizen, on the other hand, gleefully urged Conrad to "Lay on, Mc-Duff" so long as his attack was on the board and not the College. The College, he exclaimed, "is the People's Institution [which] will live and carol out its glorious future usefulness . . . ." The western members on the original board, he believed, had really tried to get a western man appointed to the faculty but not being "familiar with the beauties of forming combinations" for voting purposes, they had been outmaneuvered on every turn. Now that two of the western board members, the only true farmers he affirmed, had been replaced on the board, he too feared the consequences as did Conrad.

The relevance of these charges to the actual situation that existed is in considerable doubt. The most immediate effect was to cause a further polarization of the community around the state-college-state-control concept as against the state-college-local-control concept. Conrad's editorial served to give the adherents of this latter group, smarting over the extent to which their control of the Preston and Olin Institute had been "swept away," some points around which they consciously or unconsciously could marshall their arguments and grievances. Unhappily, President Minor's entire administration suffered irreparable harm from some of the zealots of this latter group. Ironically, Conrad himself when he later became president of the College came under immediate local criticism, perhaps more intense than any other president of the College has ever had to endure. To add to the irony of events, W. H. F. Lee, whom Conrad had attacked in his editorial, became a member of the Board of Visitors during the latter's tenure as president. Using the local attack on Conrad as a starting point, Lee and his cousin, Governor Fitzhugh Lee, were instrumental in getting Conrad replaced as president by the identical "major general" to whom Conrad had disparagingly referred in the editorial.

Ignoring both the attacks and the advice thrown its way by the press, the Board of Visitors met in Richmond on February 11, 1873, for the purpose of completing its appointment of a faculty for the College. A decision was reached to employ two persons instead of one to teach agriculture and mechanics. The candidates once more were numerous, and the pressure for each one was great; but after some deliberation, the board appointed John W. C. Davis, of Hanover County, and M. G. Ellzey, of Fauquier County. Surprisingly enough, considering the sectional rivalry of the time, the press expressed approval of both appointments, although some confusion developed as to the title and duties assigned to each. It was reported that Davis had been elected to fill the "chair of agriculture," while Ellzey had been elected to fill the "chair of mechanics." The catalog for 1872-73, on the other hand, listed Davis as professor of agriculture and mechanics and Ellzey as professor of natural history and analytical chemistry. The catalog of 1873-74 showed yet another arrangement of titles and listed Davis as professor of chemistry, technical mechanics and drawing, while Ellzey was listed as professor of agriculture and natural history. This shifting of assigned duties, particularly in agriculture and mechanics, was typical of the College in its earliest years as it sought both to create and to implement applied sciences in these two areas.

Little is known of Ellzey's background other than that he possessed an M.D. degree and, according to Conrad, was of a mechanical turn of mind. Immediately after Minor's election to the presidency of the College, Ellzey had applied to him for a position on the faculty. Minor forwarded his name to Ruffner along with a cautiously worded endorsement of the application. It is not known whether Minor's endorsement carried any weight with the board. It probably did not, since the board jealously guarded its prerogative to examine and select all faculty members. In fact, the available records indicate the probability that Minor was never consulted with respect to any faculty members employed during his tenure as president.

John W. C. Davis, the second member of this first team ever employed to teach agriculture and mechanics at the College, had participated in the program of agricultural education getting under way at the University of Virginia under Professor John W. Mallett. His appointment to the faculty received wide acclaim in the press of the state, which surprisingly, perhaps, paid more attention to the fact that he was the son of a Methodist minister than it did to his professional qualifications. One editor even advanced the observation that since Davis had lived with his minister father in numerous sections of the state, he really should be thought of as a son of Virginia rather than as the son of any particular section.

With the announced completion of all faculty appointments, the focus of attention concerning the new college shifted for a period of time from the legislature and the Board of Visitors to the College itself.

Since the board had elected to open the College before it hired anyone to teach agriculture and mechanics, the school upon opening closely resembled the typical liberal arts college. This feature probably saved its life during the earlier critical years of struggle to become a real agricultural and mechanical college in fact rather than in aspiration only. The struggle toward the achievement of this objective was a long one carried on in an environment filled with a mixture of frustrations, disappointments, triumphs, petty achievements, heroic sacrifices, and eventual success. In this respect, the development of the Virginia Agricultural and Mechanical College differed but little from the development of land-grant institutions in other states. The major differences in the development of the land-grant colleges as they moved toward a common goal arose in nearly all instances from circumstances unique to the several states in which the institutions grew to maturity. Certainly the Virginia Agricultural and Mechanical College was no exception to this pattern of development.

When the first class enrolled in the Virginia Agricultural and Mechanical College in October, 1872, the only building on the campus was the original one occupied by the Preston and Olin Institute. This building stood at the extreme eastern end of the present campus on the small hillside immediately overlooking the present Main Street of downtown Blacksburg. One could stand in the front door of the building and see the full length southward of Main Street. Conversely, as one approached the College from the south and topped the hill near the present town hall, this lone building loomed up as if placed squarely across the road, blocking all further progress. Apparently no shrubbery whatever had been planted to relieve the bare lines of the building or of the head-high public hitching rack standing immediately below it. No wonder students coming to the campus or returning to the campus in the middle of the winter coined descriptive terms of the building, perhaps best left unrepeated. Samuel P. Withers, who entered the institution at the middle of the first academic year wrote of his recollection of his first view of the College. After a three-hour ride from Christiansburg in an open hack on a windy and bitterly cold February day, he saw the lone building standing in the distance. "The architect who planned it," wrote Withers, "must have been a genius, for it was classic in its ugliness!" Other visitors, who came at more pleasant times of the year, were much kinder in their appraisal of this lonely old landmark, which before its destruction by a disastrous fire in 1913 suffered an almost incredible number of faceliftings and alterations, internal and external.

During October, 1872, a total of forty-three students enrolled in the College. The legislature in establishing the school had provided that a number of free scholarships equal to the number of members of the Virginia House of Delegates be granted to the students in the state. The recipients of the scholarships were to be recommended by the superintendents of schools for each county. If no one applied from a particular county, the faculty could grant the scholarship to an applicant from another county. These scholarships proved to be an excellent recruiting device for a number of years. At the same time, probably because of the unusually high rate of turnover in the offices of county superintendents of schools, these scholarships were never adequately developed on a statewide basis. As a result, the faculty soon found itself filling unused quotas with applicants from counties or cities whose quotas had been filled. This development led to an unusual amount of pressure on the president of the College by politicians and other prominent citizens on behalf of applicants from their particular communities. In addition to using up much of the president's valuable time in correspondence, this twist taken by the administration of the scholarships helped to pull the College into a political patronage system, which for a time threatened the school's very existence.

In all probability, the first year's enrollment of 132 was larger than had been expected, for even this number overtaxed by far the meager facilities of the Preston and Olin building. Therefore, in presenting his first report to the Virginia General Assembly on July 9, 1873, President Minor stated that the building was totally inadequate and unsuited for the purpose it was serving. The classrooms were poorly lighted and poorly ventilated. Furthermore, a lack of space made it necessary to use one room as a combination office and library, while another served as the reading room. The little equipment available had to be stored in closets, while several lectures had to be presented "in simple chambers of one window each." As a remedy, Minor expressed the hope that the legislature would appropriate for at least three years the same amount given to other state institutions of learning. Ruffner, in his annual report as state superintendent of public instruction echoed Minor's pleas. At the time, Ruffner was receiving almost unprecedented acclaim for his herculean accomplishments on behalf of public education; consequently, when he spoke the public listened, although it did not always accept or follow. Deploring the introduction into the curriculum of the ancient languages (Greek and Latin), which he held to be an "incongruity" in a college of agriculture and mechanics, he nonetheless expressed his complete approval of everything else accomplished during the first year. Fully aware of the "mutterings of sectionalism" and the unrealistic expectations of accomplishments with respect to the College held by so many "gentlemen-farmers," Ruffner wrote: "It would be most unreasonable to expect matured results, or even very definite forms of instruction in so recent an institution, and one embarking on a new course in which there are but few safe precedents, and being compelled to handle heterogeneous materials."

Continuing, he wrote of the College:

> Already its success has succeeded all reasonable expectation, and indicates a real, though perchance undefined, desire among the producing classes for some form of education which will address itself directly to their daily life. But the college is now laboring under embarrassment which not only cramps its present movements but absolutely forbids growth much beyond its present dimensions. Its only school building is now crowded and is thoroughly unsuited for its present purpose, and I see no hope of obtaining suitable accommodations except from a state appropriation. What a pity it would be to see this promising school checked . . . in its usefulness for the want of necessary buildings! Considering the peculiar objects of the school, its wide field, and its great possibilities . . . I do not see how anyone can doubt the wisdom and the economy of giving it the means of erecting such buildings as its growth demands.

The sentiment expressed in this report was repeated over and over for the next century as the College grew and expanded its effort to develop an education which "addressed itself directly to the daily life of the people."

Surprisingly enough, considering the financial plight of the state, the legislature responded affirmatively to the appeal and on March 27, 1874, appropriated $45,000 to be used for buildings.

The board was both delighted and surprised with this appropriation. In 1873, at the urging of Ruffner, it had purchased the Edward and John Black farm of some eighty acres connecting the five acres of the Preston and Olin site with the college farm. This purchase, criticized by some, turned out to be a most valuable one, for it provided the College with adequate building sites upon which most of its major buildings and all of its dormitories were erected for the next half century.

With the money in sight for buildings, the board met in Blacksburg in June, 1874, and drew plans for locating and erecting two academic buildings, two faculty homes, and a home for the president, to be constructed in that order. Ruffner was unusually excited and optimistic concerning the physical growth of the College. He was thoroughly familiar with the practice often followed by wealthy individuals of making "handsome" bequests and donations to colleges of their choice. As a member of the Board of Trustees of Washington and Lee University, he was also aware that such aid was usually generated and improved by a carefully and honestly planned approach to individuals with interests in harmony with the interests and objectives of the college. In his opinion it was the responsibility of the president of the College to take the lead in generating such support. Encouraged and stimulated by the action of the board in planning and locating the new buildings, Ruffner wrote to President Minor urging him to start a campaign for the solicitation of such additional funds. Cautioning Minor that the letter was "just a chat for the private ear of your executive committee," he proceeded to suggest names of supposedly wealthy agriculturists and industrialists whose interests probably paralleled aspects of the College's program. These individuals, he implied, if properly approached, would no doubt be happy to donate something worthy of themselves and the princely fortune which the state had poured into their laps. One of these individuals, he felt, was already prepared to lead off with such a donation.

It would appear that President Minor was unable to prepare the proper kind of "flattering unction" urged by Ruffner on behalf of the Virginia Agricultural and Mechanical College, for nothing at all came from this proposal, although most, if not all, of the potential donors listed by Ruffner did make "handsome" donations to older educational institutions in the state. The fledgling College had to pass through the dangerous period of childhood and the stormy period of adolescence to the vigorous strength of manhood before it was able to command this type of responsive support.

In the meantime, plans for the two academic buildings proceeded so successfully it was decided to hold a public ceremony for laying the cornerstones during the commencement exercises in August, 1875. Reporting this event, Minor said, "The cornerstone of the new building was laid with Masonic rites and great rejoicing, the whole neighboring county, and many from distant parts of the state assembling, in spite of the heavy rains, to witness the ceremony and hear the addresses."

The first building, known simply as the First Academic Building throughout its entire existence, was occupied in October, 1876, while the second one, designated throughout its lifetime as the Second Academic Building, was occupied some six months later. With the completion of these buildings, the expansion of the physical plant, which never came to an end during the first century of the institution's existence, was off to a most auspicious start.

These two buildings, the first major ones to be constructed by the Virginia Agricultural and Mechanical College, became in every sense of the word the true hub around which most of the major, and even minor, activities of the College revolved at one time or another for the next three quarters of a century. Both buildings were in continuous use involving a fantastic variety of services and programs until they were removed in 1957—the First Academic to make way for the present Rasche Hall and the Second Academic to make way for the present Brodie Hall. It is doubtful that there is living today a pre-1957 alumnus who does not entertain nostalgic reminiscences of events connected with one or the other of these buildings and the professors who held forth therein.

With the appropriation made at this time and a smaller one in 1877, three faculty houses, a president's house, and several minor buildings were erected. The president's house, completed after considerable litigation with a local contractor over the brick, is presently standing as a part of Henderson Hall, which houses the infirmary. Of the three faculty homes erected, one stood on the site of the present Newman Library; another stood on a site about half-way between the present Memorial Chapel and Patton Hall; and the third was located on a site adjacent to the southwest wing of the present Shultz Hall. Old photographs show these early faculty homes laid out like the typical small village home of the day; that is, surrounded by a plank fence with outbuildings and lots arranged presumably for a cow, a pig, chickens, a horse, and a garden. The story of the conversion of these old buildings to conform to the demands of the developing program of the College is an interesting, albeit incomplete one. The building erected on the site of the Newman Library was converted into lecture and laboratory rooms for agricultural instruction and later torn down to make way for a chapel, the forerunner of the present library building. The building between the Memorial Chapel and Patton Hall, after serving as a faculty home for a number of years and partially surviving a serious fire, was converted into an administration building which housed the office of the president, the registrar, the treasurer, and other officials until the erection of Burruss Hall in 1936. From 1936 until its removal in 1950, this lonely relic of the past served a variety of programs for the College.

The building located adjacent to Shultz Hall was used by faculty and then converted into quarters for the commandant of cadets until its removal to make way for landscaping the grounds around the present Shultz Hall.

Since few letters or written reminiscences of early days at the College have survived, the best picture of the activities at this time must be derived from the catalogs, President Minor's reports to the General Assembly, and the college magazine, the *Gray Jacket,* established by the students in 1873. In his first report, Minor stated that instruction in manual labor did not begin until late in the spring of 1873 because of delay in gaining possession of the farm. He might also have added the delay in securing a professor of agriculture. The manual-labor feature greatly bothered the early faculty. All agreed that the agriculturist or mechanic should possess the mechanical skills of his trade, but it was soon discovered that most of the boys attending the school already possessed these routine skills. What new "labor" could be assigned them which would be educational and illustrative rather than merely repetitious? In spite of the absence of a satisfactory answer to the question, all physically able-bodied students were assigned manual tasks and were reported to have carred them out faithfully. In fact, it appears that much necessary routine work on the farm, in the shops, and on the campus was done by the students in the name of manual labor. The results, whether educational or not, turned out to be pleasing to the majority. After completing the assigned tasks, the students could continue these or other duties for pay at an hourly wage and thereby help meet college expenses. The public, especially the agricultural press, was convinced that this manual-labor feature guaranteed the longed-for practical education, while the College administration was happy to get a number of small buildings erected or repaired, furniture made for the dormitories, and farm roads and fences constructed. The major casualty of the system was the productivity of the farm, which did not respond as expected to student labor confined to afternoon hours.

President Minor was particularly happy that the students working for the College at wages from seven to twelve cents per hour could meet most of their college expenses. In fact, one gets the impression from his annual reports that Minor was more concerned with keeping college costs to students as low as possible than he was with developing a proper curriculum in agriculture and mechanics. In effect, he seemed to be saying, "cheap enough for the poorest, and then, and then only, good enough for the proudest." His efforts were so successful he was accorded the honor not only of imitation but of some jealousy as well from some other colleges in the state.

Beginning with the second session, the opening date for the College was set for August 13 with classes to be held until December 22. Instruction was to resume on February 24 and continue until the second Wednesday in August, 1874. Two major reasons were given for this policy of having a winter instead of a summer vacation. First, it was believed that farm operations could be taught more successfully through a complete growing season; and secondly, it was believed the winter climate in Blacksburg was too severe for students from eastern Virginia. As can be imagined, this surprising concern for eastern Virginians was seized upon with great glee by the western "hillbillies" to the great discomfiture of the former group. Before long, numberless sophomores expressing deep concern over the plight of freshmen with such weak constitutions thought up and rigidly applied all sorts of original schemes "guaranteed" to build constitutions rugged enough to survive the severest of Blacksburg winters. Most of these schemes included the common denominator of cold water dashed in the face of the sleeping freshmen in the middle of the night.

The plan of winter vacation was no more successful at the Virginia Agricultural and Mechanical College than it had been at land-grant colleges in other states. After earnest solicitation from faculty and students, it was abandoned in 1881 in favor of the conventional academic year. The sophomores, or intermediates as they were called, while happily accepting the change in holidays, professed even greater solicitude for the welfare of the freshmen thus exposed to the rigors of Blacksburg weather and immediately expanded their "constitution-building" schemes to include all freshmen on the campus. It was not long therefore before the practice of "sprinkling water" in the face of sleeping freshmen became a tradition which, of dubious value in building strong constitutions, nonetheless persisted with varying degrees of efficiency until World War II. It is doubtful indeed that any cadet prior to this wartime period completely escaped the experience of being awakened in the middle of the night by a sudden application of cold water dashed in his face. The health-building advantages of such a practice perhaps had best be left a topic for alumni reminiscences.

The original plan for the College adopted by the board envisioned minimum entrance requirements. In fact, no specific standards were set for prospective students for a number of years. The *Catalogue* merely stated, "The applicant must be at least fourteen years of age, but the faculty may dispense with this requirement in favor of one who has a brother at the requisite age entering at the same time." The next year the minimum age was changed to sixteen, with the same provision. This flexible admissions policy, absolutely necessary at the time because of the embryonic system of public secondary education in the state, presented the College with unexpected problems arising from the make-up of the student body. In the first place, it resulted in an unusually wide age spread, in one instance reported to range from fifteen to forty years of age, within the student body at the same time. It brought together for instruction lads of fifteen and sixteen away from home for the first time and battle-seasoned ex-Confederate veterans. Most baffling of all, it brought together students from every spectrum of the state populace with academic backgrounds ranging from that of about the fifth or sixth grade to that of the student well-prepared to enter the best educational institutions in the country. This particular situation, while not differing greatly from that of all the early land-grant institutions, meant that Virginia Agricultural and Mechanical College resorted to many trial and error approaches before a reasonably satisfactory solution was found.

One approach was through the formation of a preparatory department at the beginning of the 1877-78 session under the guidance of Thomas N. Conrad, erstwhile candidate for president. This department was formed to provide students with poor academic backgrounds an opportunity to improve in basic courses sufficiently to enter college courses. The program included a one-year course of study in arithmetic, English grammar, geography, diction, elocution, and penmanship. Other approaches, such as individualized instruction, personalized programs of study, differentiated assignments, remedial instruction in terms of demonstrated needs, variations in class size, and differentiations in the diplomas and certificates awarded on completion of programs of work were tried in an effort to meet the wide range of differences found in the early student bodies. The results may have been frustrating, but certainly no fault can be found with the efforts made by the pioneer faculty members to adapt the Virginia Agricultural and Mechanical College to the heterogeneous needs of students who came knocking at her doors.

During the earlier years, the College was divided into three departments: the Literary Department and the Scientific Department, which included the traditional courses, and the Technical Department, which included agriculture and the mechanical arts. All students were required to take courses in English grammar, and the senior class was required to study history and English literature. In the catalog descriptions of courses offered in these departments, the instructors, after describing the course content, nearly always added the observation that modifications were made depending on the qualifications and the needs of the student. An optional provision was made for students wishing to do so to study the classical languages, and all students wishing a diploma were required to take either French or German.

Although the catalog stated that no student could change his course of study unless such action was approved by the faculty, such approval apparently was quite easily obtained, and just as easily abused, it should be noted. Students properly prepared through previous study or experience were granted permission to pursue the more advanced courses without taking the basic courses, thereby antedating by a number of years the current practice of granting advanced standing to certain students on the basis of test scores or high school records. Special students, not desiring a graduation certificate, were allowed wide latitude in their selection of courses, while all students except those physically disabled were required to take instruction in military tactics in each year of residence. The student body was not, as sometimes erroneously reported, organized on a strictly military basis during the earlier years. This development was to come later at a serious crisis in the life of the College.

President Minor was of the strong opinion, as was Ruffner at a later date, that the military drill was very valuable in teaching obedience, promptness, and neatness, and in preparing students for possible future duty as soldiers. Minor was especially convinced that the program developed in those who were farm boys a manly carriage and manner which removed the rustic awkwardness "apt to be caused by rustic training or hard labor." He did not believe, however, that the College should be organized on a strictly military basis such as that of the Virginia Military Institute or West Point. This attempt to hold the military feature to a minor role in a state whose social and political life was dominated by ex-Confederate officers and gentlemen who, if not having earned a military title, had one assigned to them anyway by the populace got Minor into deep trouble somewhat later.

When the College opened in 1872, there was an almost inconceivable shortage of equipment: no maps or charts, no laboratory or apparatus, a limited number of tables and chairs, no furnishings for the few dormitory rooms, insufficient blackboards, and no library at all. The Board of Visitors recognized the shortages but felt that with the aid of private and public benefactors many of the truly pressing needs on the farm and in the shop could be met. As a matter of fact, one can almost believe some of the board members welcomed the shortage of a library and the more sophisticated scientific equipment as a safeguard against the College's developing as a "literary" instead of as an agricultural and mechanical institution.

The board's faith in the generosity of public and private benefactors paid off with respect to equipping the college farm and to a less extent the mechanical department. General William Mahone, owner of the Atlantic, Mississippi, and Ohio Rail Road, now the Norfolk and Western, granted free transportation over this line for freight consigned to the school. Since this line connected with several steamship lines, particularly to northern manufacturing centers, the saving in transportation costs to the College was considerable over the next several years. Ruffner, while pleased with Mahone's action, felt that the welfare of the "people's college" would in turn contribute sufficiently to the welfare of Mahone's railroad to justify even greater support from Mahone. In a private letter to President Minor, Ruffner asked him if he could not lay a "flattering unction" on Mahone for even greater support. Any "flattering unction" which Minor may have prepared fell on unresponsive ears, it seems, for Mahone even then was engaged in what was to be a losing battle to retain control of his beloved Atlantic, Mississippi, and Ohio, the very initials of which he is reported to have said, meant "All Mine and Ophelia's . . . ." (Ophelia being his wife's name). Ironically, within a few years, Mahone's political followers, in one of the greatest to-the-victor-belongs-the-spoils sweeps ever known in Virginia, swept Ruffner out of office, took over the College, and replaced the Board of Visitors, the faculty, and even the janitor with individuals of their political following.

As noted, the donations to the farm were generous. This generosity was not without its drawbacks: the farm manager soon found himself saddled with so many different breeds of farm animals, all donated, that the farm began to take on the aspects of a veritable Noah's Ark. The slowly developing, unregulated fertilizer industry donated samples of its products, which in the hands of the unskilled workers, student and otherwise, killed as often as aided the crops to which applied. Individual farmers, completely ignorant of the principles of plant genetics and soil adaptation, readily sent seeds from their favorite garden and field crops. These seeds planted side by side produced results often as surprising to the farm manager as they were infuriating to the proud donor. All in all, the college farm was not prepared physically or scientifically to become "the people's farm" with such rapidity.

Besides, no decision had been made as to just what function the college farm should fill. Should it be developed as a model farm, an experimental farm, a research farm, or as a general purpose farm upon which the boys could perform manual labor and at the same time produce meat, milk, and other produce for the mess hall? Should a separate farm manager be hired? If so, how should his responsibilities relate to those of the professor of agriculture? These were just a few of the questions facing the faculty. In a letter to Minor as early as June, 1874, Ruffner exclaimed, "But oh, that farm, that farm—what shall we do?" Since most of the faculty, the students, the Board of Visitors, and all the farmers were more or less familiar with farm operations, answers to Ruffner's question became more than plentiful and equally confusing as more and more individuals volunteered solutions to the perplexing problems. J. Seddon Harvie, employed in 1873 as farmer, left in 1874, as did J. W. C. Davis, who had been employed to teach agriculture but had been switched to mechanics seemingly against his wishes. The circumstances surrounding their departure, while not clear, certainly did nothing to enhance the College in the eyes of the powerful Lewis E. Harvie, or of the equally influential faculty members in the department of scientific agriculture at the University of Virginia from whom Davis had received not only his training in agricultural education but also unstinted praise and recommendations concerning his fitness for the professorship of agriculture at the new College.

Following the departure of these two individuals, it was decided to divide the responsibility for the farm between Ellzey and S. K. Jackson, M.D., who had been employed to succeed Davis. This decision placed all instruction in agriculture and mechanics in the hands of medically trained individuals, a practice not at all unusual in the early land-grant colleges. Jackson was assigned responsibility for instruction in chemistry, technical mechanics, and drawing, in addition to his responsibilities on the farm. Chemistry, he announced through the catalog, would be taught "with a view to the probable practical use which may be made of it in after life." In life, during college at least, as soon as the laboratory was completed, the students would be taught "Chemical Manipulation," but in the meantime they would be taught "Chemical Reactions" which they would be required to produce in the classroom. The students, he advised, "are practiced in analysis by furnishing them with factitious preparations, such as imitations of mineral waters, soils, alloys of metal, etc., the ingredients of which they are required to discover."

Jackson's catalog description of his work as professor of mechanics and drawing is such a revealing presentation of the College's pioneering effort to move into the new field of mechanical education that it is here given in its entirety as Jackson gave it under the heading of TECHNOLOGY.

> This department [Technology] is one of the peculiar features of this institution which entitles it to the appellation of an Agricultural and Mechanical College, and the establishment of which was one of the conditions of the land grant by Congress.
>
> Its very wide scope precludes more than a mere enumeration, here, of the subjects embraced. Though it is the practical application of science to art, the principles of the sciences applied are taught as well.

Up to this time facilities have been furnished to pursue the following course in the study and practice of the arts enumerated below:

Drawing—Geometrical Projections, Intersections, Development of Surfaces; Drawings of Machinery, and working drawings for Machine Construction.

Architectural Drawing—Plans and Elevations of Buildings; Ornamentation, etc.; Conventional Coloring; Shading and Shadows; Perspective, linear and isometrical.

Topographical Drawing—Using the conventional Signs and Scales adopted by the U. S. Coast Survey; Isometrical Drawing; Lettering; Engineering Drawing; Projections of the Globe, etc.

Mechanical Engineering—The source of power; its development in the prime movers, viz: Animals, Hydraulic Motors, Steam and Caloric Engines, Electromagnetic Machines.

A large number of models, kindly presented by the U. S. Patent Office, furnish interesting illustrations of many of these applications.

Architecture—In addition to the Architectural Drawings alluded to, lectures are delivered upon the materials employed, viz: Stone, Brick, Wood, Concrete, Mortars, Cements, Paints, etc. Upon Masonry and Stone Cutting; Foundations, Arches, Domes, Stairs, Bridges, Walls (retaining and enclosure), Ornaments, etc., Upon Carpentry; Joints, Molding, Framing, Bracing, Trussing, Roofs, Stairs, etc.

Metallurgy—Furnaces are supplied for Cupellation, Fusion, etc. The electro-deposit of metals is practiced in the Chemical Laboratory.

Printing—Two presses and a full supply of type furnish abundant practice in this important art.

Photography—Apparatus for practicing this art has been supplied, and photographic specimens will be prepared for illustrating the various departments.

Pyrotechny—Instruction is given in this art, and students are stimulated to practice it by a promise of a display at Commencement.

Telegraphy—Regular instruction is given and opportunities afforded for constant practice. The growing importance of this art is recognized as becoming second only to Chirography, and great prominence is given to it in the Technical Department of the Institution.

The Work-Shop—is provided with an 8 horsepower steam engine, lathes, circular and vertical saws, forges, work-benches and tools, enabling students to select any branch of industry they may prefer or for which they may evince talent.

Dr. Jackson then concluded his description of his work with the following statement: "From the above enumeration, it will be seen that students are acquiring some art, which, while in college, assists materially in defraying their expenses, and which, immediately upon their entrance upon life, will yield them an ample support."

Jackson's description of his work not only reveals his philosophy of education but also indicates the embryonic beginning of several departments of engineering at the University today. His instruction in pyrotechny took an unexpected, although not necessarily surprising, turn. It appears that student progress in this interesting subject was too rapid and their youthful impatience too great to wait commencement as the time to display their mastery and ingenuity in this field. After one particularly spectacular, albeit officially unapproved, pyrotechnic display in the middle of the night, during which not only the commandant but some prominent citizens of the town as well were reported to have "exploded" louder than the biggest firecracker, all formal instruction in pyrotechny came to an end. The students ever since, though, have resorted to "pyrotechnic displays" as both approved and unapproved extracurricular activities.

In addition to his teaching duties, this pioneer in technical and engineering education shared responsibility with Ellzey for the college farm. In this capacity, he was responsible for the proper location, erection, and repair of all fences; the location, construction, and upkeep of all campus roads and bridges; the repair of all campus buildings; the operation and repair of all farm machinery; and the installation and supervision of the farm drainage system. In addition to these prescribed duties, it appears this professor, having a "mechanical turn of mind," also was called upon to supervise or assist in the selection and installation of numerous mechanical devices ranging from a doorbell for the president to kitchen sink pumps for wives of the faculty.

For the sake of modern educators greatly concerned with work loads, didactic hours, consultative responsibilities, concentration in one's specialty, and similar problems, perhaps the only reference to this enterprising individual made outside of the catalog should be recorded—"Dr. Jackson soon resigned."

With the other half of the team selected to teach agriculture and mechanics, it was an entirely different matter. Ellzey, though trained in medicine, set to work to prepare and organize his courses and content as he saw fit. Described as a brilliant lecturer in the classroom but taciturn, moody, and sparse of words outside, this individual deserves more credit as a pioneer in agricultural education than he has received. The catalog description of the material to be covered in his area of natural history and agriculture was even more encyclopedic in nature than the one enumerated for technology under Jackson, but Ellzey chopped things down to size and organized and created lectures manageable in size and sufficiently restricted in scope to meet the needs of organized classes studying agriculture. In addition to his work on the campus, Ellzey conducted the *Stock Department* in *The Southern Planter* for a number of years. In this capacity, this intrepid pioneer entered into discussions of topics in agriculture which if presented in any depth today no doubt would engage a large portion of the staff of the College of Agriculture.

In addition to his work in agriculture, Ellzey, much to the secret and amused ridicule of the students, started collections of objects for his natural history museum. In this connection he addressed appeals to "friends of the College" all over the state for "such objects as will illustrate the resources, the natural production, and the Indian history of the country." Considerable success followed this appeal, but unfortunately, some of his successors did not believe relics of the past had any usefulness for youth of the day as they prepared for life tomorrow; hence, they either discarded his collection entirely or otherwise allowed it to deteriorate and disappear from the scene.

It appears that Ellzey did not approve the decision to assign part responsibility for the practical operation of the college farm to his office. It is not clear whether he wanted complete control of the farm or the opposite, complete freedom from any responsibility for it. At any rate, it appears that instead of resigning as Jackson had done, he began moving sub-rosa within both the board and the faculty to effect a change. He got the change. Before the year was up, the board decided to employ not only a successor to Dr. Jackson but a farm manager as well. General William R. Boggs, a graduate of the U. S. Military Academy, was appointed professor of technical mechanics and drawing, while Colonel Norborne Berkley was appointed farm manager under the title of farmer. In the shifting of duties, chemistry was separated from the chair of technical mechanics and drawing and assigned to Ellzey, making him thereby professor of agriculture, chemistry, and natural history. Berkley assumed full responsibility for the farm, and Boggs took over responsibility for buildings and grounds in lieu of chemistry. These assignments were adhered to for the next several years, although the board continued to debate and discuss as it groped uncertainly for an adequate organization and a staff competent to teach that which had never been taught.

Mention was made of the fact that donations from individuals helped equip the college farm with livestock, machinery, seeds, and tools. The same source was depended upon for library materials, which were housed in a small room set up for V. E. Shepherd, who at one time or another served as treasurer, secretary of the faculty, librarian, professor of German, French, Latin, modern languages, and bookkeeping, and in between these duties found time to write to many former students apprising them of college affairs. So unsmiling, though, was Shepherd in the performance of his duties, students built a legend that he had been Jefferson Davis' private secretary, who, upon Davis' arrest, had sworn never to smile again. It was commonly reported amongst the students that he had broken his oath only once, but whether upon the receipt of a book for his library is not known. Books, however, did come in, 501 volumes of them the first year, since many state and national agencies seized the golden opportunity to donate documents and reports which had been collecting dust on their shelves. The Presbyterian Board of Richmond sent 80 volumes of their collection, and the City Mission Society of Richmond sent 50 prayer books.

The students were not particularly impressed with the results. Consequently, most of the publications henceforth collected Blacksburg dust instead of that of their point of origin. President Minor, on the other hand, was able to report that "a library has been commenced." The first actual monetary expenditure for the library was in 1878, although what the money purchased is not clear, since the financial report merely recorded "library $39.10." From this small expenditure, the library has continued to grow to its present position of prominence.

As already indicated, facilities for room and board were practically nonexistent on the campus when the College first opened its doors. Most students, therefore, were forced to find such accommodations as they could in the town. In this instance the town was not ready for the College; but a number of individuals, notably Amis, Hawley, and Caldwell, opened portions of their homes to students. In most instances the students moved in and fitted into the family routine as if they were in fact a part of the family. Thus began a practice continued to some extent even to this day, which has resulted in many warm lifelong friendships, to say nothing of the numerous more permanent alliances fostered by Dan Cupid.

Even with the private homes, the accommodations were insufficient and, in Minor's opinion, too expensive for most of the students. He was particularly concerned with what he considered to be an excessive cost of food in private homes and the public establishments in Blacksburg. To meet this problem, he erected not one but several "messes" with a kitchen attached to each one. These buildings, constructed almost entirely with student labor, were of the simplest type, rough construction completely devoid of any aesthetic design or appeal. So was the food served in them. Minor, while admitting that the food was simple and plain, defended it as nourishing, ample, and absolutely necessary to keep costs within reach of the great majority of students for whom the College was intended. Student complaints, with a remarkably familiar ring, developed at once. Efforts equally familiar in tone were inaugurated by Minor to solve the complaints; but try as he might, a permanently satisfactory solution to this problem of providing a mess which would satisfy the subjective opinions of desirable and undesirable, properly and improperly prepared food evaded Minor as it has evaded every administration from that day to this.

The shortage of boarding facilities did not go unnoticed by enterprising business men of Blacksburg. Therefore, it was not long before rooms, apartments, and buildings specifically constructed (it would be debatable to say designed) for students began to spring up near the campus. Perhaps the most significant of these buildings was Lybrook Row, known to many alumni yet living. This structure, a long one-storied building of many rooms, stood on the site presently included in the lawn of the Episcopal Church. During its early days, "Lybrook Row," according to Professor E. A. Smyth, was known "by a less euphonious name, doubtless in keeping with the actions of its inmates." Since several names, depicting possible aberrant behavior and all of them less euphonious than Lybrook Row, were applied to this building at one time or another, the particular "less euphonious name" that Smyth had in mind is not known. Perhaps it is just at well.

For years the students in "Lybrook Row" took their meals at Luster's Hotel, a huge old rambling frame structure which stood on the site of the present First National Exchange Bank. Since this hotel was so close to the entrance of the campus, the post office, and Main Street, it was inevitable that its lobby in the winter and its broad veranda and well-shaded lawn in summer would become the popular meeting place in the early evenings for the town fathers, the nearby country squires, and to a more limited extent the faculty members. From this vantage point, it was possible in addition to arguing the political questions of the day to cast an appraising eye on the activities of the College and the administration, and at the same time pass critical judgment on the behavior of the students. It was not long, however, before the activities of the administration and of the students threatened to push politics completely, albeit temporarily, out of the picture and leave only the actions of the faculty and students as a topic of conversation. Before this unusual development took place, though, the College had completed several years of existence and had started a pattern of commencement or celebration with which to mark the completion of each year's work.

The final exercises which marked the end of the first year were held over a period of four days. The exercises began on Sunday, July 6, 1873, with all events centered around religion, highlighted by a sermon delivered in the Methodist Church by its pastor, William Harris. According to Ruffner's diary, the Board of Visitors convened at the White Sulphur Springs on Monday, but it also appears that the College facilities were thrown open for the inspection of the general public on this date. Evidently, Tuesday was utilized by the board for official inspection of the College. It would seem that the institution as a whole made a favorable impression on the board, with the Literary Department excelling the other two departments. This should not necessarily be surprising. In fact, it was to be expected, since this department was following established procedures in courses offered and methods of instruction. The Scientific and the Technical Departments, on the other hand, especially the Technical, were pioneering in blazing new trails in education and had few precedents to follow.

The highlight of the celebration was the arrival of Governor Gilbert C.

Walker on Wednesday. Minor had been particularly eager to have Walker visit the College, since he felt that one of the school's chief weaknesses was one Walker had "voted to fasten on us." Without naming the "chief weakness" Minor had solicited help from several sources to encourage the governor to visit the College. If he would only visit us, Minor had written, "I defy him to see our work and not call it a valuable one."

The governor, having arrived in Blacksburg, went almost at once to the Methodist Church, where at noon he addressed an overflow audience on the subject "The Present and Future of the Agricultural and Mechanical College in Connection with General Education." This address, in which faint echoes of Ruffner's philosophy were audible, had little if any effect on the College beyond the possible elevation of hopes and aspirations far beyond anything it would attain within the next quarter of a century.

During the same day, the governor inspected the physical plant of the College and in the afternoon "after the heat of the day" reviewed the student military unit. This review, observed by the governor, the board, the faculty, and "a large assembly from the surrounding countryside," brought a happy end to the College's first year of existence. Even Thomas Conrad, who published the governor's address in the *Montgomery Messenger*, was satisfied with the results, although he did seize the occasion as an opportunity to denounce by name all members of the Board of Visitors who had not been in attendance.

The first commencement exercises at which diplomas were awarded took place on August 12, 1875, at 11:00 a.m. On this occasion twelve students—six in agriculture, three in mechanics, and three in agriculture and mechanics—were awarded diplomas. This date is also a memorable one in that amidst appropriate ceremonies the cornerstones for the First and Second Academic Buildings, the first major construction on the campus, were laid.

All of the early commencement speakers were well-known Virginians. Most of them were accomplished orators, and at least one had served on the Board of Visitors, and others were to serve at future dates. Being men of a practical bent, nearly all of the speakers devoted their attention to some topic dealing with the practical concerns of the time and then concluded their presentations with the usual exhortations customarily given by older men to younger men on such occasions.

The newspapers reported the activities in glowing terms and heaped praise on the College and its work. The public addresses delivered on these occasions were often singled out for special comment, and the large audiences were usually described as "appreciative" or "attentive." One young lady from Lynchburg gave a slightly different and perhaps more accurate impression, from youth's standpoint, at least, of one early commencement. Writing to the sister of one of the students, this young lady after modestly admitting an "affair of the heart" concerning one young man "so handsome in his uniform" continued: "All of the young men looked so handsome in their uniforms as they marched and drilled, but they nodded and slept during the long, tiresome speeches."

By 1877, commencement-speaker Robert Beverly, after entertaining the audience with his prophecy that graduates of the Virginia Agricultural and Mechanical College one day would help solve the problem of navigating in the air as successfully as on the water, pronounced it as his opinion that the College, as "an experiment in our state," was now an "assured success."

It would seem from reading the published reports of the College and its work that Beverly had every reason to be so optimistic. Enrollment had increased from 132 to 224. The press and the people in sympathy with the aims of agricultural and mechanical education were openly supporting the school. New buildings, considered ample for the most pressing needs, were available or in sight. The assured income, though small, was in line with that of most colleges of the state and superior to several. The manual-labor feature helped convince the farmer that the instruction met his almost fanatical demand for a practical education, while the unusually low cost of attending the school helped convince many that the Virginia Agricultural and Mechanical College was truly for the people. A series of rapidly unfolding events within a very few years, however, convinced many that the administrative officers of the College were not sufficiently "of the people" and "by the people." This feeling was fostered, at first apparently un-wittingly, by Thomas Conrad through the columns of the *Montgomery Messenger.*

Conrad, who as noted had assumed the editorship of the *Messenger* following his failure to secure the presidency, kept a watchful eye on the activities of the College, especially at commencement time. Often he reported in glowing detail the portions of the programs which met with his approval and damned with faint praise the portions which did not. His method of expressing disapproval for personalities involved was more direct, to the point, and blunt. Thus we find him lashing out at board members Anderson, DeJarnette, Lee, Sutherlin, Taylor, and Tidball for not attending the first commencement, and at the Con-federate hero, John W. Daniel, the "Lame Lion of Lynchburg," for his tardiness in attending to a speaking engagement at the College. Even an "amende honor-able" that he sometimes (but not often) felt compelled to make usually was worded adroitly enough to leave no doubt of his real opinion or intention. In his comments, he seemed to go out of his way to make it clear it was not the College itself but the people running the College that he was criticizing. Thus, we find him on one occasion writing, "Whilst our contempt for the partisanship exhibited by the Board of Visitors is well-understood, let it be equally known our unfeigned appreciation of the institution. It is not the creature of their creation but the state's. We recognize it as the people's . . . ."

Whatever Conrad's motives may have been, his editorials began to convince many local residents that the mistakes, the problems, and the difficulties faced by the College grew from ineptitude and inefficiency of the board and faculty. Unfortunately, strong dissension and division of opinion occurred in the faculty, which tended to reinforce and spread this idea at the very time the state was undergoing an almost traumatic economic and political change. As a result, the College was caught up in a socio-political-economic storm which brought its early success and growth to an abrasive crawl and imposed on it one reorganization after another.

4

Minor, Buchanan, Conrad, and Political Interference

1878-1886

WHEN THE VIRGINIA AGRICULTURAL and Mechanical College opened its doors in 1872, the Board of Visitors had not established any clearcut organizational plan of administration which could be used as a guide by either the faculty or the board. It should be remembered that during the early years the board was pioneering as greatly in its search for principles with which to guide the new land-grant college as was the faculty in its search for content and methods of instruction suitable for the institution.

As one consequence of the blurred, or in some instances missing, guidelines to serve as a frame of reference, individual faculty members, and in some instances board members, began acting unilaterally in proposing solutions to problems facing the College. Adding to the confusion, they acted in the same manner in executing their proposals. Individual faculty members contacted board members directly instead of through President Minor or the rector of the board. Debts were contracted by individuals without prior authorization from Minor or the treasurer. It is an understatement to say that this faculty practiced complete academic freedom long before the term academic freedom became a magic wand with which to keep administrators in line or with which to silence the public. Beyond having a daily schedule of classes set at the beginning of the session, each professor had almost complete autonomy as to course content, grading system, reports, class attendance during the year and before and after holidays, time and type of examinations if he wanted to give any, and text materials, if any, to be purchased by the students. Judging from one of Minor's reports to the board after the system had been in operation for six years, the results of this academic freedom carried on in such a permissive climate approached academic chaos rather than academic utopia.

The most immediate consequences resulting from the lack of guiding principles in this climate of permissiveness occurred in the area of student discipline. Student behavior does not appear to have been greatly different at the Virginia Agricultural and Mechanical College from what it was at other institutions in the state, but the circumstances were somewhat different. Because of the absence of sufficient dormitory space on the campus, a large number of students had to find rooms in town, the enrollment having reached a surprising total of 255 by the end of the fourth year of the College's existence. Some degree of control could be maintained over the students in the dormitory, but similar control proved difficult over students widely scattered in town. Then, as now, many student groups rented entire houses for their living quarters. It was not long before complaints with a decidedly modern tone began to be registered with the administration concerning student behavior in these locations.

As additional complaints poured in, the faculty became divided over the best solution. One group headed by General Lane proposed reorganizing the College along strictly military lines, thereby bringing the students under twenty-four hour supervision. This proposal alarmed Minor and Professor Martin, who felt this idea had been rejected by the legislature. Unfortunately, Minor's attempts to exercise leadership in resolving the differences of opinion served only to harden the lines separating the two groups. Rumors of dissension began to spread throughout the community and then over the state. One night all of the new kerosene street lights just installed on Blacksburg's Main Street were either destroyed or "mysteriously" removed. This destruction and other acts of vandalism were charged to but never proved against the students. Blacksburg's town fathers were justifiably indignant but insisted that the solution to the problem rested with the College. Certain prominent Methodist leaders, apparently still smarting over the treatment accorded the Preston and Olin Institute, began to line up with the faculty group demanding a military organization for the school. Faculty members acting independently began writing to individual board members, warning them against fellow faculty members. Thus, Professor Martin wrote to Ruffner, warning him to watch out for Lane, Carroll, and Shepherd. Ruffner, while keenly interested in the College, especially the development of its technical aspects, did not want to get involved in the internal dispute he saw developing. In fact, he had already suggested that since his activities on behalf of the College had aroused some jealousy from the other colleges, it might be advisable that he, as state superintendent of public instruction, be dropped from the board. Since this suggestion was not followed he continued to receive letters advising him of the developments and seeking his advice and influence.

As the situation became more critical, the Board of Visitors, following President Minor's suggestion, adopted a set of rules and regulations which hopefully would clarify responsibilities and establish lines of administrative communication and authority. But the faculty members proved to be more than reluctant to give up the autonomy of action they had seized during the period of no administrative guidelines. Minor's attempts to operate under the clarified rules and regulations met with instant rebuff from the pro-military faction and only token support from the anti-military group. More and more letters purporting to discuss the affairs of the school began to appear in the press. The *Christian Advocate* attacked what it claimed to be the lack of discipline in the school but concluded by exclaiming, "But what folly in the farmer to send his son to learn the art of agriculture to a school where the President came not from the plantation with its experience, but from an Episcopal Seminary in Tennessee, and who knows less of practical farming than hundreds of negro foremen in Virginia." Many attacks, some with overtones reminiscent of the legislative struggle over the location of the College, began to spring up against certain features or personnel connected with the school. President Minor became the target of the pro-military group, which demanded his ouster to be followed by a strict military organization for the school. Lane, nicknamed "Gamecock" by the students, has been characterized as the champion rooster in the military cockpit, but Martin in a letter to Ruffner claimed the trouble between Minor and Lane had been fomented by Ellzey, "whose powers for mischief you well know." B. Johnson Barbour, also in a letter to Ruffner, added Thomas Conrad's name to the trouble-makers when he wrote, "I have looked upon Professor Conrad as *among* the chief fomentors of all the troubles at Blacksburg—foiled in obtaining the Presidency in the start (as you well know) he retired full of gall and bitterness . . . ." Barbour claimed that through his paper in Christiansburg, Conrad had pounced on every little mistake at the College and spread it abroad. Conrad had especially attacked all persons he felt stood in his way. Continuing his castigation of Conrad, Barbour said, "When in an evil hour he was admitted to the faculty instead of seeking peace . . . he kept up the same traits and systematically sought to widen the breaches already existing." Conrad had even accompanied the students on a "calathump," Barbour claimed, and had seized the occasion as an opportunity to mimic and in "sundry ways" ridicule Minor. The "calathump," a noise-making orgy during which the participants used tin pans, horns, cow bells, firecrackers, or any other noise maker that imagination suggested, was sometimes a deliberate effort at annoyance and sometimes an effort at celebration. It nearly always took place at night, often with the professors as the surprised victims. The participants usually surrounded the "victim's" house and at a given signal, according to a report in one newspaper, struck up hideous music which "made the night resonant with sounds not be excelled this side of the infernal regions." Barbour did not identify the intent of the calathump he claimed Conrad had attended with the boys, but his disapproval of Conrad's action was obvious.

However accurate or inaccurate these charges may be, the fact is that trouble between Minor and Lane deepened until it was brought to a head in an unexpectedly dramatic fashion before a meeting of the faculty.

The president of the College and his professor of military tactics got into a fist fight.

A full account of the "collision" was requested by the board and given by Minor. According to this report, dissension had existed for two years before it erupted into an open fight because of Lane's attitude and hot temper. At a faculty meeting on March 23, 1878, called at Lane's request, Lane had made a speech which in Minor's opinion was most discourteous and untrue. He charged that Minor wanted to set himself up as "the great I am of the College," and as the speech progressed, Lane became so excited and angry that he lost control of himself. Minor stated that he wanted to reply to Lane but realized that Lane was in no condition to settle their differences at this meeting.

Minor called a faculty meeting on March 25 with the hope of solving the problem, but Lane immediately took the floor and spoke at length with much heat, excitement, and abuse toward Minor. When Lane finally relinquished the floor, Minor began to read a carefully prepared statement but was forced to stop from time to time because of Lane's loudly voiced interruptions. The presiding officer ruled Lane out of order, but Lane "very loudly and resentfully uttered, 'Order, the devil; this is a question of veracity.' " Continuing, Minor reported of Lane, "He rose from his seat and advanced on me, and demanded with loud offensive and threatening tones and gestures, whether I meant to impeach his veracity. I answered to the effect that if he would have it so it must be so. He then shook his fist in my face, grinding his teeth and crying aloud in rage and I struck him."

Public sentiment in Blacksburg and Montgomery County was outraged. At the insistence of certain leaders, the sheriff of the county had both individuals haled into court, where after an abundant supply of dirty college linen had been aired in public, both men were found guilty of disturbing the peace.

Conrad wrote to the rector of the board and to other board members, reporting the incident and warning that even greater danger was ahead if immediate steps were not taken to rectify the situation. The rector released the letter to Minor, who immediately denied any personal plan or intention for a "bloody encounter." Following the receipt of Conrad's letter, the executive committee of the board met with the faculty and at the repeated insistence of C. W. Button, the publisher of the *Lynchburg Virginian* and member of the Board of Visitors, secured a dubious professional reconciliation between Lane and Minor.

A meeting of the Board of Visitors was called for August. By this time the press had given much attention to the trouble in the College. Even the reactionary editor of *The Southern Planter* had taken time out from his bitter attacks on Ruffner and the public school system to urge the faculty at the College to get together on the matter of discipline. "A house divided against itself has never yet been known to stand very long; and there is nothing to show that this college will be an exception to the rule," he warned.

When the board met, Minor gave the most complete report of the College's activities for the session he ever gave during his entire administration. Not only did he give his report; he also included reports from faculty members pertaining to the operation of each aspect of the college program. According to Minor, this was the first time he had required the faculty to report directly to his office. Prior to this date, each faculty member apparently reported only to the rector of the board. In preparing his report Minor clearly shaped it to show the work of the College as an implementation of the basic guidelines laid down by the Board of Visitors within the board's interpretation of the intent of the legislature. In effect, he seemed to be saying that if his administration of the school was in error, it was up to the board not only to say so but also to show wherein he had departed from the basic plan adopted by the board itself. He freely admitted that internal dissension existed within the College, that he had even seen it coming, but that under the rules and regulations insisted upon by the board he had been power-less to do anything about it. At this point, he reminded the board of the numerous times it had failed to inaugurate certain changes in the internal administration of the College which he had suggested. Before concluding his lengthy report of the work for the session, Minor attached a brief review of the history of the institution. This review focused on many of the problems which the College had faced and overcome during its first few years, but in a sense it attempted to accomplish more than that. It attempted to show that much of the attack focusing on the discipline of the school was in reality an extension of many of these earlier problems.

In concluding his report, Minor referred to the damaging, and in his opinion inaccurate, reports about the College which had begun to appear in the press. At the same time, he made it quite clear he suspected that many of these reports had originated with certain faculty members unwilling to abide by the board's directives. As a remedy he recommended, in fact almost urged, that the board conduct an investigation to determine the authors of the articles and then take necessary steps to see that dissatisfied faculty members reported to the board before spreading their complaints "abroad through the press or otherwise."

A full account of the "collision" with Professor Lane was presented in a separate report. After reporting the actual events of the encounter, Minor related several instances of Lane's behavior to strengthen his argument that the actual physical encounter grew from Lane's ungovernable temper and his unwillingness to cooperate with Minor in executing directives laid down by the board. Once more Minor concluded his report with an earnest plea for the board to make a full investigation of the entire matter.

Minor's "Retrospective Sketch" which he included in his report on this occasion is worthy of considerable attention, not only because it gave an excellent summary of the development of the College under his direction, but also because it made the board members slow down in their tentative plans to replace Minor and organize the school on a military basis.

After referring to the "commendation of nearly all and the hearty support of every section of the state" hitherto given the College Minor continued:

> The gentlemen of the Board have surely not forgotten how general was the conviction, when the long fight in the General Assembly for the Land Scrip was over, that the thing had been buried, that the Legislature had insured a failure in placing the school where it would be remote from a large part of the state, inaccessible by rail, with a climate and soil as far as possible from an average of the state, deprived of all the advantages of the already established courses of instruction and means of illustration which our old colleges would have afforded, had the Land Scrip been assigned them. None of the gentlemen now in the Board know of other difficulties that beset the College—of the strong disposition to make it as much as possible like other colleges with the usual complement of Latin and Greek literature, and only such show of conformity to the needs of farmers and mechanics as the law might absolutely require (a blunder which has caused most of the failures in these experiments)—of the difficulty of getting students from the large malarious sections in Virginia to spend the winter on top of the Alleghany . . . and later of the need to teach and lodge the crowds of youth . . . in a single house utterly unfit for the purpose and inadequate for the numbers,—of the struggle to supply to these numbers lodging and food at rates within their reach. But by due diligence remedies were found for these and many other evils.

Continuing his "Retrospective Sketch," Minor then devoted his attention to the developments in the College program which, although he did not know it, were the basis of much dissatisfaction then and later. After alluding to the legislative changes which sought to remove sectional bias from the board, he reported

> . . . the fact was recognized that if the school was to do anything peculiar to a technical school, it could not do all that the classical schools do besides. . . . The natural ambition of Professors to rival in scholarship the other colleges of the state, was laid aside—the fact was recognized and acted on that the state had elsewhere made ample provision to train its sons for the learned professions, and to provide scientists who might analyze her soils or detect poisons, and such engineers as might plan her railroads or project her mines, such military officers as might serve her in time of need—that our task should be to train practical workingmen who should till her farms rather than theorise about scientific agriculture, build rather than plan her houses, construct rather than supervise her railroads, sink rather than project her mines, and rather be guided intelligently by the analysis of others than make analyses themselves.

To accomplish these ends, Minor wrote:

> The courses of instruction were shaped strictly to suit the actual needs of the youths who came to us, the Professors doing themselves such preparatory teaching, however elementary, as met the wants of the students. As soon as experience showed what the curriculum should be, it was adopted, and the standard of graduation was fixed not to conform to that of other Colleges, but to such attainments as our plain poor youths coming from the public schools [which were just getting started in Virginia] could with diligence attain to in the course of three years or four.
> Our students are encouraged to seek the honour of a diploma not placed so high as to be beyond their reach . . . though it does not place itself in competition with diplomas of our best classical colleges and universities.

Minor then concluded his review with the observation:

> Beyond question young farmers and mechanics have found the place congenial to them, have believed that it was conducted in their interest and have sent and carried back home such accounts of us, as have made their Delegates and Senators to the General Assembly ready to grant the College such support as has been shown to be necessary for its progress.

The effect of the total report was to stun the anti-Minor faction and to amaze the remaining members of the board. The erstwhile easygoing Minor had become thoroughly aroused and clearly had tossed the problem into the lap of the board for action. The board just as clearly was not ready to act. A lobby from the county appeared before the board at the same meeting and introduced speakers, letters, and "everything down that could be used to influence the action of the Board and induce them to remove Dr. Minor." Some of Minor's statements relative to his encounter with Lane were challenged; whereupon Minor immediately wrote a letter to the board, offering to produce evidence "and witnesses which none of you may be able to shake" to support every point of his allegations. Colonel Ronald and Colonel "Bob" Preston, presumably anti-Minor, were reported to have been "inescapable" from the members of the board, while Ellzey, Lane, and Conrad were "always on hand."

Apparently no written defense or investigation of Lane's conduct was ever entertained by the board. Professor Martin attributed this omission to the fact that the "gentlemen charged [by Minor] did not wish the matter to be inquired into . . . preferring to lie under the charges rather than have the matter exposed." Whatever the reason, the board preferred not to make a full investigation of the matter. Since it had in its possession a stiffly worded letter from Lane addressed to "Dr. C. L. C. Minor, Blacksburg, Va." which concluded with the statement, "I am willing to continue the faithful and conscientious discharge of my duties in the Va. Agr. & Mechl. Col. & in all official intercourse with you to treat you with proper official courtesy," it felt the College could continue to operate under the watchful eye of the newly elected rector, who resided in nearby Giles County.

Professor Charles Martin was of the cynical opinion that the real reason for no action was based on the hope that the governor would replace the three board members whose terms on the board would expire on January 1, 1879, with members favorable to a military organization. He expressed this opinion to Ruffner and at the same time gave his personal account of the efforts made at the board meeting to get Minor replaced. Martin claimed that Minor and his friends remained gentlemen thoughout the entire unhappy discussion. "On the other hand," he wrote, "if you can recall the frantic efforts of Preston and Ronald at the White and Yellow Sulphur in the summer of 1872, [to secure the presidency for Conrad], you can understand the whole matter. No Board was ever more carefully, constantly, persistently, even eagerly, and almost frantically . . . waited on, lobbied, and bowed to . . . than the one here in August last." Martin wrote that Wharton, Ellzey, Lane, "and others," foiled in their effort to remove Minor, were now supposed to be supporting the move to induce the governor to appoint pro-military men to the board to replace those whose terms expired on January 1, 1879. This new board, Martin reported, was then supposed to replace Minor with Conrad, Ellzey, or Sullins.

The board's act to postpone action to resolve the dispute proved to be fatal to the board and nearly so to the College. Public discussion of the "discipline" at the College and of the "split" in the faculty continued with mounting fervor in the press. In early January, 1879, a bill was introduced and passed in the state Senate, providing for the dismissal of the entire Board of Visitors for the school. The bill was sent to the House, which delayed immediate action on it. This delay in the House gave the public time to act. It did so. With a surprising unanimity, editorials and letters to the press appeared attacking the proposed bill as politically motivated, unfair, and condemning the board and faculty without proper investigation. The *Richmond Whig*, in an editorial attacking the bill, asked the question, "Is it possible that such a matter can pass?" The House decided it was not possible, and after much discussion the bill was dismissed in February of the same year.

The action of the legislature alarmed the board into action. Rector Eggleston set up committees from the board and charged them to investigate thoroughly the affairs of the school. Once more this body showed extreme reluctance in replacing any faculty member suspected of airing College linen in the press. It was later made clear that the board was confused and divided over whom to replace. A "card to the public" was released to the press on August 13, informing the public that the board had made a thorough investigation of the institution and was now satisfied that the conditions were good and were improving. The "differences" heretofore existing had been "happily adjusted," the announcement stated, and "in the future harmony and cordial co-operation will distinguish all connected with the management of the college." In the opinion of the board, the admittedly severe decline in enrollment was not attributable to the disputes which had gone on in the College but to the serious economic conditions in the state.

This "card" was too little, too late, and in the eyes of some too inaccurate to to solve the problems facing the College. As events later were to demonstrate, the board itself was divided on the report. On January 1, 1879, General Fitzhugh Lee had been appointed to the Board of Visitors. He is supposed to have started an immediate agitation for an organization along military lines in the hope that such an organization would solve the disciplinary problems which had caused so much trouble. General W. B. Taliaferro and Judge John A. Meredith, members of the board, are supposed to have supported him. Regardless of the paternity of the military sentiment, on the same day the board decided to release "the card to the public" it also decided to reorganize the College along strict military lines; however, it did not publicize this fact. Instead, it appointed a committee to draw up and submit a plan of reorganization for the school along the new lines. This plan was to be submitted to the board at its meeting in November, 1879. Before this meeting could be held and a definite plan of reorganization announced, public speculation and rumors about the College and the intentions of the board had created an apprehensive, even explosive state of mind in segments of the public.

The release in November of the proposed reorganizational plan did create an explosion, most of it in opposition but some in support of the plan. Most of the ire was directed at the proposed military feature. Letters with a decidedly familiar ring in this day of campus protest against ROTC appeared in the press. Demands for legislative investigation sprang up from many directions. Inconsistencies between the information "foisted on the public" in the "card" of August and the justification given for the plan of November were held up as illustrations of the inefficiency and irrationality of the board. The board does seem to have been vulnerable on this point. In August it had insisted that the decline in enrollment had been due to the economic conditions of the state. In its November defense of its proposed reorganization along military lines the board had stated, "After careful inquiry, the Board came to the conclusion that this marked decrease in the number of students is due to a defective organization of the College, and an inefficient system of discipline."

The plan of organization proposed by the board in November, 1878, deserves far more attention as one of the important documents in the history of the Virginia Polytechnic Institute and State University than it has ever received. Not only did it set the major direction the military feature of the College would follow for almost a century, but it also contained the first statement ever issued by a Board of Visitors expressing its belief and desire that the College should be developed on a broad rather than a narrow interpretation of the Morrill Act. "The terms of the endowment," it concluded, "do not confine the teachings of the College to such branches only as relate to agriculture and the mechanical arts . . . If the College shall be so organized, and we do not mean to say it is not now so organized, as to teach all the classical and scientific subjects, as well as such as relate more immediately to agriculture and mechanics . . . such a course of instruction will promote the liberal as well as the practical education of the industrial classes."

Agreeing that the leading object of the College was to teach the branches of learning related to agriculture and mechanics, the board also held:

> It was not intended, nor can the inference be deduced from the language used in the act of endowment, that only degrees relating to agriculture and mechanics should be conferred, nor that diplomas or symbols of proficiency

are to be given for a lower degree of attainment in the several schools of learning taught in the College than is required to obtain a diploma in the same
school in other colleges of the state. The diploma conferred by the College
should represent as high a degree of attainment as one obtained in any other
college in the same school whether technical or educational.

The degrees should not be confined to agricultural and mechanical instruction, but should likewise be awarded for distinction in those courses of study
necessary to prepare the student for other professions and pursuits in life.

A review of the report of the College prepared by Minor and accepted by the
board in the summer of 1878 will reveal just how radical a change of direction and
organization the board was proposing. Evidently it felt that Minor and Martin,
the chief opponents of a military organization, might not support the new proposals with the efficiency desired; therefore, at the November meeting Professor
Martin was replaced with Thomas Conrad and the announcement made that
Minor would be replaced at the December meeting.

When the board proceeded at its meeting on December 10, 1879, to implement the proposed reorganization by removing Minor and replacing him with
Dr. John Lee Buchanan, howls of protest directed against the board erupted all
over the state. At the same time, it is both a significant fact and a tribute to the
man that no attack was directed at Buchanan, who came to the presidency of the
Virginia Agricultural and Mechanical College from the presidency of Emory and
Henry College.

Apparently Minor remained as president until the end of the fall semester
which ended just before Christmas. Buchanan hesitated for some time before he
accepted the presidency. He visited Blacksburg during the winter vacation, when
he inspected the College and met many of the leading citizens. Finally, after considerable pressure from the board and some leaders in Blacksburg, he accepted
the office and entered upon his duties with the beginning of the spring semester
about March 1, 1880. For reasons completely beyond his control, his tenure was a
short one.

From the time of its first proposal to reorganize the College until after
Buchanan's assumption of the presidency, the attacks on the Board of Visitors had
been carried on either by editorials or letters to the press. Large numbers of these
letters and editorials concluded their attacks with impassioned appeals to the
legislature to investigate the College, the board, or both. Conditions in the state
were ripening for such appeals to be heeded.

It was inevitable that the College would be caught up in the politics of the
era. The Democratic-Conservative Party had controlled the offices of the state at
the time the institution had been organized; and as one result, members of that
party had been appointed to the Board of Visitors as well as to faculty posts. At
the very time the Minor-Lane altercation brought the trouble at the College to
public attention, the Democratic-Conservative Party was being challenged by a
group know as the Readjusters. Made up of individuals from all political parties
of the state, this group of people stood for adjusting or scaling down the huge
bonded indebtedness of the state, even if it meant partial repudiation of the
bonds. In the words of C. C. Pearson, the Readjuster Movement originated as
"a protest of the plain people against the very honest but also very narrow and
unsocial minded regime which came into control as a result of the Civil War and
Reconstruction." Many of its most articulate members came from leaders closer to
the great masses of people than to the Virginia aristocracy. Using the debt question as a spring board, the Readjusters had mounted a program of proposed social

reform which carried tremendous appeal for the "plain people" of the state. In the state election of 1878, the Readjusters had won control of the legislature, while in 1881 they not only retained control of the legislature but elected a governor as well. Once in office, many leaders attempted to organize their movement into a state party and found appealing the possibility of using the public school system and the College as political plums. Since the legislature controlled the appointment of county and city superintendents of schools who in turn controlled the nominations of youth from their respective counties or cities to receive free tuition at the Virginia Agricultural and Mechanical College, this school loomed as an unusually juicy plum. In campaigning for office, some of the Readjuster candidates openly pledged "if elected to put all administrative departments of the state in sympathy with the people." As far as possible, this purpose was carried out in the 1879-80 session of the legislature and was extended and completed in the session of 1881-82. As Matthew Page Andrews expressed it, "Not in time of peace had Virginia ever experienced such wholesale removal of officials in favor of a party in power."

The troubles at the College plus the clamor in the press gave the Readjusters a ready-made excuse to start an investigation in an effort to put the school in "sympathy with the people."

By December 18, 1879, a movement was started in the legislature by Senator J. E. Eskridge, a Readjuster from Montgomery County, to have an investigation made of the Virginia Agricultural and Mechanical College. At first some of the press supported the idea of an investigation on the grounds that justice to the replaced Minor and Martin demanded it. When later developments made it quite obvious that the real purpose of the investigation was to fill board and faculty positions with Readjusters, most of the same press excoriated the investigation with a vehemence soothing only to one whose trust had been betrayed.

At the time of his election to the presidency, Dr. Buchanan was well aware of the Readjuster sentiment. Although a Democrat by bent, he had the warm support of powerful members in the Readjuster camp. Furthermore, he was a native of southwestern Virginia, a Readjuster stronghold. There is considerable reason to believe that he discussed the matter of the presidency of the College with Readjuster leaders from the western part of the state and secured their support before he finally decided to accept the position. Whatever his reasoning, he accepted the presidency and immediately entered upon his duties.

The immediate reorganization of the College under Buchanan was not so drastic as had been anticipated. The most noteworthy academic change was to abolish the preparatory department and place the responsibility for this work under the professor of English. Even this change had been recommended by both Minor and Martin. As an economy move, the board reduced salaries of the faculty and assigned the duties of treasurer to V. E. Shepherd with no additional pay. Additional supervisory and administrative authority, earnestly requested by but denied to President Minor, was granted to the president. The most significant change had to do with the highly controversial military feature. Even this change was anticlimactic following the furious uproar which met the announcement that a change would be made. In an obvious effort to soothe public feelings, a letter was distributed to the press on March 6, one week after Buchanan took office, describing the new plan as follows:

Under the new plan students are required to rise at 6:30 instead of 8 o'clock as heretofore. Instead of roaming at will through the town all hours of the day and night, as heretofore, they are not allowed to leave the college limits except at a certain hour in the morning and a certain hour in the afternoon. At study hours, from 7:00 p.m. to 9:00 p.m. the students are required to be in their rooms, and a teacher is in the building. Heretofore there never was a study period.

The military [military instruction] is as it always has been; the same drill, an hour in the afternoon for five days of the week, nothing more, and the same as it has been from the beginning of the college, all statements to the contrary notwithstanding.

Thousands of alumni today can testify that many features of this simple reorganization affecting student life survived in the College for years. In fact, many alumni today will argue that the "good old Tech spirit" had its origin in the ingenious zeal with which students cooperated to outwit persons authorized to enforce regulations growing out of this earliest plan.

Buchanan's election to the presidency and the attending circumstances produced some surprising developments. It did not reduce the attacks on the administration of the College, but it did give rise to some denominational fears. "Citizen," writing to *The State,* excitedly charged that the Board of Visitors had fired all the Presbyterians connected with the College. Now the Presbyterians, so "Citizen" believed, had a right to be represented in a state institution. In addition to the unjust treatment afforded the Presbyterians, claimed "Citizen," the haste with which the board had replaced the fired members tended to destroy all confidence in the board. "Ought the legislature to allow such doings by the Executives it has charged with the management of the college?" queried "Citizen."

Since Professor Charles Martin, the replaced Presbyterian on the faculty, was rather well known in Presbyterian circles, it is possible this outburst by "Citizen" may have sparked some of the editorials which appeared in the press denouncing the treatment accorded Martin. A few minor murmurs of discontent emanated from the Episcopalian camp over the treatment received by President Minor; but since General Lane, reportedly an Episcopalian, was still on the faculty, this denomination apparently confined its discontent, if any, to personal contact with Episcopalian members of the legislature. There is scant evidence either to support or deny this charge.

The Methodists, especially the group in Blacksburg which had been sniping at Minor, seem to have been delighted with the changes made by the board. Thomas Conrad, their champion, had been elevated to a full professorship on the faculty, while the presidency now rested in the hands of a staunch Methodist, the former president of the Methodist Emory and Henry College. At long last everything seemed to be going their way. A letter bubbling over with pleasure and felicitations for the College, the community, and the people of the state, was sent to *The Richmond Dispatch.* The Board of Visitors was lauded for the part it had played in securing Buchanan and in launching such a wise reorganization of the College. According to Veri, the writer of the letter, Buchanan had been most cordially received in Blacksburg, while every member of the faculty was "charmed with the man." "It is to be deplored," continued Veri, "that while there is such delightful feeling now existing *inside* that there should be any person *outside* to produce the impression upon the public mind that there are schisms in the College." But certain persons have thought other certain persons have been badly treated, concluded Veri. As a result of these unfair and unfounded opinions, some "murmurings" had found their way to the legislature and had caused some individuals in that body to start thinking in terms of an investigation. Such an investigation was entirely unnecessary now, thought Veri, but if held would really help the College, because it would prove to the people how well it was now getting along.

This account drew an immediate attack from the editor of the *Dispatch,* who denounced the entire letter as an effort to throw sand in the eyes of the legislature. After making it quite clear that no attack was intended on Dr. Buchanan, the editor restated his convictions that the actions of the board in replacing Minor and Martin did need to be investigated by the legislature. The editor was particularly concerned to hear an explanation of how the board had determined that Conrad was competent to replace the scholarly, experienced Martin on the faculty. Practically every point of Veri's letter was ridiculed by the editor, who claimed that Veri seemed to be saying of the board, "Alas! that such immaculate public functionaries should be so little appreciated." The editor clearly wished that the "murmurings" which Veri said had found their way to the legislature would swell into a roar. He got his wish, but even he was not prepared for the actual roar which ensued.

As the turmoil continued to swirl around the hapless College, free advice, which one individual caustically characterized as worth what it cost, was offered from all sides. If a military school was wanted, grumbled "Tax Payer," shift the land-grant fund to the Virginia Military Institute which was already established as such. Another writer advocated leaving the College strictly alone both academically and financially. In the eyes of this individual, the school was not a state institution, since it had been brought into creation as the result of a federal, not a state, grant. Any state appropriations in addition to the $61,250 already spent on the College would be totally indefensible, he argued.

Perhaps the most unusual solution to the problems faced by the College then or at any other time in its history came from a researcher into the resources of southwestern Virginia. His solution was to turn the College into an asylum! To accomplish this solution, he proposed that the land-grant money be transfered to Emory and Henry College and that this institution be converted into a state agricultural and mechanical college. He believed that this could be done to the happiness and satisfaction of all groups concerned, since the state was seeking a suitable location for an asylum in southwestern Virginia, since Emory and Henry owed the state a large sum of money, and since the College at Blacksburg was doomed to failure anyway because of economic and other conditions in the state. In his opinion, the state could obtain Emory and Henry by cancelling the existing debt and selling the college farm at Blacksburg. In his mind the remaining acreage and buildings at Blacksburg would be more than adequate for the asylum. The buildings and the campus at Emory and Henry and a combination of the faculties of the two colleges would produce one strong successful institution from two weak and apparently failing ones. In his opinion, the asylum would draw more people to Blacksburg than the College! This being the case, the new institution would need far more employees than the number required by the College; therefore, the local farmers would be able to sell more produce to the asylum than to the College. This proposal was given no consideration whatever; but since it was published in a book bearing the interesting title of *Resources of South-western Virginia,* it has been discovered and rediscovered periodically ever since.

Whether it has proved to be an amusing or a painful discovery ususally has depended upon the state of mind of the reader at the time of discovery.

As previously noted, Senator Eskridge of the Readjuster group from Montgomery County initiated a movement in the legislature on December 18, 1879, to investigate the affairs of the College. Action on this proposal was slow at first but gained momentum as the Readjusters grew in legislative confidence. Finally on January 31, 1880, a joint resolution of the House and Senate was approved whereby a special committee was to be set up to go to Blacksburg to "inquire into irregularities, etc. of the agricultural and mechanical college."

Three days later a Readjuster caucus was held, reportedly behind closely guarded doors, but an enterprising reporter, or reporters, probably hostile to the Readjusters, managed to find out, or at least claimed to have found out, what went on during the meeting. Concerning the proposed investigation of the Virginia Agricultural and Mechanical College, the reporter noted, "Mr. Bailey said that he and Mr. Farr were on a sub-committee appointed to go to Blacksburg to investigate the conditions of things there. The management of that institution had, it was represented, done gross injustice to some Readjuster. Mr. Bailey wished to know if they went up there [to Blacksburg] and did their work, and would bring a bill which would make the institution respect the rights of the party, could he have the assurance that the caucus would sustain the bill?"

The *Dispatch* does not record the answer given to Mr. Bailey but did record, "It is understood that the sub-committee will not go to Blacksburg."

This report on the proposed action of the Readjuster caucus focused statewide attention on the College once more. Letters and editorials both defending and attacking the Readjuster proposal and the Readjusters in general filled the press. The program being undertaken by Dr. Buchanan and his faculty was almost completely ignored. Consideration of ways and means to promote agricultural and mechanical education received scant attention. Control of the College became one of the symbols of victory sought both by the Democrats and Readjusters. As one result, the College became the football in a game of politics during which both sides sought to control the ball by some dubious interpretations, modifications, and executions of the rules of the game played without any referee.

Ignoring the fact that President Buchanan had been in office less than two weeks, the House Committee on Schools and Colleges recommended a complete reorganization of both the board and the faculty of the Virginia Agricultural and Mechanical College. A minority report by the Democrats on the committee strongly opposed this recommendation on the grounds that the recently appointed board and faculty could solve all the troubles besetting the school. After rather heated exchanges of opinion which one newspaper claimed were too undignified to be called a debate, the legislature approved a resolution on March 3, 1880, removing the Board of Visitors as of June 4, 1880. The resolution further provided, "It shall be the duty of the governor, as soon as practicable after the passage of this act and prior to the close of the present session of the General Assembly, by and with the advice and consent of the Senate, to appoint a new board of visitors whose terms of office shall commence the fourth day of June, eighteen hundred and eighty. . . ." The wording of this provision of the resolution is worth remembering because the Democrats saw in it a possible means of circumventing the Readjusters.

In addition to the just-mentioned provisions, the resolution directed the new board to hold a special meeting on June 7, 1880, for the purpose of removing any or all faculty members, the said removals to take effect August 12, 1880, at which time the board was to select new faculty members and complete its reorganization of the College.

Abram Fulkerson, distinguished Readjuster senator representing Washington and Smyth Counties, the latter being Buchanan's native county, made a desperate effort to get an amendment to the resolution permitting the removal of all officers and faculty at the College except President Buchanan, but the eastern faction refused to support him in the effort. As a result, through no fault of his own, Buchanan was faced with the prospect of being removed from the office of president less than two weeks after he had assumed it.

Governor Fred W. M. Holliday signed the resolution on March 9, 1880, but apparently he thought he had spotted a way to foil the Readjusters. Holliday had visited the College on numerous occasions during its happier days; but being the astute politician that he was, he had not become deeply involved with the recent disputes swirling about the hapless institution. The dispute now, however, had clearly developed as a political one between the Democrats and Readjusters. Holliday was a Democrat. Instead of appointing the new board at once he did not find it "practicable" to do so until one hour before final adjournment of the legislature, and by this time it was too late for the Senate to confirm or reject the nominations.

The political strategy of Holliday's action at this time has been ably presented by Buchanan's biographer, John B. May, through an interpretation which is in harmony with the known conditions of the time. According to May, Holliday realized that the Readjuster Senate would refuse to confirm his appointments unless the appointees were drawn from the ranks of the Readjusters. The Democrats hoped to win control of the next Senate. Then, too, the legislature would not convene again until the fall of 1881. In this time the board could complete the reorganization of the College. If the new legislature should be Democratic, the newly appointed board would remain in office. If the Readjusters kept control of the legislature, perhaps they would fear the political consequences of an attempt to reorganize the school for the third time in a period of less than four years, especially if the present board had succeeded in winning the support of the people. This interpretation of Holliday's strategy certainly seems to be a valid one; but be that as it may, Holliday underestimated the determination of the Readjusters to control the College and overestimated the ability of the new board to reorganize the College and win the support of the people in so short a time.

The new, unconfirmed board nominated by Holliday met in Blacksburg on June 7, 1880, as required and made a clean sweep by vacating all the offices of the College effective at the close of the current session, which the board at the same meeting moved from August 12 to June 12. Obviously, faculty tenure was as unheard of at the Virginia Agricultural and Mechanical College as it was in other institutions of that day. One conclusion which has been drawn from the action of the board in shortening the school year is that the board was eager to begin the reorganization of the College.

At its June meeting, the board determined to invite applications for all faculty positions, which it planned to fill on August 12. In the meantime, a meeting was called for June 30, at which time the College was to be reorganized. The direction to be taken by this reorganization baffled the board. After all, what directions remained to be taken? The first board's rigidly restricted curriculum had been rejected. Both a pro-military and an anti-military organization had come under bitter attack. The proposal to put the literary department on an equal footing with that of agriculture and mechanics had been rejected. The limited finances available ruled out the establishment of a comprehensive university, even if the action of the legislature had not. Political factors ruled out public admission that the demand for reorganization in truth rested on political reasons rather than on any genuine dissatisfaction with an administration which had been in office less than four months.

Finally, after much agonizing over the matter, the board issued the following statement which in effect reversed the direction of the College set by the immediately preceding board in 1879:

"This Board conceives that it was not the design of the Assembly, or of Congress to establish here a military school, an academic college, or a university, but an institution whose primary function should be to turn out scientific farmers and mechanics, so far as a school may serve that purpose, and whose secondary object should be to accompany that special training and teaching with a liberal general education as may consist with and conduce to the primary aim." The military feature was to be reduced "within the narrowest limits consistent with the Federal law."

The June action of the board in vacating all offices at the institution completed the removal of every member of the pioneer faculty which had helped launch the College in 1872 and guided its destiny for the first eight years of its existence. In view of the circumstances surrounding their dismissal, it seems to be unfair to claim, as is sometimes done, that this group failed in its objective of establishing an agricultural and mechanical college. Be that as it may, the board, having settled upon a statement of guiding principles for the school, set about selecting a new faculty.

John Lee Buchanan was offered the presidency once more but, to the board's surprise, declined the offer, whereupon Colonel Scott Shipp was elected as president. Colonel Shipp had been commandant of cadets at the Virginia Military Institute since 1862 and had been in command of the cadets in the well-remembered battle of New Market. He had been approached concerning the presidency by one board member at the time of President Minor's impending removal but had declined to permit his name to be considered because of his respect for Minor. Now with both Minor and Buchanan out of the picture Shipp was willing to accept the presidency. On August 17, 1880, he had written to Ruffner, whom he knew personally, informing him that he had received official notification of his appointment to the presidency, along with instructions to meet with the executive committee of the board in Blacksburg on August 25. Colonel Shipp, a strong-willed individual of firm convictions, expressed complete agreement with Ruffner's curriculum proposals for the school first drawn up in 1872. At the same time, he expressed some disappointment that the board was insisting on opening the College before "a scheme of organization [had] been thoroughly designed by the faculty." Apparently Shipp had not realized that none of the Boards of Visitors had ever permitted the faculty to design "a scheme of organization" for the school, and that this board would not prove to be an exception.

The assignments for each of the faculty elected on August 12, 1880, indicate rather clearly the reorganization executed by the board at this time. The assignments follow: Colonel Scott Shipp, president and professor of mental and moral philosophy; John Hart, professor of English literature, to be in control of the preparatory department and to teach Latin and French if needed; Martin P. Scott, M.D., professor of chemistry, natural history and agriculture, to be in charge of the portion of the farm to be laid off for purely experimental purposes; J. E. Christian, A.M., professor of mathematics and natural philosophy; Colonel W. W. Blackford, professor of mechanics and drawing, to have charge of the workshop and to be superintendent of grounds and buildings; E. S. Tutwiler, farm manager; and John Gardner, treasurer.

In line with the board's determination to reduce military training, no one person was assigned responsibility for the military tactics, but it was assumed Colonel Shipp would add this instruction to his other duties.

Colonel Shipp had a different idea. When the executive committee of the board showed the proposed plan of organization and assignment of responsibilities to Shipp and his faculty at the August 24 meeting, apparently it was the first time Shipp had seen it. Details as to the actual happening at this meeting are not available, but it seems rather clear that in the warm discussion which followed, Shipp realized that the board, not the faculty, would take care of the details of the "scheme of organization" to be followed by the College. The strong-willed Shipp resigned at once, as the board reported, "before entering upon his duties." Regardless of whether Shipp's tenure as president is measured by the two weeks between his appointment as president on August 12 and his resignation on August 25 or by the one day spent in Blacksburg as president, his tenure still stands as the shortest one for any president of the College during its first century. Following his resignation, he returned to the Virginia Military Institute, where he enjoyed a lifetime career of exceptionally distinguished service to that institution.

Shipp's resignation on the eve of the opening of the College created both consternation and disarray in the board, which, with the exception of Ruffner, was completely inexperienced in planning a college. Ruffner was offered, and immediately declined, the presidency, whereupon the board appointed Professor John Hart as acting president. Hart had not sought and apparently did not want the job, for he knew what others had yet to discover. He knew he was not an aggressive administrator. He accepted the role of acting president, expecting to be relieved within a short time, as soon as the board selected another person to serve as president. To his surprise, the board proved unable to find such a person for nearly a year, and Hart found himself reluctantly presiding over the College as acting president for the entire session of 1880-1881, perhaps the darkest session ever experienced by the school.

Professor V. E. Shepherd, who had been replaced in the June reorganization was called back to the faculty in September to assist Hart and to take charge of the work in the preparatory department. The faculty assembled at this time was an able one with some outstanding individuals on it, but in reality it never had a real chance to demonstrate its ability. The economic conditions of the state plus the attacks on the College administration which had been swirling about in the press and in the legislature combined to reduce enrollment drastically. The few students who did matriculate were found to be woefully deficient in academic preparation. The state was in arrears in payment of money due the College;

therefore, there were no funds available for anything whatever beyond the barest minimum essentials. For periods of time even these essentials had to go unmet. Carefully prepared, progressive plans prepared by Dr. Scott for coordinating instruction in agriculture with the farm had to be by-passed or postponed for lack of funds, as did the unusually progressive plans for the mechanical department prepared by General W. W. Blackford. This latter individual also prepared and initiated a long-range plan for campus landscaping and beautification which was followed for several decades after the departure of this energetic individual from the campus. Many of the larger shade trees on the campus owe their origin to Blackford and his zeal to make the campus attractive.

The military feature plagued this faculty as it had all previous faculties, albeit in a different manner. It had no champion other than the requirement in the Morrill Act. This situation had not been anticipated but had been brought about by the resignation of Colonel Shipp. General Blackford had served with distinction during the Civil War with J. E. B. Stuart but did not feel qualified to teach military tactics. Besides, this highly competent individual already had his hands more than full with other assigned duties. None of the remaining faculty had any military training. Faced with this perplexing situation, the board resorted to a strategy which many subsequent boards found useful in dealing with the puzzling problem of military tactics. It handed the problem to someone else, in this instance to Acting President Hart, who in turn handed it to the students. Several of these students had received instruction under former Professor Lane. One of these, therefore, was named acting commandant, and the others were designated as officers. This group, according to the board, managed all drill throughout the session of 1880-1881 with commendable "zeal and diligence, and with all the efficiency it was reasonable to expect."

Unfortunately, the board did not operate with the same zeal and diligence in seeking a president to replace Shipp. Instead of prosecuting a vigorous search for a president, the board decided to go along with Hart until it could find a man with all the qualifications it sought. The board recognized certain possible dangers inherent in this plan but felt that these threats could be prevented if the executive committee exercised, "a prudent watch and care over the institution." The public felt otherwise, and the board was soon subjected to strong criticism for its apparent delay in securing a president.

In early September, after the College got off to a decidedly dubious start under the new, inexperienced faculty, Ruffner was once more offered the presidency. He rejected it at once but after considerable urging agreed to give it consideration if the board would raise the salary to $2500 and authorize him to visit other land-grant colleges in the country to study their programs of organization and operation. The board accepted this proposal at once but in so doing had to delay yet longer in filling the office of president. This delay, not being fully understood and appreciated by the public, caused even more denunciation of the board and did nothing to enhance the College in the eyes of the people.

In the meantime Ruffner spent nearly a month visiting eleven land-grant colleges in the eastern United States and collecting written information about others. The voluminous report of his travel and study which he prepared upon his return showed an interesting cross section of the development of land-grant colleges and in content antedated many conclusions and generalizations which twentieth century students of the land-grant movement would make. The report set forth a

number of principles which seemed to be developing as guidelines for the colleges, but his study did not reveal any one pattern toward which the colleges
seemed to be moving. On the contrary, he reported that "there is exhibited surprising contrariety of sentiment in respect to the meaning of the [Morrill] act of
1862. . . . A legislature or a college board may find some clause in the act which
will seem to favor almost anything that may be wanted." "It is very certain," he
added, "that the thing demanded by the public of the technical college is the
technical feature." The problem of achieving this technical feature, he noted,
was one which had to be studied by each state in order to secure a program
adapted to the needs peculiar to that state. "These colleges," he wrote, "must
work among the people, not above them. The people must understand the college, and love it, and be proud of it and thus only can you have a prosperous and
useful college."

Ruffner's report both stimulated and disappointed the board. It stimulated
them by enlarging their vision of the possibilities of development open to land-
grant colleges. It disappointed them because the report did not reveal a blue print
for the development along any of the paths opened up. But, most important of
all, the board was disappointed by Ruffner's decision following the delivery of
the report at the November, 1880, meeting of the board: once more he declined
the offer of the presidency.

There can be no doubt of Ruffner's interest in the presidency of the College.
Neither can there be any doubt that the reason for his declination can be stated
with one word, *politics*. Prior to undertaking his visit to the land-grant colleges he
had written to numerous acquaintances and members of the board, seeking their
opinion of the possible political consequences should he accept the presidency.
All these individuals wholeheartedly endorsed him for the office but admitted
political difficulties lay ahead for him regardless of whether he accepted the presidency or remained superintendent of public instruction. Major D. A. Grimsley,
a member of the board from Culpeper Court House, after discussing the situation concluded his letter with the statement, "Doctor, if the place [presidency]
suits you and you can without great sacrifice accept it, then for the good of the
institution do so, but what will become of the [public] schools I do not know."
Richard V. Gaines, influential member of the board from Charlotte County, wrote
to Ruffner at the same time and expressed his conviction that Ruffner was the
best qualified man in the state or elsewhere for the presidency. At the same time
he warned that the Readjusters would be in full control of the next legislature
and would try to oust Ruffner from any position he might hold at the time. The
Readjusters, warned Gaines in a prophetic note, would be satisfied with "nothing
less than one who is a tried and faithfull ally—qualifications and experience will
count for nothing in that fight." "I think you are more popular with the people
than you are with the politicians," wrote Gaines. "The former all support you
but the latter are afraid of you." Since Ruffner by this time was thoroughly disgusted with the way politics was creeping into his beloved public school system
and the administration of the College, he declined the presidency and began at
the same time to think in terms of relinquishing his public school work. He continued as ex-officio member of the Board of Visitors until the winter of 1882,
when, learning that the Readjusters were in fact planning to oust him from
office, he resigned as state superintendent of public instruction. The resignation
of this unusual man, the father of technical education at the Virginia Agricultural

and Mechanical College, permanently terminated his connection with the College, although it did not terminate his distinguished career as an educational leader in the state.

Ruffner's rejection of the presidency forced the board to adjourn once more before selecting a president, and this apparent vacillation and delay increased the criticism being directed at the board. *The Richmond Dispatch* claimed that everyone now agreed that the proceedings were a farce. Other accusations were less kind. Rumors, charges, and countercharges flourished in Blacksburg and throughout the state. Professor V. E. Shepherd, a moderate Readjuster, is supposed to have written to a friend stating that the board, being afraid of Thomas Conrad, would probably be forced to elect him president. Since Conrad was an ardent Readjuster, this rumor did not go unremembered by the Democrats when a year or so later Conrad did in fact become president.

For reasons known only to itself, the board made no public effort to secure a president until it met in Blacksburg in May, 1881. At this time the presidency once more was offered to Dr. John L. Buchanan. To the great surprise of nearly everyone and seemingly to Buchanan himself, he once more accepted the offer and for the second time became the president of the Virginia Agricultural and Mechanical College. He was unable to enter upon his duties until August 14; therefore, Professor Hart continued as acting president until the close of the academic session on August 11.

The action of Buchanan in accepting this appointment was puzzling. He had been dismissed as president in June, 1880, had refused reappointment in August of the same year, but accepted the office in May, 1881, nearly one year after being removed. It appears that the board, after a year of trying to operate the College under the "prudent watch and care" of its executive committee, had convinced Buchanan it was now ready and willing to leave the operation of the College to the president. Evidently Buchanan was convinced that the legislature would not involve the College in politics again. He was wrong.

William E. Cameron, a Readjuster, was elected governor in November, 1881, after a heated campaign. His entrance into office in January, 1882, placed the state government firmly in the hands of the Readjusters, who were determined to fill all appointive public offices in the state with members of their own party. The Democrats wished to fill all such offices with Democrats. This latter group resorting to more subtly sophisticated methods than the observably crude, direct methods used by the Readjusters in achieving their objective, lost several battles, but in the decade ahead won the political war and completely annihilated the Readjusters, driving them into either the Republican or the Democratic Party. The hapless College, although reorganized and placed under a president from the Readjusters-dominated Southwest Virginia, was not long to be left alone by either political party.

The act approved on March 9, 1880, directing the governor to appoint a new Board of Visitors for the College, included the provision that such appointments were to be made "by and with the advice and consent of the Senate." The appointments by Democratic Governor Holliday were made as the legislature was adjourning and therefore had not received the "advice and consent" of the Senate. Immediately upon Cameron's entrance to the governorship, the Readjuster-controlled Senate notified him that it had rejected the nominations to the board made by Governor Holliday in April, 1880. Cameron thereupon nominated a new

Board of Visitors, all Readjusters, and sent the nomination to the Senate on January 17, 1882. The Senate on the same day confirmed these nominations to the board, which met reportedly on the same day and without further ado removed "the president, professors, and other officers" who had been appointed by the preceding board. These incumbents having been removed, the board then proceeded "to fill vacancies by electing a president, a faculty and other officers" for the College. By resolution, the newly elected president was instructed "to take charge of the College at once, ascertain its condition, and report a plan of reorganization." The ubiquitous Thomas Conrad, who had been by-passed on four previous occasions, at last achieved one of his big ambitions. He was selected by the board for the presidency of the Virginia Agricultural and Mechanical College.

Thus, because of the unsettled political conditions of the time, Dr. John Lee Buchanan had been removed from office for a second time as a result of the actions of the Readjusters. By a peculiar turn of the wheels of fortune and of politics, the legislature in 1885 elected Buchanan as state superintendent of public instruction. He assumed the duties of this office on March 15, 1886, and thereby became ex-officio member of the Board of Visitors, which one week later voted to oust Conrad from the presidency of the Virginia Agricultural and Mechanical College. In 1894 Buchanan assumed the presidency of the University of Arkansas and, according to the historian of that institution, was largely instrumental in developing that school into a university.

The board which placed Conrad in office made other faculty changes. Professors Scott, Christian, and Shepherd were reappointed, with Shepherd being promoted to professor of Latin and modern languages. Judge John Gardner was reappointed as treasurer; William Grim was employed to replace Professor Hart; and General W. W. Blackford was released, not to be replaced until the next year. Eli Tutwiler, farmer, was released and his position abolished. C. H. Hitchcock was employed as the first professor of geology and mineralogy, while William B. Preston was made professor of physics and military tactics. This reorganized faculty assumed responsibility for the College in the middle of the academic year at the beginning of the spring semester.

The Readjuster segment of the public was pleased with the results achieved by the action of the legislature but at the same time was a bit shocked by the callous speed with which it had acted to correct the "Bourbon inefficiency and lack of sympathy for the masses" allegedly existing at the College. A number of letters defending and condemning the action appeared in the press. The general condemnation can be summed up in a letter published in *The Richmond Dispatch,* of January 26, 1882, as follows:

> Messrs Editors: The first and most important act of the new Board of Visitors of the State Agricultural College, i.e. the designation of a new president—has been marked by a precipitation which is scandalous; a shock to the friends of that useful institution, and an intimation of purposes in connection with it [at] which every ally of sound education stands aghast. An Act of the Assembly dismisses the old Board and authorizes the Governor to appoint a new one. This he does promptly; and then actually before their names have had time to appear generally in the newspapers of the state, and really as we supposed, before they could come together, the new Board meets, ejects Dr. Buchanan, the incumbent, elects Mr. Conrad president, and sets him to work to "complete the reorganization." It is not the purpose of this note to exalt the outgoing or to depreciate the incoming head of the college. The former is reputed an able officer, and the latter a Readjuster with zeal appropriate to an eleventh hour convert; but we have nothing to say on this score. If the late

president was unworthy and the new one unobjectionable we should still lift up our voice. Conceding for the sake of agrument that Mr. Conrad is altogether fitted for the post for which he has been selected, how did the Board find it out? It has been customary for the Visitors, when a new professorship was to be filled in one of our institutions to advertise for applicants months in advance and on an appointed day to select the best from those whose names and testimonials were before them. That wise precedent has in this case been contemptuously disregarded. It seems to have been sufficient that the aspirant was an active politician of the dominant party,—and before it was possible that his relative, to say nothing of actual fitness could be ascertained he was put into it. It is notorious that most of the State Agricultural Colleges of the country have been killed by politicians. Is it possible that ours is to have the same ignoble fate?

In spite of the political bias motivating the appointment of the Board of Visitors, its membership included some able and outstanding leaders, although one member in later years was never able to recall the correct name of the College. Of the board members, James C. Taylor of Christiansburg deserves more than a crumb of remembrance. As attorney general of Virginia he had served ex officio on the Board of Visitors which organized the College in 1872. Since then he had watched the developments in the new College with an anxious eye. When trouble had erupted during Minor's administration, Taylor felt that most of the trouble had developed because of the inexperience of both the board and the faculty with problems involved in establishing a type of college completely new to Virginia. In view of the tremendous obstacles which Minor and the board had overcome, he did not think Minor should be replaced. "Indeed sir," he had written, "I think we are compelled to look with great charity upon any mistakes that may have been made either by himself, the Board, or the Faculty."

Taylor had been the recipient of a few barbs from Conrad's pen at the time the latter was editor of the *Montgomery Messenger,* but apparently politics had served as the great healer in this instance, for Taylor as Rector of the Board of Visitors supported Conrad and gave him more latitude than that allowed any preceding president in developing the College.

Thomas Nelson Conrad, the third, fourth, fifth, or sixth president, depending upon how and where one starts counting in the previous rapid succession of presidents, undoubtedly was the most colorful and controversial person ever to hold the office of president during the first century of the existence of the College.

A native of Fairfax Court House, he had received his A.B. and A. M. degrees from Dickerson College in Pennsylvania. During the Civil War he had served as chaplain and later as scout [spy] with the Confederate forces operating mostly in northern Virginia. In this latter capacity he had operated on numerous occasions in Washington and its environs behind enemy lines. His feats of derring-do as self-described in his book *A Confederate Spy* would do credit to a modern TV thriller series. One recounted incident, which almost ended in disaster for Conrad, occurred when he was arrested as a suspected accomplice in the assassination of President Abraham Lincoln. As he was being led to prison the crowds in the streets in Washington thought he was John Wilkes Booth and tried to lynch him. His guards protected him, but even so he was pelted by rocks and sticks before he reached the safety of the prison walls. After several days of imprisonment he was able to prove his innocence and was released.

In 1871 Conrad had come to Blacksburg as president of the Preston and Olin Institute. His activities following the conversion of that institute into the Virginia Agricultural and Mechanical College have already been noted.

Upon his assumption of the presidency in February, 1882, he had been in-

structed by the board to "take charge of the College at once, ascertain its condition, and report a plan of reorganization." He accepted this charge with enthusiasm and executed it with a thoroughness and an attention to detail which
must have surprised the board itself. Even after discounting his personal bias and
the obvious effort to make a good case for the Readjuster take-over of the institution, Conrad's report of the conditions at the College as he claimed to have found
them is revealing. The report follows:

> The condition of the College, as ascertained by a careful examination and
> close inspection was deplorable. The workshop, the practical part of the
> Mechanical Department, was closed, and its costly engine had slept the sleep
> of months. The farm, the practical part of the Agricultural Department, was
> without proper organization, and had been for years. The Military, one of the
> most attractive and useful features of the College, had been shoved into a corner
> and paralyzed. The Boarding Department, by incompetent management, had be-
> come so objectionable that students went into town for their meals, and that
> at an expense exceeding the published figures in the catalogue of the Col-
> lege. . . . The condition of the College was astounding in another particular—
> its want of proper equipment after an existence of ten years.
>
> Though the resources of the College have been ample and unfailing, yet the
> College had not been provided with the ordinary equipment of a Modern
> Educational Institution.
>
> Think of a Laboratory without a drop of water! A department of Agricul-
> ture, without even a seed! A department of Mineralogy, without a mineral!
> And of Botany without a plant! and you have the College as we found it. Think
> of a State College without a Library, and that after an existence of ten years!
>
> Think of a "model farm" and no dairy; no piggery; no hennery; no vine-
> yard; no nursery; not even a garden, and you have the "College Farm" as we
> found it. Think of two large College buildings 45 × 135 and three stories high,
> without a drop of water on the premises! Think of a $30,000 farm without an
> ear of corn in the crib, or a bushel of wheat in the bin, or a ton of hay in the
> barn, and you have the "College Farm" as we found it in February 1882!
>
> Such was the condition of things when we took charge of the College. The
> only department of the institution in a creditable shape was the academic.
> This had been efficiently sustained by the professors in their respective lecture
> rooms. But for this the College would have been a total wreck.

Such was the official report, whether biased or not, of the Virginia Agricultural
and Mechanical College at the end of its first decade.

The new administration with Conrad as president set about reorganizing the
school at once. This administration for the first time in the existence of the College brought it one thing vitally needed; namely, a harmonious faculty and Board
of Visitors: a relationship not at all surprising, considering the firmly established
policy of the Readjusters followed in replacing personnel not in full agreement
with them.

In the reorganization which followed, the board adhered rather closely to the
guidelines laid down by the preceding board of November, 1878. Instead of restricting the institution to training scientific farmers and mechanics and making
all literary training subordinate thereto, this board conceived that the "great
purpose" of the College was "to promote the liberal and practical education of
the industrial classes of the state." The course of study, the board decided, should
begin "where the Public Free Schools end . . ." and continue to degrees of applied
science. Even this latter restriction was quickly removed when the board meeting
in 1882 decided to offer the A.B. degree in the literary and scientific department,
beginning with the session of 1882-83.

The College was organized into four academic departments, listed in the catalog as Agricultural Department, Mechanical Department, Literary and Scientific Department, and Business Department. This last department was justified as being one designed to meet one area of practical needs of the industrial class. The curriculum in this embyro department destined in time to grow into one of the significant colleges within the land-grant university, was organized as follows: Junior Year—Penmanship, Commercial Arithmetic, Single Entry Bookkeeping; Intermediate Year—Double Entry Bookkeeping, Business Forms, Elements of Mercantile Law, and Political Economy.

Since Conrad's administration not only saw the fruition of several practices begun by earlier administrations but also witnessed the beginning of many new practices which influenced the College for the decades ahead, his administration is worthy of further examination.

In addition to the A.B. degree, first offered during the session of 1882-83, the curriculum was expanded for the session 1883-84 to lead to the degrees of Civil Engineering and Mining Engineering. Students desiring one of the three new degrees now being offered were required to pursue four years of study rather than the hitherto customary three years of study required for the "Graduate of Agriculture" or "Graduate of Mechanics" diploma. The requirements for these latter diplomas remained the same. The long winter vacation was abandoned during the session of 1881-82 in favor of the more traditional summer vacation, and the college year was changed from two semesters to three quarters about the same time.

The few additional courses added to take care of the new degrees being offered were added to the faculty teaching loads which were already staggering if evaluated by today's criteria. The faculty was reported as carrying day-long loads. In 1882-83 J. E. Christian, professor of mathematics, reported that he had taught seven classes per day for the entire session and eight classes during part of the session. This veritable work horse had taught arithmetic, elementary algebra, advanced algebra, synthetic geometry, descriptive geometry, trigonometry, conic sections, differential and integral calculus, surveying, demonstrative mechanics, and astronomy! He did feel that the "battered and broken benches" (not desks) in his lecture room which afforded the student no facilities for writing or taking notes "embarrass both students and professor." Happily for Christian, Conrad had details of students go to the shop and make enough desks (not benches) to remove this embarrassment.

During the session of 1882-83 the library was moved to the second floor of the Second Academic Building and described in the following manner: "The large room, known as the 'ball room' has been fitted up quite tastefully for the Library and Museum. A choice library for reference as well as for circulation, has been purchased. Large annual additions will soon make it the most complete library in the State for scientific and agricultural purposes. The library will be open at stated hours for the accommodation of students and others."

The museum greatly impressed the editor of *The Southern Planter*. He reported that it was displayed in several glass cases arranged in the center of the room. These cases contained samples of varieties of grain and seeds, varieties of wood, and specimens of different kinds of ores. The editor was firmly convinced that such a display was of great educational value, since, as he believed, the students could gain a practical as well as a theoretical knowledge of the objects.

Borrowing from his departed friend Ellzey, Conrad urged the public to help build the museum by sending in "such specimens as will illustrate the ores, minerals, fossils, coals, insects, fishes, etc. of this and other states.—The College will cheerfully pay all freight charges."

With the opening of the 1883-84 session Robert J. Noell, who had been principal of the preparatory department, was promoted to instructor and librarian, succeeding V. E. Shepherd in this latter position. During the same session the library was allocated $2,229.96, the largest appropriation it had received to date and the largest it was to receive for some time, as it turned out. This entire sum was spent for books, apparently from the fields of fiction and poetry, with scientific works completely neglected. Having given the library this one generous appropriation, Conrad turned his energies in other directions and permitted the library to languish with an appropriation of $15.35 the next session.

Conrad took over the management of the farm, which he determined to develop as a "model farm for the average farmer" and at the same time as a demonstration farm for the students. "It is not an *experimental* farm or station," he wrote, "nor was it so intended. This is a matter for the future, requiring an entirely different outfit."

Conrad's idea of the role of the college farm in producing scientifically trained farmers was set forth at some length in the following revealing statement:

> The College farm proposed to demonstrate to the young men of the College and to the Virginia farmer, that farming in Virginia conducted upon scientific and business principles will pay. . . .
> Wheat, corn, oats, and hay, the usual crops, are systematically cultivated and are harvested by the most improved machinery. The reaper and binder, and the steam thresher, for the wheat and oats; the planter and the sulky plow for the corn; and the mower, the tedder and the rake for the hay, accomplish much in educating the student to intelligent and skilled labor, whilst the horsepower at the barn used for cutting fodder for stall-fed cattle, and hay and straw for horses and colts, so forcibly exhibits the relief to human muscle by applied mechanics that the impression is never lost. To walk after a shovel plow from sunrise to sunset is very different from taking a seat upon a sulky plow and driving a pair of quick stepping horses the same length of time. To swing a grass blade, with bended form, from "early morn to dewey eve" is very different from driving a mower the allotted time. Farming thus becomes scientific, and labor skilled and remunerative.

The major thrust of Conrad's reports concerning the college farm had to do with its prosperity under his management as contrasted with its dismal showing under special farm managers employed by previous admistrations. All features of the farm's operation under his management were pictured in roseate terms. Even the report of heavy inroads upon the hogs and pigs caused by cholera was preceded by the boast that "no inferior animal of any kind, from a short-horn to a shepherd dog, is allowed to remain upon the farm."

Conrad seems to have made the operation of the college farm a financial success for the first time in its troubled history, but some of the state's leaders, familiar with the developments in scientific agriculture beginning to unfold at other land-grant colleges, were not impressed. These individuals, probably expecting too much from the school with its limited resources, felt that the College was not developing a truly scientific program in agricultural education. Unfortunately, the annual reports filed by Martin P. Scott, professor of agriculture and natural history, did very little to dispel this feeling.

Martin P. Scott, M.D. had been hired by the Board of Visitors in August, 1880, as "Professor of Agriculture, Chemistry etc." to replace the departed Ellzey. He had assumed his responsibilities with abounding energy, and at the very first opportunity afforded him had started turning out astonishingly long annual reports. Most of the reports included brief accounts of the activities of the year, interwoven with long encyclopedic discourses on various phases of agriculture. These reports, which make interesting reading for the student of agricultural history, demonstrated a wide-ranging familiarity with the general field of agriculture and at the same time revealed a deep seated curiosity about some more restricted areas which Scott attempted to investigate by experimental work. His report dealing with a conserving type of agriculture as contrasted with an exploiting type, toward which, he warned, "every contrivance of modern civilization has been pressed into service," no doubt would find a more sympathetic audience today than it did when he wrote it nearly a century ago.

The overall make-up of Scott's reports was decidedly more philosophical and inspirational in nature than it was scientific. As one result, some of the leaders who began to sense an absence of scientific principles in Conrad's management of the farm began to feel the same way, although to a much less degree, about Scott's work as professor of agriculture.

In the reorganization of the College undertaken during the spring of 1882 neither Conrad nor the board seemed to know what to do with the mechanical department. Following the departure of Professor Blackford after the reorganization, the position of professor of mechanics was left vacant until filled by Floyd Davis for the session of 1883-84. In the meantime, Conrad reported that the department had been in successful operation by having the students make all repairs and improvements needed in the barracks. In addition to these repairs, all "repairs needed on the farm—repairing of plows, gates, buildings, shoeing of horses, etc. etc. [had] been made by the mechanical students."

Even as Conrad was writing this report, a groundswell for more effective education in technology was developing in Virginia. Unfortunately, neither Conrad nor the board got the message, although Conrad in his next report did express the hope that the day was not far distant when the mechanical department would be able to train men in the "mechanic arts." He believed it would take a $15,000 appropriation to accomplish this objective. Following the appointment of Davis to the faculty, the work in this department was organized around physics and analytical chemistry, with one course in theoretical analytical and applied mechanics.

Perhaps the most significant change brought about as a result of the reorganization during Conrad's administration was in the role assigned to the military feature of the College. The board favored military training and, in the words of Conrad, planned to "give it that prominence its importance required."

Prior to his dismissal from the faculty by the board in June, 1880, James H. Lane had begun to organize the military program along lines similar to the organization at the Virginia Military Institute, where he had once served as assistant instructor in tactics. Lane's successor, William Ballard Preston, also a graduate of VMI, continued to develop the program along the same lines as far as it was practical to do so. The cadets were organized into a well-disciplined and well-trained unit consisting of two companies with a full staff of cadet officers. Since all students were now being required to live on campus, military rules, regulations, and schedules were gradually extended to cover more and more aspects of the students' daily life. Cadet officers, working under the supervision of the commandant, were assigned increasing responsibilities for enforcing rules of conduct in the dormitory, which Preston always referred to as the barracks, and in the Mess Hall, which the boys dubbed "Hall of Disappointment." Conrad admitted the food was plain but insisted it was "substantial and well cooked." One cadet, as the students were beginning to be called, described the chief bill of fare, over which the cadet officers were supposed to preside to enforce "genteel" conduct, as "tough beef and cold potatoes in the fall, cold potatoes and tough beef in the winter, and both at the same time in the spring." Conrad tried a variety of solutions for the Mess. On one occasion he set up three Messes. One, the Farm Mess, provided food at $5 per month; another, the college Mess, at $8 per month; while the third, known as the Hotel Mess, charged $10 per month. In spite of the three choices the complaints continued unabated.

In addition to extending military control into the barracks and mess hall, Preston strengthened the instruction at drill and recommended that in addition to drill a class in tactics "be permanently grafted upon the curriculum so that *thorough* tactical knowledge may be imparted to officers and privates alike."

In 1876 a band had been organized by the citizens of Blacksburg under the direction of a "Professor Weiss of Tazewell, recently come from Bavaria, Germany." This organization had furnished music for some of the military events held on special occasions, but this group, dubbed Gabriel's Horn by the students, had broken up during all the recent upheavals at the College. In 1882, however, Conrad had secured a ten-piece cornet band, which he said contributed much to the interest of the drills and dress parades. This second group immediately was renamed "Gabriel's Horn" in spite of the objections advanced by one individual who argued that the name should be "Gabriel's Horns," plural, since the group never succeeded in playing together as one.

As an economy measure, the Board of Visitors in 1884 requested the Secretary of War to detail a military officer to take charge of military tactics at the College. This request was granted, and Lieutenant John C. Gresham of the Seventh United States Calvary, reported for duty in July, 1885. Apparently Preston was dropped from the faculty until his reappointment in 1886 as treasurer and farm director. Greshram, a graduate of Richmond College and of West Point, used the latter school as a model for the regulations and discipline he set up for the College. The cadets were given thorough training and instruction in guard duty and guard mounting, military communications, drill, dress parades and reviews, and in bayonet exercises. Artillery drill was introduced by using the two pieces of artillery and ammunition secured from the War Department. This drill proved to be quite popular not only with the cadets but with many of the local residents as well, or, as tradition has it, with the boys, the dogs, and ex-Confederate artillerymen from miles around Blacksburg.

Gresham recommended that all cadet officers and non-commissioned officers be required to buy Emory Upton's *Infantry Tactics* and that all privates buy Hugh T. Reed's abridgement of this book. As Preston had felt before him, Gresham also felt the students should be required to attend military classes two or three times a week for instruction in addition to that received on the drill field. This proposal had to await future developments, but the lines along which the basic military program would be expanded in the future are clearly discernible in the programs developed by Preston and Gresham during Conrad's administration of the College.

For a time it seemed that the reorganization of the College executed by the board and Conrad in 1882 would succeed. In addition to the expansion of the curriculum already noted, the board drew up plans for a School of Veterinary Science, and appointed G. H. Spooner, of Charlottesville, to take charge of it on January 1, 1886. Student enrollment jumped from 78 to 185 but dropped off to 98 during the session of 1885-86. Student morale rose to a high level and caused the editor of the *Gray Jacket* optimistically to predict that "a glorious future awaits our present Alma Mater if left to pursue its present prosperity." R. R. Farr, a Readjuster who had been appointed to replace W. H. Ruffner as superintendent of public instruction, wrote enthusiastically of the work at Blacksburg and reported through the press: "President Conrad seems to be solving the problem of how to mix learning with labor. Visit the college farm and you would think his students were all laborers; look into the college workshops and mill and you would think they were all mechanics; note their military bearing and evolutions on the parade and you would think they were all veteran soldiers; notice their gentlemanly deportment and you would be satisfied with the morals and discipline of the institution . . . the college deserves the hearty support of the people of Virginia and seems to be receiving it."

Conrad's annual reports, although filled with obvious political bias, indicated considerable growth and progress in all areas except in the physical plant. In this area he had been unable to secure any help whatever from the legislature, which during his entire tenure as president was involved in a bitter struggle between the Democrats and the Readjusters. The same Democrat-Readjuster struggle which had swept Conrad into office later swept him out of office and caused yet another reorganization in the hapless college. The political struggle between the Conservative-Democrats and the Coalition-Readjusters which occurred during the earlier part of the decade of the 1880's has never been equaled before or since in Virginia with respect to the pitch of emotionalism, excitement, fervor, and bitterness it reached throughout the state. The state elections of 1883 and 1885 were particularly spirited and reached into practically every hamlet and village as well as into the larger towns and cities in the state. The campaign of 1883 was particularly spirited in Montgomery County, which was represented in the legislature at the time by Readjusters. President Conrad entered into this campaign on the side of the Readjusters. The actual extent of his political activities is not known, but it was sufficient to arouse the ire of a number of citizens presumably of the Democratic Party, which had won the county and the state election by a small majority.

Following the convening of the 1883-84 session, A. M. Lybrook, representing Patrick and Henry Counties, introduced a resolution in the Senate proposing that the entire Board be appointed by the Senate instead of by the governor. This proposal would have by-passed the Readjuster governor and placed the appointment of the board in the hands of the Democratic-controlled Senate. The proposal was turned over to the Senate Committee on Courts of Justice, where it evidently died, since nothing come from it. In the meantime, a group calling themselves "respectable citizens of Montgomery County," (the word *respectable* being a term the Democrats were applying to themselves with telling effectiveness throughout the state) sent a list of grievances against Conrad to the House, "praying the General Assembly to rescue the Virginia Agricultural and Mechanical College from the mire of partisan politics."

The charges against Conrad were spelled out as follows:

1. With absenting himself from his post of duty for about two months during the late campaign for political purposes.
2. With using the wagons and teams, belonging to the college farm, to convey Negro and other voters to county conventions and other political assemblies.
3. That with his consent either expressed or implied, the teams of the college farm were used to convey the colored band of Blacksburg to a political meeting, held at night, a distance of eight or ten miles.
4. With using the patronage of the institution in furtherance of partisan ends.
5. With making the college a part of the political machine of the state.
6. With using his executive authority over students as a means of oppressing and damaging private individuals for personal and political reasons.
7. With discharging students from positions of emolument within the gift of the college, and filling their places with political workers of his own political faith.

It is perhaps noteworthy that no mention or attack of any kind was made upon the program being followed at the College. As a result of these charges, the Committee on Schools and Colleges was authorized and directed to investigate the charges and the affairs of the institution.

This committee obviously did not relish its task. After much delay and obvious dragging of the feet, it reported that the stenographer had been unable to transcribe all of the evidence presented at the several stages of the investigation; therefore, the committee had been unable "to properly consider or pass upon the charges preferred against Mr. Conrad." This report was accepted by the House and the matter dropped, but not forgotten.

In the meantime, the terms of office for three members of the board expired on January 1, 1884. Governor Cameron, realizing the improbability of being able to secure Senate approval for the appointment of active Readjusters to the board, appointed and received Senate approval for three new board members known either to be Democrats or at least acceptable to the Democrats. The Readjuster members, meanwhile, retained a controlling majority on the board, but the terms of office for all of this group expired on January 1, 1886. The heated political conditions of the time made it inevitable that if the Democrats retained control of the legislature and at the same time elected a Democratic governor to take office January 1, 1886, Democrats would be appointed to all vacant positions on the board. If this eventuality became a reality, Conrad's known Readjuster affiliation and his alleged political activities could be expected, in accordance with the political climate, to bring an end to his administration as president. All of these possibilities and probabilities became realities. In the state elections held in the fall of 1885, the Democrats increased their majority in both houses of the legislature and at the same time elected Fitzhugh Lee as governor.

This election marked the end of the Readjuster Party as such, since even in this election most of the membership moved into either the Republican or the Democratic Party, where it remained.

It has been reported over and over that the Democratic-controlled legislature which convened in December, 1885, removed the Readjuster-controlled Board of Visitors of the Virginia Agricultural and Mechanical College and appointed a new board in order to return the administration of the College to the Democrats.

Such a drastic measure was not necessary, however, and was not followed, since the appointees to the board made by Governor Cameron in 1884 were either Democrats or acceptable to the Democrats and the terms of office for the remaining Readjuster board members would expire on January 1, 1886. Fitzhugh Lee was inaugurated governor on January 1, 1886, and immediately nominated W. H. F. Lee, J. D. H. Ross, Waller Redd Staples, and Charles E. Vawter, all Democrats, to fill the vacancies on the board.

The board with these new appointees met on January 23 and elected Judge Waller Staples of Christiansburg as rector to succeed his fellow townsman, James C. Taylor, whose term of office on the board had expired. At this same meeting the board appointed Ross and Vawter as a committee to prepare and present to the board at its next meeting to be held March 23 a plan of organization and operation for the College. Before this March meeting John L. Buchanan, the individual twice removed from the presidency of the College by Readjuster action, had succeeded R. R. Farr as state superintendent of public instruction and therefore had become an ex-officio member of the Board of Visitors. Since neither Fitzhugh Lee nor his cousin W. H. F. Lee had escaped Conrad's scarcastic pen or tongue when they previously had served on the board, Conrad certainly could expect no support from this direction. In fact, because of the unusually bitter partisan politics and bitter personal attacks which characterized politics of the period, Conrad could expect no support of any kind from the Democrats. He got none.

At its March 23 meeting the board resolved that it was its duty to see that the College provided a "broad, liberal, practical, industrial education in the line of agriculture and mechanic arts." Then, in a statement obviously aimed at the public, the board observed that to accomplish this mission the board would have to be "untrammeled and free to select the very best men available . . ." for the faculty and staff. With this statement as its justification the board then announced the removal of all the faculty and officers of the College, July 1, 1886. At this point the board injected something new into the administrative guideline for the College. It announced it would elect a new president and in "conjunction" with this individual determine the "offices to be filled" and the salary scale to be followed. The president-elect was to be allowed $250 travel expenses to visit and study other colleges for ideas concerning the operation of land-grant schools and report his findings to a subcommittee of the board. This subcommittee and the president-elect were then to report their joint conclusions to the full board on May 28. The board would then elect a faculty. This procedure marked the first time any Board of Visitors, publicly at least, ever permitted a president to advise with the board concerning the organization of the College and the selection of a faculty.

In addition to these decisions, the board adopted a resolution forbidding all officers of the College to engage in partisan politics for any political party, beyond voting for the candidates of their choice. At the same meeting, the board once more laid down the rule that all official communications to the board by the faculty must come through the president of the College. Following these decisions, the board went into executive session and elected General Lunsford Lindsay Lomax as president-elect to assume office as president on July 1, 1886.

Apparently, not firing Conrad at once but allowing him to finish the year as president was the only action taken by the board which caused any surprise. No official report or catalog of the College was published for the academic year

1885-1886, but it seems that Conrad finished the year and then before relinquishing his office, demanded and received receipts for all machinery and college-owned livestock which might walk, run, or otherwise mysteriously disappear from the college farm. Following his removal from the presidency of the Virginia Agricultural and Mechanical College, he accepted a position as professor of agriculture and chairman of the faculty of the Maryland Agricultural College. Upon his death on January 5, 1905, his body was brought back to Montgomery County, where he was interred with military honors under the direction of the Corps of Cadets. In June, 1912, a group of alumni paid a final tribute to this controversial but colorful individual—the only one ever to serve as president of the Preston and Olin Institute and of the Virginia Agricultural and Mechanical College—by unveiling a marble memorial tablet in the old library building.

Chapter **5**

The Lomax Administration

1886-1891

GENERAL LUNSFORD L. LOMAX, who entered upon his duties as president of the Virginia Agricutural and Mechanical College on July 1, 1886, was a graduate of West Point in the class of 1856. At the time of the outbreak of the Civil War he was an officer in the Federal army but felt his duty was to his state. Writing to his classmate George D. Bayard he said, "I cannot stand it any longer and feel it my duty to resign. My state is out of the Union and when she calls me for my service I must go. I regret it very much and feel that it [is] almost suicidal." He resigned his commission and entered the Confederate services. Following the war, as a distinguished Confederate veteran, he had a wide acquaintanceship with the powerful "Confederate Cult" in Virginia politics, regardless of whether the members of this cult were now supporting the Democrats or the Republicans. He had been an applicant for the presidency during the summer of 1872 when the College was being organized; but it is not known whether he had been considered for the presidency at any time during the numerous reorganizations the school had undergone since then. At the time of his appointment to the presidency, he was engaged in farming in Fauquier County, but had had no experience whatever in operating an educational institution. Lomax was a popular man, but his

121

appointment as president might well be attributed to his long friendship with
the new governor, Fitzhugh Lee, Lomax's classmate at West Point, and with W.
H. F. Lee, who Conrad claimed wanted a place for Lomax on the first faculty.
Regardless of the source of his support, it is easy in retrospect to see that rough
days lay ahead for the College as it continued its struggle to establish a program
acceptable to itself and to the people of the state.

Even as Lomax assumed the presidency, the great rural population of the state
was beginning to recover somewhat from the deadly lethargy into which it had
dropped following the Civil War. Partly as a result of the work of the National
Grange and partly as a result of the development of the Farmers' Alliance movement in the state, a new sense of rural power and a demand to be heard were
developing in Virginia. Political realignments brought new forces and stirred
new hopes and demands. A few politicians were beginning to spend more time
looking at the present and future and less to the past. A rejuvenating sense of
power, of strength, and of optimism was definitely in the making. As one student
of the period expressed it: " 'Worth, not birth' began to assume greater importance in determining place. Slowly and painfully the 'new Dominion' began to
find herself and to rebuild from the wreckage of the war. Young men . . . without
losing respect for the past were beginning to look more and more to the future."

As one result of this awakening, a slowly increasing dissatisfaction with the
current status of many public services, especially public education, began to
develop. Clearly the people were asking for something better, but just as clearly
had to wait for new leaders to channel this energy into acceptable programs.

The Virginia Agricultural and Mechanical College, as the people's college,
was caught up in this swirling discontent and demand for a better day as it too
awaited a leader or leaders to show the way. Unhappily, Lomax with all of his
sterling qualities was unable to convince the people that he was this leader.

Well before Lomax had assumed the presidency, certain demands for improved technical education which affected the Virginia Agricultural and Mechanical College had sprung up in the state. In February, 1884, Mr. Absolom Koiner
of Augusta County had introduced a resolution into the state Senate lamenting
the lack of facilities in the state for instruction in the "higher departments of
mechanical arts, in connection with applied science." To remedy the situation,
he asked that a committee be appointed to "inquire" into the mechanical department of the Virginia Agricultural and Mechanical College and to report on
whether a school of technology might not be developed in connection with the
College. If it was found to be "inexpedient" to establish such a school at the
Virginia Agricultural and Mechanical College, he wanted the committee to
investigate the "feasibility" of establishing such a school at some other college in
the state. Not only did he want the committee to make an investigation, but he
also wanted it to present a bill to the legislature which, if adopted, would establish the school of technology.

Koiner's resolution is particularly noteworthy in that it marks the first time
that the mechanical-education facilities were ever singled out for legislative
attention. Prior to this occasion all proposals affecting the college program had
concentrated on the agricultural program or facilities. Koiner's resolution was
referred to the Committee on Public Institutions and Education but apparently
got lost because of the intense legislative battles raging between the Readjusters
and the Democrats. In fact, some individuals interpreted Koiner's resolution as

another effort on the part of the Democrats to get under way an investigation
of Conrad's administration of the College. Certainly the timing of the resolution,
coming as it did in the midst of the attack on Conrad being mounted in both the
Senate and the House, did little to dispel this opinion. Subsequent events, however, more than proved Koiner's sincerity of interest in technical education.

In April, 1885, Koiner was invited to address the State Farmers' Convention
meeting in Richmond. He had done his homework. As a result, he captivated
his audience with his presentation of the benefits to be derived to the state from
a technical college or a school of technology. His address touched off a series of
rapidly unfolding events. Charles E. Vawter got the floor and proposed a resolution asking the legislature to consider establishing a department of technology
either at one of the existing schools in the state or as a separate institution. In the
somewhat warm discussion following Vawter's resolution, Richard V. Gaines of
Charlotte County, a former member of the Board of Visitors for the Virginia
Agricultural and Mechanical College, introduced a lengthy resolution urging the
establishment of several technical schools, with one to be at Richmond, operated
in conjunction with the State Department of Agriculture. This one was to have
an "experimental station." The resolution further recommended that the military
and "academical" departments at the Virginia Agricultural and Mechanical
College be subordinated to its industrial features, "and that the sciences be taught
with a direct application to the arts which are exemplified in the field and in
the workshop."

Gaines' resolution touched off even more discussion but was finally referred
to the Convention's Committee on Education and Technical Schools. This committee after considerable deliberation reported back a resolution which among
other features included Gaines' proposals concerning the Virginia Agricultural
and Mechanical College; but even more surprising, considering the hitherto
almost fanatical demands by the farm groups for a practical education, the
resolution strongly urged that the College raise its admission requirements. As
one step in this direction, the resolution carried a proposal that all state students
be required to pass an entrance examination administered by the State Board of
Education. The committee then further resolved "that a School of Technology
be established at such a place as will offer the greatest inducements." In conclusion, the resolution urged each member of the convention to bring the
subject "plainly and personally before the people of Virginia."

The proposal that a school of technology be established at the place offering
"the greatest inducements" touched off a spirited debate which for a short time
threatened to develop along sectional lines similar to some of the earlier debates
in the legislature concerning the disposal of the land-grant fund. One proposal
followed another in rapid succession after Mr. Radford, of Montgomery County,
offered an amendment proposing that the convention ask the legislature to make
an appropriation to increase the facilities at the Virginia Agricultural and
Mechanical College for education in technology. Finally in an obvious effort to
stave off a deadlock, the convention adopted a resolution to appoint a committee
of five to memorialize the legislature to establish a school of technology in one of
the state institutions. Charles E. Vawter was appointed to this committee.

Strangely enough, President Conrad seems to have made only a token effort
to take advantage of this rather broad-based support for improved technical
education. Actually his reports indicated some hostility to the idea of an agricul-

tural experiment station. In spite of his coolness, the agitation for technical education and an agricultural "experimental" station continued to develop and to receive considerable publicity in the press. It was obvious that these two topics would receive attention in the legislature which was to convene in December, 1885. Almost immediately following Fitzhugh Lee's inauguration as governor in January, 1886, Koiner renewed his efforts for a technical school. This time he introduced a resolution in which the Board of Visitors of the Virginia Agricultural and Mechanical College was respectfully requested to develop the institution into a thorough school of technology with an experimental station of agriculture as soon as possible. Since the Board of Visitors, including the four members just appointed by Governor Lee, had announced its intention to meet at once and since it was commonly understood that this board was going to reorganize the College anyway, Koiner did not push for the passage of his resolution but upon his motion had it tabled. Some of the members of the board got the message, but unfortunately some did not.

Following this action in the legislature, the demand for an agricultural experiment station became separated from the demand for a school of technology and began to pick up support. The legislative debates revealed the existence of a considerable difference of opinion as to the best location for such a station and as to its proper function once it should be located. These divergent opinions boded ill for harmony between the station and different sections of the state; but the legislature, in obvious anticipation of federal funds to support the work, passed an act on March 1, 1886, establishing an agricultural experiment station at Blacksburg, "the same to be maintained by appropriations made by the Congress of the United States." Since no federal appropriation was available, the station was not formally organized until after the passage of the federal Hatch Act of March 2, 1887. In the meantime the program, function, and work to be undertaken by an agricultural experiment station became a topic for debate, discussion, and speculation by farm groups, agricultural societies, and politicians. Unhappily, these discussions produced more division than vision concerning the station and created additional problems to be faced by the College.

Following his appointment to the presidency, Lomax began an immediate study of the land-grant college programs. He spent some time visiting the Mississippi Agricultural and Mechanical College, which under the direction of General Stephen D. Lee was receiving wide acclaim in the agricultural press of the country as a successful agricultural school. In addition to this visit, he seems to have spent some time in Washington interviewing and meeting with governmental officials connected with agricultural programs. Following these activities and some correspondence with officials at other land-grant colleges, Lomax met with the board in May to participate in the reorganization of the Institution.

At this meeting Professors Scott, Christian, and Morton were re-elected and W. B. Preston re-employed, but this time as treasurer and farm director. President Conrad and Professors Shepherd, Davis, Jones, and Aylor were released permanently, while Fielding P. Miles was employed as professor of chemistry and geology, and W. H. Graham was employed as professor of bookkeeping and stenography and as librarian. Difficulty was encountered in finding persons agreeable to all board members to fill the chairs of agriculture and of mechanics. Finally, it was decided to let Scott continue as professor of agriculture and natural history as originally intended. James H. Fitts was appointed professor of mechanics but not until sometime in July, while the chair of veterinary science which was supposed to have started on January 1, 1886, was temporarily dropped. Scott continued in his dual role as professor of agriculture and natural history until June 9, 1887, when his son-in-law, William B. Preston, took over the duties as professor of agriculture.

The College was returned to the semester system, while the preparatory department was returned to the curriculum under the designation of the fourth group. The students in this group were those not prepared to take regular college courses. They were given instruction in arithmetic, algebra, history, spelling, geography, penmanship, and bookkeeping. The members of this class paid no fees, tuition, or room rent and were allowed to obtain their books at wholesale.

A non-diploma business program was offered for those who planned to engage in commercial activities. This program included commercial arithmetic, bookkeeping, stenography, telegraphy, and typewriting. Special classes in these subjects plus one in "Munson's System of Phonography" were also offered.

The preparatory department was defended as necessary because of the poor college preparatory work being received by the majority of students applying for admission. The business department which had been started by Conrad was continued, because it was believed this program provided an important segment of the practical education needed by the industrial classes. The special classes offered in these business courses were set up in an effort to extend the opportunities for a practical education in this area for worthy students not planning or not able to pursue a regular course of instruction. This feature of the curriculum soon came under strong attack by board members Vawter and Barton, who objected to its inclusion in the regular curriculum. They felt that too many students took these special courses merely to avoid the military training and the more rigorous academic courses in science, mathematics, English, and the languages. The results of the course, they argued, were detrimental to the achievement of a desirable academic climate on the campus and at the same time damaging to the reputation of the College throughout the state. Since the students in these special courses did not pursue the traditional academic courses, such as English, Vawter and Barton believed these students remained as illiterate upon leaving college as they had been upon entering it. In Vawter's opinion producing these illiterate alumni was absolutely inexcusable as far as the institution was concerned.

The board retained the degree program as it had been established under Conrad but substituted a B.Sc. degree for the A.B. degree. At the same time, responsibility for the Department of Civil Engineering was assigned to the chair of mathematics. This board, as had the boards at all the preceding reorganizations of the College, attempted to clarify the question of the purpose of the school. Finally it agreed that "the leading object of the College . . . is to teach the principles and the applications of Science." The board decided that the purpose of the courses of instruction was "to give prominence to the sciences and their applications, especially those that relate to Agriculture and the Mechanical Arts, . . . and at the same time the discipline obtained by the study of the languages and other sciences [was] not to be neglected."

This statement of objective and purposes lulled the advocates for a school of technology into a period of silent and somewhat suspicious watchfulness. They would give the new administration a chance, at least, before renewing their demands.

As it turned out, the problem of locating and organizing an agricultural experiment station occurred during the lull. The agricultural segment of those demanding a school of technology thereupon became so enthusiastically and aggressively involved in advancing demands and offering advice concerning this new venture that the cause of a technical school was pushed into the background to simmer for the next few years without becoming either hot or cold.

It is difficult to get an accurate picture of the conditions of the College at the time Lomax formally took over on July 1, 1886. The tendency to use the annual reports to downgrade the work of previous administrators and faculty and at the same time exalt the present officials, so conspicious in Conrad's reports, was dropped by Lomax in favor of a more objective (but less colorful and revealing) type of reporting. Actually, by the end of his administration, he was submitting annual reports for publication which consisted of little more than statistical summaries of the year's work. Even Dr. Scott's voluminous essays designed to enlighten the public concerning the numerous subjects this loquacious and versatile individual taught were omitted from the printed reports.

In truth, it would appear that the College was not in so flourishing a condition as pictured by Conrad's reports. William B. Preston, who assumed the responsibilities of treasurer and farm director, reported in some detail the run-down condition of the college farm. In a startling contrast that virtually contradicted some of Conrad's claims, Preston reported that "in order to replace the farm upon its old footing of fertility and beauty there must be spent for the next few years a considerable sum of money. There is an utter lack of modern appliances which must be supplied, as well as a good amount of repairing [to be] done to fences, buildings, and roadways." Lomax testified under oath, in a case arising nearly a year after he had resigned from the presidency, that the College when he took charge had an indebtedness of $4000 with only thirty-five students enrolled. This number reached 110 before the end of his first year. During this same case Alexander Payne, a former board member, testified that Lomax upon assuming the presidency had found the financial accounts of the college in a "wretched condition," which the board had been unable to untangle, but that Lomax had been able to bring order out of chaos by the way he handled the finances of the institution.

The heat of political strife which had dominated Virginia politics and caused such constant changes in the Board of Visitors, removal of faculties, and academic reorganizations between 1878 and 1886 began to cool rapidly soon after Lomax became president. Actually, his administration was the first one in the history of the College to be free from political interference: a freedom all the more remarkable if consideration is given to the increasing concern which the rapidly developing Farmers' Alliance in Virginia was voicing for an improved agricultural education.

Early in 1887, Lieutenant John Gresham resigned as commandant of cadets in order to return to duty in the field, and William B. Preston was asked to complete the unexpired term. Preston did so, thereby finishing the year as farm director, treasurer of the College, and commandant of cadets. He was succeeded in this last-named capacity by Lieutenant John T. Knight, who continued as commandant until the end of 1889-90 session, at which time Knight was succeeded by Lieutenant J. A. Harmon, one of the most popular of the earlier commandants.

Lomax presented a request for building funds to the first meeting of the legislature following his inauguration as president. Governor Lee, who previously had served on the Board of Visitors, was quite sympathetic to the request and in his message to the legislature expressed the hope that the body would be "generous" toward the college. In standards of the time it was generous, and on March 5, 1888, the legislature appropriated $20,000 for a new barracks and $4,000 to be used toward converting the Preston and Olin building into a shop.

No major buildings had been erected on campus following the erection of the Commencement Hall, or Pavilion, completed in the summer of 1879 during President Minor's administration. Minor considered this building as the "architectural ugly duckling" on the campus. The original plan called for its location between the First and Second Academic Buildings; but as Minor pointed out, this plan would mean placing a long, low one-story frame structure between two-story brick buildings. Acting on his own initiative, Minor located the structure on an extreme corner of the campus near the present junction of Main Street and the northeast corner of the mall. He had rushed construction of this sixty-by-ninety-foot wooden building in order to have it ready for the 1879 commencement exercises, since he firmly believed that the Methodists were planning to deny the College the use of their church for commencement purposes.

Thousands of alumni yet living can draw their own conclusions concerning this "architectural ugly duckling," since this sturdy old building before being torn down in 1940 served at one time or another as a drill hall, a commencement hall, a mess hall, a machine shop, a gymnasium, an auditorium, Cotillion and German Club dance hall, community hall, and on numerous occasions as a gymnasium and recreation hall for the Blacksburg High School.

Lomax used the legislative appropriation of 1888 to erect the building known for years as Number One Barracks but now called Lane Hall in honor of James H. Lane, first commandant of cadets. The bricks for this building were made locally; and as one admirer of trees lamented, "the handsome grove that stood west of the experiment plots beyond the Price's Fork Road was sacrificed for burning the bricks."

This building drew enthusiastic praise from the students, the faculty, and the general public. The editor of *The Southern Planter* pronounced it "an ornament to the grounds" of the College, while Lomax happily reported that the seventy-four rooms in it had been completely furnished and were heated by steam and that the building had water closets and hot and cold water bathrooms. The day of the bucket brigade to the common pump was drawing to a close.

Upon the completion of Number One Barracks, the students immediately moved into it, thereby vacating the Preston and Olin building which was then remodeled into a shop and continued as such until it was completely destroyed by fire one early morning in June, 1913. This loss removed the last man-made link connecting the college with the parent Preston and Olin Institute. Since the college had already, by necessity, started expanding its physical plant to the westward, no new structure was erected on the site of the burned building. The site was smoothed over as the extreme eastern portion of the campus over which U.S. Route 460 now passes. The hemlock tree currently used as a Christmas tree by town and gown is within a few yards of the site of this building within which the Virginia Polytechnic Institute and State University got its start.

The students found life in Number One Barracks much more pleasant than it had been in the old dormitory. They also found an increased opportunity to

invent unauthorized extra-curricular activities, many of which, with the passage
of time, came to be looked upon by the students as traditional privileges or rights.
The fact that the faculty thought otherwise merely added an element of caution
and zest to the performance of the activity. Three such activities which "bothered"
the administration for years may be mentioned. Two had to do with water delivered to the barracks under a modest head of pressure. An hydraulic ram located
near the site of Derring Hall pumped water into a tank located in the tower of
Number One Barracks. From this tank the water flowed by gravity to the bathrooms located on the ground level. It is not clear whether a faucet was installed
in the hallways at each floor; but if not, the students could still get all the water
they wanted from inside the building without going to an outside pump. It was
not long before some of the residents on the third floor "discovered" the pleasur-
able excitement of dropping a paper bag filled with water upon the head of an
unsuspecting pedestrian on the pathways surrounding the building. Since the
number of windows facing the pathways made it extremely difficult to detect the
culprit, or culprits, the practice as well as the aim of the students showed remarkable progress. In one instance it was reported that a particularly officious cadet
officer simultaneously received "three direct hits on the head and one ricochet
off his rear," as he unwittingly "strutted in front of the barracks." The faculty
took a dim, or as one punster expressed it, a "damp" view of the practice, especially so following several instances in which some of its unsuspecting members
had also been "bagged from above."

Specific rules were passed forbidding the practice, and stringent penalties,
usually in the form of demerits, were prescribed for violators; but the practice,
albeit in a reduced form, spread to the new barracks after they were built and
survived far into the twentieth century. Many an alumnus can testify to the
accuracy of these "water bombs" or in his mind's eye recall the graceful curved
trajectory they made as they sailed far outward from some undisclosed upper
story window and then curved downward straight as an arrow to land with a
surprising "plop" on or near the unsuspecting victim. Happily this crude form
of humor, stubbornly clung to for so long, practically disappeared when the College became affluent enough to install screens on all barracks windows.

The second tradition growing from the installation of water in Number One
Barracks was an "inside" one more difficult for the authorities to control. Sufficient
running water was available for the first time to afford crude hot and cold showers
in the baths on the first floor level. One night a group of upperclassmen, for reasons never recorded, made all the freshmen go to the shower room and alternately
march back and forth between a warm and a cold shower. For some inexplicable
reason this practice became popular with the sophomores as a means of "keeping the rats (freshmen) in their place without touching them," and was passed
on from class to class for the next four or five decades. No doubt many an alumnus
today, long since having risen to executive positions of power and authority, would
find himself reduced to temporary shivering submissiveness if someone should slip
up behind him and in the authoritative voice possessed by the VPI sophomore of
that day bawl out, "Rats to the shower!"

The third practice which developed in Number One Barracks was far more
bothersome than the first two mentioned. It had to do with another approach to
the treatment of freshmen, or "rats" as they were called. It does not appear that
hazing originated as a result of the erection of the barracks. On the contrary, hazing had been in existence in one form or another for a long time. The physical

arrangements of the hallways, rooms, stairways and entrances in the barracks permitted a lot of student visitation, authorized and unauthorized, to occur with little or no necessity for going outside the building. For the upperclassmen, where some camaraderie already existed, this situation created a fertile environment for the incubation and application of "extra-curricular controls" over the behavior of the freshmen. Once such a control had been applied a few times, it usually progressed rapidly, in the minds of the students at least, into the category of a practice absolutely necessary if the objectives of the military program were to be achieved. Succeeding generations of students, having been subjected to the "control" while freshmen, upon becoming upperclassmen tended not only to consider the practice from the military viewpoint but also tended to look upon the administration of it as an inherent right to be jealously guarded and protected.

This process, certainly not unique to the Virginia Agricultural and Mechanical College, survived in the environment of this campus until well into the twentieth century and gave birth to an unusually large number of practices which became traditions in the Corps of Cadets. On the other hand, some of the practices resulting from the process often outlived their usefulness, got out of hand, or developed into thinly disguised programs of hazing. Efforts to correct these situations usually resulted in a conflict or tug-of-war between faculty and students.

The first practice resulting from this process which got under way in Number One Barracks was known as "bucking" the student. An official publication in condemning the practice explained that "bucking consists of two or more old students taking a new one by the hands and feet and striking him against a post or wall, or holding him up while others paddle him with bayonet scabbards, pieces of plank, etc." The practice most likely had begun prior to the student occupancy of Number One Barracks; but once introduced in this barracks, under the conditions described, the practice soon came to be looked upon as a military necessity to be administered by the students as a right in order to "keep the freshmen in his place" and (contradictory though it was) "to make a man out of him." "Bucking" definitely was contrary to college regulations, but Lomax seems to have made little if any effort to stamp it out. As a result, it flourished and the reputation of the institution suffered.

Succeeding administrations were far more successful in eliminating, or at least controlling, this practice than was Lomax, but some form of pseudo-military student-right hazing continued to plague the College for years following its origin in "Old Number One."

The memory of the effect of the three bothersome activities which originated in "Old Number One" has been more than offset by the memories of other more pleasant events which revolved around this building during its more than three-quarters-of-a-century service to the College. With the construction of additional barracks, Number One came to occupy its present central position in the upper quadrangle. For years the flag, unfurled to the wind from atop the flag pole projecting straight upward from the tower on this building, dominated the skyline not only from practically every point on the campus but from the town and countryside as well. In the halcyon days of the Farmers' Alliance, and later of the Populist movement in the state, a drawing of the tower and its flagpole came to represent colleges in numerous cartoons attacking or defending ideas promulgated by these two organizations.

For years all cadet military functions originating on the upper quadrangle from reveille to retreat, from breakfast to supper, formed facing or near this building. On ceremonial and formal occasions the commanding cadet officer and his full staff stepped forth briskly from this building to take command of the corps. The bell in the tower with its rope extending to the cadet guard room below was used at various times to signal such important events in the life of the cadets as the arrival of mail, the beginning and end of classes, the call to quarters, the release from quarters, the changing of the guard, and taps at the end of the day. At one time the building housed the campus bookstore, which sold everything from popsicles for the hungry to souvenirs for girl friends. Benches in the bookstore were provided on which the upper-class cadets might sit while awaiting the sorting of the newly arrived mail in the student mail room just across the hall, but "rats" were forbidden by one of the student-originated "controls" to use these benches for any purpose. For a long time all incoming telephone calls and telegrams had to pass through the facilities set up in this building, while for years the ranking cadet officer was allowed his choice of rooms in Number One. Truly this old building became number one for far more reasons than being the first barracks to be erected on the campus.

The physical improvements to the campus resulting from the erection of Number One Barracks and from the conversion of the Preston and Olin building into shops received much favorable comment throughout the state. Surprisingly however, much of this comment served to reinforce the slowly developing conviction that the College was not developing satisfactorily as a school of agriculture and mechanics. In the midst of this growing dissatisfaction the Board of Visitors underwent some significant changes. General W. H. F. Lee resigned in order to enter Congress, and four new members widely known in state political and social circles joined the board on January 1, 1887. This board elected as rector J. Hoge Tyler, a resident of Pulaski County, who later moved to Norfolk. Tyler made a popular rector but soon resigned in order to make what proved to be a successful campaign for lieutenant governor on the same ticket with P. W. McKinney, a former board member, as a candidate for governor. Tyler's place on the board was then filled by J. Thompson Brown, of Bedford County, and C. E. Vawter was elected rector. The team of Vawter and Brown was one of the most successful ones ever brought together on the Board of Visitors in the nineteenth century.

Vawter, as superintendent of the Miller Manual Labor School, in Albemarle County, which had an endowment and income far in excess of that of the Virginia Agricultural and Mechanical College, brought to the board some desperately needed experience in educational administration. In addition to his practical experience, he possessed a deep-seated conviction, almost fanatical at times, that a statewide system of education properly attuned to the conditions, wants, and needs of the people was desperately needed in Virginia and the South. Of even greater importance, perhaps, is the fact that he was in a position to give time and effort toward the achievement of such a system. Becoming a member of the Board of Visitors, Vawter immediately launched an earnest effort to identify and clarify the place and mission of the Virginia Agricultural and Mechanical College as a part of the state's system of education. It is quite significant that the frame of reference within which he worked during his entire tenure on the board was dominated more by his concept of needs existing in a state-wide system of education for Virginia than it was by any interpretation of the requirements and implications of the Morrill Act.

Vawter, the educational architect, competent and articulate as he was, found an able ally in J. Thompson Brown, also an able and articulate administrator in his own right. Brown, like Vawter, devoted a great deal of his own time and energy to promoting the cause of the College and in trying to improve its image, which in the eyes of many rural leaders needed drastic improvement.

In spite of the work of Vawter, Brown, and the other board members, dissatisfaction with the College continued to grow, especially in the rural areas, which were developing a sense of new power and demands. Following the passage of the Hatch Act, the Virginia Farmers' Alliance made an attempt to persuade the legislature to move the Agricultural Experiment Station from Blacksburg to Charlottesville. The legislature refused to accede to the demand, however, and on February 29, 1888, passed the legislation necessary to accept the provisions of the Hatch Act and at the same time to establish the station at Blacksburg under the control of the Board of Visitors.

Following this action, R. T. W. Duke, a prominent leader of Albemarle County, who had been one of the prime movers to get the station moved to Charlottesville, published a strong appeal to "all farmers to come forward now in support of the station at Blacksburg." Many leaders in the Alliance refused to do so. They felt doubly rebuffed. Not only had they wanted the station to be located in Charlottesville, but they had also demanded that it be put under the control of "practical farmers." Rebuffed, as they felt, the leaders in this organization then started a vigorous campaign to get a law on the statute books to require that the Board of Visitors be fully representative of the practical farmers of the state. This campaign was well enough received by all the sub-alliances, which were springing up with amazing rapidity in the state, to cause the Democratic party to include a plank in its platform recommending that all state agencies dealing with agriculture be directed by "practical farmers." Great difficulty arose in the Democratically controlled legislature, however, when it undertook to translate its campaign pledge into practice. No agreement could be reached on the meaning of the term "practical farmer." So much argument and discussion developed on this point at one time that one disgusted member finally offered a resolution directing the sergeant-at-arms to eject from the floor any person who started a discussion of the meaning of the words "a practical farmer."

In spite of the obvious difficulty of definition, the legislature on March 6, 1890, passed an act requiring that "only practical farmers shall be appointed as visitors of said College until the number of such farmers on said board shall amount to not less than six." This act was amended on March 1, 1892, to require the governor to appoint the board members "from farmers, mechanics, and graduates of the College."

In the meantime, four vacancies on the board had occurred on January 1, 1890. When the governor's choice of men to fill these vacancies became known, a strong protest went up, mostly from Alliance workers, arguing that all of the proposed nominees were not practical farmers. This alleged defect was rectified when two nominees either withdrew or were dropped and were replaced by men known to be active in or at least highly regarded by the Alliance. With the confirmation of these nominees, one of whom held a high position in the State Alliance, this organization and *The Southern Planter* threw their support to the Board of Visitors of the College. Within the next few years the Alliance at the state level merged into the Populist movement, which rather quickly dissipated its energies in state and national politics and soon ceased to be an influencing factor in the life of the College.

By 1890, the dissatisfaction with the College as an agricultural school, as a mechanical school, and as a technical school, which had been slowly developing throughout the state and which was being fed by the rural organizations, especially the Farmers' Alliance, reached its peak. The complaints this time were noticeably different from earlier complaints which had kept the school so long in a state of considerable turmoil. The element of personal attack on the president and board members was largely missing. On the contrary, the board and especially President Lomax were held in high regard throughout the state. It was the program of the College and its results which were under fire. The attack was especially heavy on the newly established Agricultural Experiment Station for not accomplishing immediate results having immediate application for the "practical farmers" of the state. The criticisms, most of them based on expectations whose fulfillment would have required not only a fully staffed station but an extension service as well, hurt the College.

William Ballard Preston, who in addition to being professor of agriculture, had been appointed director of the Experiment Station in March, 1888, tried to refute some of the criticisms and at the same time explain the program being undertaken at the station. Unfortunately, his efforts reported in *The Southern Planter* served only to deepen the conviction that the station was spending its time "illustrating and working the fads of the professors" instead of dealing with the practical problems of the everyday farmers. Preston, unlike many of his colleagues of the day, knew when to resign and did so on June 12, 1890. This resignation brought an official end to the connection with the College of this individual, who within a period of less than eight years had served as professor of physics, professor of military tactics, professor of military science and tactics, professor of English literature, commandant of cadets, professor of agriculture, director of the Agricultural Experiment Station, treasurer, and director of the farm.

Following Preston's resignation, Lomax, against his better judgment, was appointed acting director of the Experiment Station during the time the board studied the problem of organizing and articulating the work of the station with the instructional program of the College. In July of the same year, W. D. Saunders was appointed director of the station to succeed Lomax. As Harold N. Young tactfully expressed it in his detailed study of the Virginia Agricultural Experiment Station, none of these men had special training for the directorship.

In filling the vacancies on the board in 1890, Governor McKinney, a former board member, reappointed C. E. Vawter, thereby making it possible for the first time in the history of the College for an appointed board member to serve two consecutive terms. This reappointment of Vawter was a most fortunate one. Following his election as rector of the board, he turned attention to the discontent with the College being manifested in the state. Vawter urged that, instead of any immediate replacement of the president or any of the faculty members as advocated by some, a thorough study of the College and of the proper mission it should be filling in the state be made first. The study was made, apparently with considerable thoroughness. All members of the board were fully familiar with the demands for a technical education and with the dissatisfaction with the current instruction in agriculture. They also were in full sympathy with the rural unrest which was rapidly crystallizing into a potent political force in the state. In view of all of these factors and the information derived from a study of developments at other land-grant colleges, the board reached the tentative conclusion that the best solution would be to reorganize the College on a two-track system of agriculture and mechanics. It was believed the additional financial support to be derived from the Hatch Act and the second Morrill Act would enable the board to make the College "a true agricultural and mechanical school that Virginia would be proud of."

The proposed two-track system was submitted to the faculty for "views of the professors on the subject." To the surprise of the board, some of the faculty had unusually strong views in opposition to the proposal. President Lomax, who objected to the plan, wrote to a number of college presidents on the subject and then appealed to the governor, who had been on the board at a time it was attempting to develop the literary degree. In his appeal to the governor he requested him to get an opinion from the attorney general concerning the legality of restricting the offerings of the College to agriculture and mechanics. Lomax was of the opinion such a restriction would be illegal. The attorney general agreed with him, whereupon Lomax turned all of his correspondence with the several college presidents and with the attorney general over to Vawter and, in his words, "argued with him and gave him my views with reference" to the proposal. Lomax summed up the argument between himself and the board in the following words: "I looked at the College as a stepping stone from the free school. If we had money enough for professors in any branch that a poor boy wanted to study, I thought it was our duty to give it to them. These other gentlemen [the board] thought we had a plenty literary colleges, and that we were breaking these down. My view was they had to take care of themselves, as we took care of ourselves . . . ."

As the discussion continued, the board began to think in terms of developing a technical school in which as much emphasis as possible would be given to all the sciences having bearing on agriculture and mechanics. All accounts agree that Vawter was the leader in this development. By drawing upon his experiences in setting up and administering the curriculum in his school, he was able to convince the other members of the board that such a plan would expand rather than restrict the offerings of the College in the areas of service into which it had already entered. He was especially successful in showing how such a plan if adopted could aid both the struggling Experiment Station and classroom instruction in agriculture.

He was less successful in convincing Lomax and several faculty members of the wisdom of the plan. Lomax was held in high personal regard by all the board members; but as the discussions continued, more and more of the members began to feel that Lomax did not have the qualifications needed in order to lead the school in the proposed new direction. While the board was yet contemplating the best plan of action to follow, an incident occurred on the campus which hastened its final decision.

During the latter part of Lomax's administration the "bucking" system to which reference has been made, got out of hand. The degree-bound upperclassmen developed keen resentment against the presence on the campus of the non-degree students in the special courses and in the preparatory department. The presence of these students on the campus, they felt, lowered the dignity and prestige of a true college. As one remedy for the situation, the upperclassmen resorted to their favorite method of "control": namely, "bucking" the unwelcome individuals. The remedy produced more disastrous results than the disease it was expected to cure. One individual insisted that he had been "bucked" more than one hundred times within the period of one year and after each bucking was so sore he could not sit down for a week. Apparently no one bothered to determine just how one hundred weeks of not being able to sit down could be achieved in the fifty-two weeks of a normal year; but this oversight made little difference, as rumors depicting the student body as one dominated by rude, uncouth rowdies with low morals and low background spread over the state.

These rumors, which reached a peak about 1890, were confirmed in the minds of many by an incident which occurred in December of that year. A group of students held a party in Number One Barracks, presumably to get into the proper "spirit" for the coming Christmas holidays. Unfortunately someone with the aid of one of the janitors apparently had secured some liquid "Brush Mountain Spirits" with which to aid the cause. Before the party ended, the celebrants had broken doors and window panes, including the entire sash; had smashed tables, beds, and chairs; and had thrown both smashed and unsmashed furniture out of the upstairs windows. This wanton destruction of property, coming as it did in the midst of all the other discussions and criticisms swirling around the College, convinced the wavering board members that the time indeed was at hand for a change.

By the time the board had assembled in Richmond on January 15 for its first meeting of 1891, some of its members were so aroused they wanted to fire the entire faculty and start over again. Vawter counseled against this action and urged the board first to clarify its own thinking as to the function of the school and then to determine which members of the faculty, if any, should be removed. This line of action was agreed upon and the date of April 7, 1891, set as the time for final action. In reporting its action at this January meeting, the board reported in part as follows:

> The board was convinced that the school was, in many particulars, not accomplishing for Virginia what it should do. That in no true sense of the word could it be called an "agricultural college," that as an agricultural institution, both as regards the station and the college, the State of Virginia would be but little poorer, or scarcely feel the loss, were its existence blotted out; that its leading object, as the law directs, was not being accomplished; that there were evils there that should be corrected; and that there were habits and customs there that should be changed.
>
> The board decided that the prime object of the college was not to furnish a cheap low-grade collegiate education; that its object was higher, its mission was grander; that if it did not rise to the true dignity of its requirements . . . there was no place for it in the educational system of Virginia. The board knew that Virginia sadly needed and was loudly calling for true technical education; that such was the demand for it that our young men were going North to get what Virginia should give them at home. . . . We did not wish to dwarf the study of our mother tongue, of the modern languages, or of the sciences. But we did intend to make the college what it should be—a true agricultural and mechanical school that Virginia would be proud of.

At the meeting on April 7, it became clear that Lomax would be removed. At this point Vawter requested that Lomax be permitted to resign from the presidency and at the same time be asked to consider another position at the College. The members held Lomax in such high personal regard that they agreed to this somewhat unusual procedure, but Lomax preferred to resign and did so immediately. The board thereupon appointed Professor John E. Christian as acting president to complete Lomax's unexpired term and at this same meeting decided to release Professors Graham, Morton, and Scott at the end of the academic year. These individuals were released, because the board did not believe they had the training needed to fit into the newly proposed program for the school.

Following the resignation of General Lomax as president, the board launched an immediate search for a successor. Vawter again took the lead and wrote to a number of college presidents all over the South, asking for names of possible candidates. Charles W. Dabney, a native Virginian, serving as president of the University of Tennessee, immediately answered Vawter's inquiry to him by suggesting the name of John M. McBryde, president of the University of South Carolina.

In addition to having been a practical farmer for a number of years in Albemarle County, where Vawter was now living, McBryde, according to Dabney, had "done as much fine work in scientific agriculture as any man has done in the last five years." "I believe he [McBryde] would make your agricultural and mechanical college a success at last," wrote Dabney. At the same time that Dabney wrote to Vawter, he also wrote a personal letter to McBryde in which he told him more about the Virginia Agricultural and Mechanical College and some of the recent happenings there. According to Dabney, Vawter was the "leading spirit" among those who planned to make the school "a straight out agricultural and mechanical college of the right kind."

Following this correspondence, the receipt of additional testimonials as to McBryde's fitness for the presidency and a personal meeting between McBryde and a committee of the board in Richmond on April 28, the Board of Visitors unanimously elected McBryde as president of the Virginia Agricultural and Mechanical College on May 7, 1891.

McBryde assumed his duties at the College on July 1 of the same year; but before he had been able to do much more than hang up his hat, the Board of Visitors came under another intensive legislative investigation, which for a while once more threatened the hapless institution. This investigation occurred during the first year of McBryde's administration; but since the subject matter of its inquiry resided almost entirely in the administrations preceding his, he was not drawn into the ensuing discussion. The investigation itself brought little if any new information to light concerning the College but marked an important milestone and turning point in the development of relationships between the College and the legislature.

Following their dismissal from the faculty to take place at the end of the spring term of 1891, Professors Scott and Graham sought reinstatement. Failing in this effort, they thereupon attacked the Board of Visitors and on February 10, 1892, presented written charges against them to the Virginia Senate Sub-Committee on Public Institutions and Education. Today most of the charges and the ensuing explanations are far more interesting for the information revealed as to the operation of the College than they are in showing any dereliction of the board, which was charged with (1) illegal expenditure of money, (2) improper expenditure of money, and (3) dismissal of professors without charges being made against them. Each charge was followed by a listing of board actions which allegedly supported the claim.

To support the claim of illegal expenditure of money, it was charged that the board had used funds from the Morrill Act of 1862 and of 1890 to erect an electric light plant and a water supply plant. Not only had the board spent money for these purposes, but it also illegally had spent Morrill Act funds, claimed Scott and Graham, for such things as constructing a shop, erecting a boilerhouse and smoke-stack and then had pulled down and re-erected the same. It had repainted, repapered, and installed bathrooms [plural] in the president's house for President McBryde. It had erected a stable for President McBryde's horses. It had erected a privy. It had converted a former machine shop into a mess hall and had converted a coal house into a lecture room. It had altered, repaired, and converted a lecture room into a chemical laboratory. It had paid insurance on a building, and last but by no means least it had started the construction of a gymnasium.

As to the improper expenditure of money entrusted to its care, the board, according to the charges, had permitted Professor Theo P. Campbell to leave for Europe before the close of the session 1890-91 and had paid him while absent for services not rendered. It had paid General Lomax on his resignation his salary for the remainder of the academic session for services not rendered. In paying General Lomax his salary for July [after he had resigned on April 7] and Dr. McBryde his salary for the same month, the board had paid for two presidents instead of one. It had also paid Dr. McBryde his July salary as director of the Experiment Station, while at the same time it was paying W. D. Saunders for the same position. In concluding their charges of improper expenditure of money, Graham and Scott charged that the board had approved the expense account of John E. Massey "from Alabama to Virginia, and not to attend a meeting of the executive committee" either. Circumstances surrounding this latter charge were never explored so fully as were the other charges leveled against the board. John E. (Parson) Massey, as state superintendent of public instruction, was ex-officio member of the Board of Visitors for the College. He had led an eventful political life first as an ardent Readjuster but had broken away after a strong fight with William H. (Billy) Mahone, the major leader in the Readjuster movement, and had affiliated with the Democrats. For this alleged defection he was heartily disliked by Mahone's followers in the Republican Party. Mahone, during this period under discussion, had been steadily losing his political influence in the state but still retained powerful political connections with the national Republican Party in power under President Harrison. It is quite likely, but not proved, that Mahone's known dislike for Massey and certain other members of the board, plus his known influence in Washington had some effect in causing this charge to be made against Massey. The specter of Mahone's power in Washington, whence the funds under dispute flowed, did not go unnoticed by the Democratically controlled legislature.

Actually, Massey, in his early seventies at the time, was planning to marry an Alabamian and had gone to Alabama a few days before his intended wedding ceremony. While there he received a telegram telling him of an outbreak of typhoid fever and the death of one student and a professor at the College. Rumor had it that most of the students were leaving school for fear of the fever. Hearing this, he had postponed his wedding (so he claimed) and ridden to Blacksburg to investigate the affair and see to the "improvement of the sanitary conditions." Following this inspection, he had returned to Alabama and claimed his bride. Upon his return to Richmond he had submitted a statement of and received payment for the expenses incurred in the unexpected side trip to Blacksburg. Some of his political enemies—and they were legion—thereupon claimed that Massey had charged the College for his bridal trip.

In further support of their case against the board, Scott and Graham prepared lengthy written statements in which numerous additional charges of maladmin-

istration of the affairs of the institution were leveled against the board. By implication both Scott and Graham, especially the latter, created the impression that
they intended to seek a federal investigation of the manner in which Virginia had
been spending the federally-derived funds for the College. Faced with the foregoing list of charges, the implied threat of a federal investigation, and an aware-
ness of Mahone's influence in Washington, the legislature decided to act. A joint
committee from the Senate and the House was set up and directed to investigate
the situation. The committee set to work at once by inviting the board to present
a written statement dealing with the charges. Upon receipt of this reply, which
answered the charges in some detail, the committee conducted an oral examination of all persons involved. The investigation, thereupon, took a surprising and
totally unexpected turn. It became a parade of many problems which had be-
deviled the College from its founding. The effect of two decades of political interference, of rapid turnover of board membership, of summary hiring and firing
of faculty, and of the total absence of an annual state appropriation for the College passed in quick review before the amazed committee.

Testimony was heard concerning the demoralizing effect on the faculty "who
stood hat in hand, waiting to depart" each time a new governor was elected or a
new board appointed. Ex-President Buchanan brought chuckles to the committee by his description of the precipitate and arbitrary action of the board in removing him from the presidency. He had been on official business in Washington when, as he expressed it, a new Board of Visitors had been nominated on
Tuesday, confirmed on Wednesday, and made a clean sweep of all offices at the
College on Thursday, leaving him to find out about it through the newspapers
on Friday. A replaced professor admitted that he had accepted a professorship of
English because at the time it had been offered to him he had been engaged
in farming "and that was hard work." This admission did little to enhance "book
learning" in the eyes of the farmers, or to raise doubts as to the board's wisdom
in replacing this individual.

As the investigation continued, the old confusion between broad and narrow education which had plagued the College came into sharper focus. Three
main views became identified: one, that the College should teach rule-of-thumb
farming and shop work; two, that the College should aid the poor, the children
of farmers and of industrial workers, to obtain a college education; and three,
the College should teach the application of science to agricultural, mechanical,
and related interests.

While the investigation did not reveal it fully, the school in actuality had
started out under view number one, had stumbled rapidly toward number two,
and under Lomax had been fumbling along in an effort to incorporate both
points of view into its program. The investigation did reveal that the personnel
replaced by the board at the April 7, 1891, meeting had supported the second view
in strong opposition to the board's support of the third position. As questioning
of the individual board members continued, the unanimity of their conviction
that the College as a school of technology should and could make a more significant contribution to the state than it had ever made became quite apparent. The
board's behavior, alleged to be illegal, improper, or unfair, was calmly, forcefully, and unanimously defended by its members as legal, proper, and completely
free of bias and unfairness. In all of its deliberations leading to the disputed behavior, the members argued, the board had been motivated by its determination
to develop the College into a high grade school of technology. Not once did a

member of the board waver from this position. Rector Vawter was especially convincing in both his written and oral presentation.

Claiming that he was the first person ever to have erected an electric power plant in the entire South, he readily admitted having used his influence with the Edison Company to get an electric plant installed at the College. How could a college teach the principles of power-plant operation, he wanted to know, without a power plant to operate, or the applications of electricity without any electricity to apply. As for the installation of a waterworks system to supply the shops —yes, he had supported that too when he had observed the wasteful system being employed of hauling the needed water in carts. Everyone ought to know, he slyly added, that it was much cheaper to let water run in a pipe than it was to haul it.

Vawter's defense of the money paid T. P. Campbell while he was in Europe was an excellent indication of the new approach the board had adopted in its effort to build an effective faculty. According to Vawter, Campbell was a "pretty square-speaking and a first class fellow" who had approached him one day and said, "Captain Vawter, I want you to tell me what you think of me as a professor at Blacksburg College." Vawter answered, "You have asked me a square question, and I will give you a square answer. I think you are a fine teacher and I think you are a fine gentleman; I think your influence there is for the building up of the College, but I do not think you know enough about modern languages to be a professor of modern languages." Campbell: "Thank you. Would you advise me to resign?" Vawter: "No, I would not. If I were in your place, I would fit myself in the best way; I think I would go to Europe and spend the summer there where you could talk the language." Campbell had followed his advice and immediately requested a leave of absence to study in Europe during the following summer. His leave had been granted, and he had departed for Europe two months before the end of the academic year. The board had paid him for these two months. Vawter had defended the payment on the ground that many institutions followed similar practices. Since Campbell had spent the summer "fitting himself to do better work for Blacksburg College," the College would get its money back. Vawter continued, "I am willing to stand for that; charge it to my reputation." As it turned out, Vawter's reputation was in good hands. Campbell completed his studies in Europe and returned to serve the College as professor of modern languages and subsequently as academic dean, dean of the college, and dean of the faculty for a combined total of nearly forty years.

The remaining charges against the board were either shown to be inaccurate or were faced frankly and defended by Vawter and the other members of the board as essential for the welfare of the school and, in their opinion, perfectly legal. One development relating to the financing of the College during the earliest days, although not directly involved in the charges, is worthy of passing attention.

Since the Morrill Act of 1862 stipulated that none of the income from the sale of the land scrip should be used for the erection or maintenance of buildings, the early administrators soon found themselves with buildings to be maintained but with no money for the job. Not only had the legislature failed to provide an annual appropriation for the College, but it also had passed a law requiring the board to grant free tuition privileges to 200 state students. The administration therefore could not look to student fees to be of much help. But as Buchanan expressed it, the wind sometimes came along and blew a roof off and "greatly embarrassed" the president whose immediate job was to get the roof replaced and afterwards find the money as best he could.

The system he had used to raise money for repairs, explained Buchanan, essentially was the same as that followed by his predecessors. Some of the professors had been provided with houses built on the campus with state funds, while no houses had been available for other staff members. In these cases, professor A with free housing was paid $1500 per year, while professor B without free housing was paid $1500 plus $150 for house rent. Both professors were entered on the books as receiving $1650 per year, but the $150 charged to professor A was put into a general fund to be used for repairs, upkeep, and so on. If by chance it cost $150 to repair professor's A's house, then nothing went into the general fund from this account, but hopefully houses occupied by professors C, D, and E would not require repairing at the same time.

Buchanan confessed that the question of legality of this practice had worried him at first, but the action of the legislature in readjusting Virginia's debt had more than convinced him that the practice was sound, and in fact too conservative in raising needed funds. Upon receipt of the proceeds from the sale of the land scrip, Buchanan explained, Virginia had invested the money in state bonds at six per cent interest per year. This transaction had almost doubled the original capital investment. In the tumultuous Readjuster period, the college bonds were not "re-adjusted," nor was the interest scaled down to the three per cent rate to which most of the remaining state bonds had been adjusted. As a result of Virginia's having continued to pay six per cent interest to the College and three per cent interest to other holders of state bonds, many officials held that the three per cent difference represented a state annuity to the College which the board could use to meet college expenses not chargeable to the land-grant fund. This interpretation had been accepted by members of the board who insisted they had carefully seen to it that the sums expended as a result of this practice never exceeded the three per cent figure. The board apologized to the investigating committee for not being able to give an accurate report concerning all the money expended during the year under dispute but claimed the major fault lay with the records having been kept by the displaced bookkeeper who was now preferring charges against the board. Since the investigating committee had before it the statements of two expert accountants, one of whom had sworn that the College financial records were well-kept and accurate, while the other had sworn that the same records were poorly kept, misleading, and at places inaccurate, the committee, prudently, it seems, steered its investigation into another direction and let the matter of an exact accounting drop.

As the investigation proceeded and history of the struggle made by earlier administrations to keep the College going continued to unfold, the similar efforts being made by the administration under investigation began to stand out in sharp detail. It gradually became abundantly clear that this board under Vawter's leadership had clarified its thinking concerning the mission of the College, had formulated a program of action designed to achieve this mission, and now believed it had employed a president and the nucleus of a faculty competent to carry the institution toward this mission. Any failure to move in this desired direction, it was implied, would be the result of further legislative interference and foolish nit-picking.

Vawter was particularly effective in getting this idea across without actually stating it. In concluding his remarks he also reminded the committee that he and other members had consented to serve on the board only after the earnest solicitation of the governor and other interested friends. What Vawter did not say at this stage probably carried more weight than what he did say, for every member of the committee knew full well that "other interested friends" included all of the major leaders in the rapidly burgeoning Farmers' Alliance movement.

Following its investigation, the committee found itself unable to agree on a report to the legislature. A majority report which was a political masterpiece in its attempt to avoid a full agreement or disagreement with either the plaintiffs or defendants was prepared. A more forthright minority report also was presented, expressing full vindication of the Board of Visitors for its past actions and full confidence in its ability to develop the College in the future. Both reports agreed that the reorganization effected by the board was a good one and deserved continued support. When both reports were taken up by the Senate on March 1, 1892, the majority report was rejected by a vote of 15 to 13, whereupon the minority report supporting the Board of Visitors was adopted without a dissenting vote. For the first time in the history of the College a legislative investigation into its affairs had resulted in vindication and, in effect, a vote of confidence for the Board of Visitors.

In general, the response to the Senate action was favorable, but a number of people were left puzzled and uneasy. W. F. Massey, of North Carolina, father of Arthur Ballard Massey who later served VPI with distinction as professor of biology, wrote to H. M. Magruder, of Albemarle County, Virginia, asking him about the situation at the College. Magruder was one of the outstanding country-gentlemen leaders active in Virginia on behalf of agriculture. As such he had taken a strong, almost bitterly outspoken, stand against the agricultural education program of the College and the Experiment Station as it was developing prior to the reorganization of 1891. His reply to Massey's inquiry represents one of the best contemporary answers showing how the gentlemen-farmers looked upon the changes taking place at the College during the period of reorganization:

> It would seem to an outsider that chaos was about to return at least so far as this institution is concerned, and yet I believe there is a purpose and a most commendable one behind all this which is slowly but surely being worked out; and if the guiding minds are continued in authority for the next three years, this school will become one of such a high grade for technical instruction in scientific and practical agriculture and mechanics, that it will be a source of pride to Virginia and an object of emulation to her sister states.
>
> You ask what it all means? It means that agriculture and mechanics, *real, practical, modern* agriculture and mechanics are to be taught and taught by men who are capable and zealous to make this College what its name implies and what its revenues enable it to be.

Unhappily Magruder died before he had an opportunity to see his prophecy fulfilled but not before he had been given an opportunity to submit a plan for expanding agricultural research and its benefits throughout the state.

With the legislative inquiry out of the way, the rural leadership, convinced that the College was at last safely entrusted to "practical farmers," and the Populist movement engaging the restless politicians, the reformers, and the self-appointed guardians of the "people's college," the Virginia Agricultural and Mechanical College for the first time in its troubled history entered into a period of freedom from outside pressures. From this point of view, McBryde had a freedom never enjoyed by Lomax or any of his predecessors.

Following his resignation from the presidency, Lomax worked in Washington, D. C., on the compilation of official records of both Confederate and Union Armies. He died in 1931 and was buried in Warrenton, Virginia.

Chapter 6

The McBryde
Administration
1891-1907

T HE COLLEGE BEGAN a new era on May 7,
1891, with the election of John McLaren
McBryde to the presidency as its fifth president in nineteen years.

McBryde was born on January 1, 1841, in Abbeville, South Carolina. After
a short period at South Carolina College, he entered the University of Virginia,
where he completed his formal education. At the conclusion of the Civil War,
during which he had served the Confederacy in the army and in government
service in Richmond, he had engaged in farming, first in Buckingham County
and then in Albemarle County, Virginia. In Albemarle, he had been active in
organizing and promoting farmers' clubs and had served as a trustee of the Miller
Fund, which had been used to help establish the school of agriculture at the
University of Virginia. During this time, he had published numerous articles
which led to his appointment as professor of agriculture and botany at the University of Tennessee. From Tennessee, where he made an outstanding record,
he had gone to South Carolina College. Two days after his arrival at this institution he had been elected chairman of the faculty. In May, 1883, he had been
elected president. In 1886, he had declined an offer to direct the Texas Experiment Station, while in 1887 he had declined to accept the presidency of the
University of Tennessee. By 1887, he had helped reorganize the College of South

Carolina into the University of South Carolina. This achievement had aroused the enmity of many church leaders and rural groups. The denominationalists feared that the University would attract students away from the church colleges, while the rural groups feared that agriculture would not be given sufficient support in the new University. In a movement of the populace, somewhat similar to the upsurge in Virginia under the Farmers' Alliance and the Populists, rural South Carolina had begun demanding a practical school of agriculture for the practical farmers. Many leaders attacked the University on the grounds that the program of agriculture which McBryde had developed was not and never would be practical. Benjamin R. (Pitchfork Ben) Tillman had led the attack. His oratorical ability to awaken popular support had been used with such telling effectiveness against McBryde and the University that the legislature in 1891 had decided to remove all agricultural work from the University and locate it at the newly established Clemson College. This action on the part of the legislature had greatly disturbed McBryde and undoubtedly influenced his decision to accept the presidency of the Virginia Agricultural and Mechanical College, which was offered to him officially on May 8, 1891, by means of a letter from Rector Vawter. This interesting letter follows:

> The Board of Visitors of the Va. A and M College met at the office of the Supt. of Edu. in the City of Richmond yesterday, May 7, at 8 p.m., and unanimously elected you President of the College, and Professor of Agricultural Chemistry, and Director of the Experiment Station at a salary of $4000.00 and a house—$2500.00 to be paid from the college funds and $1500.00 from the station fund. Your salary & duties to begin July 1, 1891. I am further directed by the board to say that they desire your plans to be submitted to them before they take any further action in reorganizing the College, and that the existing chairs and incumbents shall be conformed to such plan as may be adopted by the Board, and that they wish to cooperate with you in securing for the College two or three additional men of first class standing for professorships, and they wish a concentration of effort to make a first class school of Applied Science with Agriculture and Mechanics the prominent features; and they further desire that station workers, as far as possible, shall be also teachers in the College. They further direct me to say that the position of President shall be most clearly defined and strengthened; that he shall have the ear of the Board, that he shall be their channel of communication with the faculty, and that all estimates for appropriations shall be submitted by him, and all bills be approved by him before being paid; and that all recommendations from members of the faculty shall come through him, with his approval or disapproval, and reason therefor. Let me add, that the Board unanimously and heartily concur in your ideas as indicated in the above instructions, and desire most fully and cordially to cooperate with you in your great work. Kindly advise me, officially, of your acceptance of the position to which you have been elected by the Board. I am yours, very truly,
>
>   C. E. Vawter—Rector

The announcement of McBryde's appointment to the presidency of the College for the most part was enthusiastically received in the state. The editor of *The Southern Planter* was particularly happy about the appointment and congratulated the board, the state, and particularly the farmers that McBryde had accepted the office. After reviewing McBryde's accomplishments in glowing terms as an educator, administrator, and agriculturist, the editor of this publication expressed the conviction that having such an individual as president of the College, director of the Experiment Station, and professor of agricultural chemistry would convince the farmers that the College now was truly concerned with the problems of agriculture. When the midsummer announcement was made of the appointment of Professors Sheib, Smyth, and Niles, the *Planter* waxed even more enthusiastic. The appointment of Edward E. Sheib, Ph.D. (Leipsic) as professor of English, history, and political economy spoke well for an institution devoted to technical training, held the *Planter*, while the appointment of Ellison A. Smyth, Jr., "of the younger generation of scientific workers," a graduate of Princeton, as professor of biology was a guarantee of thorough modern training in this subject. The fact that E. P. Niles, D.V.M. (Iowa A and M), who did accept the appointment as adjunct professor of veterinary science, was credited with the achievements of his brother W. B. Niles, D.V.M., who had been offered but had declined the appointment, apparently went unnoticed, so great was the excitement being generated by the reorganization of the College and the advent of professors with specialized training for the work they were to pursue.

The break in the practice of appointing only native Virginians to key positions, a practice so deplored by Ruffner, did not go entirely unnoticed, as evidenced by the *Danville Register* in the following editorial:

> All other things being equal, home talent should be given the preference but the board of visitors of the Blacksburg college think differently. . . . The board of visitors on last Thursday selected for professors, men from South Carolina, Iowa, and Germany. We can but look upon the performance as an outrage. If the board means to say that competent men could not be found in Virginia to fill the vacant chairs, then the board speaks falsely, but if it means simply to put on style by going to other states and foreign lands for professors, then the members of the board have made themselves flunkeys and asses, that ought to be kicked out of the positions they occupy.

The board answered this complaint by presenting a list of prominent Virginians serving as presidents and faculty members in out-of-state colleges and universities and a list of non-Virginians serving with great distinction at the University of Virginia. . . . "In the great commonwealth of education—of letters and science—state lines have long since been obliterated," concluded the board. Here the matter rested even after Martin P. Scott, one of the replaced professors in the reorganization of the College, attempted to raise it again when in his charges against the board he ominously observed, "Virginia students have been expelled from a Virginia college by South Carolinians and Yankees. This should be a subject of inquiry. . . ." The failure of the *Register's* complaints and of Scott's direct appeal to state pride to call forth an avalanche of supporting letters and editorials in the press may be taken as an indication that the times in Virginia truly were changing.

Immediately after becoming president of the Virginia Agricultural and Mechanical College, McBryde began to plan the reorganization of the curriculum as requested by the Board of Visitors. This plan when completed and submitted to the board in July, 1891, was remarkably similar in philosophic outlook to the plan prepared by W. H. Ruffner upon the opening of the College in 1872. The proposals for implementing the philosophy, however, reflected the benefits of the two decades of experience, knowledge, and progress which had been achieved by the land-grant colleges since that date. McBryde's full report, a few excerpts of which follow, became the very foundation stone of the modern VPI.

I am convinced that the true development to be given to such schools [land-grant schools] should lie in the direction of technology. They should be made, as far as our social and economic conditions will allow, more and more professional and technical. This field . . . is virgin, the demand for such training is great and increasing, the line of work is definite and clear cut. . . . The stressing of the technological features adds comparatively little to the cost of running our agricultural and mechanical colleges. The men and materials demanded, in accordance with the terms of the acts of endowment . . . are sufficient to send out, well equipped for their life work, not only agriculturists and mechanics, but analytical chemists, and civil, mechanical, and mining engineers as well. A small additional outlay would enable them to train architects, biologists, mineralogists, geologists, electrical engineers, horticulturists, viticulturists, etc. It must be remembered, however, that these men are to be trained not only as specialists, but as citizens. . . . It is not only possible . . . but proper for these schools to educate men for manufacturing and commercial purposes. . . .

Following this presentation, McBryde presented lengthy recommendations including among others the business operations of the College, the duties and responsibilities of the president, gradations or ranks to be established within the teaching force, priorities for needs facing the school, policies for improving the grounds, and an outline of courses of study to be followed.

McBryde proposed seven four-year courses, each leading to a Bachelor of Science, and two shorter courses leading to a certificate. All courses were to be grouped under one or the other of the two heads of agriculture and mechanics. Under the heading of agriculture, the student could earn a Bachelor of Science degree in agriculture, horticulture, or applied chemistry; while under the heading of mechanics, he could earn a degree in civil engineering, mechanical engineering, electrical engineering, or general science. The short course in agriculture led to a certificate in practical agriculture, and the short course in mechanics led to a certificate of practical mechanics. The work in these two latter courses was to be offered for those not prepared for or not wishing to take the longer courses. The work in these two short courses was to be carefully laid out and supervised by the faculty in order to protect the quality of the regular four-year courses. Apparently, McBryde was determined to prevent these short courses from becoming the playground which Vawter thought similar courses had become under Lomax. The degree program in general science was switched from the mechanical to the agricultural department within the year and was never returned to the former department.

In the freshman year, the required courses, whether leading to a degree or a certificate, were about the same. These courses consisted of basic work in mathematics, history, English, inorganic chemistry, physiology, and bookkeeping. McBryde provided core courses for all students long before the term *core* came into common usage in higher education. All students working toward a degree were required to take such "liberal" courses as mathematics, English, French, German, general and constitutional history, psychology, political economy, and ethics, while the preparatory or sub-collegiate course was available for applicants unable to meet the requirements for admission to the freshman class. Laboratory work was required in every department, while compositions and other written exercises were required for the first time in English and modern languages.

The required work in the shop or field was held to be instructive and therefore was not paid for. At the same time, McBryde organized and continued on a better basis the earlier practice of paying students for "uninstructive" manual

Above: The entire V.A.M.C. campus in 1880. The two large buildings at left are the First and Second Academic Buildings, occupied in 1876 and 1877. The group of buildings at far right includes the President's Home, built in 1876 and now part of Henderson Infirmary; the "Pavilion"; the Steam Laundry; and, at far right, the Preston and Olin Building. Below: The Preston and Olin Building in 1882, showing touches of student pranks.

Above: Campus in 1897. From left are Second Academic; First Academic (tower of Number One Barracks showing above roof); Barracks Number Two (now a part of Rasche Hall); a faculty home; Old Commerce (Commencement/German Hall); the foundry smokestack. Below: Entomology laboratory in 1897.

V.A.M.C. faculty composite of 1878 shows President Charles L. C. Minor in center and, from top, clockwise: M. G. Ellzey, who taught chemistry and agriculture; General Boggs, who taught mechanics; V. E. Shepherd, first college librarian, who also served as treasurer, secretary for the faculty and Board of Visitors, and proctor; Thomas N. Conrad, teacher of English and later third president of V.A.M.C.; Charles Martin, teacher of English and ancient languages; Gray Carroll, teacher of mathematics; and General James H. Lane, professor of mathematics and foreign languages and first head of military tactics. Minor, Lane, Martin, and Shepherd were the first four appointees to the V.A.M.C. staff.

Opposite page, top: V.A.M.C.'s graduating class of 1888; bottom: V.A.M.C.'s 1894 football team, "Champions of Southwest Virginia" with a 4-1 record. The coach was J. A. Massie.

William A. Caldwell of Craig County, at left, was the first student to enroll at Virginia Agricultural and Mechanical College. By the end of the first academic year he had been joined by 131 other students, all from Virginia. Enrollment zoomed to 255 in the 1875-76 session, but facilities did not keep pace (see below), resulting in three-man rooms with makeshift triple-decked beds.

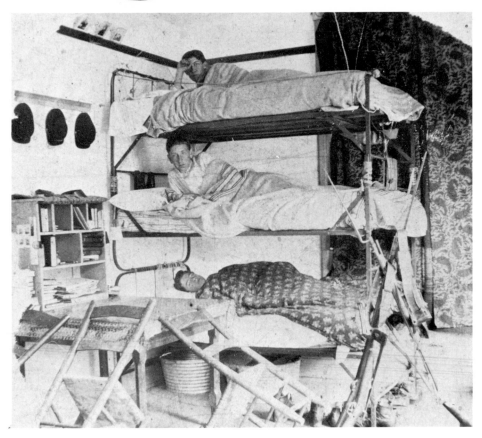

Extra-curricular activities really blossomed in the 1890s. Above: The cadet band in 1898 when it volunteered as a unit for the Spanish-American War. Below: The Thespian Club in 1896 included Ellison A. Smyth (back row, second from left), professor of biology for whom Smyth Hall is named; Lawrence Priddy (center, reading newspaper), one of only three persons who have received honorary degrees from VPI; and O. M. Stull (facing Priddy's newspaper), creator of the word "Hokie" in his "Old Hokie" yell.

Above: The college had its own forge shop in 1898 to produce farm and shop implements and to serve as a laboratory. Below: The cornerstone laying ceremony at the Y.M.C.A. Building (later called Old Military and now the Student Personnel Building) on June 20, 1899. The building was the first to be built through alumni donations and cost $20,729. Lawrence Priddy '97 headed the drive for funds for the Y.M.C.A. Building and later the Memorial Gymnasium.

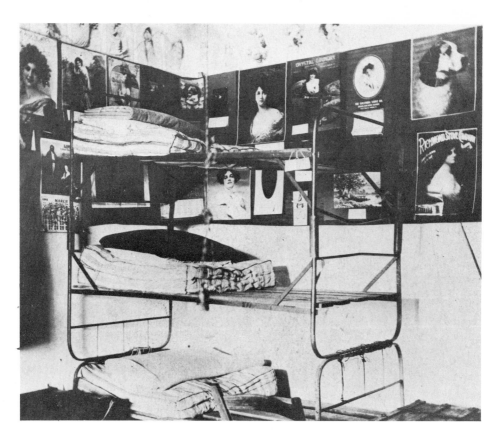

When John M. McBryde took office in 1891 there were only 150 students and 60 dormitory rooms at the college; 14 years later there were almost 300 dormitory rooms and an enrollment of 728, the highest achieved until 1919-20 when enrollment hit 757. Many students still had to live in three-man rooms in 1905, as the above photo attests. Below, a traditional winter pastime on the drillfield—a snow battle—this one in 1905. Note the Chapel under construction in right background.

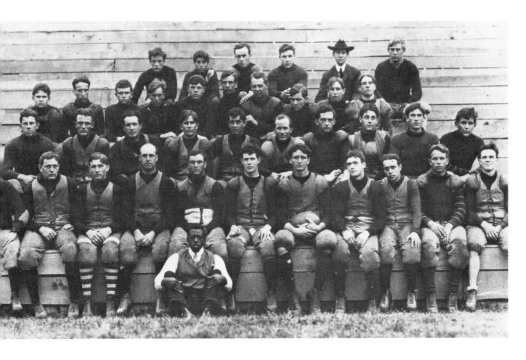

Above: the 1905 football team, "Champions of the South" with a 9-1 record, was coached by C. P. "Sally" Miles (top row, far right) and starred Hunter Carpenter (front row, fifth from left), Tech's only athlete to be named to the National Football Hall of Fame. Below: The first Tech football team to be called "Gobblers," the 1909 squad that compiled a 6-1 record for its coach Branch Bocock.

Above: Tech cadets in the Corps artillery battery practice their firing skills on campus in 1906. Batteries were made a part of the Corps structure in 1893 and were phased out in 1948, two years after the first Air Force Squadron was added to the structure. Below: The cadet Battalion marches on the drillfield in 1917 in the West Point-type dress uniforms. The Corps was changed from a Battalion to Regiment in 1922.

Above: Preston and Olin Institute Building (after conversion to shops building) and part of downtown Blacksburg in 1907. The building, destroyed by fire in 1913, stood where the dual portion of Main Street at College Avenue now traverses. Below: The old Alumni Gateway in 1915 (shortly after the Preston and Olin Building burned) also stood at the intersection of College and Main. Note the electric street light at upper left of photo.

Above: Tech's first Glee Club was organized in 1894. Here is the 1911 version, decked out in its "uniform." Below: Two students study while another reads "The Virginia Tech" in a dormitory room in 1924. The student newspaper was an organ of the Athletic Association until the student body took control in 1931. The name was changed to "The Collegiate Times" in 1969.

Above: The 1920 Rat Parade snakes into downtown Blacksburg. Below: Barracks Number One (now Lane Hall) in 1928.

Although most of Tech's cadets did not approve of the "invasion," 12 women students were admitted to Virginia Tech for the first time in September 1921. In the next 50 years that number grew to 3,500. The first coeds to graduate, above, received their degrees in 1925. From left: Mary Brumfield (M.S. degree); Ruth Terrett, Lucy Lee Lancaster, Louise Jacobs, and Carrie Sibold (all B.S. degrees). Until the 'Thirties student dramatic productions featured all-male casts, below, or all-female casts in the case of Tech's ostracized coeds who also had to publish their own yearbook, "The Tin Horn," several years before allowed representation in "The Bugle."

Above: Tech's 1928 Athletic Council was composed of, from left: J. E. Williams, C. P. "Sally" Miles, Frank W. Peake ("All-Southern" selection), Louis O'Shaughnessy, and Carol M. Newman. Williams, Miles, O'Shaughnessy, and Newman have had campus buildings named for them. Below: Cadet cheering section in old Miles Stadium in 1928 shows off a "VP" monogram above cheerleader Billy Steele's raised arms. Tech's "VP" monogram was changed to the current "VT" in 1958. Cadet "hat tricks," using white cap covers, have taken the place of the white shirts to spell out messages to football crowds.

The first five presidents: Charles L. C. Minor (1872-79); John L. Buchanan (1880-81); Thomas N. Conrad (1882-86); Lunsford L. Lomax (1886-91); John M. McBryde (1891-1907).

work. This latter provision proved to be very, very popular and became one of the practices continuing to flourish even in this day of affluence.

To carry on the instruction in his proposed program, McBryde recommended the establishment of the following positions: professorships in mathematics and civil engineering, mechanical engineering, horticulture, entomology and mycology, English, history and political economy, biology, and veterinary medicine; adjunct professorships in modern languages, physics and electrical engineering, general chemistry, mineralogy and geology, agriculture, analytical chemistry; assistant professorships in mathematics and military tactics; and instructorships in bookkeeping, wood-work, and machine-work.

In time, VPI was to embrace all of the recommendations made by McBryde at this July, 1891, meeting and to add additional courses under his guiding hand. The board's adoption of McBryde's plan was an unusual event in the history of the College. It marked the first time any Board of Visitors permitted the school to operate under a plan drawn up by the president and faculty. In all previous reorganizations, the boards had jealously guarded this prerogative and taken it unto themselves. They had determined the purpose of the College, drawn up the curriculum, hired the president and faculty, and then ordered them to put the curriculum into operation.

Thanks to Vawter, McBryde not only had an opportunity to plan the curriculum but also had the privilege and responsibility of selecting his faculty. The passage of the Hatch Act in 1887 and of the second Morrill Act in 1890 gave McBryde more than double the money available to any previous administrations with which to operate the College. While all of these funds had to be expended under specific restrictions, McBryde administered the money and the programs it financed so effectively that he eventually generated additional funds from the state legislature with which to supplement federal funds. It would be a long time, however, before the state funds equaled the federal funds.

In spite of the laudations in the press, the session of 1891-92 had scarcely begun before McBryde and his newly organized faculty faced a crisis. As the time for the opening of the session had approached, a number of letters complaining about the "bucking" and hazing which had gone on during Lomax's administration began to be received by the president, members of the board, and the faculty. The new president was nonplussed about the matter but took it up with the faculty, and a decision was made to get the situation under control. It appears likely that the faculty became over concerned. During the first week of the session, the president explained the situation to the students in assembly, reminded them of the stringent regulations against all forms of hazing, and made a strong appeal to them to cooperate with the faculty in putting an end to all forms of it. Following this appeal, he held personal conferences with all seniors and cadet officers and urged them to use their influence with fellow students to give up the practice. To McBryde's surprise, he found that bucking the freshmen, who by now were referred to by upperclassmen as "rats," had become a tradition in the eyes of the students. Three regular buckings were administered during the year: one in the fall to celebrate the issuance of uniforms to the "rats," one in the early winter upon the return of the students to campus after the Christmas holidays, and one in the late spring to celebrate having survived the winter. In addition to the "regular" buckings administered according to a strict student-developed protocol, there were a number of "irregular" ones administered under a protocol and timing subject only to the whims of the upperclassmen. The seniors promised McBryde they would try to reduce the severity of the buckings but doubted if they could stop the practice entirely. They were correct. All of the "rats" were given "irregular" secret buckings but in an admittedly milder form. The faculty was greatly disturbed but could not identify the culprits. Just at this time, a series of events starting with a perfectly innocent prank brought the faculty and students into sudden confrontation.

It all began when a student dropped a bag of water on two fellow students as they passed under his window in Number One Barracks. In retaliation, they slipped into his room during the night and while he slept painted a mustache on his upper lip. Taking advantage of the fact that the victim was a heavy sleeper, the artists did a thorough job, using some form of waterproof ink or dye. The next morning at reveille the unsuspecting victim jumped out of bed at the last minute possible, donned his uniform, and rushed out to roll call, only to be met with howls of unmilitary-like laughter. The cadet officer in charge, feeling that his dignity and authority had been grossly affronted, ordered the surprised but mustached "rat" to go wash his face. The bewildered action of the "rat" following this order served only to increase the hilarity of the spectators to such a point they had to be dismissed without a complete roll call. The incident probably would have ended here had the mustache not been waterproof. When the "rat" discovered that his newly acquired mustache would not easily wash off, he decided to keep it and showed up in class with his new adornment. The professors were not amused, or at least they professed not to be. Besides, all of the faculty was under some tension concerning hazing anyway. An investigation followed; and in spite of the protestations of all involved, the faculty decided that an indignity had been visited upon the body of the student receiving the mustache and as such came under the heading of hazing. All the students directly concerned with the affair, even the recipient of the mustache since he had thrown water out of the barracks, were put on one month's strict probation. The severity of the punishment angered some of the upperclassmen who felt the new administration was infringing unfairly on student rights.

Everything ran smoothly until the day arrived for the "rats" to don their new uniforms, which at that time were being made for the College by a firm in Richmond. Uniform day was a "regular" bucking day, but the "rats" having received an "irregular" bucking during the first two weeks of college rebelled at the idea of receiving the "regular" one. This rebellion in turn infuriated some members of the upper-class who determined to buck the "rats" by force. A near riot ensued in the barracks and spread to the drill field, at that time immediately back of Number One Barracks. The official report records that "a disgraceful scene of riot and disorder followed, and a dangerous conflict was only prevented by the ringing of the bell for return to quarters." In the investigation which followed, the upperclassmen involved "not only admitted that they were of the bucking party the night before, but boldly defended the practice, declaring that they had been bucked, and that the new men should be bucked; that as bucking was an established practice here it should be continued. They expressed no regret, made no apology for the disorder created and the disobedience of regulations, and no promise for the future." Faced with this unhappy situation, the faculty voted to place all of the participants on conduct probation for the remainder of the term.

President McBryde held personal conferences with all of the students involved in the affair and explained the faculty decision to each one. In spite of his best efforts, however, student resentment rose to a fever pitch. An "unauthorized" meeting of the students was held and a set of demands drawn up for presentation to the faculty. This set of demands was duly presented to McBryde, who reviewed them carefully with the student committee and explained in detail why he did not believe the faculty could accept them. At the same time, he agreed to call a faculty meeting and present the student demands to it for consideration. In the meantime, students had sought out individual faculty members to enlist their support on their side of the controversy. To their surprise, they found the faculty solidly behind McBryde. By the time the faculty met to consider the first set of student demands, the students had held a second unauthorized meeting and had prepared a second set of demands which they presented to the faculty while it was in session. The faculty found the second set as unacceptable as the first had been but decided to give every student desiring it an opportunity to be heard. All Saturday classes were dismissed, and the faculty spent the entire day considering the situation but postponed a final decision until Monday. Great excitement prevailed on the campus over the weekend, during which many of the student leaders sought out and consulted with individual faculty members. These members rejected all neutrality and lined up solidly behind McBryde. On Monday before the faculty had assembled, the students directly involved held another meeting and voted to withdraw the resolutions in which they had defended their right to continue the practice of bucking and condemned the faculty for trying to stop the practice. Since the objectionable resolutions involved had been signed by a number of students, the faculty insisted that the set of resolutions withdrawing the objections would have to include at least the same signatures. All day Monday was given over by the faculty to hearing individual students present their points of view. Some students confessed that in the excitement of the student meetings they had voted one way or the other without really knowing what they were voting for. These the faculty "let off with an admonition to vote more carefully and understandingly in the future." Finally, after an all-day session devoted to hearing individual cases, the "student demonstration against the faculty" was brought to an end by the unanimous vote of the faculty to permit five of the demonstrators to resign without penalty, to dismiss six with the understanding they could be readmitted, and to expel one for his action in the matter and his bluntly expressed unfavorable opinion of the faculty.

This entire incident, occurring as it did less than two months after the opening of the session, was quite disturbing to McBryde and his newly organized faculty. The Board of Visitors, fully aware of the charges of hazing, rowdyism, and disorderliness at the College, gave its emphatic and hearty approval to the "prompt, effective, and decisive action taken by the faculty to suppress misconduct and disorder, and enforce discipline." In the opinion of the board, the "affair was a crisis in the history of the school—its turning point as to its future usefulness and success as an educational establishment. Upon the way in which it was to be dealt with depended the question whether the authorities or the students were to govern." The action of the faculty, the board reported, now "gives to every Virginia parent the assurance and pledge that their sons shall be protected from maltreatment or insult, and surrounded with helpful and healthy influences and safeguards." Happily for VPI, the board's interpretation of the faculty action was fully accepted by the people of the state. Of even greater importance, it was accepted by the students, one of whom was reported to have said that henceforth it would be safer to haze the faculty than to haze the "rats!"

This entire situation, unhappy and trying as it was, in actuality enhanced McBryde's prestige as a president and at the same time tended to strengthen the College in the minds of the people. Before McBryde and his faculty could do much more than give a sigh of relief over the satisfactory settlement of this episode in college administration, the legislature had decided to conduct the investigation of College affairs growing out of the charges of Scott and Graham. This investigation did not directly involve McBryde or any of his faculty, but obviously its outcome would affect their relationship with the school. McBryde did not become involved, publicly at least, with the investigation, although *The Southern Planter* credited him with having rendered "invaluable assistance" to the board at the time. This legislative investigation was not without its ironic aspects for President McBryde. One of the charges leveled at him in South Carolina was that he had promoted liberal education at the expense of agricultural education. In Virginia one of the charges against his program was that it promoted agricultural and mechanical education at the expense of liberal education.

The resolution of the student demonstration and of the legislative investigation turned out to be quite helpful to the institution. McBryde's tactful conduct in both instances strengthened his position of leadership with students, faculty, board, and legislature. The board's conduct in both instances and especially its articulate presentation of previous troubles which had beset the College, along with its equally articulate expression of its aims and hopes for the future, created in the legislature an entirely new understanding and appreciation of the institution. The radical reorganization of 1891 and the ensuing investigation of 1892 were the last of the kind the College faced during its first century of existence.

The remainder of the session of 1891-92 was used by McBryde and his faculty in strengthening the academic program and planning improvements in campus surroundings and student life.

The hydraulic ram pumping water from behind the site of the present Derring Hall proved to be unsatisfactory and was replaced by another system which piped water by gravity from a spring on the northeast edge of town to a tank located just back of the Preston and Olin building. Water from this wooden tank, which is yet remembered by older alumni, was pumped to another tank located in the tower of Number One Barracks (Lane Hall). Freezeups, breakdown of pumps, and pranks at the spring perpetrated by local youth often caused the rebirth of bucket brigades to cisterns and wells located at different places on the campus. Student-organized retaliation on the local youth suspected of tampering with the water supply often relieved the tedium of college life but did little to improve town and gown relationships. In addition to the new water system, McBryde was able to secure much new equipment for the shops, the laboratories, the classrooms, and the farm. This equipment greatly pleased the students and led the editor of the *Gray Jacket* to proclaim that the shops were now the best in the South, if not in the nation. This youthful exaggeration was exceeded only by the youthful enthusiasm which swept the student body as change after change continued to take place under its watchful eye.

McBryde was the first president of the College to encourage the formation and growth of numerous student activities. In this undertaking, he had more than able assistance from his faculty, especially Professors Smyth, Anderson, and Sheib, and Commandant Harmon. It is worth noting that in the session of 1891-92 an athletic program was begun, publication of the *Gray Jacket* resumed, and the following college yell adopted:

Rip Rah Ree!   Va., Va., Vee!
Virginia, Virginia!
A.M.C.

Black and cadet gray were adopted as the College colors. In making up athletic uniforms, sweaters, caps, and so on these colors were presented in alternate stripes instead of in solid blocks. The results were startling, and "unpleasantly suggestive," a conclusion which can be readily confirmed from photographs of the first football team of 1892. Within a few years the colors were changed to the present burnt orange and Chicago maroon.

Some pick-up teams made up of students started baseball at VPI in 1877 by winning the first game 53-13 against Roanoke College. Apparently this score still stands as a record. No serious effort was made to develop organized teams in any sport until 1891. With McBryde's approval and support, an athletic association was organized in September of that year with J. A. Massie ('92) as president. The major efforts of this organization during its earlier years were concentrated on football first and baseball second. Tennis received "some attention, and a tennis association was formed," but no attention was given to track or "field-day exercises" until 1896.

Football, once it got a start, emerged rapidly as the most popular sport. Its start, however, was slow. At the urging of a few interested students and faculty during the fall of 1891, a number of students assembled "on the undulating combination of hills and valleys that lay back of Barracks No. 1" to play pick-up games of the new sport. The story of the long trail from these pick-up games played without a rule book, coach, uniform, or a standardized ball to the highly specialized type of game played today amidst the plush surroundings of Lane Stadium is beyond the scope of this narrative, but even so these earlier efforts deserve some attention.

In the fall of 1892, largely through the efforts of Professor W. E. Anderson, Professor E. A. Smyth, and cadets H. B. Pratt and J. W. Stull, VPI's first football team was organized, with Professor Anderson playing right tackle and serving as captain and Professor Smyth as "trainer" and business manager.

In the words of the 1903 *Bugle*, "It was not football and yet we had some fun. . . . Suits were ordered, footballs of various descriptions bought and general enthusiasm prevailed." One of the footballs described as "Camp's Foot Ball" was purchased from Harper and Brothers, Publishers, for $1.25, a price some players thought exorbitant.

Recruiting players and maintaining player morale proved to be a problem then as now. It was necessary to go into barracks every day and beg men to come out to play, since the men who played one evening were disgruntled because they were not immediately placed on the first team and refused to come out the second evening. A second team, therefore, had to be "secured every evening by threats, coaxing, promises, and appeals."

The description by one of the participants of how football got under way the fall of 1892 is interesting to recall in this day of athletic scholarships, specialized coaching assignments, and wildly cheering crowds packed into million-dollar stadiums.

> There was no idea of team play; whoever got the ball—by luck—ran with it; no one knew anything about interference, and tho' we had a system of signals, it was a question of luck how each play went . . . the boundaries of the field were marked off with a plough, as also the 25-yard lines. The field was not as smooth as the bed of the new Blacksburg railroad, but ran up and down hill, with interesting little hollows which hid the play from spectators on the other side of the field.

The first game arranged with St. Albans of Radford and played on the Blacksburg campus ended in a 14-10 victory for VAMC, but the game proved to be a revelation to the team. St. Albans, though heavily outweighed by VAMC boys, was captained by a Yale graduate who demonstrated clearly that football was a game of skill and tactics as well as one of strength, weight, and staying powers.

Largely as a result of the demonstration of skill and tactics displayed by St. Albans, the team of '93 started off "with a determination to really learn the game." Professor Smyth, after studying a book of rules, took the leading role as tutor. As a result of his efforts in this undertaking, he came to be known as "the father of modern football at VPI."

In an effort to help the struggling team, Dr. McBryde took a portion of the horticultural gardens presently included in the eastern end of the drill field and had it converted into a playing field for athletics and military drill. The field had been only partially completed for the '94 season. As a result, the boys played on the raw red earth from which many small stones protruded. Undaunted, however, "the boys spent every minute in the pauses of the game in gathering stones off the field." According to a rumor one player had gathered a stone but wanted to use it on the opposite team instead of throwing it off the field. The player's school was not identified.

Scheduling difficulties were often encountered then as now, but scheduling was usually carried out in a strictly informal manner and seldom far in advance as witness the following letter.

Emory, Virginia
Dec. 5/92

Manager of Football-ball-team
Blacksburg
Virginia

Dear Sir:

We would like to play your team a game of foot ball next Friday the 9th on our grounds.

We will pay half of your expenses, that means half of the expenses of 14 men.

Answer immediately so we can advertise the game.

Your Respt.
Edgar George.
Sec. of Asso.
Emory
Va.

(We expect you to get reduced rates.)

Not only did scheduling of games present problems; finding athletic facilities off campus also was difficult. In response to an inquiry from Smyth, A. L. Lancaster of the Norfolk and Western Railroad Company reported on November 8, 1892, that there was "no ground enclosed about Roanoke suitable for foot ball," but, he said, a field owned by the Jennett Land Company upon which the Cricket Club played could be secured. At the same time, Lancaster offered the team the use of the club rooms of the Roanoke Athletic Association. "In case any of the boys wanted to take a bath after the game," he wrote, the club rooms would come in handy, since they were "fitted up with the latest improvements."

McBryde was unable to help the team financially beyond encouraging friends, faculty, and students to make donations. Amateur plays and "Theatricals" were given on behalf of the team, but until about 1902 most of the financial support for football came out of the pockets of Professors Smyth, Sheib, and Vawter. By the close of the season of 1902, however, the caliber of the teams and the caliber of the opposition played had reached such a level that the "gate," often collected by passing the hat amongst the spectators, left a small cash balance.

Before the end of McBryde's administration, football had become thoroughly entrenched at VPI. Indeed the outstanding record against both state and out-of-state teams established by the end of his administration had gone a long way toward establishing VPI as among Dixie's football elite. The long rivalry with VMI started with a 6-10 loss in 1894 and a 24-0 victory in 1895. No games were played with VMI in '97, '98, and '99 because of a fight after a baseball game in the spring of '96 in Roanoke. Following the resumption of the rivalry in '00 victory see-sawed back and forth between these two teams often enough to develop this series into one of the most interesting in the state. Rivalry with the University of Virginia also started during the period, with Virginia sweeping the first eight games beginning with the one in 1895. Tech won the 1905 game, following which no more games were scheduled with the University until 1923. This absence from the schedule immediately following a Tech victory gave the Techmen a real opportunity to hurl taunts at their sister institution. Columns in the *Tech* indicate that the opportunity was not lost.

Succeeding generations of Techmen long discussed the individual accomplishments of the McBryde-era athletes who did so much to get athletics started at VPI. One of the athletes, Hunter Carpenter ('02), was honored in 1957 by being named to the National Football Hall of Fame. Another great athlete of the era, C. P. (Sally) Miles ('01), before his death in 1966 was known to thousands of alumni as "Mr. VPI" for his numerous outstanding contributions as athlete, coach, athletic director, teacher, dean, and friend.

With the mounting importance of all athletics during his administration, Mc-Bryde felt that a point had been reached beyond which students could not control and manage the program unassisted. James H. Gibboney ('01) thereupon, at McBryde's request, drafted a plan for a permanent manager of athletics. This plan placed the management of athletic affairs in the hands of a graduate manager to be appointed by and responsible to an Athletic Council. The plan went into effect in 1903-04 with Gibboney himself as graduate manager. This plan, although modified from time to time, was the basic one around which athletics developed at Tech for the remaining decades of its first century of history. At the same time the Athletic Association put its revised plan into effect, it also started *The Virginia Tech* under the editorship of Professor J. B. McBryde, son of President

McBryde. The *Tech* remained as the official organ of the Athletic Association until it became the official organ of the student body in 1932.

To paraphrase a statement of *The Bugle,* by the end of McBryde's administration, athletics, thriving upon the superb tonic of a number of victories, had come to Tech to stay.

Lieutenant John A. Harmon, Commandant of Cadets appointed under Lomax, grew in popularity. Encouraged by McBryde, he introduced innovations into the military life of the cadets and was largely instrumental in encouraging the formation of the first drum and bugle corps, which he began to use in the marching formations to and from the mess. The mess had been moved by McBryde from the basement of First Academic Building to the wooden building which stood for so long near the extreme eastern edge of the campus on a site now included in the entrance to the campus mall. The next year the mess was moved to the Pavilion, or old gym, which also was located near this site. Since the cadets roomed in Number One Barracks (Lane Hall), an excellent opportunity for instruction in marching now presented itself as the cadets moved to and from meals. Lieutenant Harmon had taken full advantage of this opportunity and had decided to enliven it with the drum and bugle corps. The decision delighted everyone concerned and a number not concerned. The editor of the *Gray Jacket,* in an enthusiastic report on the situation, announced that the merry peal of the drum and bugle corps "has been sounded over the campus and throughout the city of Blacksburg. No doubt it has added greatly to the military feature of the college."

The first use of the organization for the march from barracks to mess was reported to have "stirred within the boys a feeling like that which animated their old forefathers of Revolutionary times." The occasion attracted a large crowd which lined the walk and broke into loud cheers as the drum and bugle corps strutted by to the tune of "Dixie." This cheering plus the excitement of the tune was too much for the cadets to resist, and they too took up the song as they swung along in the march to the mess. As the last of the cadets marched by, the small boys lining the path of march "fell in" and brought up the rear, followed by their dogs which "dashed madly about and added to the happy uproar with their delirious barking." Everyone went home happy, while a definite boost had been given to a rapidly developing esprit de corps in the student body, which during the year began to take the first groping steps toward a permanent Corps organization.

In June, just before commencement, Lieutenant Harmon took the Corps as a military unit to Roanoke to participate in the decennial celebration of the city. One of the major orators of that celebration was John E. Penn, whose activities on behalf of establishing the Virginia Agricultural and Mechanical College have been related. His presentation dealt with the past history of the Big Lick-Roanoke community. It would be interesting indeed if we could know what this founding father thought as he watched the parading Corps of Cadets of the school which his activities had done much to create.

McBryde was a strong advocate of campus beautification. He reviewed and added to W. W. Blackford's original plan for campus improvement and then volunteered to supervise the implementation of the plan. He particularly wanted more shrubbery and trees placed around the campus and adjacent to college buildings. In the execution of this part of his improvement program, he received valuable assistance from Professor E. A. Smyth, Jr. McBryde and Smyth deserve credit for planting more than two thousand ornamental trees, some of which have survived successive encroachments of campus construction and today lend shade and dignity to areas once bleak and barren.

To help improve the appearance of the campus, McBryde bought "a pony lawnmower with which to shave the grass." Apparently this was the first such machine ever seen in the community and attracted almost as much attention as the cadet parades at the commencement which in 1892 was held in a tent erected near the present Henderson Hall.

Rain at commencement time was as much a problem then as now, it seems, for a rainstorm which occurred during the Sunday services "necessitated a liberal use of umbrellas among the audience" in the tent. Unverified tradition has it that the tallest member of the graduating class held an umbrella over the minister and his Bible during the sermon. It may or may not be significant that McBryde secured as minister for the occasion the editor of the *Christian Advocate,* the paper which the students under Lomax had accused of unfair bias toward the College.

Following the Sunday rainstorm, the weather cleared; and the commencement exercises continued. Dr. Lafferty, the Methodist who had preached on Sunday, was followed by Dr. A. E. Owens, a Baptist who spoke in the evening to the YMCA. On Monday, Mr. Robert Snavely ('76), quite prominent in the Farmers' Alliance, spoke to the alumni. Hal D. Flood, senator from Appomattox County, spoke to the literary societies on Tuesday; and Colonel A. S. Buford, well-known businessman and "eloquent speaker" from Richmond, was Wednesday's speaker. Faculty members with denominational affiliations not represented by the major speakers were used extensively in opening and closing the ceremonies by prayer. The German Club held a final ball which lasted into the "wee sma' hours of the morning." With representatives of the churches, the alumni, the Farmers' Alliance, the politicians, the business world, and the socially inclined given a chance to participate in the commencement, it is no wonder the editor of the *Gray Jacket* pronounced the occasion, "one of the most entertaining in the history of the College."

During the early years of McBryde's administration, the fate of the College clearly shifted from factional politics in the legislature into the hands of the Board of Visitors and the faculty. Many individuals helped bring about this situation, but McBryde as president has been accorded the major credit. The Agricultural Experiment Station helped matters by its publication of bulletins having practical value to the farmers and by numerous articles published in *The Southern Planter.* In the earlier days, members of the station staff engaged in a number of off-campus activities which today would be assigned to the Extension Division workers. The work of William B. Alwood in experimental research and with farm groups over the state is particularly noteworthy. It is difficult to determine whether Alwood helped the College most by his research and publications or by contacts with farmers and rural legislators in the state. But certainly, in the words of H. N. Young, "Alwood was a giant among the early pioneers at the Virginia Station."

Very early in his administration McBryde undertook a campus building program. As student enrollment increased, he began asking for the money for appropriations with which to erect dormitories. But increased enrollment also required an increased number of faculty members who, McBryde pointed out, absolutely could not find satisfactory housing "in the village" of Blacksburg. To meet the situation he proposed building both dormitories and faculty homes. At the time, very little grading had been done on the campus. Number One Barracks had been built on a ridge which extended down toward the present Duck Pond, where it leveled out into the small flat surrounding Solitude. To the front, this ridge sloped rather sharply toward the present College Avenue, while to the rear it sloped much less sharply back toward the present power plant. Both the front and the back of this ridge were further broken up by smaller hollows and ridges, but the entire area to the west of Number One Barracks sloped with a deceptive steepness toward the Duck Pond end of the campus. To the east of First Academic Building, the ground sloped downward into a rather flat north and south hollow and then ascended in a gradual slope up to the street level of the entrance to the present Mall.

In 1892, the section of the campus west of Brodie to the general site of Williams, thence north to Derring and then back to Major Williams was a wheatfield. The area in front of Rasche and Brodie extending to College Avenue was a hayfield, and the area generally westward from Robeson was an orchard. The present drill field was much smaller and had been laid off in garden plots for the horticulture department and the experiment station. Strombles Creek, which had not been enclosed, extended along the entire southern edge of the drill field and in the spring of the year turned the area between the present Davidson and Price Halls into a swampy morass. No buildings of any significance were south or west of the circular drive now enclosing the drill field.

McBryde was successful in persuading the legislature to appropriate money or to issue bonds for a number of college buildings during his administration, although he was not satisfied with the number of faculty homes he was able to have erected. In 1894, Number Two Barracks, the old section of Rasche Hall, was built; and Number Three Barracks, the old section of Brodie, was erected in 1900. In 1902, Number Four Barracks, the old section of Shanks Hall, was completed; and in 1904, Number Five Barracks, the old section of Major Williams Hall, was completed. The location of these buildings was such that they formed a quadrangle with Number One Barracks (Lane Hall) in the center. These dormitories provided the only on-campus housing for male students until 1929.

In the summer of 1894, a "boulevard" was constructed from a point midway between the stone steps of the present Student Personnel Building and the northwest corner of Brodie Hall in a southwesterly direction toward the present Duck Pond. The land was graded, and Faculty Row gradually came into existence along this road. Most of these houses faced in a southerly direction toward the drill field. Many of them had lots fenced off in the rear which were used for family gardens or for sheds within which to house a cow or a horse. The development of Faculty Row as a housing project for the staff presented the administration with some unexpected problems. An order of social prestige was soon established for each house. As one result, McBryde and succeeding presidents often were besieged with requests for reassignments of houses as professors sought to better the position of wives and family in the campus peck order. In other instances, younger staff members having been assigned a house of low peck order boosted their ego by adding such conveniences as furnaces, kitchen sinks, closets, bay windows, porch railings, and the like. Oftentimes at a later date, these individuals, if planning to sever their connection with VPI, would present the administration with an unexpected bill for the improvement. The bill was usually accompanied by a promise to "remove the said improvement if it was not satisfactory." McBryde objected very strongly to the practice, but he usually recommended the payment of the bill, since, as he said, securing satisfactory homes for the faculty in the town was almost an "utter impossibility."

Perhaps the most serious result growing from the development of Faculty Row and other on-campus housing for faculty was the tendency of such housing to separate the faculty, particularly in its social life, from the leading citizens of the community. This separation definitely tended to alienate the two groups. Since many of these citizens were descended from old Virginia families and had extensive connections throughout the county and the state, the exclusion from campus social affairs felt by this group often expressed itself in lukewarm support, or open hostility, to local legislation which appeared to benefit the College more than the county. There is considerable evidence to support the belief that the construction of a hard-surfaced road from Christiansburg to Blacksburg was delayed for a number of years because the daughter of a local citizen had not been invited to a party in a Faculty Row home.

Since these homes often had attractive young ladies growing up in them, it was not long before Faculty Row Boulevard was subjected by the students to an usual variety of marching formations, band serenades, and survey parties, to say nothing of the casual hikes from the barracks to Solitude and back. Later, as the campus expanded westward, Faculty Row was swallowed up house by house by such buildings as McBryde, Holden, Norris, Pamplin, and Burruss, whose tunnel rests astride the old Faculty Row.

In 1901, a large three-story brick building was erected on the site of the present addition to Shanks Hall to be used for a science hall. This building, quite modern for its time, unhappily was destroyed by fire in February of 1905. Without waiting for an appropriation from the legislature, the board immediately rebuilt on the same site, and the resulting building was used as a science hall until 1927 when it was remodeled into a dormitory. This building was removed in 1957 to make room for an addition to Shanks Hall.

During President McBryde's administration, the college erected some sixty-seven new buildings and renovated six old ones. Some of these buildings which survived the onslaught of progress long enough to become landmarks in the eyes of older alumni may be mentioned for "auld lang syne."

All of the administrations before McBryde's had experimented with ways in which to improve the mess system. Early in his administration, McBryde addressed himself to this problem and during the summer of 1894 saw the completion of a combination mess hall and commencement hall. This building was located near the present junction of Main Street with the north corner of the Mall, near the Pavilion, or old gymnasium. It was greatly enlarged in 1904-05 with four floors added to one addition. The first floor was used as a mess, and the second floor was used for commencements, assemblies, and entertainment. For a number of years at a later time the College YMCA provided weekly movies in the second floor assembly room. The movies were usually held immediately after supper and became so popular with the cadets that a system of strict military formation for leaving the dining room had to be inaugurated in order to prevent dangerous crowding on the stairway to the second floor. The movies were silent, but the cadets were not; they offered free advice to the stalwart heroes and the beautiful queens of the not-so-silver screen.

This building known to succeeding generations of students by such names as Commencement Hall, Mess Hall, German Hall, and finally as Commerce Hall, was torn down in 1957 only after a thorough inspection showed it could no longer be kept or made safe for occupancy. Whatever its name, this building was the mecca for thousands of alumni who upon returning to the campus wished to pay tribute to mess stewards Shultz and J. J. (Pop) Owens.

The present Student Personnel Building was completed in 1901 as a building for the College YMCA. This building, the first on campus to be built from native stone, was paid for from donations raised from private sources. The idea of a "Y" building originated with William E. Dodd ('98), later to become a distinguished author and professor of history at the University of Chicago and ambassador to Germany during President Woodrow Wilson's administration. The funds for the building were secured by faculty and students with Lawrence W. Priddy ('97) taking the lead. Priddy "traveled north and south" soliciting funds for the building. On one occasion he attempted to call at the home of a wealthy New York philanthropist, only to be turned away by the haughty butler. The undaunted Priddy thereupon rented formal attire and the next day dressed in patent-leather shoes, striped trousers, Prince Albert coat, top hat, gloves, and carrying a cane presented himself before the same butler, who immediately admitted him to the house. Priddy got his donation. At the ceremonies celebrating the laying of the cornerstone for the "Y" building, Priddy humorously was introduced as "the most insistent, persistent, and consistent beggar ever turned out by VPI." Alumni who remember this same individual's efforts in raising funds for the World War I Memorial Gymnasium will echo an admiring but fervent assent to this description of this unusual individual.

The publicity given to the ceremonies at the laying of the cornerstone had one interesting and unexpected result. One individual wanted to know if it was legal for the Board of Visitors to grant permission to a religious organization to occupy a building and hold religious services on the campus of a state school. This was a surprising and startling question in the context of the times. The particular individual did not challenge the legality of the action; on the contrary, he was in favor of it, but he wanted to be sure all monetary contributions to the "Y" would be used for the "Y." The matter was put before the legislature, and this body on February 3, 1900, while the building was yet under construction, decided that the agreement between the board and the YMCA of the Virginia Polytechnic Institute was legal. To remove all doubt, the legislature then passed a special act ratifying and confirming the agreement which the board had made with the YMCA. This action proved to be a momentous and fortunate one for the College, since it is doubtful if any non-instructional organization in the history of VPI made as many significant contributions to its growth and welfare as the YMCA.

Years later, in 1937, the "Y" offices were moved to Squires Hall and the "Y" building assigned to the military and other departments. As a result, the building was called the Military Building until the location in it of additional offices concerned with student personnel led to its present name.

To provide more room for academic instruction, the administrative offices were moved from First Academic Building to a building then located at the present north corner of the drill field about halfway between Newman Library and Patton Hall. At the time, the drill field had not been graded; in fact, most of it was in vegetable gardens. Since the grounds sloped rather abruptly from this building southward toward the garden plots which later became a part of the present drill field, the hill beside this administration building became a favorite spot from which to watch parades and athletic events after they were moved from behind Number One Barracks to the drill field.

Unfortunately, the building burned in February, 1900, the same year the administrative offices had been moved into it. Since the fire occurred at night, many records, including most of the minutes of earlier Boards of Visitors, were lost. Following this fire, the administrative offices were moved to the commandant's house, which older alumni will remember as standing on a site just east of the First Academic Building (now Rasche Hall). At this time, the plank fences surrounding the commandant's house were removed and the grounds thrown into the campus. In 1904, the administrative offices were moved back to a house rebuilt on the site of the one destroyed by fire in 1900 and remained there until 1936, when they were moved to Burruss Hall. In 1950, the old building was torn down to make way for an enlarged drill field and the approaches to the World War II Memorial.

As the College continued to develop under Dr. McBryde's effective supervision, more and more buildings were needed. Happily, the legislature recognized these needs and cooperated in trying to meet them. Only two more of the numerous buildings erected under McBryde's supervision will be mentioned.

In May, 1905, a stone building erected for a chapel was completed on the site now occupied by Newman Library. To erect this building, one of the original faculty homes built by President Minor was torn down. At the time of its demolition, it was being used for classrooms by the department of agriculture. This stone chapel and some of its rooms probably housed a greater variety of activities or services than any other building of its size on the campus. In addition to being used for daily chapel, it or a part of it was used at one time or another for a tailor shop, a dwelling, faculty room, Board of Visitors room, dance hall, gymnasium, kitchen, student activities room, arsenal, storage room, coed social room, classroom, and finally a library. It was converted to this latter usage in 1914, at which time it was glowingly reported that its facilities could be altered from time to time with sufficient ease to provide adequate library space "for the next fifty years." This happy prophecy proved to be in error, however, since the building burned even as it was being removed in 1953 to make way for the present Newman Library.

To provide for the expanding program in agriculture, an agricultural hall was erected and occupied first in 1907. This building known to generations of students as the Aggie Hall was the first of the numerous buildings to be erected around what is now known as the agricultural quadrangle. It has undergone a number of remodelings and is now known as Price Hall, named after Harvey L. Price, dean of agriculture from 1908-1945. As the field of agriculture expanded, necessitating the erection of new buildings in the area of Price Hall, this building came to be looked upon as the "capital" of agriculture in Virginia. With the erection of Hutcheson Hall, so named for John Redd Hutcheson and his brother Thomas Barksdale Hutcheson, most of the administrative offices concerned with agricultural programs of teaching, research, and extension were gradually shifted to this newer building. As a result, the "capital" for state agriculture was moved to this building, where, if there is such an entity as a capital for agriculture, it will be found today.

One additional physical landmark erected during McBryde's administration will be remembered with mixed emotions by thousands of alumni and probably by some parents of alumni as well. To replace the water system using the tank back of the Preston and Olin Building, which had proved to be inadequate for the rapidly expanding College, McBryde had an entirely new system installed. Water from a huge spring on land purchased in the vicinity of Lane Stadium was pumped to a huge tank erected some 130 feet into the air on the hill where the Coliseum now stands. Since this hill was approximately thirty feet higher than the highest building on the campus (as practically every student survey party had to prove) the combined elevation of the hill and the tank provided sufficient head to put water under pressure into every building. The tank of 50,000 gallons capacity stood on four strongly fabricated metal columns, one of which was constructed to make a ladder leading up to a platform which encircled the tank. Another ladder starting from the platform led up the side of the tank and over the edge to the very top. Climbing this tower, erected under the supervision of Professors Patton and Randolph, for whom Patton Hall and Randolph Hall have been named, stood as a perpetual challenge to every venturesome freshmen. As school spirit, and especially class spirit, increased, one particularly enthusiastic freshman, or "rat," not only climbed the tower one moonlit night but also took a bucket of paint along and in huge numbers painted his class numerals on the side of the tank visible all over the campus as well as from much of the countryside. At the same time, he advertised his low opinion of the sophomore class by use of appropriately insulting references also painted on the tank.

The next day, the sophomores after a number of excited conferences with each other decided upon a method of retaliation. They decided to use the authority allowed them as sophomores, to hold special semi-military formations of freshmen at times which did not conflict with regularly scheduled activities. This time the decision was reached to hold such a formation on Sunday afternoon and march the freshmen to the water tank, where, under the supervision of the sophomores, the freshmen would be required to hold a mock funeral marking the demise of their class numeral as it was painted out and replaced by that of the sophomore class. Following the triumphant appearance of the sophomore numeral, the freshmen were to stage a scene of rejoicing and jubilation to celebrate the privilege of "looking up at the numeral for the class of select men."

As it happened, both classes had some unusually witty speakers to assume the various roles demanded by the occasion. These speakers held forth to the delight of all, with the "rats" gaining a decided edge with their sly thrusts at the sophomores in the forensic activities of the day. Despite their underdog role, the "rats" enjoyed the occasion as much as the sophomores, if not more, and visited a repeat performance upon next year's "rats." From that time forth, a variety of activities involved in getting class numerals on and off the water tank engaged the earnest efforts of succeeding generations of freshmen and sophomores for years to come. Fortunately no one ever fell from the tower, although in succeeding years some of the activities on the ground degenerated into flagrant cases of hazing. When the always questionable authority to hold special freshmen formations was at last diverted from the sophomores, the on-ground ceremonies at the water tank were discontinued; but class numerals continued to appear on the tower year after year. Finally, in an effort to reduce the hazard involved in painting the tower, a high fence was built around the entire base of the supporting columns and a barricade built on the ladder. This precaution succeeded to a limited extent; but in 1957 when workmen appeared on the scene ready to remove the tank, one final class numeral had been painted on it the night before and toppled to the ground along with the tank as it came crashing down. Thus ended a half-century-long practice which perhaps should never have started anyway.

Ever since its opening in 1872, the College had been plagued by lack of adequate health facilities. College physicians had been employed, but in spite of their best efforts (one bitter critic said because of their best efforts) epidemics of varying degrees of severity occurred almost annually. If the disease causing the epidemic was one of the more serious ones, the students usually fled the campus and went home, regardless of regulations to the contrary. During the latter years of Lomax's administration an epidemic of typhoid fever had threatened a temporary closing of the school. McBryde hoped to prevent any such recurrence. In addition to securing and protecting a better source of water, he began the installation of a sewerage system. Unfortunately, lack of knowledge concerning the proper installation of sewer lines created a number of immediate problems and laid the foundations for future threats of lawsuits for a number of years before the old lines could be replaced. In addition to better water and sewerage McBryde wanted an infirmary. The legislature was reluctant to make an appropriation for this purpose, however; therefore, McBryde converted campus residences to this purpose for a number of years. Finally, a decision was made to build a new home for the president and then completely remodel his old home into a permanent infirmary. This was done, and the president's home located in the Grove was completed and occupied by McBryde in 1902. With the completion of the president's new home, his older one was remodeled with the addition of two stories to serve as wards and then used as an infirmary. In 1951, the infirmary was enlarged once more after having been named Henderson Hall in honor of Dr. William F. Henderson, college surgeon and consulting physician, 1890-1935. It was to this infirmary that Miss Anna G. Hannas came in 1906 to preside for the next thirty-nine years as superintendent of the infirmary, nurse, confidante, mother to the homesick, and friend to all. Hundreds of alumni, who remembered her strict professional bedside manner which changed into a warm outgoing personality in the "parlor" of her apartment attached to the infirmary, literally beat a path to her door at homecoming and other occasions of their return to the campus until her retirement in 1945.

McBryde's achievements in the physical growth and development of the College, which have been only partly recounted here, are all the more astonishing in view of the two decades of struggling existence experienced by the school prior to his administration. Even the students became caught up in the headiness of being a part of a growing institution and presented extravagant reports proclaiming the progress and achievements of the College. The newly introduced technical work proved to be especially exciting to the students even if it was not always understood by the parents. Thus, one student greatly alarmed one mother when, after giving an enthusiastic description of the newly equipped shops, he added that the College was now equipped to offer the best class in "forgery" to be found in the country.

Although McBryde's contribution to the physical growth and development of the school was phenomenal, the programs of education he established in agricultural and mechanical education and the foundations he laid for additional instruction in, "such branches of learning as are related to agriculture and the mechanic arts," were of far greater significance. The decision to develop a school of technology with emphasis on agriculture and mechanic arts removed the internal controversy which had plagued previous administrations in their groping struggle to establish an acceptable mission for the College. In organizing the degree programs under the headings of either agriculture or mechanics, McBryde secured the wholehearted support and endorsement of every major segment of public sentiment in the state. In stressing the fact that the College as a school of technology was filling an expressed need in the state, he secured the support of educational-industrial organizations which had started clamoring for such a program about 1885. In his approach to the teaching of agriculture and mechanics by differentiating these broad fields into their integral parts and providing instruction for each resulting part, he widened the opportunity for student selection of programs in each field. In addition to expanding student choices this approach also laid the foundations for further differentiation into additional courses as new knowledge was developed and acquired in each field or subdivision. McBryde's insistence on developing sound programs in the subjects "related to agriculture and mechanics," plus his interpretation of what these subjects were, laid the foundation for the development of such fields as physics, chemistry, geology, English, modern languages, economics, and several branches of biology. While the official publications continued to use the term mechanics, the degree courses in this area were listed as degrees in engineering; therefore the designation of mechanics was soon dropped in favor of the more appealing term of engineering.

In 1893, McBryde was offered the position of assistant secretary of agriculture in President Grover Cleveland's administration. It happened that this offer was publicized at a time McBryde was scheduled to make a trip to Baltimore. While there, he decided to stop over in Washington on his way back to visit the Department of Agriculture. The newspapers reported this visit, and rumors immediately spread that he was planning to accept the new position. In spite of McBryde's insistence that he was not leaving, the rumors continued to persist until some of the papers reported in detail his trip to Baltimore and the side trip to Washington as a courtesy call. With the realization that McBryde had turned down a position of national renown and chosen to remain at the College, the chorus singing his praises and expressing approval of his reorganized program swelled to a new pitch. The editor of the *Gray Jacket* expressed deep gratification that "our beloved president" had decided to stay at the College. McBryde for his part seemed unaware of all the speculation as he continued his efforts to build a technical school. In catalogs and press releases, the following statement was placed before the public over and over: "The sciences, especially those related to Agriculture and the Mechanic Arts, hold in this College, in strict accordance with the acts of Congress from which it derives its income, the foremost place. Large provision is made for instruction in their principles and applications to the industries of life."

A number of people upon reading this statement and upon an examination of McBryde's organization of the College, saw that he had in fact combined in one institution agriculture, mechanics, and scientific technology. The name Virginia Agricultural and Mechanical College indicated instruction in the first two fields but ignored the last one. With general realization of this fact a movement was started to bring the name of the College into greater harmony with its actual program. Regrettably the records concerning this movement are not available, apparently having been lost or burned in the fire of 1900, which destroyed the administrative building. According to the *Gray Jacket,* however, it is quite clear that the need for a name change had been widely discussed, on the campus at least, before any definite conclusion or proposal had been reached. Finally, an agreement was reached to request the legislature to include the words "Poly-technic Institute" in the title. In the absence of definite information, it is hard to assign responsibility for the suggestion; but it probably came from McBryde, although it could have come from Rector Vawter just as well. A bill was intro-duced into the state Senate by Senator Henry L. Maynard ('80) of Norfolk, Vir-ginia, proposing the change. Maynard's bill was enacted into law on March 5, 1896, thereby making the official name of the College Virginia Agricultural and Mechanical College and Polytechnic Institute.

According to Henry A. Wise ('98) Dr. McBryde held a special assembly to announce "to the student body the change in name of the college." Continuing, Wise wrote, "It was understood at the time the [name] Virginia Agricultural and Mechanical College had to be carried as a part of the name in order to continue to receive the grant that the college was receiving from the federal government."

As every alumnus knows, the name by popular usage was immediately short-ened to Virginia Polytechnic Institute, which in turn became Virginia Tech or simply VPI.

The editor of the *Gray Jacket* was delighted with the change of names and felt that the alumni would be happy too when they realized that the College could now compete more favorably with the other schools not only in curriculum and placement of graduates but also in the recruiting of new staff members. Then, in the same editorial, as if embarrassed by his own enthusiasm, he solemnly reminded the staff and his fellow students that a name alone would not make a college great. Greatness, he proclaimed, would depend upon a great many addi-tional factors, not the least of which would be student reaction and effort.

No information is available as to any catalytic effect the name change may have had on academic performance, but in the realm of student activities it was stimulating. Athletics, particularly football, were beginning to gain in popularity, but the original College yell previously quoted was no longer suitable. A student contest was held, and O. M. Stull ('96) won a prize for his new yell, the now famous Old Hokie. Stull successfully incorporated the desirable parts of the new name into his yell which in the original ran thus:

Hoki, Hoki, Hoki Hy!
Tech! Tech! V.P.I.!
Sola-Rex Sola-Rah
Polytech-Vir-gin-i-a! !
Rae, Ri, V.P.I.

In after years, Stull chucklingly admitted that the words he used had no hidden or symbolic meaning whatever, but had been thought up in an effort to get attention. This effort was successful, as thousands of persons attending Tech's athletic contests over the past three quarters of a century can testify.

With the new name, a new yell, and a new athletic field slowly developing on the sites of the old cabbage and bean patches, new college colors seemed desirable. The Corps, with the help of Dr. Sheib and others, after much investigation came up with Chicago maroon and burnt orange as a suitable combination with which to replace the old black and gray. These colors were adopted as the official college colors in the fall of 1896 and were first worn in a football game with Roanoke College on October 26, 1896.

During the same year the motto "Ut Prosim" translated from Latin to mean "That I Might Serve" or "That I May Do Good" was adopted, while the college seal which the Board of Visitors made official in 1963 was put into use. Unhappily, records concerning the circumstances surrounding the origin of the motto and the seal have not been located; but it is well known that McBryde and his son John were adept in designing seals and suggesting mottos.

With the passage of time, the use of the words *Agricultural and Mechanical College* passed so completely out of all usage except in official documents, that many alumni, sports writers, and other residents of the state were unaware of the full official name of the school. It is desirable to anticipate events a bit here and to record the fact that in 1944 the legislature dropped the words *Agricultural and Mechanical College* and officially made the name what common usage already had made it, namely Virginia Polytechnic Institute. In 1970, following spectacular development and growth in the College, the name of the school was changed once again in order to secure harmony with the actual program being conducted by the institution. This time the name was altered to read Virginia Polytechnic Institute and State University.

McBryde had continued to plan and forge ahead toward the development of a technical school even as all of these exciting "births" had taken place. In 1891 he had started a program of graduate study which in its inception was little more than a year's additional work in at least three courses. Each student was permitted to work out his program with the professor of his choice, completely unfettered by graduate program requirements or regulations. Fortunately, the number of graduate students was quite small and the resulting ratio of one student to one professor was quite successful in preparing a number of students who upon completion of their graduate work went on to achieve distinguished careers as teachers, researchers, scientists, and business executives. The graduate work continued in this rather loosely organized fashion until the creation of a graduate department in 1907, with William E. Barlow as dean.

As early as 1891, financial aid was given to some graduate students selected to serve as assistants where they were needed. As the student enrollment increased, more and more fellowships were awarded with the understanding that the recipient would teach a specified number of classes. At first, the president evaluated this plan as helpful to both VPI and the student. After a thorough trial of ten years, however, he did not look upon the plan so happily. Most of these student teachers, he reported, were more interested in preparing for their non-academic careers than they were in preparing for their teaching, which they looked upon as temporary. Few, if any, wished to remain at VPI on a permanent basis but left upon receipt of the first promising outside offer, sometimes in the middle of the year. Nearly all of the fellowship recipients left at the end of the first year, just as they were beginning to be of some real value as teachers.

Furthermore, reported McBryde, there was another even more serious problem. In the early years, these graduate students had taught freshman classes; but as the enrollment and the curriculum had expanded, it had been necessary to assign them to teach the more advanced courses. This practice, McBryde believed, had made the undergraduates unhappy and restless and at the same time was extremely dangerous to the reputation of the College. As a solution to the problem, McBryde advanced three possibilities for the board's consideration. First, he indicated the possibility of rigidly restricting enrollment growth, strengthening the existing programs, and returning graduate students to teaching freshmen classes. McBryde objected strongly to this proposal as a solution on the grounds that deliberately planning to strengthen the status quo instead of planning for solid growth and expansion would lead to retrogression and deterioration. As a second possibility he pointed out that the board could apply to the legislature for more financial assistance to enlarge the physical facilities needed to keep up with the steady increases in student enrollment. The increase in enrollment for the session of 1902-03, McBryde believed, was larger than that of any other school in the South. As one result, the College was now seriously overstrained in all of its efforts.

As a third possibility, which in reality was a part of his second one, McBryde suggested the hiring of six to ten well-trained young men who planned to make teaching their life work. These young men would replace the graduate students as teachers, especially in the upper classes. McBryde wanted them hired with the distinct understanding that opportunities for promotion and advancement awaited them if they performed satisfactorily.

The board accepted the second and third possibilities with far more enthusiasm than did the legislature, which was still more inclined to vote for investigations than appropriations. Enough money was secured, however, to make a start in the direction of McBryde's third proposal, and he immediately began to replace the graduate student teachers with permanent ones. He soon found, though, that he was unable to attract enough young men from other colleges and was forced to depend upon outstanding students from his own institution.

While the tendency toward inbreeding which McBryde's policy promoted cannot be denied, neither can the magnificent contribution to the College made by so many of his VPI-trained recruits be overlooked. This fact can be emphasized dramatically by a casual examination of the performance of such of his recruits to the faculty as W. M. Brodie, W. G. Conner, A. W. Drinkard, H. H. Hill, J. S. A. Johnson, Claudius Lee, C. P. Miles, H. L. Price, F. L. Robeson, J. W. Watson, and others.

As the Virginia Polytechnic Institute continued to grow in course offerings, in faculty, in size of the student body, and in the affections of the people, it began to experience an onset of growing pains. The legislature had been rather generous in its appropriations for the erection of dormitories, but it had not contributed to the support of the necessary auxiliary agencies with the same degree of generosity. The student enrollment, officially reported as 150 when McBryde assumed the presidency in 1891, had climbed to 727 by 1903-04. Charles E. Vawter, who as an educational administrator on the Board of Visitors had been a tower of strength in helping McBryde, had resigned from the board for reasons of health in 1899. He had been succeeded as rector by J. Thompson Brown, an able, competent individual but one with no experience in educational administration. The board, under Brown, backed McBryde wholeheartedly; but it just as wholeheartedly waited for him to lead the way and plan for the future. But McBryde was getting bogged down in attending to the rapidly increasing administrative details less onerous when the College was smaller. He needed help; but as he admitted to the board, he was not sure as to which of the many problems needed it most.

He was particularly concerned about the developments within the Corps of Cadets which he believed if not corrected would cause trouble later. He was absolutely correct. In 1891, the Corps, as McBryde pointed out, had been housed in Number One Barracks, with seventy-four rooms, all under the supervision of one commandant. Now, in 1902, there were four separate barracks with more than two hundred and fifty rooms to be supervised. Because of unusually heavy demands for admission to the College, McBryde added, many of the rooms had three or even four occupants. In spite of this tremendous increase, one man as commandant was still expected to supervise the barracks, provide instruction in military science and tactics, and supervise the general conduct of the Corps twenty-four hours of the day. In 1898, Lieutenant Shanks, the commandant of cadets, had been ordered to duty in the Philippines and had been succeeded by A. T. Finch, ('92). Finch had resigned in 1900 and had been succeeded by J. S. A. Johnson, ('98), who had been appointed as assistant professor of mechanical engineering and military science and commandant of cadets. As the work load had increased, young instructors, graduates of VPI, had been employed as instructors and part-time assistants to the commandant of cadets.

McBryde was complimentary of the devotion and effort put forth by these civilian commandants of cadets, but he felt better results might be obtained if he had a military career officer as commandant. The students felt the same way and said so in the columns of the *Gray Jacket*. Although not a graduate of a military school, McBryde was inordinately proud of the Corps of Cadets, which he proudly displayed by arranging trips for it to Buffalo, New York; St. Louis, Missouri; Charleston, South Carolina; and Norfolk, Richmond, and Roanoke, Virginia. During the Spanish-American War the Corps had tried to volunteer as a unit but had not been accepted by the United States Government. Commandant D. C. Shanks, however, before leaving for the Philippines, according to W. B. Harper ('99) asked J. P. (Pete) Harvey, leader of the VPI Band, "to prevail upon the band to join the Second Virginia Regiment of Volunteer Infantry as regimental band." The band, said Harper, was not allowed to go as a unit, but most of its cadet members resigned from school and enlisted individually. In addition to the cadet members, said Harper, "We picked up some players from town and also from Christiansburg." Following the War Harvey and most of the band members and other cadets who had enlisted in the army returned to the Blacksburg campus.

The return of veterans to the Corps did not add an element of tranquility to barracks life.

McBryde became convinced that in order to promote further growth of the Corps and to provide proper supervision of barracks living conditions and conduct, the time had come to employ several full-time assistant commandants or a full-time commandant with several part-time assistants. Several years passed before he was able to put his ideas into full operation, however, and by that time a number of disciplinary problems erupted on the campus.

In order to help solve some of the increased academic-administrative problems caused by the growth of the College, McBryde with the full support of the board, created the office of dean of the faculty and appointed E. A. Smyth, Jr., to the post in 1903. In 1904, he effected a more thorough administrative plan by organizing the College into four departments, each with its own faculty and dean: academic department, Professor T. P. Campbell, dean; scientific department, Professor William M. Patton, dean; agricultural department, Professor A. M. Soule, dean. At the same time, McBryde relinquished the direction of the agricultural experiment station to Soule, while J. S. A. Johnson continued as commandant of cadets and E. A. Smyth, Jr., as dean of the faculty. This group of five deans and the commandant was then organized into an executive council; but unfortunately, neither the faculty nor the students knew what duties this new organization was expected to perform. Neither did the executive council.

The first results were both unhappy and unexpected. As McBryde reported it, Professor Alwood resigned because he had not been appointed director of the Experiment Station, and Professor R. C. Price resigned because he had not been appointed dean of the scientific department. As a result, said McBryde, "their friends endeavored to create, and with some success, prejudice against the new organization given to the administrative department, by circulation of all kinds of injurious reports—all without foundation in fact." "One of the instructors who had been removed from the college also endeavored to give trouble," he added.

Alwood's resignation had been particularly distressing to McBryde, since it had resulted from complete misunderstanding between the two men. Alwood, one of the truly great scientists of early VPI, after more than a decade of dedicated service, had become greatly discouraged over lack of financial support for his research. About a year prior to his resignation he had gone to McBryde to discuss the situation. In the lengthy discussion and planning which followed, Alwood got the impression he was in line for the directorship of the station and perhaps for the deanship of agriculture. McBryde, on the other hand, got the impression that Alwood did not want either the directorship or the deanship. With the announcement of the appointment of Andrew Soule as dean of agriculture and director of the Agricultural Experiment Station, Alwood had immediately demanded an explanation from McBryde regarding the change of plans. McBryde's surprised answer and detailed explanation had been unsatisfactory to Alwood, who immediately protested to the board and then resigned.

By way of an interesting epilogue it may be added that Alwood, having left the institution, continued his career but never lost his love for VPI. During his lifetime he donated a number of valuable books and papers to the library and kept in close touch with VPI and one of his early proteges, Harvey L. Price, dean of the school of agriculture. As an old man in his eighties, Alwood wrote to President Burruss in 1943 to request that if possible a VPI cadet bugler be allowed to blow taps at his, Alwood's, funeral. "I listened to taps so many years at VPI that I would like those, to me, beautiful notes to be sounded on the occasion," he wrote. Burruss promised to honor the request if possible. As it turned out, John R. Hutcheson was president when Alwood died, but knowing of the request he saw to it that it was honored by personally providing transportation for a cadet bugler to attend the services.

Just why Professor R. C. Price had resigned because he had been passed over for a deanship is not entirely clear, but along with his resignation he too had written a strong letter of protest to McBryde and to some members of the Board of Visitors.

The young instructor who had been released at the time of the administrative reorganization had protested bitterly to McBryde, the board, and the students. He had secured a number of affidavits from this latter group attesting to his fitness as a teacher and with McBryde's permission had appeared before the board. His popularity with the students had led some of this group to demand his restoration to the faculty. In addition to these disturbances, some of the farmers who had worked with Alwood in the Farmers' Institute were expressing unhappiness over his departure. The results of McBryde's efforts to put the growing institution on a broader administrative basis seemingly had created more problems than it had solved.

The second result from the administrative reorganization was equally unexpected and unhappy. The group of newly appointed deans, exercising their new authority with the zeal of earnest neophytes, found unused, obsolete, or long-ignored rules and regulations affecting such matters as class absences, sick reports, conduct, and admissions to senior standing. Having discovered these rules which many students, as well as the professors, had never heard of, the deans proceeded to apply them with what the students thought was an unbecoming rigidity or even unfairness. As one result of the sudden application of these old rules, it was belatedly discovered that "quite a considerable percentage of the class, which is the largest Senior Class we have ever had, were so far behind in their studies that they had no chance of graduation." This element of the class, McBryde believed, had been disloyal and ever ready to stir up trouble at the first opportunity. The opportunity came in December when a member of the Junior Class played a prank which today probably would go unnoticed beyond a laugh, but which at the time was interpreted by the executive council as "an outrageous breach of discipline."

Using straw from two student mattresses and pieces of a gaudy uniform salvaged from a Tech Minstrel show, plus some pieces of a discarded cadet uniform, a comically dressed effigy purporting to be the commandant had been hung from the electric wires running between two barracks. A vigorous investigation which succeeded in publicizing the incident in the state press, identified the guilty student, who forthwith had been punished. His classmates, however, according to the official report, had been inclined to believe the student's "gross misstatements to the effect that he had not had a fair trial but had been treated with contumely by the Faculty." The Junior Class met at once and issued a demand that the faculty rescind its action by the next afternoon. When the next afternoon had passed without the faculty's having met to consider the demand, the class, already disturbed over the new application of old regulations, withdrew from College at once. All those leaving the campus were thereupon dismissed by the faculty.

Charges and countercharges, letters, explanations, and visits to and from irate parents helped create for McBryde one of the most unhappy Christmas seasons he ever spent. Finally, most of the students were readmitted after the Christmas holidays but under conditions which many parents felt were unnecessarily humiliating. The entire situation had a surprisingly depressing effect on McBryde. The newspapers of the state had given the incident widespread publicity, and one paper succeeded in giving the impression that the student immaturity displayed in the matter was second only to that of the faculty, which, in the opinion of the paper, had created the unpleasant situation and then passed it on to Dr. McBryde to solve. Several prominent citizens in and out of the state expressed the same opinion but in tones less restrained than those of the papers. The students felt the trouble had arisen from the ineptness of the council of deans. There is evidence to indicate that privately McBryde felt the same way, but publicly he backed the deans and the faculty to the fullest. J. Thompson Brown, rector of the board, backed the action of the faculty which followed after the receipt of the student ultimatum, but felt that the action of two of the deans had really precipitated the student action. He had the board adopt a resolution urging that any group student protest in the future be referred immediately to McBryde rather than to the council of deans.

Following the readmission of most of the students after the Christmas holidays, the furore gradually died down, but McBryde was left with the unhappy thought that his phenomenal success in building the College to its current eminence might prove to be a Pyrrhic victory. VPI now definitely was too big for him to attend to all the administrative details to which he had devoted so much time in the past; but his efforts to organize and assign administrative responsibilities to others had caused dissension in the faculty, unrest in the student body, and some alienation of support in the state. For more than a decade, he had been receiving literally hundreds of letters from parents who sent their sons to "McBryde's College" to be looked after by McBryde. Efforts on his part to assign responsibilities to others for student welfare were quickly resented by many parents, who just as quickly wrote to him and told him so. But what was he to do now that the student body was getting so large?

The excitement and ill will created by the incident of student unrest had hardly subsided when on the night of February 23, the new science hall was completely destroyed by fire. McBryde had been receiving a number of anonymous letters, both threatening and insulting in nature, ever since the Junior Class episode. When the fire occurred, he had suspected arson committed by a person from this group but was never able to confirm his suspicion. He did report to the board, though, that the fire if not of incendiary origin had been caused by carelessness on the part of somebody with no authority to be in the building late at night. The fact that the building had been closed all day February 22 for Washington's birthday created enough speculation in the newspapers to cause a Baltimore detective agency to offer to conduct a veritable cloak-and-dagger secret investigation of the fire—provided the detectives were paid $100 and expenses in advance.

To add to McBryde's growing problems for the year, Professors Patton and Randolph, who had been helping plan and design many of the new buildings being erected on the campus, disagreed sharply over the architectural details for one of the larger buildings. Each man clung to the conviction that his design was superior to that of the other. An outside architect had been brought in but instead of resolving the problem had added to it by rejecting both plans and submitting one of his own.

Finally, McBryde, after complaining that he had been completely worn out in trying to resolve the differences between the two men, passed the problem on to Rector Brown for arbitration.

To add to the unhappy events of the year, Professor Patton died just before the close of the session.

In spite of the discouraging events of the year, McBryde was able to report continued expansion of the physical plant, the addition of new courses, and the adoption of a degree program in practical geology. At the same time, his annual report for the session of 1904-05, for the first time in his long career at the College, took on a depressed note and ended with the statement, "I may add in closing that my health has suffered seriously this session."

Any recovery of his strength which McBryde may have enjoyed during the summer of 1905 was quickly lost with the opening of the session of 1905-06. The College opened on September 21. On September 24, a group of four students were detected in an episode which the faculty interpreted as hazing. As a result, the students were denied permission to re-enter school. The father of one of the students thereupon intervened on behalf of his son and tried to persuade the faculty to rescind its action. The prominence of the father, Judge George L. Christian of Richmond, and of his counsel, United States Senator John W. Daniel, of Lynchburg, and of other individuals who became involved, caused a considerable stir not only in Blacksburg but throughout the state as well. When the faculty refused to rescind its action, Judge Christian immediately appealed to the Board of Visitors and requested that body to set aside the faculty action. Faced with this demand, the board agreed to hold a hearing on the matter in December, but in the meantime asked McBryde to prepare a full report on the entire situation for the board's use.

McBryde's efforts to comply with this request, while at the same time carrying on the duties of the president, proved to be too great a burden for his already declining health. As a result he became greatly depressed and decided he had better resign as president and seek less burdensome work. The Board of Visitors, however, was not about to give him up if it could help it. Meeting in December, this body fully supported McBryde and the faculty in the Christian case and proceeded to grant McBryde a six-month leave of absence for rest and recuperation.

Following this action of the board, McBryde left for an extended trip to Jamaica, and Judge Christian prepared a strong appeal to the legislature, requesting that body to reinstate his son at VPI.

The legislature to which Judge Christian addressed his appeal, after some hesitation, appointed a joint committee of the House and Senate "to investigate the Christian, Eubank and Salley case, and any other matters at the college, which may seem proper . . . and report on the results of their investigation to the next General Assembly." This investigation was not undertaken until July, 1906, by which time numerous rumors concerning almost every aspect of the College were flourishing. Upon his return to the campus in June, McBryde found himself faced not only with the frustrations of legislative investigation into the Christian affair but also with the possibility of an investigation into "any other matters at the college" which the investigative committee deemed proper. The events and rumors which had developed during his absence made it impossible for him to know the scope of the investigation which was to take place.

Events other than those directly connected with his administrative duties at VPI had also contributed to his frustrations and disappointments which seemed to pile upon him so rapidly beginning in 1904. In March, 1901, McBryde had been elected to the first Board of Trustees for Sweet Briar Institute, in Amherst County, Virginia, and at the first meeting of that board had been "appointed to every committee." During the summer he had been offered the presidency of the institute at a salary of $5000 and a house. There is no doubt whatever but that he had been greatly tempted to accept the offer; however, he had asked for a postponement of his answer "until he could see his way clearly." As a result, according to the Sweet Briar historian, *The Lynchburg News* was kept on the run following reports 'from the best authority' of Dr. McBryde's intentions." Confusing reports that he had accepted the presidency, that he had not accepted the presidency, that he planned to accept the presidency, that he planned not to accept the presidency, that he did not know what he planned to do, and finally that he planned to remain at VPI but would conduct the business at Sweet Briar as well, appeared in both state and out-of-state papers.

J. Thompson Brown, the rector of the Board of Visitors for VPI, was in Richmond when one of the first reports "from the best authority" appeared in the press, stating that McBryde planned to accept the offer. Brown rushed to his hotel room and wrote a twenty-page letter to McBryde in which he resorted to cajolery, flattery, promises, threats, pleadings, and outright begging in an effort to dissuade him from leaving VPI.

The board members, according to Brown, could not think of McBryde's leaving and remain calm. For the sake of the board, of the College, and of the state, wrote Brown, "do not leave us now." The faculty adopted resolutions expressing its support for him and urged him to remain as their leader, while letters poured in urging him not to move. One alumnus wrote, "You and VPI are inseparable in the eyes of the students. The growth of VPI is a wonder all over the country. The state needs VPI and VPI need you." Then revealing a bit of the campus politics, this alumnus reminded McBryde that rumor had a certain professor working for the presidency if McBryde left. "May the Lord deliver us from it," he concluded.

McBryde in a letter to his son John confessed his uncertainty as to the best course of action to follow but did say he felt obligated to remain at VPI for a while at least. The Sweet Briar board apparently did not push him for an answer but elected him as chairman of the executive committee and gave him authority to act as "superintendent of the plans, the material, and the equipment of the institute and [to be] the authoritative manager of all the property in the hands of the trustees." "For this he received an annual salary of $2,500 a year and he earned it," wrote the Sweet Briar historian. The VPI president had set about providing the physical basis for the creation of the newly chartered Sweet Briar Institute with the same zeal, energy, and enthusiasm with which he had been achieving such phenomenal success in building VPI. For fear the building made from bricks from the red Sweet Briar clay might prove to be ugly, "red splotches on the landscape," he had barrels of Sweet Briar clay shipped to VPI, where test bricks were burned to determine the final color. The results were satisfactory; whereupon, he arranged for the bricks necessary for the building program he proposed at Sweet Briar to be burned on the Sweet Briar campus. The assistance of Professor William M. Patton was secured in constructing a lake and in the laying out of the campus roads, while a "horticulturist from VPI" laid out the Sweet Briar orchards. In the formulation of his plans for the campus McBryde never wavered from his belief that the best was none too good for Sweet Briar. Unfortunately, this conviction, plus the fact he could not be on the Sweet Briar campus to supervise the execution of his plans, created a situation in which expenditures and unexpected costs greatly exceeded appropriations. Besides, by the middle of 1905 the

expected endowment of $500,000 for the new institute had turned out to be some-
what less than $200,000. In the midst of the mounting problems at VPI, McBryde
saw that the matter of finances at Sweet Briar was emerging as one with which
he would have to grapple mightily whether he accepted the presidency or not.

While he was engaged in projecting plans for the establishment of Sweet Briar
Institute, he became involved in yet another episode which caused him some embarrassment and unhappiness before it ended. In 1903, his name was mentioned
as being in the forefront of those being considered for the presidency of the University of Virginia. Pressure developed at once for him to remain at VPI. The
faculty addressed a resolution to the Board of Visitors, expressing full confidence
in him and urging the board to do everything in its power to keep him at VPI.
Letters once more flowed in from friends and alumni pledging him full support
and urging him to remain with the College. At the time, he had not been offered
the presidency, but it had been "discovered" by the newspapers that influential
members of the Board of Visitors of the University of Virginia had visited Mc-
Bryde in Blacksburg and were "supposed" to be promoting him for president.

On April 19, 1904, the rumors became a reality, and the Board of Visitors of
the University of Virginia offered McBryde the presidency of that institution but
conveyed the information to him only. McBryde immediately requested and received time to think about the matter, but in the meantime the press gave wide
publicity to his supposed election. After much thought, McBryde wrote a long
letter to Carter Glass, member of the Board of Visitors of the University of Virginia, declining the appointment. He expected his letter, which set forth in full
his reasons for declining the offer, to be read to the full Board of Visitors and perhaps released to the press. Glass, on the other hand, after writing a warm letter
of appreciation to McBryde for his great work at VPI, dropped the matter and
resumed the search for a president.

No official statement concerning the offer of the presidency to McBryde was
released by the University of Virginia, but the press engaged in much speculation
about the entire matter. J. Thompson Brown, rector of the Board of Visitors of
VPI, felt that this speculation in the press was hurting both McBryde and VPI,
but in his contacts with McBryde and Glass he got the impression that the latter
did not want the fact that McBryde had been offered but had declined the presidency to be publicized until after a president had been named for the University
of Virginia. Following the public announcement of the appointment of Edwin A.
Alderman as the president of the University of Virginia, a number of VPI alumni
and friends felt that McBryde's true involvement in the matter should be clarified.
One zealous individual claimed to have discovered that the official records at the
University of Virginia not only did not include McBryde's long letter explaining
his reasons for declining the presidency but did not even mention the fact that he
had been under consideration for the office. J. Thompson Brown immediately
wrote to Carter Glass, urging that now since a president had been appointed, a
public acknowledgement of the fact that McBryde had been tendered but had
declined the presidency of the University of Virginia was due both McBryde and
VPI. In the same letter, Brown also expressed strong surprise that McBryde's
letter to Glass in which he had set forth his reasons for declining the presidency
had neither been read to the board nor entered into the official records.

Glass, in reply, explained that he did not feel that any benefit would result
from publicizing the original offer to McBryde. As for the matter of records, wrote

Glass, none of the efforts made by the board to get a president appeared in the official minutes, since all of the action taken by the board had occurred in executive session with no secretary present.

Brown was none too happy with Glass's explanation but decided not to pursue the matter, publicly at least. A short time later excerpts of McBryde's letter to Carter Glass appeared in the press, but by whose authority was not stated.

McBryde was quite unhappy with the turn the offer had taken but made no public effort at the time to clarify his position. In a personal letter to his son Charles, whom he addressed with the nickname of "Saint," he discussed the offer and his refusal and he concluded by saying, "I am greatly saddened by my decision—ten years older."

At the time the board had granted McBryde the extended leave for rest and recuperation, it also appointed Professors E. A. Smyth and T. P. Campbell to serve jointly as president on the campus. At the same time the rector, J. Thompson Brown, was designated as the official head of the College. Brown entered upon the discharge of his new duties with a combination of trepidation and enthusiasm. He immediately foresaw the difficulties he might encounter in attempting to interpret the College's needs to the legislature which would be in session during McBryde's absence, but he also welcomed the opportunity for the experience, since he at the time was toying with the idea of running for the office of commissioner of agriculture. At the time McBryde had been granted the sick leave, rumors were still circulating that he planned to leave the presidency of VPI for that of Sweet Briar. Brown had gone to McBryde and had requested a written statement from him declaring his intentions, which Brown could use if it appeared these rumors were about to hurt VPI. After all, McBryde had had nearly five years in which to make up his mind. McBryde thereupon wrote a letter to Brown stating that he planned to remain at VPI and had no intention of moving to Sweet Briar. For reasons known only to himself, he asked Brown to release the letter to the public only if in Brown's judgment it seemed best to do so.

In January, the newspapers began to report "from the best authority" that McBryde upon his return from Jamaica would move to Sweet Briar and relinquish to Rector Brown the presidency of VPI. Brown quickly discovered that this report was pleasing only to the supporters of Sweet Briar. Upon further investigation, he became convinced the newspaper report had originated either on the Sweet Briar campus or "from people at least near those in confidence of Sweet Briar." The report threw Brown into a dilemma. He quickly saw the demoralizing effect it was having on the VPI faculty, and he greatly feared the effect it might have on the legislature, which was being petitioned by Judge Christian to investigate the College anyway. Acting on his own initiative, he called the executive committee of the board into session to consider the matter. Dr. McBryde's son Bolton, a member of the VPI faculty, was called into conference. Bolton, through his mother, had learned of his father's decision to remain at VPI and after a thorough discussion of the matter agreed that it might be advisable to release McBryde's letter to Brown in which he stated his intention to remain at VPI. Brown thereupon released the information at once, to the consternation, dismay, and even anger of the Sweet Briar Board of Trustees. The timing of the release could not have been worse in so far as McBryde's future relationship with Sweet Briar was concerned. The Sweet Briar trustees had just discovered how far McBryde's expenditures for the Sweet Briar campus had exceeded the board's appropriation.

The trustees had been "horrified and they said so in writing." They had stripped McBryde of most of the authority he had been assigned and replaced him as chairman of the executive committee during his absence "or until further notice." It was while this action was still fresh in their minds that Brown had announced that McBryde "had no thought whatever of going to Sweet Briar—he wants to stay at VPI as long as he can be of use." Any sense of remorse which may have been developing amongst the Sweet Briar trustees over the treatment accorded a sick man in his absence quickly died with Brown's announcement.

As a result of these developments, which took place during his absence in Jamaica, McBryde returned in June, 1906, to a College facing a legislative investigation, a faculty rapidly polarizing into factions, a declining student enrollment, and a board at Sweet Briar very unhappy about, if not openly hostile toward, the way he had handled a project so dear to his heart.

Upon his resumption of duties at VPI in June, 1906, he quickly solved his problem with Sweet Briar by resigning from the board of trustees, but letters to his family revealed the depth of his feeling and the drain upon his emotions caused by the unhappy incident. He was not able to solve the problem of the pending legislative investigation brought about by Judge Christian's appeal with the same dispatch. When he began planning for the investigation and for the next year's work, he was dismayed by the faculty attitude which had developed during his absence. Many members of the faculty, apparently aware that McBryde's state of health would not permit him to remain much longer as president, were beginning to maneuver for personal advantage or were lining up with those who were so doing. Some of the Experiment Station staff had become thoroughly aroused over the promotional techniques Andrew Soule, the new director, was employing. Even Harvey L. Price, an easy-going, amiable, pleasant individual, had joined with other staff members in writing a hot letter of protest against what they considered to be Soule's self-promotional techniques at their expense.

A behind-the-scene struggle between certain faculty members and the State Board of Agriculture which had been smoldering for a number of years was threatening to break out into the open, while rumors were rife that the political hatchet was about to fall on the rector and certain other board members who reportedly had not supported Governor Swanson ('86) in his campaign for office in 1905. To add to the general uncertainty, the state of Virginia was in the midst of one of the most dramatic campaigns in its history for an improved system of rural education adapted to rural needs. Leaders in this campaign were openly challenging VPI to throw its resources back of this movement, but unhappily some of the faculty members interpreted this challenge as a threat to their on-campus programs and were dragging their feet.

Within a month after his return to the campus, McBryde realized his health would not permit him to remain much longer as president. Outwardly he carried on his duties as usual, but privately he expressed his great discouragement to members of his family. In a letter to his son John, written just a few days before the legislative investigation of the Christian charges was to begin he said:

> I am doubtful about writing to you, I am so worn out and depressed. I have gone through enough in the last month to kill an ordinary man and it has certainly nullified greatly the effect of my rest. I find treachery and disloyalty on all sides. I do not know whom to trust. I do not know the scope of the

investigation which begins Monday. I only know that a great trial awaits me and that I am in no condition to meet it. I have no rallying power—my age explains it. . . . This session, I realize must be my last. The Christian matter and the pending investigation is greatly impairing the prospects for another session. We must face a heavy falling off in students.

The "great trial" which McBryde dreaded opened on July 23 with the arrival on campus of the legislative investigation committee. At the very first session of the committee a petition was received from Judge Christian requesting that the investigation of his charges against the faculty in connection with its action against his son be dropped; after his presentation of the original charges, he wrote, he had learned that his son and the others charged had in fact been engaged in hazing as accused by the faculty.

Upon receipt of this petition the committee immediately dropped this matter from the agenda. But under the legislative mandate to investigate ". . . any other matter at the college which may seem proper" the committee decided to explore some of the rumors and charges which had developed during McBryde's absence from campus.

Advertisements were placed in the paper announcing the committee's readiness to hear any and all complaints against the College or any member of its staff. The only result was one letter complaining that the college dairy was selling its products in town. A local carpenter who had been particularly effective in spreading rumors of waste, excessive costs, inferior workmanship, and even hints of graft in connection with the College building program, was summoned to appear before the committee but apparently preferred to leave town rather than do so. With no one willing to appear before it to register a complaint, much less back up any charges against the school, the committee proceeded to spend a full week visiting the farm, shops, laboratories, dormitories, and mess hall. In addition, it interviewed the president, deans, department heads, faculty, other college officials, and prominent citizens in Blacksburg. The result of the investigation was a complete vindication, actually an accolade, for the ailing McBryde's administration of the school. In the opinion of the committee, the College had spent every dollar of its appropriation wisely, had developed a program adapted to the needs of the state, and if given proper support from the legislature would render even greater service to the state in the future. One alumnus, happy over the praise given VPI as a result of the investigation, promised to do everything in his power to make such investigations an annual affair.

McBryde naturally was happy over the outcome, but realized he could not stand the strain of another session as turbulent as the two he had just passed through. In the meantime, some of his friends with his consent had started a movement designed to get a retirement pension awarded to him from the Carnegie Foundation for the Advancement of Teaching. One requirement for his award called for affidavits from individuals who could and would attest to McBryde's contribution to the field of education. The list of individuals who supplied these affidavits for McBryde reads like a list of Who's Who in Education, Business, and Jurisprudence in the South at the time. The president of practically every major institution of higher education in the South attested to McBryde's contributions not only in Virginia but throughout the South. A number of college presidents frankly admitted they had shaped portions of their programs after the one McBryde had developed at VPI, while J. A. C. Chandler, later to be identified so

closely with the College of William and Mary, went to great length to show what
the polytechnic feature being developed by McBryde at VPI was doing for Virginia.

The joint efforts on his behalf were successful, and at the meeting of the Board
of Visitors in October, 1906, McBryde announced that he had been awarded the
retirement pension. At the same meeting he submitted his resignation as president
to take effect at the end of the session. The board accepted his resignation with
extreme reluctance, but the people balked. In sickness and in health, in youth
or in old age, the people wanted McBryde. Letters and telegrams which must have
been especially welcome after the trying experiences of the past two years, poured
in, urging him to remain at VPI. Governor Swanson wrote to him, pledging him
his full support if he decided to remain, but McBryde knew when to retire. At
the board's request, he agreed to serve until the following September but with
his usual tact and courtesy turned aside all pleas that he remain as president.

Outwardly, McBryde's final year as president was a happy one. The agricultural hall (Price Hall) was completed in January, thereby enabling him to move
toward his long-cherished goal of providing permanent homes for the work developing in the department of agriculture. A minor argument concerning the
use of this building was quickly settled when the board sustained him in his decision to use the basement for a creamery instead of assenting to the request of
the animal husbandry department to use it as a stable fitted for stock judging.

An unusually comprehensive exhibit depicting the work of the College was
displayed at the Jamestown Exposition, where it received high praise in the press
and from thousands of visitors. The commencement exercises for 1907 were held
on June 2, earlier than usual, in order to permit the Corps of Cadets to visit the
exposition, where after numerous parades, drills, and visits to the exhibits, the
Corps was dismissed for the summer. Favorable publicity was brought to the
institution as a result of the exhibits; the performance of the cadets also was
pleasing particularly to McBryde, who felt such publicity would help counter-
act the adverse attention brought to the institution in connection with the recent
hazing incident. The behavior of the students during the session of 1906-07 was
gratifying to all, especially so in view of the turbulent behavior of the past two
sessions. McBryde felt that much of the improvement in student behavior grew
from the reorganization of the military department under a full-time rather than
a part-time commandant. J. S. A. Johnson, who had been serving as commandant
on a part-time basis, had reminded McBryde on a number of occasions that he
desired to relinquish his military responsibilities in favor of his teaching duties
in the mechanical engineering department. On June 9, 1906, he reminded the
board that he had no ambitions or plans for a military career and therefore would
like to resign as commandant and be permitted to devote full time to his teaching
duties. The board accepted his resignation; whereupon, the War Department detailed Captain G. H. Jamerson, who was appointed full-time commandant. Johnson, or "J.S.A." as he came to be known by the students, assumed full-time teaching duties in the department of mechanical engineering with such notable success
that in 1966 Johnson Hall was dedicated in his honor.

On the surface, affairs at the College were moving smoothly. Beneath the surface however, affairs were in a turmoil, and McBryde knew it; but as retiring president there was little he could do to improve conditions.

Andrew Soule as dean of agriculture and director of the Experiment Station was a promoter and showman to the very core. His activities on behalf of his department had alarmed many of the faculty, who felt that the agricultural department under Soule was about to swallow up everything in sight. Even before his arrival on campus, Soule had requested a horse, a stable, a saddle, and a buggy for his personal use. In addition, he had visited the College and picked out a site for his proposed home and submitted his personal plans for a college house to be erected upon it. D. O. Matthews, superintendent of grounds, who had acquired an enviable reputation for his ability to get the "best house for the least money" had objected to the cost involved in executing some of Soule's ideas, and McBryde had been called upon to arbitrate the matter. McBryde's decision had not been too pleasing either to Soule or Matthews, who henceforth kept a wary eye on each other. Soule had entered upon his work with unusual enthusiasm and vigor. By numerous public addresses and articles in the press, he had quickly identified himself with practically every organization in the state working to promote agriculture.

The farmers loved him, but it soon dawned on many of the leaders that Soule's proposals would take money and more money. By 1906, he had greatly over extended the work in his department and was bluntly reminding the board and the public that without more money for new positions and better salaries, VPI was rapidly degenerating into a second-rate institution. An institution, he warned, useful only as a training ground for ambitious young men who would remain just long enough to get experience and then move on to other institutions with better salary schedules.

His efforts to get increased financial backing for his programs took an unexpected turn. Many farm leaders interpreted his statements as a charge that the agricultural programs at VPI were being discriminated against in the distribution of funds available to the College. McBryde indignantly rejected this interpretation and compiled figures for the board which showed that if any discrimination existed financially, it greatly favored rather than injured the agricultural department. The engineering faculty became greatly disturbed lest Soule's arguments should result in reduced financial support for engineering, but the board showed the most surprising sensitivity of all. This body wondered if Soule were casting aspersions on its good judgment. Finally, the board adopted a resolution by which it notified Soule that reports were "flooding in" from all quarters that he was being disloyal to the board as a result of his actions. No "cease and desist" order was given to promoter Soule, who merely softened his wording but kept up his agitation for his beloved program.

In April, 1907, he resigned to accept a position at the University of Georgia and immediately demonstrated the validity of his conviction concerning the VPI salary schedule by taking a number of the faculty with him at an increase in salary. His departure did not restore the harmony longed for by the board, for in spite of McBryde's effort to prevent it, the seed of suspicion and distrust which Soule had unintentionally sowed between the agricultural and engineering departments had fallen upon fertile ground and was growing vigorously by the end of McBryde's administration. Soule's departure also contributed another element to the unrest seething below the surface. It created two more vacancies on the faculty, the deanship of agriculture and directorship of the Experiment Station. There were eager applicants for both places.

When McBryde's impending retirement was announced, the board appointed a committee headed by Joseph D. Eggleston, to seek a new president. Before this committee had time to act, the Alumni Association met and passed strong resolutions urging the committee to find an outstanding person with both educational and administrative experience. The newspapers took up the search and suggested name after name of prominent and not-so-prominent Virginians. Then after having put the name before the public, the same papers literally filled column after column describing the reactions of alumni and board members to the supposed candidates.

The committee in the meantime conducted its search so quietly that the impression got abroad that it was not trying to find a successor. Even McBryde became disturbed and privately expressed the fear to his son John that the board expected him to remain as president. What the public, including McBryde, did not know was the fact that the committee, with the low salary it could offer had been unable to interest a number of top flight individuals it was contacting concerning the position.

At its regular meeting in January, 1907, the board conferred upon McBryde the honorary degree of Doctor of Science and elected him president emeritus, thereby making him the first person ever to receive either one of these honors from VPI. When the board adjourned without having named a new president, the press after congratulating the board for its action toward McBryde, resumed its speculation concerning the office. By this time, the situation on the campus had become tense and was getting worse. The rumor spread that Rector Brown and board members Robertson and Watkins would be replaced by persons supposed to be supporters of Governor Swanson. Professor T. P. Campbell was reported as being an active candidate for the presidency, while Professor Meade Ferguson was supposed to be seeking faculty support for the positions vacated by Soule. The alumni were reported as vigorously opposed to both men, and the faculty was reported as being "vigorously divided into pro, con and neutral camps on everything." McBryde, in an unhappy vein, wrote, "The atmosphere here now is vile with wretched scandal and slander, . . . everything is at sea—the faculty is split into bitter factions." Even the board, McBryde said, was divided into two factions.

As the speculation continued, the name of Paul B. Barringer, a member and former chairman of the faculty at the University of Virginia, began to appear more and more in the press. It was noted that Barringer certainly was not making any public effort to secure the presidency, if indeed he was a candidate. At the same time, it was noted that his name did not stir up the opposition which the names of so many other prospects evoked. In addition to his seeming acceptability to all factions, his tenure as a faculty member and chairman of the faculty at the University of Virginia gave him the twin credentials of educational experience and administration being demanded by the alumni. With these facts before it, plus very strong endorsements of Barringer for the presidency secured from faculty members at the University of Virginia, the committee headed by Eggleston decided to act. On May 30, 1907, it recommended, and the board elected Paul Brandon Barringer as president of VPI. Since Barringer was unable to report for duty until September 1, McBryde was requested, and agreed, to remain in office until that date.

Dr. McBryde's administration brought phenomenal success and some disappointments and failures. Upon his retirement, his successes were summarized over and over in the press, in college bulletins, at alumni meetings, and in letters to the editor. His disappointments and failures were ignored or submerged by the outpouring of heartfelt tributes from alumni and friends. To these individuals Dr. McBryde was VPI. He had headed the College at a time when many people who were denied an opportunity for anything beyond the simplest rudiments of an education for themselves were awakening to the hopes of something better for their children. These people sent their sons to McBryde, and he took them in in numbers beyond the capacity of the College to care for them properly. In 1903, he had informed the legislature that with adequate facilities the enrollment would go well beyond the one thousand mark. This was an unheard-of college enrollment in Virginia, not to be achieved at VPI for two decades, but there is no reason whatever to doubt the accuracy of McBryde's prediction.

Not only did the people expect McBryde to attend to the academic instruction of their sons, but they also expected him to attend to other duties as well. The following excerpts gleaned from letters addressed to McBryde reveal but a small sampling of these duties the people had been assigning to the president of their land-grant College by the time McBryde retired:

"My son has decided to come to *your college*. Please teach him what is needed to become a mech. engr."

# # #

"My two boys left this morning for your college. Charles is a husky boy and will get along. William is in poor health. Please see that he wears his hat and coat when the weather is bad. . . ."

# # #

"Will you please stop my boy's Spanish and put him in Latin as he is not interested in it and wants to give it up. If I had been consulted at first I should have said Latin instead of Spanish."

# # #

"I am very much surprised at not getting the bills of what my son needs from the officials. As it is I do not know what the money is spent for."

# # #

"I have just received my son's report and see that his professor is surprised. So am I, please explain."

# # #

"Please use the enclosed money to buy my boy a new uniform. Please see that it fits him and let him have it before he comes home Easter."

# # #

"My boy is coming to your college today. Please give him a sunny room on the second floor and help him choose a good roommate."

# # #

"Please tell all the store keepers up there not to let my boy start a charge account. I won't pay any of them. Don't let my boy write to anybody but his home folks. It will take his mind off his work. I noticed he was charged with fourteen letters by the treasurer. I want this stopped at once. I want him to stay at college winter and summer, not do any running around and get his mind off his work. Dr., I can't hear about my son's conduct . . . he is a boy that if he

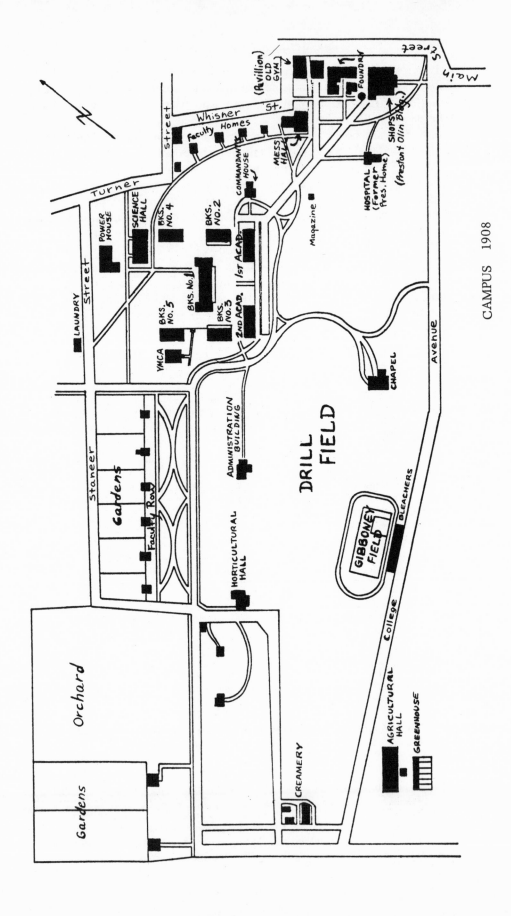

CAMPUS 1908

can get with the right company he will be a useful man. He has no father. Oh, Dr., please talk to him and help him to choose his associates. . . ."

# # #

"When my son left home I told him I did not want him to play foot and base ball. Please look into the situation and let me know. It is not that I do not trust him, I just want to know. . . ."

"P.S. Don't tell him I asked you."

# # #

"My son joined the Y.M.C.A. and goes to the meetings but I do not know if it does any good. Where does he go after the meetings? Please let me know but don't tell him I asked."

# # #

"You may remember I dropped out of school last year. Since that time I have been working with a survey party in the mountains of West Virginia. I have slept on pine tops and eaten corn pone and bacon until I have come to the conclusion that the best thing I can do is to return to V.P.I. next session and study a little more calculus and football. Can you help me?"

# # #

"I am sending you five dollars in case the corps goes on from Buffalo to Niagara. If the corps goes I want my son to go along. Please do not let him have any of this money to spend frivolously on side shows and the like. I do not want him to develop spendthrift habits. Thank you for making it possible for the corps to go to Buffalo."

# # #

"Please buy my boy the things he needs for his room. 1 wash basin 20 to 25¢; 1 pitcher 22-30¢; 1 slop bucket 30-35¢; 1 mirror 15-25¢; 1 mattress $1.25 to $1.50; one water bucket 15-23¢."

# # #

"I have just heard that my son has gotten a great many demerits. I am very surprised because he is a good boy. I told you not to let him run around with the wrong crowd. Please let me know at once what you can do about it. I want him to be an engineer not a soldier. Do you think it is fair to let demerits keep him from becoming an engineer?"

# # #

"Please send me a catalog of your college. Is the experiment station in Blacksburg? If not where is it?"

# # #

"Herewith I mail you two worms and the acorns in which I found them. . . As I use fried acorns in my experiments I should like to know of what insects the worms derive and beg you to kindly communicate to me this."

# # #

"My son is 12 ½ years old but he is quite good in his books. Can he get into your college?"

# # #

"No doubt you get a lot of letters from fathers telling you all about the fine qualities of their sons. Well I love my son very dearly but so far as books are concerned I have not discovered any fine qualities yet. Will you take him in your school and see if your professors can find any?"

\# \# \#

"I write to ask you about my son. I waked up in the middle of the night with a feeling that something was wrong with him. The last time this happened to me, when I got up the next morning, I found a member of the family was very ill. Please send me a telegram at once about my boy."

\# \# \#

"Your school is supposed to build character so I am sending you my son. I do not want him to smoke, chew, cuss, loaf or run around. He does all of these things now."

\# \# \#

"I sent my son some money. He writes that he got it but doesn't know what he did with it. Please check and let me know."

\# \# \#

"I have just received my son's report. I do not understand a thing on it. Do you? If so please explain it to me and make it simpler next time."

\# \# \#

The records indicate that McBryde answered all of these letters apparently to the satisfaction of the writers. It is no surprise that following his retirement John McBryde soon came to be called the father of VPI.

Following his retirement, McBryde bought the Stanger farm, presently included in McBryde Village, and lived in the large frame house he had erected immediately across the Price's Fork Road from the campus entrance to the Green House Road. He died on March 23, 1923, while visiting one of his sons in New Orleans, but not before he had been accorded signal honors at the Golden Jubilee celebration of the College held in 1922.

Chapter 7

The Barringer Administration

1907-1913

PAUL BRANDON BARRINGER was born in Concord, North Carolina, on February 13, 1857, of distinguished ancestry. His college-preparatory work was done at Kenmore University School, Amherst Courthouse, Virginia. A graduate of the University of Virginia with an M.D. degree, he also studied at the University of the City of New York and for two years in Europe, where he did further work in medicine. After engaging in farming and the practice of medicine near Charlotte, North Carolina, he joined the staff at Davidson College, from which school he moved to the chair of physiology at the University of Virginia. From 1895 to 1903 he was chairman of the faculty there, the highest executive office then within the gift of the University.

Barringer came to the presidency of VPI with high recommendations from various sources, especially from many of his colleagues at the University of Virginia. One professor reported that he had "executive ability amounting almost to genius," while another faculty member singled out for praise his demonstrated ability to deal with students and faculty in such a way as to draw out the best in both. Others spoke in glowing terms of his broad culture, warm personality, familiarity with Virginia conditions, and noted success as a teacher. Professor S. C. Mitchell, a highly respected leader in the movement for a better system of public education in the state, spoke in glowing terms of Barringer's ability to

183

lead the state in the development of agriculture and manufacturing. The Alumni Association pledged its "cordial and earnest support to . . . the newly elected president, Dr. Paul B. Barringer," whom it described as one "who is widely known as an eminent educator, and a cultured gentleman of the highest type, a broad-minded man, of splendid personality, proven executive ability, and superior educational qualifications." *The Virginia Journal of Education* carried a long article praising Barringer for his demonstrated accomplishments as a gentleman, scholar, and administrator and for his potential for developing VPI to even greater usefulness to the state. Professor R. H. Hudnall wrote to the alumni and said:

> With the characteristics of the educator, Dr. Barringer combines the qualities of the man of practical affairs. In dealing with men he shows tact, and good, sound common sense, discriminating judgment, and business capacity of a high order. He is greatly interested in the social, industrial, and economic problems of modern life. He knows how to bring things to pass. He is aggressive, yet conservative; quick in grasping a new situation, yet calm and deliberate in action.

Dr. Barringer assumed the duties of his office on September 1, 1907, amidst a veritable chorus of praise from all sides. Before his first year had been completed, this chorus ended with dramatic suddenness, caused by events many of which were not of his making.

At the time Dr. Barringer assumed the presidency, Virginia was in the midst of the greatest agitation for better public education, particularly in the rural sections, the state has ever witnessed. The work of the Farmers' Alliance and the Populist movement had more than paved the way, but the work of the Southern Education Board and the General Education Board deserve the credit for focusing attention on public education. After a number of well-advertised conferences and an exciting campaign in May, 1905, a governor and a legislature friendly to education had been elected. At the same time, Joseph D. Eggleston had been elected state superintendent of public instruction. Under his dynamic influence, the legislature of 1906 had enacted legislation which embarked the state on a remarkable program of high-school construction and development. As one result of this legislation, high schools in rural villages and small towns sprang up with breath-taking rapidity. In 1905-06, there were 74 high schools in the state. This number jumped to 218 by the end of the 1907-08 and climbed steadily until it reached 448 in 1913 and 575 in 1918.

Since Virginia was overwhelmingly rural, it was only natural that a demand for agricultural education should grow as her rural schools increased in number. The State Farmers' Institute, organized in Virginia about 1904, became particularly active in agitating for an improved scientific education in agriculture. This organization, under the leadership of such men as T. O. Sandy, Westmoreland Davis, W. H. Mann, and others, argued that science had made the industrialist successful; now farmers could become successful if they learned how to apply science to farming.

Davis and Sandy not only preached the doctrine of scientific agriculture but demonstrated it as well—Davis at his plantation, Morven Park, and Sandy at his farm near Burkeville in Nottoway County. By 1910, this organization, largely as a result of Westmoreland Davis' efforts, had become a potent force in Virginia politics.

Organizations and agencies in addition to the Farmers' Institute urged better schools and better rural conditions. Attempts had been made to enlist the institutions of higher education in the cause. Dr. McBryde had been invited to participate in the state program which got under way during his administration, but he had been prevented from doing so because of his health. Andrew Soule, however, had published a number of articles dealing with agricultural education in public schools and had appeared before a number of the rapidly developing teachers' associations in the state; but there was a general feeling that VPI was lagging in the effort to improve rural life. The University of Virginia, on the other hand, under the dynamic leadership of President Alderman, was rapidly emerging as the champion of improved rural conditions.

The legislature in the decade beginning with 1906 caught the spirit and became more than generous in enacting legislation which directly and indirectly affected public schools and VPI. It was careful to see that such generosity did not spill over into financial affairs, however.

One of the most dynamic leaders of the educational renaissance sweeping the state was Superintendent Eggleston. A fluent writer and a dynamic speaker capable of adapting his presentation to his audience, he succeeded in creating a vision of better things in the minds of thousands of rural leaders. Eggleston wanted a school system in which the rural schools served as community centers for their particular communities. He wanted his teachers trained not only in the usual academic subjects but in the skills of rural community leadership as well. His canvass of the state prior to his election as superintendent of public instruction had convinced him that Virginia schools needed to develop programs in agricultural education, manual arts, and domestic science. He wanted these programs set up as a part of the offerings in comprehensive high schools rather than in separate schools. Such separate schools, he argued, were undemocratic and unworthy in that they tended to separate rather than integrate the population. Almost immediately after his becoming superintendent of public instruction, he began looking for ways and means to introduce agricultural education into the rural schools. He was a strong supporter of the program at VPI but did not believe the program was reaching enough people; neither did he believe VPI was identified closely enough with the total movement for an improved rural life in the state.

When Barringer became president, he was thoroughly familiar with the developments in the state on behalf of improved education. Indeed, he had participated in the important Conference for Southern Education which had been held in Virginia in 1903. He was even more familiar with the efforts being made by E. A. Alderman, Bruce D. Payne, and others at the University of Virginia to promote better rural life through better rural education. Barringer correctly identified these efforts as an outgrowth of the Southern Education Board Movement, which he preferred to call the "Ogden Movement" after its chief promoter, the wealthy philanthropist William H. Ogden of New York. He approved of the activities of the University but at the same time worried constantly lest these activities encroach upon the field of endeavor that he believed rightfully belonged to VPI. It soon developed that a worried or aroused Barringer was a fighting Barringer whose most effective weapon was his ability to express his ideas "in terse and husky Anglo-Saxon."

He was in complete agreement with the opinion being echoed and re-echoed over the state that agricultural education held the key to the future prosperity of Virginia. He was also in agreement with Eggleston that the program in agriculture at VPI was not reaching enough people, but he went one step further; he did not believe the program itself was on college level.

Acting on this belief, Barringer unintentionally committed his first blunder as president. He announced to one and all his determination to develop the agricultural side of the College until it was at least on a par with the engineering side. At the same time, he announced his determination to "wipe out everything which did not contribute to industrial education." Since industrial education was not a clearly defined field, the expression of this latter determination posed a threat which faculty members, by the exercise of the simplest imagination, could extend in any direction.

The faculty in the department of engineering was already unhappy over what it considered to be the favored position given to agriculture under the tenure of Soule. When the engineering faculty approached Barringer concerning his plans, he interpreted their attitude as one of hostility toward agriculture and notified the Board of Visitors to this effect. At the same time, his explanation of his real intentions made matters worse instead of better. Denying that he planned to downgrade engineering, he readily admitted that he planned to build up the agricultural rather than the engineering program. Indeed, said Barringer, he hoped this determination would be "shouted from the housetops." It was, with the dean of the department of engineering leading the "shouters." Not only did he lead the shouters, but he led a program of mild guerilla warfare against Barringer for the next half a decade.

Before the faculty in the department of agriculture had time to do more than recover from its surprised delight over Barringer's statement of preferred position, a series of events occurred which annoyed and then divided this faculty into hopeless factions that greatly nullified any psychological effect Barringer's statement might otherwise have given this group.

The first event was not without an element of humor. Immediately after the opening of the 1907-08 session, it was discovered that the location of the agricultural hall (Price Hall) on the lower end of the campus made it extremely difficult for the students having classes in the "Aggie Hall" to get to their next class on time if the class met in the First or Second Academic Building, or the Science Hall, located on the upper end of the campus. If a professor held his class overtime, the difficulty assumed the proportions of an impossibility and provided an opportunity for everybody to complain. They complained, and Barringer soon found himself with protests "pouring in from all quarters" that the professors in the agricultural department were holding men overtime. Barringer immediately wrote to Dr. W. J. Quick, who had succeeded Dr. Soule as dean of agriculture, instructing him to see that all professors in the department "provide themselves with time pieces of such regularity as will enable them to conform to the ordinary time table of the institution." "I have ordered a large whistle for the Power House," said Barringer, "that can be heard all over the grounds, and if a man will set his time with this, there is no reason why his watch should not be made to conform." Barringer was as good as his word, and the whistle he installed could be heard not only all over the grounds but over most of the town as well. Within a short time, this whistle came to be the unofficial arbiter of correct time for the campus, the town, and much of the surrounding community as well. When its use to signal time was discontinued during President

Hahn's administration at the earnest petition of students residing in dormitories close to the power plant, the event was noted by the older residents of the community with the sadness characteristic of the parting from a dear friend. The students, on the other hand, who had felt that they were being lifted out of bed by the early morning blasts of the whistle, sang a song of praise to Hahn for his willingness to adjust to the times by discarding an obsolete custom.

Since the whistle merely provided the opportunity for all the staff to coordinate their timepieces, some lapses of memory continued to cause some professors to hold classes overtime. Finally, this excuse was removed when the central clock, designed and installed by the "mechanical genius" of Professor Claudius Lee ('96), was arranged to connect all buildings with a system of electric bells which could be set on the hours of the day. Before this arrangement had been made, however, many of the agricultural faculty had received an unmerciful ribbing and an unusual collection of nondescript watches, alarm clocks, hour glasses, and even sundials as fellow faculty and students joined in to help them make their timepieces conform. While this bout with time had been taking place, other events far more significant for Barringer and the College were in the making.

When Barringer arrived in Blacksburg on September 1, he found that no successor had been employed to replace Soule as director of the Experiment Station. John Spencer, professor of veterinary medicine, had been appointed as temporary director pending the appointment of a permanent director. In the meantime, Dr. Walter J. Quick had been appointed as professor of animal husbandry and dean of the department of agriculture. Barringer and Quick arrived on campus at about the same time and found that all the staff except one herdsman in the department of animal husbandry had resigned to go to Georgia with Soule. Since most of the college farm was under the supervision of the animal husbandry department, something had to be done at once. A. B. Spencer ('05) was employed as associate professor of animal husbandry, chiefly because he had served as assistant in this department, and H. S. Peyton was employed as farm manager or superintendent. The herdsman, a Mr. Winston, was planning to follow Soule to Georgia but was persuaded to remain in order to help the newly appointed staff become familiar with the program. The work of the Experiment Station was divided between Spencer and Quick, pending the appointment of a permanent director. Barringer met with all of the five individuals involved and attempted to explain their new duties and responsibilities; but having just come on the job himself, he was unable to do more than outline general responsibilities. By Christmas, the result was a six-way clash of professional opinions as to what was to be done and who was to do it; but the confusion was just beginning. In order to reduce expenses, Barringer decided to sell some of the 300 head of livestock on the college farm. The sale was held, but in some way a number of scrub animals with decided blemishes had been sold as pure breeding stock. To make matters doubly embarrassing to Barringer, a man trained in medicine, it turned out that a number of the cattle sold were infected with tuberculosis. The reaction of the shocked public was swift and bitter. The College refunded the purchase price for all diseased animals and faced lawsuits from the purchasers of others. An attempt was made by the board to fix responsibility for the fiasco, but the effect succeeded only in generating additional charges and countercharges.

Publicly, Barringer tried to minimize the incident as of small consequence; but privately, he began to plan for ways to replace the individuals he believed to be responsible for the incident. He wrote to a number of college presidents in surrounding states, asking them about the policy they followed in replacing "dead wood" on the faculty. He got absolutely no help from this source beyond vague statements that faculty dismissals usually were preceded by advance notices of "several months." President Venable, of the University of North Carolina, facetiously suggested that the only "safe and sure" method by which to replace unwanted faculty members was "to pizen" them. No record of Barringer's reaction to this method is available.

Dr. S. W. Fletcher became director of the Agricultural Experiment Station in February, 1908, thereby relieving Spencer and Quick of their responsibilities in this division; but by this time, these two individuals were at odds with each other. By spring, the differences having developed among Quick, A. P. Spencer, John Spencer, and Peyton had caused herdsman Winston to resign and had convinced Barringer that a change in personnel was needed if the agricultural program was to grow. Acting on this conviction, Barringer suggested to the board that Quick and A. P. Spencer be replaced. The board accepted his proposal at its June meeting, and in an effort to get the farm department operating efficiently also authorized Barringer to make further changes in the personnel of the department. The press in reporting the action of the board inadvertently made it appear that the board had given Barringer a completely free hand to replace any personnel in any departmet of the College as he saw fit. This erroneous report sent a shock wave of sizeable dimension through the faculty, even causing some of the senior professors, including the popular Smyth, to start making discreet inquiries about openings at other institutions. Barringer made no effort to correct the news report until nearly two years later, at which time he confessed that the report had "created a devil of a situation" on the campus. He had not attempted to correct the report, he said, since he had made it a rule not to get involved in newspaper controversy.

Before the time for Quick's departure arrived, four new members had been added to the Board of Visitors. This board, following a strong appeal from Quick, rescinded the action of the previous board in releasing him and decided to give him another chance. Then, within less than a month, the board reversed this action and decided to release him on September 1, 1908. At this time, H. L. Price was appointed dean of the agricultural department. Quick resigned at once but then presented a bill for the work he had done as director of the Experiment Station prior to the arrival of Dr. Fletcher. The United States Department of Agriculture refused to pay this bill on the grounds that it had no record of Quick's having served as director; thereupon Quick brought suit against the College for payment. The representative of the United States Department of Agriculture declined to be drawn into the controversy but decided to withhold federal funds from the Experiment Station until it was firmly established that all such funds had been, and would be, expended legally. Barringer disagreed strongly with Quick and said so in one of his typically blunt letters but had to settle by paying a portion, at least, of Quick's claim.

In the meantime, Barringer was facing trouble from another direction. At the same time he had recommended the replacement of Dr. Quick, he had also recommended that R. A. Marr be replaced as dean of engineering. Marr

objected, and the board sustained his objection on the grounds that any dissatisfaction with his department grew from inadequate equipment rather than from
his alleged deficiencies as a teacher. Following this "victory," Marr reportedly
launched a program of guerilla warfare against Barringer but disguised it as a
campaign for the welfare of the engineering department. Barringer's first year
in office certainly had not started off very auspiciously with his faculty. His second year was little if any better and once again started with events which he
could not foresee.

He held another reduction sale of livestock, which boomeranged again.
This time it was found that some of the hogs sold had been infected with hog
cholera prior to the sale. Once more the College was faced with lawsuits and
angry demands for refunds of money. Such refunds were made right and left,
and the reputation of VPI diminished rapidly.

While these events had been taking place, Barringer had been caught up in
another series of developments which he had nothing to do with starting. The
developments skyrocketed him to a temporary pinnacle of popularity with students and alumni and just as suddenly plunged him into the role of the scape-
goat responsible for a colossal failure.

During McBryde's administration, VPI had entered into an arrangement
with the State Board of Agriculture to conduct a geological survey of the state.
For some reason the relationships between VPI and the Board of Agriculture
had not been too cordial, and the Board of Agriculture had withdrawn its financial support of the survey. Following this withdrawal of support, a bill had been
introduced and passed in the state Senate to provide $10,000 per annum for
such a survey. According to Wyndham B. Robertson, a member of the VPI
board, the proposed survey was to be conducted jointly by a committee made up
of representatives from the VPI board and the State Board of Agriculture. Robertson explained to Barringer that he had gone to Richmond to support the
Senate bill but failed to consult the representatives of the Board of Agriculture.
As a result, said Robertson, the Board of Agriculture "took grave offense and
instead of assisting I think the Commissioner of Agriculture, if not the entire
Board, fought it." At any rate, the bill was held up in the House and did not
pass.

Dr. T. L. Watson ('90), professor of geology under whom the survey had
been started at VPI, had resigned during the session of 1906-07 to move to the
University of Virginia and had been succeeded as head of geology by Dr. R. J.
Holden. On December 13, 1907, Robertson wrote to Barringer, setting forth
these developments and then said:

> Now Professor Watson is on the faculty of the University of Virginia, and
> the University of Virginia I am satisfied will try this session to get an appropri-
> ation for such a survey. The VPI having originally suggested this matter,
> and having then the man, Prof. Watson, to make this survey, it seems to me
> the VPI ought not willingly to permit the University of Virginia to step in
> and steal its thunder. We at least ought to be recognized and have a repre-
> sentation and proper credit. This is the way it strikes me. I simply call your
> attention to this matter that whatever steps may be determined upon should
> be taken in time to effect some results.

Barringer's "steps" were sudden, terse, devoid of all subtlety, and taken
"in time to effect some result," although not the one expected by either man.
Alderman's activities at the University of Virginia on behalf of the movement for

better rural conditions had already aroused Barringer's suspicions. Barringer reasoned that if Robertson's information was correct, it meant that the University of Virginia was in fact planning to move into the domain he had staked out for VPI.

A few discreet inquiries soon convinced him that a bill was to be introduced into the Senate by G. T. Rison of Chatham to establish the geological survey at the University of Virginia. Having verified this fact, Barringer set to work. He appealed to the students to spread the word that the University was attempting to steal something that belonged to VPI; at the same time, he urged them to get their parents to contact members of the legislature. Some of the students reacted to this information with a fervor more appropriate for a football game than a legislative matter. They wrote passionate letters of appeal not only to parents but to every farmer whose address they could secure. Many of these individuals caught the excitement manifested by the students but swamped Barringer instead of the legislature with mail. One individual assured Barringer that the geological survey was of doubtful value to the farmers if left at VPI; if moved to the University of Virginia, it would be of no value to anyone, he said. Others wrote, urging Barringer "to hold on to whatever it is you have, don't let the university have it." Other letters, expressing sentiments strikingly similar to those expressed nearly three quarters of a century earlier in connection with the geological survey undertaken by William Barton Rodgers, poured in on the swamped Barringer. It is not known how many letters, if any, the "farmers" wrote to members of the legislature.

Barringer secured more favorable results from the alumni and friends to whom he addressed the following letter:

> During the present session of the Legislature, Senator Rison, of Chatham, will introduce a bill (see enclosure) to transfer and establish at the University of Virginia, the Geological Survey of the State, recently begun at the Virginia Polytechnic Institute.
>
> An examination of this bill will show that it proposes, not only the removal of the geological work proper, but the introduction there of such work as the "examination of soils and study of their adaptability to particular crops," and other allied forms of investigation strictly industrial and best done at industrial institutions.
>
> No friend of the University of Virginia, knowing its history as a school of pure learning, high literary standards and cultural aims, even in learned professions, but must deplore this attempt to mingle bastard industrialism with other catch-penny adnexa recently added to its curriculum. I have but recently come to the Virginia Polytechnic Institute, and I wish the opportunity, untrammeled, to harmonize and work out the great industrial problems belonging to its field. This move is really more political than anything else. It is now, "but the camels nose in the tent"—but unchecked this and every other state school will soon be found as "trailers to the Ogden kite."
>
> I ask your earnest consideration of the real aim of this move.

Many alumni gave "earnest consideration" to this letter and began a concerted effort to influence the legislature not to support the proposal. A long letter was addressed by Barringer to Senator Rison, in which Rison's bill was attacked point by point as unwise, unnecessary, and unwelcome. This letter concluded with the following blunt assertion: "This proposal to create such an 'enterprise' at the University of Virginia seems to me as simply the beginning of an ill-disguised move to finally concentrate all work of a scientific nature in the state at the University of Virginia, and make this, as well as all other state institutions in the state subservient to it."

Other letters written by Barringer indicated that he was enjoying to the fullest the controversy he was stirring up. To Wyndham Robertson he wrote: "Our alumni look to us to fight this thing to a finish," while to another acquaintance he said, "We have been having a very interesting fight here, on the attempt of our friend Alderman to grab our geological survey. He may succeed, but when he gets it he will know he has been fighting." Letters with a direct sectional appeal and carrying a plain warning that this bill was but the beginning of an effort on the part of the friends of the University to steal from VPI went to different parts of the state; at the same time other letters, reminiscent of the post-bellum debate on locating the agricultural school, went to many leaders. The students were delighted with "Oom Paul," as they familiarly called Barringer; alumni backing appeared to be solid. It began to appear that Barringer's one-man campaign conducted largely by his "command of the ability to express his ideas in terse and husky Anglo-Saxon" would succeed, but at this moment the campaign collapsed. The Board of Visitors did not share Barringer's determination to keep the geological survey at VPI.

The realization of this fact dismayed Barringer, but the board, perhaps with greater prudence and understanding of the political situation, decided it would rather switch than fight. After several conferences, it entered into a compromise: if the legislature would provide for the establishment of a professorship of mining engineering at VPI, and appropriate funds to wipe out a part of its debt, then VPI would withdraw its objection to the location of the geological survey at the University of Virginia. Barringer did not like the proposed change but confined the expression of his strenuous objections to the board members. His counterproposal was to go after both the professorship and the survey. What Barringer did not know and what he did not learn until several years later was the fact that the astute rector J. Thompson Brown, had conducted his own private poll of the Senate and had decided it would be futile to oppose the location of the survey at the University of Virginia. Besides, Brown and several board members had parted political company with the leadership in the State Board of Agriculture and feared that a political fight would do VPI more harm than good. The political fodder that the diseased cattle episode provided to anyone hostile to VPI did not go unrecognized by the board either.

The compromise bill was passed by the legislature and approved on March 13, 1908. President Barringer accepted the defeat gracefully and proceeded to write to alumni and friends, explaining what had happened. No attempt was made to inform the alumni of his opposition to the outcome beyond his branding it as a compromise. On the contrary, the entire tone of the communication was optimistic and constructive, but the alumni were not consoled; furthermore, a small but powerful group refused to be consoled. Instead of giving Barringer the support he requested, many alumni, soured by the loss of the geological survey to rival University of Virginia, began to watch his administration with an over-critical eye, ready to seize on anything and everything he did which in their opinions was not in the best interests of VPI. The day the legislature established the geological survey at the University of Virginia marked the beginning of an alumni revolt against Barringer which plagued him for the rest of his days at VPI. He recognized the alumni hostility at once but felt it grew from excessive loyalty to the institution. Early in 1908 he wrote to Eggleston, "The devotion of the alumni of this institution is to me of a peculiar nature. At the University we had an academic-like affection, but here it is a personal matter if you touch the Virginia Polytechnic Institute. It is a loyalty I have never seen, but it produces a bitterness which had best not be."

To another acquaintance he expressed the conviction that loyalty of some alumni was so great that it caused them to confuse proposals for change and growth at the College with an attack on the College. The problem of introducing needed change, he wrote, was often hindered rather than helped by excessive alumni loyalty. This charge was tartly answered by one alumnus with the observation that it was the responsibility of a college president to provide intelligent leadership rather than bullheaded dictation where alumni were concerned.

Regardless of the responsibility for the unusual events which unfolded during Dr. Barringer's first year at the helm of the College, the unhappy fact remains that the year ended with less harmony than it had begun. The split in the faculty, evident during the last year of McBryde's administration, had widened; a segment of the alumni had been alienated; the dean of agriculture had been forced out over his protest; the dean of engineering had been threatened; the United States Department of Agriculture was demanding a more accurate accounting of Experiment Station funds; officials in the State Board of Agriculture had been alienated; powerful political figures had been miffed; the operation of the college farm had been reduced to near shambles; and the tenure of every professor was thought to have been placed solely in Barringer's hands. The greatest plus in his favor was the fact that most students liked him and did not hesitate to say so. These students felt that Barringer was the unfortunate victim of circumstances during his first year. The records seem to support this opinion. The records also support the belief that Barringer's personality did little to help his cause. He was simply too blunt, forthright, and outspoken in presenting his views to avoid ruffling the feelings of those who might differ with him. He recognized this fact but seemed unable or unwilling to do anything about it, although he never deliberately departed from being courteous. In a letter of apology to Governor W. H. Mann, Barringer once said of himself, "While in some ways a blunt man in speech and manner, I am never knowingly guilty of a breach of courtesy." On another occasion in answer to a board member complaining that the impression was "getting around" that Barringer was not in favor of military training at the College, he frankly stated that he did have strong doubts about the value of such training "and as I dissemble poorly the community is obliged to see it." Perhaps the most significant appraisal of self made by Barringer is to be found in a letter he addressed to Woodrow Wilson during the latter's campaign for the presidency of the United States. After suggesting a somewhat risky stratagem for Wilson to consider in an effort to woo the Negro vote, Barringer concluded, "I think it pays to do the bold thing—when the proper thing, and then let the multitude think what they blamed please." Certainly Barringer's warmest admirers and strongest critics would have to agree that he tried to follow this conviction in his administration of the Virginia Polytechnic Institute.

If Barringer felt any discouragement over the results of his first year in office, nothing in his official reports or correspondence showed it. On the contrary, these reports sounded a note of confidence and optimism, almost exuberance, over the prospects facing the College. Early in the session of 1907-08, he had appointed Dr. W. E. Barlow as dean of the graduate department and had secured Professor O. C. Burkhart to fill the newly created chair of mining engineering. In addition to these accomplishments, he had spent the year studying the overall situation in the College and planning for future growth and developments. Before the end of the first year in office, Barringer knew exactly what he wanted VPI to become under his direction. He wanted a high-grade industrial college devoted to agriculture and the mechanic arts. His examination of the College convinced him that the agricultural program was quite weak; at the same time, his study led to a dark suspicion that the engineering department was not developing the real mechanical-arts function appropriate to land-grant colleges. Since the state seemed to be in such a dire need of agricultural education, he decided to pursue a policy of maintaining the engineering department at its current level of operation and to concentrate on the building up of the agricultural program.

Obviously, in order to accomplish his objective, he had to operate within the framework of his times; and these times, especially with respect to education, were in a ferment. The Cooperative Education Association, organized in 1904 primarily to capitalize on the interest in education created by the Southern Education Board and the General Education Board, had been unusually successful by the time the legislature met in January, 1908. Largely as a result of the strenuous efforts of the first-named association, this legislature devoted an unusual display of interest to the cause of industrial education in general and to agricultural education in particular. Legislation was enacted leading to the establishment within each congressional district, of one high school specifically organized to teach agriculture, domestic economy, and manual training. These schools were to be conducted under rules and regulations to be prescribed by the State Board of Education and the president of VPI. This same legislature, after a prolonged struggle to locate one normal and industrial school for women, reached a compromise by locating, not one but two such schools and by unofficially promising to locate a third one at Radford. The first two were to be located at Harrisonburg and Fredericksburg respectively. It was generally assumed that at least one, if not all of these schools, would teach agriculture to the girls enrolling in them.

Since the College of William and Mary had been taken into the state system of higher education in 1906, the sudden addition of two new institutions in 1908, with the almost near certainty of a third to be added in 1910, alarmed some of the conservative members of the legislature. This alarm was heightened when proposals were made to establish a normal training department at each of the single high schools to be selected to teach agriculture within each congressional district. If these proposals became realities, the state would be faced with ten additional state institutions. In the face of this alarm, cries of excessive multiplication of colleges, excessive duplication of effort, and of excessive numbers of governing boards began to be heard. To cope with this situation, which admittedly was becoming confused, the legislature appointed a commission to study the educational program developing so rapidly in the state. As one part of its responsibilities, this commission was to investigate the state's program of higher education. The directives to the commission were not clear, but it was commonly understood that one of its objectives was to discover unnecessary

duplication of work between state institutions and to recommend possible con-
solidations of programs where practical. Barringer suspected that one member
of the commission was none too friendly toward VPI.

In addition to the possible effect of legislative activity on VPI, Barringer
knew of another development having direct effect on the College. VPI had come
under strong attack at a meeting of representatives of the newly developing high
schools. This group felt that because of its low admission requirements and the
work of its preparatory department, VPI was competing with high schools and
defeating their efforts to strengthen their college preparatory offerings. Barringer
felt the same way and did not hesitate to say so as he set about reorganizing the
College into an industrial institute.

Beginning with the session of 1908-09, the school was organized into the following departments: department of agriculture, department of agricultural experiment station, department of applied sciences, department of engineering, and the
graduate department. This latter change put the graduate program on the same
administrative level enjoyed by the other departments.

The board accepted Barringer's recommendation to drop the preparatory
department, but his blunt appraisal of this department as being totally unworthy
of the time and attention of a real college deeply wounded the ego of many alumni
who had taken advantage of this department in order to get into VPI. Others, who
had attended only the preparatory department, felt that their status as alumni of
VPI had been degraded and cheapened by Barringer's remarks. At the same time
he dropped the sub-freshman or preparatory work, he also dropped the general-
science degree program. Barringer did not say so publicly, but privately he
expressed the belief that the general-science program, not being a "bread-winning" one, would be considered by the newly appointed commission to study
higher education as a duplication of work. In a letter to A. H. Rosenfeld ('04), who
had moved to Argentina, Barringer, discussing the dropping of these two programs, said, "I have wiped out every degree course here except technical ones.
There are no longer any courses in General Science or things of that character,
as I felt that we should concentrate on the bread-winning courses and do only
college work. I have wiped out the sub-freshman work also. This created more
animosity than I expected, but in the future I feel that it will be best." The thing
that Barringer did not write, and perhaps did not know, was the coincidental fact
that the group feeling the greatest animosity over the dropping of these two
courses was the same group which had experienced the greatest emotional upset
over the loss of the geological survey to the University of Virginia.

At the same time he dropped the two just-mentioned courses, he persuaded
the board to increase the entrance requirements in English and mathematics. As
Barringer forcefully pointed out, he wanted the College to take full advantage of
the increase in the quality and number of high schools in the state in order to
upgrade its own program. Throughout his administration, Barringer worked to
upgrade the admission standard at VPI. In a letter to Thomas S. Pritchett, President of the Carnegie Foundation for the Advancement of Teaching, Barringer
expressed his utmost contempt for the college preparatory value of the vocational, industrial, and "bob-tailed" science courses getting under way in the high
schools. Work in such courses, he argued, represented only paper credit. He
wanted good solid work in English, history, and mathematics; and he wanted it in
that order. Furthermore, he wanted the colleges to force the high schools to improve their offerings in these areas by refusing to accept their graduates until they

did so. Pritchett answered Barringer to the effect that in his opinion schools like VPI should exercise caution as they raised entrance requirements in terms of Carnegie units, lest they unintentionally close the door to the very people for whom the College was intended. Following receipt of this communication, Barringer moderated the speed with which he pressed for higher standards, but he did not yield one whit in his determination to achieve this goal for VPI.

To upgrade the instructional program in agriculture, Barringer continued the two four-year courses in the school of scientific agriculture. One degree was given in agriculture, and the second was given in horticulture. In addition to these programs, one called the farmer's winter course of one month's duration was organized in the winter of 1907. The work of this course was entirely practical. A third program known as the school of agricultural apprentices was organized and offered for the first time during the session of 1908-09. This was a two-year course definitely set up to meet the demand for instruction in practical agriculture. As first organized, a student upon successful completion of the work in this course could enter one of the regular four-year programs in scientific agriculture. After one year's operation of the program, Barringer found that most of the enrollees were using the program as a sub-freshman stepping stone into one of the regular four-year programs and were not interested in agriculture at all. At the same time, he realized that this program would be duplicated by the agricultural instruction he was helping to set up in the congressional-district high schools getting under way in the state. Barringer was determined that VPI under his administration would never again be accused of teaching work on the high-school level. The next year, therefore, he reduced the apprentice course to one year, eliminating all work which might be counted toward college admission, and made the course into a rigidly practical one.

During the reorganization of 1908-09, the class schedule was changed to four fifty-minute morning periods with a three-hour laboratory period for the afternoon. This schedule was so popular it became the basic one followed long after Barringer's retirement from the presidency. At the same time this schedule was set up, the executive council of deans was abolished in order, Barringer said, to permit him to come into closer contact with the students.

This change succeeded in bringing him into contact with the students, but Barringer quickly realized the College was making contact with only a small part of the agricultural community of the state. In an effort to improve this situation, he threw his support back of the movement for more district or field experiment stations, which he believed could be operated as a combination experimental and demonstration farm. With respect to these stations, he was in accord with the following description by S. W. Fletcher, director of the Experiment Station: "The Experiment Station plots should be a popular meeting place for farmers of the state, and would be if they were more accessible. The only practicable way to improve this situation is to take the Experiment Station to the farmers by means of these temporary experiment plots, which we call 'District Experiment Stations' and by cooperative experiments." The results from these earlier district stations were mixed as far as benefits to farmers were concerned, but definite as far as Barringer was concerned. He became convinced that off-campus agricultural education, whether it involved experimentation or demonstration, achieved the best results when conducted under the supervision of a trained worker, preferably a VPI faculty member.

As another method of extending agricultural education to the people, Barringer supported the "moving schools of agriculture" which had been started during McBryde's administration as a cooperative project between VPI, the State Department of Agriculture and Immigration, and some of the railroads. These "moving schools" consisted of special trains fitted up by the VPI staff as agricultural laboratories and hauled over the state by the railroads, particularly the Southern and the Norfolk and Western. The schedules for these trains were carefully worked out in advance in cooperation with local leaders who assumed responsibility for advance publicity and made all local arrangements. Under this plan, the arrival of an "institute train" in many communities became a great local event at which bands played, educational speech-making flourished, and huge picnic lunches did not go unnoticed. Barringer was so enthusiastic about these trains that he explored the possibility of getting the Virginian railway to build a spur connection into Blacksburg in order to move an "institute train" over that line. His desire to get an additional rail line for his movable schools backfired on him. Some of his discussions supporting an expansion of the schools onto additional lines were reported by one newspaper as a strong attack on the schools supported and hauled over its lines by the Norfolk and Western Railway. Patrons along this line were greatly shocked and angered by the report. So was L. E. Johnson, president of the railroad and member of the VPI Board of Visitors. Johnson wrote a warm letter to Barringer, offering to withdraw the railroad's support of the schools, since Barringer deemed them inferior to the ones supported by the Norfolk and Western's "competitor." Not only had the statement hurt the railroad, claimed Johnson, but also had made it appear that he, Johnson, had made improper use of both his position on the board and his position as president of the Norfolk and Western Railway. Barringer answered Johnson at once and attempted to convince him that the news report was due to a reporter unfriendly to VPI and to the Norfolk and Western and not to any criticism he had made of the Norfolk and Western movable schools. Barringer's report satisfied Johnson, who thereafter continued to support the schools and at the same time gave his full backing to Barringer's administration of the College. Since this correspondence was not released to the public, many alumni and "grass roots" supporters of the College and of the "institute trains" continued to harbor resentment against Barringer for what they thought was an unfair attack on the Norfolk and Western movable school.

Barringer also was active in trying to bring the resources of VPI to the aid of the agricultural education programs getting under way in the public schools. He was none too successful in this endeavor for a number of reasons. In the first place, Barringer, and especially some of his faculty in the department of agriculture, saw parts of this public school program as a threat to the practical side of the VPI program. The legislation which made it possible to launch instruction in agriculture in the public schools had been pushed vigorously by Joseph D. Eggleston, state superintendent of public instruction. Eggleston saw to it that this legislation made it possible for VPI to cooperate with the total program, and mandatory to participate in the high school program. Unfortunately, the leadership at VPI seemed devoid of imaginative ideas in this new venture and largely contented itself with a minimum compliance with the legislative mandates. Eggleston, on the other hand, proved to be a dynamic, aggressive, imaginative leader, who grabbed everything in sight that faintly resembled agricultural education and attempted to introduce it into his school system. As a result, he found himself faced at once with a shortage of teachers trained in agriculture and immediately wrote to Barringer for help. Referring to the agitation to teach agriculture in the new normal schools and institutes, Eggleston asked, "Is it possible we will have to depend on women to teach agriculture?" Barringer thought not; he was sure such an "unfortunate situation" would not come to pass if Eggleston would provide funds for VPI to operate a summer school especially organized to train persons to teach agriculture in the public schools.

In support of his summer-school proposal, he informed a skeptical Eggleston that VPI could take care of 2,000 students, since, "we have the equipment and if necessary we can get a few spell binders from the outside." This "spell binder" approach was not what Eggleston had in mind; besides, he did not have the money for such an undertaking. His confidence in the competence of VPI to train teachers of agriculture was further reduced when he heard that Quick, dean of agriculture, before his dismissal, had argued that special training was not needed to teach agriculture. All that was needed, according to Quick, was a "simple book on agriculture" which any teacher could buy. Dean H. L. Price, who succeeded Quick, seems to have kept silent on the subject, although in later years he admitted that he had been opposed to the idea of preparing agriculture teachers at VPI. S. W. Fletcher, director of the Agricultural Experiment Station, was in favor of a comprehensive program to be worked in cooperation with other state institutions of higher education. By the time Fletcher had formulated his ideas, however, Eggleston had reason to believe that Barringer's interest in preparing teachers of agriculture was motivated more by a desire to prevent the University of Virginia from preparing such teachers than it was by any sincere interest in the work. Eggleston, who had worked mightily to pour oil on the troubled waters churned by the geological survey episode, did not want to precipitate another incident between the two institutions.

Undoubtedly, the greatest error and lack of imagination manifested by Barringer and his faculty in agriculture was the failure to see the potential and the significance of the farm demonstration work and its closely allied boys' and girls' club work which Eggleston was promoting with effective vigor. The evolution of this extension work in Virginia has been told and retold. Briefly stated, it started after Dr. H. B. Frissell of Hampton Normal and Industrial Institute told Eggleston of the demonstration work getting under way in Mississippi under Seaman A. Knapp. Eggleston was impressed with what he heard and arranged a meeting with Governor Swanson and others to hear Dr. Knapp outline the program in more detail. Eggleston in later years seemed to have some difficulty in recalling the names of the participants in this conference, but he did remember Governor Swanson; E. A. Alderman, president of the University of Virginia; S. C. Mitchell of Richmond College; John S. Bryan, wealthy business-man and newspaper publisher of Richmond; Jackson Davis, editor of *The Southern Planter*; George W. Koiner, Commissioner of Agriculture; Mrs. B. B. Munford of Richmond, an active member of the Cooperative Education Association; and T. O. Sandy, a progressive farmer living near Burkeville. Apparently, no representative from VPI attended the meeting. It is not known if one was invited.

As an outgrowth of this meeting, T. O. Sandy was employed as the state agent, and the first farm demonstration work in the state started in 1907 in three counties within traveling radius of Burkeville. Sandy chose Southall Farrar as his assistant and assigned him the responsibility for developing the boys' corn clubs in the state. About the same time, Sandy chose Miss Ella G. Agnew to develop the girls' garden, canning, and poultry clubs. In 1910, she "became the first home demonstration agent in America and the first woman to serve as a field worker of the United States Department of Agriculture."

In 1910, the legislature formally created and strengthened the congressional-district agricultural high schools it had started in 1908 and at the same time made it possible for these schools to conduct both demonstration and experimental work. Sandy went along with this idea of expanding his work, but Barringer dragged his feet. He saw these programs as interfering with the College's field experiment stations, the movable schools of agriculture, the school of agricultural apprentices, and the first year of college instruction in agriculture. Eggleston, on the other hand, was delighted with the developments. He did everything within his power to promote work for the adults. At the same time he made repeated overtures to VPI authorities to assume more responsibility for promoting the work. When it became clear that these authorities were only lukewarm toward these programs, Eggleston went full speed ahead without them. With or without VPI, Eggleston, Sandy, Frissell, and others were determined to have the demonstration work. This determination was ably supported in the legislature by W. H. Mann and others.

By 1910, that part of the spirit for educational revival which had been channeled into the support of agricultural education, had produced a confused picture in Virginia. This development was not at all surprising, considering the fact that agricultural education programs were being sponsored simultaneously by the Virginia Polytechnic Institute, the State Board of Agriculture, the General Education Board, the State Board of Education, and the Cooperative Education Association. The resulting confusion was threatening the entire movement. To help remedy this situation and at the same time to provide an agency for receiving and disbursing the money being given to the state by the General Education Board through the United States Department of Agriculture, Eggleston proposed that the state form a United Board of Agriculture to coordinate the work and oversee the disbursements of funds.

Unfortunately, by this time the professional relations between Eggleston and Barringer were rather cool. Matters between the two men had not been helped any by a news release out of Blacksburg reporting on a meeting of the Board of Visitors. According to this report "State Superintendent Eggleston was not present nor has he been present at a meeting for more than two years." Eggleston was furious and wrote to Barringer, demanding to know who had prepared the report of the board meeting; such a statement, claimed Eggleston, was a stab in the back by some one at Blacksburg. Barringer had partly soothed Eggleston's ruffled feelings by telling him that the article was an elaboration by the local correspondent, E. R. Price, "whom the boys call Flopsy." "Flopsy" was a harmless fellow, said Barringer, who got paid by the yard and therefore had to pad his reports. He never wrote with malice or animus, Barringer insisted; therefore Eggleston could be sure that no stab in the back was intended. Then Barringer got in a sly thrust at Eggleston.

It was reported, he said, that at the meeting in question Price "lay on the grass out in front of the Board Room . . . and heard a good deal more than the [official] report covered." Having thus implied that Eggleston's long absences from the board meetings had indeed been a matter of discussion overheard by Price, Barringer offered the dubious consolation that Price was a wild sort of young fellow whom few took seriously. "Remember," said Barringer, "that a wild horse kicks without regard to the points of the compass." Barringer's estimate of Price proved to be as faulty as his estimate of farm demonstration work, because "Flopsy" Price, as professor of journalism, editor of the *Extension Service News,* and local correspondent for many state papers, came near becoming a campus "institution" "without regard to the points of the compass" as any professor that ever served VPI.

When Barringer first heard of the bill in the legislature proposing the creation of a United Board of Agriculture, he casually mentioned the bill in a circular letter to each board member. He had not been consulted concerning the proposal, but instead of getting information concerning it he pointedly stated, "I know nothing of the facts beyond the rumor that Governor Mann is behind it." "A cursory investigation," he said, had convinced him that the proposal, if accepted by the legislature, would be of uncertain value. If Barringer had made more than a "cursory investigation" of the matter, undoubtedly he would not have written such a letter. Not only did the proposal have the backing of Governor Mann, but it also had the backing of "every friend of VPI in the House and Senate," according to one supporter. In addition to having this wide base of support, the bill embodied ideas identical with some which the Board of Visitors had already endorsed.

When Eggleston, who in reality was the father of the United Board proposal, received Barringer's letter, he immediately sent to each board member a letter in which he deplored the fact that Barringer, after admitting that he knew nothing of the facts, had seen fit to pass judgment upon the merits of the bill. Turning to a defense of the bill, Eggleston wrote:

> I beg to assure the Board of Visitors that the bill, in my judgment, will be of immense help to the Virginia Polytechnic Institute and that so far as I know every friend of that institution in the State Capitol is heartily in favor of it. I feel sure that when the members of the Board of Visitors have read the bill they will agree that it will help popularize the Virginia Polytechnic Institute throughout the State of Virginia. It places the adult demonstration work in the hands of that institution. The demonstration work now being done by the U. S. Department of Agriculture through Mr. T. O. Sandy and others will under this bill receive $10,000 for this work and this amount, in addition to what is now given by the U. S. Department of Agriculture, will be spent through Blacksburg. The Board of Visitors at its last meeting endorsed identically this idea . . . .

In spite of this thinly veiled opportunity for VPI to move toward the leadership of the agricultural demonstration work in the state, Barringer preferred to follow his own program, although he realized that he had made a mistake in his analysis of the United Agricultural Board bill. He therefore attempted to extricate himself by means of the following letter to Eggleston:

> Your circular letter just to hand, and in reply I will say that I am afraid you have treated my comment too seriously. I stated frankly that my examination was cursory, and went no stronger than *believe* on the rest of it. A more careful examination convinces me that the bill is the original matter put into organic form, minus the spirit of rivalry that I had hoped for from the independent workings. Of course, a platform is a place to get in on, and if you think there is more likelihood of an appropriation in this than the other, I am for

it. I hardly cared to send the bill [to board members] without some comment, but I am sorry you took that comment so seriously.

Eggleston accepted this somewhat confused explanation and continued to support the bill for the United Agricultural Board, until the legislature created such a board in March, 1910. Following the passage of this bill, Eggleston was both puzzled and disappointed by the fact that Barringer made no effort to have VPI assume the leadership in the farm demonstration work; instead, Barringer pushed his movable schools of agriculture with increased vigor and thereby began to lose the support of the "farm demonstrators."

Although Barringer had been working vigorously to develop the agricultural program, he had not been neglecting other facets of the college community. The source of the College's water supply was safeguarded by appropriate masonry, and a cooperative arrangement was started between the town and the College to share a water and a sewerage system. A concrete walkway was laid connecting Number One Barracks with the Mess Hall. This latter walk, once it was lined with trees and shrubbery, came to be known as "The Long Walk," or as "Lovers' Lane" by generations of cadets, most of whom got their first military experience at VPI by marching to and from mess over this walkway.

A mining engineering building was erected close to the site of the present power house and a dairy and horse barn erected on the site presently included in the parking lot to the west of the Coliseum. Barringer wanted to erect a library, but neither the legislature nor the board seemed interested in such a project. Unable to get an appropriation of money for this purpose, Barringer wrote to Lawrence Priddy, who had been so successful in raising the money for the "Y" building, to solicit his help in trying to get a donation from Andrew Carnegie. Priddy said that he had visited Carnegie on behalf of the "Y" but that Carnegie had informed him he was not interested in Christian work or in making donations to state-supported schools. Upon receipt of this information, Barringer wrote again to Priddy, suggesting that they approach Carnegie anyway. At this point, he asked Priddy if he thought it would help matters with Carnegie if he, Barringer, sought to enlist the aid of some prominent New Yorkers whom he knew personally. Priddy did not think so; but while he and Barringer throughout this exchange remained cordial, he would have been less than human if he had not noticed Barringer's readiness to use "prominent New Yorkers" to get what Priddy himself had failed to get.

Barringer did not give up his efforts to secure outside funds for the institution, although he did abandon the idea of a new library. In May, 1910, he wrote to the wealthy Thomas Fortune Ryan, soliciting his interest in the school. This letter to Ryan is so revealing of Barringer's thinking that it is given in its entirety:

> I have been the president of the Virginia Agricultural and Mechanical College "VPI"—for nearly three years, and from the day I landed here it has been a fight against inertia, conservatism, and antagonism to change and I am thoroughly weary of the job.
> You have the power to change this into a practical school of agriculture, rid it of its moss-back methods, and take it to the people.
> If you have any inclination to listen to arguments along this line, I should be glad to write to you further or confer with you and give you all the information I possess.

Ryan, who was an active behind-the-scenes power in Virginia politics, apparently was not inclined to listen. At least there is no record of any reply to this unusual approach. In another appeal to a wealthy philanthropist, Barringer referred to the Virginia Polytechnic Institute as "an industrial school for poor boys of the state." This appeal got no money whatever but brought rich rewards in resentment from all alumni who heard about it.

As Barringer began to develop the short courses and the special courses in agriculture, he began to encounter some difficulty in fitting these courses around the military requirements. After struggling with the problem for about three years, he recommended to the board that the military requirements be suspended for all except the freshmen and sophomore classes. "I am convinced," he wrote, "that the duties of a soldier as demanded here cut down the capacity for class-room work at least twenty-five per cent. The question for us, therefore, seems to be—Can we fulfill the demands of the United States Government and yet increase the opportunities of our men for obtaining more out of their technical course than they now obtain?"

Barringer informed the board that he had tried to get some information about military practices from the presidents of other land-grant institutions but that for the most part they had not been interested in discussing the matter. They had long since "determined that when these schools pass high school grade, they have got to cut out military of the senior year and even of the junior, except where especially desired." As for the present situation at VPI, Barringer said, "Believing that the best way to get rid of a bad law was to enforce it, I have for the past two years held the seniors to the general military regulations, with the result that they are continuously pressed for time for study."

Barringer's recommendation for such a drastic change in the military feature of the school shocked the board, which, after some discussion, referred the matter to a committee for further study. Before the committee had reached an agreement on the matter, the board got another shock. In 1912, the State Farmers' Institute recommended that the name of the College be changed from the Virginia Agricultural and Mechanical College and Polytechnic Institute back to the original name of the Virginia Agricultural and Mechanical College. At the same time, this institute recommended that the military feature be reduced to the minimum required by law.

Barringer in an I-told-you-so report to the board, expressed his full sympathy with both resolutions but felt it was too late to do anything about the name change. The first change in name should never have been made, he said; but since it had been made, the monogram "VPI" had become known throughout the whole country. Any change now would hurt, he warned. At long last, Barringer was beginning to respect the power of the alumni, some of whom, he knew, had been fighting him every step of the way. As for any revision of the military, he contented himself with reminding the board of his previous recommendation and repeated his conviction that experiences in the better land-grant colleges "show that scholarship and military are really incompatible, unless you have one instructor for every ten men, as they have at West Point, etc." The board considered the matter at some length and then recommended that no change be made in the military feature.

In actuality Barringer was against the entire concept of training in "military tactics" as required in the Morrill Land-Grant Act. Not only did he investigate the extent of military training being carried on in the land-grant institutions of the country, but he also tried to get the presidents of these institutions to unite in support of a movement to have Congress remove the military feature from the land-grant act. Not getting much support from this source, he solicited the help of the Carnegie Endowment for International Peace. As a result of the military feature, he wrote, "In these land-grant colleges . . . Militarism with all that it implies is thus begotten in . . . young men at a very susceptible age. . . ." Not only did the military feature promote an unhealthy militarism, he wrote, but it also interferred with what he considered to be the true mission of the schools. He believed:

> The work of these schools is made incongruous by the military teaching. We are called upon to send men out to the fields with a proper bucolic spirit of the husbandryman, and men to the forests with a true spirit of conservatism as their chief asset, and yet we make all worship first, in their susceptible years, at the temple of Mars. It not only militates against their technical proficiency in the gentle arts, but ruins the spirit.

In another letter to the same group he wrote, "Aside from the peace element in it, to improve our men technically for the new warfare, the warfare of conservation and industrial improvement is good business. . . With the intuitive foresight of youth, the boys themselves already see this new relation in its true light, and they are nearly all 'down on military.' "

Barringer received no help from this source either but, although against the military feature, announced his intention to enforce the requirement rigidly as long as it was a requirement. Records indicate that he carried out this intention to the fullest extent.

Whether because of or in spite of his aversion to the military feature is not clear, but President Barringer took the lead in extending self-government to the students. Following the adoption of a constitution by the Corps of Cadets in 1908, he encouraged the officers in this organization to formalize an honor code which could be used as a guide for conduct and regulation of student behavior. Rejecting faculty supervision of the enforcement of the honor code as "undesirable paternalism not to be tolerated" he encouraged the students to assume increasing responsibility for regulating their own affairs. This blending of the honor code, to be enforced by an honor court made up of cadets, into the organization of the Corps of Cadets, proved to be a most significant event in the history of student life at Tech. The principle of an honor system as a guide for personal conduct soon became one of the Corps' most cherished ideals and continues so to the present day. As the student body grew, the same principle was extended to the civilian students, who in 1941 set up their own honor court. An interesting feature of the honor code is the fact that during the years the students have largely determined the conduct which would constitute a violation of the honor code. Today violations consist of lying, cheating, stealing, and failing to report a suspected violation.

In spite of his aversion to the military feature, Barringer was proud of the Corps of Cadets and the appearance it made in public. Beyond his support of the honor system he was a bit skeptical about the Corps as a character-building agency and immediately denounced as an "insult" a claim that the Corps was necessary in order to accomplish such an objective. He left unanswered the question of who or what was insulted. Out-of-state Corps trips were discontinued, but numerous trips in the state were taken. In November, 1910, the Corps, en route to Norfolk, stopped over in Richmond to be reviewed by President Taft and to escort the President to the auditorium. Following the return of the group to Blacksburg, Barringer received a letter from Adjutant General W. W. Sale, reporting that some of the cots used by the Corps in the Richmond Armory were "missing," the implication being that the cadets had carried them off. Barringer fired a letter back to Adjutant General Sale, agreeing to investigate the matter if the word "missing" was changed to "misplaced." "Everyone must know that a Corps of Cadets marching out under arms in broad daylight could not carry off gold metal cots," he wrote.

President Barringer kept an open door policy toward the students, and they took full advantage of it. Undoubtedly, this policy was a drain on his energies, but it enabled him to keep in close touch with student wishes and developments. Oftentimes he was able to inaugurate programs or changes in conformity with these wishes. For instance, on learning that some students would not wear their uniform when at home for the holidays because the uniform was similar to that adopted by some of the preparatory schools, he immediately agreed to student-requested changes which made the VPI uniform "different." On another occasion, he agreed to let the German Club, organized in 1893 as a student social club whose primary function was the promotion of student dances, pay for and lay a special hardwood floor on the second floor auditorium of the Mess Hall. In return for this effort, the German Club was given some voice in determining the use of the building. The club exercised this "voice" so effectively it was not long until the name "German Hall" was given to the auditorium and in time extended to the entire building. As dances grew in popularity, each sponsoring organization had to secure permission from the German Club for the use of the floor. This practice, complained Barringer, soon convinced the students that they now owned "the whole building and the grounds around it." As a remedy, he proposed that the board refund the cost of the floor to the club and assert its full authority over the building. The board refused to do so, and the club continued to grow in stature and conviction of its control over the building. This situation was not resolved until during the early years of Dr. J. A. Burruss' administration, at which time the money was repaid to the German Club and the College took control of the German Hall once more.

Many of the students felt that six days were entirely too long a period of time to devote to commencement exercises. Barringer agreed. He presented a blunt recommendation to the board that the exercises be reduced, preferably to one day. The board was properly surprised and appointed a committee to study the matter. This committee finally recommended and the board agreed that the program should be reduced to three days. To help relieve the boredom of one of the longer commencements, which all students were required to attend, Barringer consented to a student request to make the sham battle, which had been a regular commencement feature for a number of years, into one larger than usual. According to student reports, one battle was a huge success, punctuated with the rattle of musketry, the roar of cannon ("we used only one"), the groans of the wounded, the yells of the charge, and the excited barking of all the dogs in Montgomery County which had converged on the field of battle but had refused to take sides. Small boys had darted everywhere picking up expended shells, while mothers on the sidelines, anxiously wringing their hands, had lent an unexpected touch of realism. Horses tethered in the grove surrounding the president's home had panicked, and some broke free. One dashed madly across the edge of the field of battle, drawing a careening buggy behind him. He parted company with the buggy, however, when he sailed across Stroubles Creek and the buggy did not. One squad of "soldiers" had been reported as missing but had been found resting in the shade of the apple trees back of Faculty Row, where some of the young ladies had fled at the first sound of battle. It was found that this squad had prudently conserved its ammunition; but it had not been determined whether this had been done as a precautionary measure in case it should be needed to protect the ladies or whether it had been done to protect the rifles from excessive cleaning. Other "soldiers" had not been so reticent in their use of ammunition, for as Barringer sheepishly informed the board, the military department had spent so much money on blank cartridges, "and other things of kindred value," it needed $250 additional money to pay for the event.

Athletics during Barringer's administration began to draw increased attention and support from the students. Track had been inaugurated as an intercollegiate sport in 1906. Basketball was inaugurated in 1908. Instead of having a coach for each sport, however, one man coached football, baseball, basketball, and track. Instead of a recruiting program the coach "took whatever came his way and did the best he could with it." Coach Branch Bocock did well indeed with the material that "came his way." In 1909 he won the "championship of the south" with a 6–1–0 record in football, losing only the game to Princeton University 6 to 8. He had a perfect record in basketball. In 1910 he had a 6–2–0 record in football, losing only to Navy, 0 to 3, and to N.C. State, 3 to 5. Once more he made a clean sweep of all basketball games.

Prior to 1909, VPI had been playing Navy in a series of games. Because of a misunderstanding in scheduling, graduate Manager C. P. (Sally) Miles dropped Navy from the 1909 schedule. The Navy "Football Representative," Lieutenant F. D. Bevier, immediately wrote to Barringer, protesting the action. Pointing out that Navy had agreed to pay a $500 guarantee which was "a sum greater than any guaranteed any other team except Princeton," Lieutenant Bevier continued:

> . . . We are willing to allow this amount, owing to the importance of having a good game at this time. I cannot tell you how important this game is to us, and we feel that we have not been quite fairly treated in the matter. Our game with your team has always been a good hard clean game and has been looked upon as a sort of a fixture on our schedule. I sincerely hope that the game can be played this year and that it will always be held as in the past years.

Dr. Barringer, after a thorough investigation which convinced him that the mix-up had occurred as a result of an oversight on the part of the Navy rather than on the part of Miles, declined to intervene. Indeed the records show that Barringer, while keeping fully informed as to athletic developments, on numerous occasions declined to intervene in the affairs of the Athletic Association on the ground that "the games are played by the students, not the faculty."

In 1909, the students wanted a better athletic field and presented their request to Barringer. He immediately granted their request and made arrangements for the athletic field started by McBryde to be enlarged and graded. The horticulture department, which had been using a part of this field, completed its move to the area north of the present Derring Hall and continued to develop an orchard on the site presently used as a student parking lot. The athletic field, a part of the present drill field, was then enlarged, graded, smoothed, and planted in grass. At the same time, the name "Sheib Field" was superseded by that of "Miles Field" in honor of C. P. (Sally) Miles, who had taken the lead in getting the improvements under way. Miles Field continued to be used for all outdoor athletic events until 1926, when Miles Stadium, located immediately south of the War Memorial Gym, was dedicated.

Barringer's administration was marked by a continuous effort to improve the physical facilities and surroundings for both the faculty and the students. Nearly every report to the board referred to some needed or suggested improvement, but lack of finances kept him from accomplishing very much in this direction. Many of his proposals for the improvement of physical facilities were ahead of the times both for his board and for the community of Blacksburg. His proposal that the board authorize the construction of a college swimming pool is said to have shocked two of the members into "stunned silence," from which one member did not recover until the next day. This is a highly dubious description of the board's reception of this proposal, but the rejection of it is a matter of record. When the building erected during McBryde's administration for a chapel and auditorium had proved to be unsatisfactory as a chapel, Barringer had permitted the students to use it as a gymnasium and had made arrangements for brief chapel services to be conducted in the mess hall each morning at breakfast. This switch of usage and service, traditional to the building, disturbed some of the alumni and local ministers who saw the change as a tendency toward excessive worldliness. This feeling of worldliness was aggravated by the fact that Barringer's broad social philosophy of life permitted him to accept as normal much student behavior which others, with a much more restricted philosophy, looked upon as a sign of moral depravity.

The minister's conference of Blacksburg was especially concerned with what it believed to be "a growing spirit of worldliness in this community." In an effort to do something about the situation, this body addressed a written protest to Barringer, protesting the lack of proper chaperoning of young ladies attending the dances, the number of dances, and the decline in emphasis given to "literary and other entertaining features, during the entire session and especially at the commencement."

Barringer answered the protest fully, completely, and bluntly. Many of the visiting girls did indeed stay at local hotels, he admitted, but it was mostly because of "a local prejudice which exists here against girls that dance, and as a consequent refusal on the part of many to take them into private houses." If the ministers felt that some of the girls attending the dances were of an undesirable character, he argued, then the problem was purely one for ministerial treatment. A letter to the girls' "home advisor" might be of value. "I don't know how far you care to go in this line," he wrote, "but if you can build a fire, or even make a smoke, in the rear of some of the divorcees and grass widows that attend these functions, you will be doing this community a great service. If you can't do it, you certainly can't expect me to."

If the ministers really thought the girls were unsafe in the hotels, he said, "you should take the matter up with some of the adamantine-hearted sisters of the community who shut their doors in real, or pretended, horror on these girls, and see to it that in common charity they open up both their consciences and their homes."

As for the decline in interest in the literary societies, it was a world-wide decline, he wrote. People were no longer influenced by oratory and the spell-binding style of speaking. "That day is gone—the simple direct form of address, which is most attractive when showing evidence of, so called, cultivation, has done the business." "The poet, the orator, the literary society and the last year's bird nest are all gone, and though we charm ever so wisely, we cannot bring them back."

Barringer had written much more and in the process demolished the points, inferences, and innuendos, expressed and unexpressed, in the ministers' protest. Upon receipt of his letter, the ministers became as angry as their calling would permit and passed the letter to some local alumni, whose calling permitted a much greater freedom of expression. This group of alumni was already greatly disturbed over the loss of the geological survey to the University of Virginia, the dropping of the general-science program, the upheaval that had occurred in connection with the college farm, and with the rumors that the commission appointed to study higher education in Virginia was about to recommend that the engineering work at VPI be transferred to the University of Virginia. Dr. Barringer's publicly avowed determination to build up the agricultural side of the college program accentuated this latter fear.

The receipt of Barringer's letter to the ministers added another cause for worry. Maybe the moral tone of the College was deteriorating as claimed. By the spring of 1909, the combined fears of this group became so great that the Alumni Association's Welfare Committee decided to conduct an investigation of the College. This investigation convinced the chairman of the committee that the College was indeed deteriorating under Barringer. Upon the election of this individual to the presidency of the Alumni Association, he immediately attempted, but failed, to get the association to adopt a resolution calling for Barringer's removal from office. Following this failure, the president of the Alumni Association, with his Welfare Committee, continued to press the Board of Visitors all summer long to remove Barringer. Finally the matter broke into the press with such intensity that the board decided to hold a special meeting to hear the charges being made against Barringer by the Welfare Committee. At this meeting held in Richmond on January 13, 1910, the board was presented with a printed pamphlet of more than fifty pages containing the Welfare Committee's charges. The board then decided to give Barringer two months to formulate his answer to the charges.

By this time, some of the politicians wanted to get into the controversy, but their efforts to get a legislative investigation under way were not successful beyond giving the affair more publicity of dubious value to VPI. Instead of waiting until Barringer had prepared his answers to the charges, the Welfare Committee made its report public in early February. The newspapers summarized the report, saying that the committee charged Barringer with: violating the rules of the institution; lack of tact and initiative; making speeches not creditable to the institute; ignoring department heads in administering the affairs of the institution; carelessness and laxity in discipline and failure to exercise moral restraint; repeated issue of erroneous and misleading statements and unwarranted deductions; and not having watched progress of legislation during the last session of the legislature. Actually, this summary oversimplified and unduly condensed the charges by omitting many that appeared to be of a trivial nature, for, as one alumnus stated it, the committee apparently blamed Barringer for everything done by anyone connected with VPI which had disappointed the committee or any of its members.

Following the public issuance of the charges, the chairman of the Welfare Committee kept the matter agitated by an open letter to the alumni in which he presented his side of the controversy. In this letter, he also criticized the board for not having earlier responded to his demands that Barringer be ousted.

He concluded his letter with an appeal to alumni for cash support to defray the expenses of prosecuting the case. The major effect of the letter was to split the Alumni Association, with the majority of the chapters in the state supporting Barringer.

The student newspaper, *The Virginia Tech,* had supported Barringer during the entire controversy. This paper under the editorship of Cadet C. Taylor Adams had poked fun at the committee from the very beginning and by its satire, ridicule, and pointed barbs had stirred one of the local members of the Welfare Committee into a perfect frenzy of determination not only to oust Barringer but to force him to punish the staff of *The Virginia Tech* as well. Following the publication of the Welfare Committee's report, the *Tech* gave what turned out to be a most accurate description of it when it said: "To the outsider and to one unfamiliar with conditions here or at other colleges, [the charges] may appear of weight, but to us and to everyone who is in a position to view the matter from inside, they are chiefly a series of petty grievances and trivialities which have either been twisted about or elevated to false importance by the committee."

The excitement over the approaching hearing, which was set for March 25 in Blacksburg, was increased when it was learned that Richard Evelyn Byrd, speaker of the House of Delegates, would represent the Welfare Committee and that Judge Daniel Harmon, of Charlottesville, would represent Barringer. The prominence of the members of the board which included the president of the Norfolk and Western Railway, also added to the interest.

On the day of the hearing, the board decided to hear the charges one at a time but declined to permit legal counsel to argue the case for either side. The Welfare Committee protested the exclusion of legal counsel, but Barringer professed his readiness to meet the charges in any manner and under any conditions. He appeared to be jovial, at ease, and confident. He was confident. Upon receipt of the written charges, he had prepared a carefully worded explanation, refutation, or justification for all of his conduct which was under fire, but he had not stopped with a defense of his conduct. On the contrary, using his command of both "terse, husky Anglo Saxon," and his familiarity with the actual events leading to the charges, he made many of the charges look ridiculous. In the process, he did the same thing to most members of the Welfare Committee.

One of the charges made by the committee was that Barringer, in dropping the general-science program and moving to restrict the College to agriculture and engineering, was violating the intent of the land-grant colleges. In support of this charge, the committee presented indisputable evidence to show that most land-grant colleges were seeking to expand rather than to restrict their programs of service to the state. Barringer made no attempt to deny the trend toward the broader interpretation of the land-grant act. He merely pointed out that the commission, appointed in 1908 and continued by the legislature in 1910, to study higher education in Virginia, almost certainly would not permit

VPI to expand its offerings along this broader path. To Barringer's credit he did not use to his advantage the unpublicized fact that even as the hearing was being held, he was making a strenuous fight before this commission not to expand offerings but to hold on to part of the program VPI already had.

The hearing against Barringer continued for two days, and then the board announced it would render a decision at its next formal meeting, which was to be held in April. This delay gave the papers ample time to report, dissect, discuss, and evaluate the hearing. They did so, but the conclusions were contradictory, with some papers calling for Barringer's resignation, some supporting him, and others claiming that the entire situation had "resulted in a fiasco." The Board of Visitors met in Richmond on April 19 and voted to dismiss the charges against Barringer. In the majority report supporting its decision, the board made a special effort to heal wounds and unite all factions in promoting the welfare of the College. The sincerity of the Welfare Committee was readily acknowledged and future cooperation from this group was invited. At the same time the board made it clear that it was cooperation not dictation that was needed. Two members of the board voted against the majority report and filed a minority report in which most of the charges against Barringer were sustained. These two reports were also aired in the press, to the discomfiture of many friends of the College.

Following the board's report, peace of a sort returned to the campus, but Barringer made no effort to improve his relationships with the alienated alumni. In fact, it would appear that after this hearing Barringer made no effort to improve his relationships with anyone, alumni or otherwise, if in Barringer's opinion that person stood in the way of the program he had mapped out for VPI. Since one of Barringer's greatest weaknesses was his complete confidence in this program, it was inevitable that he would stir up opposition.

In August, 1911, an alumnus who had been removed from the faculty by Barringer informed the board that Barringer had been "countenancing immorality" at the College and that an investigation should be made. The board acted at once and appointed a committee, with at least one member known to be hostile to Barringer, to investigate the matter. Specific charges were not aired to the public, but it was generally understood that they had something to do with Barringer, the YMCA, and sex. This investigation was put into better perspective recently by O. R. Magill, who after a distinguished career in YMCA work in China returned in 1955 to Blacksburg to live. Magill, who was "Y" secretary at VPI in 1911-12, said he had invited Dr. Barringer as an M.D. to present some lectures on sex education to members of the "Y". Barringer, according to Magill, presented a few lectures which today probably would put the students to sleep but at that time had created a sensation. Apparently, the disgruntled alumnus took this incident and coupled it with another equally absurd incident and preferred the charges against Barringer. The committee investigated the matter fully and completely and then voted unanimously that the sensational charges of "immorality being countenanced at the institution were without foundation."

By this time, some newspapers in the state were beginning to intimate that the attack on Barringer was the beginning of a campaign to replace him with someone else. One paper even intimated that the "inspirers of the new bits of malice probably have picked someone else for president."

By November, 1911, Barringer had begun to hear rumors that he was being persecuted to make way for someone else. He thought he knew who "someone else" was. He wrote at once to Superintendent Eggleston and mentioned the fact that he had heard rumors to the effect that he, Barringer, was being persecuted to "make way for personal or political favorites." Then coming bluntly to the point he wrote, "The underground talk of some of your political friends has allowed many people in this state to get the idea that this reference was to you." Eggleston never answered Barringer's letter, nor would he discuss it years later when asked about it.

Beginning with January, 1912, Barringer's cup of woe really began to overflow. Without acknowledging Barringer's tremendous struggle to promote agricultural education at the College, numerous agencies and organizations in the state had mounted an almost hysterical demand for more agricultural education. The Farmers' Institute, although commending VPI, adopted a resolution urging the school to set up a course which would be absolutely practical but which would at the same time require the usual college entrance requirements for admission. This resolution really upset Barringer. Just what could the College do, he asked his board, to spread the word abroad that the College with the exception of the admission requirements, had just such a practical course as the institute was demanding. He felt that the alumni certainly could not be expected to spread the word around, since most of them were not interested in agriculture. Continuing, he rather bitterly observed, "The mere fact that I have accented the needs and the interests of the agricultural side of the college during the past few years, has already won for me the bitter antagonism of most of the non-agricultural alumni, which now, as we see, constitutes some ninety per cent of the whole body." On another occasion he rather bitterly observed that the harder the farmers yelled for agricultural education the faster they sent their sons to VPI to study engineering.

The events that upset Barringer the most during his entire administration began to unfold in the legislature which met in January. For one thing, the appropriation for the movable schools of agriculture, so dear to Barringer's heart, was cut out. Barringer had attempted to get the appropriation restored and had gone to the people with a letter urging them to bring pressure to bear to get the cut restored, but the attempt had failed. The United Agricultural Board had been reorganized by the legislature and in its new form not only declined to support the movable schools but also insisted that it could not reimburse VPI for the expenses of such a school conducted a previous year. Barringer had written a strong letter of protest to the governor in which he accused the governor of never having "appreciated the interest taken in this work by the farmers of the State." He had closed his letter with the assurance to the governor that the farmers would no doubt take the matter up in the next legislature. It turned out that the governor was decidedly more annoyed than assured.

Before Barringer had recovered from the loss of the appropriation for his movable schools, the Senate proposed a cut of $5,000 in the annual appropriation for VPI. Upon hearing of this proposed cut, Barringer went to Richmond immediately and bluntly accused some members of the legislature of using the cut as a means of attacking him personally and of attacking Montgomery County and VPI directly for electing a Republican instead of a Democrat to the House of Delegates. He claimed he got some confirmation of both charges and an agreement to restore the cut. The House did vote to restore the amount, but the Senate was adamant; and the cut was not restored.

When Barringer reported the loss of revenue to the rector of the board, L. E. Johnson, he announced that he could get along some way, but for the first time in his administration at VPI his report took on a decidedly pessimistic tone. Of the loss in revenue he said, "I am much disheartened, however, at the result, and general lack of interest in public and press. If we cannot get a Board meeting soon, I don't know what we will do. Wade [the treasurer] is much worried and I am likewise. I want counsel and backing, some authority to do things."

Before the board had an opportunity to do anything about the situation, Barringer heard another rumor. The governor, according to the rumor, was planning to appoint to the Board of Visitors a man known to be strongly anti-Barringer and thought by Barringer to be morally and ethically unfit for the honor. This was more than Barringer could take. Throwing caution and discretion to the wind, he fired off a letter to the governor, asking him to delay the appointment until "you consider well the following facts." Then he listed the reasons he thought the individual was unfit for the appointment. He concluded the letter with the suggestion that the governor could show it to the individual in question if he was in doubt. The implication was more than clear. If the governor appointed this man, Barringer intended to release the letter himself. The governor's real intentions were never revealed; but to the surprise of many persons, he did not appoint the individual to the board. Barringer was still winning the battles, but he was just as surely losing the war.

Other incidents with a certain element of humor continued to plague Barringer and at the same time add to his strained relations with "Farmer Governor" Mann. Any telegrams intended for Blacksburg were delivered to the station in Christiansburg and then telephoned to Blacksburg. The telephone service was questionable, to say the least; and as a result, the intended message frequently underwent a change of meaning in the process of its telephoned delivery. On one occasion, the governor sent a telegram to Barringer, requesting an immediate shipment of material on bee keeping. To his surprise, he got some suggestions on bookkeeping. Since the governor's administration was under fire for its alleged weakness in accounting for state finances, it is not difficult to understand his reluctance to accept Barringer's explanation that his secretary had heard *bee keeping* as *bookkeeping* over the telephone. About the same time, the governor notified Barringer by wire of an important meeting he was arranging for the thirteenth of the month. Barringer showed up on the thirtieth. Once more the embarrassed Barringer had to explain the operation of his telephone to a somewhat irate, and perhaps skeptical, governor. It turned out that his absence from the meeting had blocked immediate action on a matter the governor wanted to pass but which Barringer wanted to drop.

In 1910, Governor Mann appointed Captain Micajah Woods to the Board of Visitors. Woods lived in Charlottesville and long had been identified with the interests of the University of Virginia. Publicly, Barringer expressed strong approval of the appointment; privately, he said it was a "red flag to the old guard" alumni who were already accusing him of showing favoritism to the University of Virginia graduates on the staff. Captain Woods died before he had a chance to prove his worth on the board, but someone made the governor privy to Barringer's private statement.

Even some of Barringer's most sincere efforts to be helpful boomeranged on him at times. As president of VPI, he shared responsibility for developing the congressional district agricultural high schools which, as pioneering undertakings, were busily repeating many of the mistakes made by VPI during its earlier days. Some of these schools purchased farms and happily set about stocking them with machinery and livestock necessary for the usual farming operations. In an effort to be helpful, Barringer offered to ship each school a pure-bred bull calf and did ship one to the school at Burkeville. From this point onward, the record becomes mixed with emotions, facts, and perhaps fiction. It seems that the students took to the bull and the bull took to the students. After a few skirmishes from which the bull emerged the victor, some of the larger boys entered the ring as toreadors. The bull continued to be victorious. At this point, the parents intervened; and T. O. Sandy, who was in charge of the demonstration work at Burkeville, wrote to Barringer to know if he could dispose of the bull, since he was a "troublesome animal to have around our school." Barringer readily assented to the disposal; but in the period of delay caused by the red tape involved in disposing of state property, the bull reportedly achieved a spectacular victory by tossing one of the would-be toreadors over the fence. Whatever the true story may be in connection with what some have claimed to be a "lot of bull," the fact remains that a number of people accused Barringer of sending an "undesirable animal" to the school. A number of the farmers were reported to have expressed the same opinion in much earthier language.

Accenting the irony of the situation is the fact that Barringer and T. O. Sandy did not see eye to eye on the value of the farm demonstration work which Sandy was advocating so effectively. It is easy today to see that Barringer made a mistake in his first appraisal of this work, but it was not so easy to see his error at the time. Finally, when he began to realize the value of the work, he was unwilling to admit that Sandy was the best man to direct it. For reasons that have never been fully explained, these two men just did not like each other. Sometimes they let their feelings show, usually with unhappy results for both. One such incident took place in Richmond in the spring of 1912.

Barringer had gone to Richmond to attend a meeting of the Board of Visitors. The meeting turned out to be a long and disappointing one for Barringer, who, during the meeting, realized he had lost his movable schools of agriculture, while Sandy had won support for his demonstration work. After the meeting had adjourned, Sandy approached Barringer and informed him that the governor would like to talk to the two of them together concerning their work. Barringer, who had heard numerous rumors to the effect that the governor planned to appoint Sandy to the Board of Visitors in order to "get Barringer," gave Sandy a blunt answer to the effect that everything had been settled and that he did not have anything he wanted to discuss with the governor. Barringer's answer lost none of its bluntness in Sandy's retelling it to the governor, and the governor took offense. In early June, Barringer heard about the governor's reaction and immediately wrote a letter of apology to him, but in the same letter managed to get in a dig at Sandy and a chiding for the governor for using Sandy as a messenger.

Governor Mann answered Barringer's letter, assuring him that "your explanation is entirely satisfactory, and I absolve you from all suspicion of discourtesy." But by this time, disturbing rumors were assailing Barringer from all directions. Newspapers in various sections of the state were editorializing and openly predicting that Eggleston would be the next president of VPI. Opinion as to the wisdom of this move was divided, but it was becoming clear that the College's effectiveness was being hurt by the publicity. The Board of Visitors to take over in July would be dominated by the new members to be appointed by Governor Mann to replace those whose term of office had expired. Barringer was getting rumors and anonymous letters indicating that Mann planned to "pack the board" with appointees friendly to Eggleston. Other rumors left Eggleston's name out of consideration but confirmed the belief that Mann was going to return to the board the members known to be opposed to Barringer. When the new nominees to the board were named, Barringer was relieved to note the high caliber of the men, all of whom were known to be friendly to himself. Especially gratifying was the fact that Rector L. E. Johnson had been renominated to the board. But, just as Barringer was concluding that rumors of his impending replacement were unfounded, L. E. Johnson, after a conference with the governor, resigned from the board and declined reappointment. Rumors immediately started circulating to the effect that the governor did indeed expect the new board to replace Barringer and that Johnson, who had supported Barringer, would have no part in the proceedings.

Upon hearing these latest rumors, Barringer wrote to Johnson in an obvious attempt to find out if he thought the governor had packed the board for "certain purposes." Johnson's reply is not available; but in the meantime, Barringer had heard from other sources that some of the new members of the board did expect him to tender his resignation at the first meeting of the newly organized board. Taking all of these factors into consideration, Barringer on July 2, 1912, addressed the following letter to the Board of Visitors:

> I am one of those who believe that confidence and its resultant harmony, between any governing board and its executive officer is absolutely imperative. To this end during the seven or eight years in which I was the chief executive officer of the University of Virginia, I gave the Board their regular opportunity to determine if such a condition existed by presenting, every two years, my resignation. It was my intention to do this at the end of my second year at VPI, but I was not given the opportunity. I could not think of resigning, when, at practically every meeting, some trumped up charge reflecting upon me as a man and as an executive officer was presented.
>
> In spite of the fact that the opportunities for making good at the Virginia Polytechnic Institute have so far been meager, I now present my resignation to take effect on this date.

The board at its meeting on July 10, after some discussion, accepted the resignation but asked Barringer to continue as president until July 1, 1913. In accepting the resignation, the board said in part:

> In accepting this resignation the Board desires to place on record its appreciation of the able services of Dr. Barringer during his incumbency as President of this Institution and to express the high personal regard in which he is held by each member of this body.
>
> Despite the fact that President Barringer's administration has been conducted under peculiarly harassing difficulties the Institute has made decided progress in many lines of endeavor; and the financial management is particularly to be commended.

Barringer asked for a delay before answering the request to remain as president for the next session; then on July 13 he agreed to serve for the period requested. In his letter of agreement he wrote:

> I am much troubled, however, by the continued barking of certain organs of the State press. For years I have borne this with scant rejoinder, but I feel that I will do myself a great injustice if I allow these insinuations to continue without rebuke. I wish, therefore to say to you, as Rector of the Board that I feel that my acceptance of this responsibility, under present conditions, must in no wise be considered as tying my hands if this should continue.

In his letter of acknowledgment Rector Brown concluded with the statement, "I trust you may not be subjected to any further annoyance from inconsiderate and pestiferous persons in or out of the press."

Both Barringer and Brown got their wish. Following his decision to retire from the presidency Barringer's administration entered into a year of relative peace and quiet. Alumni attacks, whether through the Board of Visitors or through the Alumni Association, came to an end. Many alumni began to realize for the first time that Barringer's concept of the role of VPI as Virginia's land-grant college was almost radically progressive when contrasted with most of the concepts being advanced by many leaders in the strident demands sweeping the state for better education for an agricultural society. While struggling to build up the agricultural side of the program, Barringer at least was willing to fight to hold on to the engineering program. Many of the rural leaders, on the other hand, wanted to scrap this aspect of the College and, in the words of Henry S. Pritchett, convert it into "an outright agricultural college, or possibly an agricultural trade school, with low entrance requirements, giving only such instruction in mechanics as is involved in the right teaching of agriculture." The report of the Education Commission which functioned from 1908 until its final report in 1912 went but little beyond this idea when in its report to the legislature it recommended that VPI become a combination of (1) a school giving two years more or less of practical agricultural training and elementary shop practice in the mechanic arts; and (2) a college of agriculture and mechanic arts associated with an experiment station "and starting from the same entrance requirements as other college departments." The mechanic arts aspect of the program was to "include a two-years' course of collegiate grade in engineering." The report concluded with the observation that the function of the Virginia Polytechnic Institute should be exercised in three directions:

(a) In the further development of the four years in agriculture, based ultimately upon requiring a full four-year high school course for admission, and leading to the degree of bachelor of science in agriculture
(b) Thoroughly elaborated and differentiated short courses covering one, two, or three years, winter courses, etc., in agriculture and mechanic arts, requiring less than the full high school course for admission
(c) The expansion of its extension and institute work for both farmers and mechanics.

The rural awakening set in motion by the Farmers' Alliance and the Populist Movement, which made it possible for Vawter and McBryde to develop a polytechnic institute in the first place, now was threatening to choke off its own offspring.

Barringer was in full agreement with the idea of building up the agricultural program, but he was equally strong in his opposition to any reduction in the engineering program. In a letter to Johnson before the latter's retirement from the board, Barringer had warned him of the possible loss of the last two years of the engineering program. Barringer, the fighter, wanted to get organized to resist the movement, since he believed "the only really serious argument for moving the engineering school from here" was the colossal egotism of one member of the engineering faculty, whose replacement he had already recommended. Johnson, obviously alarmed over the prospect of Barringer's going to war over this issue, or any other issue, had urged Barringer not to take any action but to leave it up to the board.

Since Barringer resigned from the presidency shortly after the issuance of the commission's formal report, the decision about any action relating to it fell to others. One far-reaching effect of this report, however, was to help crystallize the concept in the minds of Virginians, that the major function, if not the only legitimate function, of a land-grant college, was to promote programs of agricultural education. By 1912, this concept had become so strong that the College, and Barringer, had come under criticism because of the success being achieved by the department of engineering.

Although Barringer had urged everyone to "shout from the housetop" his determination to develop the agricultural side of the College, he had not neglected the engineering work. Many graduates in engineering had been particularly successful not only in the United States but in many foreign countries as well. The department of electrical engineering under Professor S. R. Pritchard had been particularly successful in turning out graduates in great demand. Barringer was highly pleased with this result and in supporting his request for more funds for all of the engineering work had singled out the department of electrical engineering as the one "making us the most reputation." Even this success was turned against Barringer by one individual who claimed that VPI was likely to be better known in Schenectady, New York, than in rural Virginia. Another farm group, in its incessant clamor for practical agricultural education, said that VPI was the best agency in the state for taking boys off the farm, educating them, and sending them out of the state. Barringer was aware of these charges but declined to reduce his support of the engineering program.

In 1912, he presented some statistics to the board which showed that approximately ten per cent of each graduation class for the past twenty years had been in agriculture. The other graduates had been in engineering or one of the "non-breadwinning" courses, such as general science. Barringer and his board thought this ratio was deplorable for a state in which more than three-fourths of the people earned their living from agriculture. Barringer thought the cause of this unfavorable ratio grew from a failure on the part of the College to "spread the gospel" to the farmers about the school's program. Some of the leading dailies thought the cause rested with the College's having given undue emphasis to the development of engineering at the expense of agriculture. Not one voice was raised in the press or elsewhere in the state to advance the idea that perhaps the people, the ones who had sons to be educated, wanted their land-grant institution to be more than a college of agriculture.

The remedies proposed by Barringer and the press also differed. Barringer wanted to set up comprehensive programs of scholarships for boys in agriculture who would promise to stay in Virginia. In addition to this solution, he proposed strengthening the four-year degree programs by raising the entrance requirements to fourteen units and then expanding the short courses in several directions to take care of boys not interested in, or not prepared for the four-year program. In addition to these approaches, he wanted the College to plan cooperative programs whereby the farm demonstrators would recruit students for the department of agriculture.

The newspapers, once Barringer's planned retirement became known, proposed a more direct remedy for the imbalance: secure a nationally-known person with proven experience in the development of a college of agriculture. The papers were more than generous with this type of advice but remained strangely silent on the question of where the money would come from to pay such a person.

Having tendered his resignation, Barringer did not retire to his tent to sulk. On the contrary, he continued active direction of the institution and at the same time proposed a number of developments for the board's consideration. His "terse and husky Anglo-Saxon" gave way to a gentler, if less colorful, style which tended to soothe rather than ruffle tempers. Under his persuasion, the board agreed to require fourteen units of high school work for admission during the 1914 session. The board accepted his proposal to establish a professorship of forestry and to establish programs in chemical and agricultural engineering. This latter program was unique in that it was to be a five-year program conducted cooperatively by the department of agriculture and the department of engineering. The financial situation at the College forced a modification of this program before its actual introduction, however. The same financial conditions forced the postponement of his proposals to convert the chapel-auditorium into a library, to secure more equipment for the department of engineering, to hard-surface the new road running from the newly erected alumni gateway to the front of the academic buildings, to remodel the dairy barns, and to erect a new building for the department of engineering. At the same time Barringer made these proposals, he repeated his suggestions that the military requirements be dropped for juniors and seniors and that the commencement program be reduced to one day. The board rejected both of these proposals as it did his proposal for a summer school, which he made at about the same time.

During Barringer's last year in office, J. S. Cates, newly appointed editor of *The Southern Planter,* wrote to him asking for information about the program at VPI. Cates had just come to Virginia and therefore knew very little about the developments at the College. Barringer immediately sent him a detailed, but confidential, report on his administration of the College. This report makes an interesting valedictory for this remarkable individual's effort to have VPI keep faith with the clamorous demands for agricultural education in harmony with the conditions of the time. This report follows in part:

> While each state is justly expected to make its contribution to the number of scientific men at work on this the greatest of all the arts—agriculture, it was clear to me that the dissemination of the benefits of the Virginia Polytechnic Institute could not be made through the medium of the four-year scientific graduates alone. To this end, we began a farmers winter course of one month, and an apprentice course of one or two years.
> At the request of the Farmers' Institute we have . . . changed the name of this apprentice course to a young farmers' short course. . . . The difficulties in getting a man to come in mid-winter to a storm swept plateau 2200 ft. above

the sea, and off the main railroad line, is very great. The type of farming
adapted to this region is unlike that of any part of the state except the southwest. As a result it has not been as popular as we had hoped, but we determined
to stick to it in the belief that a change of spirit would come. We have absolutely
changed the spirit of the place, as far as scientific agriculture is concerned. This
line of work is now the pride of the students, as you can find out by writing
to recent graduates. . . . I have been much gratified by the change of spirit.

[In our admission requirements] We have risen from 2 ½ units (Carnegie)
in 1907 to 14 units (Carnegie) in 1914, and have ten units (Carnegie) enforced
already . . .

An improvement in scholarship, an improvement in agricultural interest,
and putting the place on a good financial foundation has been my aim. Any
member of the board will tell you I found this place in 1907 with a floating debt
of $34,000 and a bonded debt of $25,000 on an income of $125,000 a year. This
was largely occasioned by loss of from eight to ten thousand dollars on the farm,
and other losses in our economic plants. I got the legislature to pay off the floating debt, and I have paid off every dollar of the bonded debt, and today we
have a balance of $20,000 to our credit in cash for improvements which will be
made largely along lines of the fundamentals—physics and chemistry, and
proper agricultural lines. I have done nothing to break down the engineering
department we had here, but I plainly stated that I did not intend to add anything to it until the agricultural department built up to equal standing in
patronage and teaching force.

As you will see by reference to the papers sent, the alumni of the last twenty
years here are about 90% non-agricultural and ten percent agricultural. Quite
a number of these graduates in agriculture, as you will see, are not pursuing
their calling, so the truth is the spirit of the place was something like 95%
non-agricultural. This body of non-agricultural men have been the source of
my undoing, as they were not in sympathy with my plan for the upbuilding
of the other side.

[Barringer then reviewed the charges of pro-agriculture, anti-agriculture
brought against himself by the Alumni Welfare Committee and then concluded:]

The above is given simply as an illustration of the anti-agricultural spirit
which I have had to fight for five years, but I have about completed an absolute
change in spirit here, in spite of their machinations.

In conclusion, I will leave for my successor, whoever he may be, a house
swept and garnished, and strong in finances. The farm and every other economic
plant here now pays, if we except the Mess. I am glad to be relieved of it, and
would not continue under any possible conditions, but I do not want to go
out leaving the public under any misapprehensions as to what has been done.

Even this last wish was partly denied to Barringer. In the midst of his
last official commencement exercise, fire completely destroyed the original
Preston and Olin building in which VPI had started. "Misapprehensions" developed at once in the minds of many individuals as to the significance of the fact
that the fire started near midnight on Friday, June 13, 1913. Some individuals
argued that the fire was an omen of bad luck visited upon the board for permitting Barringer to leave. Others saw the fire as an omen of bad luck for the
incoming president, Joseph D. Eggleston, who had been elected to the presidency by the board on March 13. A few shook their heads and muttered darkly
about arson, revenge, and the irresponsibility of the younger generation. The
majority rejected all of these theories and accepted the fire as an unfortunate
occurrence. Barringer leaned toward this latter camp but declined to make
any comment relative to "misapprehensions" concerning the significance of the
number 13.

Barringer, upon turning the presidency over to his successor, Joseph D. Eggleston, on July 1, 1913, returned to Charlottesville to live and resumed the practice of medicine until his death in 1941. At the suggestion of some alumni who were students during his administration, the present Barringer Hall completed in 1962 was named in his honor by the Board of Visitors.

Chapter 8

The Eggleston
Administration

1913-1919

J OSEPH DUPUY EGGLESTON, JR., who assumed the presidency of VPI on July 1,
1913, was born on November 13, 1867, in Prince Edward County, Virginia. He
graduated from Hampden-Sydney College in 1886 with the A.B. degree. Following his graduation from college, he entered educational work and taught
public schools in Georgia, North Carolina, and Virginia. From 1891 to 1900
he served as superintendent of schools in Asheville, North Carolina. In 1902,
he was placed in charge of the editorial work of the Bureau of Publicity of the
Southern Education Board with headquarters at Knoxville, Tennessee. In this
capacity, he made a close study of educational conditions and problems not
only in the southern states but also in other states of the Union. Excessive eye
strain forced him to give up this work, whereupon he returned to his home in
Farmville, Virginia. After a short period as superintendent of schools in his
home county, he became active in the campaign for better public schools
which began in the state about 1904. In 1905, he made a vigorous campaign
for the then-elective office of superintendent of public instruction and won by a
large majority. Under his vigorous leadership in this office from 1906 until his
resignation on December 31, 1912, the public school system, especially the rural
high schools of the state, made unprecedented and hitherto undreamed of

219

progress and advancement. On January 1, 1913, he became chief of Field Service in Rural Education in the United States Office of Education, but resigned this position six months later to accept the presidency of VPI.

On July 10, 1912, when Dr. Barringer had presented to the board his resignation from the presidency, rumors were being widely circulated that Eggleston was to be the next president. These rumors had led to the expression of a difference of opinion regarding Eggleston's fitness for the position. Some alumni were known to be strongly opposed to the idea. It was a matter of record that Eggleston's strong, vigorous, dynamic leadership in behalf of public education had aroused some opposition on the part of several conservative members of the state legislature. It was also known to some of the new board members that "underground rumors" were being spread abroad that Governor Mann, who had assumed office in January, 1910, expected them to elect Eggleston as president. In making his appointments to fill vacancies on the board, Mann had returned J. Thompson Brown and J. B. Watkins after they had been dropped from the board by Governor Swanson. With Brown's return, the other members immediately elected him to his former position as rector. Brown was fully aware of the rumors abroad concerning Eggleston; therefore, when he appointed the committee to seek a successor to Barringer, he included both pro- and anti-Eggleston men on it. The fact that three of the four members on the committee to select a new president were Mann's appointees did not go unnoticed in the rumor mill, however.

During the period the committee was searching for a successor to Barringer, VPI was subjected to an unusually critical examination of its past, present, and future by the press and by discussions and letters published in the press. Few if any new ideas were advanced, but the net result was a further crystallization of the idea that the major function of the school was to promote agricultural education.

As reports began to spread that the committee was contacting educational leaders all over the country in search of a president, the agitation against Eggleston began to fade. The agitation for a "big-name president" faded even faster when board and alumni became aware of the salaries needed to attract the big-name prospects. With the 1913 spring meeting of the Board of Visitors rapidly approaching and no president having been named, a small groundswell of support actually began to develop for Eggleston. There is no evidence to indicate that he made any campaign for the office. In fact, by the time the board met in Richmond, it was rather well understood that Eggleston had said he would accept the presidency only if it was offered to him by a unanimous vote of the board. He did not plan to attend the spring meeting of the board to hear of its vote or to press his candidacy. If it was true that Eggleston demanded a unanimous vote before he would accept the presidency, he got his wish. The board meeting in Richmond on March 13, 1913, unanimously elected him president of VPI. Eggleston arrived in Richmond the next day but surprised everyone by asking for time within which to consider the offer. Before the week was ended, he surprised no one by accepting the offer.

The board in releasing the announcement of his appointment went to great lengths in reviewing its activities leading up to his final selection. "Thousands" of letters had been written to individuals all over the United States, so one report had it. Committee members Brown and Watkins had spent considerable time visiting and traveling outside of Virginia, seeking a person with qualifications superior to those possessed by Eggleston. Committee member Smith frankly confessed that he had tried to find a man better suited for the presidency than Mr. Eggleston but had failed in the search. No matter which way it turned, reported the committee, or what criteria it set up, Mr. Eggleston always emerged as the best man for the job. Strong letters endorsing Eggleston for the presidency had been received from Dr. Wallace Butterick, secretary of the General Education Board, and from Dr. P. P. Claxton, U. S. Commissioner of Education. Other well-known educators who had endorsed Eggleston included Dr. E. A. Alderman, president of the University of Virginia; Dr. S. C. Mitchell, professor of history at Richmond College; Dr. H. B. Frissell, principal of Hampton Institute; and Dr. George H. Denny, who had just moved to the presidency of the University of Alabama after a highly successful tenure as president of Washington and Lee University. Faced with such overwhelming evidence and support, the board reported it had voted unanimously to offer Eggleston the presidency.

The announcement of Eggleston's acceptance of the presidency was received with enthusiasm by his supporters and a cautious wait-and-see attitude from the more skeptical. Pleas that the new president be given a chance echoed and re-echoed over the state. *The Southern Planter,* which under the ownership of the wealthy Westmoreland Davis was rapidly emerging as a powerful advocate for the rural interests, was disappointed with the choice, but at the same time urged that all unite back of the new president. The *Planter* wanted a man with more technical experience in agriculture. This publication, after commenting that "VPI has been kept at turmoil when it should have been at work," warned its readers that if the election of Eggleston failed to bring success to the College the legislature would have to intervene.

Eggleston, who was certainly no stranger to the campus, arrived in Blacksburg on June 25 and immediately set out to win friends and influence alumni. He succeeded in both endeavors. Although possessing the fiery zeal of a reformer and the dauntless spirit of a sincere missionary, Eggleston also knew how and when to listen. Perhaps of greater importance, he also knew how and was more than willing to give credit and recognition to others for their participation and achievements in programs for which he was responsible. Immediately upon his arrival in Blacksburg, he visited on the campus and in the town, where he "shook hands and spoke to everybody in sight and was nearly smothered with kindness."

His first official act was to create the office of dean of the general faculty and then to appoint his old acquaintance, Theodore P. Campbell, to the position. This appointment proved to be a happy one for the faction-ridden faculty, which, after a series of meetings, began to manifest a community of interests essential to the College's welfare. *The Southern Planter* in a second editorial appealing for support of the new president reviewed the fact that every president prior to Eggleston had someone "dead set against him as soon as he took office." It was impossible for the school to do the best work under these conditions, pleaded the editor; therefore, the people of the state were urged to support the new president and not to start another fight. Just as it appeared that the people might follow this advice, an ugly cloud suddenly appeared on the horizon.

Governor Mann made an indiscreet statement which was published in the

Richmond Times-Dispatch to the effect that he had brought about Dr. Barringer's resignation from the presidency in order to secure harmony amongst the various agricultural agencies in the state. Whether correct or not, this statement was more than Barringer was willing to bear in silence. In a lengthy letter to the *Times-Dispatch,* Barringer denounced the governor in no uncertain terms and then revealed his account of the events which had brought about his resignation.

According to Barringer, his close friend Judge Daniel Harmon of Charlottesville had told him that he had been informed by J. G. Ferneyhough, who was acting as a special messenger for Mann, that unless Barringer resigned the presidency at a designated time, the governor was going to appoint to the Board of Visitors some men known to be unfriendly to Barringer. After discussing the matter, Barringer wrote, he and Harmon had held a meeting with Ferneyhough at which time Ferneyhough had confirmed the original statement. Furthermore, he had informed them that the governor would agree not to appoint the men known to be unfriendly if Barringer would agree to tender his resignation at the first meeting after the board was changed. Barringer was also told, he said, that his resignation would be accepted by the new board and that he would be asked to continue in office for one year. The entire scheme, claimed Barringer, had been politically motivated in order to get the governor's political friend, Eggleston, appointed to the presidency and to get the work of the United Agricultural Board placed under the jurisdiction of the College.

Faced with this situation, Barringer had written, it had not taken him long to decide that he would make the sacrifice, "for the sake of the college and of the state, and also for my own peace of mind." Further, he said, "to remain in office with such an enemy in the capitol was unwise." Therefore, he had agreed to resign. Eggleston's resignation as state superintendent of public instruction, in Barringer's view, was merely designed to get him off the Board of Visitors and make him eligible for the presidency.

Barringer's letter made the headlines of most of the state papers, and the public braced itself for another assault on VPI. Eggleston and Mann refused to comment publicly; but the rector, J. Thompson Brown, in a public letter denied that the board had been influenced or pressured to elect Eggleston president. According to Brown, the board had heard that Barringer planned to resign. The request for him to serve one extra year, he wrote, had nothing to do with Eggleston's candidacy but had originated with Brown, because he believed the extra time would give the board an opportunity to make a thorough search for a new president. Since the board knew about the rumors connecting Eggleston with the presidency, Brown wrote, he as rector of the board, in appointing the committee to search for a successor, had purposely put two men on it who were known to be opposed to Eggleston. The committee had made a long, thorough search for a president, Brown concluded, and had come to the unanimous conclusion, without pressure or influence from the governor or any one else, that Eggleston was the man. The board upon hearing the full report had agreed with the committee, and Eggleston had been elected by unanimous vote. Furthermore, said Brown, the resolution of appreciation which the board had extended to Barringer upon his resignation certainly should be interpreted by everyone as a sincere reflection, on the part of the board, of no animus whatever toward Barringer.

Brown's letter was given much the same attention in the press that had been given to Barringer's, but whether by design or chance most of the headlines identified the circumstances as an attack on Governor Mann rather than as one on Eggleston and the VPI administration. No committee of alumni rushed forward demanding Eggleston's resignation; and since Governor Mann, in addition to being popular, was about to conclude his term of office, no politician appeared on the scene, ready and eager, to make political hay from the contretemps. Personal letters between Mann and Eggleston indicate that both men were disturbed because of the possible effect the affair might have on VPI; but as the summer passed with no more letters from Barringer, their fears began to subside. Mann, who had good reason to know the power of Barringer's pen, wrote to Eggleston in the fall, expressing the hope that since no more letters had appeared from a "certain gentleman," Eggleston would go ahead with his program. Here the matter dropped, publicly at least, but there is strong evidence to indicate that this unhappy incident caused several members of the legislature of 1914 to vote unfavorably on legislation affecting VPI finances.

If there was one thing Eggleston did not need, it was a prod from the governor to get on with a program for VPI. In fact, before Governor Mann left office, he was practically begging Eggleston to "slow down" in presenting his proposals and requests to the legislature for approval.

Immediately following his official assumption of presidential duties, Eggleston visited every department on campus and held a "sympathetic interview with every faculty member in sight" concerning the work and the needs of the College. He was utterly aghast at the inadequate facilities available to the staff with which to carry on its work; but the staff was delighted with the concern Eggleston showed for their work, surprised with his requests for their suggestions for improvements, and amazed when many of these suggestions became realities within a month.

In 1913, Eggleston's appointment of Professor L. S. Randolph as dean of engineering to replace Professor Marr, who had resigned, pleased most of the engineering faculty, while his known interest in and enthusiastic support of agriculture pleased the faculty in agriculture. His appearance "in appropriate costume" [not described] at a student pep rally and his forthright proposal delivered at the first student assembly for all to join together in getting funds for an athletic field house more than endeared him to the students. His "pep talk" given before the Blacksburg Board of Trade so aroused this body that it forthwith nominated him for president, an honor he tactfully declined until the next year. Although a Presbyterian, his proven willingness and ability to go into the pulpit of any denomination and hold the congregation spellbound with his skill in applying biblical teachings to modern problems endeared him to the local ministers' association. His humorous objection to mess steward Ellison's grinding and advertising mess hall scraps for sale as "VPI Beef and Bone" set everyone, including the board and the enterprising Ellison, to laughing. By Christmas, 1913, Eggleston had the entire Blacksburg community on his side. He was not so sure about the alumni, the state press, and the upcoming legislature; but he bought a new typewriter, hired an additional secretary, and set to work.

A Richmond paper in describing Eggleston once said, "Sometimes he has not hesitated to take the bit in his teeth and ride over ancient predilections. A good many people believe he will do the same thing if he goes to Blacksburg." This is a good description of the approach Eggleston used in preparing and presenting VPI's financial needs to the legislature in 1914.

After holding a series of faculty meetings and conferences with members of the board, he drew up a statement for the legislature, setting forth the financial situation and needs of the College. In his statement, Eggleston attempted to establish the following points: one, the Virginia Polytechnic Institute was a part of the state's system of higher education, and as such it had its own mission to fulfill; two, this mission was concerned primarily with the development and promotion of scientific education in agriculture and the mechanic arts in harmony with the needs of the state; three, since the state was overwhelmingly agricultural, any failure on the part of the state to support agricultural education would be disastrous to the people; four, the College had a staff of men ready, willing, able, and eager to provide Virginia with the high quality education she desperately needed and deserved in agriculture, engineering, and the supporting technical sciences; five, unless the College secured increased financial support, it absolutely could not go forward in fulfilling the mission assigned to it by the state, and in fact, if such financial assistance was not forthcoming, the school would deteriorate into a hollow shell; six, the legislature of 1912 while increasing the annuity of every other state college, "because of a misunderstanding" had reduced the annuity for VPI $5,000; seven, this act was unprecedented and unheard of in the entire history of the state of Virginia; eight, technical education, which the state had assigned to VPI, was more expensive than the traditional academic education; nine, Virginia, a great agricultural state, was falling far, far behind neighboring states in support of her land-grant colleges [at this point Eggleston introduced figures which presented dramatic evidence to support this statement]; ten, VPI was spending less per student than sister institutions in the state; eleven, in spite of pleas to the contrary the state was in an excellent financial condition not only to support VPI but to support the entire system of public education. As far as VPI was concerned, he concluded, this was the time for the state to spend some money if it wished to make some money.

In addition to sending his report to members of the legislature, he also sent either the full copy or a modified form of it to alumni and asked them for their reaction. All alumni who "reacted" by writing to Eggleston immediately received cordial follow-up letters from him thanking them for their replies, even though their replies may have been negative or critical. This second letter to the alumni was usually accompanied by an appropriately modified form of a circular which had been prepared by Eggleston and Dean T. P. Campbell. The financially related affairs at the College were vividly portrayed by these circulars, one of which follows:

My Dear Sir:

I am enclosing a detailed reply to your very kind letter of Jan. 14th. I appreciate greatly the readiness to serve the institution which this letter exhibits, and I feel sure that you can be of very great service to us.

Now, as to the information which you desire:

First, the amount of money received from the United States Government that is applied to the instructional work of this institution is $33,333.00. The value of our plant, as a whole, including buildings, grounds and equipment, is $750,-000.00. The fees that are received from the students are $4,435.00. You will understand that in this last item is not embraced what is paid for board, lights, heat, etc., since this all goes out again. The above amount includes tuition and matriculation fees.

We have received from the state legislature annual appropriations as follows:

1903-4	annuity	.$ 30,000.00
1904-5	annuity	40,000.00
1905-6	annuity	45,000.00
1906-7	annuity	55,000.00
1907-8	annuity	56,000.00
1908-9	annuity	60,000.00
1909-10	annuity	60,000.00
1910-11	annuity	60,000.00
1911-12	annuity	60,000.00
1912-13	annuity	55,000.00
1913-14	annuity to March 1st	36,666.00

Special appropriations:

1904-5, $165,000.00 for building and equipment

1905-6,   35,000 for Agricultural Hall

1906-7,   25,000.00

1907-08 (the year of Dr. Barringer's coming here) 34,000.00 to pay off indebtedness brought over from former administration

1908-9,   10,000.00 for equipment,

since which time we have received nothing from the legislature in the way of special appropriations, the only money received being annuities as listed above. It should be noted that so far from receiving an increase of appropriation, during the last two years our appropriation has been reduced $5,000.00, from which we have suffered and are suffering now.

The total number of students here today is 521, and of this 462 are Virginia students; in other words, about 90%. This is a larger percentage of Virginia students by far than is to be found in other state institutions of the same scope and standing as this.

There has been discovered recently a new method of testing soils for the quantity of lime necessary to improve them. This is information that will be valuable and vital to our farmers. Had we $3,000.00 a year to apply to this purpose, we could furnish information to numbers of these farmers daily. As it is, we have not a dollar for this purpose, and cannot do this work. The person who requests work of this nature to be done rarely appreciates the fact that we have no money, and the refusal to do the work almost invariably is the occasion of dissatisfaction with the institution.

We have a college library, but we have not a dollar to devote to the library. Not a cent is appropriated to it by the board; the only fund we have is a small fee of $2.00 a session from each student. This does enable us to buy a few books, but so meagre is the amount the committee has to use that in endeavoring to appropriate a sum to each department of the institution for technical books and magazines, it is enabled to *give the magnificent sum of $23.00 a year to a department.*

We have not a dollar to pay traveling expenses for any purpose. Calls come to us frequently for experts to go out into the state, and we are unable to send them; though we have the men, the ability, and the willingness, we have not the money. Our professors are debarred, even the heads of departments, from attending the conventions of their associations, by means of which they could get in touch with their work and receive many new and valuable ideas, because the institution has no money to pay expenses.

We have not a sufficient number of residences on our campus to house our faculty. We have not a dollar to devote to building houses. The quarters provided for our professors are very inferior to those provided by other institutions in the state. The professors are elected to these positions, come with their families, but when they reach here we are unable to furnish them houses on the campus, and they are unable to rent houses in town. At the present moment, there is but one house in town not occupied, and this an indifferent one. This is a hardship and an injustice to the professor and his family, and as you may well imagine causes no feeling of contentment or satisfaction.

In order that this letter may not go to too great a length, I shall say in brief that our whole income is today used in supplying the absolute needs of the institution, in instructors, in laboratories, in shops, in lecture-rooms and in equipment, and even as it is we are not able to provide adequately for the number of students we have. In several of the departments the classes are so crowded that both the professor and the student are dissatisfied with their work. This is fatal, and should be remedied. In the laboratories, where only two men should work at a desk, we are often forced to put three, the unfortunate result being that not one of them gets the benefit from this work which he is entitled to expect. You may readily see, therefore, that the securing of this additional annuity of $15,000.00 is vital to the life of this institution. We have reached a period when we must supply our needs and advance, or we must go to pieces.

There is every indication of an increased attendance of students here next session. I have in my possession letters that indicate that we shall have even a larger percentage of increase than we have had the past year. If we do, this will make the number of students so large that it is absolutely impossible to handle them with our present appropriation. The result is inevitable. After reaching a fixed number which we are able to accommodate, which is perhaps about 550, then we shall have to turn students away from our doors. I feel quite sure that both the people of the state as well as the members of the legislature will deplore such a state of affairs. In asking for the increase in our annuity then, we are only calling upon the legislature to give us sufficient funds to forfend the occurrence of such a state of affairs.

Please do not imagine that I have overdrawn the picture, for I have not. I have painted it in far lighter colors than truth would justify me. Since you are a graduate of the VPI, I am sure that you will appreciate the circumstances.

I hope that I have furnished you such information as you need for your . . . use. If there is anything omitted that you desire, I hope you will write me at once, and I shall take pleasure in giving you any information that you may want.

Please let me call your attention to the fact that in the above amounts is included the money that was appropriated for the restoration of the Science Hall, which was burned by fire, and that, therefore, this is not to be regarded as new money at all.

Please let me assure you of my very warmest personal regards and of my best wishes for you and your family during the coming year.

Eggleston's reference to the new method of testing soils for their lime content was a shrewd one. An unprecedented demand for this service had developed in Virginia as a result of the agitation and victory in the legislature by the farm groups demanding state owned and operated limestone-grinding plants. The prospects of an increased supply of a soil "sweetener" in the form of ground limestone had increased the demand for soil testing; at the same time, a controversy had developed relative to the merits of ground limestone versus burnt limestone as a soil "sweetener." Whether a "limegrinder" or a "limeburner" the farmer was clamoring for soil testing.

Editorial comments on VPI's request for funds, especially if unfavorable, got much the same treatment as that extended to alumni. A letter from Eggleston would go to the editor, thanking him for his interest in the school. This letter would include an explanation of the mission of the College and illustrations of how it was attempting to fulfill this mission. Whenever possible, the illustrations would be taken from college activities having particular significance for the community served by the editor's paper. If a request for assistance had come from the area served by the editor's paper, a copy of the request went along with the letter. If the request for assistance had been turned down by the College because of lack of finances, several copies went to the editor. But Eggleston did not stop with the editor; he sent copies of his reply to influential leaders in the editor's particular community and to the members of the legislature representing the community. Running through all of this correspondence which went out over the state was the idea that the people expected VPI to develop a program in agricultural education, that VPI wanted to develop a program in agricultural education, but that VPI with its current financial resources could not develop a program in agricultural education in keeping with the scientific advances of the day. Having made these points, Eggleston's letters invariably closed with a nicely phrased plea for help in resolving this dilemma.

Instances of hardships faced by specific departments or divisions in the College were singled out for attention. The difficulty faced by the department of mechanical engineering in trying to operate the entire department on an annual budget of $200 was forcefully presented to members of the legislature and others by the simple expedient of circulating in one packet copies of (1) a letter from Charles I. Wade, treasurer, to Professors Randolph and Johnson, notifying them that they had exceeded their annual appropriation of $200 by $58.95 and informing them that, "I cannot pay any further bills," (2) a letter from Professor Randolph to President Eggleston enclosing an urgent request for an additional appropriation of $150 with which to "pay off this deficiency and keep everything running," and (3) a letter from President Eggleston to Professor L. S. Randolph in which Eggleston in reply to the request for the extra money had said, "I beg to say that there is no money on hand, and I see no way of providing this sum unless the Executive Committee authorizes me to borrow it."

The following comment from Eggleston accompanied this packet of letters:

> Here is a sample of what comes to my office a good many times during the session. It is an illustration of the pitiful straits in which each of the departments here finds itself on account of the inadequate financial support given this institution.
>
> The absurdity of allowing an important department only $200 with which to keep up all breakage and repairs in equipment, do correspondence, and pay postage is apparent.

Alumni response to Eggleston's approach was immediate, positive, and constructive. Letters in support of VPI appeared in the press, editors were cajoled, and "legislators were helped to see the light." J. Ambler Johnston ('04), with Eggleston's blessing and Eggleston's ammunition, appeared before a surprised legislative committee which "listened attentively" as he told them what VPI meant to young men in Virginia who wanted a technical education. Alumni from out of the state wrote encouraging letters to Eggleston and to members of the legislature. Unfriendly editorials dropped in number, while a small pro-VPI groundswell was reported to be developing in the House of Delegates.

Eggleston was happy with the response given to his efforts by the alumni. Apparently, most of the alumni were happy with the response given to their efforts by Eggleston. In fact, everybody was happy, it seemed, except some of the more conservative members of the state legislature. This group had become sincerely alarmed with the rapidly increasing cost of the educational institutions, agencies, and programs which the legislature had created since 1906. Since this group was in control of the key appropriation committee in the legislature, Eggleston did not get the appropriation he had requested. He did succeed in getting a modest appropriation to help replace the shop equipment which had been destroyed in the Preston and Olin building fire, and he did get the $5,000 cut in the annuity restored.

He was disappointed with the results but more puzzled than discouraged. His faith in the value of VPI's contribution to the economic progress of the state was so great that he simply could not understand why the state gave what he considered to be such niggardly support to the institution. After considerable reflection, he came to the same conclusion that Barringer had reached: the people were not getting the message either as to what VPI was doing or was capable of doing. Unlike Barringer, however, Eggleston believed the alumni could help to get the message to the people.

In reporting to the board the action of the legislature toward the College, Eggleston adopted a positive approach. Instead of berating the legislature or any member of that body for its failure to help the school, he informed the board that in his opinion neither the legislature nor the people really knew much about the real work of the College. The remedy, insisted Eggleston, was a year-round program designed to keep VPI and its program before the people. The ones to undertake this program, said Eggleston, were board members, the faculty, and the alumni. It was a waste of time, effort, and patience and was unrealistic, he argued, to seek alumni support only during the time the legislature was in session. Intelligent support was needed every day of the year. To be intelligent such support had to come from informed alumni. Every effort, therefore, should be made to keep the alumni informed and interested in the total program of the College. To this end he advised the startled board that each member should be willing to meet with alumni chapters on invitation to discuss college problems.

Following his report to the board, Eggleston arranged for H. H. (Bunker) Hill ('09), chemist in the Agricultural Experiment Station, to devote part of his time to alumni work. Hill was provided with both clerical and financial assistance with which to do this work and proceeded to make excellent use of both as he helped build in the hitherto divided alumni a new spirit of loyalty and unity.

The faculty responded to Eggleston's plea to become "walking, talking, living ambassadors," ready to carry the VPI story wherever and whenever their duties carried them into the state. Some members of the board, on the other hand, balked at "speaking in public." The resourceful Eggleston switched tactics with these individuals and by dropping a word here and offering a suggestion or two there soon had these individuals attending alumni smokers, banquets, and other meetings either as his guest or as the guest of some prominent alumnus.

It is difficult to determine if Eggleston's efforts were successful in giving the people a better understanding of the programs at VPI, but his efforts were quite successful in laying the foundations for a strong and appreciative alumni association. One alumnus commenting upon Eggleston's work at this time wrote, "He was . . . always ready to take the alumni into the confidence of the College, and by so doing he was largely instrumental in welding that body together and bringing about the present spirit of loyal unity."

Eggleston's disappointment over the action of the legislature with respect to his financial request for the College was more than offset by his jubilation over its action in placing the farm demonstration work at VPI. In January, 1914, the United Board of Agriculture and the Board of Visitors of the College had united in a petition to the legislature, requesting that the United Board be dissolved and that the cooperative demonstration work be conducted by VPI.

Discussion of this proposal in the legislature had been seriously delayed and influenced by the uncertainty as to the fate which awaited the Smith-Lever bill which was being debated at the same time in the Congress of the United States. This bill, whose passage seemed imminent, would provide federal assistance for the demonstration work and require that such work be conducted through the agricultural college. The major provisions of the federal measure were well known but of course would not become certain until final passage by Congress. Eggleston had become alarmed lest the legislature, in awaiting some final action by Congress on the Smith-Lever bill, fail to act on the petition to put the demonstration work at VPI. He also knew he was in a delicate position. His enthusiastic support of the farm demonstration work was well known in all circles. The rumor that his appointment to the presidency was a political one, motivated in part as a scheme to move the demonstration work to VPI, was also known. Now if he became too active on behalf of the proposal to move the work to VPI, he ran the risk of raising a howl of political I-told-you-so opposition. If he remained inactive, he might lose his beloved demonstration work, or see its transfer to the College delayed for at least two more years. Faced with this situation, Eggleston, whenever the occasion demanded it, reiterated what was already known; he favored moving the demonstration work to VPI. Publicly at least he left to others, particularly the outgoing Governor Mann and the incoming Governor Stuart, the problem of rallying legislative support for the transfer. His plan was successful, and the legislature on Friday, March 13, 1914, passed the legislation necessary to place the cooperative demonstration work at VPI.

Eggleston had not secured the financial support he had requested from the legislature; but perhaps more important for the years ahead, he had met and passed the test of appraisal imposed by a conservative legislature on a progressive leader.

Upon the adjournment of the legislature, Eggleston called a faculty meeting and assessed the situation. As usual, he adopted an optimistic tone. A good college, he said, depended upon several factors, the most important being good teaching, good buildings, and good equipment. As a result of the legislative action, VPI to become an even greater college must continue to depend on its buildings and superior teaching. Begin this teaching at once, he urged; to await fully equipped classrooms and laboratories would be to await until "the angel Gabriel blows his horn." Turning to the transferred demonstration work, he congratulated the faculty on the opportunity "to make the state of Virginia the campus for the Virginia Polytechnic Institute." At this same meeting, he urged the faculty to join in a concerted effort to interpret VPI to the people in the state.

He was a little less optimistic with his board in discussing the action of the legislature with respect to its failure to increase the financial support of the College. This failure continued to puzzle Eggleston. To his way of thinking, everything VPI did, especially in its program of agricultural education, added dollars to the state's economy and dignity to rural living. The fact that others did not view the college program in this manner, he attributed to a lack of understanding on their part. As one remedy, he urged the board to continue its effort to inform the people about VPI and its program. It was all the more important for the board to do this now that the demonstration work was to become a part of the college program, he insisted. This demonstration work, he happily told the board, was being eagerly received by all the faculty in the department of agriculture. If anyone does not like this new work, he bluntly observed, "we will get rid of him at once." He kept his word.

S. W. Fletcher, director of the Agricultural Experiment Station, was not enthusiastic about the demonstration work "as now conducted in this state." He believed, as Barringer had believed, that the agricultural substations scattered over the state represented one of the best methods for carrying on the work. Early in March, 1914, before the legislative action transferring the demonstration work to VPI, Fletcher had hired as workers for his substations several of T. O. Sandy's best farm demonstrators but had not informed Eggleston of the action. Sandy, however, wrote a strong letter to Eggleston, protesting that the demonstration work was being undercut by Fletcher's action in hiring the demonstrators at salaries which he, Sandy, was not allowed to pay. The records indicate that Eggleston, upon receiving this information, resorted to what for him was most unusual behavior. He lost his temper. He went further. He translated his temper into a long blistering letter to Fletcher in which he excoriated him for his actions in the matter. Having thus partly relieved his feelings, he left the letter on his desk, locked his office, and walked furiously up the hill to his house in the grove.

Eggleston knew full well that friction or a rupture between VPI and the demonstration workers might be fatal to the legislation even then shaping in the legislature to transfer the work to VPI. The next morning when he returned to the office, he resorted to the typical Eggleston approach; he penciled on the letter to Fletcher the comment "written but not mailed," put the letter in the file, and then composed a firm but perfectly courteous letter to Fletcher, outlining the policy he should have followed in the past and would be expected to follow in the future. At the same time, he wrote to Sandy reassuring him that the Experiment Station would not compete with him in the hiring of workers.

Following the location of the demonstration work at VPI, the plan for administering the program was not clear. On April 3, the board at Eggleston's suggestion adopted a resolution, "that there be elected a man who shall be denominated Director of the Station, Director of the Agricultural College and Director of the Agricultural Extension Work." The resolution specifically stated that H. L. Price would be kept as dean of agriculture, but no mention was made of Fletcher. Upon hearing of this resolution, Fletcher, after several conferences with Eggleston, tendered his resignation to take effect July 1, 1914. In his letter, Fletcher stated that his resignation had been caused "by those in charge of the demonstration work in the state." Eggleston wrote to him at once, denying this charge, and stated, "Your resignation was asked [for] on the ground you did not fit into the plans for reorganization contemplated by the Board of Visitors and the President." In this same communication, Eggleston went out of the way to stress the fact that the board was not criticizing Fletcher's conduct of the experiment stations.

Eggleston's message was abundantly clear. As a result, word soon spread over the campus that if one wanted to stay at VPI he had better not criticize "Joe Eggleston's demonstration work."

The resignation of Fletcher and the passage of the Smith-Lever Act to go into effect July 1, 1914, necessitated some administrative changes at the College. At the request of his friend, David Houston, Secretary of Agriculture in President Wilson's Cabinet, Eggleston agreed to serve as acting director of Demonstration and Extension Work. W. J. Schoene was appointed as acting director of the Experiment Station, while H. L. Price continued as dean of the department of agriculture. T. O. Sandy and Ella Agnew continued as state agents for their respective parts of the demonstration program and remained in Burkeville pending further administrative organization and clarification of the work and the arrangement of suitable quarters for them in Blacksburg.

During the session of 1913-14, an alumni gate opening onto the campus at a point closely adjacent to the present intersection of College Avenue with Main Street was completed. A curving driveway was constructed from this gateway, passing north of Henderson Hall and up the hill until it passed in front of both academic buildings (now the site of Rasche and Brodie). After passing these two buildings, it curved sharply to the north and then branched into a "Y" with one branch passing by the YMCA (present Student Personnel Building) and the other branch curving westward down Faculty Row. This drive was joined in front of the second Academic Building by a branch road which meandered southward by the library and the field house. Another branch road joined it in front of McBryde Hall and led to the Administration Building, which stood on a site about half way between present Patton Hall and the Memorial Chapel. This alumni gateway provided the main entrance to the campus until it was removed in 1936 in order to widen Main Street.

During this same session some sixty acres of land, in the vicinity of the old high school building, Donaldson Brown Continuing Education Center, and the University Club, were acquired by the College. During the same period, the library was moved from the Second Academic Building to the stone chapel-auditorium-gymnasium building. The library remained at this location except for a temporary location in the First and Second Academic Buildings during the construction of the present Newman Library. The construction of the alumni gate and roadway had begun in Barringer's administration. Barringer had also inaugurated the movement which led to the purchase of the land mentioned and to the relocation of the library.

Other events which helped make Eggleston's first year in office a happy one have been ably summarized by Smyth as follows:

> The defunct "Gray Jacket" later "The Skirmisher" was resuscitated under the name of "The Firing Line"; and the Monogram Club was formed. . . . During this session two thirds of the enrolled students were members of the YMCA with Mr. R. W. Owens as secretary. . . . The world's record in butter production was broken by a Holstein cow of the VPI dairy herd. The farmers' winter course was attended by about double the number of the previous year. At a meeting of the Corps in March it was decided to build the long needed athletic house on the athletic field, and work thereon was begun immediately.

This last event deserves further attention. Eggleston wanted to establish a department of physical education but was unable to do so because of financial stringencies. To Eggleston, the three "R's" were merely tools to be used in developing a "sound body, an active mind, and the spirit of civic service, of good fellowship." "We shall no longer call a child educated," he said, "when he acquires arithmetic and adenoids; history and hookworm; algebra and astigmatism; cube root and consumption; Caesar and spinal curvature. Education must be a development of the whole life." He was firmly convinced that physical education was one tool necessary for the achievement of this objective. He had discussed the importance of "physical culture" with his board, but his theories in this field were too far ahead and finances too far behind the times to make any progress with this body.

In the fall of 1913 at a student assembly he vigorously supported Coach Branch Bocock's suggestion that the students and faculty join together in raising funds for a "field house" to be used until better facilities could be secured. The students in addition to the money pledged outright, requested that a special fee of $5 to be used for the building be collected from each student at the time of registration. The board, after a persuasive presentation from Eggleston and the students, agreed to the proposal, and construction of the house was begun immediately. The building, which stood on a site about twenty-five yards south of the present Newman Library, was completed during the session of 1914-15 and put into immediate use.

While Eggleston was urging the board, the faculty, the alumni, and the students to speak up for VPI, he was busy doing the same thing. One of his most successful ventures was the injection of better organization and clarification into the confused picture of agricultural education with which the College had become involved. As a result of his often humorous explanations and descriptions, the blurred lines distinguishing experimentation, research, teaching, demonstration, and extension became much sharper and more logical. As a result of his addresses, pamphlets, and newspaper articles, the farmers, the bankers, the industrialists, and the business community in general began to get a better understanding of the responsibilities assigned to the Experiment Station, the resident teaching staff, and the extension staff. Happily, much of this understanding began to rub off on the agricultural faculty; and this group began to work together with a harmony reminiscent of the earlier days of McBryde's administration.

Eggleston's real love was his agricultural extension program. He preached this program constantly. Once again he was far ahead of the times with respect to the possibilities he saw in the extension work. While he recognized its importance as a factor in increasing farm production, he thought its real importance rested in its powers for improving all aspects of rural living. To accomplish this purpose, he wanted the VPI on-campus program expanded in such directions as rural economics and rural sociology and then to have the "demonstrators" carry and help apply the results of this expansion to the rural communities. In an article in *The Southern Planter* in which he outlined the developing program in agricultural education, he concluded his discussion of the extension program with the declaration that ". . . it is our desire and our purpose to make the state of Virginia the campus of this agricultural college, and to answer promptly and effectively every reasonable call that is made by any one who wishes to improve conditions on the farm."

Having presented a picture of what the College was doing, Eggleston in this same article, projected a rosy picture of what he hoped to do. Then he concluded with the following observation: "All of this will take time, and patience, and money. Let me assure you that we have on hand a large stock of patience; that we have on hand a large stock of time we wish to utilize promptly, but we are woefully lacking in money. The financial condition of this agricultural college is serious. It cannot hope to be what it should be unless it receives better support at the hands of the state."

From reading the official records, checking the newspapers, and reading student accounts, it appears that the gregarious Eggleston did indeed make the state his campus as he went about explaining VPI to the people.

As his first year in office drew to a close, he consented to a return to the more elaborate commencement program frowned upon by Barringer. This decision delighted the alumni and led to the publication of a Commencement Number Bulletin, which gave a detailed account of the commencement activities and published in full both the baccalaureate sermon delivered by the Reverend D. H. Rolston and the address delivered to the literary societies by the popular Dr. John Calvin Metcalf.

The happy occasion began on Friday night with the juniors entertaining the seniors at the junior-senior prom, the sophomores entertaining themselves at the sophomore banquet held at the Blacksburg Inn, and the "rats" entertaining everybody with their ingenious schemes for avoiding all upperclassmen. Saturday morning was given over to military exercises and competitive company drills. Saturday night was enlivened by literary competition and debates between the Lee and the Maury literary societies. Sunday morning was given over to the baccalaureate sermon, which all cadets were required to attend. The YMCA held religious services open to the public on Sunday evening. A chorus made up of students and faculty under the direction of Professor Harry Gudheim sang at both of these services.

Monday morning saw "a change in the program" in that the Cotillion Club gave its final dance of the year. The cornerstone of the new shop building which had been officially named the "McBryde Building of Mechanic Arts" [at the suggestion of Eggleston] was laid amidst impressive ceremonies Monday afternoon. Monday evening Dr. J. C. Metcalf addressed both literary societies on the topic, "Idealism in Southern Literature." At ten o'clock the same night, the German Club gave its final dance for the year. Tuesday was designated Alumni Day. Allen T. Eskridge on behalf of the alumni presented the Alumni Gateway to the College, "and President Eggleston received the gate in the name of the Virginia Polytechnic Institute." The general alumni association met at 10:30, conducted some business, elected officers, and heard alumnus G. L. Fentress, speaker of the day, deliver an address on "Tendencies in Modern Educational Development." Following this address, the alumni were entertained at a luncheon in the dining hall. Tuesday afternoon was given over to the annual sham battle, which according to the bulletin "was one of the very best ever given here, and the crowd was considerably augmented by two excursions from Roanoke, each train bringing ten coaches loaded to the limit with passengers." At seven o'clock, Governor Henry C. Stuart arrived by train and was greeted with the governor's salute of seventeen guns as soon as the train came in sight. Upon debarking from the train, he was escorted by the entire Cadet Corps and band to the home of Dean T. P. Campbell, where he spent the night. On Tuesday night, after the arrival of the governor, there was an alumni smoker, "an illumination of the campus, a band concert, and the senior prom." On Wednesday after an imposing procession, made up of the graduates, the Corps, the faculty, and the alumni, had been seated in the auditorium, Governor Stuart addressed the graduates, and President Eggleston awarded medals, announced honors, read cadet promotions in the military department for the next year, presented certificates to the special students in agriculture, and "conferred degrees upon the fifty-six graduates, making them a brief talk on their duty to the College . . . and closing with the formal announcement that the session was at an end." The session may have been at an end, but the exercises were not concluded until after the benediction and the group singing of "Auld Lang Syne."

Even the singing of "Auld Lang Syne" did not bring an end to the activities, for "the social features of commencement week had a glorious ending Wednesday night when sixty-five couples danced the final ball until daylight . . . and [at which] three hundred guests were served supper in the dining hall soon after midnight."

The entire affair was considered to be so successful that a decision was made to put on a special drive to get more alumni to return for the next commencement program. The Blacksburg Chapter of the Alumni Association took over most of the planning, but Eggleston's hand can be clearly discerned in the background. Some success was achieved in increasing the number of alumni returning to the next exercise, but rainy weather interfered with most of the outdoor activities. The talks to alumni and graduates revolved around loyalty to Alma Mater. One speaker gave what he confessed to be an "emotional" talk on loyalty to VPI. In a choked voice he described his feelings upon receiving an invitation to return to the campus. "During all the years that I had been away from Blacksburg," he said, "during all those years when I had never forgotten, I had not been forgotten." The alumni present at this commencement exercise were caught up in a fervor of loyalty. Promises, if not vows, were made to get more alumni back for a reunion at the 1916 commencement exercises, and plans for accomplishing this objective were made. Of even greater importance, these plans were carried out. Most of the work was done by the alumni, but Eggleston happily cooperated and "sicked them on" with their plans.

Alumni day was set for Tuesday, June 13, for the 1916 commencement. The program got under way Friday with a formal guard mount and retreat parade by the Corps. On Friday night during the usual junior-senior prom and the sophomore banquet, "the 'rats,' as usual, took to the woods and country, and many did not show up until late the following day." Rain on Saturday morning caused the cancellation of the customary military activities and gave the sophomores a chance to recuperate from their interesting activities of the preceding evening. Time-out was taken on Saturday afternoon to cooperate with the Montgomery County School Board in laying the cornerstone for the Blacksburg High School building. Dr. C. M. Newman was the chief orator on this occasion, while the band furnished the music. It was known to very few people then and to even fewer now, that the idea of this building, which VPI eventually purchased in 1965, had originated with Eggleston.

A touch of sadness was added to the program by the death of Professor Hudnall on Sunday; but at the insistence of the family the exercises planned for Tuesday and Wednesday were carried through. Tuesday was the big day for the alumni, the College, the town, and the community. Two special trains were run from Roanoke and one from Richmond for alumni from the eastern part of the state. This latter train was welcomed at the station by a military salute from the guns of a squad of cadets especially trained for the occasion. Following this welcome, the surprised alumni were escorted to the campus by the band and Corps. The townspeople joined in the celebration by putting out welcome banners and opening their homes to the visitors. "Alumni money was valueless in Blacksburg on June 13," so great was the hospitality extended the visitors, said the official report.

To the surprised delight of everyone some four hundred, instead of the expected two hundred, alumni showed up. Following a luncheon in the Mess Hall the alumni adjourned to the walkway outside. Here they were organized into companies, with each alumnus going to his company of cadet days. Then with the band in the lead, they marched to the drill field, where they put on their own parade before the assembled Corps of Cadets. Some completely original and unexpected executions of military formations and military protocol took place before the bug-eyed cadets, but this group being in military formation had to contain its amazement as best it could. Following the parade of the alumni, the overworked band then led the Corps in its version of what a parade ought to be. Since no competition was involved, no winners were announced, and everybody retired in high spirits to the hillside to watch the sham battle.

By this time, a huge crowd had assembled on the grounds. In addition to the arrivals by the special trains, visitors from adjoining communities and counties had "swarmed into town on foot, on horseback, in wagons, and in automobiles." The alumni were given special seats on the porch of the Field House, which overlooked the site of the impending battle. To add a touch of realism, tree branches had been cut and piled on the site in such a way as to represent trenches; while over in one corner of the field, a flag indicated that the Red Cross was ready to care for the wounded. Within a few minutes, the battle got under way and "raged back and forth for a considerable time before the victors vanquished their adversaries." A touch of realism in greater keeping with the times than most realized was added in that "a number of young ladies volunteered as Red Cross nurses and took good care of the wounded."

Following the restoration of "peace" to the campus, the alumni were entertained at a banquet in the newly opened, but unequipped, McBryde Building of Mechanic Arts. Thousands of students would never know this building as anything other than a shop building fitted with lathes, forges, foundries, saws, planes, and other machinery which in operation filled the air with clanging noises and covered the operator with grease and grime. But on the night of June 13, 1916, the west end of this building was:

> . . . beautifully decorated and transformed into a rustic bower. Cedar trees were planted around the columns, and streamers of orange and maroon were draped along the ceiling and walls, which were also decorated with evergreens, while the floor was covered with fresh green grass. An old fashioned rail fence built around the whole group of tables completed the rustic setting and helped lend the necessary outdoor touch to the surroundings. Japanese lanterns shed soft, subdued light over the scene, and an orchestra filled the air with strains of inspiring music.

All speeches for the occasion revolved around the development of VPI.

Eggleston, with some nicely turned phrases, brought the group to its feet in a standing ovation for President Emeritus McBryde, who was present for the affair. Then with his own deft touch and happy choice of words Eggleston focused the warm emotions of the occasion on the problems faced by VPI in getting state-wide recognition and understanding of the program and possibilities for contributing to state welfare.

Following this "most-pleasant-in-the-memory-of-all" banquets, the alumni were invited to the Field House for the final ball, where "as usual the report of a cannon in front of the Field House indicated the opening of the dance, and not until the morning cannon was fired did the merry crowd disband."

The officers of the Alumni Association were overjoyed with the success of the commencement and of the attendant alumni reunion. Plans were immediately started to recruit not two hundred but a thousand alumni for the next reunion. A spirit of camaraderie and cooperativeness with the administration of the College burst into full bloom. One alumnus, who had steadfastly opposed Dr. Barringer, now sought and secured, by unanimous vote, his election to honorary membership in the Alumni Association. Committees were appointed with reckless extravagance to work toward the achievement of goals, some of which, in the eyes of one alumnus at least, were equally extravagant. This individual, confessing himself to be a "little hayseedy," felt that the effort to establish a billiard room in a proposed alumni house was too extravagant for an industrial institution established for "an industrial class of people." Confessing that "I do not believe in a billiard room but my city friends do," he nonetheless pledged his cooperation in the effort to secure one. At the same time he warned, "We would get more support from the state if we called it a Rest Room." Having thus salved his conscience, this "hayseedy" individual threw his full support to this and other "extravagant" objectives.

Before the numerous committees set up by the alumni had a chance to do much more than get organized, the uncertain conditions caused by World War I brought their activities to a grinding halt. The one outstanding exception was the committee set up to cooperate with Eggleston, the faculty, and the board in promoting the interests of VPI before the people and before the legislature. This committee, heavily sprinkled with faculty members, caught a part of Eggleston's vision as to what VPI could do for the state if adequately supported by the state; it also accepted his belief that the people of the state should be "educated" as to what VPI was doing before they should be asked for financial support. As a result of the activities of this committee and the enthusiasm generated by the 1916 alumni homecoming, the legislature of 1918 was better informed on the activities and needs of VPI than any other legislature meeting during the first half a century of the College's existence.

In the meantime, Eggleston had not been devoting all of his energies to the alumni. In 1915-16, at his suggestion, the faculty reorganized the general-science program which Barringer had "wiped out" because it was not a bread-winning one. Under Eggleston's version, the program was to be "more broadly elective" than the one which had been dropped. Curiously enough, Eggleston defended the course on almost the same grounds on which Barringer had attacked it. Eggleston wanted to offer some work in nonvocational science. At the same time this course was organized, the departments of English, economics, foreign language, history, and mathematics were organized into an academic department with Professor C. M. Newman as dean.

In mid-1916, W. J. Schoene relinquished his work as acting director of the Experiment Station in order to return to teaching and to his duties as state entomologist. He was succeeded as director of the Experiment Station by A. W. Drinkard ('06), whose appointment to this office received the hearty endorsement of the U. S. Department of Agriculture, *The Southern Planter,* and prominent alumni in the state. At the same time, Jesse M. Jones was appointed as director of the extension department, thereby relieving Eggleston from his duties as acting director of the work. Quarters for this developing program were completed on the campus, whereupon T. O. Sandy and Ella Agnew moved to Blacksburg from Burkeville. Henceforth, all extension work supported in part from Smith-Lever funds was directed from the VPI headquarters.

With the extension work located at the College, the need for better communication to points outside of Blacksburg became imperative. Eggleston set to work on this problem and after a "year and a half" of hard work succeeded in getting a telegraph office located in one corner of the Field House in October, 1916. Prior to this date, Blacksburg had to depend upon uncertain telephone service to its nearest telegraph office, located in Christiansburg since the telegraph line built by the students in the seventies had fallen into disuse. As the day for the opening of the office drew near, Eggleston heard that the operator was disgruntled with the idea of locating in Blacksburg. He immediately wrote to members of his board and suggested that it might be a good public relations gesture if, on the day of the opening of the office, each member sent a telegram of congratulations addressed to the operator, while he in Blacksburg sent one of a similar nature to the manager of the company. Evidently the public relations move was successful. At least the office remained in Blacksburg.

From the students' standpoint the most exciting "instant communication" with the outside world was by means of the "wireless station" erected during the 1915-16 session by Professor C. E. Vawter and some of his students. In addition to amateur communication and the receiving of official weather reports, this station also received the official Arlington time signals. It was not long before the students devised an ingenious system whereby the incoming time signals were relayed to the power plant operator, who upon receipt of them blew the big whistle installed there by Barringer. The ability to regulate one's timepiece by signals directly from Arlington afforded much comfort to the precision-minded scientist, and provided a topic of conversation for the host entertaining out-of-town guests.

The legislature of 1916 increased the college annuity by $5,000, appropriated $25,000 for the first unit of a proposed new academic building, and gave $51,000 for the demonstration work. In discussing these appropriations with the board, Eggleston said, "While we did not come out badly, the state is still niggardly in its support of this important institution." On another occasion he complained that "however crying the need, however necessary an improvement, however desirable an expansion, we are constantly met by our treasurer with the cry 'no funds.' " As the inflation of the approaching war began to be felt, the financial condition of the College became increasingly difficult. Eggleston was particularly unhappy over his inability to hold his younger staff members. "We get a young man here and train him," he wrote, "and he makes a reputation and instead of being able to advance him in his work, we are so straitened in circumstances that other institutions step forward and get the men we have trained. It is disastrous to the state, and it is a pity it does not see it." To Eggleston's puzzled disappointment some members of the legislature persistently blocked his requests for sufficient money to complete and equip McBryde Hall (as the building came to be called). After twice having had to stop construction on this building for lack of funds, the board finally borrowed enough money to complete the building sufficiently for occupancy in the session of 1916-17.

In actual fact the circumstances surrounding the erection of McBryde Hall had stirred up considerable controversy, which although carried on behind the scenes was constantly threatening to break into the open. The relatively unknown firm of Carneal and Johnston had been chosen not only as architects for the new building but also as architects to submit a general plan for the future development of the entire campus. The selection of this firm of young architects had shocked and disturbed a number of alumni, not because they knew anything detrimental about the firm, but because they did not know anything at all about it. One prominent alumnus wrote a long letter to protest to Eggleston in which he said in part:

> For the life of me I do not understand how the business men who are on the Board could think for a minute of making any such selection. Both of these young men are young and inexperienced, and on their own admission have never undertaken any such task. This is a far-reaching undertaking, and the very best engineering architects should be selected for this important work.
> As a loyal graduate of the Institute, I protest against any such selection, and unless the Board takes some steps to secure the services of more experienced men I shall make some public statement on the subject with the hope of creating public sentiment that will force them to make a more wise selection. Do not understand this letter to be in the nature of a threat to either you or the Board, but I do wish it understood that I am bitterly opposed to any such unbusinesslike procedure and shall make my views known publicly if forced to do so.

Eggleston had partially calmed the fears of this particular alumnus by assuring him that "any scheme" submitted by Carneal and Johnston would be carefully reviewed by the board and by "a consulting architect of wide reputation and recognized experience." Since it was known that Carneal and Johnston had been recommended by Eggleston's good friend, the internationally known architect Ralph Adams Cram of Boston, the impression seemingly spread that Cram was to be the "consulting architect of wide reputation." It is not known whether Cram was actually consulted, but J. Ambler Johnston, the junior member of the Carneal-Johnston firm, in later years admitted that Cram and his firm "had quite an influence on our way of thinking."

The second controversy arose when it was announced that instead of locating McBryde Hall on the site of the burned Preston and Olin building, a home on Faculty Row would be demolished and the new building erected on this site. To many people in the Alumni Association and to a few powerful members of the legislature this action was interpreted as a complete lack of business acumen on the part of Eggleston and the Board of Visitors.

The lack of confidence in the business ability of the board and of the president was underscored when it was learned that the building would be of stone quarried on the campus and "laid up by former stone workers in the community," under the direction of D. O. Matthews, superintendent of grounds. Not only had the board been unwise in the selection of an unknown firm of architects, and in the location of the building, wrote one alumnus, but now it was compounding its errors by entrusting the workmanship of the building to a group of inexperienced workmen under the direction of a foreman also inexperienced when it came to a building of such magnitude as this one was to be.

In instructing Carneal and Johnston as to the type of architecture to follow, Eggleston informed them that he wanted the new building to be the prototype of a new VPI. "He wanted to depart from the poverty stricken factory type of Lack of Architecture hitherto employed and wanted this new structure to express the character and type of education for which it was created." Carneal and Johnston's answer to this challenge was the McBryde Building of Mechanic Arts. Thousands of alumni can decide for themselves whether this building met Eggleston's instructions.

The impressiveness of the building when completed quieted most of the discontent in the ranks of the alumni, but it had not convinced certain members in the legislature that Eggleston knew how to get the most building for the least money. One member of the legislature even commented that the building proved that Eggleston knew how to build for ornament, but not for use. Shortly after the completion of this building the rumor spread, with some basis in fact, that the long range plan for campus development included the replacement of the First and Second Academic Buildings and the replacement of all the barracks on the quadrangle with more ornate buildings, matching in style the architecture of McBryde Hall.

This wholesale departure from the "poverty stricken factory type of Lack of Architecture hitherto employed" was too much for some members of the legislature already convinced that Eggleston was too inclined to build for ornament. As one result of this development, Eggleston never did succeed in getting any significant increases for building purposes from the legislature.

There is a happier note. The erection of the McBryde building marked the beginning of a long and happy association of the firm of Carneal and Johnston with VPI from that day to the present. It also influenced the style of architecture followed on the campus for the next half century. Years later J. Ambler Johnston wrote:

> The building [McBryde] was dedicated in 1914, the artistic features were lauded, pictures were taken, articles were written then forgotten.
> Thirty or more years later a party would go to VPI and graduate and never see or understand this early effort to lift VPI out of the appearance of a trade school cow college, yet its spirit has gone on. The McBryde building did what Dr. Eggleston wanted; it set the pace for everything since.

It is a real tribute to Eggleston the man that the early circumstances surrounding the erection of the McBryde building were not used against him by any except the small group in the legislature. And this group confined its opposition to rejecting his pleas for large sums of money for capital improvement.

With the exception of the financial situation, Eggleston had every reason to feel encouraged as he entered the session of 1916-17. The alumni were giving him enthusiastic support; the faculty was supporting him and working harmoniously within itself; the legislature was beginning to give a grudging support to his beloved extension program; the press was far less hostile and in

most instances favorable; even the student body was "doing as well as could
be expected." The board declined his recommendation that secret fraternities
be allowed a trial period but approved his proposed course in industrial physics
and even more wholeheartedly approved his appointment of the popular E. A.
Smyth as dean of the department of applied sciences to succeed the deceased
R. J. Davidson.

Many of the matters which the college community considered to be important faded into insignificance as the nation was drawn into the First World
War. VPI's response to the war effort drastically affected not only Eggleston's
developing program but the entire college community as well. As America
approached the war, the students at first were uncertain in their attitude toward
it. A number of debates occurred between the advocates of pacifism and isolation and the forces of preparedness and militarism; but as the war swept closer,
the campus was caught up in a fervor of patriotism. Many students began
dropping out of school to join the armed forces. In November, 1916, the board
authorized Eggleston to apply for a unit of the Reserve Officers Training Corps
to be established at the College. The application was approved, and an infantry
unit was established on January 5, 1917.

The establishment of ROTC programs at VPI did not disrupt the academic
program, since the College was already devoting more time to military training
than that required by the new program; in fact, the only difficulty faced by the
College in adjusting to ROTC seems to have been that of finding suitable housing for the additional military personnel required by the program. Captain S.
W. Anding continued as commandant but was succeeded in March by Captain
C. C. Carson. To assist with the expanding military program, the War Department in March, 1917, detailed to VPI Sergeant M. J. Bresnahan, "who was
considered the best drill sergeant in the army." In time, Bresnahan became one
of the best known and most popular noncommissioned officers ever assigned to
the ROTC unit at VPI.

As the war fervor increased, Captain H. E. Keller ('17) volunteered to give
military training to all men on the campus and in the community. Large numbers turned out at his call and marched and countermarched up and down the
drill field and over the streets of the town. Persons having had previous military
training could apply to certain military centers for a period of training, which
if successfully completed entitled the applicant to a commission in the armed
services. Cadets, especially seniors, took full advantage of this opportunity
prior to the establishment of the ROTC at the College. On May 12, 1917,
seventy-five seniors embarked at one time to Fort Myer under this plan. The
band escorted them to the train, a Hokie was given, and then as the train
pulled out, "music and cheers subsided into a quiet good-bye told in the waving
of hands and handkerchiefs. Tears in the eye showed the deep feeling of those
who were going and those staying behind."

The faculty voted to award degrees to all seniors in good standing at the
time they volunteered for military service. At the same time, the session was
shortened to end on May 31, without the usual commencement exercises or
alumni reunion.

At this commencement, Eggleston, in keeping with the urgent plea of
Secretary of War Newton D. Baker, urged all students under twenty-one years
of age to remain in college. To do so, he said, was a patriotic duty and respon-

sibility. Continuing, he warned: "President Wilson says that the world must be made safe for democracy. True. But, if democracy is destroyed it will be destroyed not by autocracy but by itself. It will be destroyed by individuals composing it insisting on their so-called rights and slacking in their duties."

In urging that the College continue its program for all of those not old enough for military duty, he cautioned: "It cannot be too often or too emphatically or persistently said that if the colleges and universities of this country were closed during the next half dozen years, the loss to this country in efficiency, in leadership, in culture, in wealth, in practically everything that goes to make a nation worthwhile would be so colossal that the nation could not recover from it in a century of time."

By 1917, the activities of the VPI alumni in the war effort were getting almost daily attention in the press. Eggleston was pleased with the contribution being made but at the same time was a bit unhappy that the recognition had to be achieved in such a manner. Commenting on this recognition, he said:

> It has seemed necessary for a distressing condition to arise to accentuate the peculiar efficiency of the Virginia Polytechnic Institute. In a time of stress and danger, the country calls for men prepared in one or more of three lines: military, agriculture, and engineering. When the government called for men trained militarily, VPI said at once, "We are ready," and the War Department is finding out at Fort Myer and elsewhere that VPI was ready.
>
> When the government called for engineers, VPI said, "We are ready," and the government is finding out the truth of this statement also.
>
> When the government sent out a distress call for greater food production and looked around for men to organize and direct the men and women, boys and girls, in the first line of defense it turned to VPI in so far as Virginia is concerned, and VPI said, "We are ready," and today VPI has in this state an organization for greater food production that two prominent government experts say is the best in the South, and one of the most efficient in the whole country.

When President Woodrow Wilson appointed Herbert Hoover as United States Food Administrator in 1917, Eggleston immediately wrote to Hoover, offering him the services of the entire agricultural extension organization in Virginia. This body of men and women had already been doing much of the work that had to be done to increase the production, preservation, and conservation of essential foods. Eggleston believed the "war would probably be won or lost before a new field organization could function." To Eggleston's surprise, he got no acknowledgement of his offer. What Eggleston did not know was that a director of, or Federal Food Commissioner for, the state was to be appointed, but Senators Martin and Swanson, not Eggleston, would be Hoover's advisers as to the appointee. In due time, Elijah B. White of Leesburg was appointed commissioner and immediately attempted to set up an organization in the state with headquarters in Richmond. Running into some problems, he immediately consulted with Eggleston, who repeated the offer he had made to Hoover. The offer was accepted by White, and in the words of Eggleston, "the transition was easy." The resulting activities of the extension workers in promoting food production and conservation received unstinted praise from the press in the state, one daily paper closing its tribute with the observation that "the people of Virginia should be very grateful to VPI for what it is doing for them as well as for America."

The session of 1917-18 was an unusual one for the College in many ways.

The student body was larger than expected, but whether in spite of or because of the war was not known. December and January were bitterly cold, with the thermometer registering zero or below fourteen times. December 30 established a new record of −27 degrees and caused an unusual number of plumbing casualties on the campus and in the town. The prolonged cold spell placed an alarming strain on the heating system, which proved inadequate to heat some of the barracks. This condition caused the boys to write many letters claiming they had to wear their overcoats while in their rooms. Eggleston immediately commiserated with the boys and asked for copies of the letters in order to show them to the finance committee of the legislature. At the same time, he was experiencing difficulty getting sufficient coal for the College. To help solve this problem, the resourceful Eggleston immediately leased the entire output of two coal mines in nearby Brush Mountain, employed labor to operate them, and bought two trucks to haul the coal to the campus.

By January, 1918, the financial situation at the College had become desperate because of wartime inflation and normal depreciation of buildings and equipment. Faculty salaries were so low that several staff members had gone elsewhere and others were preparing to leave. All buildings on the campus needed repair. Many had not been painted for thirty years. Equipment was reported as worn out, and pleas for repairs to faculty homes had piled up on Eggleston's desk. Even the resourceful superintendent of grounds, D. O. Matthews, who reportedly knew how to get five dollars return for every one dollar appropriated, was issuing dire warnings of impending breakdown.

Faced with this situation, Eggleston and his board decided to make a concerted appeal to the legislature for increased financial assistance. The strategy of the appeal used was the same essentially as that of 1914 and 1916. The approach used was more massive. Once more the College was pictured as a part of the state's system of higher education. This time its function as a land-grant college was stressed. The program, especially the agricultural portion, which VPI had developed in an effort to achieve this function was explicitly spelled out. All features of this program were presented as facing immediate collapse unless aid was forthcoming. As a land-grant institution, said Eggleston, "VPI is the worst supported agricultural and mechanical college in the United States, both as to annuity and as to buildings and equipment . . . . Unless immediate measures are taken for very substantial increases . . . nothing can save the institution from collapse. What can be done?"

Eggleston and the board generously provided the legislature with a simple answer to this question: (1) increase the annual appropriation to the College from $71,000 to $160,000 and (2) make a special appropriation or permit the College to sell bonds for new buildings and equipment to the amount of $400,000.

With this appeal before the legislature, Eggleston, the board, the faculty, the Alumni Association, and the students went to work to convince the individual members of the legislature of the justness and worthiness of the cause. Press releases and pamphlets were prepared and distributed; questions about the College, its buildings, its programs, and its plans were invited from the public and the press; and comparative statistics were spread before the public to emphasize different aspects of the college program. The following information was given wide publicity with telling effect:

Annuity from the State to VPI is now $71,000, the lowest annuity of any land-grant college in the South and on a par with Rhode Island whose land-grant college gets the same annuity as ours. Rhode Island can be put in Pittsylvania, Halifax, and Charlotte Counties and not fill them. North Carolina's land-grant college gets from the State an annuity of $122,500; South Carolina $230,-000; Georgia $220,000; Alabama $115,000.

Salaries of full professors at VPI have been raised $200 in 22 years. The salary is now $2,000. New Mexico is below this, giving $1,800. The University of Virginia professors get $3,000, and VMI professors including perquisites . . . a little over $2,600. The professors in these institutions are not overpaid. They earn what they get and more. Is there any reason why VPI professors should be discriminated against?

Alumni President J. W. Stull and Alumni Secretary H. H. Hill led the alumni attack. Hill was fantastically effective. Apparently he not only knew the alumni, but he also knew the names of fathers, brothers, uncles, and business and political associates of alumni. Using this knowledge with consummate skill, he saw to it that these individuals received written or verbal information about VPI's program and needs. If he discovered a spark of interest, he tried to fan it into a flame. If he discovered hostility, he generated and directed "Eggleston's eloquence" toward it.

The legislature's reaction to this all-out appeal, in the words of Eggleston, "was a memorable one" and resulted in "an exciting contest." This legislature itself was a memorable one on at least two counts. In the first place, it was characterized by a bitter factional fight between "Farmer Governor" Westmoreland Davis and the so-called organization Democrats. In the second place, it marked the end of the process by which the state budget for the coming biennium was prepared by the legislature from separate bills drawn up and presented by separate House Appropriations and Senate Finance Committees. After 1918, the state budget for the coming biennium was to be prepared by the governor and transmitted to the legislature, which could then increase or decrease the proposed funds on listed items. Unfortunately, some of the VPI faculty inadvertently got caught up in the factional fight which developed in the legislature. The second "memorable" development, while not an unhappy one by any means, did mean that VPI would have to make a number of changes from top to bottom in its system of keeping financial records.

After a prolonged discussion in the legislature, the request for a special appropriation or a bond issue was defeated by parliamentary maneuvering on the part of the small group whose opposition was so puzzling to Eggleston.

Of the new money requested, the legislature approved sums totaling approximately $102,000.

Rector Brown was jubilant. He ended his telegram to Eggleston conveying the good news with a "Hip Hip Hurrah!" T. P. Campbell ended his telegram of congratulations to Brown with a "three cheers and a tiger." Eggleston was out of town and unavailable for comment.

The bombshell fell four days later. An irate governor called the legislature back into session to rework the state budget, which, according to his figures, exceeded all available revenue. Included in the budget cuts he recommended was a sizeable one for the VPI appropriation. The resulting special session was an especially acrimonious one; but a compromise was eventually reached, which in so far as VPI was concerned reduced its request for new money $10,500.

Eggleston was highly pleased with the result but felt that "a small handful" of legislators had continued to show prejudice against VPI. For reasons not entirely clear, he immediately wrote to the presidents of all state institutions seeking specific information as to how each one had fared in the special session. The answers he received varied from straightforward detailed presentations to masterpieces of evasions and generalities. But once more it appeared that VPI had suffered the greatest cuts. General E. W. Nichols of VMI after supplying the requested information which showed almost no cuts for that school twitted Eggleston with, "You asked for the earth with New Jersey thrown in and you got all except New Jersey! Aren't you satisfied!"

If Eggleston was satisfied, J. W. Stull, president of the Alumni Association, was not. He wrote a letter to Eggleston in which he bitterly denounced the tactics that "a few senators" had used to defeat the bond issue by preventing it from coming to a vote. Stull wanted to expose the tactics for all the state to see.

Eggleston immediately wrote a soothingly optimistic letter to Stull, claiming victory out of defeat. "We have come out of this fight with far more strength than when we went into it," he wrote. "We have not been defeated. We have in reality won the victory, but the fruits of victory have been withheld from us for two years, as far as the bond issue is concerned. Our consolation is that we could not build under present conditions anyhow, because labor and materials are too high." Eggleston then thanked Stull for the splendid support the alumni had given to the effort made before the legislature and then suggested to him that plans be begun at once for getting such support organized for the next legislature two years away.

Eggleston's claim that the College came out of the fight stronger than it was at the beginning was probably correct. Newspapers from all over the state seemed to have gained a better insight as to what VPI was trying to do. More important, perhaps, they showed a much better understanding of what it could do. The same change was manifest with a large number of the legislators. Letters and public statements began to appear which echoed the sentiment expressed by R. Holman Willis, of Roanoke, who said, "My interest in VPI came through my work in the General Assembly. I became convinced that for every dollar spent, the State comes nearer getting one hundred cents worth of education than from any other similar work to which she contributes." Outside the legislature there is no gainsaying the fact that the experience created a sense of unity and loyalty in the Alumni Association. Eggleston's immediate use of a portion of the new money to raise faculty salaries and wages paid to labor on the campus did not cost him any friends either. He had lost the battle, but he appeared to be winning the war for recognition.

In the spring of 1918 after the adjournment of the legislature, the State Board of Education acting as the State Board of Vocational Education decided to assign the responsibility for training of teachers for the Smith-Hughes vocational agriculture in the secondary schools to VPI, the University of Virginia, and the College of William and Mary. The plan provided that the students spend two years at VPI studying technical agriculture and two years at either one of the other two schools to study pedagogy and other required courses. Eggleston felt that all of the work should be located at VPI but told the board the decision to spread the work had been made to prevent "friction and squabbling over the appropriation" made by the federal government. At the same time he advised the board not to be too concerned about the matter, since in his opinion the state plan was not sound and therefore all teacher-training work in agriculture would eventually be located at VPI. His prophecy was fulfilled before the plan had a tryout. The Federal Board of Vocational Education rejected the plan outright and insisted that the program would have to be placed at the agricultural college. The state board thereupon entered into a cooperative agreement with VPI to train the teachers for the Smith-Hughes vocational agriculture.

A department of agricultural education was organized with Dabney S. Lancaster as head. The appointment of Lancaster, who transferred from the department of animal husbandry, was a most fortunate choice for both the College and the public school system of the state. At the time of the passage of the Smith-Hughes Act, the picture of agricultural education in the state at the secondary school level was a confused one with overlapping agencies conducting overlapping programs, often in the same school. The entire situation was fraught with possibilities of friction and misunderstanding. Just as the college staff in agriculture had looked with some suspicion on the introduction of the agricultural extension work, so now the extension staff tended to look with suspicion on the introduction of Smith-Hughes work. Lancaster, working in close cooperation with Eggleston and members of the State Department of Education, was able to clarify responsibilities and allay most of these fears and suspicions and thereby help lay the beginning of one of the most successful cooperative programs ever developed in the United States between a state board of vocational education and its land-grant college.

The real change on the campus occurring during the war period began in May, 1918, when a detachment of 226 soldiers arrived for special training in some of the vocational areas. The men were quartered in Number Three and Number Five Barracks under the direct command of Major John C. Skuse, assisted by Lieutenants Standrod, Bell, and Taylor. A surgeon, dental officer, and quartermaster were attached to the unit, and a portion of the campus was organized as a typical military post. Dean Campbell served as director of the instructional program, with the instruction carried on by the following men: Professor Parrott, bench work and carpentry; Professor Connor, machine work; Professor J. M. Johnson, forge and foundry; Professor Robeson, radio work; Professor McKesson and Mr. D. O. Matthews, concrete work. In addition to the regular staff, Messrs. Nickle, Barker, and Wilson were recruited to help with instruction in radio and mechanics. To be sure the men understood what the war was all about, Dr. Drinkard gave a series of lectures on "War Issues."

The first detachment left the campus at the end of July, and the second detachment of some three hundred men began their training on August 1. This group completed its program and departed around October 1. On account of these two detachments, the opening date of the College was set for October 1, 1918, but all new students were instructed to report on September 1 for special military training.

With the arrival of these detachments on the campus, the YMCA assumed a character of which its founders never dreamed and put on a program unprecedented in its history of usefulness at VPI. A red triangle banner was run up in front of the "Y" building, and Dr. C. M. Newman, who had been appointed camp secretary of the post, started a program commensurate with the military routine.

Athletic goods and indoor recreational equipment were secured from the National War Work Council. A victrola with a supply of modern records was placed in the recreation room. A small canteen was set up adjacent to the lobby. One room was converted into an attractive hostess room, where the boys could entertain their mothers, wives, and sweethearts. Nightly programs were arranged: group singing on Monday, movies on Tuesday, Bible classes on Wednesday, stunts and concerts on Thursday, movies again on Friday, recreation of a general nature on Saturday, and religious services on Sunday.

The residents of the entire community joined the "Y" in the effort to "make Blacksburg a home away from home for the boys." The young folks of the community joined their talents with those of some of the "boys" and helped stage talent shows, plays, skits, and novelty dances which startled the audiences and reinforced the old folks' conviction that the young folks were headed for perdition. Many ladies of the community exhausted their talents and war-rationed family larders in baking goodies for the boys. Others invited the boys into their homes for Sunday dinner and supplied them with fried chicken and Blacksburg hospitality. When at last the day came for "the boys" to leave, the ladies of the community provided each one with a boxed "dainty home-made lunch for the trip." According to rumor, many boxes also contained a "dainty home-written note" to cheer the soldier on his way.

All in all, the war during the summer of 1918 made a not-altogether-unpleasant impact on the VPI community.

Happily for the College, Paul N. Derring, who had assisted Newman with the "Y" program from its inception, was elected general secretary for the YMCA in November of the same year and kept alive for the next four decades the spirit of "Y" services and innovation which was generated in the summer of 1918.

If the summer of 1918 was a pleasant one on the campus, the fall was just the opposite. In August, the War Department organized the Students' Army Training Corps for the preparation of future officers. After much entanglement in red tape and general confusion, a unit of 550 men was assigned to VPI with October 1 set as the beginning date. This program, in contrast with the summer program, was of collegiate grade designed to give special training as requested by the armed services. VPI was requested to give training, or courses, for the: (1) Engineer Corps, (2) Signal Corps, (3) Chemical Warfare Service, (4) Quartermaster Service, (5) Ordnance, (6) Medical Corps, (7) Infantry, (8) Artillery and Machine Gunnery, (9) Transport and Tank Service, and (10) Air Service. By special request a modification of the regular mechanical engineering course was set up to provide training for a naval reserve unit assigned to the campus by the Navy.

After the course outlines supplied by the authorities in Washington had been adjusted sufficiently to satisfy the professional ego of the faculty, some confusion and contradictions developed concerning the admission of individuals to the program. Would students already enrolled at VPI be admitted? Would new students applying for admission to VPI be admitted to the program? Did the Army, the College, or the draft board control admission?

All students having applied for admission to VPI had been instructed to report on September 1 for special "catch up" military training. These students began reporting before the admission policies and qualifications for the SATC had been fully clarified, or at least understood by the college officials. At this stage, the only point on which all records agree is that confusion reigned.

Some of the newly arrived students were found to be too young, some too old, and others too deficient in academic training for the program. Some individuals arrived via the draft boards. Others arrived in defiance of the draft boards. Others just arrived. Altogether, most of the arrivals on the campus during the entire month of September seem to have been either unauthorized or unorganized. Exodus from the campus took place during the month in the same manner.

Finally, amidst all the confusion, the official SATC unit got under way when, according to the 1919 Bugle, "six hundred and more" were sworn in on October 1, 1918, at 12 o'clock. At the same time, the "old dearly beloved blue and gray vanished as if by magic, off the campus for khaki and olive drab." The same source says, ". . . the old four-year Tech courses completely disappeared. Two-year courses replaced them. None of the old courses remained. . . ."

Just as the confused turmoil of September was fading into memory and instruction in the new program was getting under way, influenza hit the campus and spread like wildfire. All instruction except outdoor drill was suspended. Assemblies inside buildings were eliminated. The Field House was converted into a hospital, ten additional nurses were secured, the Navy detached a special surgeon to help, and physically able students were recruited as orderlies. More than two hundred cases had to be cared for at one time. Nine deaths occurred, and many special students not in the SATC went home.

Class work finally got under way on November 3, but the "false armistice" of November 7 created an emotional orgy which dulled the reception of the real armistice four days later. Rumors of impending demobilization swept the campus immediately following the armistice. Interest waned in all class work. The eternal verities of mathematics and English could not compete with the eternal emotions of going home. Youth impatiently awaiting demobilization tagged the SATC as meaning "Straggle Around Till Christmas." Even the faculty longed to get rid of the SATC and "have the college curricula placed on their pre-war basis." Demobilization took place between December 5 and 12, but no boxes of "dainty lunches" sped the departing "boy soldiers" on their way.

Classes were continued until the end of the quarter for all students desiring to remain, but the faculty decided to start the session of 1918-19 over again, beginning with the morning of December 31 and to extend for six months. This period was to be divided into three terms of two months each. Boys returning from service would be admitted at the beginning of each term.

The SATC program was the only one undertaken during Eggleston's entire administration which he curtly described as "a dismal failure." Private letters indicate that he had strong reservations about the morality involved in drafting boys and sending them to college to study programs dictated by the War Department. Whatever his reservations may have been, Eggleston joined his faculty in its pleasure over returning the curricula to the pre-war basis.

If the college community was unhappy over the outcome of the SATC, it was more than happy with the significant, almost spectacular, war record being made by VPI alumni. H. H. (Bunker) Hill ('04) acting as alumni secretary voluntarily undertook to collect and record information about the alumni military activities. The comprehensiveness of his report discourages more than the presentation of a few generalities here.

All told, VPI had 2297 alumni under arms and nearly five hundred additional engaged in essential war work. It furnished 639 commissioned officers to the army. At ten of the various training schools and camps every VPI man who entered received a commission, and the percentage of successful candidates [for a commission] at all camps was 98. Forty-two per cent of all VPI alumni were in military service. Ten men were killed and twenty-six wounded. Nine were decorated, and twelve were cited for bravery in action. Of the many noteworthy individuals, four deserve special mention. Two of the four were brothers, Colonel Julian E. Gaujot and Captain Antoine A. M. Gaujot.

Julian attended VPI in 1889-90, and Antoine attended in 1896-97. Antoine had received the Congressional Medal of Honor for bravery shown at San Mateo, Philippines, in 1899. In World War I, he participated in three battles and received three bronze leaves. Julian had received the Congressional Medal of Honor for action during the Madero revolution of the Mexican Border campaign in 1911. He received two bronze leaves on his service ribbon for action in two major World War I offensives.

Earle D. Gregory, the third individual deserving special attention, was the first native Virginian to be awarded the Congressional Medal of Honor. His official citation as recorded in *The Virginia Tech* reads:

> Earle D. Gregory, sergeant, Headquarters Company 116th Infantry—
> For conspicuous gallantry and intrepidity beyond the call of duty in action with the enemy at Bois de Consenvoye, North of Verdun, France, October 8, 1918. With the remark, "I will get them" Sergeant Gregory seized a rifle and a trench mortar shell, which he used as a hand grenade, left his detachment of trench-mortar platoon, and advancing ahead of the infantry, captured a machine gun and three of the enemy. Advancing still farther from the machine-gun nest, he captured a 7.5 cm. mountain howitzer, and entering a dugout in the immediate vicinity, single-handed captured 19 of the enemy.

In addition to this honor, he also was awarded the Medaille Militaire, Medal of the Legion of Honor, Croix de Guerre, and the Montenegrin Order of Merit. Gregory was wounded in battle but recovered and following the war completed his work at VPI, graduating in 1923. This much-decorated hero entered the Corps without a murmur of protest, and, according to *The Virginia Tech,* became known to every member of the Corps as one of the most popular cadets. In May, 1963, VPI's crack cadet drill team was renamed the Gregory Guard in his honor.

The fourth individual deserving special attention was Major Lloyd W. Williams of the class of 1907. To Williams has been attributed one of the more famous quotes of World War I: "Retreat? Hell, No! We've just come!" There seems to be no doubt whatever but that Williams' conduct and statement led to the quote. Whether he used these exact words has never been officially established. The story as borne out in the official records was that a French major, moving with his battalion along a dark road and believing that a general withdrawal had been ordered, told Williams to follow. Williams reported the incident to his commander in the following words: "French drawing back through us. French major ordered me to withdraw with him. Told him to 'go to hell.'"

A few days after this incident, Williams died after being gassed and wounded in a battle near Chateau-Thierry, France, when the Germans were making their strong drive toward Paris.

A Distinguished Service Cross was later sent to Williams' parents at Berryville in honor of their son, the first Virginian known to have been killed in World War I. In 1957 the Major Williams Hall was named in his honor.

The transition from a wartime to a peacetime basis, which began with the "regular" academic session on December 31, was not a smooth one. Professor Randolph had resigned as dean of engineering and professor of mechanical engineering and had been succeeded as dean on September 1 by S. R. Pritchard. Professor J. S. A. Johnson had succeeded Randolph as head of the department of mechanical engineering, and in December Major John Skuse, who had been in command of the SATC had been appointed commandant of the Corps of Cadets. A number of instructors had been employed to fill the positions temporarily vacated by the staff members who had left the College for military service. With the war over, this group of temporary employees wanted a definite understanding as to their status for the remainder of the session. A few of these individuals resigned at once to seek employment elsewhere. Some of the staff having entered military service wanted to return to teaching at once, some of this group did not want to return at all, while a few individuals dragged their feet without committing themselves one way or another. Some of those having returned to teaching after a period of military service resigned at once upon discovering the "peck order" which now prevailed in the faculty as a result of promotions in rank which had taken place during their absence.

The most surprising and upsetting event of the session, however, took place on January 24, 1919: Dr. Eggleston resigned as president, his resignation to take effect at the end of the session. In his letter of resignation he thanked the board for the cooperation and kindness it had manifested toward him but said he had decided to accept the presidency of Hampden-Sydney College.

Eggleston's resignation, which caught most of the public by surprise, was received with dismay from most quarters. Telegrams and resolutions from alumni poured in, urging him to remain at VPI. The faculty joined with the alumni in trying to persuade him to change his mind. Governor Davis wrote him a personal letter pledging him his full support if he remained. But Eggleston remained adamant in his determination to leave. The Board of Visitors, therefore, accepted his resignation but asked Harris Hart, board member, to prepare a resolution of acceptance to be released to the press. Hart drafted such a resolution and then secretly showed it to Eggleston to see if it met with his approval. Eggleston altered a word or two in order to make the resolution a bit less laudatory, whereupon the resolution was released to the press and spread upon the minutes of the board.

Eggleston never made any public statement to explain his resignation, but a careful examination of his official reports and correspondence indicates that contrary to the image he was presenting to the public, he was becoming quite discouraged. For one thing, he was discouraged with his inability to get the mass of people in the state and the conservative element in the legislature to accept an enlightened vision of the contributions a land-grant college could make to the state if properly supported by the state.

In addition to what he considered to be the lack of understanding of the real potentialities of a properly supported land-grant college, he was also bothered by frequent newspaper rumors that VPI was to be consolidated with the University of Virginia. Publicly, Eggleston brushed these rumors aside as too insignificant for his attention. Privately he wondered why the rumors persisted.

He was also upset because of certain conditions which had developed within the student body during and after the war. Some rowdyism and considerable hazing had broken out. Complaints had been made to Governor Davis, and Davis, refusing to give any names as to particulars, was putting considerable pressure on Eggleston to correct the situation. The baffled Eggleston had done the best he could to correct the situation but had informed the governor that without more information concerning the alleged hazing nothing more could be done about it. Davis did not agree with this point of view and had said so. Unfortunately, a particularly flagrant case of hazing had occurred about the the same time, and Eggleston, although absent from the campus at the time, had been blamed for the occurrence.

The attitude of the Board of Visitors toward Jesse Jones, director of the Agricultural Extension Service, was another factor bothering Eggleston. For reasons which were never clarified some of the board members were not satisfied with Jones' work although Eggleston was satisfied and said so. There is some evidence to indicate Eggleston suspected that the board's attitude toward Jones was politically inspired as a result of some developments in the struggle between Governor Davis and his political opponents.

Eggleston's biographer, Dr. Edward Overton, of the University of Richmond, advanced an additional factor to explain Eggleston's resignation. He felt that the move was influenced by a religious change that came over Eggleston and helped create within him the desire to spend the rest of his professional career in a church oriented college. Certainly some of Eggleston's conversations with older students at Hampden-Sydney College tended to confirm this opinion. Whatever his real reason or reasons, Eggleston declined to withdraw his resignation.

With Eggleston's resignation a settled fact, the board appointed a committee to seek a successor for him, and Eggleston set about his final six months as president with his usual show of ebullient optimism. In February, the ROTC program was organized, and units of coast artillery, infantry, and engineering were established at the College. In June, Eggleston happily told the board that: "The report of the U.S. Army Inspector was most flattering and resulted in placing the Virginia Polytechnic Institute on the list of twelve distinguished colleges in the country. I should add that this is the first time in its history that it has obtained such rating."

At the same time Eggleston reported this event, he also announced the appointment of John R. Hutcheson to succeed Jesse M. Jones, who had resigned as director of the extension service. Eggleston was strong in his praise of Jones, but he also expressed his strong conviction that Hutcheson would make an excellent director. Hutcheson proceeded to fulfill Eggleston's prophecy by filling the office of director with distinction until he resigned in 1945 to accept the presidency of the College.

As the time for the close of the session drew closer, plans were developed for an extensive alumni homecoming to be held on Tuesday, July 1, as a part of the commencement program. On June 12, it was announced that Julian A. Burruss ('98) had been elected president to succeed Eggleston and planned to attend the commencement program. Burruss' election was pleasing to most alumni and helped swell the attendance at the final exercises.

Very few innovations were planned for this particular commencement. The cadets wore their khaki uniforms which blended in with the uniforms worn by many of the visiting alumni. The usual military maneuvers were engaged in by the cadets and watched with a more than usual critical eye from many alumni. One alumnus even remarked on the lack of actual relationship between the drills learned by the cadets and the skills needed in the big war "over there." This same alumnus, however, sat on the front row and gave rapt attention to the remarks attendant on the unveiling of a monument erected by the class of 1919 to "Our Dead Heroes Over There." To the present day, all cadets salute in memory of the dead as they pass this monument, which stands at the junction of the walkway leading from Lane Hall with the walkway passing in front of Brodie and Rasche Halls.

Eggleston's last official act as president took place on July 2, 1919, when he awarded diplomas and addressed the graduating class. At the same exercises, he was presented a gold watch by the student body and a silver service by the faculty and others of the College. Much pleasant comment was caused by the fact that a past president, McBryde, and future president, Burruss, were on the stage with President Eggleston while he presented his valedictory to VPI. President-elect Burruss was particularly attentive while Eggleston, in proclaiming that VPI was on the threshold of a new era of development and usefulness to the state, said:

> The history of the Virginia Polytechnic Institute has always been one of struggle. . . . No one knows it better than the honored Rector of this Board, who . . . has wrought so ably to relieve her of the fetters of poverty.
>
> And, oh, what a pathetic struggle it has been to educate the citizens of this state to grasp this conception and to act upon it for their own good and for the good of their children! What heartbreaking years they have been—for what can be more heartbreaking than to be compelled to use up from sixty to seventy percent of one's energies and thoughts to overcome indifference and opposition and sheer inertia, in order to get from thirty to forty percent of actual constructive results! Why does humanity fight its own advancement!
>
> To me nothing could be more pathetic than to have witnessed in this struggle for advancement—yea, for the very life of this institute—the great loss that has come to the people of the Commonwealth because V.P.I. has been denied her opportunities for serving those she desires to help, and could so well help if only unfettered.
>
> But we can thank God and take courage. Two years ago . . . I said that it seems necessary, before an institution can come into its own, that it shall be baptized in blood shed by her sons in public service, and that it seems necessary for such a background to be built before its real worth is recognized by the public. The background is here.

Eggleston then reviewed the contribution to the war effort made by the college and returned to his conviction that as a result of this effort a new day awaited VPI. "A new era for VPI—and this era made by sons of VPI. . . . Has the cost in money to the State for the upbuilding and maintenance of this institution been too great for the result obtained? The question answers itself. . . . The verdict is already written. Well and nobly done."

Whether Eggleston's belief as to the forces which would cause the new era to develop was correct or not may be debated. His prophecy of a new era of service and development proved to be correct, however, for VPI did indeed enter into a new era of growth and development in its second half century of life beginning shortly after the close of World War I. Just how much Eggleston's administration contributed to the launching of this new era is hard to determine, but certainly one fact stands out in joyous relief; for the first time in the troubled history of the College, a departing president left behind him a board of visitors, a faculty, a student body, and an alumni association united in a spirit of harmony and good will toward the College, and more important, toward each other.

Following his retirement from the presidency of VPI, Eggleston returned to his beloved Prince Edward County and immediately entered into his duties as president of his alma mater, Hampden-Sydney College, filling this office until his retirement in 1939. Following his retirement, he continued to live in Prince Edward County, where he devoted most of his time to historical research and writing until his death in 1953.

Chapter **9**

The Burruss
Administration

1919-1929

J ULIAN ASHBY BURRUSS, who succeeded Eggleston to the presidency of VPI in 1919,
was born in Richmond, Virginia, in 1876. He entered VPI in the fall of 1894
and received a B.S. degree in civil engineering in 1898. As a student, he was
editor of the 1898 *Bugle*, captain of Battery E, president of the YMCA, and was
active in other student organizations. In 1906, he received his A.M. degree from
Columbia University after studying at Richmond and Harvard. At the time of
his election to the presidency of VPI, he was in the midst of his program for the
Ph.D. degree, which he received from the University of Chicago in 1921. His
earliest professional work was at Normal College, Waleska, Georgia, and at
Searcy (Arkansas) Female Institute. He also taught for a short period at Speers-
Langford Military Academy. In 1901, he returned to Richmond as principal of
the Leigh School. In 1904, he was appointed director of manual arts for the
Richmond City public schools; and in 1908, he was elected first president of
the Normal and Industrial School for Women (now Madison College) at Harrisonburg, Virginia. In this latter capacity, he took the lead in organizing the
curriculum, laying out the grounds and buildings, selecting the faculty, and
establishing a system of financial accounting for the institution. As a result of
his work at Harrisonburg, he also became familiar with the several agencies

working to improve conditions surrounding rural life in Virginia. Perhaps of even greater importance, he developed some understanding and skill needed in working with the legislature and other governmental agencies.

Following the announcement of Eggleston's resignation as president, Burruss discussed the vacancy with a number of prominent alumni and then decided to make himself "available" for the position. At the same time, he knew full well the furore that might erupt if he, while president of one state institution, became an active candidate for the presidency of another state institution. With this touchy situation in mind, he decided to leave the promotion of his candidacy before the board and before the public in the hands of friends. His classmate J. G. Ferneyhough ('98), State Veterinarian, volunteered to take the lead with this group. He did a superb job. The alumni had been agitating for a long time to get more of their members on the Board of Visitors. Ferneyhough with able assistance from L. T. Price ('01) and H. M. Smith ('77) took advantage of this desire and succeeded in converting it into suggestions that an alumnus be appointed as president. At the same time, Ferneyhough strongly resisted all suggestions that the Alumni Association or any of its chapters publicly endorse Burruss or anyone else. If an alumnus wanted Burruss for president, insisted Ferneyhough, let that alumnus, as an individual, say so to board members or anyone else, but under no condition should organized pressure be directed toward the board on Burruss' behalf. A number of alumni followed Ferneyhough's suggestion and saw to it that Burruss' credentials were thoroughly placed before every board member. Some alumni went a step farther and saw to it that professional weaknesses in other alleged candidates also were discretely called to the attention of the board. The board made no public statement; but it became a matter of public knowledge that the search for a president was being conducted both inside and outside the state.

As the summer approached, Burruss found himself in a difficult position. He had been offered a summer instructorship at the University of Chicago, and the time was rapidly approaching when he would have to accept or reject it. He confided his dilemma to his friend Ferneyhough, who immediately wrote back and assured Burruss that his election as president was a foregone conclusion. Burruss had his doubts; consequently, when June arrived without any commitment from the board, he accepted the Chicago instructorship. Then on June 12, 1919, Burruss was unanimously elected president of VPI.

Before accepting the presidency, he contacted the board and found that it was willing for him to fill his instructorship at Chicago and report for duty as president on September 1. He thereupon notified the board of his official acceptance of the presidency, and Rector J. Thompson Brown agreed for the second time in his career to serve as acting president during the absence of the president.

Upon completing his summer at Chicago, Burruss reported for duty September 1 and plunged immediately into the problems of administering VPI. He had written to an alumnus and stated, "If elected to the presidency of VPI, I pledge to devote my entire energy and effort to its promotion and upbuilding." Burruss kept this pledge. Fortunately for everyone concerned, the period of good will left by Eggleston, plus the elation of the alumni over having an alumnus as president, gave him a chance to devote his energies to the College rather than to overcoming factional prejudice or jealousy. Incredible as it may seem, Burruss was the first man during the first half century of the College's existence to assume the presidency with the unanimous backing of all major groups concerned with the College's welfare.

Burruss also was the first man to bring to the presidency a background of experience and professional study in school administration, curriculum, and school finance. Even as he assumed the presidency, he was in the midst of completing his doctoral program of study at the University of Chicago in these areas. Invaluable information was being acquired as he completed his doctoral dissertation, which bore the lengthy title of "A Study of the Business Administration of Colleges Based on an Examination of the Practices of Land-Grant Colleges in the Making and Using of Budgets." In early 1919 he had served on the study committee set up by Governor Davis to help draft a budget system for the state of Virginia. In correspondence with LeRoy Hodges, the governor's personal secretary, concerning this particular study, Burruss had confessed his strong, almost compelling, interest in matters concerning school administration, finance, accounting, and surveys. In the same correspondence, he had expressed the desire to use this interest some way in service to the state. Burruss got the fulfillment of his wish when he became president of VPI, for the College needed help in every one of these areas.

From the administrative standpoint, VPI was floundering when Burruss assumed the presidency. The same condition prevailed, but to a lesser extent, with the curriculum program which had been disrupted by the war. Eggleston had succeeded in creating an atmosphere of harmony and goodwill, but he had not succeeded in establishing an effective administrative organization. Neither had he succeeded in establishing a clear-cut sense of direction for the College. Perhaps it was just as well that this real situation was known only to a few individuals, one of whom was Governor Davis.

As a part of Davis' effort to put all state institutions on a sound business basis, he had directed Dr. William H. Allen, director of the Institute for Public Service, New York City, to make a survey of VPI as one of the important state agencies. Allen's report submitted to the governor on March 6, 1919, was not released to the public until much later and was shown to Burruss only after he had been in office nearly three months. By this time, Burruss had made his own survey of the situation and was in almost complete agreement with the parts of the report concerning the administration of the College.

According to Allen, the institution's conception of its duty and opportunity had been altogether too limited; the president [Eggleston, who had resigned] was not enthusiastic about the future of VPI, but was apologetic, "even disparaging, with respect to its possibilities as a separate institution; its location; its plant"; the dean of the college who had been assigned too many of the president's responsibilities, had little conception of what Virginia should be doing through VPI; a thorough-going reorganization was needed from top to bottom, including the condition of the halls, the business offices, the roadways, the school, and the catalogs.

Allen concluded his report with an unusually long list of suggestions for the College to follow in securing a better administrative structure and curricular program in harmony with the conditions of the time. He also showed little sympathy for the complaint so constantly voiced about the location of the College in Blacksburg. "It is true that the location is very inconvenient," he reported, but "it is also true that Blacksburg is where the institution is . . . if the board will not go to Blacksburg to meet," he said, then the governor should select "members who will attend at Blacksburg." The reason for having six deans "to take care of a little over five hundred [students] at a time" intrigued Allen. He could not justify this many but "passed the buck" by suggesting that each dean be required to justify his office. His recommendations as to instruction were blunt, succinct, and to the point. He believed that VPI was a state college of agriculture, engineering, and applied science, created to serve the interests of the state. In the College's instruction, Virginia's special interests should "be emphasized in all courses—Virginia's chemistry, Virginia's geology, Virginia's geography, Virginia's economics, Virginia's agriculture."

Burruss was not willing to make all of the instruction so "Virginian," but he wholeheartedly embraced and promoted the philosophy that VPI was a state college of agriculture, engineering, and applied science, created by Virginia, he said, "primarily and specifically for the education of Virginians in those phases of agriculture and mechanic arts which Virginia needs for the development of Virginia's resources." Burruss repeated this philosophy over and over in a variety of ways. To his faculty he said, "Above all, it must be kept in mind at all times that our *first* duty is to Virginia, to train Virginians to work for Virginia and this is intended to be along agricultural and industrial lines." On another occasion in discussing the feasibility of altering a certain course to bring it into harmony with national trends he observed, ". . . it might be proper to raise a question as to the propriety of using Virginia's money to supply a type of training which can not be clearly shown to be necessary for Virginia's own development." This latter concept became the criterion by which Burruss passed judgment whether or not to approve additions of new courses or curricula for the College. Fortunately for VPI, his idea as to what contributed to the agricultural or industrial development of the state was rather comprehensive and tended to enlarge rather than shrink with the passage of time. Burruss' idea of his land-grant College as being one of agriculture, engineering, and applied science devoted to the development of Virginia's agriculture and industry was reiterated over and over in bulletins, in press releases, in reports to the alumni, in reports to the legislature, and in circulars to agricultural and industrial groups. Since this idea also was in harmony with the prevailing convictions of Virginia leaders, it soon came to be accepted by many as the only permissible function to be fulfilled by VPI.

It has been recorded that Eggleston, on assumption of the duties of president, bought an extra typewriter and hired an extra secretary. Burruss went him two steps better. He bought an extra typewriter, a mimeograph machine, and a printing press. He installed the typewriter in his study at home, the mimeograph in the administration building, and the printing press (rented in 1921 and purchased in 1923) in the basement of the First Academic Building. He used the typewriter to communicate with individuals and to draft rough copies of his reports, the mimeograph to communicate with faculty groups and the board, and the printing press to communicate with the alumni and the general public. The results were startling but satisfactory to the faculty, the board, and the alumni. The general public did not express an opinion.

Within two months after assuming the presidency, he had a "General Report" prepared which must have amazed the board with its thoroughness, objectivity, attention to detail, and proposals for development of the College. In addition to this "general information" he submitted his proposed budget for the coming biennium. For the first time in the history of the school, the budget had to be prepared in conformity with the budgetary regulations set up by the state and submitted to the governor's office before the convening of the legislature. Burruss had taken the general budgetary headings required by the state, but for the sake of clarity had divided many of these headings into subdivisions conforming to the work being undertaken at the College. Where necessary, each division or subdivision was accompanied by a "message" in which an attempt was made to explain or justify the item. This budgetary procedure, more or less routine today, had enabled the board for the first time to see the total college program spread before it in terms of dollars and cents. After some discussion the board approved the budget, whereupon Burruss had copies of the budget and the message mimeographed and delivered to the faculty. The faculty reacted in much the same manner as the board, and both groups sat back in eager anticipation to await the action of the governor and the legislature.

Burruss then submitted his budget request to the governor, who seems to have been delighted with its format but a bit uncomfortable with its size in terms of money. After some conferences involving Burruss, the rector, and the governor, a compromise budget was agreed upon which involved considerable reduction in the original amount of money requested but included substantial increases over the amounts appropriated for the past biennium. By the time the governor submitted this budget to the legislature for its consideration, many alumni, particularly those who had participated in the 1918 legislative struggle for funds, had become keenly interested in the outcome. When the requested budget won the approval of both the House and the Senate with no difficulty whatever, this group of alumni was overjoyed. The chairman of the Alumni Welfare Committee wrote to Dr. Lawrence T. Price, president of the Alumni Association and reported, "Not once in the session were we accused of lobbying for VPI. Everything went smoothly. As a matter of fact the budget system, the Governor's friendship, the interest of Colonel [LeRoy] Hodges in VPI, and the splendid work done by President Burruss is what carried us to victory."

At the same time Burruss had been preparing the budget, he had been studying the total operation of the school. He discovered that the faculties in agriculture and engineering had been attempting to revise their curricula in an effort to make them more relevant to the changed conditions following the war but had become bogged down. Using his knowledge of curriculum building, he immediately prepared voluminous materials and guides for developing curricula and courses suitable for a college of agriculture, engineering, and applied sciences specifically organized to serve the needs of Virginia. By overworking both himself and the mimeograph, he soon had this guideline material beautifully organized and placed in the hands of a surprised faculty. Before this group had an opportunity to recover from its surprise and decide that it too was overworked, he had prodded it into making rather drastic reorganizations in the major curricular offerings.

The work in agriculture was organized into areas of specialization; and degree programs were offered in agronomy, animal husbandry, dairy husbandry, horticulture, and agricultural education. A combined program called agriculture and home economics was offered to students having completed two years of satisfactory work elsewhere. The major changes in the engineering program consisted in the modification and updating of four-year programs in chemical engineering, civil engineering, commercial engineering, electrical engineering, mechanical engineering, mining engineering, and industrial education. The designation of general science was dropped and in its place four-year programs were offered in applied biology, applied chemistry, applied geology, and applied metallurgy. A pre-medical course of two, three, or four years was also offered as were a number of short courses, a two-year course in practical agriculture, and a short course in linotype machine operation.

While leading the movement to reorganize the curricula and the administrative staff, Burruss had been busily engaged in studying the business affairs of the College. Once more he turned out a voluminous report which surprised, in fact shocked, the board. With a delicacy for the sensibilities of others, which few persons indeed knew he possessed, he laid bare a picture of confusion, overlapping responsibilities, duplication of effort, inaccurate cost accounting, and hidden debt. Reiterating that it was the system that was at fault, not any one individual, he used his training and experience in administration and finance to pinpoint trouble spots and to propose remedies.

Cautiously he reminded the board that the glowing accounts of the physical improvements to the campus attributed to Eggleston had not told the full story. Many of these improvements, he pointed out, had not been paid for. For example, the McBryde Building of Mechanic Arts not only had not been paid for but had not been completed. Worse than that, he reported, this building, the most imposing one on the campus in appearance from the outside, was totally unfit for its purpose on the inside. The high vaulted rooms, Burruss reported, were much more suitable for a cathedral than for a shop. Not only was the building unpaid for, unfinished, and unfit, it was so poorly constructed, he said, that the simple matter of trying to prevent the roof and walls from leaking and flooding the rooms after every rain would be a perpetual drain on college finances. Burruss saw no immediate solution to the problems faced in connection with this building but suggested that he be allowed to start an accumulation of funds with which to complete, alter, and repair it over a period of time. So much hostility had already been created in the legislature in connection with attempts to fund this building, he said, it would be unwise to request any more funds from this source. Time proved Burruss to be correct in all of his opinions concerning this building. After repeated attempts to keep it in effective use, it was torn down and a new McBryde Hall was nearing completion on the site in 1971.

Burruss did not stop with just one illustration of false prosperity inherited from Eggleston's administration. In fact, by the time Burruss completed his report to the dismayed board, he had rather conclusively shown that by an accurate system of accounting, most of the major physical improvements made on the campus during the previous administration remained to be paid for. Even the "eternal college farm" was placed before the board as a business enterprise losing money because of confused responsibilities and poor accounting.

After having painted this rather gloomy picture of the indebtedness of the College, Burruss directed his attention to a consideration of causes and solutions. Once more he shocked the board. The major cause of the difficulty, he reported, was not so much one of insufficient money as it was one of improper expenditure, supervision, and accounting for the money which was available. According to Burruss, VPI had expanded its program so rapidly that in terms of money it was now the largest educational institution in the state. The administrative organization, however, had not kept pace with the educational expansion; the administrative organization and supervision was particularly weak in all areas concerning the expenditure of college funds, he reported, but was glaringly defective in the area of plant upkeep and improvement. At this point, Burruss summarized for the board some of the non-instructional activities for which the College assumed responsibility. This summary proved to be an eye-opener not only for the board but for all who read it. It is not likely to put one to sleep today:

> . . . VPI has numerous commercial and semi-commercial departments, which it is compelled to maintain by reason of its location in a very small community. It must lodge a large majority of its students; it must house a large part of its instructors and officials; it must feed practically all of its students; it must manufacture the larger portion of the clothing for its students; and it must maintain its own shops and working forces for carpentering, painting, wallpapering, bricklaying, plastering, concrete and cement work, plumbing, steam-fitting, electric work, etc., for in the village none of these may be found on any adequate scale. It must supply the entire community, college and village, with electric current for lights and power; it must supply all the water that is used in both college and community; it must supply the sewerage system for both college and community; and whatever needs there may be for a steam laundry the college must supply—for none of these utilities is found in the surrounding community. Whatever articles in wood or in metal, whatever repairs or replacement of parts, are needed for immediate use, must be made in our carpentry shop, our forge, our foundry, our machine shop. Our sick must be cared for entirely by the college infirmary for there is no other hospital for many miles. Being an agricultural college we must conduct a farm of considerable size, a large dairy and animal husbandry plant, and a creamery. It has even been necessary to operate a coal mine for several years. While all of these utilities bring in considerable revenue, none of them can be conducted on a profit-making basis. . . . The fact is, because of the large number of commercial or semi-commercial activies at VPI this situation is not comparable with any other institution in Virginia but must be considered as a different type of institution.

After completing this summary, Burruss directed his analytical mind toward the manner in which the College had been and yet was going about taking care of "a plant valued at nearly two million dollars." The results, he felt, were a reproach to the College, the state, and the members of the faculty with technical training in agriculture and engineering.

As a step toward improvement in the handling of the non-instructional activities, Burruss recommended that the office of business manager be created and the duties of this office be coordinated with the duties of the treasurer. This latter office, he felt, should be moved to the campus from Christiansburg, where it had been located simply because Charles I. Wade, the highly efficient treasurer, happened to live in that town.

Above all, he said, the business manager should expect to relieve the president of many time-consuming chores which, under the existing organization, took up so much of the chief executive's time. "The fact is," said Burruss, "under the present conditions of organization the conscientious president attempts here the impossible." Continuing along this line, he said:

> Indeed to fulfill properly the position of president of this college under the present form of organization, one must needs have the qualifications not only for conducting a large college offering a great variety of instruction, resident and non-resident, with research work, but also for managing an immense boarding

establishment, a steam laundry, a hospital, a clothing factory, an electric plant, a water system, a sewerage system, a plumbing shop, a paint shop, a forge, a foundry, and a machine shop, a farm, a dairy herd, a creamery, and a coal mine. Details concerning all of these are being constantly brought to the president, and the time and energy of the highest paid employee of the institution is consumed indiscriminately in approving orders for a few bushels of coal, in hearing complaints about a torn shirt in the laundry, in ordering a kitchen sink repaired, and so on ad infinitum and ad nauseam.

Dr. Burruss got his business manager. Indeed, he got his business manager and all of the other organizational changes which he had suggested at the end of his first year devoted to the study of the College. Only a few of the major changes will be mentioned.

For instructional purposes, the institution was organized into three divisions: a school of agriculture, a school of engineering, and another division designated as the college. All applied science and other courses needed but not directly related to agriculture and engineering were assigned to this latter division.

In addition to a dean for each one of these schools, the organization provided for a commandant of cadets, a health officer, and a business manager. The individuals occupying these positions, together with the president, made up the nucleus of the Council of Administration for Burruss' entire administration.

In reorganizing the faculty, the deanships of the general faculty, the graduate department, the academic department, and the applied science department were abolished. T. P. Campbell, who had been dean of the general faculty, was appointed as dean of the college. The men who had occupied the other deanships returned to full-time teaching and, according to their testimony, did so willingly and happily.

The directors of the Extension Division and of the Agricultural Experiment Station were put under the office of the dean of agriculture. This office was also given additional responsibility for coordinating the work in agriculture. After some persuasion from Burruss, H. L. Price, the incumbent prior to the reorganization, accepted the position of dean of agriculture. S. R. Pritchard continued in the office of dean of engineering. This office was given additional responsibilities in anticipation of the establishment of an Engineering Experiment Station and an Engineering Extension Division. The head of each department within the three colleges was designated as the adviser to students in the particular department; and, perhaps as important as any administrative step ever made by Burruss, the duties, lines of authority, and responsibilities of the entire staff were set forth in written and graphic form.

The office of college surgeon was abolished in favor of a full-time health officer. Shortly thereafter, W. A. Brumfield, M. D., was employed to fill this office. Upon arrival on the campus, Brumfield immediately reduced the number of daily admissions to the infirmary by the simple expedient of changing the daily sick call from 8:00 a.m. to 4:00 p.m. Brumfield came to VPI with an enviable record in coping with problems in public health; but, according to his way of telling it, he met his Waterloo at VPI. He had never been able, he reported to a group of sophomores, to diagnose the baffling diseases which beset the VPI cadets and sent them to the infirmary on the day the department of physics held its tests.

In May, 1922, E. C. Miller took over the responsibilities of business manager of the College. Part of his duties involved enforcing regulations prohibiting students from owning and operating automobiles on the campus and from having unauthorized electrical applicances, such as radios, irons, and toasters in their rooms. In addition to these duties, Miller, whom the boys nicknamed "Ducklegs," was responsible for protecting the college apple orchard from "rats" operating under the "Apple Expeditionary Force" with orders from the sophomores to "collect and bring to my room by tomorrow morning a laundry bag full of apples." In the enforcement of the responsibilites Miller was unequivocal, direct, and blunt. If he found an unauthorized automobile, he impounded it. If he found an unauthorized iron or radio, he confiscated it. If he caught a "rat" with a laundry bag full of apples, he took both the apples and the laundry bag. The automobile, radio, or bag would be returned to the student at the end of the year if the student had nerve enough to reclaim his property, but by that time the aversion to the penalty had been transferred to the hapless Miller. As one result of these occurrences, the name "Ducklegs Miller" became anathema to thousands of students who never had an opportunity to know the real Miller.

Burruss' extensive reorganization introduced a hitherto missing quality of efficiency into the business management of the institution. He was so successful in effecting financial savings that he soon paid off all old debts and embarked on an extensive program of repairs and improvements to the entire physical plant. His wiping out of old debts led one alumnus to comment that Barringer wanted improvements, Eggleston got them, and Burruss had to pay for them, an observation not altogether incorrect.

As one part of his reorganization program, Burruss set up continuing faculty committees to study and make recommendations for the improvement of many aspects of the College. Many of the resulting recommendations reflected ideas having been articulated by Dr. Barringer at an earlier date. For example, Barringer's idea of a swimming pool was expanded into a proposal for a lake suitable for "boating and swimming in the summer and skating in the winter," to be constructed on the lower end of the drill field. According to the committee, this objective could easily be reached by building a high dam from a point now included in the picnic area just below the president's house, north across Stroubles Creek to a point near the present entrance of the golf course.

This proposal was drastically modified when one professor with considerable foresight caustically observed that such a venture would start out as a lake, turn into a swamp, and wind up as a mud hole contaminated by pollution carried down from all of Blacksburg every time it rained. The idea of a lake was never completely abandoned but culminated about a decade later on a greatly reduced scale, in the present Duck Pond. The pollution prophecy has also been fulfilled.

Another committee thought the grazing of ponies, horses, and cows on the campus should be restricted. The problem of cows on the campus had plagued Barringer, who with his trouble with Quick and the sale of defective cattle yet fresh in his mind, had received the following tactful letter from Professor Smyth:

Mar. 31st, '11

Dr. P. B. Barringer, Pres'd't.
V.P.I.

My Dear Doctor

I do not know whether I may be extending the bounds of professional propriety as a campus resident, nor to whom I should properly speak in the following matter, but have concluded to write you, trusting that you will pardon me if I speak where silent resignation would be more becoming.

The res gestae concern the bovine nomads that like an all-devouring horde infest the lower part of the campus, and not content with the grass on the farm side of the campus, are emboldened to "carry the war into Africa" and nibble at the front shrubbery and growths by the houses; in particular doing damage to the alfalfa by my house, upon which I am depending for milk production later in the season; their droppings on the walks are not in the best of good taste either.

I am well aware, that in a community like ours, the individual must sink his feelings for the general good, and so I trust you will not consider me as out of order in making this mild and submissive—I hardly care to call it a—protest.

If the matter is as it should be, I cheerfully acquiesce, and ask that you will consider this letter as not written.

I could not find time to see you in your office, though I do not like the formality of a written communication; and I must apologize for adding in any way to the burdens and annoyances to which you are constantly subjected.

Very sincerely and respectfully yours

Barringer had issued instructions restricting the cows to certain areas of the campus, but during World War I it was decided that if sheep could graze on the White House lawn, cows could graze on the VPI campus. With the war ended and the shortage of food no longer acute, many faculty, especially those not owning cows, felt that the time had come to ban them from the campus. Burruss agreed and immediately inaugurated a policy which eventually restricted all livestock to the college farm. He was less successful, however, in his effort to persuade the Blacksburg town council to banish livestock from areas of the town adjoining the campus.

Continuing to work with and through faculty committees, Burruss strengthened and developed the College in a number of ways. A chapter of Phi Kappa Phi, a national honorary scholarship fraternity was established in December, 1921; admission requirements were raised to fifteen units and then almost immediately to sixteen units; a new system of credit-hours, quality credits, and grading was inaugurated; and a system of student orientation and guidance was begun. Certificates of merit in agriculture were authorized by the Board of Visitors in 1923 at Burruss' suggestion, and the Institute of Rural Affairs was begun in 1929.

The summer school, which had operated intermittently ever since 1904, was strengthened and organized on a quarterly basis to harmonize with the remaining three quarters of the academic year. The duties of the registrar's office were placed under the dean of the college, and the athletic activities were brought under the direct supervision of the college authorities.

The most significant innovation introduced by Burruss was the admission of women to VPI, beginning in September, 1921. Barringer had wanted the doors opened to women as early as 1908 but had to content himself with the hope that such an accomplishment would "take place in the near future." Eggleston had permitted women to attend certain short courses held mostly during the summer, but Burruss wanted them admitted on an equality with men. His report to the Board of Visitors advocating such admittance was thorough, persuasive, and lengthy. Briefly, these were some of his arguments. The war period had liberated women in many ways and had opened to them many fields of work "from which they are not quick to retire." The extension of suffrage to women had doubtless strengthened women's position in industry. "Women workers . . . are here to stay." The extension of suffrage had made women full citizens of Virginia and of the United States. To exclude women, now full citizens, from an institution supported by federal and state funds would probably be illegal since the land-grant acts made "no distinction as regards sex." Continuing, he added, VPI already had in operation many of the courses needed by women working in the extension service, industry, and agricultural laboratories. It would be more economical to admit women to VPI than to provide technical and agricultural training for them at some other state institution. It would be easy to provide living quarters for the few women who probably would enter within the next few years; and if necessary, the president's home could easily be converted into a dormitory for women. The Board of Visitors had complete authority, he claimed, to admit women, although later it might find it necessary "to ask the General Assembly to make special appropriations for this purpose."

At the conclusion of Burruss' presentation, the board voted unanimously to admit women to all courses except military for the next session, beginning in September.

The Corps met the announcement of this plan with public howls of protest and secret feelings of pleasure. When September arrived, five full-time and seven part-time coeds arrived with it. This small number of girls called for a lot of public I-told-you-so's plus an even greater number of discussions in the barracks. The editor of *The Virginia Tech* risked censure from his fellow students when, with tongue in cheek, he wrote, "The making of VPI a coed school failed to bring many members of the fairer sex within her walls, but it produced remarkable results in other ways. VPI has the largest enrollment of cadets in the history of the school."

The cadets continued to protest the invasion of VPI by the women and predicted dire consequences for school spirit, athletics, academic standards, and school traditions. The discovery one day of a "rat coed" nonchalantly sitting atop of the water tower did nothing to allay the concern for traditions. Fears about academic standards also received unexpected and unwelcome confirmation, but not in the manner expected. Within a short time, one of the coeds walked off with the highest academic honors. Dr. Burruss' announcement of this fact at commencement exercise drew mixed applause from the cadets. This applause quickly swelled into protest when Burruss undertook to use the occasion to congratulate the institution for having admitted women. This protest threatened to break into pandemonium when the surprised Burruss advanced to the front of the stage, and shaking his finger at the equally surprised cadets, accused them of being jealous of the coeds. This demonstration subsided as suddenly as it had erupted, when the cadets observed that the commandant not only was not amused but was raking the boisterous cadets with a steely eye. Following the restoration of quiet, the mood of the cadets changed; instead of booing at the mention of the coeds, they began to applaud. Since applause was a more accurate expression of the real feeling the cadets had toward the coeds anyway, applause soon became much more prevalent than hostility. As one alumnus, reviewing the early history of the cadet attitude towards coeds at VPI expressed it, "Our hostility gave way to a desire to applaud, our desire to applaud gave way to a desire to accept, and our desire to accept the coeds, soon gave way to a desire to embrace them." "Women workers" were indeed at VPI to stay.

Coed enrollment did not increase rapidly, probably more because of the highly technical curricula than because of any real anti-coedism on the campus. Neither was there a noticeably rapid increase in the privileges extended to the coeds as students. The military traditions built up in an all-male school for half a century could not be broken over night. The coeds were not allowed on the upper quadrangle, even to enter the College Bookstore located in Number One Barracks (Lane Hall). Occasionally one would deliberately set foot on the forbidden territory, probably to "bait" the cadet guard walking his post in front of Number One. Such an invasion was usually met with a yell, "Women on the Quadrangle." Immediately all barracks windows facing the quadrangle would be thrown open and filled with cadets ready with free advice to the coed, the guard, or both. If the guard did not know what to do about the "invasion," he called the corporal or sergeant of the guard. Usually one or the other of these individuals knew how to handle the situation. If not and the coed seemed inclined to argue her right to intrude on sacred ground, the officer of the guard, a cadet senior was called. From this point on the action usually became original but never dull for the spectators as the officer of the guard attempted to persuade the coed of the error of her presence on the quadrangle.

Coeds had to skirt the quadrangle to get to classes in the old Science Hall located on the site of the present Shanks Hall. In her diary, one coed described the walk to the Science Hall as follows:

> We had to go back of barracks to some of our classes and thus see and hear most everything nice little girls shouldn't see and hear. 'N funny thing, seemed like the boys always needed fresh air as we came by—up went the windows and down came the water (in paper bags), as that seemed to be their chief indoor sport. Along with the water came squeaky voices yelling and saying silly things to us.

Membership in the several clubs was denied the coeds as was participation in the student publications. Although the coeds were conscious of their isolation from campus activities, in general they were not much disturbed by it. They soon organized their own amusements. Dubbing themselves the "Turkey Hens," they organized their own basketball team and charged the cadets a stiff admission fee to their games. The cadets retaliated by rooting for the opposing team. But they did attend. Denied representation in *The Bugle,* the coeds issued their own year book, the *Tin Horn.* A delightful take off of *The Bugle,* the *Tin Horn* got more space in *The Tech* than did *The Bugle* itself.

Continuing their own independence, the coeds soon organized their curricular and extracurricular organizations, such as science, chemistry, biology, business, dramatics, and glee clubs. By 1930 there was a Women's Student Organization. In 1934 a Women's Student Union was organized, but in 1939 the women students joined the Civilian Student Union. Shortly after its organization the Women's Student Union requested coed representation in *The Bugle.* This request was flatly rejected, but opposition weakened rapidly. Finally a group picture of the Women's Student Union was permitted. The next year full representation in *The Bugle* was extended to all senior coeds.

Perhaps one of the most unusual holdouts against coeds was in the male dramatic club. Not being allowed to participate in dramatics with the men, the women formed their own club and staged their own plays. One year the men gave their play with cadets playing the women's roles. The women gave their play with coeds playing the men's roles. Ironically the men borrowed costumes from the coeds, and the coeds borrowed costumes from the men. Gradually the absurdity of this separation became apparent, and the two groups began producing plays together. In 1935-36 the two groups cooperated in forming the Tech Players, the forerunner of the Maroon Mask, which was formed in 1938.

By the outbreak of World War II any remaining discrimination against coeds was more a matter of custom than of conviction. The dramatic exodus of men from the campus during the war spelled an end to even these lingering customs. A few firsts remained to be won by the coeds in the period following the war, but by that time the coeds as usual had won the battle and had earned the right to equal status with the men.

As the year 1922 approached, a decision was made to hold a semi-centennial celebration commemorating the first fifty years of the College's life. Numerous committees were appointed and extensive plans were made and duly publicized.

When these plans became known to the Corps, a small hitch developed. It had been decided to hold the celebration in conjunction with the annual commencement exercises, but certain dates had been rearranged. Instead of scheduling the events on the previously announced dates of commencement, it had been decided to start the exercises on the last day of senior examination week, which always came one week earlier than the examinations for underclassmen. Then after the celebration and commencement had been completed, the underclassmen would be given their regular examinations. This approach, if followed, would permit the regular session to close on the previously announced date. The three underclasses did not think this plan was at all satisfactory and said so in a petition to Burruss, requesting that they be allowed to take their examinations at the same time seniors took theirs. Burruss refused their request; the three classes thereupon appointed a committee to appeal to the Board of Visitors. Earle D. Gregory, of World War I fame, was chosen as chairman, and a letter was directed to the rector of the board, requesting that the examinations be given early. This letter was a psychological masterpiece as much in what it did not say as it was in what it did say. Professing complete loyalty to VPI and to the purpose of the semi-centennial celebration, the letter with a complete absence of overt hostility against anyone, pointed out the difficulties the three classes would experience in putting forth their best efforts to make the celebration a success while at the same time operating under the worry of examinations yet to come. One paragraph was a clincher for alumni members of the board:

> After participating in such events as take place here during the final exercises . . . a student is unfitted, both physically and mentally, to pass his examinations. For example when one has attended a drill in the morning, a speech or exercise followed by another drill in the afternoon, and a dance at night, each day for a week, one is in no frame of mind for serious application, and neither three days nor a week is a sufficient length of time for a return to normalcy.

The records do not indicate any board action, but Burruss saved face, and the situation, by allowing himself to be overruled by the faculty, which agreed to give examinations early.

The celebration, immediately named the "Golden Jubilee," was held May 28-30, 1922. To accommodate the expected crowd, a huge circus tent capable of seating more than three thousand persons was erected on the eastern end of the parade grounds. In an effort to prevent any recurrence of disastrous results such as had occurred in the leaking tent used in the commencement of 1892, this tent was given a special waterproofing treatment of paraffin. Such precautions were unnecessary, for the weather proved to be ideal for the occasion. Pup tents were erected on the campus to house students who surrendered rooms to returning alumni. Orange and maroon banners and welcome signs lined the Main Street of Blacksburg—all three blocks of it, said one report. A sign made of light bulbs welcomed the guests at the Alumni Gateway entrance to the campus. Electrically lighted Japanese lanterns lighted the curving roadway and walks from the campus entrance to the barracks. Boy scouts at the registration booth, located on the campus across the street from the present Corner Drug Store, eagerly waited to do their daily good turn by guiding or otherwise helping visitors. Automobiles from town and gown alike met all trains at Christiansburg and provided free transportation over "the dusty nine miles to Blacksburg," Exhibits and open houses were held in all of the college departments, and alumni "from Maine to California, from Canada to the Gulf" poured into Blacksburg in a steady stream. Military policemen, "a startling innovation for Montgomery County, according to old citizens," were present to direct the traffic and handle the happy crowds.

During the "College Day" ceremonies, messages of congratulations and felicitations were received from sister institutions, learned societies, and governmental organizations. Governor E. Lee Trinkle welcomed out-of-state visitors and then by careful phraseology managed to deliver the political platitudes customary to such occasions in a manner pleasing to all. E. A. Alderman, president of the University of Virginia, after delicate allusions to its founder, Thomas Jefferson, and the fact that the University had just celebrated its hundredth anniversary, welcomed VPI as a younger brother. "The elder and the younger brother," he said "both have a right to look along the paths of the new century . . . with an unclouded conscience and a quiet spirit, and to challenge the records of the Nation's service for proof that their sons have served well the state and kept their honor clean." Then Alderman proceeded to pay the following tribute which could not fail to stir a note of sympathy in the minds of all familiar with the half-a-century-long story of VPI.

> In a larger sense than the University [of Virginia], the Virginia Polytechnic Institute began its life in an era of disillusion and transition, of self-denial and suffering. It stirs the spirit to think how you have triumphed over your difficulties. I congratulate you out of a sincere mind on the courage of your career, the wisdom and steadfastness of your aim, and the strength and glory present as you stand here today, poised on the threshold of a new era, secure in the affection of the Commonwealth and the loyalty of your sons.

Alderman, who represented the state institutions, was followed by President Henry Louis Smith, of Washington and Lee University, who brought greetings from the private institutions of the state. Smith became so carried away that he discarded most of his "penned" speech and devoted most of his time to a consideration of the kind of education needed in a democracy. In the process, he congratulated VPI for promoting the very kind of education which would most likely protect democracy from Russian Bolshevism. Smith was followed by William Oxley Thompson, president of the Ohio State University. Thompson brought greetings from the land-grant colleges of the country. Declaring that "the world do move," Thompson traced the advances in the country brought about as a result of the work of the land-grant colleges during the preceding half century. Then, Thompson, a native of Ohio, born and reared in that state, brought gasps of surprise from the audience with his ringing endorsement of the League of Nations, which President Warren G. Harding, also a native of Ohio, was fighting. Thompson then prophesied the day would come when the "United States . . . will give to the entire globe the mandates and wise counsel that its leaders have learned in colleges, in universities, and institutions of the character of VPI." The evening session of "College Day," presided over by former president Eggleston, heard C. A. Cobb, editor of the *Southern Ruralist*, laud the value of agricultural products, warn against the imposition of a high tariff, and assert that the time had come for the agricultural colleges to give more attention to the man behind the plow than to the plow. At the same evening session, Homer L. Ferguson, president of the Newport News Shipbuilding and Drydock Company warned of trouble ahead for the peacetime shipbuilding industry because of the federal government's short-sighted policy in this field. Dr. Charles R. Stockard, professor of anatomy at Cornell University, concluded the session with a discussion on the role of technical education in applied science. Apparently, Stockard made no startling pronouncements or prophecies, since the newspapers merely mentioned his address.

Tuesday, May 30, was designated as Alumni Day, with every event of the day, except the cadet parade, in charge of alumni. Even this event was infiltrated by a few alumni who slipped into ranks of cadet companies and tried to prove that one could go home again. One or more representatives for every year of the College's existence were present at the morning exercise to give a year by year account of the development of the College. One hundred per cent of the class awarded graduation certificates in 1875 were present. Major John T. Cowan of Montgomery County, the only surviving member of the first Board of Visitors, received ovation after ovation as he moved from group to group. Long standing mysteries surrounding a number of college high jinks of an earlier day supposedly were cleared up in the convivial atmosphere and reminiscences of the day.

Enthusiasm and high spirits continued to mount and, apparently for some, reached a somewhat unsophisticated peak at the luncheon prepared by J. J. (Pop) Owens and served in the college dining hall. A "jazz orchestra" featured at this affair provided many of the alumni their first contact with the "jazz age." The results were surprising, if not startling. Exposure to the saxaphone and the trumpet lowered inhibitions. Before long Rip, Rah, Rae was competing with Hokie, Hokie, Hi; college songs and class yells long since forgotten were revived. For a period of time, it appeared that the mess-hall pranks of the previous half century would be re-enacted and squeezed into the period of one hour as many gray-haired alumni sought to relive the "good old days."

At the business session following the luncheon, Lawrence Priddy proposed to the assembled alumni that they raise $50,000 toward the erection of a "war memorial hall" in the form of a gymnasium with quarters for visiting alumni. According to one report, Priddy "handled the crowd like a combination of

Billy Sunday and a jewelry auctioneer" and secured pledges of $72,742 within seventeen minutes. Priddy was immediately re-elected president of the Alumni Association and instructed to continue the campaign for the memorial hall. At the evening session, the alumni heard United States Senator Claude Swanson ('77) condemn the newspapers as the "cause of the country's present degenerating condition." He rejoiced, however, that "such men as this institution produces will promise a good future." The connection between Swanson's opinion of the press and his opinion of VPI graduates was not made clear in the press reports. Major W. P. Tams ('02), president of the Gulf Smokeless Coal Company, warned of the growing arrogance of John L. Lewis but quickly warmed to the task of eulogizing the product of VPI as men who "will give an inestimable value to their alma mater's reputation."

The commencement address on Wednesday was delivered by William E. Dodd ('95), distinguished professor of American history of the University of Chicago. Having urged the alumni to permit the administration to infuse new blood into the faculty of the College, Dodd directed most of his attention to national affairs, which he found to be in a sad state and likely to become sadder, one reason being the influx of new blood brought about by immigration from European countries to the United States. Dodd's proposed remedy was for the South to produce more leaders such as Woodrow Wilson and to send them North.

The entire celebration was reported by the newspapers of the state. Several eastern Virginia dailies, for the first time in the history of VPI, sent special reporters to Blacksburg to cover the affair. These reporters not only covered the main events but also wrote a number of human interest stories which, although in a light vein, reflected a subtle warmth, almost an affection, for the College, seldom if ever manifested in the press coverage of earlier days. The arrival of one wealthy alumnus in his private railroad car, which he kept parked on the siding at the station and in which he entertained fellow alumni and guests, got less notice than the alumnus of the class of '76 who by invitation served as drummer for a number of military formations. Antics of over-exuberant alumni instead of being condemned as motivated by too much "Brush Mountain Dew" were pictured as manifestations of desirable school spirit. All in all, the occasion seems to have turned out as a happy ending for one period and an equally happy beginning for another in the history of VPI.

Privately, Burruss seems to have been a bit disturbed over the semi-carnival atmosphere which had intruded itself into certain portions of the Jubilee program. Publicly, he felt that the affair had created good will with the alumni and the public which should be utilized at once. But before he had a chance to take full advantage of this spirit, an incident occurred which threatened to undo the good will created by the Jubilee and at the same time to affect adversely the reorganization program of the College which Burruss was promoting. Since the incident grew from roots deeply imbedded in the traditions of the Corps of Cadets, it deserves more attention than it otherwise would get.

The Corps of Cadets, organized as a formal body during the session of 1891-92, had been assigned responsibility for supervising certain aspects of student-body life. In 1908, with Barringer's encouragement, the Corps had drawn up a constitution which in effect provided for a form of student self-government for the nonmilitary aspects of student life. This part of the Corps authority was administered by an executive committee of fifteen students elected by the cadets. This executive committee was assisted by a sub-executive committee also made up of cadets. The original constitution had been approved by the college authorities but from time to time since its adoption had been amended by the students. Oftentimes, these amendments had not been submitted to the college authorities for approval or disapproval, but with the passage of time this fact came to be overlooked. As one result of this evolutionary growth, a number of Corps regulations affecting both the behavior of the "rats" and the concept of hazing had come into existence but had never received administrative sanction.

Presidents McBryde, Barringer, and Eggleston had been troubled with specific instances of hazing of freshmen and had appealed to the leaders in the Corps to help stamp out the practice. In each case, the Corps had responded favorably and had agreed to eliminate the particular act branded as hazing, but other acts not having been specifically banned had grown up almost immediately. During the wartime distractions of Eggleston's administration, the situation had become quite serious. In the spring following the demise of the SATC program, two students had been arrested by civil authorities for a flagrant case of hazing. Eggleston was absent from the campus at the time, but Dean T. P. Campbell, assisted by other faculty members, had called the Corps officers together, and they had agreed to extend the honor system to ban certain forms of physical hazing. At the same time, the college authorities approved certain extensions of regulations concerning the government of "rats." These regulations extended and strengthened the authority of upperclassmen, especially the sophomores, over the conduct of the "rats" at all times they were not attending class or observing call to quarters. Any upperclassman could post the name of a "rat" violating one or more of these regulations on a bulletin board, or "rat trap," located adjacent to the guard room in Number One Barracks. At stated intervals, these names were collected and all "rats" having had their names posted a certain number of times within the interval were summoned before the sub-executive committee for a "trial." If adjudged guilty, the "rat" was assigned a certain number of "penalty tours," which meant that he had to don full-dress uniform and spend a specified length of time for each "penalty tour" in walking back and forth on the pathway or walks in front of Number One Barracks. During each tour, the "rat" was to assume a "braced position," look straight ahead at all times, and speak to no one. The "braced position" varied slightly over the years, but in general it meant holding the head up, eyes focused straight forward, chin pulled back, stomach in, and chest out. The arms were held rigidly downward with the fingers pointing down and the thumb of each hand pressing against the outside seam or stripe in the trousers.

Within a very short time, the "rat regulations," the military regulations, and regulations which had developed out of traditions became a maze of contradictions for some, inconsistencies for others, and varying degrees of confusion for all. During the happy confusion of the "Jubilee" the "rat regulations" became just about whatever the sophomores decreed them to be. One regulation which had grown from tradition decreed that all "rats" must get out of town on the night of the sophomore banquet held annually as a part of commencement week. Some "rats" during Jubilee week, however, had violated this "regulation" and remained in town. Since the culprits would be sophomores before they could be punished by the usual procedures, the sophomores had caught the "grossly fresh rats" and had shaved portions of their heads. The papers had reported the incident but in general had passed it off as a harmless illustration of exuberant college spirit. The boys apparently felt the same way, but some of the parents were not so sure about the matter and had expressed their doubts to Burruss. Burruss was upset but hoped the matter of freshmen-sophomore relations would quiet down next year. He was disappointed.

In the fall of 1922, three students had been dismissed for conduct which they argued was permitted by the "rat regulations" which had been published in the YMCA handbook in the section devoted to the Corps of Cadets. The administration, on the other hand, looked upon the action as hazing. This incident served to bring to Burruss' attention the fact that the Corps was operating under a number of student-made regulations which had never received either faculty or board approval. Burruss brought this fact to the attention of the board at its January, 1923, meeting and at the same time reviewed the developments which had brought about the situation. At his suggestion, the board adopted a resolution reasserting the fact that the final authority for adopting rules and regulations affecting all student behavior rested with the board; furthermore, such authority could not be and had not been delegated to the Corps. At the time the board adopted this resolution, Burruss was in the midst of studying the total problem of student behavior but was not ready to make any specific recommendations for changes. His delay precipitated a near crisis.

During the same session, one freshman after having walked off a number of penalty tours for infractions of student-made "rat regulations," turned nonconformist and rebelled against the system and refused to obey any more of the regulations. After a full trial, the Corps committee thereupon dismissed this nonconformist from the Corps of Cadets as being "an undesirable student." The student appealed the decision to the college authorities, who after a lengthy investigation refused to uphold the action of the Corps' executive committee. This committee thereupon resigned its office. As soon as this fact became known, feelings ran high in the Corps, and the officers and noncommissioned officers resigned their offices en masse, their resignation to take effect on the afternoon of the next day unless the faculty rescinded its action in failing to support the student executive committee.

The faculty met at once and declared the threatened resignation of the officers to be an act of insubordination and defiance of higher authority. Thereupon it unanimously adopted a resolution to dismiss any officer or noncommissioned officer who did not withdraw his resignation before 4 p.m. the next day. Following this action, Burruss sent the following telegram to the parent or guardian of every cadet involved in the affair.

> Your son defying college authority. If he persists dismissal will result. Your cooperation suggested.
>
> Julian A. Burruss, President

Burruss was swamped with the "cooperation" he got. Letters, telegrams, and parents filled with varying degrees of advice, anger, and worry poured into Blacksburg. One parent remained at home but wired, "Son twenty-seven years old. Veteran of numerous campaigns. Suggest son able to care for self." The newspapers helped broadcast the incident. One reporter got a copy of the Rat Regulations as published in the YMCA handbook, or "Rat Bible," as it was called and managed to make many of the regulations appear not only ridiculous but contradictory and childish. In the meantime, the faculty met with individual students, groups of students, and a full assembly of students.

The differences between the responsibilities as an administration-appointed officer in the cadet regiment and as a student-elected officer in the Cadet Corps were clarified. Many cadets for the first time saw the distinction between military regulation set up by college officials, Corps regulations, and "rat regulations" set up by the students, and pseudo regulations set up by tradition. To the lasting credit of the cadets involved, they recognized that they were indeed in the wrong. They thereupon withdrew their resignations, the nonconformist cadet was permitted to transfer to a nonmilitary day-student status, and the crisis began to subside almost as rapidly as it had risen.

But Burruss was left with a number of irate parents and highly disturbed alumni with whom to deal. He put his typewriter and mimeograph into use once more. A personal letter was sent to all persons who had written or wired to him during the affair, and a mimeographed form letter was sent to all others. These letters heavily favored the administration's position in the matter but also were conciliatory enough in tone to help sooth ruffled feelings. Some of the major dailies also helped matters by congratulating the cadets for their good sense in withdrawing their resignations. The cadets were not sure whether they had won a victory or had been clobbered; but after some grumbling about the telegrams which had brought their parents into the matter, they settled down into the late spring routine of college life.

As a result of this flare-up, the faculty and students appointed committees which worked together and revised the Corps' constitution and its included "rat regulations." This revised constitution was approved by the faculty and the Board of Visitors and provided the framework for the operation of the so-called "Rat System" for the next decade.

Burruss was so thoroughly shaken by the entire affair that he appointed a faculty committee to study student life on the campus and to make recommendations for improvement.

At the same time, he started a re-examination of the administrative organization he had set up for the College and came to the conclusion that its major weakness rested in the division relating to the management of students. For one thing, he said, too many responsibilities in this area fell to the president. This conclusion was probably correct. McBryde, Barringer, and Eggleston had welcomed such responsibilities at a time when the total college program was much simpler. But all three men had experienced difficulties with student life at one time or another. Even Eggleston, the genial mixer, had experienced some difficulty in his contacts with student groups. And, Burruss was no genial mixer. He was the exact opposite—a reserved man, happiest when buried in his office and dealing with plans, budget, and buildings, while communicating with his faculty by means of self-typed memoranda.

Burruss' attempts to influence student behavior by the customary use of inspirational talks at assembly usually turned out to be painful affairs for everyone concerned—especially Burruss. Following one presentation which the students thought to be particularly inept, he had received a number of anonymous letters, presumably from cadets, which along with other things ridiculed his points, belittled his position, suggested that he "get in touch with the times," and reminded him that VPI was not Harrisonburg. Some of the letters after attacking his position offered constructive suggestions. What the writers of these letters probably never learned was the fact that Burruss, with an objectivity seldom associated with such a situation, took these letters and a copy of his assembly talk and extracted from both some suggestions for administering student affairs. He also kept these letters in a special file which he labeled as his "Bug File."

Burruss' conviction that his organization was weak with respect to management of student life had received strong re-enforcement for several years as a result of the unusual enthusiasm with which certain "traditions" were celebrated by the cadets, presumably the sophomores. One "tradition" which had developed over the years was to hold a sophomore banquet on the evening following the completion of spring quarter examinations. During the same evening, the juniors entertained the seniors at the annual junior-senior prom, but the "rats" were supposed to get out of the barracks, in fact get out of town. Before leaving, however, they were supposed to carry their used mattresses or "hays" to the drill field to be used later on in the evening by the sophomores in a bonfire to light up their post-banquet activities. As one final "proof" of physical readiness to assume the strenuous responsibilities of the sophomore, the "rats" upon returning to barracks after "sophomore banquet night," were expected to sleep on bare slats or the floor until the end of the session, usually three days away. Following the banquet, usually held in one of the town hotels or the college mess, the sophomores by tradition returned to the campus, lit the bonfire made from the mattresses, fired a salute to the class, and after a lot of cheering and playing of pranks on each other, broke up into various-sized groups to play pranks on anybody according to the dictates of passing whim. By the early twenties the salute to the class had "progressed" from the firing of a cannon to the firing of dynamite. This salute was achieved by firing charges of dynamite equal in number to the class numeral. The pranks for the most part revolved around schemes for "redecorating" the barracks and walkways of the quadrangle. The redecorating was not always confined to the quadrangle but often spread to adjacent areas. Thus, the proud owner of an Angus bull, which was grazing in a lot adjacent to the present site of Randolph Hall, looked out one morning to discover that the face of his prize bull had been painted white during the night. Professor Rasche, or "Bosco" as he was affectionately known to the students, on a similar occasion had looked out to discover that his riding horse had been painted by the students to resemble a zebra. This latter event, it may be added, precipitated a feud which in time became legendary between "Bosco" and sophomores.

The redecorating of the quadrangle was usually achieved by means of paint, farm machinery, and livestock. The paint was usually applied to the tower and front of Number One Barracks, to the walkways, to the cannon, or to any other surface, object, or moving creature catching the fancy of the students. The farm machinery was collected from the countryside, brought to the campus, and placed on the stoops to the barracks or disassembled and lifted piece by piece to the roof of Number One Barracks and then reassembled. The livestock, usually cows, was brought to the campus and placed inside the barracks, usually in the room of the "tightest" cadet officer, and left for the night. The details varied from year to year, but each celebration tended to fall into the related pattern.

By 1923, Burruss had become alarmed over the sophomore banquet night and other activities which usually occurred during the spring quarter. One freshmen class faced with the necessity of getting out of town for the banquet night, decided to go to Roanoke in a body to hold a celebration of its own. Just before the train bearing the group pulled out of the "Huckleberry" Station, two or more upperclassmen (the exact number and class designation is still being argued in alumni circles) greased the Huckleberry tracks on the steepest grade just out of Blacksburg. Since the train hit this greased section of the track before it had reached normal speed, never very high on the Huckleberry anyway, it came to an abrupt halt. The freshmen, discovering the cause of the delay, jumped off the coaches and pushed the train over the hill. Having overcome this obstacle, they remounted the train and proceeded to Roanoke, where they held their celebration unmolested by the sophomores.

Burruss reviewed the total situation of student conduct and decided that most, if not all, of the hazing and other undesirable action was being caused by a lack of proper administrative supervision and direction of student life. As a possible solution for the problem, he suggested that the board employ a dean of men to work in the area of student activities. In support of this suggestion, Burruss then drew upon his training in school administration and presented to the board an outline of his concept of the duties of a president and of a dean of men.

In retrospect, it is possible in this outline to see a reflection of Burruss' unhappy experiences in dealing directly with the students. "The president," he reported, "is not and cannot be . . . in close touch with the students, and it is hardly fair to him or to them that he be forced to pass on matters which are of necessity rather foreign to him." The duties he assigned to the dean of men made it perfectly clear that Burruss expected henceforth to deal with the students as far as possible through the dean rather than directly.

The board accepted Burruss' recommendation, and Dr. Henry F. Holtzclaw, former dean of the school of commerce and marketing of Oklahoma Agricultural and Mechanical College, was secured for the position. Holtzclaw's appointment was surrounded with difficulties from the start. In the first place, he had not applied for the deanship. He had applied for a position as instructor in economics following a shake-up in the faculty at Oklahoma Agricultural and Mechanical College. Burruss had met Holtzclaw in Memphis, Tennessee, and had persuaded him to accept the job at VPI under the title of professor of economics, dean of students, and dean of the school of business administration. Since instruction in business administration was just getting under way at the College, Holtzclaw found himself faced not only with responsibility for developing the office of dean of students but also with the responsibility for developing a school of business administration. The development of this latter program required not only preparing some new courses but also regrouping, under his administration in the new school, some of the older courses. Before Holtzclaw had been in office a week, he found himself having to deal with the occupational hazards of resentment, resistance, and rebellion which seem to lie in wait for all deans, especially new and inexperienced ones. There seems to be no doubt whatever but that most of the faculty affected by his appointment to a triple role developed a resentment against the new dean. Some let their criticisms of Holtzclaw filter through to the students in various ways. As one result, it was not long until these criticisms spread into the barracks, where they found a receptive audience, especially among the upperclassmen, who increasingly resented Holtzclaw's attempt to get them to modify certain interpretations of "rat regulations." These students conceived it to be their responsibility to instruct the new dean on "how things are done at VPI" rather than to have the new dean instruct them on needed modifications in ways of behaving. There is considerable evidence that some older faculty members sympathized with the students as they constantly used the traditional concept of the Corps' authority to baffle the new dean.

The following letter to Holtzclaw is one of the less baffling ones he received from officers in the Cadet Corps:

> Corps of Cadets
> Virginia Polytechnic Institute
>
> Dean H. F. Holtzclaw
> Blacksburg, Virginia
> My dear Dean Holtzclaw,
>
> At a meeting of the Executive Committee held on May 2, 1924, [names of four cadet sophomores listed] were tried for sprinkling water in the faces of freshmen who were in bed. After hearing the testimony of several freshmen and the four sophomores the Committee voted that it did not consider sprinkling water on freshmen as hazing. A case similar to this one was tried some time ago and was dropped.
>
> Very truly yours,
>
> _____, Chairman
> Executive Committee

Holtzclaw could not understand why sprinkling water in the face of sleeping freshmen was not hazing. Neither could the faculty, but it expected Holtzclaw to stop in one year what it had not been able to stop at all.

Student unrest and discontent became particularly noticeable during the session of 1923-24. The barracks were overflowing, with most rooms having three to four cadets crowded into them. The Field House burned in November, leaving only the Old Pavilion to be converted into a gymnasium. VMI won the Thanksgiving Day football game, played in a driving downpour while the Cadet Corps watched from the open-stands side of the field. To add to student woes, a number of professors, stung by Burruss' comment that often there was a "softness to be found in certain types of college teachers," altered their grading systems and recorded more failures than usual.

The sophomores adhered rigidly to the letter of the "rat regulations" but blissfully ignored the spirit and thereby succeeded in keeping the "rats" in a state of considerable uncertainty. Unable to await sophomore banquet night, some of the sophomores began to fire salutes to the class in a highly disorganized manner. Occasionally a junior or senior would slip out in the dead of the night and fire off a salute to his class. A group of more daring "rats" revived the scheme of converting each class salute into one for their own class. Thus if the first salute ended with twenty-six explosions, the freshmen would add one extra to make twenty-seven. The sophomores retaliated by placing a secret guard at the entrance to all barracks in order to keep the freshmen from slipping out to add an extra explosion. The freshmen met this challenge by tossing lighted sticks of dynamite from barracks windows. Fortunately, the only casualties from this highly irresponsible conduct were hundreds of panes of window glass, the smooth surface of concrete walkways in the front of Number One

Barracks, the tennis courts behind Number One Barracks, and the student contingent fee.

Unknown to the students, both Burruss and the faculty were burning the midnight oil in an effort to find a solution to the unrest. Equally unknown to the students, and probably surprising to many alumni, was the proposed remedy reached by Burruss and the faculty. As a solution, they proposed to abandon the four-year military system, do away with the Cadet Corps, convert the barracks into dormitories, reorganize the student body on a strictly civilian basis under a civilian student government, and convert the mess hall into a dining room, or commons.

The report of the faculty committee supporting these proposals follows in part:

> The committee has inevitably been brought to the conclusion that many of the evils of our student life are the more or less direct results of the military system of discipline and are in a measure inherent in such a system; it has also taken cognizance of the following facts; that of the forty-eight land-grant colleges VPI is one of the three having a full four-year course of compulsory military training and one of two having four years of barracks life; that we are now receiving a more sophisticated class of students who are inclined to chafe at military discipline; that the attitude of the army officers detailed to institutions such as VPI has materially changed since the World War, these officers regarding themselves primarily as instructors in ROTC courses and not enforcers of military discipline, that except for the government academies, no large institution of college grade has an absolutely strict system of military discipline. . . .

Burruss was in agreement with this report but did not push the board to adopt the proposed changes. Instead, he summarized the problem and urged the board to decide on some permanent policy with respect to student organization. He made his position abundantly clear in the following statements:

> It is far from clear, even though we secure the necessary funds to greatly enlarge the physical plant and teaching staff, how we can hope to enlarge the student-body if it continues to be organized on the present military basis. Indeed, even with the present enrollment, it seems that we are attempting the impossible. We are trying to do something that no standard college in America, so far as we have been able to ascertain, is even attempting to do, unless we include the United States military and naval academies. . . . To put it bluntly the arbitrary military system of government of students in college is archaic, and any institution that has the temerity to try to continue it must suffer under almost insuperable handicaps in its effort to grow and to maintain a place in the group of standard colleges . . . it is difficult for one to convince himself that young men trained under a despotic system in their formative years are receiving the best preparation of citizenship in a democracy.

In concluding his report to the board, Burruss noted that the board, whether it dropped the military system or not, would definitely have to limit enrollment unless additional barracks were secured. Burruss wanted the enrollment limitation to be secured not by barring new applicants for admission but by adopting and enforcing more stringent academic and conduct standards for remaining in school. The best approach to improvement of academic standards, he argued, was through a program designed to improve instruction. Some of his proposals for securing this improved instruction have strikingly modern overtones. He wanted:

1. Deans and department heads to make annual evaluations of teaching efficiency of all instructors

2. Regular conferences on the improvement of instruction to be attended by all the staff
3. Visitation by department heads to other colleges to study methods of teaching
4. Supervision of the teaching being done by young instructors
5. Statistical studies of grade distribution by departments
6. Reduction of inbreeding in the employment of new faculty
7. An open-end salary schedule which would enable the president in consultation with the deans to reward special achievements of faculty members.

Burruss realized the far reaching effect his report might have for the College. To the board he said:

> In what has been said in this report and in the report of the faculty committee on student life, have been laid bare some of the sore spots in the operation of this institution. . . . We have no desire to shirk our responsibility, but we feel that we ought to know just how far the Board is willing for us to go. . . .

The board did not know just how far it was willing for Burruss to go. It did conclude, as the prior board under Barringer had concluded, that it could not give up the Corps of Cadets. It therefore modified the military requirements by making the first two years mandatory with the last two optional. If a student wanted to take ROTC work, he had to remain in the Corps all four years. If his freshman and sophomore record was deficient in any way whatsoever he could be barred from junior and senior military training. This latter change was a significant one. As Burruss expressed it, "It is true that juniors and seniors will not be required to take military,—yes, but neither will military be required to take juniors and seniors."

These changes were announced to go into effect during the session of 1924-25, but for the next several years, most students were very reluctant to get out of the Corps after spending two years in it. As the student enrollment increased, however, more and more students began to seek civilian status for their last two years, and thereby began a slow build-up of the civilian student body.

In the meantime, Dean Holtzclaw—with more than a strong hint from Burruss—decided not to return. His work in business administration was continued by being distributed to the three remaining colleges, and the office of dean of students was abolished. Dean T. P. Campbell resigned as dean of the college, and Professor J. E. Williams was appointed as his successor. The responsibilities which had been assigned to the dean of students officially were transferred to the office of the dean of the college. Unofficially, Burruss expected these duties to be divided between Williams as dean of the college and Paul Derring as secretary of the YMCA. Both men more than measured up to the responsibility thrust upon them. Both men had a deep interest in people. And, as one alumnus expressed it, both men had the ability to win friends and influence students.

In the re-examination of his administrative organization with respect to student life, Burruss had discovered that the YMCA program was already filling an important function in student life and activities. In 1919, the YMCA gymnasium had been remodeled into a banquet hall and kitchen, a conference room, and a room for shower baths. In 1924, extensive repairs and improvements had been made on the second, third, and fourth floors. In 1920, the position of assistant secretary, and 1923, the position of YMCA hostess and office secretary had been created. The YMCA handbook, begun in 1894 and commonly referred to as the "Rat Bible" until it acquired the more sophisticated title of "Guidon" in 1934, was practically indispensable as a means of introducing new students to Tech songs, yells, "rat" regulations, and traditions. By 1924 the "Y" building was well on the way to becoming the center of student life and activities. Under the direction of Paul Derring, and with Burruss' encouragement, it became just such a center. In 1937, the "Y" offices were moved to the Student Activities Building, now Squires Student Center, where the program continued to grow and expand under Paul Derring and his assistants.

John E. Williams as dean of the college proved to have an unusually wholesome and stabilizing influence on the students. Even before he became dean he had the respect, admiration, and trust of the students. In 1911, President Barringer had reported to the Board of Visitors that Williams had "the confidence and esteem of the students, who come to him probably in larger numbers for advice and counsel than to any other professor on the grounds. He is fully on to his job." The intervening years had more than confirmed Barringer's evaluation. Williams was particularly adept in directing the energy of the angry, frustrated, or rebellious student into constructive lines of behavior. While he could be "old steel eye himself" if the occasion demanded, his approach was usually reassuring and disarming, as witnessed by the following typical note in his own handwriting, sent to one student:

> Mr. John _____
> Dear John:
>   Some quiet afternoon, and at your convenience, will you please drop by my office to discuss a matter of mutual concern.
>
> > Sincerely yours,
> > J. E. Williams, Dean

The startling contrast between this type of approach and the typical brusk, terse commands more common in a military environment usually got immediate attention. So did the student reports of the ensuing interview with Williams. Before long the barracks resounded with colorful, and no doubt exaggerated, descriptions of such occurrences. Students, aware that a fellow student had received a "quiet afternoon" invitation often gathered in his room to hear his account of the meeting. On one such occasion a student returning from his "interview" put on an act for his fellow students awaiting his return. Rushing into his room be began to pack as if for a trip. In answer to queries he said, "I have just come from an interview with Dean Williams. He told me to go to Hell. He made the prospects sound so pleasant my only regret is he didn't tell me sooner. I'm in a hurry to get started so I can make up for lost time. Get out of my way." There are a number of alumni today who, while admitting that this act probably was not original with the student, nonetheless will insist that the act did reflect Williams' ability to inspire students to new ways of behavior.

Following his revamping of the military program and the delegation of responsibilities for student life, Burruss took another look at the total administrative structure he had organized to carry on the work of the College. With the exception of the military program, he liked what he saw; and he was more than willing to try out the new military features. If every man carried out the duties assigned to him in the organization, he informed the board, there was now no reason the College should not move forward more rapidly than ever. Burruss was correct. His organization and the men in it, for the next decade at least, "purred like a nicely tuned automobile" and gave VPI an unusual impetus upward and onward.

At the opening assembly for the session of 1924-25, Burruss happily described his completed administrative organization to the student body. With a competent official now looking after every major aspect of the College, he informed the students, the president could henceforth devote most of his time to the broader aspects of running the institution and building a greater VPI. This would mean, he said, that the president would have to spend a lot of his time working out of the sight of the student. He would be available to them to a limited extent, he reported, but for the most part he would work with them and they with him through the deans or other designated officials.

To most of the students, after the assembly, Burruss seemed an aloof and reserved man. In truth, he was a reserved man, but he was also a planner, a thinker, and a builder.

With Williams and Derring moving steadily into the picture, much of the student unrest manifest in previous sessions began to die out in 1924-25. The conditions in the barracks continued to be crowded, since very few students when given the opportunity to do so really wanted to get out of the Corps. In fact, Burruss reported that the threat of being denied admission to the Corps on the grounds of unsatisfactory academic or military conduct had brought about marked improvement in both discipline and academic performance. He was still unhappy with the military system and bluntly repeated to the board that "this institution is attempting to do what no other institution in the United States is attempting. It seems that we are attempting an impossible task."

The incident that had once more goaded Burruss into this pessimistic view was the sophomore banquet night held in June, 1925. The sophomores had decided to "put on a celebration bigger and better than anything ever seen on this campus." If they did not succeed it was not because they did not try. Even the sophomores were embarrassed the next morning when they viewed the results of their night's handiwork in the light of day. One participant in the affair painted the following general picture:

Cows bawled disconsolately from fourth story barracks windows. Farm wagons, disc harrows, and grain drills adorned the roof of Number One Barracks. A horse-drawn hearse and a skeleton (borrowed from I. D. Wilson's biology laboratory) rested on the stoop roof. All the rolling equipment normally left overnight at the Huckleberry Railroad Station rested in surprising locations around the quadrangle. Huge roadside signs leaned drunkenly against stoop columns. Two steam rollers from a nearby highway construction job stood facing each other as if engaged in a bull fight, as indeed they had been the evening before under the guidance of two embryo engineers. A huge grocery-delivery truck headed downward into one of the basement entryways. Pigs ran squealing and grunting into and out of barracks. A hive of bees took over one entire top floor, and a riding-horse trotted nervously up and down a second-floor hallway. A fully-assembled fire hose reel teetered atop the ridge pole of one barracks building and threatened to come crashing down with every passing breeze. The quadrangle had the appearance of a cross between a junk yard and a farm implement show, while garishly painted pictures, slogans, signs, and caricatures of professors and "our prexie" covered walls and walkways. A sheet bearing the class numeral painted in the middle and a skull and cross bones in each corner had been run up the flagpole on top of Number One Barracks and the rope then cut. Two roosters perched on top of the tower to Number One Barracks and from time to time crowed lusty defiance to one and all as the college crew arrived to start cleaning up the mess.

Several irate farmers refused to come and claim their cows or farm machinery but sent bills instead. Some came to the campus and claimed their property but sent bills as well. One big construction company sent a bill for time lost from highway construction while its foreman "hunted for the steam roller carried to the campus." One farmer armed with a shotgun, arrived on the campus just in time to see his prize heifer jump through an upstairs window on to the stoop roof. He declared to one and all his intention to shoot everyone in sight and a few not in sight if his heifer was hurt in the process of getting her down from the roof. Fortunately, she was lowered safely to the ground. Finally, most of the mess was cleaned up and the commencement activities resumed, but Burruss knew that something would have to be done before another commencement rolled around. He got help from an unexpected quarter. The sophomore class the next year voted to hold the annual banquet but to forego most of the other activities. The class was aided in reaching this decision by the activities of Dean Williams, Paul Derring, "Pop" Owens, the college steward, and others. The decision was supported by most of the leaders in the Corps, the officers of the two upper classes, the faculty, and many alumni whose exploits while cadets were still being told on the campus. The appalling cost of the preceding banquet night, which the administration had successfully passed on to the sophomore class before permitting it to enroll as juniors, did nothing to discourage the decision either.

The decision to drop the destructive aspects of sophomore banquet night is difficult to explain, but the decision seems to have been symbolical of an important change in the attitude of the Corps of Cadets. As one alumnus—known to have helped put at least five cows in the barracks—expressed it, the attitude of the Corps seemed to undergo a subtle change in 1925-26. Continuing, he said, "We became less hostile, less negative. We seemed to be groping for ways to make our activities more constructive and less destructive for the greater VPI which just about everybody seemed to be talking about." "Speaking for myself," he said, "the behavior of the spring quarter of the preceding years which culminated in the destructiveness of sophomore banquet night, absolutely did not fit into the spirit or the image of the new VPI. I believe others felt the same way."

Whatever the reasons for the modification of sophomore banquet night may have been, the decision itself marked an important turning point in the life of the institution. Pranks, oftentimes destructive, continued to be played, it is true, but on a smaller scale and not as an organized class activity.

The "spirit of lawlessness," as Burruss described it, slowly receded, and the administration shelved its proposals for a drastic overhaul, even elimination of the Corps of Cadets. As one result of the change, a lot of hitherto wasted energy was caught up in more constructive channels and did in fact contribute to a greater VPI.

Burruss was elated with the changed attitude in the Corps of Cadets. In fact, he was modestly elated with the progress being made in all aspects of the college program. In 1923-24, VPI, for the first time in its history, had been

fully accredited by the Association of Colleges and Secondary Schools of the
Southern States. Burruss was greatly pleased with this achievement but reported
to the board that faculty salaries would have to be substantially improved before
the College could get accreditation from certain national agencies. It will come
as a distinct surprise to many faculty members who served under Dr. Burruss,
as well as to many alumni, to know that the question of low faculty salaries and
faculty welfare engaged Burruss' almost continuous attention from the day he
took office until the day he retired from the presidency. The records do not make
it clear whether his interest in faculty welfare grew more from a concern for
what low salaries would do to VPI or more from a concern for the welfare of
his co-workers. Certainly, both concerns manifested themselves in his reports
to the board, but Burruss the introvert never let either one manifest itself very
strongly to his faculty.

Aside from the administrative and curricular reorganizations of the College
which he had set in motion by 1924, Burruss' skills manifested themselves most
effectively in the physical development of the school. Starting with a plant which
was in an admittedly rundown condition, he inaugurated a program of renovation, repair, and improvement which by the mid-twenties had wrought a trans-
formation in the appearance of the campus and in the efficient use of practically
every building. In 1921, an apartment house for extension workers was completed
on a site immediately south of and across the road from the present Newman
Library. This building later was used as a women's auxiliary dormitory before
being converted into office space. Unfortunately this building was destroyed
May 29, 1971, by a suspected incendiary fire following a series of student demonstrations protesting certain restrictions placed on visitation in women's dormitories. The present Sandy Hall, built originally as headquarters for the agricultural extension workers, was completed in 1924.

When Burruss accepted the presidency in 1919, Governor Westmoreland
Davis had advised him to develop a long-range plan for additional campus
buildings. Burruss did so, and during the first five years of his administration he,
along with faculty committees, board members, landscape gardeners, and representatives of the architectural firm of Carneal, Johnston, and Wright, developed
a long-range plan for the physical development of the campus. It was decided to
recondition and preserve the brick buildings on the quadrangle and preserve its
integrity as such; second, it was decided to develop a new plant of stone structures to the west of the quadrangle. In describing this western portion, Burruss
said in part:

> The plan contemplates a central recreation and drill field, approximately
> three times the area of the old athletic field, which forms the eastern end. This
> expanse is to be left open forever, and around it are to be grouped the buildings
> of the new plant. These structures are [to be] designed in the modified Tudor
> type of architecture, with walls of limestone quarried on the campus.

The first building to be located and erected in keeping with this plan was the
World War Memorial Gymnasium, dedicated with elaborate ceremonies on
October 23, 1926. This building represented the culmination of efforts begun
in 1919 by the Alumni Association to memorialize VPI men who had lost their
lives in World War I. Lawrence Priddy ('97) deserves the major credit for
successfully raising funds from alumni and others for the erection of this building.

Miles Stadium, which stood immediately south of the memorial gymnasium,

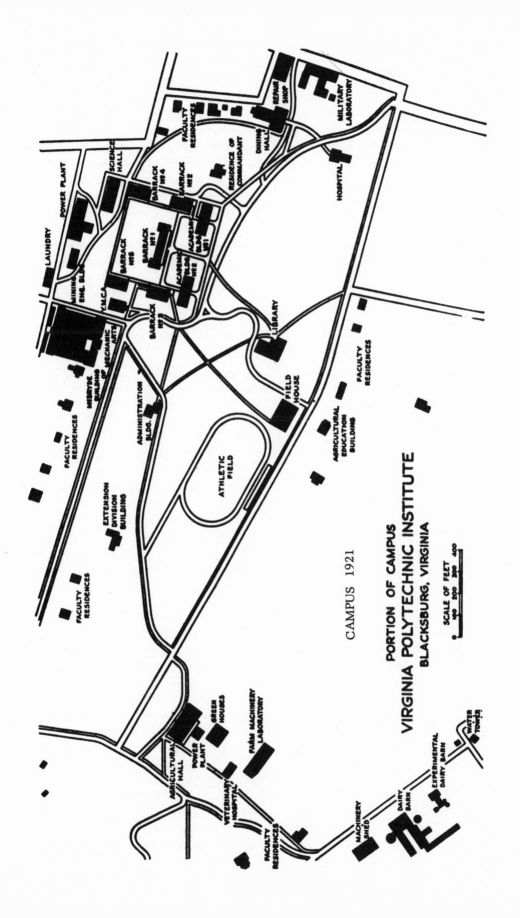

CAMPUS 1921

PORTION OF CAMPUS
VIRGINIA POLYTECHNIC INSTITUTE
BLACKSBURG, VIRGINIA

SCALE OF FEET
0 100 200 300 400

was also dedicated on October 23 with elaborate ceremonies, followed by a football game with the University of Virginia. VPI's cup of joy really overflowed on this day, for she got a gymnasium, a stadium, and a football victory over the University of Virginia all in one day. Miles Stadium, named for C. P. (Sally) Miles ('01) director of athletics, was financed almost entirely by the Athletic Association under Miles' direction. The dedication of this stadium on a site which was in the middle of a cornfield in 1923 excited the imagination of the students and younger faculty members, who saw great days ahead for the College. The more conservative members of the VPI family on the other hand shook their heads and issued dire predictions of financial difficulty ahead. The stadium was too big, they said, and would never be filled to its capacity, variously estimated to be six to ten thousand people. In 1964, when this stadium was torn down to make way for student dormitories, pencil trays were made from the wood of its seats. A tray with the following message in it was mailed to each alumnus:

> Here is a little piece of VPI for you—a pencil tray made from the seats of Miles Stadium. This familiar structure has given way to desperately needed dormitories.
>
> Just as the wood seems richer for its years of weathering service, so with VPI as it changes to meet the needs of Virginia's youth. Keep this remembrance with our very best wishes.
>
> T. Marshall Hahn, Jr.

In 1926, the first section and in 1929 the last section of Patton Hall, named for Professor William M. Patton, were completed. The front section of Davidson Hall, named for Professor R. J. Davidson, was completed in 1927. Additional sections were added to this building in 1933 and in 1938. In 1926, largely due to the efforts of State Senator R. J. Noell ('82), the legislature made it possible for the College to borrow money to erect additional dormitories.

This "new" money, and some increased legislative support, plus the obviously successful operation of his administrative reorganization of the College, cheered Burruss tremendously. His annual reports for the next few years took on an unusually optimistic tone as he devoted more and more energy to building his "greater VPI." Barracks Number Six, now included in Major Williams Hall, was completed in 1927, and the remodeling of the Science Hall into Barracks Number Seven was finished the same year. This structure was torn down in 1957 to make way for a portion of Shanks Hall. In 1929, with a strong assist from Burruss, the members of the University Club, which had been organized in 1925, floated a bond issue and erected their clubhouse on its present site.

Following the completion of Miles Stadium, the old bleachers which had stood on the south side of the drill field were removed, and work was begun on grading and extending the field westward. This work was done under the supervision of Professor R. B. H. Begg ('99), head of the civil engineering department, and some of his seniors in civil engineering. Before the project, which involved moving huge quantities of earth, was completed, the rains made the drill field a veritable lake of mud and water. The cadets immediately dubbed the area "Begg's Lake" and then had a field day advancing facetious explanations of alleged engineering mistakes responsible for the mud. Some of the proposed solutions advanced by the same group were thought to be amusing by everyone except Begg and his senior cadets.

Before the end of his first decade in office, Burruss' absorbing interest and faith in buildings, budgets, and bulletins as instruments for achieving a greater VPI were clearly manifest. He felt that he had been particularly successful in using the third instrument to get VPI, its program, and its potentials before the public, especially the industrial public. He firmly believed, and just as firmly reminded the board, that Virginia was on the threshold of a new era in industrial growth. With all his heart he wanted VPI to contribute significantly to this development, but he was worried lest supporters of the institution, including some alumni and even members of the board, might not develop an intelligent interest in this new challenge. Reporting to the board in 1927 he said:

> If all who are interested in the institution would but familiarize themselves with facts concerning it, what it has done and why, and what it hopes to do and why, and set forth these facts to others, a brilliant future would be assured.
>
> The institution is so much bigger and more permanent than any individual connected with it, that it would be absurd for one's vision of its present aim and its future to be dimmed by personal considerations and attitudes. This institution has throughout its history apparently suffered more than any other institution in the state from misleading statements made, and damaging attitudes assumed by individuals who by right ought to be, and frequently do pose as being, among the most loyal and enthusiastic supporters of the institution. If we can but get people to see facts, facts undistorted and unexaggerated, we can wipe away misunderstanding as to persons and things and enlist as enthusiastic and helpful supporters, representative men in every section of our state and country.

Burruss' faith in facts as a molder of opinion received a rude shock before the year ended. In early 1927, the legislature had authorized a survey of higher education to be made in Virginia. At the same time it had appointed a commission to review the survey findings and then to make recommendations to the legislature based on this review of the findings. These recommendations had been made, but in Burruss' opinion many of the ones affecting VPI had almost completely ignored the facts which had been included in the survey committee report. Furthermore, the recommendations, if enacted into legislation, not only would have greatly restricted VPI's future growth as a technical college, but would have taken away important instructional segments already in existence and almost universally assumed to be a part of the program intended to be developed by land-grant institutions.

He prepared a lengthy detailed report for the board. In this report Burruss, a skilled practitioner in drawing conclusions from statistical presentations of survey data, took the survey report and presented what he considered to be glaring discrepancies between the information in the report and the commission recommendations. Without actually saying so, Burruss made it clear to the board that he suspected deliberate discrimination against VPI on the part of some members of the commission, only one of whom had ever been in Blacksburg. He was particularly upset over the following two recommendations:

> 1. That the University of Virginia be given the field of all graduate instruction or work beyond that for the baccalaureate degrees, and that no work of graduate standing or credit be offered at any of the other state institutions.
> 2. That at the Virginia Polytechnic Institute all work of the nature of liberal arts be eliminated. Practical courses in business administration and home economics should be given only as a preparation for more efficient lines in the fields of agriculture and mechanic arts, for which professions Virginia Polytech-

nic Institute was established. These courses should never be expanded into major departments of instruction in competition with the University of Virginia or the College of William and Mary. The pre-professional courses for law, medicine, pharmacy, and chemistry should not be given at Virginia Polytechnic Institute except as regular courses in agriculture and mechanical arts offer these professional prerequisites.

There were numerous additional recommendations in the commission's report which, in Burruss' opinion, would injure VPI if enacted into legislation. Having reviewed the alarming possibilities posed by the commission's recommendations, Burruss and the board anxiously awaited the introduction of legislation designed to implement the commission's recommendations. Portions of this legislation when introduced were even more unfavorable to VPI than had been the commission's report. Faced with the unhappy situation created by the proposed legislation, Burruss and the board opposed its passage in the legislature and were successful in eliminating or modifying the most objectionable features.

Burruss was disturbed lest the opposition he had organized against the commission's legislative program be misunderstood. Acting on his shocked but firm faith in facts as a molder of opinion, he prepared a brief bulletin entitled "Information for Alumni and Friends" and gave it wide distribution over the state. In this bulletin he pointed out that before the survey staff report, because of its size, had been printed and made available to the legislature, the commission's bills had been introduced into the legislature and that this body had proceeded "to consider them in the absence of the facts contained in the survey report." "The survey staff report being favorable to the Virginia Polytechnic Institute," he continued, "and the commission's report being in serious measure unfavorable, this institution was placed at a decided disadvantage before the General Assembly." "Under the circumstances there was nothing for us to do but to oppose as strongly as possible the undesirable recommendations of the commission."

With respect to the legislation introduced to prevent duplication of curricula, Burruss reported:

> To the supporters of this institution it appeared that [the legislation] was framed to take away from us important types of service which we have been for some years rendering to the State, as an attempt to protect other institutions from duplication by this institution, while making no provision for protecting our college from duplication by other institutions in fields generally recognized as belonging to us.

After some further discussion of the commission report, Burruss directed attention to the aims and the attitudes of VPI, which he described as follows:

> The Virginia Polytechnic Institute is interested only in serving the State and fulfilling its obligations to the Federal Government, which are jointly responsible for its establishment and operation. It does not ask that anything be taken from any other institution and given to it; it does not ask that it be left with anything that is not needed by the State; but it does believe it to be its duty to protect the State from the loss of any service which is valuable in the development of the State and which this institution may be rendering as efficiently as, or more efficiently than, any other institution, and where no financial saving can be effected.
>
> The Virginia Polytechnic Institute does not aspire to be a university, or a liberal arts college. It has no desire to enter into the recognized field of any

other state institution. Its ambition has been, and now is, to develop a genuinely efficient technical school, offering instruction of standard college grade to resident students, conducting research in its own restricted fields, all to the end that it may forward in every way in its power Virginia's agricultural and industrial advancement. Agriculture, industry, and business comprise the definite and generally recognized division of human endeavor for this type of college. We simply want to develop our present field of service and to raise our work to the highest possible standard. To this end it is necessary that we secure a high grade of professors and research workers, and adequate equipment for our present activities. This will engage our thought and effort rather than the possible entrance upon new fields of work. What we need now is intensive strengthening of our existing departments.

Virginia has entered upon a marvelous new era of economic development. Her program of progress depends in great measure upon the development of agricultural, industrial, and commercial interests. Not only are the utilization of our natural resources and the production phases of agriculture and industry important, but also the distributing, marketing, and business phases in these fields are more important than ever before. The Virginia Polytechnic Institute is contributing in a valuable way to these; it is our proper field of work; and we should be allowed to continue it.

This is one of the clearest, most complete statements Burruss ever made concerning the aims of VPI. It was generally accepted by the legislature and the people and became a rather inflexible frame of reference within which the institution developed for the next two decades and by which it was heavily influenced for the next four decades.

Immediately after issuing this bulletin for the general public, Burruss issued an executive bulletin to the faculty apprising it of the legislative action. As one result of these developments, he said, it would be necessary to eliminate any work of a solely liberal arts nature. At the same time he instructed all department heads to "scrutinize mercilessly its work [to determine] beyond doubt what contribution it is making to the agricultural, commercial, and industrial development of the Commonwealth of Virginia." The departments able to show the greatest promise of rendering valuable aid to the state in these areas, he promised, would receive the lion's share in the distribution "of college funds now available." It is perhaps noteworthy that several faculty members more interested in pure science than in applied science left at the end of the year following receipt of this executive bulletin.

While Burruss had been happily engaged with his buildings, budgets, and bulletins, the faculty had not been idle. The Engineering Experiment Station had been established in 1921 and had been followed by an Engineering Extension Division during the session of 1923-24. Burruss was unhappy with the funding of these agencies, which, he said, were being kept alive largely as a labor of love by some of the faculty. But try as he might, he was never able to get the financial support for these two agencies which he thought they should have. With his full support and encouragement, the engineering faculty revised its curriculum during the session of 1927 to conform to the recommendations of the Society for the Promotion of Engineering Education. This revised curriculum went into effect for the 1928-29 session. In 1928, S. R. Pritchard resigned as dean of engineering and resumed his teaching duties in the department of electrical engineering. He was succeeded as dean by Earl B. Norris, who came to VPI from the position of dean of engineering at Montana State College.

The school of agriculture had also revised a number of its curricula and made significant advances. In 1925, Walter S. Newman ('19) state supervisor of agricultural education, in a conference on the campus with H. W. Sanders ('16), H. C. Groseclose ('23), and E. C. Magill, suggested the development of a state-wide organization for boys enrolled in high school vocational agriculture. Sanders, Groseclose, and Magill were on the faculty of the department of agricultural education, while Newman had just moved from a position on this staff to his position as state supervisor. After much cooperative work and planning which involved numerous teachers of vocational agriculture in the state, this organization was perfected under the name of Future Farmers of Virginia. Within a very few years, the Virginia program grew into the National Future Farmers of America (FFA) organization. The evolution of Newman's idea, into the Future Farmers of Virginia and then into the Future Farmers of America, involved the cooperative endeavors of numerous workers in the field of agricultural education in the state. As one result of this cooperative endeavor involving so many different people, numerous claims of credit for this or that feature of the organization soon developed not only in Virginia but on the national level as well. The spectacular growth and success of the FFA, which H. C. Groseclose, with the help of Newman and others, incorporated under the laws of Virginia on September 5, 1928, has done nothing to reduce these claims or clarify the picture.

If written records, memoranda, minutes, and letters on file in 1951 in the department of vocational education at VPI are rigidly followed instead of oral reminiscences, the following facts seem to be well established concerning the origin of the FFA at VPI: Walter Newman originated the idea of an organization of farm boys enrolled in vocational agriculture; Sanders, Groseclose, and Magill agreed with the idea. Magill and Newman asked Groseclose to draw up a plan for the organization; Groseclose originated the name Future Farmers of Virginia; and with the help of numerous teachers of agriculture drafted a tentative constitution and procedural plan for conducting meetings. The FFV organization was an immediate success in Virginia. Walter Newman, at the request of Robert D. Maltby, southern regional agent for vocational agriculture, explained the Virginia plan to attendants at the Southern Regional Conference of Vocational Agricultural Workers in San Antonio, Texas. These workers liked the organization and determined to set up similar ones in their respective states. The VPI staff was deluged with requests for further information about the Virginia organization. H. C. Groseclose, as itinerant teacher trainer in vocational agriculture, responded to these requests with out-of-state visits and letters. Walter Newman and H. C. Groseclose, working with the staff of agricultural education service of the Federal Board of Vocational Education in Washington, drafted a tentative constitution for a National Future Farmers of America organization. This constitution was based on the Virginia plan which had evolved from Newman's suggestion. The constitution, with a few minor changes, was adopted in Kansas City on November 20, 1928, as the constitution for the National Future Farmers of America organization.

The story does not end here. Groseclose was the first man to be elected as executive secretary and treasurer of the national FFA. As a result of his early work in Virginia, his early contacts in the Southern Region, and especially his early work with the National FFA, he soon came to be called the founder of the FFA in Virginia and in the nation. This development upset Groseclose, who for a short period of time wrote a number of letters to workers in the field of vocational agriculture both in and out of the state denying that he was *the* founder of the organization. These denials got little publicity. Consequently, to this day there is a tendency to ignore the work of Newman, Sanders, and Magill and to credit Groseclose with creating and founding the FFA.

While the department of agricultural education was busy developing a significant program of vocational agriculture for rural youth, the Agricultural Extension Division under the direction of John R. Hutcheson was also expanding and developing its program. The nature of the work continued in the direction started by Eggleston. It moved out from the College and became established in the counties, where the county agents and home demonstrators soon allied themselves with local units of national farm organizations, or with any organization working for the betterment of rural life. In 1929 Miss Maude Wallace succeeded Mrs. M. M. Davis as state agent for home demonstration work. This appointment proved to be a most fortunate and a most propitious one for the next thirty years. During this time, Miss Wallace, with able assistance from her staff, developed the home demonstration work in Virginia to a high level of effectiveness and efficiency. Shortly after her retirement from active duty in 1958 the new home economics building, at the request of members of home demonstration clubs throughout Virginia, was named Wallace Hall and dedicated in her honor during the fall of 1968.

The Extension Division throughout the decade of the twenties was a strong supporter of the Farmers' Institute and its program. In 1928, Hutcheson conceived the idea of the Agricultural Conference Board which was organized chiefly by the efforts of B. Morgan Shepherd with behind-the-scenes support from Westmoreland Davis. In 1929, the first Institute of Rural Affairs met on the campus in conjunction with the Farmers' Institute. The Institute of Rural Affairs had received the full endorsement of the Farmers' Institute, *The Southern Planter,* and Westmoreland Davis; in fact, Davis contributed a thousand dollars to initiate the annual meetings of this organization. The warm support of Davis and of his *Southern Planter* given the Institute of Rural Affairs nearly boomeranged on the College, for as Kirby in *Westmoreland Davis* stated, this support "sparked alarm within the state political organization." In a letter from Senator Carter Glass to Governor Byrd (quoted by Kirby) Glass wrote, "If the College in Blacksburg is to continue to be exploited for the political advantage of men like Westmoreland Davis and others . . . the fewer functions transferred to it from other established bureaus, the better it might be." Fortunately, this sentiment did not break into public print, but persons attending sessions of the Institute of Rural Affairs, after the first session, noted and remarked on Hutcheson's carefully phrased disclaimers of political motives in so far as the Extension Division was concerned. There also is a possible but unexplored, thread of relationship between this political fear and the drastically restrictive aspects recommended for VPI by the education commission's report to the legislature in 1928.

The institution's athletic program had been curbed drastically during the war years of Eggleston's administration, although the football team of 1918, under Coach C. A. Bernier ('14), had gone undefeated. In 1920, Bernier resigned as graduate manager and coach, and with Burruss' endorsement the office of graduate manager was combined with that of director of athletics. C. P. (Sally) Miles was then elected to fill these two offices, and S. B. Sutton was employed as football coach, and W. L. Younger ('20) employed as basketball coach. Burruss was highly pleased with Miles' appointment and immediately wrote to him, pledging him his full support in the effort to develop a sound program of athletics. How well Miles responded to this pledge has been told and retold both during and after his tenure of this office which he filled until returning to teaching in 1935.

For years a member of the old and now defunct South Atlantic Conference, VPI became a charter member of the Southern Conference when that, then far-flung, sports body was formed in 1921. Earlier in 1920 a system of mass athletics embracing compulsory physical education classes and an intramural sports program had been installed. This program, as thousands of alumni can testify, has survived in one form or another until the present time, although the compulsory feature has been modified.

Coach Sutton resigned after one year, and the job of rebuilding Tech's football program fell to Coach B. C. Cubbage and his assistant, Younger.

Wrestling and tennis became intercollegiate sports in 1921 and were recognized by the Athletic Association the following year. Wrestling became popular under Coach George Herring, a member of the staff in the department of animal husbandry. Boxing was started independently by Roy Harman ('26) and Karl (Dick) Esleek ('27) and later made a major sport. It has since been dropped from this category.

The first full scholarships to prospective athletes were offered in 1925. Whether as a result of these scholarships is not known, but the freshmen teams of 1925-26 went undefeated in football, baseball, basketball, and track. Andy Gustafson succeeded Cubbage as football coach in the mid-twenties, and his famed "Pony Express," with the great Frank Peake, alternately "cheered and chilled" the football faithful for the remaining decade of the twenties. In the meantime Younger moved on to Davidson College, and basketball suffered eighteen consecutive losing seasons and two break-even seasons under a number of coaches, including Younger, who returned to Tech in 1933.

Under Miles' supervision additional seats were added to the stadium and other physical improvements made to the athletic plant, but a number of wealthy alumni wrote to Burruss, complaining that Miles was too conservative "in money matters" for VPI to develop a real athletic program. When the depression of the early thirties hit the campus, however, Miles' earlier conservative policy helped keep the athletic program in a healthy state.

As Burruss approached the end of his first decade as president, he cast a backward look over the results of his stewardship. In general, he was pleased with what he saw. In addition to the growth and changes noted, the resident faculty had doubled in number; student enrollment had more than doubled; degrees granted at commencements had gone up nearly four times; degree curricula had increased from six to twenty-four; instructional departments had increased from twenty-three to thirty-one; the number of courses had risen from 238 to 376; the staff of the Agricultural Experiment Station had increased from twenty-nine to forty-two, and its work had been extended particularly in agricultural economics, agricultural engineering, home economics, and rural sociology; the staff of the Agricultural Extension Division had increased from 154 to 183; salaries and wages had increased on the average of sixty per cent; additional homes for faculty had been built; a new sewerage plant had been built jointly with the town of Blacksburg; and a number of buildings had been erected for the college farm. With respect to the operation of the farm, which had plagued the College from the day of its founding, Burruss wrote, "It is probably too much to hope that our plant and livestock will ever be up to such standard that there may be found nothing whatever to criticize adversely; but it is confidently believed that there is much more to commend than to censure." Burruss gave much of the credit for the fine condition of the farm to Professor T. B. Hutcheson and Professor R. E. Hunt.

In addition to the improved condition of the farm, physical growth and improvement was evident all over the campus. New roadways had been built and in some instances macadamized; much landscaping had been completed; park lights had been erected on the main campus and the wires put underground; and the power plant had been enlarged. This last improvement called for the erection of an unusually large smokestack which upon completion led to two unexpected problems; the stack belched forth quantities of black smoke and fly ash which polluted much of the surrounding territory, and it offered an irresistible target to cadets wanting to practice rifle marksmanship from barracks windows.

Burruss noted many additional improvements which he felt had resulted from the cooperative efforts of the faculty, administration, YMCA, and the Corps of Cadets. He was particularly pleased with the administrative organization which he had developed for instructional purposes. In 1927, he had dropped the idea of a school of business administration. Instead, he organized a department of business administration with Professor T. W. Knote as head and put it under the supervision of the dean of the college. In 1928, departments of architectural engineering, ceramic engineering, wood technology, and publications had been established, and provisions had been made for conducting a series of industrial surveys. Progress had been made toward the adoption of faculty standards to comply with the standards of accrediting institutions, and sizeable increases had been made in the student loan and scholarship fund.

Burruss was particularly pleased with the relationships existing between the Corps and the administration. He gave the faculty, especially Dean Williams and Major W. R. Nichols, the commandant, most of the credit for the improved conditions; but by 1929 he himself had greatly altered the tone of his numerous memoranda and letters to the student leaders. Burruss would grant interviews to students and faculty, but he much preferred to communicate with them by means of memoranda and letters, which he often typed rather than dictated. When he really exerted himself, he could write letters which were conciliatory, persuasive, and vitally constructive. In the late spring of 1925, he had used all of these traits and more with the officers of the senior class in connection with the commencement program.

During the Golden Jubilee Commencement of 1922, the faculty and the graduates had worn academic regalia for the first time in the history of the school. The reaction had been so favorable that it was decided to continue the practice. In 1924, just a few days before commencement, it was discovered that the caps and gowns which had been rented would not arrive in time; therefore, they could not be used. In order to prevent such an occurrence again, the College had bought its own caps and gowns with the intention of renting them to future graduating classes. A few days before commencement, 1925, Burruss sent the necessary instructions to the senior class, explaining the procedures for picking up caps and gowns, forming the academic processions, and so on. To his amazement, he got a brief note from the class president, informing him that the class had not been consulted regarding the matter of academic regalia and did not plan to wear them at commencement. The note had ended with the following statement, "We think the class should be given a voice in this matter, and I would be very glad to hear from you or even come down and talk the matter over with you and hear your side of the question."

Burruss immediately answered this note with a long letter disclaiming any intention of trying to dictate to the class. Using a conciliatory tone, he pictured the use of the academic attire at commencement as a time-honored custom whereby the faculty tried to honor its graduating students for their academic achievement. The academic attire, said Burruss, was now being used at commencement time by nearly all, if not all, major colleges and universities throughout the United States. Since VPI had at last achieved the distinction of being a recognized standard college, the administration had assumed it would continue the practice of using academic attire first begun in 1922. If the seniors did not want to wear the regalia, however, under no conditions would the administration try to force them to do so. Burruss then ended his letter with an earnest plea that the class reconsider the matter and let him know its decision as soon as possible.

While awaiting the class decision, Burruss sent a copy of his letter to Dean Williams along with the following note:

> I am puzzled and disappointed in the enclosed letter from Mr. ———. It seems very easy for the best motives one has to be misunderstood. I have gone into the situation rather fully in the accompaning memorandum. I shall be grateful if you will think over the matter, and advise me as to the best way to handle it. It hurts a fellow to get a letter expressed this way, when he is trying with all his powers to do what is for the best interest of the College and build it up to be a real college and not a trade school or preparatory academy. Cudgel your good judgment a little over it and let me know what you think.

The official records end at this point, but photographs indicate that the class of '25 did reconsider the matter and decide to wear the customary caps and gowns for commencement. Perhaps of greater importance, an official memorandum from Burruss provided for a faculty committee to work more closely with students in planning future commencement programs.

In spite of the phenomenal growth the College was showing on all fronts, Burruss began to be discouraged during the session of 1927-28. In a personal letter to a friend he wrote, "I am putting my whole life into my work at the College but the work has now expanded so greatly I must have some assistance." With the exception of a trip to attend a Rotary Convention in Denver, Colorado, Burruss had not had a vacation in seven years, and the pace was beginning to affect his health. Perhaps the real reason for his discouragement rested in what he considered to be a rather cool reception of his vision of a greater VPI. Following the discussion of the Education Commission's Report of 1928, Burruss had seized upon the recommendations concerning VPI which the survey committee had made to this commission and had proposed a long-range program of growth and expansion which would implement these recommendations. "This College," Burruss had insisted, "has now reached a stage in its development when its focus should be shifted from the material side to the human side, from considerations of physical plant to considerations of men and service." He wanted the College to move from the narrow concept of an agricultural and engineering school to a broader concept of a school devoted to the promotion of the agricultural, engineering, commercial, and industrial interests of the state. To this end he wanted to update and expand instructional, research, and extension programs in all of these areas. To accomplish these overall objectives, he argued, new courses should be offered and variations permitted from the fixed salary schedule in order to attract outstanding men to the faculty and to reward outstanding faculty performance. The time had come, he said, to seek for staff members, men well and favorably known "in their professions, with more than a local reputation."

When Burruss had unfolded to the board his "visions and plan for a greater VPI" as he liked to call it, the board had accepted his recommendations but with far less enthusiasm and understanding than he had hoped to get. Publicly, Burruss continued to press for a greater VPI. Privately, he began to have his doubts. He was particularly concerned with the attitude of two of the most influential board members. One of these, he implied in a private letter, seemed to be more interested in a leak in the roof of Patton Hall and the other in a new bull acquired by the college farm than in considering the VPI of the future. To add to Burruss' discouragement, a movement begun by a few prominent alumni to get the Board of Visitors to increase Burruss' salary came to naught. Burruss knew that the governing boards for all of the remaining state educational institutions had made strenuous efforts, with some success, to get increased salaries for their presidents. As far as he knew, his board had not made any particular effort on his behalf. He interpreted this lack of aggressive effort on the part of the board as equivalent to a vote of no confidence in him as president. This interesting situation was resolved by a series of even more interesting developments, which began outside of the state. The press of Oklahoma announced that Dr. Burruss was being considered for the presidency of Oklahoma A & M College, and the press in Virginia immediately broadcast the story throughout the state.

Upon reading the news story, one of Burruss' best friends and trusted supporters on the board wrote to him, urging him not to leave unless he felt that his period of usefulness at VPI was at an end. In this same letter, he urged Burruss to give him a completely frank, personal expression of his feeling about continuing as president of VPI.

Burruss responded to this letter with one of his own in which he poured out the accumulated frustrations and disappointments of the past few years. The central theme of his letter was that he had no real desire to leave VPI; but now after nine years in the presidency during which time he had devoted his entire energy every day and oftentimes far into the night to the building of a greater VPI, he felt that he did not have the confidence or full support of his board. A small minority, he believed, not only did not support him but was in fact hostile to his efforts to build VPI into anything other than the small agricultural and mechanical college it had been when he had assumed the presidency. Furthermore, this narrow vision of VPI, he believed, extended to some of the board members' concept of the duties of the president. These members, he stated, seemed to think that he as president of the institution promoting the largest and most complicated educational program in the state but with the smallest administrative staff should continue to do work which any competent clerk or stenographer could do just as well, "perhaps even better." As for his leaving

VPI, no, he had not made any plans to do so, but in view of the present situation he did feel that he owed it to himself and to his family to begin following up on some of the numerous "feelers" he had been receiving concerning his availability for the presidency of other colleges.

This letter was not publicized, but evidently some of its contents became known to the board, for this organization began to give Burruss more support in his effort to implement his plan for a greater VPI. *The Roanoke Times* in an editorial entitled "Virginia needs Him" urged him to stay on at VPI. Within the year, a number of the board members, prominent alumni, and citizens had let Burruss know their sentiments with statements such as the following: "To me it is simply marvelous the way that institution has grown under your administration, and as a humble graduate. . . I wish to say how grateful I am over the success of the institution." A member of the board wrote, "The improvement in the institution since Dr. Burruss was made president has been phenomenal. It is hard to realize the wonderful changes that have taken place." E. Lee Trinkle, former governor, wrote, "I would hate beyond expression to see Dr. Burruss leave Virginia, and I hope developments will not take place that will lead him to do so but—out of common justice—I must admit that whoever gets him, if he does leave, will be most fortunate."

These manifestations of confidence cheered Burruss tremendously, and if anything, he devoted even more energy during the session of 1928-29 to getting his program under way. First, he conducted an extensive recruiting program for new faculty. In this endeavor, he was successful in recruiting many faculty members well known in their time and more than pleasantly remembered by many alumni today. Included in the list of these faculty recruits were many who devoted the remainder of their professional life to VPI: E. B. Norris, engineering; C. R. Woolwine, health officer; C. H. Cowgill, architectural engineering; J. W. Whittemore, ceramic engineering; B. L. Hummel, rural sociology; Maude Wallace, home-demonstration work (elected in 1928, reported for duty in 1929); P. B. Dyck, physical education; A. H. Teske, horticulture; R. H. McNeil, English and publications; R. L. Humbert, economics and executive secretary to the president; H. B. Riffenburg, chemistry; P. B. Potter, agricultural engineering; B. O. Miller, economics; R. D. Michael, English and broadcasting; P. M. Reaves, dairy husbandry; P. S. Dear, ceramic engineering; and E. D. Chestnutt, mathematics.

As Burruss began his tenth year as president, *The Virginia Tech* joined in the chorus singing his praise. This organ which in 1925 had intimated that it might be better to be a "radical with a beard and a bomb" than a man without brains or courage to declare himself, did declare itself, in part as follows:

> Through [Burruss'] guidance and help the institute has grown by leaps and bounds and today it ranks as one of the fine leading engineering schools in the United States. His dream of the greater VPI is rapidly coming to realization, and each year the institute advances to a higher standard.

Having divested itself of this declaration, the *Tech* proceeded to list Burruss' activities and offices held at local, state, and national levels. The imposing list surprised many students for whom Burruss was rapidly becoming more heard about than heard or seen in the flesh. Burruss immediately thanked the editor, reminded him that any progress made had resulted from the full cooperation of the student body, faculty, alumni, and board, and sent him additional information on the new curriculums being developed to meet the expanding industrial needs of Virginia. The editor spread this information before his readers and then launched his own program for a better VPI to be achieved in part by more subscriptions to the *Tech,* better school spirit, a reformed "rat system," and fewer paths on the drill field.

Burruss was even more complimentary of the alumni activities of the past ten years than he was of the editor of the *Tech.* As a result of his review of these activities to the board this body adopted a resolution to award "three honorary degrees to alumni selected by himself [Burruss], this being in recognition of the fact that the commencement of 1929 marks the completing of the tenth year of his administration. This is authorized for this special occasion only and is not to be taken as establishing a custom." Burruss thanked the board for the "high honor accorded" him and instead of nominating three alumni, nominated only one—Lawrence Priddy ('97)—for the honorary degree.

The announcement of this honor for Priddy caused a few ripples of resentment on the part of some of the younger alumni who felt that, while students, they had been over persuaded by Priddy to buy VPI Loyalty Bonds to help finance the World War Memorial Gymnasium. The completion of this building and the passage of time soon calmed the ripples. As a result, most of these same alumni, upon reviewing "Rip" Priddy's varied support of VPI, which continued throughout his adult life, look upon him today as having been one of VPI's most loyal sons.

To deliver the 1929 commencement address at which Priddy was awarded the degree of Doctor of Commercial Science, Burruss secured F. Donaldson Brown ('02), vice-president in the General Motors Corporation. The thing that he did not know in time to prepare for it was that the executive committee of the Alumni Association planned a small celebration at commencement time to honor Burruss. Hence when at this celebration the students, the Alumni Association, and the Executive Committee paid tribute to him and presented a silver service to him and Mrs. Burruss, he insisted that he "was too overcome to make adequate response." In the response he did make he thanked his audience and immediately turned its thinking to a consideration of the wonderful opportunities in the decade ahead. In concluding his annual report to the board of 1930, Burruss wrote:

> When we look back to the situation in 1920 and compare it with that of 1930, we must recognize that the decade has been a progressive one for this institution. So much remains to be done, so many urgent needs to be met, and so many opportunities promising rich results are continually being offered us to serve our state, that it is quite discouraging at times that the resources at our disposal are so limited. Yet what has been achieved should inspire us to hope for the future.
>
> The important consideration now is not what has or has not been accomplished in the past ten years, but what is to be accomplished in the next ten years. . . . As we set our stake at 1930, we move our objective ten years ahead and reconsecrate ourselves to our high mission.

Even as Burruss wrote these words, the shadows of the "Great Depression" were beginning to creep over the state.

Chapter 10

The Burruss
Administration

1930–1945

I N SPITE OF THE DARKENING financial picture Burruss began the session of 1930-31
full of optimism. For one thing, a cloud of doubt seems to have been erased from
his mind concerning his relationships with his Board of Visitors. In spite of the
accolades he had received for the growth and development of the College, he
had continued to feel that a minority of the board was not in sympathy with
his efforts to develop VPI in areas other than agriculture. Even in this area he
felt that some of the board members had an unusually limited vision.

Dr. J. G. Ferneyhough had been appointed to the board to succeed J. B.
Watkins, who had resigned. Ferneyhough, it will be recalled, had been instrumental in getting Burruss appointed to the presidency of the College. Since
that time, however, he and Burruss had broken sharply, almost bitterly, over
questions of college policy. Ferneyhough, who as state veterinarian had crossed
swords with some of the most powerful leaders in Virginia, had a large following in the state. Burruss assumed that Ferneyhough was going to organize this
following against him and make his position intolerable. Acting on this assumption, Burruss immediately began to make plans to move to another college. In
a letter to a trustee, discussing this proposed move, Burruss once more alluded
to the tremendously increased responsibilities which now rested on the presi-

dent of VPI. He was willing to accept these responsibilities, he said, but under no conditions would he continue them in an atmosphere of distrust and controversy which he believed to be forthcoming as a result of the new appointee to the board.

Some of the more prominent alumni, including some of Ferneyhough's classmates, heard of Burruss' fears. As a result, a delegation of this group went to Ferneyhough to sound him out concerning his intentions. He immediately disclaimed any and all intentions of conducting a vendetta against Burruss. As far as he was concerned, he said, his past disagreements with Burruss had been professional, not personal. The past was water over the dam; the important thing now was to unite for a greater VPI. He planned to let bygones be bygones, he informed the group; and he hoped Burruss would feel the same way.

Burruss, when informed of Ferneyhough's position, did feel the same way. In addition to Ferneyhough's promise of support, other members of the board assured Burruss of their support and at the same time helped convince him that Ferneyhough's appointment was not an anti-Burruss move on the part of anyone. With this renewed assurance of support, Burruss dropped his plans to leave VPI. As a result, Ferneyhough lived up to his promise, and these two distinguished members of the class of '98 worked shoulder to shoulder until Ferneyhough's death about a year later.

In addition to his satisfaction with the renewed relationship with his old friend, Burruss was pleased that the legislature had made slight increases in its appropriation to the College. He used a portion of this appropriation to give modest (very modest) increases to the already modest salaries of a number of the faculty. In addition to this usage, he recruited new faculty to take care of the enrollment which had steadily increased from 477 in 1918-19 to 1659 in 1930-31. He called the particular attention of the board to the fact that during this latter session every city in the state and every county except one had one or more representatives in the student body.

Not only Burruss but the entire College started the decade in a spirit of optimism. New programs designed to aid the industrial and commercial development of the state had been launched by the Agricultural and the Engineering Experiment Stations and the Extension Division. Several types of industrial surveys had been undertaken and, in Burruss' opinion at least, had resulted in bringing VPI to the favorable attention of important industrialists and leaders in chambers of commerce throughout the state. The school of engineering was projecting exciting plans for extending its areas of service. The Alumni Association was being constructively active. The unusually constructive tone of *The Virginia Tech,* so evident by the mid-twenties, gave every evidence of being continued. The anti-military, anti-ROTC sentiment beginning to attract attention on many of the college campuses of the nation was largely absent from VPI, and no doubt its absence was pleasing to the college community. Burruss was beginning to be looked to by political, industrial, business, and agricultural leaders as one of the outstanding educators of the state.

In the fall of 1930 *The Techgram,* which had been started in 1923 in a double-post-card format was changed to a 9½ inch by 12¼ inch tabloid newspaper format. This publication in its new form was under the direction of R. H. (Bob) McNeil, director of publications, and H. B. (Puss) Redd ('21), alumni secretary. It was published bi-monthly except during July and August, with the objective of informing the public about VPI events and alumni activities. Using photographs and the nontechnical language of the newspaper, this publication was an immediate success in achieving its objective. While having undergone some recent changes in format and content, it is continuing to inform the public, especially the alumni, of college activities today.

Major John B. Maynard ('07) was appointed commandant of cadets in the fall of 1929. Maynard, an effective army officer, often took a surprisingly unmilitary-like view of some of the cadet peccadillos. To the cadets some of his responses to these peccadillos were equally surprising. As one result, the Corps soon came to be entertained with an abundant crop of anecdotes relating to encounters between Maynard and cadets or groups of cadets. There is considerable evidence to indicate that Maynard knew of this development and surreptitiously encouraged its growth by his actions at some of his unexpected encounters, often at night, with cadet mischief-makers. His rather cordial relationships with members of the Corps were in no way hindered by the fact that cadets in reporting to his office usually had to pass the desk of his secretary, the vivacious "Miss Jimmie Jamison," now Mrs. "J. B." Jones. The wide latitude he allowed "Miss Jimmie" in disposing of minor office calls did not go unappreciated by the cadets either.

Even Maynard's broad tolerance was finally taxed to the limit by some of the ingenious methods and maneuvers thought up by the Headquarters Company. This organization at one time made up almost entirely of senior privates, or "skippers," as they were more commonly called, seemed to have united behind one objective: namely, to extract the greatest enjoyment from life by spoofing everything military. Officially organized as one of the cadet military companies, the group at one time had unofficially organized itself as a sea-going naval unit led by officers with student assigned naval instead of army titles. By some ingenious method the "skippers" had secured or constructed a boat, small for the vast ocean, but huge for the dry land of a campus located amidst the mountains of southwest Virginia. Wheels or rollers had been attached to the boat, and the "skippers" enjoyed a number of practice "sailings" while they acquired their "sea legs." One day, so a story not entered in official records has it, all of the "skippers" that could do so "boarded" their vessel and following the usual route "sailed" instead of marched to mess. The arrival of this "vessel" and its subsequent "docking" at the mess hall, all carried out with supposed nautical precision, nonplussed the officer in charge, detailed for the day from the commandant's office. Not being able to recall any military regulation concerning the situation, this individual wisely did nothing, but stood by until all of the cadet soldier-sailors had entered the mess hall. Details of his report the next day to Commandant Maynard are missing, but Maynard soon thereafter suggested to Burruss that the Corps be reorganized next year with the senior privates being distributed through three headquarters batteries. By such a distribution, Maynard said, the senior privates would no doubt acquire military knowledge more valuable for the purposes of ROTC than was the military knowledge they were acquiring under the present system. Burruss thought so too, and plans were begun to phase out the Headquarters Company, certainly one of the unique organizations ever provided for cadets at VPI.

The better distribution of the "skippers" did not terminate their tradition or determination to enjoy military life by spoofing it. On the contrary, instead of this determination being concentrated in one location it was now scattered over the Corps. The result was a series of running "battles" and "skirmishes" between the "military" on the one hand and members of the Corps, presumably "skippers," on the other. These encounters, never vicious, vindictive, or obscene, helped enliven many otherwise dull days and in the process built up a plentiful stock of anecdotes which alumni have been telling and retelling with great delight ever since.

Maynard was succeeded in 1935 by Lieutenant Colonel C. H. Tenney, who proved to be a rigid disciplinarian. Prior to this appointment he had served for two years as assistant commandant. Tenney was admired by most of the cadets, who for some unrecorded reason nicknamed him "Buck." As one result of this nickname numerous jokes and cartoons built around the slogan "Buck Tenney Rides Again" became popular on the campus. Unfortunately his rigid belief in military protocol and the role to be played by the military program at VPI got him into difficulty with some of the newcomers to the faculty, who felt that the military program was incompatible with high academic standards and research. Before this problem became serious, however, he completed his tour of duty at VPI and was succeeded as commandant by Colonel John H. Cochran ('09), who served until the outbreak of World War II.

Corps morale and popularity reached a high peak in the decade preceding World War II. Indeed a number of alumni believe that the Corps reached its zenith during the period. They may be correct. Even Burruss, who at one time despaired of integrating the Corps into his "greater VPI," became one of its enthusiastic boosters. At the same time he retained his conviction that the Corps was one of VPI's unique features. In this belief he certainly was correct, for if there was one feature which came to be associated in the minds of the public with VPI during its first century it was the Corps of Cadets.

In existence as a military entity from the earliest days of the institution, the Corps was formally organized during the session of 1891-92, at which time the cadet companies, all infantry, were organized into its first battalion. In 1893 an artillery battery was added to the military structure. The company structure has remained as one organizational unit to the present day, although the battery unit was also used intermittently until it was dropped in 1948. The first organization of the Corps as a regiment occurred in 1922, while in 1946 an air force squadron was organized in addition to the army units. Currently the Corps consists of "a regiment composed of a battalion and a group, and a regimental band company." From its earliest inception each organizational unit whether regiment, battalion, group, squadron, battery, or company has had its full staff of cadet officers.

Mention has been made of the constitution adopted by the Corps in 1908. The student government features of this constitution had been encouraged by President Barringer in an effort to overcome what he considered to be an excessively paternalistic attitude of the faculty toward the nonmilitary operations of Corps life. Largely as a result of his suggestions the operation of the Corps' governing body had been placed in the hands of an executive committee made up of cadet representatives from the four academic classes. The makeup and responsibilities of this committee varied from time to time until it eventually was organized as the present cadet honor court.

Members of the Corps' executive committee were elected by the cadets, but all cadet military officers were appointed by the commandant with the approval of the president. The establishment of general overall policies and methods of operation of the Corps nearly always rested with the commandant of cadets with the cadet officers being responsible for implementation of policies and procedures. The existence of two organizations to attend to Corps affairs often resulted in some confusion and charges of conflict of interest, since offices in both groups often were filled simultaneously by the same individual. Efforts to change or prevent the occurrence of this last situation often led to exciting political campaigns on the campus; but in the public press clarity as to whether the term "Corps officer" referred to one elected by the students or to one appointed by the commandant suffered innumerable casualties.

Some variation was practiced from time to time in the matter of the academic class from which the cadet officers were drawn, but until about 1937 commissioned officers came from the senior class, sergeants from the junior class, and corporals from the sophomore class. In 1937 commissioned officers and sergeants were appointed from the senior class and corporals from the junior class. In 1938 first class privates were appointed from the sophomore class. The abrupt change in the source from which to draw officers for the cadet regiment, a move designed to extend more control over the senior "skippers," was resented by many students and resulted in some unusual confrontations between student groups and the commandant. On one occasion as the commandant arose to address the Corps assembled in Burruss Hall, the Corps broke into deafening pseudo applause which continued until the annoyed commandant gave up and stalked off the stage. At a subsequent drill period the Corps was drilled double time until, as one cadet said, "our tongues dragged the ground." The Corps took the thinly disguised retaliation in the spirit in which it was given, but Burruss working quietly behind the scene succeeded in getting the commandant transferred before more serious confrontations took place.

The commandants usually worked closely with the cadet officers and with the executive committee in trying to promote satisfactory living conditions in the barracks. As one result of this cooperative relationship a number of students each year saw many of their suggestions relating to the area of student life translated into action. It is not difficult to understand the morale building effect this result had on the students. Conversely it is not difficult to understand the demoralizing effect that sometimes occurred when the authorities were unable to grant certain requests for changes in student life. As Dean Williams expressed it, the mechanism used in dealing with the Corps was "a trifle delicate at some points and highly explosive at others."

The frustrations, failures, and shortcomings of the Corps often made the news headlines. The thing that often went unnoticed was the fact that the achievements and triumphs of the same organization got the abiding affection of thousands of cadets as they participated in its activities. It should be clearly understood that in spite of numberless gripe sessions and frequent anti-military, anti-Corps movements, thousands of students left VPI with a deep-seated, almost fanatic, attachment to the Corps of Cadets. For some individuals the attachment no doubt derived from the military features of the Corps. For others there is no doubt whatever but that the attachment derived from the pleasant emotions of a camaraderie built from associating and doing things with one's cronies and fellow members in the Corps. For whatever may have been its merits or demerits, life in the VPI Corps of Cadets provided abundant opportunities for engaging in activities with one's friends and associates in an environment that was never dull.

The activities were compulsory and noncompulsory, military and non-military, organized and unorganized. The cadet parades, Corps trips, and routine military formations were carefully planned and executed, as were the formal dances, junior-senior proms, military balls, and other formal entertainments. Many other activities, however, although repeated from year to year, were more unstructured. Much of this latter type of action was of a spontaneous, ebullient nature, often with a pleasing sense of ingenuity. Some of it, such as the earlier "come on June nights," might be called purposeful pandemonium, ardently pursued—and caught.

Each class, indeed each cadet company or battalion, expressed its own individuality as it sought to perpetuate traditional Corps and company activities. And in the process each company helped create new forms of behavior which in turn became traditional and gradually replaced some of the older behavior no longer appropriate to the new conditions. Three activities long since discontinued but once considered "absolutely essential in the making of a Tech-man" may be mentioned.

In the "rat" parade, which was usually held on a warm Saturday afternoon in the early fall, the freshmen were dressed in costumes designed and applied by the sophomores. The resulting costumes ranged from the amusing to the vulgar. Often a well-known faculty member would be mercilessly caricatured by some innocent freshman who had never heard of the professor. Well-known movie characters, male and female, as well as nationally known personages, were often presented in tableaux so organized as to heap ridicule on some campus group, organization, or event. Having been costumed on the campus, the "rats" usually circled the quadrangle and, escorted by the sophomores, paraded up and down Main Street. These events, usually announced in advance, drew crowds of spectators who lined the sidewalks as the parade "marched, shuffled, rode, and trickled by." "The public," said one alumnus of the class of '26, "enjoyed this annual event." So did most of the "rats" as they vowed to "put on" a better parade the next year.

The first snow of the winter usually meant the annual snow battle. The freshmen were divided into two groups, usually by companies, and marched to the drill field where they were formed into two lines facing each other. A bugler sounded charge, and amidst flying snowballs the two lines rushed forward to meet in the middle of the drill field. Here in the words of one participant:

> We fought with snowballs and rolled each other in the snow until we were too tired to fight any longer. Then there came yells of "rats to your holes" from every side, and tired and almost out of breath we made our way back to barracks . . . any way we could to avoid the pelting of snowballs from the hands of the old boys.

Not all of the participants fought as vigorously as this individual, for as many an alumnus will testify, the "rats" often outsmarted the sophomores by grappling each other and by mutual agreement rolled about in the snow in such a manner that first one and then the other was on top. Fooling the sophomores, however, merely added zest to the occasion.

The origin of "numeral scrubbing" is not known, but at one time every

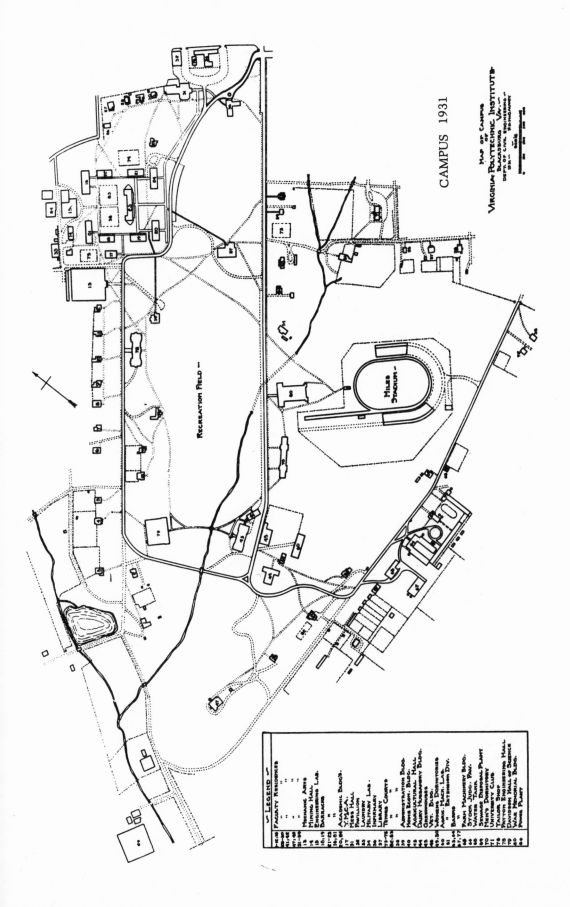

CAMPUS 1931

MAP OF CAMPUS
OF
VIRGINIA POLYTECHNIC INSTITUTE
BLACKSBURG, VA.—
DEPT. OF CIVIL ENGINEERING
1931 — 1932
SCALE IN FEET

RECREATION FIELD —

MILES STADIUM —

LEGEND —

1-38	FACULTY RESIDENCES
	" "
39-40	" "
41-42	" "
43-44	" "
13	MECHANIC ARTS
14	MINING HALL
15	ENGINEERING LAB.
16-19	BARRACKS
	"
21-23	"
30-31	ACADEMIC BLDG.
30	Y.M.C.A.
31	MESS HALL
	PAVILION
34	LAUNDRY
35	MILITARY LAB.
36	INFIRMARY
37	LIBRARY
71-76	TENNIS COURTS
38-39	" "
38	ADMINISTRATION BLDG.
40	HORT. ECON. BLDG.
41	AGRICULTURAL HALL
42	DAIRY HUSBANDRY BLDG.
46	VET. BLDG.
47-48	WOMEN'S DORMITORIES
49	AGRIC. MACH. LAB.
50	EXTENSION DIV.
	" "
37,77	BARNS
68	FARM MACHINERY BLDG.
69	STOCK JUDG. PAV.
65	WATER TANK
66	SEWAGE DISPOSAL PLANT
70	MEN'S DORMITORY
71	UNIVERSITY CLUB
78	TAILOR SHOP
79	PATTON ENGINEERING HALL
80	DAVIDSON HALL OF SCIENCE
81	WAR MEMORIAL BLDG.
82	POWER PLANT

"rat" at VPI knew the art of the practice, having learned it by "rote drill properly spaced over a learning period of nine months duration." The practice was simple, the variations numerous. Freshmen would get up for breakfast, usually Sunday, to find their class numeral painted on the sidewalks adjacent to the barracks. The sophomores would make a valiant effort to express surprised indignation at such "gross freshness" on the part of the "rats." An after breakfast formation would be announced, at which the "rats" were expected to arrive, dressed in old clothes. At this formation the "rats" were ordered to find bricks and scrub the class numerals off the sidewalk. In the midst of the scrubbing, always under the supervision of the sophomores, the freshmen would be asked if they thought water applied to the brick would help remove the paint. An affirmative answer got water in paper bags delivered from upstairs barracks windows. Negative answers got the same response. Finally after much scrubbing, along with an abundant supply of water, the numeral would disappear. The familiar "rats to your holes" cry usually given after a mock warning not to be so "fresh" the next time, brought the incident to an end. In actual fact it was never known whether the sophomores, the freshmen, or "town rats" painted the numerals, but so many were painted and scrubbed off that the effects are visible on some of the walks to this day.

Strangely enough the activities just described plus other activities such as requiring the freshmen to run errands, make up beds, sing the laundry list to the tune of "Home Sweet Home," clean upperclassmen's guns, and attend innumerable "crap meetings" called to entertain the sophomores, were not considered by the upperclassmen as hazing. On the contrary such action was often strongly defended on the grounds that it was a part of the "rat system" necessary to keep freshmen in line and at the same time make men out of them.

By the early thirties a number of the Corps leaders were beginning to have doubts about the real contributions many of the practices, as they had evolved, were making toward a better VPI. Their doubts were reinforced from an unexpected source.

In the fall of 1932, Dr. Burruss received a number of letters complaining of abuses which had grown up around the "rat system." Investigation convinced him that the charges were correct and that something needed to be done. He immediately went before the Corps and "in a speech which lasted forty-five minutes but seemed like ten" pinpointed many of the abuses which had grown up around the system. At the same time, he portrayed most vividly the evil effects these abuses were having and would have on the greater VPI. Something would have to be done to improve conditions, Burruss insisted, but it should be done by the students rather than by the administration. Having tossed the problem to the students, Burruss sat back to await results.

According to *The Virginia Tech,* which reported that Burruss had emerged from his sanctum in the administration building to present the problem, the students were both surprised and delighted—surprised to find that Burruss knew so much about what was going on in the barracks, and delighted to have him come before them to discuss the problem. The students hoped he would continue to come before them, said the editor. Such an appearance was not necessary on this particular problem, however, because the Corps after lengthy discussions, drastically modified the "rat system" in such manner that it was succeeded in 1934 by military and civilian rules for freshmen.

What the Corps did not fully realize and probably never did find out, was that even as it was struggling to modify the "rat system," a number of alumni chapters, unhappy over the first losing football season since 1920, had also declared war on the system. These chapters felt that the "rat system" not only kept prospective athletes from entering VPI but also caused an unusually large number to leave for the same reason. One chapter had even gone so far as to notify Burruss that it had appointed a committee to visit the College and make an on-the-ground "investigation" of the system. Since some members of this committee had also been members of the committee which had "investigated" Dr. Barringer's administration at an earlier date, Burruss was disturbed lest such an investigation injure the College instead of correcting the "rat system." He put forth tremendous effort, therefore, and succeeded in getting the chapters to support the efforts to improve the system rather than to investigate it.

Burruss' straightforward dealing with the alumni and with the Corps concerning abuses of the "rat system" received the approval of both groups. Thanks to his lucid, tactful, but firm letters to alumni leaders, this group got a clearer picture of how to promote the real interests of VPI by working through the administration rather than by an independent approach. This lesson having been learned, the alumni, as if conscious of their role in a greater VPI, gave increased aid, financial and psychological, to the administration.

Burruss' efforts to enlist support rather than attack from athletically minded alumni received a tremendous boost the next year by an unusually successful football season. In 1932 H. B. (Puss) Redd ('19), whose freshman football teams repeatedly had threatened to steal the show from the varsity, was appointed head coach. At the same time W. L. (Monk) Younger ('20) and S. D. (Tex) Tilson ('23) had been appointed as assistant coaches. This all-alumni coaching staff immediately turned out one of Tech's all time great teams, losing only one game 9-6 to powerful Alabama, after outplaying the Crimson Tide for most of the game. Victories over such teams as Georgia, Maryland, Kentucky, Virginia, and VMI left the Tech faithful "walking on cloud nine" and convinced them that henceforth alumni should be appointed to fill all offices at VPI. "Puss" and his staff were unable to repeat this record the next season, but even so VPI received an invitation to a post-season game to be played in Memphis, supposedly against the University of Tennessee. Athletic Director Miles wrote to Burruss listing the difficulties the team would face if the invitation should be accepted but left the door open for the administrative council to make the final decision. Then in a "confidential postscript" he advised Burruss that the coaches hoped the administrative council would reject the bid. The administrative council did just that. During this same period the College received a request for permission to broadcast football games over the radio. Miles once more objected but advised Burruss that as president of the Southern Conference he did not believe that he, Miles, should express a public opinion on the matter. Burruss felt that the idea had "possible merit" but allowed himself to be guided by Miles' opinion.

The popular Redd continued to coach until 1940, at which time he resigned to devote full time to his duties as alumni secretary.

In 1935 Younger gave up football coaching to succeed Miles as athletic director. He did continue as basketball coach for a period of years, however. In a move toward economy no additional assistance was given to Redd and Tilson as everyone connected with athletics closed ranks in an effort to overcome the lingering effects of the depression.

In May, 1936, the Alumni Association cooperated with the college officials in beginning a "Virginia Tech Day," sometimes called "High School Day," by bringing hundreds of high school students to the campus for a program of varied activities. If guards, tackles, and backfield men dominated the group of prospective Techmen visiting the campus, so much the better. The alumni also helped raise money to be used by the administration in helping students especially hard hit by the financial depression. This assistance was given especially to seniors who otherwise would have had to drop out of college. In 1937, the Alumni Loyalty Fund (later changed to the Alumni Fund) was established "to promote the progress and growth of cultural and educational advantages" at the College.

In 1931 the one-hundredth anniversary of the first reaper by the Virginian, Cyrus Hall McCormick, was celebrated on the campus as a part of the program of the Institute of Rural Affairs. In addition to distinguished visitors from the state, the out-of-state guests included Harold McCormick, son of Cyrus, and Fowler and Cyrus McCormick, grandsons of Cyrus. A portion of the program was broadcast from the campus radio studios which had been established January 6, 1930, in the War Memorial Building. An old-fashioned barbecue was served in what was then the dell back of the infirmary, and in the evening a "brilliant pageant in six scenes was held in the stadium" before an audience of 10,000 people, the largest crowd ever to assemble on the campus until that time. "The pageant depicted the evolution of harvesting machinery from the earliest days to the present." "Colorful costumes and lively dancing made a beautiful picture," reported *The Techgram*. The participants taking part in the pageant included Blacksburgers, Radford College girls, and a professional ballet of twenty girls from Chicago. Historical accuracy was assured by the supervision exercised by Mr. Herbert A. Kellar, director of the McCormick Historical Association Library, then in Chicago. A motion picture film, later in great demand over the state, was made of the production and portions of the crowd in attendance on the happy occasion. Pictures of the celebration and copies of the speeches made at the time were later published as a college bulletin and given wide circulation not only in Virginia but over the nation as well.

In 1932, the Corps assembled on George Washington's birthday "to have a modest part in the world-wide celebration of the bicentennial of Virginia's most distinguished son." Talks setting forth Washington's contributions as an engineer, soldier, farmer, and citizen were presented by members of the faculty. Following these talks the Corps formed to witness the planting, in the front of the War Memorial Hall, of an elm, Washington's favorite tree. Pranksters the following night took matters into their own hands and added a number of cherry trees to the site. Unhappily neither the elm nor the cherry trees survived. Some members of the faculty felt that the exercises honoring Washington had been too modest. Plans were started, therefore, for a more elaborate ceremony in the form of a pageant to be given during the 1932 commencement. Since the year also marked the sixtieth anniversary of VPI, it was decided to celebrate both anniversaries at the same time. Some difficulty was encountered in arranging a pageant which would honor both Washington and VPI at the same time, but according to *The Techgram,* the connection between VPI and George Washington [to be depicted in the pageant] "was clearly shown in the prologue written by Dr. C. M. Newman and spoken by the Muse of History played by Miss Maude E. Wallace." Professor T. W. Knote, the largest man on the faculty, made an impressive Washington as the symbolism of colorful pageantry wove the thin (very thin) threads of history connecting Washington with VPI into the grand finale, "The Call of 1932."

In spite of the deepening financial depression over the country, the commencement of 1932 was permeated by a spirit of optimism. *The Virginia Tech* felt that the entire student body had manifested an increased sense of maturity and responsibility. The various class nights which for years had been noisily celebrated with sharp blasts of dynamite were observed in a comparatively quiet manner with a smoker supplanting the blasting. *The Techgram* in an article entitled "Light Favorite Fag Instead of Fuses Becomes Tech Custom" credited J. J. (Pop) Owens with taking the lead in persuading class officers to "give up dynamiting in favor of a smoker." The editor of *The Virginia Tech* hailed the new method of observing class night as "a new occasion in the life of the various classes at VPI . . . prep school practice has been supplanted with a college man's way of doing things." The editor's belief that dynamiting had been completely eliminated from the campus proved to be a bit premature, but his stand did help in the movement to supplant the practice.

Burruss, in his official report to the board and in his informal report to the Alumni Association, reflected considerable satisfaction with the work of the College and with the changed attitude of the student body. At the same time, he expressed a note of concern about the effect the deteriorating financial condition of the state might have on the College. He did not have to wait long to observe the effect, for the depression arrived on the campus with the session of 1932-33.

The legislature cut all faculty salaries by ten per cent and the biennial appropriation by approximately seven-and-one-half per cent, to take effect July 1, 1932. Before the depression ended, faculty salaries had been cut a total of twenty per cent, while the annual appropriations had been reduced even more drastically. Student enrollment dropped from 1817 for the session of 1932-33 to 1561 during the session of 1933-34. Following this latter session, it started rising and continued to do so until the outbreak of World War II.

In spite of the stringent financial conditions, morale of both students and faculty remained high. Many of this latter group realized that after all they had jobs while many of their friends did not. As a result of Burruss' vigorous pursuit of economy no major college program was discontinued, although some work in home economics was temporarily suspended; in fact, Burruss approached the end of each fiscal year with a surplus of funds. On one occasion his expenditure of this surplus within the last month of the biennium created a small furor in the state. The state auditor reported that such an expenditure, while not illegal, certainly violated the intention of the regulations covering such supposed surpluses. The newspapers leveled critical blasts at Burruss for his supposed lack of sympathy with the necessity for economy during the critical financial period being experienced in the state. Burruss prepared a spirited and detailed explanation of his conduct and presented it to his board, but he issued a mild statement to the press, urging the latter to make a full investigation of the affair and then to report all the facts, not just the sensational ones. The state auditor

admitted that many of the charges of improper expenditure grew from technical differences existing between the system of record-keeping being followed
at VPI and the system recently approved by the auditor's office. A number of
individuals, including some political office holders who apparently thought
Burruss knew as much about financing as did the auditor, wrote privately to
Burruss, expressing their confidence in his ability to handle the situation. Burruss did not continue to press for vindication of his practices but invited the
auditor to visit Blacksburg and supervise the inauguration of a financial
accounting system which would be in harmony with the one being advocated
from Richmond. The auditor accepted the invitation (since he was going to
insist on the change anyway) and sent his representatives to Blacksburg, and the
new system of record-keeping and accounting was duly installed. At the same
time the auditor wrote a letter to Burruss, complimenting him for the unusually
constructive, businesslike attitude he had taken throughout the entire affair.
This letter was never given the publicity that had been given the earlier more
sensational charges of improper expenditure of surpluses. Neither was a letter
received by Burruss from General Lejeune, superintendent of VMI, advising
him that under the new accounting system "the only way to save money is to
spend it" during the period for which it is appropriated. Burruss' constructive
objectivity in dealing with this touchy situation was in strong contrast to the
behavior of a number of officials of other public agencies whose financial records
had also come under criticism from the auditor's office. As one result, Burruss'
opinion relating to financial affairs in general, and to VPI in particular, came
to be looked upon with considerable favor by the "inner circle" of guardians
of state finances at the state capitol, certainly not an unenviable position for a
college president in constant need for increased appropriations.

In January, 1934, the depression-born federal Public Works Administration
made the first of several combination grant-loans to the College to be used
primarily for the erection of new buildings. These new funds when combined
with the already existing Civil Works Administration funds and later with the
WPA funds helped finance projects which changed the face of the campus
within the next few years. The story of the struggle to secure the first PWA
grant was prepared by J. Ambler Johnston ('04) and included with other documents sealed in the cornerstone of the Teaching and Administration Building
begun with these funds in 1934. The cornerstone of this building was laid during
commencement week 1935 under ceremonies conducted by the Grand Lodge of
Virginia, A. F. and A. M. One alumnus wanted Secretary of the Interior Harold
Ickes present for the ceremony since he felt "Ickes deserves commendation for
the cleanness which pervades the PWA." Ickes was unable to attend, but the
presence of important Masonic officials helped focus favorable publicity on
VPI anyway. The story of the struggle to secure this first PWA grant as told by
Johnston, a participant, is a fascinating one as much for what it does not tell
as for what it does tell of Virginia, the New Deal, and state and national politics.
Its complete recital is beyond the province here; but according to Johnston,
ninety-nine per cent of the real work involved in getting this first grant, which
extended to all the state institutions of higher learning, was done by Burruss,
W. S. Moffett ('01), J. Vaughn Gary, W. L. Carneal, and himself, "with General
Lejeune making the hit that brought in the winning run." This last statement
was based on Johnston's conviction that just as the request for the grant was on
the verge of being rejected, General Lejeune had appealed directly to President

Above: Tech's old Library stood on the site of the present Carol M. Newman Library. Built in 1905 as a chapel-auditorium, it was used as a gymnasium from 1909-14 and as a library after 1914. It was destroyed by fire in 1953. Shown is the interior in 1930. Below: Guests arrive at Memorial Gymnasium for McCormick Day in July 1931. The event marked the centennial observance of the first successful demonstration of the reaper.

Above Cadets dine in the Old Commencement Hall in 1932. The mess was moved to Owens Dining Hall in 1938 and Commencement Hall became Commerce Hall. The building was torn down in 1957. Below: The agricultural barns in 1935 occupied the site now included in the parking lot west of Coliseum.

The picture grouping above from the 1935 "Bugle" shows scenes from Tech's first junior class Ring Dance, inaugurated by the Class of 1935 on April 27, 1934, and held annually ever since. In 1942, the Corps of Cadets petitioned band leader Fred Waring to write a popular song for their Ring Dance. The result was "Moonlight and VPI," with lyrics by Charles Gaynor, introduced nationally by the Fred Waring Glee Club on April 17, 1942, on his national radio network show. The song is always played at Ring Dance.

Above: Downtown Blacksburg in 1935. Below: Old Administration Building in 1949. This building was located at the northeast corner of the present drillfield and was used as administrative offices from 1904 until July 1936 when Burruss Hall was completed. The building was torn down in 1950.

VPI was selected by the Army in 1943 to train Army engineers through an Army Specialized Training Program. Above: The wartime student-soldiers take calisthenics on the drillfield. Below: A cadet company salutes the World War I memorial as it passes in review in 1943. Almost 2,300 Techmen were under arms in World War I, while about 7,300 served in World War II.

With the huge influx of veterans following World War II, VPI was forced to establish trailer parks around the campus perimeter to house the student families. The above aerial photo shows one of the parks in 1948 and the old college water tower, located close to the site of the present Coliseum. Below: Second Academic Building in 1949. Both the water tower and the Academic Building were torn down in the late 'Fifties.

The VPI Memorial, originally intended to memorialize Techmen who lost their lives in World War II, now memorializes all deceased Techmen. A gift of Tech alumni to their alma mater, the Memorial was begun in the spring of 1951 and dedicated in the spring of 1961. Beneath the Memorial Court is a Chapel that seats 350. The photo above shows work completed by the fall of 1951. Below is the completed Court and eight sculptured pylons representing, from left: Brotherhood, Honor, Leadership, Sacrifice, Service, Loyalty, Duty, and the University motto, "Ut Prosim (That I May Serve)."

Coeds were still under 200 in number on campus in the late 'Fifties, but they were involved in practically all phases of student life and enrolled in most curricula. Above: A coed takes notes in a mechanical engineering laboratory (at right). Below: Students in an electrical engineering laboratory in the mid-'Fifties.

The Alumni Association established the William E. Wine Faculty Achievement Awards in 1957 as a memorial to Wine, a 1904 alumnus who had served as rector for four of his 11 years as a member of the Board of Visitors. Above: The first three winners with Graham Claytor, then president of the Alumni Association. From left: George R. Powley, electrical engineering; Claytor; Paul M. Reaves, dairy science; and Robert C. Krug, chemistry. Below: The Corps at ROTC Awards ceremony, 1957.

Even though there has never been a music department at Tech, alumni and students had much to be proud of through the efforts of the Regimental Band and Men's Glee Club in the 'Sixties. The "Highty-Tighties," above, are seen marching in President John F. Kennedy's inaugural parade, the third consecutive such parade in which they took first place honors. Below, the Virginia Tech Varsity Glee Club sang behind President Lyndon B. Johnson at the nationally televised Christmas Tree Lighting Ceremony in 1969.

Tech was on the move in the athletic area in the 'Sixties in a big way. The football team won its first conference championship and participated in two Liberty Bowl post-season games. The athletic plant expanded into one of the finest in the country with the completion of a 10,000-seat Coliseum, a 37,000-seat Stadium, and a new Field House. Above: Lane Stadium, the baseball field, and the Coliseum with the campus' new high-rise dormitories in the background. Below: The Coliseum filled to capacity for the 1969 Commencement exercise.

Student life at Tech changed rapidly in the late 'Sixties, and it was sometimes difficult to keep up with the huge student body's ever-increasing needs. One long-felt need finally was satisfied with the tripling in size of Squires Student Center, above. The increase in the number of coeds to a proportion of 1-4 from a proportion of about 1-30 in a few short years changed the face of the campus in more ways than one. Below, coeds in the early 'Seventies have a watermelon party in their room in "coeducational" high-rise Ambler Johnston Dormitory.

A new, transitional architecture began to appear on campus in the late 'Sixties with the construction of academic buildings to house the College of Architecture and several arts and sciences departments. Above: Cowgill Hall. Below: Derring Hall.

The Virginia Polytechnic Institute and State University Campus, 1970.

Above left, Paul Brandon Barringer, sixth president (1907-13); right, Joseph Dupuy Eggleston, seventh president (1913-19); below, Julian Ashby Burruss, eighth president (1919-45).

Above left, John Redd Hutcheson, ninth president (1945-47); right, Walter Stephenson Newman, tenth president (1947-62); below, Thomas Marshall Hahn Jr., eleventh president (1962-present).

Franklin D. Roosevelt on behalf of the request. According to Johnston's account, Senator Harry Byrd and Secretary of the Navy Claude Swanson ('77) had arranged a meeting between Ickes and Burruss, at which time Ickes had indicated a flat rejection of the request. Continuing his report, Johnston said:

> The next day a small meeting was held in Richmond between Dr. Burruss and other friends of this measure and it was decided not to give up hope but on the other hand to organize a new method of attack.
>
> Here for a few weeks is a veil through which we cannot penetrate, but sufficient to say that the Superintendent of Virginia Military Institute, General John A. Lejeune, had commanded the Marines in France during the War when the Honorable Franklin D. Roosevelt was Assistant Secretary of the Navy, and closely associated with General Lejeune.
>
> Furthermore on December 26, 1933, General Lejeune called on the President in the afternoon and spent several hours with him and a few days thereafter the Department of Public Works announced through the Associated Press the approval of our loan.
>
> From then on to this date [December 1934] there has been a mass of routine without a single hitch of consequence.

The Teaching and Administration Building, completed in June, 1936, went by the name "T and A Building" until 1944, when by a unanimous vote the name was changed by the Board of Visitors to the Julian A. Burruss Hall in honor of President Burruss. Ambler Johnston had proposed this name as early as 1936, because it never would have been built, he said, if it had not been for Burruss. Records confirm this belief. The college administration offices were moved from the old Administration Building to the T and A Building in July, 1936, where they have remained ever since. The June, 1936, commencement exercises were held in the three-thousand-seat auditorium of this building, to the delight and comfort of the attending public. The reaction to this new building was overwhelmingly favorable throughout the entire state, although a few artists and architects are known to have argued sharply over whether the building was or was not an austere monstrosity "spelled out in stone."

By the end of 1940, Burruss' skill in generating and using funds from the federal and state agencies born of the depression had resulted in phenomenal improvements and expansion of the physical plant. The rapid growth and changing landscape was particularly surprising to returning alumni, most of whom were delighted with the change. Others, grumbling that Burruss was converting a Virginia institution into a midwestern type of college, proposed that more Virginians loyal to Tech traditions be employed on the faculty, that only alumni be appointed to the Board of Visitors, and that coeducation be eliminated. Others proposed that alumni be consulted before any old buildings be replaced by a new one, and that more regard be shown for protecting trees and the natural beauty spots of the campus. Different proposals immediately developed as to which beauty spots should be protected. Most of these proposals were made at a meeting of the Alumni Association and were referred to a committee, where, according to one alumnus, "the proposals being in such good hands they were left permanently." Burruss was fully aware of this minor grumbling and usually met it by increased urging that alumni and all concerned "get the facts, all of the facts, about what we are doing" before condemning us. To help in the dissemination of facts Burruss appeared before numerous alumni chapter meetings and "talked a greater VPI from the time he got off the train until he got back on it again."

The campus buildings erected during Burruss' administration were desig-

nated at first by some name in harmony with the usage of the building. Later, at
the agitation of *The Techgram, The Virginia Tech,* and some alumni, most of the
buildings were named for faculty members or alumni having made significant
contributions to the institution. This change of names resulted in duplication
and confusion at times, but for the buildings erected largely from depression-
generated funds the change took place as follows: The Faculty Apartments,
also known as Faculty Center, was completed in 1935 and enlarged, remodeled,
and named F. Donaldson Brown Center for Continuing Education in 1966;
East Stone Dormitory Number 1 was completed in 1935. Two wings were
added in 1939 and the entire unit was named Eggleston Hall in 1952; a wing
to the West Stone Dormitory was completed in 1939. This unit went by the name
of Stone Dormitory, or Civilian Dormitory until it was named Campbell Hall
in 1952; The Student Activities Building also known as the SAB was completed
in 1937, and named Squires Hall in 1949. This building was greatly enlarged
and renamed Squires Student Center in 1969. The Agricultural Engineering
Hall was completed in 1937 and named Seitz Hall in 1956. A new Dining Hall
in two sections was completed in 1938 and 1939 and named Owens Hall in 1952;
the Home Economics Building was completed in 1939 and named Agnew Hall
in 1949. The Natural Science Building, sometimes called "Aggie Annex," was
completed in 1939 and with a second section to be completed in early 1950 was
named Smyth Hall in 1949; the new Agricultural Hall was completed in 1940
and named Hutcheson Hall (for J. R. and T. B. Hutcheson) in 1956. The
Mineral Industries Building was completed in 1940 and named Holden Hall in
1949. Hillcrest, a women's dormitory, was completed in 1940 and immediately
given the unofficial name of "Skirt Barn" by the male students. In addition to
these major buildings, the airport hangar was completed in 1940, and the old
dining hall was remodeled into offices and classrooms and assigned to the business,
administration department. The Dairy Building, finished in 1931, was named
Saunders Hall for W. D. Saunders in 1949.

The conditions surrounding the erection of the Agricultural Engineering
Building (Seitz Hall) are worthy of more attention. Instead of letting the erection of the building out to contract, the agricultural engineering staff designed
the building and then trained transient labor in the skills of stonecutting,
masonry, plumbing, carpentry, electricity, and so on needed to erect the structure. Then having trained its own working force, the staff supervised much of
the actual erection of the building. This on-the-job training made everybody
happy. The College got a much needed building, the workmen got a paycheck
during the depression, and the state got a boost in the number of skilled workers.

In addition to the construction of these major buildings Burruss reported
that:

> A variety of other productive work has been accomplished . . . such as the
> construction of roads, walks, lakes [the Duck Pond], planting and landscaping
> on our campus. . . . We have found it possible to . . . enlarge our heating and
> power plant, with extension of our underground pipelines to all principal
> buildings.

It is quite likely that students enrolled during the period remember these
latter projects even better than they remember the erection of the buildings,
since it was these projects which led to the campus being crisscrossed with deep

ditches and mounds of raw earth, churned into a morass of deep mud in the winter and clouds of dust in the summer.

As the year 1940 began, there seemed to be a realization on the part of many that VPI had passed through an important decade. *The Techgram* under the title of "The Tremendous Thirties" noted that "the thirties for Virginia Tech were a decade of great growth and advancement. Expansion was noted in every phase of college activities—some of which will be hurriedly noted." The following activities were among those deemed important enough by the editor to be "hurriedly noted."

> Tech's enrollment more than doubled: the staff and number of courses offered were increased. The plan of offering the first one or two years of engineering work at various places in the state . . . has worked quite satisfactorily. The Engineering Council for Professional Development placed its approval upon engineering curricula. The General Education Board granted money toward development of teaching and research in agricultural economics and rural sociology.
>
> At the beginning of the decade 25 curricula were offered. This has now been increased to 31. In some cases, the work has been offered as a part of some other curriculum. The curricula added since the twenties include industrial physics, conservation and forestry, general agriculture, general science, poultry husbandry, rural sociology, ceramic engineering. An option in aeronautics was offered several years ago. Flight instruction as a part of the C.A.A. program was added as the decade neared its close. Instruction in research and wildlife conservation were started. A graduate program in power and fuel engineering was begun.
>
> The number of graduate students increased nearly three-fold and during the latter part of the decade work was offered in certain departments leading to the doctor of philosophy degree. [Agricultural economics, biology, chemical engineering, and chemistry.]
>
> Student government was reorganized. A senate was established with representation from cadets and civilian students. Last year the civilian students and the women students merged their governments into one.
>
> One of the most constructive steps taken was the establishment of the Student Finance Board. The movement for the creation of this board was led by Pi Delta Epsilon. . . .
>
> . . . the national and honorary fraternities established [at Tech] in the thirties follow: Pi Delta Epsilon, journalism; Alpha Zeta, agriculture; Phi Lamda Upsilon, chemistry; Omicron Delta Kappa, leadership; Tau Beta Pi, engineering; Scabbard and Blade, military; Sigma Delta Psi, athletic; Sigma Xi, research. A professional commerce and business administration fraternity, Alpha Kappa Psi, also was established.
>
> Summer began one of the busiest seasons with more and more groups finding it desirable to hold their meetings upon the campus. . . . To such regular meetings as the Institute of Rural Affairs, 4-H Boys' and Girls' Short Course, Virginia Association of Future Farmers of America Conference, and Masonic Schools were added during the decade the annual meeting of the Virginia Federation of Home Demonstration Clubs, . . . the Old Dominion Boys' State, the Rural Ministers' School, and the Garden Lovers' Short Course. The enrollment of the two terms of the Summer Quarter increased from about 300 to nearly 700. . . .
>
> During the stress and strain of the depression, the Agricultural Extension Division took over additional duties in helping the federal government's farm relief program. Tech has also cooperated with other agencies that have been set up during the past few years.
>
> Just as the decade was six days old, a daily broadcasting program from studios in Memorial Hall was begun. That same month saw the beginning of *Technical Topics* a monthly publication of information about engineering and

technical activities at Virginia Tech and elsewhere. Numerous engineering research reports were published as college bulletins.

Many alumni will readily agree that each event of this excellent though incomplete summary is deserving of far more attention than can be given it at this time. At the risk of ignoring other important developments, a few more may be mentioned.

Extension schools offering the first two years of the College's principal engineering curricula were established in cooperation with what is now the Virginia Commonwealth University, in Richmond, the Old Dominion University, in Norfolk, Bluefield College, in Bluefield, and Lynchburg College, in Lynchburg.

The state soil survey, begun in 1930, soon carried additional VPI personnel into nearly every county of the state. The annual horse show, begun in 1932, and held at a specially prepared site just northwest of the present site of the Coliseum, proved to be extremely popular with horse lovers throughout the state. As an ingenious method of beating the depression, a group of students requested permission to join together in renting and living in a house in the town. Burruss and Dean Williams were gravely concerned about the possible effects such a move might have on relations with the people of the community but finally consented to the request. Graduate students in fuel and power engineering provided living facilities in a house located near the power plant and immediately named the residence the BTU House. The success of the BTU House helped create a desire for more "houses" in which to live. The campus humorous publication, *V.P.I. Skipper,* became too "spicy" for the times and had to suspend publication in 1934. A minor crisis occurred in 1932, when the senior class long accustomed to elect its valedictorian and salutatorian failed to elect to either position the student with the highest academic average—a coed. Friends of the coed accused the College of discrimination against women. Burruss dug back into the records and was able to show that the senior class had not always elected as valedictorian the individual with the highest academic record. The individual having been elected then came forward and announced that he would serve only if public acknowledgement was made at the commencement exercises that the coed in question had achieved the highest academic standing. The senior class accepted this proposal and requested Dr. Burruss to make such an announcement at commencement time. Burruss agreed to do so, and the entire matter then passed off quietly as far as the public was concerned. Privately, Burruss scolded the director of publications for the publicity he had given the matter and shuddered when an old-guard alumnus demanded an end to coeducation. Working quietly through another old-guard alumnus known to be more favorable to coeducation, Burruss was able to convince the anti-coed alumnus that restricting coeducation at VPI, a land-grant college, would probably result in the curtailment of federal funds for the College. The alumnus, so the story goes, muttering "women's rights I'll never understand, but money I do understand," dropped his objections. Within a few years, the senior class discontinued having a valedictorian or a salutatorian. Alumni were divided over whether this development represented a victory or a defeat for women's rights.

In 1934, the department of agricultural education, under the leadership of Professor E. C. Magill, changed its name to that of the department of vocational education, and began a program of expansion. Later under the leadership of Professor Harry W. Sanders this department developed one of the most comprehensive programs of teacher preparation for vocational education to be found in the United States. In 1936, the Tech coeds shocked the senior class by asking for representation in *The Bugle*. The request was refused, but a very thought-provoking editorial in the *Tech* clearly showed that the sometimes pseudo anti-coed sentiment was rapidly changing to a pro-coed attitude. The spring of 1936 saw the formation of the Blacksburg Community Concert Association. This truly cooperative undertaking made up of music lovers from Wytheville to Roanoke brought an unusual number of outstanding artists to the campus before it gave way to the changing tastes and the march of time with the end of the 1968-69 series of concerts. During the same year, the Corps became so large that compulsory church attendance became a risky business. The number of cadets attending some churches threatened to leave no seats for the regular members. To solve this situation, church attendance was made optional for all juniors and seniors. This relaxation of rules was immediately followed by a petition from the Corps to the administrative council, asking its support of Sunday movies. The council acted by deciding not to act.

About this time the editor of *The Virginia Tech* discovered that the legislature had set twelve miles per hour as the legal speed limit for all roads on the campus. He immediately launched a campaign urging the cadets to secure the license number of any automobile observed exceeding this limit. Since students were not allowed either to own or operate automobiles on the campus, it was obvious to all that the editor was not asking students to report on fellow students. For a number of weeks after the appearance of this editorial, Burruss, "Ducklegs" Miller, and a number of the faculty were observed driving about the campus at a veritable crawl.

W. L. "Monk" Younger, who succeeded C. P. "Sally" Miles as athletic director in 1936, launched a successful intramural athletic program under the slogan of "Athletics for All." In 1937, enrollment in the Corps of Cadets was limited to the number which could be accommodated in the barracks. This restriction brought irate protests from students and parents alike, but, in the opinion of the commandant, strengthened the Corps next year when it could be enlarged as the result of a new barracks. During the late thirties, according to this same commandant, the VPI cadet uniform became so well known that the cadets could hitchhike to Norfolk and back any weekend they so desired. In fact, said the commandant, "it was reported that one cadet had hitchhiked to Boston and back" one weekend.

In 1938, at Burruss' request, Professor C. E. Seitz, head of the department of agricultural engineering, went to Washington to appear with others before a U. S. Senate Appropriations Committee to explain the needs for research in rural electrification. As a result of this conference the United States Department of Agriculture was granted funds to promote research in this important area, and VPI was selected as one of the institutions to start the investigation. This pioneering program started the next year under the direction of E. T. Swink and R. J. Blair of the department of agricultural engineering and has continued to this day. As a result of this continuity the department of agricultural engineering is the only one in the United States that has maintained an uninterrupted cooperative program of research in rural electrification with the USDA from 1939 to the present time.

During the entire decade of the thirties the YMCA under Paul Derring, with the assistance of a more-than-able faculty advisory board, rendered increasingly important service to the college community. Burruss, acutely conscious of the lack of proper administrative provision for student personnel services, turned more and more to Derring for help in this area. Paul met the challenge then and later in a manner worthy of a separate history in itself.

During the decade of the thirties, although he had his problems, Burruss knew more triumphs than disappointments. Essentially a shy man, as the College grew with a corresponding increase in his responsibilities, he tended to confine himself more and more to his office. Students seldom saw him except at strictly formal occasions, such as the opening assembly in the fall and the commencement program in the spring. At the former occasion he seldom departed from the customary platitudes and clichés used to welcome and advise freshmen upon their arrival at college; at the latter occasion he usually followed a stiff, set ritual. If he met a student face to face on the campus or at the post office, he usually kept his eyes glued to the ground and hurried past as if afraid the student might speak. He usually put in an appearance at the important football games but managed to give the impression that his thoughts were elsewhere. He accepted a few invitations to student-sponsored banquets but often went through the entire evening as if unaware of his surroundings. As one result of this detachment many students got the impression he was a cold, aloof individual devoid of any genuine interest in their welfare or opinion. Many of the faculty developed the same impression. These individuals, student and faculty, could not have been more mistaken. The individuals, especially the students, who had occasion to visit Burruss in his office found him to be a gentleman of kindness, understanding, and deep concern for their welfare and opinion. Unfortunately, these individuals in the student body were so limited in number that the opposite opinion usually predominated. *The Bugle* of 1933, which was dedicated to Burruss by the senior class, came close to expressing the true opinion held by those who got to know him when it described him as ". . . alumnus president, gentleman, scholar, administrator whose guiding hand has placed VPI at her present high status, who through his untiring effort as president during fourteen years, has done more toward the development of the institute than any other man. . . ." The record more than supports this high opinion.

To many people in the college community, Burruss appeared to be an autocratic, dictatorial administrator. His practice of making decisions in terms of his concept of a greater VPI helped strengthen this opinion, for when the time for decision-making arrived, Burruss was ruthless in putting "his" VPI first. This practice was so strong that it once drew a protest from his minister, who delicately informed Burruss that as an officer in the church he should put the church, not VPI first. As an interesting sidelight on Burruss, it may be added that this suggestion drew a reply in which Burruss "amazed" the minister in question with his knowledge of theology. The young man quickly retracted his charge and shifted his attack to the "rat system," which, he said, could never be accepted without protest by modernly trained ministers. Burruss accepted this latter charge and then asked the young man to join him in an effort to introduce religious instruction into the curriculum at VPI. The minister was not sure that this responsibility fell within his province. Both men, then having established a point and thereby having satisfied their egos, dropped the matter and resumed amiable relations. The minister, however, is reported to have warned his successor not to underestimate Burruss' knowledge of theology.

Burruss' decisions were obvious for all to see. The things that went unseen, particularly with respect to the decisions directly affecting personnel, were the behind-the-scene efforts he made and the concern he showed for the welfare of all college employees. The records indicate that Burruss possessed a comprehensive knowledge—in many instances a detailed knowledge—of college-employee behavior and problems. The absence of adequate provision for workmen's compensation, sick leave, and old-age retirement was a constant source of worry to him. This concern was clearly reflected year after year in his reports to the board in which he advanced numerous plans and suggestions for helping incapacitated employees or for extending aid to the family of deceased employees.

While engaged in these unpublicized efforts to help the employees, he was also sending out a constant stream of letters of commendation and encouragement to the employees for work he considered well done. The recipients of these letters included a day laborer on the college farm whose leg had been broken "by the kick of a mule," an elderly and apparently neurotic janitor who was having "family troubles," the dean of the college who was receiving accolades in the press, and many others in between these extremes of vocational levels with no claim to fame beyond a job well done. At the same time he was using his typewriter to communicate with his official family, he was also using the same medium to communicate with others. Many student-body officers, usually drawn from the senior class, were often surprised to receive a note from Burruss, congratulating them for their accomplishments. Other students often received notes from the same source but with the congratulations omitted. Newspaper editors often came in for their share of attention. If the paper published an article favorable to VPI, Burruss often wrote the editor a brief note of appreciation and usually managed to send along an additional bulletin. If the article was critical, he wrote a longer letter, seldom if ever controversial in tone, suggesting that the editor might be interested in the additional facts to be found in the enclosed report or bulletin dealing with the topic in question. Burruss on more than one occasion in trying to promote VPI wrote, "We have no fear of the facts, but the trouble seems to be to get folks to recognize and accept facts." He never did develop an understanding of the role of emotions as a motivator of behavior or a factor in the development of attitudes.

As the decade of the thirties developed, Burruss was called upon to participate more and more in the numerous efforts being put forth at both the national and the state level to cope with the economic depression sweeping the country. His time-consuming efforts in this direction were favorably received and began to get not only state but national attention. During this same period, he began to take an increasingly active part in the Association of Land-Grant Colleges and was appointed to important committees in this organization.

In 1937, he was lauded by *The Progressive Farmer* for his "great success" at VPI. In June of the same year, he was awarded an LL.D. degree from Hampden-Sydney College. Increasingly he was called upon to serve in advisory capacity upon state and national commissions, committees, and organizations. In November, 1938, he was elected president of the National Association of Land-Grant Colleges. The faculty and the Alumni Association were happy over this honor. The former group immediately launched a plan to celebrate not only this honor but also to celebrate his twenty years of service as president of VPI. It was determined that a national radio hook-up could be secured in December, 1938. The versatile faculty committee quickly adjusted to this date by deciding

to combine into one celebration the beginning of Burruss' first year as president
of the Association of Land-Grant Colleges with the beginning of his twentieth
year as president of VPI. With the cooperation of the United States Department
of Agriculture, an hour-long celebration was broadcast coast-to-coast over the
National Broadcasting Company radio system. Startled listeners and delighted
alumni heard "Tech Triumph," Hokies, bits of college history, praise for Dr.
Burruss, descriptions of work being done at VPI, and selections from the college glee club and the Highty-Tighties come wafting out of loud speakers.

The reaction to the broadcast was highly favorable. Letters and telegrams of
congratulations poured in to Burruss. Some listeners, descendants of the first
faculty employed by the College, sent in some original documents, written by
their ancestors relating incidents in the early history of the school. These documents, said the donors, might help correct some of the errors of VPI history
related in the broadcast. Since the content of the documents referred to some
unhappy incidents in the early history of the College, the papers were put into
the "locked case" in the library rather than being put in the newspaper to stir
up unpleasant memories. Douglas Freeman, distinguished editor of *The Richmond News Leader,* noted biographer, and Virginia representative of the General Education Board, was especially complimentary to Burruss. "As I have
observed the growing VPI and its service to the state," he wrote, "every year it
seems to me you grow in stature and understanding." Other letters similar in
nature were received from state and national leaders. The faculty was well
pleased with the overall effect and looked with confidence to the future. The
state was recovering from the depression; most of the salary cuts had been
restored to the faculty; the enrollment was climbing; and the legislature was
known to be favorably impressed with VPI's programs of service to the state.
Even Burruss reported to the board:

> The president of our general alumni association has been visiting chapters
> of this organization in the larger cities of the North, the middle West, and the
> Southwest. He has recently written me how impressed he has been with "the
> way in which VPI has fused itself into the industrial life of the nation." One
> can hardly go into any large city in the United States without finding representa-
> tives of this institution who are taking a creditable part in the life and work of
> the community, many of them occupying positions of outstanding impor-
> tance. . . .
> The work of members of our staff has received much publicity in the news-
> papers as well as in scientific publications recently. Hardly a day passes that does
> not bring creditable news items, and frequently complimentary editorial refer-
> ences in Virginia and to some extent outside. No institution in the state has
> received anything approaching the amount of space given in newspapers to this
> institution, yet we have not sought most of this publicity but representatives of
> the Associated Press and others have visited the institution frequently and dis-
> covered information suitable for publicatiion, usually valuable to the people of
> Virginia.
> A number of times during the year members of our staff have received special
> publicity, more frequently for research which they have completed or for some
> exceptionally valuable service which they have rendered. At the annual conven-
> tion of the American Association for the Advancement of Science, at Richmond
> in December, several of our research workers were given, in the newspapers
> reporting the proceedings, more space than was given to other scientists. . . .

After this brief allusion to accomplishments, Burruss immediately directed
the board's attention to present problems and plans for future growth. The col-

lege did continue to grow as it entered the decade of the forties, but by now its tremendously expanded growth and program had outgrown the size of the effective administrative organization which Burruss had set up the twenties. In addition to this disturbing factor, two of his deans, both of whom were on the administrative council, were in their seventies; the heads of three important departments were also in their seventies; and the span of service for the heads of seven other departments ranged from thirty-five to forty-six years. A number of the senior professors were equally advanced in age or tenure of service. Burress, in his sixties himself, recognized the tremendously increased responsibilities but does not seem to have thought of any administrative reorganization or expansion as a solution. Instead he took on more responsibility for himself and thereby violated the basic principle of administration which he had invoked so successfully in setting up his organization two decades earlier. Both outstanding alumni and the board recognized that Burruss was undertaking too much for himself. Board member J. P. Woods of Roanoke was particularly concerned. He wrote to Burruss a number of times urging him to delegate more responsibility to others or to "get whatever help you need." Finally, Burruss sent a memorandum to the Council of Administration. Since this memorandum is so revealing as to his state of mind, and more particularly since his almost total failure to implement his own proposals contained therein help explain many events of the next half a decade, this memorandum is given in its entirety.

To Members of the Council of Administration:

For several years our Board of Visitors and some of our prominent alumni have urged me to distribute the administrative work of the institution among the officials of the institution, in such a manner as to relieve me from details, and thus enable me to devote my time and attention more largely to the broader aspects and general responsibilities of the administration. The rapid growth of the institution in recent years and the expansion of its activities have accentuated the need in this connection. The large PWA and WPA projects, relations to various Federal and State agencies and to private foundations and organizations of various types, the necessity for continuous readjustment of the financial structure of the institution, and the redefining of policies and procedures relating to the numerous and various activities in which this institution is engaged, have created problems so numerous and of such magnitude, and sometimes much involved, as to demand an ever increasing amount of time and energy from the executive head of the institution. The Board of Visitors has not been unmindful of this situation, in its meetings many times attention has been directed to it. At the meeting last week members of the Board were quite insistent that steps be taken by me to change conditions, hence I feel that I must do what I can to comply with the wishes expressed by Board members, as well as by leaders of our alumni.

I am sure that you realize to some extent the heavy load which I have been attempting to carry, and it is increasing all the time. I am not complaining, but I recognize that my only hope to carry it successfully is that our college officials, committees, etc., will relieve me of a large part of the burden by taking full responsibility for the respective activities, duties and tasks assigned to them or properly falling to them, thus freeing me for work which they cannot undertake, or think they cannot do. For some time I have been gradually transferring responsibilities to others and I shall continue in perhaps somewhat greater measure to do this. Also, I am withdrawing from active participation in some outside organizations, in order that I may give all of my attention to the institution.

As I understand it, the function of the head of the institution is to establish, with the approval of the Board of Visitors, principles and policies governing the institution, and general procedures for its operation. Obviously he cannot see to the detailed carrying out of these policies and procedures, but must be content with initiation and general supervision. Other types of responsibilities, and their name is legion, must be assumed by various college officials and committees. So far as I am concerned, I am quite willing to leave interpretation and application to their judgment. If there be difference of opinion in a committee or other group, that may be fortunate, inasmuch as it serves to bring out fully both sides of any question, and action will doubtless be in accordance with the democratic custom of majority decision.

The Council of Administration is the most important agency we have in the college management, and I have the utmost confidence in it, particularly since it represents all of the principal divisions and groups in the college. It is doing an indispensable and valuable work. It will probably be expected to carry an even heavier responsibility than heretofore, and I shall continue to be very grateful for it. As for myself, I know that the Board of Visitors and my alumni friends are right, and that what they insist upon is not only best for me personally but is also what the institution itself has a right to expect and demand of me.

Very truly yours,
Julian A. Burruss, President

The records of the early forties indicate that Burruss did not clarify his intentions as to the responsibilities he planned to delegate to this council. The records further indicate that after delegating a committee or a staff member to deal with a problem, he often bypassed the committee or staff member and dealt directly with the problem himself. This behavior, in addition to creating an atmosphere of confusion, strengthened the opinion of a number of people that he was an autocratic dictator. In actuality, he was an overworked man in need of help, and at the same time he was rapidly approaching a state of exhaustion in which he could not use help if proffered. As the problems of the approaching war became more acute and finally burst forth in full fury, the note of martyrdom, even self-pity, evident in his memorandum to the council, became more and more pronounced. Instead of expanding his administrative organization as he had done twenty years earlier, he retreated into his innermost office and buried himself deeper and deeper in the mass of detail attendant upon administering the College. Almost all social invitations, whether extended by alumni, faculty, or students, were declined with the plea that "my load of administrative work is increasing all the time." To a friend he wrote, "There is so much waiting for me to do that even the suggestion of something else seems to get on my nerves even though under normal conditions it would be a delightful experience for me."

Even before the uncertainties of the forties set in, Burruss had showed signs of unusual concern lest the College end one of its fiscal years with a deficit. To prevent such an eventuality, he had imposed some restrictions which often hindered rather than contributed to the efficiency with which department heads replaced or secured much needed equipment. This fear of a deficit also dominated his consideration of proposals for new courses or expansion of old ones. In fact, there is considerable evidence to indicate that a number of opportunities to secure financial assistance to launch new programs were passed by on the grounds that such assistance would impose future financial burdens on the College.

In addition to Burruss' increasing fear of financial deficits, his fear that VPI would be accused of duplicating the work "rightfully belonging" to other state institutions also increased greatly in the late thirties and early forties. This concern was amply fed by the attitude of the state press and the legislature, which were constantly denouncing "costly duplication in the offerings of our state institutions of higher education." Although Burruss felt that in the matter of duplication of work "VPI was more sinned against than sinning," he freely exercised his rights of veto over proposals to introduce new courses if it could not be clearly shown to his satisfaction that the proposed courses were in fact needed in the curriculum of a school of applied science and technology emphasizing agriculture, engineering, and business. The application of this philosophy resulted in some interesting developments, such as the teaching of nontechnical courses like English, mathematics, psychology, sociology, history, and economics as "service" courses for the degree-granting curricula, the practice of having young instructors in mathematics enroll for courses in engineering, and the refusal to employ a person trained in psychology for fear he might teach "pure" instead of applied psychology. This latter fear was resolved by permitting applied psychology to be taught as a course in business administration, and other branches, such as general, educational, and adolescent psychology to be taught as applied courses in vocational education. The instructor in any of the nontechnical courses who could not or did not relate his course directly to the work of the agriculturist, engineer, scientist, or businessman frequently found himself in trouble with his students. When this happened, the professor seldom got sympathy from Burruss. Ironically, at a later stage in the development of VPI, many of the staff who achieved unusual success in developing the semivocational orientation of these nontechnical subjects found it necessary to reject this orientation and in lieu thereof develop the "pure" approach.

Perhaps the most significant result of Burruss' developing fear of a financial deficit and a duplication of work was the fact that VPI entered the decade of the forties with a restricted offering in the social sciences and the humanities.

By the fall of 1940, the effects of the country's preparation for national defense were being felt on the campus. On October 16, some five hundred students registered for the draft in Squires Hall under the Selective Service Act. Juniors and seniors enrolled in ROTC were exempt from this registration. By the first of the year, VPI was offering a number of defense courses both on and off campus. Since most of these courses were technical in nature, many of them had to be developed by the engineering faculty under the supervision of Dean Norris.

Although interest in the war in Europe and the increasing activities of national defense engaged a great deal of attention, the actual routine of the College was not greatly disturbed during the year. H. B. (Puss) Redd, who resigned as football coach, was succeeded by "Jimmy" Kitts, who according to the sports writers, was expected to introduce the "wide open Texas style of football" to Tech. Former president Paul B. Barringer, who, according to Burruss, the records showed was more sinned against than sinning, died in January, 1941. The students under the leadership of Omicron Delta Kappa unveiled a plaque in Squires Hall, honoring John H. Squires ('05), whose financial contributions had helped make the building possible. Burruss had participated in the unveiling, but even he did not know the full story of why Squires had developed such a strong attachment to VPI.

In 1904, Squires, a junior at North Carolina College of Agriculture and Mechanic Arts, had been suspended along with his entire class for some group or class action considered as insubordination by the authorities. When he found that he would not be readmitted to college, he wrote to Dr. McBryde, president of VPI, asking about the possibilities of completing his education "at your school." He had been quite frank about his situation at North Carolina A and M, neither defending nor excusing his conduct. McBryde contacted President Winston of North Carolina A and M, who gave his approval of Squires' admission to VPI. Following the receipt of this approval, McBryde sent Squires a telegram notifying him that VPI would accept him as a student. Squires entered school at once and from that day forward was one of VPI's most loyal and devoted sons. Upon his death he had left VPI a considerable legacy, a larger part of which Burruss had used to start construction on the student activities building, later named for Squires.

During the summer of 1941, the board increased student charges for the ensuing year but after a lengthy discussion turned down once more an oft-repeated request for a compulsory student activity fee. Unfortunately, Burruss did a far better job in presenting the pros and cons of such a fee to the board than he did to the student leaders. To the latter group, he merely reported the fact that the board had declined to authorize such a fee. His failure to communicate effectively with the students at this time proved to be a serious mistake. Many student leaders, disappointed over not having this source of revenue to help finance student-sponsored activities, erroneously assumed that Burruss alone was responsible for the rejection of their plea for the activity fee. Burruss, becoming more and more involved in administrative detail, did little to correct this erroneous conviction.

By the summer of 1941, Burruss was facing a new kind of problem. For the first time in its history the College was having to compete desperately for secretarial, skilled, and unskilled labor. The Hercules Powder/Radford Ordnance Works, which in 1940-41 had been located only six miles from the campus, needed workers of practically every classification. This plant, which at one time employed a force of more than twenty-three thousand people, had a pay scale far in advance of that authorized for employees at VPI. As a result, Burruss found himself faced with an unusual exodus of long-time employees from the campus. In addition to the loss of these employees, an increasing number of the younger faculty members were leaving for the armed services or defense-oriented work. Some of the replacements for the long-time employees proved to be anything but satisfactory. Even "Ducklegs" Miller complained to Burruss, "I employed a dark horse for janitor. He proved to be darker than I expected. He brought liquor on the campus and sold it. He took barracks property off the campus. He sold that too."

Burruss gave the board a full report of the problems being faced but warned that in his opinion much greater problems lay ahead as the College adjusted itself to make the maximum contribution to the defense effort. He was more than correct in his prophecy of greater problems ahead. Just before the opening of the fall quarter, the beloved Dr. Carol M. Newman, head of the English department and "godfather of all extracurricular activities at VPI," died unexpectedly. Newman's death plus the observation that Deans Price and Williams as well as some of the senior professors were beginning to show the effects of advancing age had a definitely depressing effect on Burruss. Without going into details, he urged the board to start giving increased consideration to plans for a better retirement system for the older or disabled faculty.

The academic year of 1941-42 started out fairly satisfactorily with the largest enrollment in the College's history to that date. For a period of time, it appeared that the major problems, in addition to those created by the shortage of help, would revolve around securing a better water and sewerage system for the College and town, finding a satisfactory solution to the pollution being caused by the "fly ash" pouring forth from the smokestack at the new power plant, and preventing the snow battles between the Corps and the civilians from developing into full scale warfare. The "headache" of how to deal with the "skippers," according to Colonel Cochran, the commandant, had been solved a few years earlier by Commandant Tenney's appointing all sergeants for the Corps from the senior instead of the junior class. This practice, said Cochran with tongue in cheek, had reduced the quality of the sergeants, but it had proven its worth by preventing the "skippers" from running the place "as they had been accustomed to do when they were concentrated in one company."

The news of Pearl Harbor, December 7, 1941, sent a shock wave throughout the entire campus as it did the rest of the country. In the week following, Burruss addressed an overflow audience of students and faculty in the college auditorium. He pledged the institution's total support of the war effort but begged for calmness and restraint on the part of all while more definite plans were being made. Until such plans had been made, he said, it was the students' patriotic duty to remain in school and prepare themselves for the stern tasks ahead. At this point, Burruss discarded his notes, advanced to the front of the stage, and in a voice strained with emotion, urged the students not to act hastily in withdrawing from college, but to wait until the proper orders had been received. He did not tell them that as a cadet captain in the Corps during the Spanish American War of 1898 he had attempted an opposite line of behavior. He had signed a petition urging that the entire Corps be allowed to withdraw from school and enter the army as a unit.

A number of students ignored Burruss' appeal and began to drift away to join the armed forces, but the majority remained in college. Accelerated programs were set up at first for seniors and finally for all students to enable them to move more rapidly toward the completion of their work. For the first time in the history of the school, degrees were awarded at a simple graduation ceremony held at the end of the winter quarter. All social activities except the senior dance were canceled for the regular spring commencement, which was dominated by "an underlying note of sadness." An important milestone was passed at this commencement in that VPI awarded its first Doctor of Philosophy degree, Nathan Sugarman of Atlanta, Georgia, having earned the degree in chemistry. This commencement exercise also markëd the end of the regular tour of duty for Colonel John H. Cochran as commandant. Burruss, announcing that he hoped Cochran could remain as commandant "until Gabriel blows his horn," had made repeated appeals to the War Department to have him left at VPI. The War Department instead of Gabriel, however, blew the horn, and Cochran was transferred, to be succeeded by Colonel Ralph W. Wilson.

During the summer of 1942, VPI entered into a full-scale accelerated program by offering a full quarter's work. A special lightweight cadet uniform was adopted, and the Corps was organized in the manner customary for the fall quarter. The ROTC camp usually held for cadets at the end of the junior year was dropped in favor of special training to be given to ROTC graduates upon their entrance into regular service. Burruss however was alarmed lest insufficient preparation to house, feed, and clothe the students had been made in the short time available between the closing of the spring quarter and the opening of the summer quarter. He was particularly upset over the effect all of the wartime activities were having on the financial affairs of the College. For the first time in his long service as a college administrator he found himself in a continuous state of uncertainty about financing the various parts of the rapidly changing educational program.

He was particularly disturbed about the operation of the VPI airport, which was being financed in part from federal funds. Earlier in the spring he had turned to Dean Norris for help in this connection. Shortly afterwards, Burruss had been disturbed over the expense accounts turned in by the director of aeronautics, which, according to Burruss, included "numerous and expensive trips, large telephone tolls, and various bothersome items which he has caused." Burruss sent a protest to Dean Norris, who had approved the travel. Norris, who by now was almost as overworked as Burruss, considered the note to be "ultra-critical." He explained to Burruss that the expenses had been incurred in an effort to cut through some of the Washington and Richmond red tape because, said Norris, "the one thing I hope to do is *once* to get a program finished on time and get the money in before the end of the fiscal year." In concluding his rather lengthy explanation of the operation of the airport, the usually imperturbable Norris in the following statement revealed the strain under which he was operating:

> I don't mind carrying responsibility when I feel that my efforts are appreciated. But this constant criticism gets me down, especially when the fault traces back to government red tape.
> When you get ready for those drastic steps which you mention perhaps you better consider my resignation as the first item.

Upon receipt of this note, Burruss immediately dispatched one to Norris in which he disclaimed any and all intention of criticizing him either personally or professionally. "All of us," he wrote, "have been under such unusual strain recently that I do not wonder that you like myself have been misunderstanding each other." Burruss then expressed his deep appreciation for the manner in which Norris had assumed responsibility for the airport. Of the director, however, he insisted, "He is a good fellow in many ways and I have no doubt he means well, but his peculiar procedures at times are quite troublesome." Then coming more directly to the problem at hand, he paid the following well-deserved compliment to his overworked dean of engineering:

> All of the remarkably fine efforts you have made, and the valuable results you have achieved for VPI are appreciated beyond measure. Don't take my "drastic steps" too seriously—may be my blood pressure was too high! When General Jackson died, General Lee said he had lost his right arm. I am far from being a Lee, but I should feel as Lee did if for any reason you should be lost to VPI—such a loss is unthinkable.
> Cheer up!

Dean Norris did cheer up and continued to work so diligently on behalf of VPI that the Board of Visitors in 1967 named one of the new engineering buildings Norris Hall in his honor.

Ironically, neither Burruss nor Norris checked up on the alleged peculiar behavior of the director of aeronautics. As a result, they were both involved at a later period in a widely-publicized, unpleasant situation in which this same director was charged with having misused state funds.

The many abnormal factors generated by the war helped create a controversial situation, which came to a head on the campus during the summer of 1942. The Corps of Cadets, sincerely believing that it had been shamefully treated by Dr. Burruss with respect to his handling of their complaints about the mess hall, organized a mass demonstration of protest. About midnight on July 27, 1942, the Corps in civilian clothes but in regular formation under cadet officers, marched to the president's home. Upon arrival, a proclamation of protest against Burruss' action was read, an effigy was burned, and at a signal from the bugler, a few minutes of "shouting, yelling, and band playing followed." Then, still in formation, the Corps marched back to barracks. Beyond this point, accounts attempting to explain why the incident happened, who was to blame for its happening, and the consequences of its having happened differ with varying degrees of divergence and emotional tones. Whatever may have been the real cause, the demonstration created a sensation. The United States was at war; therefore, to some it appeared that cadets enrolled in one of the country's largest military schools had rebelled in time of war. Newspapers and radio in and out of the state gave the incident coverage ranging from the factual to the sensational. Broadcasts from Germany reported that the students in one of the large military colleges in the United States had revolted. All in all, a fantastically large tempest was generated in a rather small teapot.

Beyond the shadow of a doubt, this is one of those events which should not have happened but which did happen. In all fairness, it can be said that fault rested with both the administration and with the Corps. Any alumnus can testify that grumbling about the food and the way it is prepared has never been a monopoly belonging to any one class or period in Tech's history. In fact, it is a matter of record that every administration in VPI's first century had to face this problem at one time or another. Many circumstances contributed to the unusual flare-up in the summer of 1942. The students had moved from the spring to the summer quarter with almost no vacation. The senior class had not undergone the maturing experience of ROTC camp. The drastically restricted travel of automobiles through Blacksburg caused by rationing of gasoline and tires practically eliminated weekend hitchhiking, and no formalized programs of recreation, entertainment, or intercollegiate athletics were in operation. Sunday movies were not available, the library hours had not been properly adjusted for the weekends, uncertainties abounded on all sides with respect to the draft, and important as any factor, the customary easy formality of the summer session had given way to the rigorous military discipline needed in preparation for war.

The high wages at the Radford Ordnance Works had lured most of the trained workers from the mess hall, 250 replacements having been hired between July 1, 1941, and June 30, 1942, for a work force of 35. Many of these newcomers were completely unreliable and just as completely inefficient and indifferent. As a result, the conditions in the mess hall had become downright sloppy, if not actually unsanitary. The deterioration had begun during Cochran's tenure as commandant. At Cochran's request, Burruss had appointed a student-faculty committee with the commandant as chairman, to hear complaints and suggest remedies. Cochran, who repeatedly stated that student "growling" about food and the mess hall was a normal "habit" which usually led to trouble only when the boys felt that no one in authority would listen to their complaints, had kept this committee busy. Apparently the committee did more listening than acting, although it did recommend that the steward, A. A. Henderson make a number of changes. Henderson had attempted to comply with practically all of the suggestions made to him not only by Cochran's committee but by some of the students as well; however, many of these attempts, because of the quality of the help, made matters worse instead of better. As one result of these "backfires," Henderson had become a little less than enthusiastic about spending any more time listening to student suggestions for improving the mess-hall conditions. He did continue to work with the authorized committee, but unfortunately many students did not know this.

Burruss had cooperated fully with Cochran's committee whenever it had sought his help, but he fully expected the committee, not himself, to take the initiative in attending to mess-hall complaints. Colonel Wilson, who had succeeded Cochran as commandant, had continued the student-faculty mess-hall committee but had not had time to inaugurate any significant changes. By this time, Burruss was seldom seen on the campus at other than strictly official college functions. Many students who did not attend these functions claimed they had never seen him at all. As one result of this seeming isolation from campus affairs the erroneous impression that Burruss was not interested in student welfare had grown both with students and younger faculty members.

By late July, student dissatisfaction with the mess hall rose to a fever pitch. A committee of five students was appointed to collect all complaints. *The Virginia Tech* reported on the student unrest and wrote a strong editorial urging immediate action toward improved conditions. *The Roanoke Times* carried a story within a few days based on the *Tech's* editorial and report. The *Times* story was not complimentary of the mess-hall situation. In midmorning before Burruss had seen the morning newspaper, he was queried over the telephone by a reporter of *The Roanoke World-News,* the afternoon newspaper. The result of this conversation, appearing on the front page of the afternoon newspaper, inflamed the students. To many of them it seemed that Dr. Burruss had deliberately denied their claims that undesirable conditions existed at the mess hall. To others, it appeared that he had used the newspaper in an effort to brand them publicly as liars. That night they executed the protest march to his home. Included in the proclamation that the students read was a demand that Burruss retract his statement "as it appeared in *The Roanoke World-News.*"

The demonstration amazed Burruss. The mess-hall committee had been receiving and discussing complaints, but according to Burruss they had not brought a single complaint to his attention. In addition to the mess-hall committee, Burruss had appointed a student-welfare committee to help deal with problems of student life. As far as he could determine, no complaint had been registered with this committee either. Since the quarterly meeting of the board was scheduled for Thursday, July 30, arrangements were made for the student committee to present its list of grievances to Burruss and then to the board. Upon receipt of the list, Burruss was surprised to find included in the grievances a number of conditions which he knew to have been corrected. This discovery when pointed out to the board influenced the attitude of this body toward the student representative when he appeared before it to present the student complaints. As a result, the board "after a lengthy discussion of the situation" left the matter in Burruss' hands for settlement, and the students continued to seethe over the entire affair.

Colonel Wilson called the senior class together on Wednesday, August 5, and read out in detail the military punishment imposed for its participation in the nighttime demonstration. After some heated discussions, the class decided "to accept cheerfully the punishment." Apparently the matter had come to an end, but in reality it had not.

Within a few days, a lengthy letter written by "a son to his dad" which set forth the students' position was mimeographed in large quantities and offered to all students for the purpose of mailing home. This letter, which was published in a number of newspapers, in actuality shifted the students' complaint from an attack on the mess hall to an attack on Burruss' administration, particularly with respect to its handling of student affairs. The Board of Visitors also came in for some slaps. According to the letter, the board all too often merely acted to rubber-stamp Burruss' highhanded dictatorial decisions. Burruss' seclusion in his office and his failure to have any contacts with student leaders was also heavily criticized.

With the situation back in the press again, a few more ominous rumbles of discontent began to be heard. Suggestions that a state institution was being used to harbor "draft dodgers" were voiced. Opinions were expressed urging that the students be inducted into service at once. Rumors that "subversive influences" were operating within the Corps with the intention of sabotaging one of the country's largest military schools began to float around. Parts of a confidential letter Burruss had written to certain department heads "leaked out." In this letter, which had absolutely no connection whatever with the student unrest, Burruss had informed the department heads that a report had come to him that "an unidentified person" had been seen photographing some of the laboratories on the campus. In his letter, he had urged the department heads to exercise the precautions necessary to protect expensive and vital equipment. The leakage of portions of this letter quickly converted the "unidentified person" into a German spy ready to foment more rebellion. Perhaps the most absurd rumor, which no one on the campus, cadets or faculty, took seriously was that the Corps planned to march on the Radford Ordnance Works and blow it up. The only effect of this rumor was to excite some of the guards at this plant, who otherwise were leading a rather bored existence.

Governor Colgate Darden, as the wartime governor, took considerable interest in the entire affair. He visited the campus several times and interviewed both the student leaders and the college officials but declined to make any public statement. Then on August 11, probably at Darden's suggestion, the Board of Visitors held a special meeting to consider the situation. Darden attended this meeting. First, he informed the board that he had just received notice from representatives of the Third Service Area Headquarters Command that investigation had convinced them that no subversive activities of any sort were involved in the Corps' conduct. Then, Darden gave the board a gentle slap on the wrist. As the result of an investigation of his own, he said that he did not understand how the president of the institute had been able to carry the load he had been carrying and that he needed at least two individuals who would take over the management and control of the various utilities. To show that he meant what he said, he forthwith promised the board that he as governor would approve additional positions for administrative help for the president.

With this prodding from the governor, the board decided that a reorganization of the administrative work at the College was needed in order to provide Burruss some relief from the "overwhelming mass of detail" with which he had to deal. The actual plan of reorganization to follow was left to Burruss. In addition to this action, the board appointed a student-life committee to meet with the president at least once a month to consider "all matters that affect student life," a mess-hall committee "with power to act," and a senior-privileges committee to study the matter of senior privileges which had been abolished as a result of the demonstration. These committees, especially the first two, began to function at once, and the campus began a slow return to relative normalcy.

This entire summer episode had a far reaching effect on VPI. The committee of students and faculty set up to study the matter of senior privileges withdrawn on "Black Wednesday" by Colonel Wilson as a part of the punishment meted out for the demonstration, was never able to reach an agreement. After a number of meetings, the committee members agreed that they could not agree and returned the problem to the board. By the time this body met again, the war conditions were of such a nature that the entire matter seemed trivial. The board therefore decided to let the matter rest. It did so until the early post-war period, when the cadets, claiming that they had had nothing to do with the circumstances surrounding "Black Wednesday," succeeded in getting the matter put on a more satisfactory basis—to them at least. The most unfortunate outcome of this committee's deliberations, however, grew from the impression, whether correct or not, that Colonel Wilson was possessed of both a narrow and inflexible view of proper and improper military life and conduct in barracks. This impression persisted and eventually helped contribute to unrest on the part of army trainees later sent to the campus. Some of the faculty members close to the situation took an even more serious view of the matter and attributed the inability to agree, to the incompatibility of military training and true education. In the postwar era these individuals were not to be found in the group supporting the Corps.

As another outcome of the summer incident, every member of the board, not just a few, recognized the almost superhuman load the growth of VPI had placed on the aging Burruss. The charge leveled at it by the students of being a "rubberstamp board" that met only to carry out Burruss' recommendations also stung some members apparently unable to defend themselves against the charge. The action of the governor of the state in coming before the board and informing it frankly that the College needed two additional administrative persons was unparalleled in the history of the institution. As a result, the board took a look at the total situation and began planning to take a more active part in the administration of the College. It did not make drastic overnight changes, but no governor since the Corps' midnight march of 1942 has ever had a need to complain that VPI's administrative staff was undermanned.

As the summer waned, a number of students resigned and entered military service. As a result of the unpleasant experiences, some of these students as well as a number of those remaining on the campus acquired a very unfavorable image of an aging, overworked president.

In retrospect, it is obvious that Burruss never regained his full self-confidence after the incidents of the summer of '42, although most of the numerous letters he received from all over the country during the controversy expressed confidence in his ability to deal with the situation and pledged full support of his actions. At the same time, many of these same letters urged him to "go before the students more often." One alumnus expressed the conviction that if he only went before the students more often they would learn to "know, respect, admire, and who knows, maybe even love you." "Certainly your integrity, great accomplishments, and personal devotion to VPI deserve such treatment from all of us," he wrote.

Burruss could not bring himself to attempt a line of action so foreign to his true nature and at the same time not in keeping with his concept of the role of a president. He continued, if anything, to remain even closer to his office, but he did throw his full support back of the committees set up by the board. Before making decisions on any student affairs he often sought, by memorandum, advice from Colonel Wilson or Dean Williams. Two memorandums, one from Wilson and one from Williams, in answer to a request from Burruss for suggestions about dealing with a problem are quite revealing. A complaint about a situation in the mess hall which Burruss knew full well had been corrected came to his attention. He immediately wrote to Wilson, asking him if he could explain why the complaint persisted. "You did correct the situation," replied Wilson, "but you took care of the entire matter yourself without letting the students know that you were doing it." The advice from Williams was even more direct. Burruss had written to him, seeking his opinion as to the best way to handle a student petition. After evaluating Burruss' position, Williams added, "I would suggest that you not try to deal with the matter from a distance, but that you invite the students to your office for a discussion." If Burruss felt that the petition had to be denied, added Williams, "explain it to the students personally, do not knock it down with a typed memorandum." Burruss' response was to arrange a regular weekly schedule of meetings with the editors of *The Virginia Tech* to discuss problems of their choosing—and to increase memoranda, many of which he personally typed to his staff.

In spite of the unpleasant publicity attendant upon the incident of the summer, VPI opened in the fall with the largest enrollment in its history to that date. The loss of faculty to industry and the armed services, plus the uneven distribution of students among the several curricula, resulted in an unusually heavy demand for faculty in some departments and a greatly reduced demand in others. To meet this situation, a number of the faculty transferred from their regular departments and burned a little extra midnight oil as they attempted to keep at least one step ahead of the students in the unfamiliar courses they volunteered to teach. The results at times were surprising to both students and faculty but in general were satisfactory.

In the midst of the preparation for the war, the students petitioned for a course in race relations, which the surprised faculty approved and offered at the beginning of the winter quarter. Early in the year, it was announced that all juniors and seniors would be called up for service at the end of the winter quarter. This announcement caused a crop of wild rumors which in conjunction with those already afloat led to the establishment of a rumor clinic. This clinic was supposed to brand rumors for what they were and to expose them in such a way as to render them harmless. Almost overnight, disputes arose over whether the clinic laid rumors to rest or created new ones in exposing the old ones.

The departure of the junior and senior classes on February 27, 1943, to enter

active military duty left a distinct void on the campus and had an even greater
sobering effect on all left behind. The regular college program was continued for
the duration of the war; but following the departure of these two classes, the war
effort received top priority at all times.

On the evening of March 10 the entire College and community took time out
to honor Paul Derring for his twenty-five years of service at Tech. During the
ceremony held in the Student Activities Building (Squires Hall), and which came
as a complete surprise to Derring, he heard himself described by President Burruss,
as "the most trusted and most beloved man on the campus," and described by
W. W. Argabrite, Mayor, as Blacksburg's "best known and best beloved citizen."
Hundreds of letters of appreciation and commendation from former students,
friends, and associates were bound and presented to him in a single volume. Perhaps the highlight of the evening came when Paul's face broke into smiles of unre-
strained joy when Professor Harry Sanders on behalf of friends, presented him
with a studio piano for his beloved "Y" chapel. The next day a number of state
papers joined in the salute to this great leader of Tech's YMCA.

During the year the cadets, with funds provided by the College, constructed an
obstacle course at the lower end of the campus. This course having been completed,
the cadets spent hours wiggling through barrells, squirming under low hung wires,
scaling an eight-foot wall, and swinging across Stroubles Creek on a rope. Naturally, par was established for the time needed to run the course. Just as naturally,
some of the coeds tried the course and found they could "run it" successfully. Perhaps not as naturally, some of them easily bettered the par having been established
by the cadets. The interest in the obstacle course and its contribution to physical
fitness became so great that a number of faculty decided to run the course. Some
did so successfully. It seems best to leave the achievements of others unrecorded.

In February, 1943, it was reported that the College had been selected for the
Army Specialized Training Program (ASTP) and would be used to train Army
engineers. Later additional war training programs, including a naval pre-flight
unit and a Specialized Training and Reassignment (STAR) unit, were added. At
the program's peak, more than two thousand soldiers were on the campus at the
same time. Despite the confusion and uncertainties surrounding the coming and
going of these units, they merged into the campus community rather well. Each
unit retained its own identity as did the Corps of Cadets, with all units under the
command of Colonel Wilson, commandant. The full facilities of the College,
including the YMCA, the gymnasium, the Student Activities Building (Squires
Hall), and the athletic fields were made available to all units. Of the several Army
units sent to the campus, the ASTP was by far the most significant as far as impact
on the College was concerned. In discussing this unit and its relationship with the
college, John R. Hutcheson wrote in December, 1945:

> With the end of this term 386 students and trainees of the Army Specialized
> Training Program will leave the campus. Only a few reservists will return to
> begin the term starting in January. This will virtually end an interesting phase
> of the life of VPI during World War II. It is with a great deal of regret that we
> bid these young men goodbye and we sincerely hope that they will take with
> them pleasant memories of this period of their army life.
>
> There have been 3,387 young men enrolled at VPI in the Army Specialized
> Training Program since it was started [exclusive of STAR and other programs].
> On March 19, 1943, 186 men began the first term, and since that time the num-
> ber has fluctuated between this low and a maximum of more than 2,000. From

the beginning these young men have entered into the life of the school. They were matriculated in exactly the same manner as students have been throughout all the years. The courses they have taken have been recorded by the registrar and full college credit given for all but the course of the N-30, or Introductory Curriculum, which were below college level. Because of previous college training and their ASTP courses, forty-six men were able to obtain their engineering degrees from VPI while enrolled in the ASTP.

Hutcheson concluded his article by reasserting that the ASTP boys had indeed participated fully in all campus activities, both academic and nonacademic. To tell the full story of the contribution of VPI and its alumni to a nation engaged in global war is impossible at this time. On the home front, thousands of alumni moved into war work in industry, agriculture, business, and government. The extension service workers were particularly active in promoting food production and the conservation program. Teachers of vocational agriculture made significant contributions not only in the promotion of more food production and community canneries but also in the promotion of farm machinery repair programs. The contribution of alumni in the armed services was equally significant and far more spectacular. Once more a quotation from an article prepared by John R. Hutcheeson in 1946 can be used to present a brief summary of this contribution.

> Although VPI has long been recognized as one of the eight leading military colleges in the United States, a high percentage of its graduates devote their lives to civilian pursuits. When a national emergency arises, the military training which they have received here enables them to fit quickly into the picture. Prior to the outbreak of World War II only 87 of our former students were serving in the armed forces. On V. J. Day some 7000 were in uniform.
>
> How well these Techmen served is indicated by the fact that 4500 of them were officers. Fifty-eight per cent of our former students were in the service and 90 per cent of our graduates were commissioned. In the army and the marine corps were 5 major generals, 10 brigadier generals, 220 colonels and lieutenant colonels, 476 majors, 1216 captains, and more than 2000 lieutenants. In the navy, the coast guard, and the merchant marine there were 1 rear admiral, 8 captains, 11 commanders, 31 lieutenant commanders, 125 lieutenants and 385 lieutenants junior grade and ensigns. Three hundred one Techmen made the supreme sacrifice, 755 were decorated, and three were awarded the Congressional Medal of Honor. I know of no land-grant college with a better military record.

Major General C. R. (Scribe) Moore ('16) was the chief engineer officer for the entire European Theater of Operations. Brigadier General L. A. (Abbie) Pick ('14) was given credit for having built the Stillwell Road from Burma to Ledo, which even before completion was dubbed as "Pick's Pike."

The Techgram throughout the entire period performed an amazing task of keeping up with the alumni in service and recording pertinent information concerning their activities. Letters from over the world poured into Alumni Secretary Redd's office, expressing surprise and delight experienced by Techmen upon receipt of copies of this publication, so ably edited by R. H. McNeil.

The three Techmen receiving the Congressional Medal of Honor aroused a deep sense of pride not only in the Tech family but throughout the entire country as well.

Second Lieutenant Robert E. Femoyer ('44), a native of Huntington, West Virginia, received the medal for action over Germany in a "Flying Fortress." He piloted his anti-aircraft riddled plane back to safety in England, saving the lives of his crew, although mortally wounded himself. He died in a hospital one hour after landing his plane on November 2, 1944. Femoyer Dormitory was named in his honor.

First Lieutenant James W. Monteith, Jr. ('41), a native of Richmond, Virginia, received the medal for action on the Normandy beachhead while leading his men out of a Nazi trap. He led his men through obstacles of barbed wire, mines, and fire to a position above shore that meant that his unit had established its objective. He was then killed in leading his men in a charge that strengthened the hard-won position. Monteith Hall was named in his honor.

Sergeant Herbert J. Thomas ('41), a native of Charleston, West Virginia, received the medal for heroism on Bougainville (Pacific Campaign) November 7, 1943. While his squad was attacking a machine gun nest, a live grenade fell in their midst. Thomas immediately threw himself on top of the grenade and was killed by its explosion but saved the lives of the men in his squad. Thomas Hall was named in his honor.

As the heroism of these and thousands of other Techmen continued to be reported, the press of the state devoted more and more commendatory attention to what one paper referred to as "The Tech Triumph." After one presentation, one state daily said of the alumni activities, "It is a record of which Virginians, alumni or not, may be proud. It is a record in keeping with the traditions of the Institute and of the State."

Although VPI channeled its energies into the war programs, it continued most of the activities conducted by and for the regular students. A special drive headed by Dr. Mildred T. Tate, dean of women and head of the home economics department, began bringing an increasing number of coeds to the campus. *The Virginia Tech* with J. Beverley Jones as editor delighted some faculty members and needled others with its editorials calling for more cultural education for the engineer. Because of the rapid departure of editors to the service, the *Tech* suspended publication at the end of the fall quarter 1944 "for the duration." The Maroon Mask was suspended by Colonel Wilson during the same quarter, because some of the actors in presenting "The Male Animal," had given unusual emphasis to the "profanity" in the script; in fact, where convenient the players had added a few choice "cuss words" of their own. The cadets and the army trainees in the audience knowing that Wilson was trying to enforce what they considered to be an extremely narrow code of "no profanity," had reacted to the stage "profanity" with howls of laughter and rounds of applause. Wilson had taken offense at such effrontery and had banned the dramatic organization. Some of the faculty who did not feel that Wilson's action was justified but who did not want to be labeled as "pro-profanity" thereupon encouraged the students and helped them write and produce plays through channels other than the Maroon Mask. Since Colonel Wilson never attended these plays, the excitement of baiting the commandant with "cuss words" died down, and home produced profanity and the Maroon Mask disappeared from the stage of Burruss Hall for the duration.

VPI discontinued football for the fall of '43 and '44. VMI, however, continued to play and arranged a game with the University of Maryland in Roanoke on Thanksgiving Day 1943. The VPI Highty-Tighties were extended an invitation, which they accepted, to attend the game. The band under the leadership of Cadet Captain N. B. Evens, according to *The Roanoke Times* ". . . did not enact their role perfunctorily. They entered into the spirit of the occasion and played the VMI school songs as lustily as they could have performed if they had been playing for their own. . . . The VMI cadets reciprocated . . . by giving the VPI yell and singing the "Tech Triumph" . . . in unison to chant the praises . . . of their keenest—and dearest—rivals."

The editor of the *Roanoke Times,* Powell Chapman, whose own son, a VPI alumnus of the class of '40, had been killed only a month before, concluded his editorial with the following comment:

> With America at war, and VMI and VPI alumni serving side by side in the armed forces of their country in every quarter of the globe it was supremely fitting that the spectators at the Thanksgiving game should be afforded this impressive and never-to-be-forgotten demonstration of the fact that the cadets of VMI and VPI, though rivals are friends, bound together by mutual ties.

The Techgram, after commenting in happy vein on the band parade and half-time maneuvers, noted that "the band members sat with VMI rooters. Whether the Techmen cheered for VMI or Maryland is a deeply guarded 'military secret.' "

A succession of young army officers were sent to the campus to serve in the several military units. On occasion, reports from cadets, parents, and faculty members reached Burruss' desk complaining of excessive adherence to military protocol on the part of the "young shavetails." These reports upset Burruss, who felt that the wartime conditions prevented him from taking any action in such cases. Once in passing one such complaint on to Dean Norris, he said in exasperation, "It does seem to be true that it is easier to get justice from a major general than from a second lieutenant." Behind the scenes Burruss made a number of efforts to make life more comfortable for the cadets. Publicly, he continued to give his backing to all constituted authorities.

With the cessation of publication of *The Virginia Tech* and of *The Virginia Tech Engineer* "for the duration," *The Techgram* assumed even greater importance as a medium of communication among the several segments of the college community, the public, and the alumni. The student body, recognizing that the rapid departure of editors to military service made it virtually impossible to continue the student publications as usual, resigned themselves to reading the more serious *Techgram* and to searching for other do-it-yourself means of entertainment.

By April, 1943, Burruss had not made any progress in implementing the administrative reorganization of the College indicated by the board's resolution of the preceding August. Reporting this fact to the board he said, "The difficulty is of course in personnel. There are numerous and sensitive personnel situations which must be handled tenderly and gradually. . . . It is necessary to proceed rather slowly in the selection of men for important positions . . . and there are very few acceptable men to be found . . . unless we can raid other institutions." Since the mess-hall situation had been settled and the College seemed to be moving along smoothly, the board did not press Burruss to speed up the reorganization. As it later turned out, this fact did not go unnoticed by certain state newspaper editors, who, while extremely friendly to VPI, nonetheless felt that the college administration from the board on down was less than agressive in adjusting to the changing conditions.

On May 1, 1943, Dean John E. Williams at the age of seventy-six died after a lengthy illness. Williams' passing removed one of the most popular, best-known, and most effective teacher-administrators the College had ever had. A number of persons recognized this fact but none more keenly than Burruss. After a heartfelt tribute to his departed colleague, Burruss announced that it would take some time to select a person to fill the vacancy left by Williams' death. Before any action could be taken toward filling the vacancy, Robert S. Moss, rector of the Board of Visitors for seventeen years, and a member for nearly twenty-five, died at his home in Burkes Garden.

The loss of these two men, both of whom had served side by side with him during his entire term as president, was a severe blow to Burruss. He felt particularly lost without having the help of Williams, who, as Dean Norris expressed it, was actually serving as director of admissions, dean of the college, and dean of students. The summer quarter following Williams' death opened amidst considerable turmoil. Units of the ASTP, the STAR, the naval flight program, and the special engineering program for girls, were getting under way at the same time instruction for the regularly enrolled students was starting. The program at the VPI airport was moving with bewildering confusion. Faculty were leaving for military service, and recruits were desperately needed to replace them in certain vital areas. Some departments were overstaffed with faculty. Other departments were understaffed. In addition to the activities connected with the several instructional programs, contracts with the War Department relative to the training of the military units had to be executed. With all of these demanding activities swirling about him, Burruss needed help more than ever. Fortunately, his highly efficient executive secretary, R. L. Humbert, proved to be a tower of strength in helping him with the government contracts. As a result, Humbert prior to his transfer to Third Service Headquarters in Baltimore soon found himself filling a vital role in connection with these contracts.

Before the summer quarter was two weeks old, Burruss realized he needed help in the office of the dean of the college. Above all, he wanted a man who could work with the faculty, the public, the students, the alumni,—and with himself. He looked about him and decided he had such a man in C. P. (Sally) Miles. He was correct, and at Burruss' request "Sally" Miles moved into the office of the dean of the college on July 19, 1943. At this point, the records become a bit confused. It is not clear whether Burruss intended to appoint Miles as acting dean pending the approval of the board or if he intended his appointment to be a permanent one. Apparently the board did not know either. But before this body could convene and get reorganized following the death of the rector so many expressions of delight and approval of Miles' appointment to the deanship had poured in from all over the state and from alumni all over the world that the board took no further action in the matter. It is known, however, that at least one of the younger board members, while approving of Miles as dean, did raise a question about the division of authority between the board and Burruss.

Before Burruss had settled the problem of a successor to Williams, another problem had arisen which kept the campus in a state of some uncertainty for some time. In May, Governor Darden had announced his proposal that VPI and Radford College be merged under the VPI Board of Visitors. No details for the proposed merger had been announced; but since the idea was in harmony with the efforts of nearly two decades to restrict and reduce the number of state-supported institutions of higher education, the proposal drew almost immediate support from the press. Burruss reacted to the report, in public at least, with surprising apathy, if not complete indifference.

In September, 1937, when a president was being sought for Radford College to succeed the deceased John P. McConnell, Burruss had written to E. Lee Trinkle, chairman of the State Board of Education, urging that board to select as president a man who would cooperate with VPI in promoting programs designed to improve rural living. Just such a man had been appointed in the person of Dr. David W. Peters. Now less than six years later with an opportunity to work for cooperative programs, Burruss felt too busy to give the matter consideration. In reply to Governor Darden's request that he serve on a commission to study the matter of consolidation of the two schools, Burruss wrote in part, "At present I am greatly loaded with duties resulting from efforts to maintain the finances of the College. . . . For the reason stated, together with a large amount of work of unusual types, I trust that it will not be necessary for me to attend any meeting at a distance in the month of July." The surprised governor wrote back and asked Burruss to notify the Board of Visitors that the study of the proposed merger was to take place.

At the regular meeting of the board held in August, 1943, Burruss, after presenting an eleven-page mimeographed report filled with statistical data and other information relating to the physical well-being of the College and the students, informed the board that *The Techgram* of August 1 had "an interesting article concerning the suggestion of the governor for the amalgamation of . . . the State Teachers' College at Radford with the Virginia Agricultural and Mechanical College and Polytechnic Institute." "Certainly we must not let prejudice direct our actions, and whatever is done must be for the welfare of the Commonwealth of Virginia," he informed the board. Beyond this rather noncommittal reference to the proposed merger, Burruss does not seem to have given the matter of an "amalgamation" much further thought, then or later. One member of the board thought the matter deserved more attention. Upon hearing that the governing board of the University of Virginia had held at least two meetings at which the matter of "amalgamation" of the University with Mary Washington College in Fredericksburg had been discussed, this individual wrote to Colonel J. P. Woods, who had succeeded the deceased Moss as rector of the VPI board, and suggested that the VPI board should meet to consider the matter. Woods did not think a board meeting was necessary, "since the matter was proceeding smoothly."

As the matter "proceeded smoothly," it was announced that John B. Spiers of Radford, able representative of Montgomery County and Radford in the House of Delegates, had been asked to prepare the bill for legislative action needed in order to consolidate the two schools. Considerable excitement developed on the Blacksburg campus when it was alleged that Spiers had promised to draft his bill in such a way as to help Radford College. When it appeared from the actual bill that one method of achieving this objective was to deny permission for all undergraduate women to reside on the Blacksburg campus, this excitement became intensified. The Corps of Cadets met and passed a resolution urging the retention of coeds at Blacksburg and even raised money to help defray expenses of a coed committee to go to Richmond to speak against this feature of the merger. Faculty members urging student moderation were immediately branded as "anti-coed." A mimeographed statement purporting to show the effect of the passage of the bill upon women's education was prepared and distributed over the state. The *Radford News Journal* added further fuel to the fire when in discussing the bill it said, "As written now it would appear that Radford State Teachers College is amply protected." Women's clubs and women's organizations over the state denounced features of the bill which they thought discriminated against women. Finally after much debate and excitement, most of it outside the legislature, a compromise, which under certain conditions permitted a few women to be domiciled on the Blacksburg campus, was reached. A bill embodying these compromises was then introduced into the Senate by Senator Leonard Muse of Roanoke and eventually was passed by both houses and was signed into law by Governor Darden on March 16, 1944.

The act changed the name of the institution from Virginia Agricultural and Mechanical College and Polytechnic Institute to Virginia Polytechnic Institute. Radford College was to be known as Radford College, Women's Division of the Virginia Polytechnic Institute. Both institutions were to be operated under the one Board of Visitors of the Virginia Polytechnic Institute. The president of the Virginia Polytechnic Institute was to become the chancellor of Radford College, which was to retain its own presidency. Radford was also "to retain as far as practicable, its separate institutional life." The bothersome question of housing of women students was partly solved by permitting women over twenty-one years of age, women residing in Blacksburg or vicinity, and graduate students, to enroll on the Blacksburg campus. An additional provision was included which permitted the Board of Visitors to permit other women enrolling in certain curricula to live on the Blacksburg campus. The Board of Visitors was to be increased to sixteen (later amended to fifteen) members, four of whom were to be women.

Additional features covering the consolidation of the two schools were included in the bill, but can be omitted here. The full board met for the first time at Radford College on June 27, 1944. Most of this meeting was given over to consideration of matters pertaining to Radford College and to plans for implementing the provisions of the legislative act consolidating the two schools. At the November meeting it was decided to adopt a committee plan for carrying on the board's work. In addition to an executive committee, a personnel and curriculum, a buildings and grounds, an agriculture, a student relations, and a rules committee were organized. The duties of each committee were defined and provisions made for special committees, one of which was listed as a committee on the consolidation of the schools. The committee plan for conducting board affairs proved to be very effective in getting the entire board familiar with and involved in the operation of the two schools. Fortunately, this plan was in operation as the College faced a number of unusual, unexpected crises within the next few years.

The major difficulty facing the board in implementing the consolidation was arriving at a decision concerning the operation of the home economics departments in existence on both campuses prior to the consolidation. This problem was turned over to a committee for study and recommendations. Neither this committee nor the board was ever able to arrive at a decision completely satisfactory to all parties concerned, but decisions were reached on this and other matters; and the merger of the two schools was continued until 1964, when by mutual agreement it was decided to dissolve the partnership and permit each school to seek and develop its own destiny.

Following the consolidation of the schools, Dr. Burruss continued his attitude of apparent indifference about the entire matter despite numerous overtures from some of his staff and from Dr. Peters of Radford to explore avenues of cooperation in areas other than home economics. A number of the staff were critical of Burruss for the way he had handled the entire VPI-Radford merger. Other staff members, closer to the administration of the College, were more tolerant. They concluded that Burruss was allowing himself to be swamped with the business and financial details of running the College. They also recognized the great contribution Burruss had made to VPI during his quarter of a century as president. In May, some members of this group had suggested that a "small banquet" be arranged to honor Burruss' twenty-fifth anniversary as president. This proposal was received with such enthusiasm that the "small banquet" was changed to a "simple dinner" to be held in the college dining hall in order to seat the more than five hundred persons, who despite the hardships of wartime travel, expressed a desire to attend.

The "simple dinner" was held on June 22, with Dr. John R. (Jack) Hutcheson serving as toastmaster. Governor Darden was in attendance. He praised Burruss for the tremendous advances that had been made under his administration. "Not only do I speak for myself," he said, "but for the nearly three million citizens of the Commonwealth when I tell you how proud we are. Your standing among our great citizens rests secure." Dr. Walter S. Newman, president of the Alumni Association, pointed out that the rebirth of constructive alumni activities came during the early years of Burruss' administration. The alumni, said Newman, had taken an increasingly greater interest in the institution as Burruss had made it an increasingly dynamic force in the Commonwealth. Dr. J. W. (Quiz) Watson, speaking on behalf of the faculty, enumerated the many advances that had been made under Burruss' leadership. At the conclusion of his remarks, he "presented Dr. Burruss with handsomely printed and bound highlights of the 1919-1944 era." The title page was illustrated by Mrs. W. H. Rasche, beloved artist of Blacksburg. Signatures of forty-one persons who had been faculty members throughout the quarter century were appended at the end of the volume. Dr. William T. Sanger, president of the Medical College of Virginia, spoke as a personal friend and as an official from another state college. Dr. Burruss had been successful, he explained, because he early developed a plan that was right and spent ceaseless effort to execute it. Then, as recorded in *The Techgram,* he made a statement which the college community would have occasion to recall within the year. "The college president," he said, "is apt to receive too much praise when things go right and too little consolation when things go wrong." Colonel J. P. Woods, rector of the board, after jesting that Governor Darden had always been sympathetic with VPI's aims, but that sympathy was not enough when money was needed, touched the highlight of the evening—he announced that the Board of Visitors by unanimous vote had named the Teaching and Administration Building the Julian A. Burruss Hall in honor of Dr. Burruss. This announcement was received with enthusiasm by the audience, and as *The Techgram* reported it, "The dinner was judged a great success."

Even before the pleasant echoes from this dinner had begun to wane, a discordant note was heard. The state auditor reported that some grave financial irregularities had been found in the operations of the VPI airport. The Board of Visitors immediately appointed a committee to make a full investigation of the entire matter. This investigation, a real ordeal for Burruss, was not only thorough but was far-reaching. While it completely absolved Burruss from any wrongdoing, the investigation also made abundantly clear what a number of persons had been suspecting for some time: namely, the ever-mounting pressure of the presidency and advancing age had taken their toll on Burruss and had been affecting his efficiency. Burruss' failure to secure the administrative help authorized by the board also was noted. The board decided to take matters into its own hands

Meeting in Roanoke on January 4, 1945, the board created the office of executive assistant to the president and named Dr. John R. Hutcheson, director of the Agricultural Extension Division, to the position. At the same time, the board granted Dr. Burruss a six-months leave of absence [the date] "to be determined by the rector and the president." Burruss and Hutcheson were directed to prepare a plan "defining their respective duties and activities. . ." under the new arrangements. Professor L. B. Dietrick was appointed acting director of the Agricultural Extension Division to serve "during the absence of Dr. Hutcheson."

The high esteem with which the board regarded both Burruss and Hutcheson was revealed by the resolution adopted and publicly announced by the board. This resolution follows in part:

> Recognizing the ardent, effective, and loyal services of our president and desiring to conserve his higher abilities and experience for the wider field of direction and supervision in the development and expansion of the institute, we do hereby establish the office of executive assistant to the president.

> Recognizing also the ability, talents, and resourcefulness of the director of one of our most important divisions, we therefore appoint Dr. John R. Hutcheson to be executive assistant to the president of the Virginia Polytechnic Institute, effective with the approval of this resolution. . . .

Dr. Hutcheson began to make immediate plans to transfer the extension work to Dietrick and to start upon his new duties. On January 8, he communicated to Burruss his availability and readiness to start planning for the division of responsibilities between the two. Before Burruss could reply and before the two men had an opportunity to confer, Burruss, on January 10, suffered a fractured vertebra in an automobile accident as he was en route home from Roanoke, where he had gone for medical advice. The board acted promptly in this unexpected emergency. On January 12, Rector Woods issued a full statement to the officials, the staff members, and the employees of VPI, informing them of the situation and announcing that Hutcheson had been requested, "to assume immediately all duties and activities of the president of the institution until such time as it is possible for him and Dr. Burruss to confer to carry out the direction of the board in the . . . resolution" [adopted by the board on January 4].

At the time of Woods' announcement, since the extent of Burruss' injuries was not known, it was commonly believed that he would be back in office shortly. Rector Woods, recognizing the touchy situation confronting Hutcheson as a result of the developments, appealed to the faculty to give Hutcheson its full support and cooperation as he gave up his duties as director of extension and familiarized himself with the duties of acting president. Hutcheson's outgoing personality and widespread popularity got this cooperative support almost overnight.

As the College began the winter quarter of 1945, however, it became clear that Dr. Burruss would not be able to resume his duties as president. The board meeting in Roanoke on May 15, 1945, recognized this fact and elected Burruss president emeritus, effective July 1 of the same year. At the same meeting, the board asked Hutcheson to continue as acting president and instructed the executive committee to bring in a recommendation for president at the August 14 meeting of the board. Hutcheson informed the board that he was not a candidate for the presidency but would accept the position "for a few years" if the board asked him to do so. By unanimous action the board on August 14, 1945, did "ask him to do so," and Dr. John Redd Hutcheson thereby became president of the Virginia Polytechnic Institute.

Perhaps one of the most fitting summaries of Dr. Burruss and his administration ever given in print is to be found in the rather lengthy resolution adopted by the board upon the occasion of his being elected president emeritus. This resolution follows:

> An era at Virginia Polytechnic Institute has closed. It was an era in which the institution made the greatest progress in its entire history. It was during this period that its student body had its greatest and most rapid growth. During this period the education program was increased many fold, and was expanded in graduate study and research.
>
> Dr. Burruss, the first alumnus president, and the late Dr. John E. Williams, dean of the college, were a great team working for a great and more useful Virginia Polytechnic Institute. Though different in personalities, the two divided the task in such a way that tremendous progress was made by the institute. Dean Williams quietly worked with the students and attended to educational matters, while Dr. Burruss devoted his unusual talents to expanding the services afforded to the industrial and agricultural interests of the state.
>
> The success of Dr. Burruss' administration was based on his persistent and tenacious adherence to objectives and ideals established during his early years at Virginia Polytechnic Institute. They remained as guiding principles throughout his administration of more than a quarter of a century.
>
> He has served his state and nation well by building a strong technical college which has graduated many men and women who are contributing much to the agricultural, industrial, professional, commercial, and scientific advancement of their country.
>
> VPI also has served most efficiently in training a great reservoir of officers for their country's armed forces. Of the 6,300 Techmen in the armed services 65 percent of them are officers largely because of the training they received at VPI.
>
> Dr. Burruss' planning, his resourcefulness, and his energy have combined to make his vision of a greater VPI a reality.
>
> It is most fitting that after 26 years of active service to VPI and the State of Virginia, Dr. Burruss should be permitted to live leisurely and comfortably close by the school he served so long, so faithfully, and so efficiently.
>
> It is most unfortunate that after such an active and useful career the injuries suffered last January should have contributed to a condition which renders him unable to again assume the strenuous duties of the president of VPI.

Dr. Burruss never fully recovered from the accident of January, 1945. Although he returned to the campus between long periods in the hospital, he avoided all public appearances, living quietly with his family until his death on January 4, 1947. The occasion of his death called forth an unusual outpouring of tributes to him by individuals and by the press. Two statements from the latter source seem a fitting farewell for this remarkable man:

> In a state which appreciates monuments to its heroes and its great men, there could be no finer or more fitting memorial for Dr. Julian A. Burruss than the Virginia Polytechnic Institute. He came to it as a vigorous educator in his prime and after 26 years of devoted service turned it over to his successor a magnificently expanded college of nation-wide reputation.—*Roanoke World-News*
>
> A great administrator he was! Virginia is debtor to him and will be for generations.—*Richmond News Leader*

Chapter 11

The Hutcheson Administration

1945-1947

J OHN REDD HUTCHESON was born on January 13, 1886, near Charlotte Court House, Virginia. After attending the public schools in Charlotte County, he entered VPI, where, as he was proud to relate, he worked his way through school. He earned the degrees of Bachelor of Science in 1907 and Master of Science in 1909. For the next two years he taught school at Middletown, Virginia, then moved to Mississippi, where he served as principal of the agricultural high school in Ellisville. During the summers of these years he served as an instructor at the University of Virginia. In 1914 he joined the Virginia Agricultural Extension Service as livestock specialist. In 1917 he was appointed assistant director and in 1919 director of the extension service by the Board of Visitors. This appointment was made on the same day that Dr. Burruss was elected president. During the more than a quarter of a century that he served as director of the extension service, he built up a national reputation as an agricultural leader. Clemson College recognized his contributions by conferring upon him in 1937 the degree of Doctor of Science. By the time he entered upon the duties as president of VPI, he had been accorded a number of national and state honors and had been elected to numerous honorary and social organizations.

Possessed of an outgoing personality, a liking for people, and a ready smile for everyone, Hutcheson was popular wherever he went. As a speaker once put it, "Jack Hutcheson to some and 'Dr. Jack' to others had the ability to walk with kings and keep the common touch—as well as his southside Virginia drawl."

In actuality, because of Burruss' illness, Hutcheson's administration began on January 4, 1945, when he was appointed executive assistant to the president. He had accepted the position of executive assistant, expecting Burruss to continue looking after the budget, buildings, and business affairs of the College while he, Hutcheson, took over the responsibilities for faculty, students, alumni, and general public relationships. Burruss' accident thrust all of these responsibilities on the unprepared Hutcheson. Yet another difficulty faced him. How far dared he go in making and implementing decisions which might not harmonize with President Burruss' policies and plans? In fact, what were Burruss' policies? Hutcheson set out to find an answer to this question and was overwhelmed with his discovery of the enormity of the amount of work Burruss had been carrying almost single-handed. He immediately appealed to the board for additional help. "If I am to continue serving as Acting President for any length of time," he wrote, "I cannot possibly handle all the business details of the Institute and at the same time look after its larger interests." To help meet the problem, he proposed that he be allowed to appoint "a well-trained business or financial manger." E. C. Miller, the currently designated business manager, he reported, confined his activities largely to the buildings and grounds. Besides, Miller wanted to retire at the end of the year.

The board reacted favorably to Hutcheson's proposal, whereupon he appointed Stuart K. Cassell ('32) as financial and business manager, the appointment to take effect March 1, 1945.

Stuart Cassell, born in Wythe County, Virginia, received his B.S. degree with honors, and his M.S. degree in agricultural economics in 1933. In 1939 he had been appointed state executive officer of the Agricultural Adjustment Administration in Virginia with headquarters in Blacksburg. In this position, he carried responsibility for general executive functions in the development, organization, supervision, and direction of all AAA programs in the state. This program had involved the handling of from $5,000,000 to $8,000,000 a year, with individual accounts being kept for more than 150,000 farmers. Cassell's efficiency and effectiveness in handling this far-reaching program had attracted favorable comment not only with Virginia officials but with federal officials as well. Hutcheson, who was thoroughly familiar with Cassell's work, wholeheartedly recommended him to the board as one who would quickly master the business and financial details involved in VPI's far-flung activities. At the suggestion of William E. Wine, board member, Cassell spent a short period of time with the treasurer and the state auditor studying the business and financial setup of the College and then proceeded to prove that Hutcheson's prediction was correct.

Hutcheson entered into his new job with vigor and enthusiasm. The college finances, he reported to the board, were in good shape but would be in trouble soon because of the declining enrollment, which in terms of regularly enrolled students fell from 3,382 in the spring of 1942 to 557 in the spring of 1944. The army trainees helped swell the enrollment slightly, but this program too was steadily shrinking numerically.

The Techgram continued its effective job of promoting good public relations by its vividly written condensations of campus activities and by its vignettes relating the activities of alumni at home and in service. Events affecting VPI reported in the state press were noted and sometimes reproduced in its pages, which went out to alumni and others. One appreciative alumnus in service, after reporting that *The Techgram* had followed him all over the world for two and a half years, wrote, "Just keep the boys informed, for *The Techgram* is read on every battlefront of a world at war." *The Techgram* was also read on the homefront in every state in the union as it went about its masthead proclaimed job of achieving "An informed Virginia Tech Alumni." If appreciative letters to the alumni secretary, H. B. "Puss" Redd, from alumni whose reunions had been discontinued "for the duration" can be used as criteria, this job was both well done and appreciated.

A few random events occurring during the winter and spring of 1945 as the College began thinking in terms of postwar problems may be mentioned. The spring quarter started with an enrollment of 411 students, with 201, the smallest number since 1893, enrolled in the Corps. Thirty-five veterans "some under the so-called G. I. Bill of Rights" returned to give the college a small inkling of things to come. Sherwood Eddy, brought to the campus by the YMCA, started furious debates by his talk entitled, "Russia, Friend or Foe?" The debates were inconclusive, but a few extremists wanted to censure the "Y" for being soft toward communism. Miss Carrie Sibold ('25) left the alumni secretary's office for temporary employment in Washington, D. C., and was succeeded by "Miss Liza" Akers. Miss Sibold soon returned to the alumni office, where she and "Miss Liza" soon became walking encyclopedias of information about Alumni affairs before their retirement in the sixties. The Board of Visitors struggled mightily to develop a working plan acceptable to all for the coordination of Radford and VPI. It succeeded only in the development of a plan. The Service Recreation Committee brought a number of professional and amateur entertainers and groups to the campus. Troupes of entertainers from nearby Roanoke were particularly cooperative in presenting performances which were always open to the public. Quin W. Stuart ('11) presented the College with a life-size portrait of Dean John E. Williams. A number of the faculty cooperated with the University of Virginia to teach off-campus extension courses. J. R. Abbitt ('21) was appointed as director of buildings and grounds to take office in July. The VPI extension in Danville, Virginia, was authorized by the board to open in the fall. A decision was made to resume football in the fall of 1945 with H. M. McEver ('29) and S. D. Tilson ('22) as coaches. The legislature authorized the Board of Visitors to create the office of vice-president for VPI. *The Virginia Tech* resumed publication in May. Cyrus Hankins ('11), president of the Alumni Association, was authorized to appoint a committee to start consideration of a suitable memorial commemorating alumni activities in World War II, and committee after committee made up of faculty was appointed to study and plan for post-war problems expected with the return of the veterans.

Hutcheson, or "Doctor Jack" as he was known to most of the campus, moved about with vigor and enthusiasm, but in keeping with his position as executive assistant to the president spoke in generalities about the future of the College. When the board, realizing the seriousness of Burruss' illness, appointed Hutcheson as acting president and at the same time elected the former to the position of president emeritus, Hutcheson felt freer to act without fear of offending Dr. Burruss. In actuality, Hutcheson's plans for VPI were nothing more than a strengthening of the college programs already begun by Burruss. He did envision the possibility of extending the influence of these programs beyond state borders, but the College was to be developed as a technical and agricultural school. "Our dream at VPI," he asserted, "is to develop the present school into the greatest technical and agricultural school in the South and one of the greatest in the United States." To accomplish this objective, he repeated over and over, would necessitate the recruitment of a strong faculty. "Teachers," he declared, "are far more important to an institution of learning than expensive buildings, modern stadiums, and up-to-date equipment." Hutcheson's philosophy was sweet music to the ears of conservative Virginia. Therefore, when he was elected president of VPI on August 14, 1945, expressions of approval were voiced throughout the state. Apparently no one thought to remind Hutcheson or the applauding press that the recruitment and the retaining of a strong faculty was in and of itself an expensive business. Hutcheson discovered this important fact for himself, however, before the end of his first year in office.

In the meantime, other incidents in the life of the College took place. On the same day the board elected Hutcheson president, it appointed L. B. Dietrick director of the Agricultural Extension Service. Since "Deet" Dietrick had been serving this agency in a number of capacities since 1923, he was able to move into his new position with a smooth efficiency which eliminated the period of uncertainty usually following a change of administration.

Shortly after the college community learned of Hutcheson's elevation to the presidency, the announcement of Japan's surrender was made to the world. Obviously this announcement had nothing to do with Hutcheson's election to the presidency, but the students reacted swiftly. They marched to Hutcheson's home and serenaded him; then they gathered near the traffic light at "the corner." Here "the madly milling crowd blocked traffic and demonstrated wildly to rival pre-Thanksgiving Day cheer-fests of yester-year." A holiday from classes was announced for the next day. The War Department granted the army students a second holiday. Needless to say, the Administrative Council quickly decided that the "second day holiday also would apply to Tech students."

Following this two-day celebration, the students settled into a period of excited normalcy as they awaited the summer quarter commencement exercises. Colonel R. B. H. Begg, speaker on this occasion, bluntly informed the listeners that although the war was over, peace had not been won. "Can we carry over into peace the energy, determination, courage, and spirit of cooperation that we used to such good effect during the war," he asked, "or are we going to slip back into our habitual attitude of selfishness and distrust of our neighbors at home and abroad, which has unfortunately characterized so much of our life in the past?" Neither the excited students nor the faculty took time to ponder an answer to this significant question as both began feverish preparation for the fall quarter to open within the next ten days.

The fall quarter got under way with *The Techgram*'s headlining: "VPI's Football, Enrollment Begin Comeback." The comeback enrollment, nearly double that of the previous quarter, looked more promising than the comeback of football. The Gobblers dropped their first encounter 14-0 to the University of North Carolina, their second 38-0 to William and Mary. Their third game, an upset 21-13 victory over the University of Maryland, was followed in quick succession by defeats from the University of Virginia, North Carolina State, and Clemson. A weak University of Richmond eleven was defeated 44-6 in Miles Stadium, only to be followed by VMI's winning the renewed "Military Classic" 7-0 on Thanksgiving Day.

A. F. (Matty) Matthews' skillful reporting in *The Techgram* of all games managed to take much of the sting of defeat out of the poor season. In fact, Matthews was so good along this line that one disgruntled alumnus insisted that his reports had VPI winning every game in all respects except on the score board.

The record of the comeback enrollment, which showed 833 regular students and 433 soldiers enrolled for the fall quarter, was pleasing for the present and frightening for the future. This record when combined with other statistics clearly forecast that VPI would be swamped with applicants for admission far beyond the capacity of the College. Hutcheson kept this forecast before the public and before the faculty as he worked tirelessly to prepare the campus for the expected avalanche. His job was formidable. The return of faculty from military service was irregular and uncertain. The dormitories had received little if any repair during the war years. The dining facilities were limited and in need of overhauling. Most disturbing of all, neither the College nor the town had living accommodations for married students.

Hutcheson was faced with another and more subtle problem. A number of the department heads and key faculty members, giants in their prime, were now aging giants unwilling to accept the fact that time had taken its toll of their vigor and vision. Dr. Burruss had struggled with this same problem and had succeeded in getting a weak retirement system set up whereby faculty members unable to perform full duties could be continued on the faculty with a reduced work load and a correspondingly reduced salary. Burruss had not been happy with the system, which he considered to be entirely inadequate, but he had accepted it as being better than no system at all. The state of Virginia was attempting to set up a retirement system covering all state employees; but during Hutcheson's administration, the state system offered almost no help to employees already beyond sixty-five years of age. Since most of Hutcheson's problems related to employees past seventy, seventy-five, and even eighty years of age, he had to solve these problems within the VPI retirement system. Furthermore, time had not depleted the energy and vigor of the staff at a uniform rate; it often was necessary for one individual seventy-two years of age to be placed in the retirement system while another individual would be retained on full salary until seventy-five or more. Someone had to make a decision as to when each faculty member went on the reduced-work-reduced-salary schedule. Burruss on numerous occasions had informed the board of how unpleasant it was to make this decision, but he had never avoided making it when he thought the interests of the College demanded it. As a result, some individuals felt that he had been both ruthless and dictatorial toward some of the older faculty. In an effort to avoid this criticism of his approach to the problem, Hutcheson personally contacted each staff member showing decreased vigor because of age and solicited that individual's preference as to his work load. To his surprise and dismay, every individual contacted replied by insisting that his health, vigor, and interest were such that he desired to continue teaching a full load. One individual, in addition to believing that the condition of his health, vigor, and interests was highly satisfactory, listed as further assets for the arduous tasks of full-time teaching, his good digestive system and a clear conscience which, he said, permitted him to sleep eight hours a day without worrying about misdeeds committed against his fellow man. The none-too-subtle sarcasm involved in this reply did not go unnoticed by Hutcheson, who at the time was suffering from an extreme case of insomnia and indigestion. The reply did not contribute to the cure of either malady.

Before Hutcheson had time to do more than identify the major problems facing the College, pressures for immediate solution to some of them began to pile up. This pressure was becoming acute with respect to some problems in the school of agriculture, which had begun to receive unfavorable publicity. In the summer of 1945, the Glade Spring Farmers' Club, dissatisfied with the work of the Agricultural Experiment Station, addressed letters of complaint to the Board of Visitors, the governor, and the Associated Press. At the same time, it was known that segments of the horticultural industry in the state were dissatisfied with the progress being made at the College in research and teaching in the field of horticulture. Ironically, some staff members in the school of agriculture had been aware of the existing situation, which they felt had resulted primarily from a lack of financial support for the Experiment Station and from an excessively conservative outlook on the part of its director, A. W. Drinkard.

Hutcheson, while defending the quality of the work done at the station, readily admitted that serious gaps existed in its program of research. Insisting that such gaps resulted primarily from lack of financial support, he surprised and shocked the critics, as well as the state at large, with statistics showing that practically every state in the union, especially the surrounding states, supported their agricultural experiment stations far better than Virginia was supporting hers. During the controversy both H. L. Price, dean of agriculture, and A. W. Drinkard, Jr., director of the Experiment Station, expressed a willingness, almost an eagerness, to relinquish their jobs to younger men. Arrangements were made to achieve this switch, and Dr. T. B. Hutcheson ('06), head of the department of agronomy, was appointed as dean of agriculture, and Dr. H. N. Young, head of the department of agricultural economics, was appointed director of the Agricultural Experiment Station. Both appointments, although announced in mid-November, were to take effect on January 1, 1946. Dean Price, already past seventy, retired under the VPI retirement plan, while Dr. Drinkard transferred to other administrative work in the station until he retired at a later date.

Dissatisfaction with the work in horticulture was partly solved when members of the Virginia State Horticultural Society purchased land adjacent to the Blacksburg-Christiansburg road and leased it with the intention of selling it to the College if the legislature made the needed appropriation. Such an appropriation eventually was made, and work was begun on the present "horticultural farm," or VPI arboretum so attractive to visitors.

In the fall of 1945, a faculty committee requested permission to arrange a suitable ceremony inaugurating Dr. Hutcheson as president. The College had been served by many presidents, said the committee, but never in its history had it held an inaugural ceremony. The surprised "Dr. Jack" thanked the committee but quickly vetoed the idea. The committee thereupon switched from an inaugural ceremony to a reception honoring the new president and his wife, the popular Eleanor Parrott Hutcheson. At this happy affair, Professor W. H. (Bosco) Rasche, on behalf of the faculty, presented President Hutcheson with an illuminated copy of a faculty resolution pledging full support of his administration. At the same time, another resolution was prepared and sent to the Board of Visitors, warmly congratulating this body for its "happy choice of Dr. Hutcheson" as president.

From the day he assumed administrative responsibilities for the College, Hutcheson adopted an open-door policy toward students, faculty, alumni, and friends. He called faculty meetings at which he discussed problems and plans for the College. He visited departments and solicited advice and suggestions from all. The telephone largely replaced Burruss' memorandums as a means of communication with individuals of the faculty. Informal receptions were given for faculty members from the Radford and Blacksburg campuses. His appearances on the sidelines at football practice surprised and delighted the football squad —and raised questions in the minds of the coaches. His frequent attendance at student social events received favorable comment from all, while his often repeated statement to alumni chapters that the aim of the administration was to make VPI "one of the finest schools of its kind in the United States" was received with the enthusiasm of a touchdown over VMI.

To many of the older faculty members, Hutcheson's activities were reminiscent of Burruss in his earlier days. To the younger members, his activities did indeed seem to be ushering in a new era for VPI. The effect on both groups was largely the same: the development of an unusual sense of optimism, in some instances almost euphoria, with respect to the immediate welfare of the College. This optimism and sense of well-being was reinforced with a sense of pride which grew from the revelation, for the first time, of the fact that many of the faculty and the alumni had cooperated extensively in the secret research which had led to the development of the atomic bomb and other scientific developments during the war.

The first real inklings of rough days ahead for the administration began to appear during the winter quarter of 1946. In the first place, of the 1,189 students registering on the first day only 370 entered the Corps of Cadets. For the first time in seventy-three years civilian students outnumbered cadets. Most of the returning veterans, to the surprise of no one, elected not to enter the Corps. Some of the returning veterans, however, did want to enroll in advanced ROTC. Colonel T. W. Munford, who had replaced Colonel Henderson as commandant of cadets in November, 1945, tried to work out a plan whereby veterans with acceptable military experience could enter the Corps at the beginning of the junior year. This plan was looked upon with considerable suspicion as well as alarm by some alumni. This alarm was greatly increased when subsequent enrollments continued to swell the size of the civilian student body faster than that of the Corps of Cadets. It was not long, therefore, before alumni chapters began passing resolutions urging the Board of Visitors to protect and enlarge the Corps.

The sudden emergence of the civilian group from a minority to a majority status also placed unusual strains on the administrative structure available for dealing with student personnel problems. Prior to the war, faculty members had been "drafted" to serve on a part-time basis as civilian student advisers, with R. P. Snead ('29) serving in this capacity in 1939-42 and J. M. Barringer serving in 1942-43. The position had been discontinued during the war and its responsibilities handled through the office of the dean of the college. Dean C. P. "Sally" Miles was upset over the idea of his serving as adviser to the returning veterans. So were a number of the faculty.

A proposal was made to employ a dean of men to take care of the situation. Dean Miles entered a mild objection by recalling the unfortunate experiences under Dean Holtzclaw. A proposal was then advanced to employ a special vocational guidance counselor to work with the veterans. Miles, once more, mildly objected on the grounds that previous employment of a director of guidance and counseling had not proved to be successful. At this point Dean Norris, as chairman of the Administrative Council, entered the discussion rather forcefully. Brushing aside Miles' somewhat timorous approach to the present by constant reference to the past, Norris pointed out that neither Burruss nor Dean Williams had been able to discharge all the duties which had piled up in their respective offices during the last few years of their incumbency. In addition to the offices of business manager which had been filled, and that of a vice-president which had been approved, Norris thought the College should proceed forthwith in the appointment of a dean of men, a director of admissions, and a director of guidance and placement. If a dean of men could not be secured, then a full-time adviser of civilian students should be appointed at once.

Hutcheson was favorably impressed with Norris' proposal but before committing himself conducted an investigation as to the salaries individuals properly qualified for the respective positions would probably have to be paid. As a result of this investigation, as he afterward ruefully admitted, he "got the shock of his life." He discovered that salaries paid VPI faculty and administrators in most instances were far from being competitive with the salaries of other land-grant institutions. This fact proved to be a source of never-ending worry to Hutcheson during his entire tenure as president. He immediately appealed to the legislature for additional financial support. This body, while providing some additional funds for the College, never shared Hutcheson's enthusiasm for the great VPI which could be built only with an adequate increase in state funds. This fact, when realized by the faculty, tended to work to Hutcheson's disadvantage. Some faculty members had succumbed to Hutcheson's intoxicating enthusiasm about VPI by assuming that the legislature would grant his every request. When the legislature did not do so, some of the faculty cooled perceptibly, and certainly unfairly, toward Hutcheson.

Faced with serious budget problems, Hutcheson realized that he would have to create new positions rather slowly. In the meantime, veterans were returning to the campus in increasing numbers as civilians. Something would have to be done at once. In order to have more time within which to explore the possibilites of a dean of men, Hutcheson established a full-time position of adviser to civilian students and appointed Earl J. Shiflet ('40) to the office.

Prior to entering the armed service, Shiflet had worked in the YMCA as student counselor with Paul Derring. A graduate in rural sociology, which at that time was administered in the department of agricultural economics in the school of agriculture, Shiflet had risen to the rank of major while in the armed services. Because of Shiflet's experiences, Hutcheson looked upon his appointment as an excellent one designed to secure desired liaison "between the offices of the dean of the college, business manager, commandant, and YMCA secretary." Many students in engineering, some of the faculty, and some of the alumni took a less optimistic view of the appointment. These individuals, in no way criticizing Shiflet personally, were quick to note that both Shiflet and Cassell, now filling offices which affected the entire school, were "aggie" graduates. This fact, when considered in connection with Hutcheson's acknowledged leadership in agriculture, generated rumors that the "ag boys" were planning to take over the College. The state press unintentionally added strength to the rumors by giving what many thought to be too heavy emphasis to the school's work in agriculture while giving little or no attention to its work in engineering, business administration, and the supporting sciences. Even *The Roanoke Times* on one occasion felt compelled to remind its readers that VPI was more than a school of agriculture. The discussions surrounding the appointment of a vice-president brought the entire matter to a sharp focus for the surprised Hutcheson.

In November, 1945, the Board of Visitors decided to appoint a vice-president for the College and authorized Hutcheson to submit to the board at its next meeting a list of names of possible appointees for the position. Working mostly through his contacts with alumni and personnel in land-grant institutions throughout the country, Hutcheson set to work to compile such a list. At this stage he received two surprises amounting almost to shock. None of the persons contacted was interested in the position at the salary offered. Secondly, some of the prominent out-of-state persons he contacted were not interested seemingly because of the "narrow gauge" interpretation and implementation VPI was giving to the Land-Grant Act. One of this latter group also had doubts about the future of a land-grant institution which was giving so much prominence to military training. After some upward adjustment of the salary to be offered, Hutcheson was able to secure a list of names which he submitted to the board at its February, 1946, meeting. The name of Dr. Walter S. Newman ('19) was on the list. Hutcheson informed the board that Newman had permitted his name to be submitted only after considerable pressure from alumni groups but in so doing had made it clear that he would not consider himself under obligation to accept the position even if the board offered it to him. It was generally accepted as a fact, Hutcheson informed the board, that Newman was in line for another important position in state education work.

In the meantime, some members of the board's executive committee had been securing information about persons whose names were known to be on Hutcheson's list. This information, when combined with the information obtained by Hutcheson, convinced the board that Newman was the best man for the vice-presidency. The board thereupon agreed unanimously to offer Newman the position and instructed Hutcheson to confer with him concerning the appointment. The newspaper account of this action merely stated that the board had established the position of vice-president and had authorized Hutcheson to find a suitably trained person for the position as soon as possible. Rumor, however, had it that the position was to be offered to Newman.

On the same day the board acted to offer Newman the vice-presidency, Hutcheson received a disturbing letter signed by the presidents of the VPI student chapters of the American Society of Civil Engineers, the Institute of Aeronautical Sciences, the American Society of Mechanical Engineers, and the

American Institute of Electrical Engineers. These four presidents, representing the majority of engineering students in the College, wanted a person with an engineering degree to be appointed to the vice-presidency. These students, displaying a not-at-all-surprising lack of understanding as to the financial and business operations of the College, also displayed an equal lack of understanding of the true character of Hutcheson and his newly appointed business manager, Stuart Cassell. The student letter, however, did reflect some of the fears which had been generated by the rumors that the "aggies" were planning to take over the College. This fear was brought out in the following paragraph:

> We should like to point out the discrepancy between the number of engineering students enrolled at Virginia Polytechnic Institute and the number of graduate engineers on the administrative group controlling the operational funds of the school. We understand this group is composed of the president of the college, the business manager, and the vice-president in charge of instruction. Neither the president nor the business manager is an engineering graduate and we sincerely feel that the needs of the engineering departments cannot be fully represented unless one of the members of this group possesses an engineering degree.

Hutcheson answered this letter at once and reviewed in detail every step taken by himself and by the board in the search for a vice-president. The committee appointed by the board to help select the vice-president, he wrote, was "made up of two alumni who are graduates in engineering, one alumnus who is a graduate in agriculture, one lawyer, and one business man." This committee, he said, was looking for a man especially trained in education, but the committee, he assured the students, would "keep the total well-being of the institution in mind in making their recommendations." Hutcheson also outlined for the students the cooperative process whereby the deans of the several divisions of the College were fully involved in determining the distribution of funds available to the institution. He did not believe any discrimination had been or would be practiced. "For twenty-five years prior to the time I became president," he wrote, "the president of the Virginia Polytechnic Institute was an engineering graduate and although I was working in the field of agriculture, I always felt that I received fair treatment from him." My special training in the field of agriculture, he assured the students, "will not prevent my giving fair treatment to the School of Engineering and the School of Business Administration and Applied Science."

The letter from these four students worried Hutcheson to a surprising degree. Knowing full well of the criticism that had been directed at Dr. Burruss for his loss of contact with the students, he had been going out of his way in an effort to establish cordial working relationships with the student group. Also, the letter might represent the feelings of members of the engineering faculty. With this latter possibility in mind, he directed the following letter to E. B. Norris, dean of engineering:

> In order that you may have full information as to certain correspondence between certain students and the President of the Virginia Polytechnic Institute, I am sending you herewith a copy of a letter which I received from these students under date of February 12 and a copy of my reply to the same.
> Under date of November 21 [1945] I wrote to you and other members of the Administrative Council for any suggestions which you cared to make regarding this matter [the selection of a vice-president]. I also asked for recom-

mendations from the President of the General Alumni Association and other alumni who are engineering graduates.

I hope very much that you and the heads of the various engineering departments believe that the present administration will endeavor to be absolutely fair to the School of Engineering in the determination of the division of operational funds. However, if at any time any member of the staff feels that I have not been absolutely fair, I should be glad if he will take the matter up immediately with me.

Dean Norris' immediate reply to this letter is so illuminating as to the campus climate with which Hutcheson had to deal for most of his administration that it is given in its entirety:

Your letter of the 14th with enclosed copy of a letter from certain students was a complete surprise to me. I certainly hope that there are no grounds for the possible inference that you may suspect me of having inspired any such effort. So far, I have found two department heads who ever heard of it, and they were shown a copy of the letter *after* it had been mailed to you.

Certainly I have no complaint over any division of funds, nor over any other phase of our relations as affecting the School of Engineering. If and when I have, you can expect a frank expression directly from me, and not in any such round-about method as might be inferred from this correspondence.

You should know, if you don't already, that ever since your appointment, and especially since the appointment of Mr. Cassell as Business Manager, the gossip of the town has been that the "Ag School has taken over VPI." Such talk is not confined to Blacksburg, but has also been made by engineering alumni from around the state.

I have tried whenever I heard any such talk to dispel any such suspicions. The situation got worse this last week when the story got around that Dr. Walter S. Newman was to be made Vice-President upon your recommendation to the Board of Visitors. This started tongues wagging about an "agricultural triumvirate." I think that this talk was the basis for the letter which you received.

If you think desirable, I would be only too glad to write the four young men who signed the letter to you. I understand that your reply was quite convincing to them, and that they are entirely satisfied with the assurances you gave them.

There are some secondary factors which may also contribute to the misunderstandings which people seem to have. As you know, the building program for the School of Agriculture is several steps ahead of that for Engineering. If we could only get Board action to indicate what areas of the campus are to be developed for Engineering and get consideration of Professor Cowgill's numerous sketches and a selection made by someone with authority, then perhaps some definite start could be made toward planning the engineering laboratory group. As things now stand, we are getting nowhere in getting space that is badly needed. The Agricultural Group is much easier to push because the locations are fixed by existing buildings which are to be connected up.

Another contributing factor to the talk lies in the unbalanced publicity which has been given to your various addresses and activities. You have had very little publicity on your interests in the engineering school, or in engineering research, but your efforts to secure greatly enlarged appropriations for agricultural research and extension from the state have been played up, along with the efforts for more dormitories.

There may be other minor factors which give people the small grounds which form the basis for gossip. Blacksburg is about the worst place I know of for the "old ladies tongues" to start wagging on the least provocation.

I hope you will believe me when I assure you that I have not only not been a party to such talk, but that I have taken every opportunity to dispel any such ideas.

Norris' explanation was readily accepted by Hutcheson, but the latter's state-wide image as "Mr. Agriculture" continued as a factor influencing his relations with faculty and students. Some of this latter group, smarting under "old ladies tongues" gossip that Hutcheson was planning to develop a super "cow college," began building up resentment not only against Hutcheson but also against much of the college program he was advocating. In face to face situations, Hutcheson could easily win over these dissident students; but as the enrollment exploded overnight, he soon found like Burruss that he simply did not have time to engage in dialogue with all the student groups eager to advise him on running the institution. Neither could he find sufficient time within which to meet with all the individual faculty members and department heads faced with unusual problems caused by the sudden influx of returning veterans. Most members of this group of faculty cooperated fully with him. A very small minority, however, resenting his agricultural image and interpreting his efforts to hold down expenditures as an affront to their judgment and a threat to their programs, made Hutcheson unhappy with sarcastic, almost insolent, letters and memoranda. Hutcheson's routine reply in most of these instances was a courteous reminder to the writer to submit his complaint or request through his dean. The deans' reactions to this development are unrecorded.

Early in the winter quarter of 1946 it became perfectly obvious that the College would have to speed up its preparations if it expected to accommodate the returning veterans seeking admission. Providing for married veterans proved to be particularly difficult, since VPI had never made any provision whatever for married students. Hutcheson wanted to erect a dormitory for this group but realized that one could not be erected in time to meet the immediate demand. A survey of housing facilities available in Blacksburg simply reconfirmed what was already known: namely, that such facilities for married students were either nonexistent or totally inadequate. Facilities for single students were not much better. As one solution to the problem, the College set up a trailer court on the site surrounding Solitude, west of Davidson Hall. Solitude was converted into a community center for the camp, and the veterans occupied the trailers as fast as they could be set up. The camp proved so successful that two additional camps were soon established in the general vicinity eastward from the present Coliseum. These courts while designated as trailer courts number 1, 2, and 3 on the official records were immediately renamed by the inhabitants to suit their own fancy. Court number one at Solitude usually went by the unimaginative name of Vetsville, but the inhabitants of number two and three, on the hill "where the icy winds of winter knew no mercy," engaged in lively debate over whether to name their camps "Cassell Heights" or "Cassell Folly" in honor of the college business manager. An appeal was made directly to Cassell, so the story goes, to resolve the debate by expressing his preference of names. The astute business manager according to one account "wowed" the audience with his quick retort that "with ignorance in trailers, 'tis folly to be wise," and declined to express a preference. This comment swung most of the support to Cassell Heights.

On March 23 it was announced publicly that Dr. Walter S. Newman had accepted the position of vice-president of VPI and would assume the duties of the office on May 15. This acceptance of the position came as a relief to Hutcheson, who had begun to fear that Newman was not going to accept the offer.

Newman, in becoming the first vice-president in the history of VPI, did not come as a stranger. Following his departure from the campus in 1925 from his work as professor of agricultural education, he kept in constant touch with campus affairs. He had served as president of the General Alumni Association for four years and on the board of directors for six years. In addition to these activities, he had been a member of the Alumni Fund Council since its inception in 1939. As a member of this council, he had familiarized himself with campus programs and student activities needing assistance from alumni funds. Upon Newman's arrival on campus, Hutcheson immediately asked him to take charge of the curricular study already inaugurated by numerous faculty committees in all the instructional divisions of the College. Newman took charge of this work at once, and while rejecting Burruss' job analysis approach to curriculum construction, nonetheless soon had the faculty busily engaged in the more difficult philosophical approach to curriculum building.

In the meantime, thousands of applications for admission to college swamped Dean "Sally" Miles' office. "Sally" Miles, or "Mr. VPI" to thousands of alumni and many sports writers, was a beloved individual in the VPI community; but even he confessed he was having some difficulty in dealing with the dean-of-the-college problems in an institution struggling to adjust to the bewildering demands of the postwar era. He found the process of evaluating transcripts and records to determine the eligibility of many returning veterans for admission to be particularly troublesome. Most of these records, complained Miles, were cluttered with psychological data and facts beyond his ability to interpret in the limited time at his disposal. He wanted some help, he said. The Administrative Council agreed with him, whereupon Dr. Hutcheson created the office of admissions, and placed Dr. Paul H. Farrier, professor of English, in charge of it in June, 1945.

The choice of Paul Farrier as admissions officer proved to be a most fortunate one. He quickly mastered the psychological data which had bothered Miles and then went several steps further by establishing some significant relations between the data and conditions faced by students at VPI. Within a short time, he also conducted some very significant studies which predicted future enrollment with satisfying accuracy. One of his greatest contributions was the calm, level-headed, helpful manner he followed in dealing with everyone having contact with the office. He could not admit all applicants, but he convinced most of them that they had received fair treatment at his hands.

Hutcheson was determined to do what he could for the returning veterans. As a result, more students were admitted than could be adequately cared for. Dormitory space was rented at the Radford Ordnance Works, and every effort made to convert some other buildings at the ordnance plant into suitable classrooms. At the same time dormitories, classrooms, and laboratories on the campus had to be renovated. New faculty had to be recruited, the power plant had to be enlarged, additions to the sewerage plant were urgently needed, and sites had to be chosen for the urgently needed dormitories and engineering laboratories. Water, sewerage, and power lines had to be extended to the trailer courts. Coal needed to be stocked for the power house; and supplies of sugar, meat, flour, and other foodstuff needed to be assured for the dining facilities. Unexpected problems were encountered at every turn. Low salary schedules not only hindered the recruiting of new faculty but increased the difficulty of holding faculty already employed. Wartime restrictions and shortages hampered essential repairs to buildings. On one occasion a simple repair job was held up for lack of nails. Firm bids could not be secured for the needed power plant improvements, because no one dared to quote prices on boilers. One packing company rejected an order for beef on the grounds that the order would consume its yearly supply and leave nothing for its other customers. Teaching materials such as books, drawing instruments, slide rules, and even chalk were in short supply. In fact, just about everything needed for the operation of the College was in short supply except applications for admission. Finally in August, 1946, it was announced that no more applications could be received for the quarter to begin at the end of September. Even this date had to be changed and the opening of the College postponed one week to complete a few last-minute preparations.

In November, Hutcheson reported to the board that approximately 3,100 students were living in campus facilities, while 900 day students were living in Blacksburg and surrounding communities "all the way from Vinton to Pulaski." Day students were permitted to own and operate automobiles but were not supposed to operate them on the campus other than to get to and from designated parking lots. Enough students ignored this regulation to cause monumental traffic jams all over the campus and at the "corner" traffic light, thereby forcing the administration to adopt more stringent regulations before the year ended.

Despite the overcrowded conditions, every effort was made to operate the College in as normal a manner as possible and continue the development of needed courses. A division of industrial arts education, with J. A. Schad as head, was established in the department of vocational education; a Master of Science degree in applied mechanics was established with Dr. Louis O'Shaughnessy as director; and an Air Force unit in ROTC was set up largely through the efforts of Colonel T. W. Munford, Commandant. At the same time efforts were continued to resume student activities, organizations, and clubs dropped or restricted during the war.

This latter effort proved to be more troublesome than expected, although the reasons were understood. Prior to the war the student life, activities, organizations, clubs, recreations, and even class work were dominated by the traditions and the military organization surrounding the Corps of Cadets. During the session of 1946-47, the civilian students, mostly veterans, outnumbered the cadets more than three to one. Student organizations and activities conducted in such manner as to comply with the military traditions, rules, and regulations could not meet the demands of the greatly changed student body. Many constitutions and by-laws had to be rewritten or amended, while the very existence of some clubs and organizations was challenged. First-year and transfer students with no previous contact with Tech traditions outnumbered upperclassmen bent on returning to the good old days. Many members of this former group were outspoken in their demands for change. The term "adjust or adjourn" used by Hutcheson in an address to the students became a byword on the campus. Many professors promptly adopted the term but just as promptly objected to its application to mores and traditions dear to their hearts.

Some friction and unrest developed as the college officials and the student leaders sought to prevent VPI from becoming a "house divided." A student-originated proposal to set up one student government to serve both cadets and civilians was soundly defeated by the students at the polls. A reorganization of the Athletic Association was achieved only after repeated attempts. Dissatisfaction with civilian housing was voiced by a decidedly vocal but even more decidedly minority group. Murmurs of protest about the service in the mess hall began to be noised abroad. Hutcheson, greatly disturbed over the direction student affairs were taking, appeared before a convocation of faculty and students and quite forcefully outlined the tremendous efforts the College had put forth and was continuing to put forth in order to provide educational opportunities for the greatest number of students, especially the returning veterans.

Frankly admitting that conditions on the campus were unsatisfactory because of overcrowding, Hutcheson just as frankly pointed out that without such overcrowding approximately one thousand students, ninety-five per cent of whom would have been veterans, "would not be in this audience today." In concluding his address, Hutcheson made a direct appeal for student cooperation in helping solve the perplexing problems facing the College as it sought to provide a quality education for the greatest number possible.

No dramatic changes occurred overnight as a result of Hutcheson's talk, but a more thoughtful approach began to emerge in the student discussions of campus problems. A number of factors as well as several faculty members contributed to this development. The work of the YMCA under Paul Derring and his newly appointed associate secretary, Alfred C. Payne, was unusually effective. "Al" Payne, who one admirer claimed had rather discuss than eat, was particularly helpful in getting veterans and married students constructively involved in campus affairs. According to one observer, before the year was up, "Al" had weekly student-faculty-administrator bull sessions going on all over the Campus. These sessions, later referred to by the more euphonious term of "dialogue," often lasted far into the night and helped all involved get a better understanding of mutual concerns. Student unrest did not disappear, but by the end of the year Vice-President Newman reported the situation as greatly improved. He attributed this improvement to an emerging student leadership in both the Corps and the civilian student body and to the creation of the office of director of student affairs which had been filled on January 1 by the appointment of Dr. Robert E. Bates, who according to *The Virginia Tech* was "to act as mediator between the entire male student body and the administration."

The creation of the office of director of student affairs represented Hutcheson's last major change in the administrative organization of the College. He now had a vice-president, a business manager, a director of admissions, a director of student affairs, and a director of buildings and grounds in addition to the administrative organization inherited from Burruss' administration. Probably as to be expected, some confusion developed as to the division of responsibilities and authority to be assigned to these new offices. The Board of Visitors, which by now was keeping in close touch with college affairs by means of its committee system, sensed this problem at once. Since Hutcheson was undergoing treatment for extreme fatigue, the board asked Newman to prepare a detailed report outlining the duties of the newly developed administrative organization.

In the meantime, other events, perhaps unimportant in the cosmic history of the College but of some significance to those participating in the transition from a wartime to a peacetime footing, may be mentioned.

Fifteen busses were employed in transporting students domiciled at the Radford Ordnance Works to the main campus. The students, renaming their portion of the sprawling facility "Rad-Tech," quickly adjusted to the situation. Library and YMCA services were provided. The cafeteria proved highly satisfactory, while the recreation hall provided facilities comparable to those in the Student Activities Building (Squires Hall) on the campus. An outdoor recreation field and tennis courts equaled the regular campus facilities. Some thirteen faculty members commuted daily from Blacksburg to teach basic courses required by all students. Special sections, some scheduled for the early nighttime hours, were provided on the regular campus for certain laboratory courses which could not be offered off campus. The nearby Radford churches cooperated in welcoming the Rad-Tech students. So did the Radford College girls, somewhat to the consternation of Radford's beloved Dean Mary M'Ledge Moffett. The only real dissident note was an occasional snow storm which left huge snowdrifts on the Price's Fork Road leading from Rad-Tech to the campus. Even this infrequent occurrence yielded some of its unpleasantness; students, faculty, and bus drivers agreed to take a holiday whenever it happened.

Old traditions continued to be uprooted on the main campus. Miss Freda Polansky became the first coed editor-in-chief of *The Virginia Tech*. Civilians instead of cadets assumed leadership of the German and Cotillion Dance Clubs. Husbands and wives often led the formal dances promoted by these organizations. Wives of the married students introduced a completely new element of cosmopolitanism into many student organizations and student-faculty-town affairs. At the same time, this group provided a welcome source from which to recruit stenographers, secretaries, musicians, and public-school teachers.

The inhabitants of Vetsville and Cassell Heights both joined in the regular campus and town activities and at the same time organized their own amusements. In political campaigns which both rivaled and "spoofed" professional politicians in baby-kissing and attention-getting stunts, the inhabitants elected "mayors" and other officials for their "towns." Working with the regular college officials, these duly elected representatives clearly demonstrated the wisdom of getting students involved in helping solve problems of mutual concern facing the College. Many of the wives of veterans on and off the campus joined their husbands in academic work. In general, the scholastic and extra-mural conduct of both veterans and wives in this and subsequent years was universally approved. The feared inability of the veterans to adjust to academic demands did not materialize. In fact, records show that the veterans received slightly better grades than the average undergraduate.

A few years after the peak of the veteran enrollment had passed, an alumni faculty member in informally discussing the impact of the veteran on the campus concluded that the veterans had made worthwhile contributions in every way except that of preserving the military traditions of yesterday. An inconclusive argument immediately developed over whether this was or was not a significant contribution.

The Alumni Association, which had become such a significant factor in the welfare of the College during Burruss' administration, continued its activities during Hutcheson's incumbency as president. A huge victory reunion and homecoming was celebrated on October 27, 1946, at which Coach Jimmy Kitts' "boys" delighted some four thousand homecoming alumni by upsetting a favored

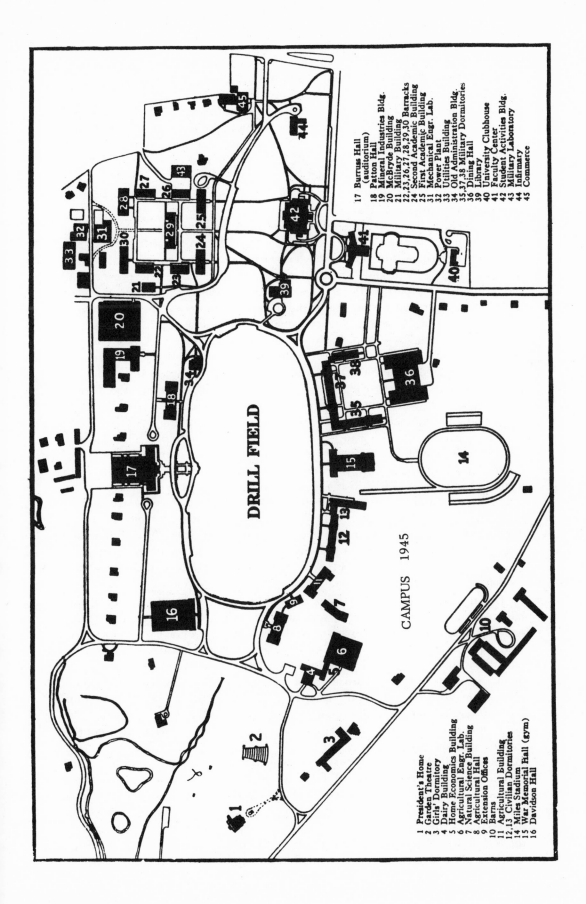

DRILL FIELD

CAMPUS 1945

1 President's Home
2 Garden Theatre
3 Girls' Dormitory
4 Dairy Building
5 Home Economics Building
6 Agricultural Engr. Lab.
7 Natural Science Building
8 Agricultural Hall
9 Extension Offices
10 Barns
11 Agricultural Building
12,13 Civilian Dormitories
14 Miles Stadium
15 War Memorial Hall (gym)
16 Davidson Hall

17 Burruss Hall
   (auditorium)
18 Patton Hall
19 Mineral Industries Bldg.
20 McBryde Building
21 Military Building
22,23,26,27,28,29,30 Barracks
24 Second Academic Building
25 First Academic Building
31 Mechanical Engr. Lab.
32 Power Plant
33 Utilities Building
34 Old Administration Bldg.
35,37,38 Military Dormitories
36 Dining Hall
39 Library
40 University Clubhouse
41 Faculty Center
42 Student Activities Bldg.
43 Military Laboratory
44 Infirmary
45 Commerce

North Carolina State eleven 14-6. At the alumni rally held earlier in the day, D. P. Morton ('11) as chairman of the alumni war-memorial committee described the memorial agreed upon by this committee. According to *The Techgram,* "the vision of a shrine that will preserve in stone our glorious motto, 'Ut Prosim, That I May Serve,' was made clear" to the alumni. The shrine was to be built on a slope at the northeast of the drill field "at the end of a mall which will form a new entrance into the campus."

At the time of the unveiling of the plans for the shrine, the proposed mall attracted more attention than the proposed memorial. Shortly after becoming president, Hutcheson had appointed a local building committee to plan physical facilities for a student body of 6,000. An outstanding architectural firm had taken this committee report and had prepared a site plan which provided for the natural growth and expansion of the existing plant. The present mall was proposed as a part of the expansion. Construction of this mall, however, would require the destruction of the major part of the woody grove which grew on the hillside and in the dell between what is now Brodie and Rasche Halls on one side and Henderson and Squires Halls and the Newman Library on the other side. Although not intended as such, the proposed mall became identified with the proposed memorial. Opposition to the mall developed almost at once on the grounds that destroying the trees destroyed one of the greatest natural beauty spots to be found on the campus. In spite of Hutcheson's repeated assurances that the plan called for replanting the area with more shrubs and trees than it destroyed, opposition to the mall continued to develop. This opposition spread to the plan for the proposed memorial, which was also drawing its share of opposition, mainly from advocates of a utilitarian rather than a spiritual-type memorial. The Board of Visitors approved both the plans for the memorial and the mall and authorized the State Highway Department to start construction on the latter as soon as possible. The Memorial Committee and officers of the Alumni Association thereupon joined forces in promoting the funding and erection of the memorial and at the same time did a good job of reconciling the pro- and the anti-utilitarian sentiment which for a period of time threatened the harmony within alumni ranks.

Jimmy Kitts had returned from military service on January 1, 1946, and laid plans to enter the gridiron wars of the Southern Conference. A puzzling season's record of 3-3-3 was partly overlooked because of a 20-7 victory over VMI before a crowd of more than twenty-eight thousand fans in Roanoke. The record was more than forgotten when it was announced that VPI had accepted an invitation to play the University of Cincinnati "Bearcats" in the El Paso, Texas, Sun Bowl on New Year's Day, 1947. Great excitement gripped the campus and the football-minded alumni as plans were made for the first state team not only in Tech, but also in Virginia history, to play in a bowl game. Cooperation in an effort to make the game a great success was received from all sources except one—the weather. An early snow covered Blacksburg and threatened an end to all football practice. Bulldozers and snow plows were used to clear a practice area on the drill field. The wind promptly covered the area with snow once more. Relief was expected from foul weather upon arrival in El Paso; but to everyone's surprise, snow, ice, and bitterly cold weather greeted the team in the Sun Bowl. The sting of the 18-6 loss to the Bearcats in the game played on a snow-and-ice-covered field was partially assuaged by the open-armed hospitality and warm reception given to the players and the visitors from Tech by El Paso alumni and press.

The team returned to Blacksburg, loaded down with interesting souvenirs, ten-gallon hats, rumors that Jimmy Kitts was being sought as coach by one of the "big time football schools," and a fund of stories at "Sally" Miles' expense. According to one of these stories, "Sally" had slipped over the border to Juarez to watch a bull fight. Instead of cheering the matador, "Sally" had cheered the bull, so the story went. Not only had he cheered the bull, but he had done so in Spanish. His actions had angered one of the matador's senorita friends who, seeking revenge, had engaged "Sally" in conversation and in the process had relieved him of his pocketbook. Beyond the bare facts that "Sally's" pocketbook disappeared and that he had to borrow money to get home, this story was never confirmed.

With the opening of the winter quarter, it was unofficially announced that Hutcheson, who had entered the hospital in December, was improved in health but was not yet able to return to full duties. Vice-President Newman, keeping in close touch with the executive committee of the board, began discharging the duties of the president and found an unusually able assistant in Business Manager Cassell. These two men working in close harmony soon had the business and financial affairs of the institution organized in a manner which proved to be quite successful in interpreting the College's financial needs to the legislature, the board, and other interested groups.

At its May, 1947, meeting, the Board of Visitors extended Hutcheson's sick leave to September 1 and named Newman as acting president for the interim. By midsummer, it was obvious to the board that the session of 1947-48 would present as many if not more problems as the session just closed. The board definitely did not want to lose the services of the able Hutcheson, but it just as definitely did not believe that Hutcheson should again attempt the arduous duties of the president. Faced with this situation, the board on August 12, 1947, adopted the following resolution, which because of its significance in introducing a new element into the history of VPI is reproduced in its entirety:

> In recognition of the devoted and faithful services of Dr. John R. Hutcheson to this institution through the years, we feel that in justice to him and the institution as well, the board should relieve him of his duties and burdensome responsibilities as president in order to promote his health and prolong his services to the institution. Therefore be it resolved:
>
> 1. That Dr. Hutcheson be elected to the position of chancellor of the Virginia Polytechnic Institute, in which position he will act as agent of the board in such matters as are delegated to him by the board.
> 2. That Dr. Walter S. Newman be and is hereby elected to the presidency of the Virginia Polytechnic Institute with full responsibility for the administration and management of the institution under such powers as are delegated to him by the board.
> 3. That the above appointments shall become effective September 1, 1947.

Fortunately, Hutcheson recovered from his illness and continued to render distinguished service to VPI, this time as chancellor. In 1948, the VPI Educational Foundation, Inc. was established by the Board of Visitors to "work toward increasing gifts and endowments made to the College." Dr. Hutcheson was immediately named president of the foundation. In 1956, he retired as chancellor and devoted all his energies to the foundation until his death on

January 23, 1962. In many different ways John R. Hutcheson made significant contributions to VPI as instructor, director of agricultural extension, president, chancellor, and president of the VPI Educational Foundation.

Chapter 12

The Newman
Administration

1947-1962

WALTER STEPHENSON NEWMAN was born at Woodstock, Virginia, July 20, 1895. After attending public schools in Shenandoah County, he entered Hampden-Sydney, from which he was graduated with the A. B. degree in 1917. In 1919, he received the M.S. degree in agriculture from VPI. From 1919 to 1922 he taught vocational agriculture at Windsor, Virginia, being one of the pioneer teachers of the state in this field. He returned to VPI in 1922 as associate professor of agricultural education and remained in this position until 1925, when he moved to Richmond as state supervisor of agricultural education. He served in this position until 1942, at which time he became assistant state superintendent of public instruction. From 1936 to 1942 he also served as state administrator of the National Youth Administration. In 1931, he received the Ph.D. degree from Pennsylvania State College. During his tenure as president of VPI, he received the honorary LL.D. from Roanoke College in 1949 and from Hampden-Sydney College in 1959. In 1920, he married Liz Otey Hoge of Blacksburg.

Prior to his returning to VPI in 1946 as vice-president, Newman's entire professional career had kept him in close contact with VPI and its expanding program. His active participation in the Alumni Association had led to his being elected four times as president of this organization. As state supervisor of agricultural education and as assistant state superintendent of public instruction, he had become thoroughly familiar with the operation of state government and its legislative process, even to the extent of being on a first-name basis with the majority of the state leaders and many local leaders.

His achievements had also made his name well known to the state press, which received his elevation to the presidency with expressions of approval. *The Norfolk Ledger-Dispatch,* after pronouncing Newman's background for the presidency as "impressive," continued: "To it must be added the fact that Dr. Newman is a man of force and executive ability, who faces up squarely to decisions and has a gift for quick understanding and appreciation of complex problems."

In commenting on the choice of Newman for the presidency by the Board of Visitors, *The Richmond News Leader* said:

> Had they looked the country over, we doubt if they could have found a man better suited than their own vice-president to assume the direction of an institution that has before it a tomorrow greater even than all the yesterdays.
>
> Many years ago, a man who had studied Virginia education for a generation remarked . . . that the school at Blacksburg in time could influence helpfully the lives of more Virginians than any other institution possibly could. That still is a challenge—a challenge the new president will meet.

With these accolades and others from the daily press ringing in his ears, Newman picked up the reins of the presidency of VPI.

Although he began his presidential responsibilities officially on September 1, 1947, in actuality he had been discharging presidential duties since Hutcheson's illness, which had begun in the preceding December. This period of apprenticeship served both Newman and VPI well. As a result of it, he had familarized himself with the institution's total program and had come to know many of the staff and department heads with whom he would have to deal. This latter information proved to be useful in helping him to select personnel for important committees which he set up at once upon his assumption of the presidency. It also helped him to meet some of the prejudices against an "aggie president" which had plagued Hutcheson during his short tenure.

Hardly had Newman moved from the vice-presidential office in the east end of Burruss Hall to the presidential office on the same floor in the west end until he began to receive unsolicited letters from a few department heads, setting forth facts thinly disguised as information an "aggie president" needed in order to understand the true importance of the letter writer's department. To the surprise of these skeptics on the staff, the new president quickly demonstrated that he had both breadth and depth of knowledge about the institution. In his reply to one individual, Newman outlined his desire to use the resources of the College to promote the growth of the institution on all fronts, with each department functioning as an integral part of the whole. He suggested to the department head the nature of some types of research and some possible shifting of priorities which might possibly generate additional funds. He followed this suggestion with an analysis of the physical facilities available to this department in comparison with the physical facilities available to some of the other departments. In terms of Newman's analysis, the department had not reached the emergency situation existing in other departments. He did not stop here. Instead, he reviewed the immediate and the long-range plans for meeting the department's physical needs as plans were realized for expanding the physical facilities of the entire

College. He was sure no loss of accreditation need be feared, he wrote, since he had already acquainted the accrediting agency with the problems faced and the plans proposed as a remedy and had been assured that the plans met with the agency's approval. Following recovery from his surprise over receipt of this type of letter, the department head in question continued to work vigorously for his own department but never again did he write the president a do-this-now-or-else type of letter. Neither did he ever make the mistake, he confided to some friends several years later, of assuming that "the aggie president didn't know his way around." Of equal significance, as one result of several similar incidents the word soon got abroad on the campus that "Walter Newman is tough some of the time, works for the total institution overtime, and is a gentleman all the time." Not a bad beginning for an incoming president.

The session of 1947-48 started off with 4672 resident students. The total enrollment for the year reached 5458, the largest ever recorded to that date. Approximately 900 students were housed at Rad-Tech, where J. E. Hardy had succeeded G. G. Dickenson as manager. Of the total enrollment, only about 1200 enrolled in the Cadet Corps; but since this number represented an increase over that of the preceding year, the opinion was advanced that "the Corps is on the way back." Unusually crowded conditions continued both as to living conditions and teaching facilities. A registration system designed primarily to get students into classes rather than to balance sections produced some results surprising to students and faculty alike. One professor with a class assigned to a room with twenty-five seats in it arrived to find more than two hundred students trying to get in. He arrived at his next class assigned to a 150-seat room to find three students awaiting him. In spite of the initial confusion, the year was a relatively successful one. The transition in administration from Hutcheson to Newman proved to be extremely smooth, a not-at-all-surprising development considering the fact that Newman had already served his apprenticeship, during which time, at the request of the board, he had prepared a detailed outline of the organization and responsibilities for all the administrative officials in the College.

The tempo of change began to accelerate rapidly as VPI approached the mid-twentieth century. Seymour Robb succeeded the retired Ralph (Brownie) Brown as librarian and immediately began an aggressive campaign for better library facilities. Surprisingly, his campaign was received with less than enthusiasm by some faculty members, who frankly admitted their preference for increased laboratory rather than increased library facilities. When Newman openly threw his support back of improved library facilities, some of the pro-laboratories group, shaking their heads, muttered darkly about the effect Newman's liberal arts degree was having on the College. The students, however, expressed approval of all advances and just as promptly forgot all about them.

Advancing age continued to take its toll of faculty members, giants in their days and almost legendary characters to thousands of students. The retirement system had been improved slightly for elderly faculty ineligible for the state retirement system, but continued to be quite inadequate. Some alumni, knowing this, quietly donated funds to the retirement system. Others expressing for individual faculty members an affection approaching that of a son for his aging father, quietly donated sizeable sums to be used as a supplement to the individual's retirement. The replacements for the retiring faculty quickly picked up the reins and made great contributions in their own right. John R. Castleman ('19), World

War I ace, replaced the ailing but still colorful "Bosco" Rasche as head of the department of graphics. D. H. (Dan) Pletta succeeded Louis O'Shaughnessy as head of the department of applied mechanics and H. L. (Herb) Manning succeeded the resigned Paul T. Norton as head of industrial engineering. Byron Cooper had already been appointed head of the department of geology to succeed the deceased "Roy J." Holden, and T. W. (Inky) Hatcher had succeeded J. E. Williams as head of the department of mathematics.

W. H. (Ham) Crockford ('32), Bob McNeil's right-hand man in publishing *The Techgram,* resigned to accept a position with the *Richmond Times-Dispatch,* and David K. E. Bruce resigned from the Board of Visitors to accept the post of assistant secretary of commerce in Washington. J. P. Woods, member of the board since 1924 and rector since 1943, died during the summer of 1948. Woods, who had provided such distinguished service and steadying influence during the uncertain period of Burruss' and Hutcheson's illnesses, was succeeded as rector by William E. Wine ('04). At the request of *The Techgram,* Wine, the first alumnus ever to serve as rector, issued a statement which concluded with the following words: "I pledge my talents and energy to preserve the greatness and honor of this Institute and to promote its usefulness to the State and Nation." Both Wine's talents and energy were abundant indeed. As a consequence, a deserved tribute is paid to this individual with the simple statement that "Wine kept his pledge."

Included in the list of long-time faculty members retiring from the scene at this period because of illness or age were such well-remembered names as H. B. Riffenburg, chemistry; W. H. (Billy) Byrne, extension; Weldon Ellis, heat and power engineering; H. H. (Bunker) Hill, experiment station; and Harry (Gudie) Gudheim, mathematics. It is doubtful indeed if there is a living alumnus who was graduated prior to 1950 who could not tell one or more delightful anecdotes related to these and other colorful characters who began moving to the sidelines by 1950.

The sessions of 1947-48 through 1949-50 saw many additional changes, some happy and some not so happy. The "football euphoria" generated by the Sun Bowl trip began to fade rapidly when first Virginia and then William and Mary won by lopsided scores. The situation grew worse when neither the alumni nor the Highty Tighties who had accompanied the team to West Point could help prevent an Army victory of 41-0. The College's football fortunes hit rock bottom when VMI, after trailing 14-7 at the end of three quarters, turned the game around and won 28-14. With such "disasters" and a 4-5-0 overall record to attack, loud cries were heard from some alumni and student groups. Charges and countercharges flew thick and fast. In the midst of the uproar, Jimmy Kitts on January 18, 1948, issued the following statement: "Due to many misfortunate happenings that occurred last year, I think it best for all concerned that I tender my resignation as head football coach at Virginia Polytechnic Institute." Some sports writers, now that Kitts had resigned, were loud in their praise of him and somewhat critical of the athletic authorities for letting him go. Dissident alumni and students not having Kitts to kick around dissipated their concern by speculation and debate as to what Kitts had meant by the "many misfortunate happenings."

The Athletic Council in the meantime set about to find a successor. In February of the same year the council announced it had found him: Robert C. (Bob) McNeish, former University of Southern California backfield star. McNeish, once described as "the handsomest coach in the Southern Conference," came to the

position with a colorful record of bowl-game experience. After impressive performances as player and coach on the west coast, he had come east to accept a
position as assistant coach to Tom Hamilton at Annapolis. He came to Tech from
this position. The big names of the people who had endorsed McNeish plus the
big-time football programs with which he had been associated acted to replace the
gloom leading to Kitts' departure with rosy visions of football prowess and sweet
revenge on state rivals. The visions soon turned into nightmares. McNeish's first
season ended with a 0-8-1 record. His second year was little better with a 1-7-2
record. His third year was the worst of all with a 0-10-0 record. Some alumni and
students started yelling for the scalp of everyone connected with the athletic
department. Free advice, in some instances worth its cost, poured in suggesting
remedies and solutions to the situation. By mid-season 1950, the unhappy Mc-
Neish, announcing that he planned to sleep for three days, resigned as coach and
headed back for the west coast. He was succeeded by his assistant, Al Learned,
who tried to turn the tide but to no avail; he wound up the season with a 63-7
loss to the University of Maryland. Even so, the team of 1950 was reported to have
set a national record—it received more kickoffs during the season than any other
major football team. Only the uninitiated received consolation from this dubious
achievement.

In the meantime, as if one losing season after another was not enough humili-
ation, the nationwide press announced that VPI, along with several other schools,
mostly in the Southern Conference, faced expulsion from the National Collegiate
Athletic Association for violation of the "sanity code" set up by this organization.
VPI, according to the "sanity code," was providing excessive financial aid to the
athletes. Most of the other schools in the nation, especially those excelling in
athletics, were reported to be operating "in compliance" with the code. VPI
alumni and friends received this news with incredulous amazement and both
demanded and awaited an explanation and a solution.

Reduced to its simplest terms, the "sanity code" stipulated that financial assistance given by a college or university to an athlete must be restricted to a job actually performed by the athlete and paid for at the wage rate prevailing in the community for similar services. At the time, VPI had a system of athletic scholarships
which provided free room, board, tuition, books, supplies, laundry, and a cadet
uniform for the recipients. A survey had indicated that while all athletes were
required to meet all academic standards set up by the College, very few could
qualify for the academic scholarships. As for providing financial aid through
jobs, a survey had quickly established that the town and the college campus combined did not have enough job openings to meet the demand. Besides, if required
to meet college expenses by employment at the wages prevailing in the community,
no time would be left for the athlete to participate in either the military requirements of the College or in athletics. Faced with this situation, VPI had reported
that it was in full sympathy with the efforts to regulate financial assistance provided for athletes but that it could not comply with the "sanity code." Upon
receipt of this report, the NCAA officials had recommended that VPI be expelled
from membership along with Boston College, The Citadel, Villanova, the University of Maryland, the University of Virginia, and VMI, who for one reason or
another also had reported inability to comply with the code.

When the story broke that these schools, not one of which was a powerhouse
in football, were in violation of the code while all of the big-time football schools

were in strict conformity, scores of derisive editorials and articles denouncing the "sanity code" and even the NCAA appeared in the national press. The gist of many of these articles was that the "sanity code" encouraged hypocrisy, while the stand of the "rebel schools" encouraged honesty and integrity in dealing with the difficult problem of financial assistance to athletes.

Newman, who had taken an active part in defending VPI from the very outset, requested and was granted permission to appear before the annual meeting of the NCAA in New York City. President Colgate Darden of the University of Virginia also requested and was granted permission to appear before the same group. When the matter of expulsion of the "rebels," as the New York press called them, came up, Darden, Newman, and "Curly" Byrd of Maryland took the lead in defending the cause of the threatened schools. After a confused three-hour debate on the floor, the motion to expel the "rebels" lost by twenty-five votes.

The consequences of this NCAA affair were mixed. VPI got more widespread coverage, most of it favorable, from the nationwide sports press than from any athletic event in its entire history. At home, the alumni seemed to settle into an attitude of "OK, we've known all along that we were honest. Now let's get going and win a few games for a change."

Following his return to the campus, Newman was deluged with alumni-mailed newspaper clippings and pictures from out-of-state papers reporting on his activities in New York. Perhaps the most gratifying thing to him personally was the number of letters he received complimenting him for his "gentlemanly stand" in helping organize a fight in favor of honesty as contrasted with hypocrisy in athletics.

With the excitement of the threatened expulsion from the NCAA fading into the background, the Athletic Council, following McNeish's resignation, conducted an aggressive campaign for a head football coach. Finally after a thorough canvass the choice fell on Frank O. Moseley, assistant coach to Paul (Bear) Bryant at Kentucky. At his own request W. L. (Monk) Younger ('20) relinquished his duties as director of athletics to Moseley and took over the duties of business manager. Moseley entered into his new work in January, 1951, and as coach-director helped start VPI on the long road to a tremendously expanded athletic program.

Among the happier events of the period was the formal inauguration of President Newman into office. At the earnest solicitation of Dean C. P. Miles speaking for the faculty, the Board of Visitors readily agreed to such a ceremony and appointed a committee to plan the details. Newman agreed to the ceremony with the stipulation that it must be kept simple. At the same time, he pointed out that no ceremony of any kind had been held for Dr. Hutcheson either as president or as chancellor. It would be more than fitting, he suggested, to inaugurate Hutcheson as chancellor at the same time he, Newman, was inaugurated as president. Hutcheson quickly vetoed this idea, but at the same time gave his enthusiastic endorsement to the plans to inaugurate Newman. For a number of reasons it became necessary to delay the actual ceremony, but the date of April 18, 1949, was finally agreed upon.

Dr. James Rhyne Killian, Jr., president of Massachusetts Institute of Technology delivered the principal address, using as his topic "The Importance of Being Useful." Pointing out that "VPI and MIT are truly sister institutions, sharing a common philosophy of education and common fields of study," Killian surprised many in the audience when he pointed out that it was in the Commonwealth of

Virginia "that MIT was conceived and the concept of technological education given new and more ample form." He was of course referring to the work of MIT founder William Barton Rogers, who while on the faculty of the University of Virginia had in 1846 prepared "A Plan for a Polytechnic School in Boston" which led to the founding of MIT in 1861. Killian probably would have been surprised himself if he had known how thoroughly William H. Ruffner had studied Rogers' philosophy and its implementation at MIT nearly eighty years before, when VPI as the Virginia Agricultural and Mechanical College was struggling to establish guidelines for its own destiny.

Following Killian's address, which in the main dealt with the problem of keeping technological education useful in the liberal sense of the word, Newman was inducted into office. The simple ceremony was conducted by William E. Wine, rector, before approximately fifteen hundred educators, public officials, and alumni assembled in Burruss Hall. Following his official induction, Newman presented his inaugural address. Surprisingly, it paralleled rather closely the idea expressed by Killian that technological education should place emphasis upon fundamental disciplines as distinguished from the "immediately applicable, narrowly conceived, practical techniques." Newman also felt, as did President Day of Cornell, that technological education should be guided by "a steadfast recognition of the broader implications and social obligations of the vocation for which training is being provided." Newman never lost sight of these two principles during his entire administration. It may be added, however, that some of his faculty never acquired insight into what he was talking about. These individuals, accustomed to teaching the "immediately applicable" considered any other approach as an unfair imposition on the students. Some of the students agreed with this point of view. In spite of the divergent opinions as to the teaching of basic principles versus the teaching of the immediately applicable, Newman's introduction of the former principle into his administration laid foundations for considerable development of this idea in the administration subsequent to his.

Departing from a discussion of the need for emphasis upon fundamental principles and a recognition of social obligations, Newman then discussed what he called certain "characteristics or aspects of this institution [VPI] as they have emerged through the years." His intent he said, was to show if possible, "their significance in the present and for the future." The mandate given to VPI throughout its history, he believed, had been "to offer instruction leading towards proficiency in the professions involved in industry, agriculture, and the field of distribution." Newman did not, at this time, propose changing this mandate. Rather he said, "In attempting to achieve these objectives, the institution should place major emphasis upon instruction in agriculture, engineering, home economics, and business administration, along with basic supporting subjects." Since major emphasis was already in these areas of instruction, no particular interest was aroused by this statement. He had close attention from some in the audience, however, when he continued: "Areas of instruction closely associated with these just mentioned should be added, but no attempt should be made to encroach upon or to duplicate areas of general education and other professional curricula receiving emphasis in other state-supported institutions of higher learning in the Commonwealth."

This latter statement was unsatisfactory to a number of faculty members in the audience. Even as Newman made the statement, a discussion was under way in the state concerning ways and means of eliminating duplication of effort in the state institutions of higher learning. A number of the faculty felt, as Burruss had at an earlier date, that in the matter of duplication, VPI was more often sinned against than sinning. To some of these individuals it appeared that such investigations of duplication nearly always resulted in building fences around VPI which prevented the institution from making available services customarily offered by land-grant colleges. More than one faculty member was strongly of the opinion that such studies merely "prevented the *people's* college from becoming the people's *college*."

The portion of Newman's inaugural address which attracted the greatest attention on the campus, however, was the part dealing with military training and the Corps of Cadets. After a brief review of the evolution of the Corps as an inseparable part of VPI tradition and of the part it had played as thousands of alumni had received their education at Tech he said in part:

> I would be derelict in my duty if I did not also comment on the fact that there is gradually evolving a changing concept concerning military life and military regulations. General Bradley, chief of staff, in speaking of the training of young men drafted under Selective Service, says: If we are to make good use of these valuable years from the lives of draftees, then we must offer them a healthy moral, intellectual, and social climate in which they will serve willingly—not resentfully because of compulsion.
>
> VPI men must receive proper training in leadership in order to take their places in civil pursuits first, and, secondarily, prepare for the defense of America when and if this is necessary. The changing times must be recognized in the life of our fine Corps of Cadets.

The hint of modifying the Corps, perhaps by dropping the compulsory feature, sent a ripple of fear throughout the Alumni Association. Within a few years, this ripple grew into a sizeable wave which for a time threatened to engulf both Newman and the civilian student body.

Newman discussed other aspects of the institution, but only one further statement he made concerning the implications of these aspects will be considered here. In discussing the development of the work in engineering and science he said:

> Despite the fact that for many years the enrollment in engineering and the sciences has constituted the majority of the undergraduate student body, and valuable research has been conducted, funds for such work in science and engineering have not kept abreast of those in agriculture. More extensive research in all technical branches is needed if VPI is to offer instruction to its students and services to the State comparable to that afforded citizens and industries in other states.

In concluding his address, Newman pledged:

> Our most earnest desire is to dedicate the complex facilities of this institution to furthering the advance of agriculture, business, and industry to preparing our youth proficiently in the vocations, and at the same time, to develop human beings informed with humility and, thereby aware of their social privileges and duties.

The history of Newman's administration clearly demonstrates that his inaugural address was not a presidential platform to be laid aside following the inauguration.

The reaction in the state press to Newman's inauguration was favorable. In general, the press expressed the idea that he had already demonstrated exceptional qualities of leadership at VPI; therefore, he could be expected to render even greater service ahead. The agricultural features of the College's program as usual were heavily emphasized in the press, but some glimmering of the fact that the College was indeed more than an "ag school" appeared here and there; thus the Norfolk *Virginian Pilot* wrote in part, "Dr. Newman . . . will find himself at home with the varied curricula of VPI. It goes all the way from animal husbandry and business administration to the doctrine in the abstruse engineering sciences and in sociology."

As for Newman the man, *The Richmond News Leader* expressed the opinion implied by the majority of the press when it said:

> Were the choice to be before the board of visitors again, we do not know a single available person who would be so well equipped in all the essentials as President Newman is. Some might have greater experience in a specialty represented at VPI and some might have more pronounced aptitude in this administrative sphere or in that. For the challenging combination of duties, Dr. Newman is superlatively qualified. We look for another great administration at VPI and for the further enlargement of its service to the life of all Virginia.

A variety of other events, changes, and innovations following Newman's inauguration enlivened the campus.

Largely through the efforts of Graham Claytor ('06) the Appalachian Electric and Power Company gave the College a ninety-acre camp site on Claytor Lake, the latter having been named for Claytor.

Some nationally recognized teachers in the field of the humanities addressed faculty and students at the YMCA's popular Religious Emphasis Week and thereby touched off warm discussions on the role of the humanities in a technological institution.

Simultaneously some alumni discovered that VPI was not recognized by the Association of American Universities and that some discrimination had been shown toward its graduates seeking admission to certain graduate schools because of this fact. Excitement rose sharply with this group when it was discovered that its rival VMI was recognized by the association. Letters were addressed to Newman, the board, and alumni chapters, demanding to know why VPI was not recognized by the agency and at the same time demanding that steps be taken to secure such recognition. It turned out that no one would or could pinpoint specific reasons why VPI was not recognized. The consensus reached was that the institution offered insufficient liberal arts courses. This conclusion in turn precipitated additional debate on the meaning of "liberal arts."

Letters from students demanding increased courses in the "humanities" were published in *The Virginia Tech*. This demand led to a discussion of the meaning of the term "humanities." Some of the answers advanced alarmed the more vocationally oriented students especially the veterans, desiring to complete their interrupted education as soon as possible. Prominent engineering alumni returning to the campus by invitation to speak to faculty and student groups unwittingly added fuel to the discussions by endorsing the fundamental disciplines approach rather than the immediately applicable approach. Not only did this group want the emphasis placed on fundamental disciplines, but it also wanted a broader offering in humanistic studies. No specific solutions emerged from all of the discussions, but the way was made easier for the adoption of the curriculum changes slowly emerging in all of the schools of the College. Perhaps of greater importance, these discussions helped pave the way for the "further enlargement of its services to the life of all Virginia" prophesied for VPI by *The Richmond News Leader.*

The peak enrollment of veterans was reached during the session of 1948-49 with more than eight hundred students at Rad-Tech and a total enrollment of all sources of 5689. Improvements in the registration procedures introduced by a committee under the leadership of Professor A. V. Morris ('23) reduced the time students had to stand in line on registration days and helped somewhat in harmonizing the size of student sections with the size of classrooms available. Student numbers instead of student names began to assume increasing importance as International Business Machine cards with mysteriously punched holes began to replace the more familiar class roll and grade report forms. Some startling information was spewed out on occasion from the IBM office on IBM cards secretly doctored by curious students or by professors annoyed with the entire procedural changes in registration and grade reporting.

Serious difficulty resulted from the effort to accommodate the two different student bodies on the one campus, but in general the relationships between the two groups were harmonious. The student radio station WUVT was begun in the spring of '48; coeds for the first time were admitted to membership in the Block and Bridle Club; and the Maroon Mask under the able direction of Professor and Mrs. J. P. Milhous startled the entire campus community with the announced intention of producing "Brother Rat," a play based on cadet life at VMI. The cadet corps at VMI cooperated with this latter venture by lending the Maroon Mask needed VMI uniforms and by sending a large delegation to Blacksburg to attend the presentation of the play, which was well received by a record attendance.

Following his appointment as president, Newman had instituted an immediate search for a vice-president. After a prolonged search, during which time some thirty individuals had been considered, the position was offered to and accepted by Dr. C. Clement French, head of the department of chemistry at Randolph-Macon Woman's College. Dr. French entered into his duties at VPI in mid-January, 1949, and almost immediately won an enthusiastic following. By working closely with department heads and faculty committees he soon had the curriculum-revision programs already instituted by Newman moving forward toward specific implementation.

At French's suggestion, a member of the staff in the department of vocational education organized a remedial reading program to be conducted for the benefit of the entire College. When it became obvious that placing this new venture in the department of vocational education would require additional laboratory space and staff for the department, a suggestion was made that the laboratory space and staff be provided and that a division of psychology be organized within the department, which at the time was already teaching a number of courses in psychology. This proposal created something of a minor crisis. Would the creation of a division of psychology, even if included within a large department, constitute a legitimate enlargement of VPI's "service to the life of all Virginia" or would it constitute unnecessary duplication of work at other state supported institutions? After considerable discussion of the matter French decided it would be "unwise duplication at this time" to establish a specific division of psychology. The remedial reading program was then assigned to the office of guidance and placement, where it was taken over and developed by John R. Anderson. The course work in psychology, however, which had progressed from its listing in the catalog as agricultural education to vocational education was changed to its more accurate designation as courses offered in psychology.

Dr. French continued his unusually effective leadership until August, 1950, when he resigned to accept the post of dean of the college at Texas A and M College. From this position, he soon moved to the presidency of Washington State College, where he continued his distinguished career as a great educational leader.

Dr. W. H. Cato succeeded D. B. Dunlevy as director of guidance and placement in midsummer, 1949. At about the same time it was announced that Dr. W. J. Schoene, entomologist in the Experiment Station; Dr. Louis (Shag) O'Shaughnessy, director of graduate studies; and Dean C. P. Miles would retire under the VPI retirement plan and assume reduced duties on September 1, 1949. At the same time, the vice-president of the College assumed the directorship of graduate studies relinquished by O'Shaughnessy and the office of dean of the college was abolished. In lieu of this latter position, a "dean of the school of academic science and business administration" was to be appointed as soon as a suitable person could be found. Within a short time, this latter name was changed to that of a school of applied science and business administration. A department of statistics incorporating the statistical laboratory which had already been established was organized to begin in the fall of 1949 under the direction of Dr. Boyd Harshbarger (M.S. '31). At the same time a course entitled "Western Civilization" was organized by a committee under the chairmanship of Dr. B. O. Miller, to be offered as a required course for all engineering students. According to one alumnus this course, dubbed by the students as the "Norris Humanities," soon had one-hundred per cent participation from all engineering students—fifty per cent supported it—fifty per cent fought it.

During the same fall quarter, the huge biology department began to divide up into specialized departments. In 1935, Dr. I. D. Wilson, "I. D." to his students, had organized the departments of botany, plant pathology, zoology, and animal pathology into a closely knit department of biology. Since that date, the growth of the department and the addition of several more divisions of biological sciences had made the department administratively unwieldy even for a man of Wilson's admittedly great administrative ability. The first specialty thought to be ready to stand on its own feet as a separate department was that of plant pathology and physiology; consequently, a new department by this name was started with Dr. S. A. Wingard at the head. The same report carrying the announcement of the formation of this new department also announced the appointment of Dr. W. P. (Wes) Judkins as head of the department of horticulture to succeed the deceased Dr. Overholser.

Femoyer, Monteith, and Thomas dormitories were completed in the fall of '49; and it was decided to discontinue Rad-Tech. All students housed there were returned to the main campus for the winter quarter. Considerable excitement and an equal degree of protest was generated in segments of the student body when it was learned that the board had determined to employ house mothers, or matrons, for the new dormitories. The board overrode student protest, however, and to the surprise of many, alumni and students as well, the use of house mothers in the dormitories proved to be quite successful.

Plans for extensive repairs and improvement to the president's home in "the Grove" were advanced and drew immediate, albeit anonymous, objections from some, presumably alumni, who frankly admitted they were opposed to all of the changes emerging so rapidly on the campus. The president's home had been considered to be somewhat of a white elephant by Presidents Barringer, Eggleston, and Burruss, the latter having at one time gone so far as to suggest abandoning it as a president's home and converting it into a coed dormitory. The board authorized the repairs to be made, however, and Dr. and Mrs. Newman upon the completion of the improvements held an "open house" which gave the faculty an opportunity to pass judgment upon the completed project.

Perhaps the most baffling problem faced by Newman during his entire administration was that of determining the best policy to follow with respect to military training and the Cadet Corps. It was obvious to most officials on the campus that the Corps was losing its appeal to entering students. Many students entering the Corps as freshmen dropped out to enter the civilian student body at the first opportunity. In addition to the veterans enrolling as civilians, the number enrolled in this latter group was constantly swelled by transfer students entering at the junior class level from the branch colleges. In fact, a little-publicized study conducted by the director of admissions confirmed that a number of students purposely enrolled in the branch schools for two years in order to avoid having to enroll in the Corps. Another study conducted by the same office revealed that a number of Virginia's superior high school graduates were refusing to enroll at Tech because of the military requirements. Studies of grade distributions between cadets and civilians, although inconclusive, tended to show the civilian students earning the best grades. An increasing number of parents were demanding to know why a student, if he wanted to study a course like agriculture which was offered in Virginia only at VPI, had to enter the Corps of Cadets to do so. The pre-war answer that it was a college regulation set up by the Board of Visitors did little to satisfy this group. Equally disturbing was the fact that a number of outstanding high school teachers of science working in the Virginia Junior Academy of Science were unhappy about the military system as represented in the Corps of Cadets at VPI. Many of this group felt that the military environment surrounding the Corps was detrimental to the continued development of the "scientific attitude" which they had tried to impart to their students. A number of these teachers bluntly informed VPI's representative working with the Junior Academy that not only would they not recommend VPI to their graduates, they would do the opposite—they would advise their graduates not go to VPI if they had to enter the Corps of Cadets.

Newman was not anti-Corps as some accused him of being, but he did not believe that ignoring the problem would make it go away. He discussed the matter with a number of alumni chapters and finally wound up by asking the officers of the Alumni Association to appoint a committee to cooperate with the Board of Visitors in studying the problem and suggesting a solution. A number of alumni chapters immediately adopted resolutions urging the board to strengthen the Corps of Cadets. One chapter even urged the college administration to conduct a rigorous examination of all prospective faculty members and to employ only those persons sympathetic to military training and the VPI traditions already built up around the Corps. The specific traditions to be perpetuated were not named. Another suggestion was made to require the branch schools also to offer two years of military training. If this was done, reported the chapter, the transfer students could then be required to enter the Corps. All of the chapters reporting or responding to the situation urged the board to take steps to strengthen the Corps. It appeared to these organizations that the adoption of a few rules and regulations by the board would accomplish this objective. President Newman, closer to the situation, had his doubts.

The overall problem of military training was further complicated, he reported to the board, by the fact that other colleges in Virginia and elsewhere were offering ROTC work without a cadet military organization. At VPI, ROTC work and the cadet military organization were so closely interrelated that the senior ROTC instructor acted as commandant of cadets. "Older alumni feel that the heart and soul of VPI is the cadet corps . . ." Newman told the board, but ". . . applicants for admission who are interested in an education and a reserve commission do not always agree . . ." he said.

The board, which was making a study of the overall program of the College, did not know what to do about the problem; but, following the precedent set by previous boards when confronted with the same vexing concern, it appointed a committee to study the matter. Before this committee could complete a report, the College entered the decade often referred to as the "fabulous fifties."

The decade of the fifties was one unparalleled in the previous history of VPI for growth and advancement along all fronts. Established programs were strengthened and new ones were launched. Student activities, student government, and student life assumed new directions. Services to the state expanded in numerous ways. The athletic program was revamped and expanded. Student enrollment fell alarmingly and almost immediately increased in the same way. Changes were introduced which put more administrative responsibility on the faculty. Expansion of the physical plant made the roar of bulldozers and the sight of construction elevators and derrick booms against the skyline a familiar part of the campus scene. Even as growth and change alternately irritated and titillated the faculty, the established schools pursued their customary courses and performed their usual duties with generally satisfactory results. It is impossible in this narrative to follow all of the developments of the fifties. Those which for one reason or another were brought to the attention of the public eye or were thrust into the deliberations of the faculty, administration, or alumni emerge here as a brief record of events which may be filled in with greater detail by alumni who lived among them.

The return of the students from Rad-Tech to the campus in January, 1950, marked a definite break with the decade overshadowed by World War II. The fleet of yellow buses dubbed by the students as the "yellow perils" and the "striped tigers," which had been used for transportation from the "outpost campus" to the main campus, was sold. The government once more took over the Rad-Tech dormitories as it resumed the manufacture of powder because of the developments in the "cold war." The number of enrolled veterans, which had reached its peak during the 1948-49 session, declined sharply, causing the total enrollment to drop from a high of 5,689 to 3,215 for the session of 1952-53. From this date, the enrollment began a slow rise, which by mid-decade accelerated almost as rapidly as it had fallen, reaching 5,747 for the session of 1960-61.

The problems concerning the Corps of Cadets did not fade away. On the contrary, they surfaced with increasing frequency, generating countless rumors in the process. Matters were brought into sharper focus when J. P. Fishburne of

Roanoke, a distinguished member of the Board of Visitors, admitted to the Roanoke Chapter of the Alumni Association that the matter of compulsory military training was under consideration. "The question," Fishburne said, "is whether military training will be required or optional for future students." At the same meeting, Fishburne questioned the right of VPI to require military training for all. If it did so, he inquired, can VPI do the educational job for Virginia of which it is capable?

The excitement caused by this statement led Newman to issue a lengthy clarifying statement concerning the military study being conducted by the board. No sudden drastic changes were contemplated by the board, he said, but the expansion of the institution in its physical plant, its course offerings, its graduate programs, its research programs, in fact its total service to the state of Virginia, made it necessary to consider some modification in the military life on the campus. The board was seeking some plan, said Newman, which would "enable the institution to continue the ROTC training and the Corps of Cadets and likewise make it possible for the institution to serve agriculture, industry, and business in the state in an ever-expanding and improving manner." This statement did not settle the growing controversy. One alumnus sourly observed that all it did was to show that "the administration" wanted to "eat its cake and have it too."

In June the board of directors of the Alumni Association joined the discussion. In a lengthy meeting with the directors Newman reiterated his often repeated belief that it was possible and necessary to modify the Corps in such a manner that it would be attractive to entering students and at the same time not interfere with the development of the institution.

Following this meeting, the alumni directors issued a nine-point statement which in effect strongly endorsed the Corps, urged its retention, denied that the Corps stood in the way of high academic achievement, and "viewed with the greatest alarm any action which might in any way weaken the Corps of Cadets." Furthermore, continued the statement, "The [alumni] board believes that any change in the basic concept of the Corps of Cadets would have a disastrous effect on the general morale, spirit, support, and cooperation of alumni." Copies of this statement were sent to "the Governor of Virginia, to each member of the Board of Visitors, to the president of the College, and to the president and secretary of each alumni chapter," as well as to the editor of *The Techgram*. The administration was respectfully requested "to advise the Alumni Association of the decision reached by the administration concerning this vital matter and to receive a committee of the alumni board prior to the presentation of its report to the Board of Visitors."

Public reaction to this statement was mixed, but the summer vacation and its attendant activities pushed consideration of the problem into the background. It was brought into sharp focus on the campus again during the session of 1951-52 when a number of civilian students, mostly veterans, started a prolonged anti-Corps agitation under the slogan, "The Corps Must Go." *The Virginia Tech* duly reported the agitation on the campus and in the spring of '52 conducted a poll of the alumni on their opinions concerning the retention of the Corps. Alumni opinion, to the surprise of no one, turned out to be overwhelmingly favorable to the retention of the organization. Vernon G. Eberwine ('17), chairman of the Board of Visitors' committee studying the situation, when pressed for a statement said that the board had "no idea" of abandoning the Corps of Cadets. "What we would like to do," he said, "is to make every possible effort to strengthen the Corps and make it more popular." Eberwine's statement, perhaps calming and soothing to alumni, did nothing at all to calm the unrest on the campus, where, as Newman reported to the board, there was "an appreciable gulf between the military students and the civilian students."

In a sincere effort to solve the problem the Board of Visitors reaffirmed its intention to operate the College with two student bodies and pledged its efforts to strengthen both groups. As one step in this latter direction, it decided to employ a full-time commandant of cadets responsible to the administration only. ROTC instruction would be continued by a staff of armed service personnel as usual, but henceforth the instruction would be organized as a department of instruction with no direct responsibilities for the Corps of Cadets. In effect the board proposed to operate the Corps under a commandant, and to operate the civilian student body under the director of civilian students. The individuals selected for these two positions would be given adequate staff and would be expected to work cooperatively in promotion and coordination of the interests and activities of both student groups. Specific plans for operating the new program were to be developed by the administration which was "directed" to take the necessary steps "to assure complete cooperation among the various departments of the Institute" in putting the program into effect.

Newman accepted the board's decision and directive in good faith. At the same time, a few murmurs from the faculty concerning academic freedom were heard on the possible intent of the directive "to take necessary steps to assure complete cooperation among the various departments of the Institute." Other individuals close to the campus felt that the directive was unfair to Dr. Newman in that it was "directing" him to achieve the impossible.

Once more summer vacation intervened to calm the Corps problem. In the meantime, it was announced in August, 1952, that Major General John M. Devine had been appointed as the new commandant of cadets and that Joseph Wiley Guthridge had been promoted from assistant director of student affairs to the position of director of civilian students and coordinator of student activities. Dr. R. E. Bates had resigned this latter position to become dean of students at Colorado Agricultural and Mechanical College. Joseph E. Hardy, dormitory manager, was promoted to associate director of civilian students and assigned increased responsibilities pertaining to dormitory life. Both Guthridge, or "Wiley Joe" to those who enjoyed reversing his given name, and Hardy were well known and popular with faculty, cadets, and civilian students. Before long, General Devine also won the respect and admiration of all these groups. Under these three men and a new set of student-life regulations adopted in the fall of '52, student-life conditions showed appreciable improvement for the next several years. Whether the Cadet Corps was increasing in stature and wisdom, however, continued to be a warmly debated question. In the fall of 1955 the board in consideration of "some general misunderstanding as to the status of the Corps of Cadets at the Virginia Polytechnic Institute," reiterated its determination to continue the Corps and the civilian student body. Notification by the Department of Defense in 1956 that VPI was included in the small number of schools classified by the department as military colleges led the board to adopt a resolution which in effect congratulated VPI for both past and present military achievements. The board was of the strong opinion that the Corps of

Cadets chiefly was responsible for the fine military showing made by the College. Credit for the "fine achievement" in being included in the "select list" was divided by the board between Newman and Devine. "In the list of colleges named by the Department of Defense," said the board, "VPI is one of only two land-grant colleges listed as a military college." Instead of filling the faculty and students with pride and joy, however, the statement strengthened the conviction of many that Tech through its Cadet Corps was clinging to a system of student organization long since discarded by most land-grant institutions. In spite of the earnest efforts of the administration and of Commandant Devine, there was no concerted effort on the part of the students to enlarge the Corps by electing to remain in it at the end of the required two-year membership.

The decade saw a number of administrative and faculty changes caused by death, retirement, and resignations. In April, 1950, the beloved dean of agriculture, T. B. Hutcheson, died very suddenly. H. N. Young, director of the Agricultural Experiment Station, was drafted to fill the position of dean while a permanent successor was sought. The search for a suitable person proved to be a long one. Finally, after an unusually thorough search for a suitable individual, Newman recommended L. B. Dietrick, director of the Agricultural Extension Service, for the position. At the same time he informed the board that Dietrick was not a candidate for the place and might not accept it even if it was offered to him. The board made some significant adjustments and clarifications of the duties of the dean's office and then unanimously elected Dietrick as dean. After considerable pressure from a number of individuals, Dietrick (M. S. '28) accepted the deanship and entered upon the duties of the office on October 1, 1952. At the same time Dietrick became dean of agriculture, W. H. Daughtrey ('27) was appointed as associate director of the Agricultural Extension Service. With these appointments completed, Young returned to his full-time duties in the Agricultural Experiment Station.

When Dean Miles had announced his intention to retire from the deanship in 1949, he had offered to serve until a successor could be found. The administration accepted this offer and began a search for a man with qualifications to serve as dean of the school of applied sciences and business administration. Since the College was under pressure to strengthen and enlarge its offerings in the humanities, the administration wanted a dean with training in one of these areas. Such a man was found in the person of Dr. George Burke Johnston, who at the time was serving as assistant dean of the college of arts and sciences and professor of English at the University of Alabama. Johnston assumed his duties as dean on September 1, 1950, at which time Miles returned to part-time teaching duties in the department of English and foreign languages.

In effect, Johnston was returning to VPI, since he had served at the College as instructor in English from 1930 to 1933, when he had resigned to return to Columbia University to study for his Ph.D. degree. He had been quite popular with faculty and students; indeed in the *Bugle* elections of 1933 the students voted him to be the "best sport" on the college faculty. Seventeen years later this "best sport," leaving behind him strong accolades in *The Tuscaloosa (Ala.) News,* returned to the campus to pick up the duties of dean of the school of applied science and business administration.

In August of the same year, it was announced that Dr. Louis A. Pardue, dean of the graduate school at the University of Kentucky, had been appointed as vice-president and director of graduate studies to succeed C. C. French, resigned. Pardue, with his Ph.D. degree in physics from Yale University, came to VPI with both administrative and teaching experience in higher education. His wartime experiences with the "Manhattan Project," which led to the development of the atomic bomb, and his close connection with the Oak Ridge Institute of Nuclear Studies, with headquarters at Oak Ridge, Tennessee, were also impressive.

The appointment of Johnston and Pardue was pleasing to most of the faculty, who felt that such appointments would bring new perspectives to the college affairs. Minor murmurs of resentment that Newman had passed over "well-qualified" faculty in the making of these two key appointments quickly died out as these two men introduced new dimensions of cooperation with the faculty in introducing new programs and strengthening the old ones.

Dean Earl B. Norris continued to serve with vigor until his retirement on his seventieth birthday in September, 1952, at which time he was succeeded by John W. (Jack) Whittemore, who had been serving as associate dean since 1943. Before his retirement, Norris had the satisfaction of seeing the number of curricula in the school of engineering grow from six to twelve, all accredited by the Engineering Council for Professional Development. Only three other schools in the country had this many. The appointment of Whittemore as dean of the school of engineering and architecture completed Newman's appointment of his top administrative officials for the decade. With the assistance of these men, namely Johnston, Pardue, Dietrick, and Whittemore, Newman recruited and promoted numerous individuals to fill faculty positions or to become heads of instructional divisions.

Improvements in the retirement system inaugurated in 1952 helped make the prospects of retirement less unattractive to faculty members. These changes did not produce any clamor for retirement, but they did help create a happier climate for the administration and for the increasing number of faculty members approaching the retirement age.

The interesting record of the faculty changes during the decade is too voluminous for inclusion here. A listing of changes in heads of departments, however, seems more than fitting as one way of saying goodbye to a group of outstanding men long identified with VPI and at the same time welcoming a group of worthy successors. The chronology of welcome and farewell is general only and in no way intended as official.

Colonel W. B. Merritt succeeded Colonel T. W. Munford as commandant of cadets in July, 1950. Merritt retired from service almost immediately after he was succeeded as commandant by Major General John M. Devine in 1952.

Professor R. B. H. Begg, colorful head of the civil engineering department, retired and was succeeded in the fall of '50 by P. H. McGauhey, who returned to the campus from Southern California, where he had been on leave from Tech since 1948. McGauhey was no stranger to the campus, since he had joined the faculty in 1927. He did not remain as head of the civil engineering department long but resigned within a short time to accept a permanent position at the University of California at Berkeley. He was succeeded by R. C. Brinker, who resigned in 1957 and was in turn succeeded by Henry C. Morris.

In the fall of 1951, R. W. Truitt succeeded A. E. Rowland as head of the department of aeronautical engineering. Rowland had resigned to accept a job in industry in Ohio.

In January, 1952, Dr. Charles K. Martin succeeded Dr. D. W. Peters, deceased, as president of Radford College. Within a very short time Martin succeeded in launching Radford College Women's Division of VPI on the greatest period of growth and expansion in its history.

During the winter of '52 Professor R. E. Hunt requested that he be permitted to give up the headship of the department of animal husbandry but to continue as teacher and adviser to students in that department. Hunt was succeeded by Professor George W. Litton, who had served as acting head of the department in 1947-48 while Hunt was on leave in Syria serving as adviser to the Syrian government. The success of George Litton with his homespun philosophy in building this department into one of the strongest at VPI warrants greater elaboration than this narrative can sustain.

In 1951, Dr. E. L. Long, assistant minister at the Blacksburg Presbyterian Church, was appointed on a part-time basis to introduce courses in ethics and philosophy, which had long since been dropped from the cirriculum. This step was taken on an experimental basis in response to overtures from certain student groups and from the Blacksburg Ministerial Association. This latter organization assumed major responsibility for financing the first year of this venture from private rather than public funds. The new courses proved so popular that a one-man department of philosophy and religion was started in 1955 under Long. He resigned to accept a position at Oberlin College and was succeeded in 1957 by Dr. Norman L. Grover, assistant professor of philosophy and religion at Hollins College. At the same time, Dr. Guy B. Hammond was added to the staff, thereby providing a two-man staff for the department of philosophy and religion.

In 1952, Henry Dekker ('44), popular young treasurer, resigned to enter business. He was succeeded by J. F. Boone ('37). According to the students, Boone spent his first year in office trying to devise painless methods of extracting college fees from all students and then developing foolproof methods of guarding the fees once they had been extracted. Certain students attest he succeeded only with the second endeavor. Nevertheless, he has served long and well.

During 1951, Mrs. Helen Holland, vivacious and talented wife of Professor Charles T. Holland, head of the department of mining engineering, took over the direction of the glee club and steered it through the difficult years of the early fifties.

Dr. Charles R. Woolwine, health officer for twenty-three years, retired in 1951 and was succeeded by Dr. C. R. Lyons, who remained until 1956, at which time he was succeeded by Dr. E. R. Irvin ('28). Dr. Lyons was the first health officer to serve in the enlarged infirmary, now Henderson Hall, completed in 1951. To the surprise of no one, the students nicknamed the infirmary the "lion's den."

In the fall of 1952, Dr. G. C. Graf succeeded Professor C. W. Holdaway as head of the department of dairy husbandry. Graf had joined the faculty in 1945. During his nearly forty-eight years on the faculty Professor Holdaway had served the dairy interests of the state in practically every way possible for a man to serve.

During the same year, Professor Paul S. Dear was promoted to head of the department of ceramic engineering, which had become vacant when J. W. Whittemore had moved up to the deanship.

Also during the year, the department of agricultural chemistry was reorganized as a department of biochemistry and nutrition. Dr. R. W. (Charlie) Engel, professor of animal nutrition at Alabama Polytechnic Institute, was recruited to head up this department. Engel quickly demonstrated not only leadership but a sense of humor as he went about explaining to faculty why he objected to having his departmental mail being addressed to the abbreviated department of "Bio. C. and Nut."

The retirement of R. W. (Bob) Bingham, also in '52, as stockroom man in the department of chemistry for forty-three years, evoked as many nostalgic reminiscences from alumni as did the retirement of any department head. "Bob" probably helped more discouraged freshmen unravel the mystery of the "known in the unknown" solutions concocted in the chemistry laboratory than any other man ever employed at Tech.

The fall of '54 saw a number of additional changes and promotions. Dr. Fred W. Bull ('33) was promoted to head of the chemical engineering department, succeeding Dr. Frank C. Vilbrandt, who gave up administrative duties in favor of teaching. The latter continued as a teacher until his sudden death in 1960.

Professor E. T. Swink ('30) succeeded Professor Charles E. Seitz as head of the department of agricultural engineering. Seitz retired during the same year. He continued to live in Blacksburg and took an active part in the development of the VPI-Blacksburg-Christiansburg Water Authority until advancing age forced his retirement from this organization.

Dr. Wilson B. Bell ('34), animal pathologist in the Agricultural Experiment Station, was promoted to fill the newly created post of associate director of the Agricultural Experiment Station.

During the same year Dr. M. V. Nevitt ('51) was promoted to become head of the metallurgical engineering department to succeed Professor H. Vance White ('26), who had died earlier in the year. Nevitt resigned in late 1955 to enter business and was succeeded in 1956 by Dr. John F. Eckel, consulting metallurgist with the General Electric Company.

During the spring of '54, Dr. Frank L. Robeson ('04) announced his intention to retire from the headship of the department of physics. Dr. T. Marshall Hahn, professor of physics at the University of Kentucky, was recruited as his successor. Hahn resigned in 1959 to go to Kansas State University as dean of arts and sciences. Dr. Thomas E. Gilmer "consented to serve as acting head" until a successor to Hahn could be found. After a considerable search Dr. James A. Jacobs, professor of physics at the State University of Iowa, was recruited to begin his duties as head of the department in the fall of 1960.

In 1955, Professor T. W. Knote, who had built the department of business administration into the largest on the campus, announced his intention to retire after thirty-five years as a faculty member. Dr. B. O. Miller declined to accept the headship of the department but agreed to serve as acting head until a successor could be found. Dr. T. H. Cox, "former government official, businessman, and teacher" with his Ph.D. degree from Iowa, accepted the headship in 1956. He resigned in 1958 to return to government service. Miller once more agreed to serve as acting head of the department until a new head could be found. In the fall of 1959, it was announced that Dr. H. H. (Bill) Mitchell, head of the business administration department at Mississippi State University, had been appointed to the position, effective in February, 1960.

Professor Clinton H. Cowgill, for twenty-eight years head of the department of architecture, announced his intention to retire at the end of the summer of 1956. Cowgill, who had played a significant role in planning for the physical development of the campus under three administrations, was succeeded by Leonard G. Currie, who came to Tech from Bogota, Columbia, where he had headed the Inter-American Housing Center since 1951.

Ill health led Professor W. A. (Bill) Murray, for nearly twenty-one years head of the electrical engineering department, to step down from administrative duties in this department in the fall of 1956. He continued to teach until his full retirement in 1959. Murray was succeeded by B. M. Widener ('25) as acting head. Widener died suddenly in 1958, at which time Professor George R. Powley ('38) was appointed acting and later full-time head of the department.

The rapid turnover of department heads slowed down in 1957 with only one occurring. Professor Harry L. Moore, head of the department of poultry husbandry, retired to accept a two-year appointment to Laos by the International Cooperation Administration. He was succeeded in February, 1958, by Dr. C. E. Howes, professor of poultry husbandry at the University of Maine.

Dr. Mildred T. Tate, head of the department of home economics since 1937, resigned, effective July 1, 1958. The resignation of Dr. Tate, a tireless advocate for the cause of women on the VPI campus, was felt by many persons to be a blow to the cause of coeducation at Tech. She was succeeded by Dr. Laura Jane Harper, however, who as acting head of the department continued the fight for wider recognition of coeds. Dr. Harper had joined the Tech staff in 1949. In September, 1960, she was made dean of the coordinated school of home economics on the Blacksburg and Radford campuses.

Dr. I. D. Wilson, after serving nearly thirty-five years as head of the department of biology, retired in January, 1958, in order to accept a two-year appointment as an educational adviser in India. Dr. F. S. Orcutt was promoted to acting head and a short time later to permanent head of this huge department which Wilson had developed.

Dr. J. W. (Quiz) Watson ('09), head of the chemistry department, retired at the end of the summer of '58 after having served on the faculty for forty-five years. He was succeeded by Dr. Robert C. Krug, a member of the faculty since 1949.

In September, 1958, Miss Maude E. Wallace retired as assistant director of the Virginia Agricultural Extension Service. Miss Wallace, who had been in charge of home demonstration work in the Old Dominion since 1929, was succeeded by Miss Lucy P. Blake, district home demonstration agent in east central district since 1948. Miss Blake had joined the extension service in 1934.

During the early summer of 1958, it was announced that Joseph W. Guthridge planned to leave to accept a post as director of placement at Georgia Tech. Marcus L. Oliver ('44) served as acting director of student affairs until Dr. James W. Dean was recruited to replace Guthridge. Dean, who was assigned the title of director of student affairs and dean of civilian students, reported for duty on March 1, 1959. Dr. Dean was the first person with extensive training in education, guidance, and student personnel administration ever employed to work with students at VPI. At the same time Dean was appointed, it was announced that Albert W. Crawford, civilian dormitory counselor since 1952, had been promoted to the post of assistant dean of civilian students.

The year 1960 had scarcely begun before the entire campus community and alumni were saddened by the death of Alumni Secretary Henry B. (Puss) Redd ('19), who had devoted his entire adult life to advancing Tech athletics and alumni services. Redd, who had served either as part-time or full-time alumni secretary since 1926, was succeeded on March 1, 1960, by Marcus L. Oliver. Oliver had been serving as assistant alumni secretary since 1949 and therefore continued the functions of the office with little or no break.

During the spring of 1960, Dr. M. Clifford Harrison, head of the department of English and foreign languages and for forty-five years a member of the Tech faculty, announced his intention to retire at the end of the summer session. He was succeeded as head of the department by Dr. Markham L. Peacock, who had joined the faculty in 1926.

After nine years as commandant, Major General Devine retired in June of 1961. Devine, certainly as popular as any commandant ever to serve at VPI, presented the commencement address in June of that year. He was succeeded as commandant by Brigadier General M. W. Schewe.

During the same year of '61, Dr. James B. Eades, Jr., ('44) succeeded Dr. R. W. Truitt as head of the department of aeronautical engineering. Dr. Truitt resigned to accept the headship of the department of mechanical engineering at North Carolina State College.

Three additional appointments completed the major additions to the faculty during the year of 1961. Dr. Archer Jones, dean of Clinch Valley College in Wise County, was named to the headship of the newly created department of history and political science, effective September 1. Dr. John F. Hosner, associate professor of forestry at Southern Illinois University, was appointed as head of the department of forestry and wildlife; and Dr. J. R. Lucas, head of the mining engineering division at Ohio State University, was named head of the department of mining engineering to succeed Professor C. T. Holland, who resigned to become dean of the school of mines at West Virginia University.

Newman's experiences convinced him very early in the decade that the great majority of people in Virginia had a decidedly limited understanding of the services the College was rendering and was capable of rendering to the state. He felt that this limited understanding helped explain the conservative stance often manifested toward VPI by the legislature and by certain newsapers in the state. Conveying this conviction to the board he urged its members to keep this possibility in mind as they made their customary contacts with people throughout the state. Without being specific, Newman made it clear that he felt the time had come for the College to involve more people in telling the story of VPI's services and needs. To Eggleston's typewriter, and Burruss' mimeograph and printing press, Newman, without announcing it, was ready to add people as a medium for telling the VPI story. A number of circumstances and developments made the addition a reality.

John R. Hutcheson, working through the VPI Educational Foundation, contributed significantly toward getting more people involved in developing the VPI story. In inaugurating the foundation, Hutcheson organized a board of directors made up of representatives from the college administration, the Board of Visitors, the Alumni Association, and from industrial leaders representing a wide spectrum of industries within and without the state. Both Newman and Hutcheson quickly saw to it that this group of highly influential people became aware of VPI's far-flung activities, needs, and potentials for even greater service.

Working through alumni, faculty, and the foundation's board of directors, Hutcheson made contact with individuals and industries having possible interest "in making an investment in Virginia Polytechnic Institute." Naturally in making these contacts the College's program, services, resources, and potentials for growth were brought into sharp focus. The full history of the foundation has never been written, but the results, while not spectacular in comparison with many older colleges and universities, were quite pleasing, even surprising to early skeptics. In addition to financial support, the more realistic understanding of the VPI program generated by the foundation activities has proved quite beneficial to the College from that day to this, and promises to be even more helpful in the future.

The official recognition of the Virginia Engineering Experiment Station at VPI by legislative action in 1950 also helped generate better public understanding of VPI's program. The Board of Visitors, at Burruss' insistence, had established the station in 1921. Under the original plan each department in the school of engineering had to carry on its research within the normal operating budget; consequently, in addition to weak financing, other difficulties were encountered in setting up research projects which cut across departmental lines. The legislative action of 1950 established the station as a separate division with a research function and a budget of its own, under the direct control of the Board of Visitors. Dean Norris, who had been director of the older station since 1932, continued as director under the new arrangement until his retirement in 1952, at which time Dean J. W. Whittemore became director. The financial record-keeping for the station was assigned to already existing agencies in the College, thereby keeping overhead operation to a minimum. The newly recognized station quickly expanded its projects, some of which involved the crossing of departmental lines, to include research on problems of particular significance to smaller industries and businesses in the state. A series of rules and regulations were set up, and cooperative programs of cost sharing on research were developed with a number of industries. In other instances the station undertook to finance the full cost of projects. Advisory personnel often were called in to help with particular research problems, or to help with the general program. As one result of this total effort the school of engineering received favorable publicity on a greatly broadened front, and an increasing number of people learned of VPI's story of service to the state.

The cooperative education program, although not organized for this purpose, also helped disseminate information about VPI. This program, put into operation in June 1952, was labeled by the students as the "earn while learning" program. It permitted the students to alternate quarters of study on the campus with quarters at work in industry. After a slow start, the program became more popular and helped the faculty learn about industry and industry to learn about VPI. This program was developed on the Blacksburg campus under the aggressive leadership of Dr. E. D. Harrison, who later became president of the Georgia Institute of Technology.

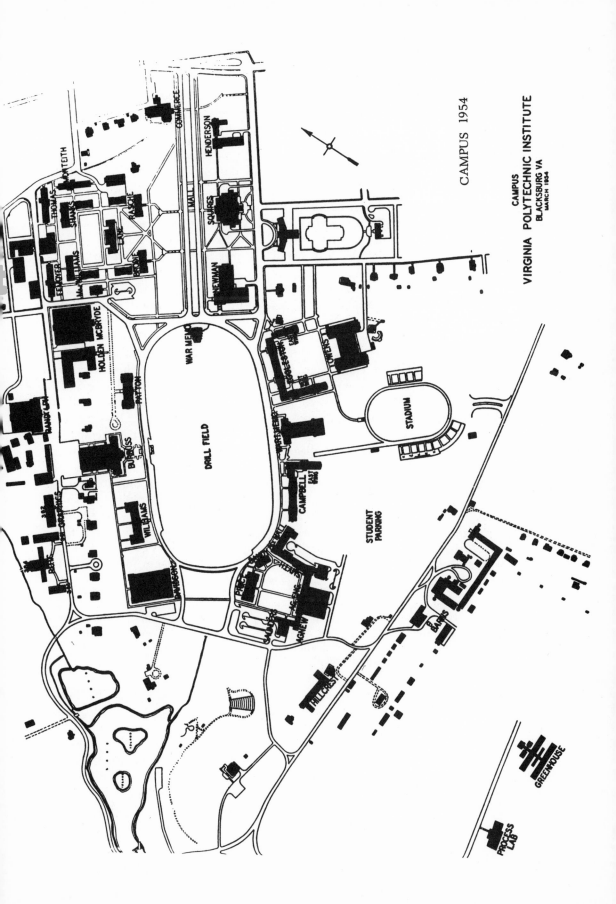

CAMPUS 1954

CAMPUS
VIRGINIA POLYTECHNIC INSTITUTE
BLACKSBURG VA
MARCH 1954

While these relatively new agencies were spreading a part of the story of VPI's service to the state, the school of agriculture was not idle. Through its programs of teaching and its state and federally supported programs of extension and research the school was in the best position of all to tell of its service to the state. Under the leadership of Dietrick as dean, Young as director of the Experiment Station, and Daughtrey as associate director of the Extension Service, the school did a superb job. The complete story would be a full history in itself. Long before the decade was over practically every organization in Virginia connected with agriculture and rural life had been given an opportunity to hear about VPI, its services, and its potentials for greater service. Perhaps of equal importance to VPI, most of these organizations before the end of the decade also were helping to generate support in the legislature for VPI's expanding services.

Newman gave freely of his time and energy to all the agencies and organizations attempting to interpret the College to the people. Already popular and widely known throughout the state because of his earlier work in public education, he was much in demand as a speaker for an unusually large variety of programs relating to the educational, agricultural, industrial, or business development of the Commonwealth. Since VPI was also concerned with all of these areas of development, Newman seldom experienced any difficulty relating VPI's program and potentials to particular problems in these areas. He spoke with a straightforward simplicity, friendliness, and earnestness that nearly always got his story across to the audience and at the same time created a feeling of empathy between the audience and the College. One well-known newspaper columnist, commenting on this characteristic said of Newman: "He has the capacity to get anyone, except probably VMI alumni, enthusiastic about VPI and its future."

Newman's effort to get more people involved in spreading the VPI story got an unexpected boost from *The Roanoke Times* and *The Roanoke World-News* very early in the decade. In late December 1949, it was announced that Newman would present a fifteen-minute program over the VPI WDBJ [Roanoke] radio network, telling of some of Tech's contributions to the state. This announcement led the editor of *The Roanoke Times* to comment:

> He cannot possibly hope to cover the ground comprehensively in a bare quarter of an hour, it goes without saying. To do that would require the [radio] station's entire time on the air from sun-up to sun-down . . . some [services] will be new to them [listeners] on the myriad ways in which the great engineering and agricultural school up at Blacksburg is serving the Commonwealth and the people.

Newman gave the radio talk, and it did indeed surprise many of the listeners. One of those surprised was State Editor William Bagbey of *The Roanoke World-News,* who immediately decided to prepare a series of newspaper articles on Tech and its program. This series prepared by Bagbey after lengthy visits to the campus, ran for more than a month in the *World-News.* The articles, each prepared as a complete feature, represented one of the most comprehensive reports on VPI ever brought together by a newspaper. Before long, other newspapers throughout the state also began to publish features on various facets of the VPI program, which before the end of the decade was touching the lives of so many people in the state.

Much of the progress achieved by VPI can be attributed to the vision and leadership manifested by its Board of Visitors. This leadership was particularly strong during the last quarter of the College's first century of existence. For one thing, the boards operating during this period began to develop a broader vision of services which a land-grant college, as the people's college, could and should render throughout the state. Along with this vision, the board members also began to realize, apparently grudgingly at first, that the accomplishment of this vision would require action and decision which would break rather sharply with some of the traditions of the past. One of the first decisions which led to the most visible break with the past involved plans for the development of the physical plant.

During his incumbency, President Hutcheson had appointed a local buildings and grounds committee to consider plans for the future development and location of buildings on the campus. Working through the firm of Alfred Hopkins and Associates, the committee completed its plan and presented it to the board in the spring of 1950. The board gave tentative approval to the plan, which provided for a "physical plant development to accommodate an enrollment of 10,000 students." Exact details were not spelled out, for some flexibility was included to provide for conditions prevailing at the future time the individual units were to be constructed.

Work was started almost immediately on implementing the plan. The old Administration Building, a familiar landmark for nearly half a century, was demolished during the summer of '50 to make way for the approaches to the World War II Memorial. The stones from this building were saved to be used in the construction of the memorial. This construction got under way in 1951 under a nonprofit contract with the English Construction Company of Altavista, Virginia. This company, with W. Curtis English ('32) as president and E. R. (Red) English ('34) as vice-president, agreed to construct the memorial at cost. Before the end of the year the State Department of Highways had also started construction on the mall. During the year an improvement project was started on College Avenue, especially the portion in front of Squires Hall. Within a very short time grading and construction was started on buildings now identified as Henderson, Williams, the power house, the meat processing laboratory, and Randolph Hall. Smyth Hall was completed in 1950, but large areas around Smyth, Femoyer, Montieth, Thomas, and other buildings needed walkways, roadways, landscaping, grading, shrubbery, and grass. A number of utility lines had to be dug up and relocated in ditches and tunnels which in turn had to be constructed, usually in new locations.

As one result of this and other simultaneous construction projects during the first half of the decade, the eastern section of the campus was torn up to a greater extent than had been known in the history of the College. At the same time the southwest, or agricultural area, did not escape disruption, since it too was torn up for the underground location of utilities, tunnels, and drains and for the aboveground landscaping, seeding, and planting of shrubbery. Building projects more extensive than the ones undertaken between 1950-55 have been completed, but the location of these projects never again required so great a disruption of the campus as that caused by the projects under way between 1950-55.

The construction projects did not contribute to improved campus morale. Rain often turned the raw dirt from the ditches and excavations, which extended in all directions, into a morass of mud. In spite of efforts to provide temporary walkways, the mud made walking difficult and treacherous for faculty and students. Vivid accounts of having "slipped and fallen into a ditch" were heard from all sides. Ditch digging machines seemed to operate with unusual efficiency. One salesman visiting the campus ignored a "no parking" sign and returned an hour later to find the only exit for his parked car blocked with a newly dug six-foot-deep ditch. Two weeks later, he got his car out of the lot, left Blacksburg, and turned the territory over to his competitor. A number of faculty, students, and at least one dean have personal anecdotes of even more colorful experiences with the mud and ditches.

The most emotional vocal reactions occurred in connection with the construction of the mall and the World War II Memorial. The mall project involved the destruction of a beautiful grove of trees. Note has already been made of the opposition which developed at once when it was learned that these trees would be sacrificed. The opposition increased and in some instances turned to bitterness as the grove disappeared leaving only raw red earth. The bitterness expressed itself in a number of ways, one of which was to denounce the administration, the school, and even the governor of the state. During much of its construction, the mall was indeed a desolate, uninspiring sight. At times even the strongest supporters of the project grew faint. One afternoon a faculty member who had supported the proposed mall from the first was joined by Chancellor John R. Hutcheson as the two were surveying the apparent desolation. Turning to Hutcheson the faculty member asked, "Dr. Jack, do you think we will ever get this spot restored to the beauty and dignity it had before construction was started on this mall?" Dr. Jack's answer is worth recalling as one looks at the mall today. "Yes, we will." he said. "It may not look that way now, but remember we will plant far more trees and shrubbery in connection with the mall than we are destroying. Not only will we achieve more beauty and dignity, but the mall will be practical as well and will achieve more beauty with each passing year for the next fifty years or more." Continuing, he added, "People are blaming me for putting the forces into operation which led to this mall. I am perfectly willing to accept the blame for the mall now if the people will give me the credit for it when they view it twenty-five years from now."

Construction, particularly grading, for the World War II Memorial went on simultaneously with that of the mall. Students residing in dormitories on the upper quadrangle in getting to the dining rooms in Owens Hall had to face the inconvenience of crossing the construction at the mall or the memorial or of making a long detour around both. A number of students found outlets to this frustration by joining others in condemning the memorial. The resulting rather widespread condemnation of the memorial placed the alumni committee charged with its erection in a perplexing situation.

The decision to erect a spiritual rather than a utilitarian memorial had been presented to the alumni at the 1946 homecoming. Following this meeting, the Alumni Association had inaugurated a fund-raising campaign, which by 1950 had secured sufficient funds with which to start construction of the first unit of the memorial. Since insufficient funds were available to complete the entire structure at one time, it had been decided to complete the structure a unit at a time. The complete memorial plan was to include a chapel, chimes, and a number of academic scholarships. Now with construction actually under way, opposition to the chapel, dubbed "Alumni Folly" by some dissident groups, seemed to be growing. Ironically, much of the opposition came from individuals who had become alumni since 1946 and from students who had not as yet become alumni. Obviously, the complaint from some of this group that they had not been consulted in planning the memorial was correct.

D. P. Morton ('11), chairman of the memorial committee, recognized the growing dissatisfaction and dedicated his efforts, time, energy, and talents to remedying the situation and to generating increased support for the memorial. It would be inaccurate to say he converted everyone to the support of the memorial, but he certainly did more than anyone else to achieve this objective. As the physical features of the memorial began to take shape, much of the student opposition began to die down. In fact, the senior class of 1956, which as freshmen and sophomores had been on the campus for a part of the time when "mud and anti-memorialism" seemed to reign supreme, made a gift of money toward the completion of the memorial. Thanks largely to Morton's dedication and untiring zeal in rallying alumni support, the final unit of the chapel was completed and with an impressive service of dedication was turned over to the College on May 29, 1960. This shrine, a memorial to VPI alumni who gave their lives in service to their country, is at the same time a monument to the loyalty and dedication with which D. P. Morton worked to provide his alma mater with a shrine that would preserve in stone the motto, "Ut Prosim."

At the same time the mall and the memorial were receiving so much attention, construction was going on at other sites. The fourth addition to Henderson Hall was completed in '51, while the meat processing lab was completed in '52. In 1952, Williams Hall and the first section of Randolph Hall were completed. Following the completion of these two buildings, classroom instruction was discontinued in Academic Buildings One and Two, for the first time in nearly three quarters of a century and the buildings converted to temporary library space. With the transfer of the library facilities to the academic buildings, the old library, a landmark for nearly half a century, was torn down to make way for a new library. This building, named the Carol M. Newman Library in honor of the former professor and head of the department of English, was completed in 1955. The community, as well as Treasurer Boone, was made happy when Paul Mellon, working through the Old Dominion Foundation, contributed a million dollars for the new library project.

To provide electricity and heat for the rapidly expanding physical plant, an addition to the power house at its present site also was completed in 1955.

During the same year, it was discovered that "Commerce Hall," the unofficial name given to the old mess hall upon its conversion to classrooms, had deteriorated to a point beyond safety and repair. This building, known to generations of students as Commencement Hall, Mess Hall, or German Hall, was then torn down and the site graded into one of the lawns adjacent to the present Shultz Dining Hall.

Long before the middle of the decade, Newman had made it clear that VPI was rapidly approaching a crisis in its need for additional dormitory space. A decision was reached to enlarge Shanks and Major Williams Halls and to replace Academic Buildings One and Two with dormitories. This decision meant that these two well-known landmarks would have to be torn down. Once more protests went up from alumni, and pleas were made to save the two old buildings. One alumnus on the faculty was particularly outspoken in his condemnation of the practice of removing so many of the landmarks on the campus. Happening to encounter H. P. C. Vandenburg ('28), campus engineer, in front of the Second Academic Building, he let Vandenburg know of his disapproval. It was a sad state of affairs, he informed the startled engineer, when a college with a supposedly competent faculty of engineers, architects, and landscape specialists was not imaginative, creative, and energetic enough to come up with a plan for preserving instead of destroying old landmarks dear to the heart and memory of thousands of living alumni. Vandenberg listened quietly and instead of arguing with the concerned alumnus, invited him to go with him on a tour of the two buildings. The professor accepted, whereupon "Van" took him from the basement to the attic of each building and pointed out one structural weakness after another which even the professor recognized as being beyond repair. Following this particular tour, this alumnus-professor became a strong convert to the policy of getting the facts before condemning the administration. A recently discovered document reveals some interesting facts and possible explanation as to the rapid deterioration of these old buildings. According to information prepared by Professor J. R. (Polly) Parrott ('83) in a memorandum to President Burruss about 1920, these buildings had never received proper maintenance. In addition to this neglect, he said, the improper extension of the basement foundation, the relocation of partitions, the cutting of windows and doorways in walls, and the subjection of the floors to overloads had caused permanent damage which would force the College to abandon both buildings in the not-too-distant future. No doubt alumni blood pressure would have been improved had this information along with the conditions of the buildings been known by all alumni at the time the destruction of the buildings was announced.

The additions to Shanks and Major Williams Halls were completed in 1957, as were the dormitories erected on the site of the academic buildings. The dormitory erected on the site of Academic Building Number One was named Rasche Hall in honor of Professor William H. (Bosco) Rasche, while the one erected on the site of Academic Building Number Two was named Brodie Hall in honor of Professor William M. Brodie. During the same year these dormitories were completed, a new Commerce Hall was completed. In 1969 this latter building was named Pamplin Hall in honor of R. B. Pamplin ('33), a loyal supporter of VPI.

Even as these buildings were being completed, other construction began. Between 1958 and 1960 the remaining houses on Faculty Row were removed to make way for classrooms and laboratories. In 1959 the second section of Randolph Hall was completed. In 1960 the first section of Norris Hall and the fourth section of the power plant were completed. A new physics building was completed during the same year and in 1969 named Robeson Hall in honor of the retired Dr. F. L. Robeson, long-time professor and head of the department of physics.

In 1954 Newman presented the Board of Visitors with a long-range plan for improving the physical facilities for the athletic and recreational programs at the College. This plan had been developed as a result of the study and cooperation of a large number of persons, he told the board. After much discussion, its members approved the plan in principle and authorized Newman to start putting it into effect. The execution of this plan called for another rearrangement of "hills, valleys, and buildings," but this time most of the rearranging was done on the periphery rather than in the center of the campus. The agricultural division of the College continued to move its barns and experimental plots farther outward and watched a baseball field emerge from a former pasture on the south side of the campus. Within a short time a golf course took shape on a part of the old college orchard and on the experimental plots used for years by the agronomy department.

During the Christmas vacation of 1957, the water tower, long a familiar landmark on the campus was removed. Bulldozers roared back and forth as they graded, leveled, and excavated sites formerly occupied by the horse-show ring, and the horse, cattle, and dairy barns, and barnyards. Washington Street was extended westward beyond the greenhouses and the meat processing laboratory; and, to the vocal regret of many, another grove of campus trees was removed. During the summer of '58 grading was begun for a field house, which was later designated as the Coliseum. This building proved to be such a big undertaking it required several years to finance and complete. The campus heard much debate for and against the Coliseum during the interval, but fortunately no sharp split occurred.

As a part of the homecoming program during the fall of 1958, D. P. Morton ('11), on behalf of the Alumni Association, presented the College with a memorial carillon. The installation of this carillon, Morton reminded the audience, represented the completion of one phase of the memorial concept agreed upon by the alumni in 1945. The carillon and the console were installed in Burruss Hall, where both remain today. Mrs. M. C. Harrison was appointed as official carillonneur and from that date until the present has delighted many campus gatherings with her concerts.

In addition to the major construction projects during the "fabulous fifties," programs involving extensive repairs and renovations to existing buildings also were carried out. As a part of this program, all of the old barracks on the upper quadrangle, with the exception of Lane, were renovated and tied together into four "corner" units with Shanks at the north corner, Rasche at the east, Brodie at the south, and Major Williams at the west. For the sake of older alumni, it may be added that just outside the old quadrangle group Monteith is located east of Shanks, Thomas just north of Shanks, and Femoyer slightly northwest of Major Williams. Barracks Number One (Lane), with its familiar tower and flagpole, still presides, albeit in somewhat shabby gentility, in the middle of the old quadrangle.

The decade also witnessed the further expansion of the campus into the state by the improvement of facilities at the agricultural substations and by the acquisition of additional land. In 1949, Paul Mellon gave the College some farm land in Fauquier County, which with additional financial help from Mellon was developed during the fifties into a forage research station. In 1954 the McCormick family gave VPI "Walnut Grove," the farm in Rockbridge County upon which the invention of the reaper had taken place more than a century earlier.

In 1954-55 the VPI-Blacksburg-Christiansburg Water Authority was organized and, as one wag expressed it, started detouring a portion of New River through the two towns and the campus. The arrival of this water on the campus in 1957 helped solve one problem each administration had faced every year from the day the College had first opened. No longer could sophomores hope to get an unexpected holiday by ordering the freshmen to go around at night opening all water faucets, hoping thereby to drain the reservoirs. Relegated to the past also

was the necessity sometimes faced by the administration of limiting the supply
of water to the barracks.

The period of Newman's administration also was one of unprecedented academic change, growth, and expansion at both graduate and undergraduate levels.
These changes and growth came about as a cooperative effort on the part of the
faculty and administration to keep the College's program of service abreast of the
changing conditions of the state and the changing demands in the fields of science
and technology. As a result of the growing realization that "man can not live by
science alone," as one professor put it, the period also saw the beginning of a
strong effort to strengthen the offerings in the humanities and to broaden the
base of the social sciences.

A few of the more significant academic developments of the period may be
noted briefly.

During the session of 1948-49, representatives of the State Department of
Education requested the department of vocational education to develop programs
for the preparation of teachers in business and home economics education.
This request posed a number of problems, since undergraduate instruction
in both of these areas was already being offered on the Radford campus.
Finally, after a number of conferences, it was agreed that the home economics
education program on the Blacksburg campus would operate at the graduate
level only and would be offered in cooperation with the Radford College faculty.
This arrangement proved to be only partially satisfactory; therefore, the board
in 1951 created a "unified" department of home economics with a division of
technical home economics to be located on the Blacksburg campus and a division
of home economics education [teacher preparation] to be located on the Radford
campus. The two divisions were to be operated by co-chairmen, with all graduate
work in both divisions to be centered on the Blacksburg campus. Dr. Pardue was
appointed as coordinator "in order to secure the greatest degree of coordination."
Honest opinions still differ as to how much effective coordination Dr. Pardue was
able to achieve under this arrangement.

At the same time the program in home economics education was being developed, a program in business education at the graduate and undergraduate level
was also organized for the Blacksburg campus. Women students, however, were
allowed to enroll in this program only at the graduate level. This program of
business education developed as a cooperative one between the department of
vocational education in the school of agriculture and the department of business
administration in the school of applied science and business administration.

As a result of the addition of the programs in home economics education and
business education and very shortly thereafter the addition of a program of
teacher-preparation in trades and industries and of one that is currently known as
distributive education, the department found itself in an unusual administrative
position. Although located in the school of agriculture, the head of the department had to operate administratively through the offices of the dean of agriculture
and the dean of applied science and business administration. At the same time,
he had to operate the program in harmony with the decisions made in connection
with the Radford-VPI merger and with the decisions made by the director of the
graduate school. To complicate matters further, the cost of a large portion of the
program of teacher-preparation in vocational education was reimbursed by the
state board of education operating through its division of vocational education.

Rules and regulations covering this reimbursement had to be observed.

Early in the fifties, Miss Martha Creighton, professor of home economics education in the department of vocational education, clearly foresaw the difficulties this administrative arrangement carried. At the same time she feared the possible effect such an arrangement might have for the future. As a remedy she, in consultation with other staff members in the department, prepared and presented to President Newman a proposal that the department be reorganized either as a school of education or as a school of vocational education. Newman rejected the proposal on the grounds that the trend was to consolidate existing departments rather than to expand them into schools. Neither did he foresee difficulties arising in the cooperative financing of the program in teacher education.

As it developed, Miss Creighton was overly concerned with respect to the financing of the program, since the state department of education continued to discharge its responsibility in this respect. She was more nearly correct with respect to administrative complications. Before the end of Newman's administration, the department of vocational education was operating under the offices of the dean of agriculture, the dean of the school of business, the dean of the school of science and general studies and the dean of the school of home economics. The fact that the department by the end of this period had developed a program of teacher-preparation for all of the major areas of vocational education offered in public schools is a tribute to the spirit of cooperation manifested by Professor Harry W. Sanders, who served as head of the department of vocational education from 1940 to 1962.

Fortunately the growth and development of new programs in other departments took place with much less administrative involvement. In 1951 the Board of Visitors approved the Master of Education degree. For a number of years work on the Blacksburg campus toward this degree was restricted to the vocational areas. Students wanting to work toward this degree in areas other than the vocational were expected to register under the supervision of the Radford faculty.

The addition of the master's degree program to many of the already existing curriculums was extensive. Without describing any of these additions, it is well to pass on to some of the other new program developments.

In the fall of 1951, the department of applied mechanics began offering work leading to the Ph.D. degree. The department of biochemistry and nutrition, organized in 1952, absorbed much of the work of the older department of agricultural chemistry, which was no longer listed as a separate department.

In the fall of 1953, a Ph.D. degree was begun in geology. During the same year the "Earle B. Norris Research Professorship" was established in the school of engineering in honor of Dean Norris upon his retirement. Dr. E. George Stern, research professor of wood construction, was appointed to this position.

During the session of 1953-54, the branch instruction in ROTC was discontinued in favor of a more general program, one for Army ROTC and one for Air Force ROTC.

In 1955 a distinct department of extension education was begun in the school of agriculture. During the same year a department of philosophy and religion was established in the school of applied science and business administration. The board also agreed to drop the name dairy husbandry in favor of the name dairy science. At the same time, it voted that the name of the geology department would be changed to that of geological sciences.

The year 1956 proved to be a crucial one for future curriculum development. The Board of Visitors, as a result of Newman's reports and the keen insight of many of its members, realized that VPI had developed just about as far as it could go in engineering and agriculture without strengthening its offerings in supporting work, most of which was administered in the school of applied science and business administration. The specific steps to be taken to strengthen this work were not defined at the time, but the board agreed to the principle that a strong school of applied science and business administration was needed "to support work in engineering and agriculture." Dean G. B. Johnston and his faculty in the school of applied science and business administration were more than ready to cooperate in strengthening and developing work in this school. A master's degree program in nuclear physics was begun before the year was out, and one at the same level was started in mathematics in 1957. At the same time, extensive plans were begun to expand and develop other programs.

During the year 1956, the board also agreed to the principle of developing a program of teacher education in the trades and industries but left the specific development of the program to the administration and the department of vocational education. The curriculum in the area was begun in 1959.

In 1956 the board also authorized the degree of Bachelor of Architecture to be operated in the school of engineering and architecture.

The separate departments of English and foreign languages were combined in 1958 into one department of English and foreign language. During the same year the board approved the inauguration of Ph.D. degree programs in agronomy and in aeronautical engineering. Somewhat reluctantly, it seems, the board also returned to the perplexing problem of setting up a curriculum in home economics which would be satisfactory to the interests on the Radford and the Blacksburg campuses. After listening to a strongly worded report from the committee of the board which reviewed the efforts beginning in 1945 to coordinate the two programs, the board agreed to create a school of home economics out of the two departments on the separate campuses. A dean was to be employed for the new school, and a committee of disinterested persons qualified in home economics was to be selected to help study the situation and to make suggestions relative to the proposed new school. The faculties at "VPI and Radford," the board said, were not to be allowed to influence the dean while the study was being made.

The study was launched before a dean was appointed, and after a considerable time an announcement was made that the new school of home economics would begin in the fall of 1960-61. Dr. Laura Jane Harper, acting head of the department of home economics at Tech, was appointed as dean of the school to take office upon its opening.

The creation of this school called for the formation of new departments. Four were formed at once: three on the Blacksburg campus and one on the Radford campus. The three on the Blacksburg campus were formed chiefly by the grouping of courses already having been organized under Dr. Mildred Tate before her resignation from the faculty. A department of home economics education was formed on the Radford campus under Dr. Ruth Hackman. On the Blacksburg campus a department of clothing, textiles, and related arts was organized under Miss Oris Glisson. A department of foods and nutrition was formed in July, 1961, and placed under the headship of Dr. Marian Moore. The newly formed department of management, housing, and family development was placed under Miss

Mary Settle in November of the same year. The appointment of Miss Settle completed the initial organization of this school, the first one in the history of VPI to be organized and launched with an all-female staff. This development occurred almost exactly four decades after the admission of the first women to VPI.

Seven new programs got under way or were authorized in 1959. The Ph.D. program in agricultural economics, which had been authorized in 1947, got under way; a Master of Architecture degree was approved and a department of forestry and wildlife, a department of entomology, and a department of veterinary science were carved out of the older biology department. A faculty committee was appointed to administer the department of forestry and wildlife while a head was being sought. Dr. J. M. Grayson ('35) was appointed as head of the new department of entomology, and Dr. D. F. Watson was appointed head of the department of veterinary science.

The creation of the department of veterinary science completed a unique program of instruction in veterinary work. For a number of years, beginning during Dr. Burruss' administration, organizations in the state had urged VPI to establish a department or school of veterinary medicine. The VPI administration had responded favorably to such proposals but each time had pointed out the high cost such a program would entail. A number of appeals had gone to the legislature to authorize the College to establish such training. The legislature for its part had approved the establishment of such a program on several occasions but just as steadily had failed to appropriate the necessary funds. Finally in the period just prior to 1949 a cooperative program had been worked out with the University of Georgia and later with Texas A and M as well, whereby properly qualified students at VPI with the approval of VPI officials could transfer to one of these schools and complete their work for a veterinary degree. The state of Virginia through VPI paid a portion of the VPI students' expenses after they transferred to the out-of-state institutions. The new department meant that Virginia residents now had an additional option in veterinary training.

During the same year of 1959, a Ph.D. program was authorized in horticulture and a Ph.D. program in mathematics approved to become effective as soon as possible under the national defense act of 1958. These conditions were met, and the program in mathematics was launched in 1961.

During the decade, Newman, a part of his faculty, and some members of the Board of Visitors became increasingly aware of the fact that VPI was lagging far behind sister land-grant institutions in the development of work in the humanities with which to round out the changing programs in the more technical areas. This deficiency also had been pointed out both by accrediting agencies and by individuals invited to the campus to help study proposed curricular changes and programs. The deficiencies in these areas, Newman informed the board, not only weakened the overall programs in the technological areas but also unduly restricted the opportunities for students at VPI to get the well-rounded college training increasingly necessary in the changing world. The social-science area also needed development, he said, if VPI was to keep abreast of the broadening demands on the College.

It is too close in time for definitive evaluation, but it would appear that the last half decade of Newman's administration witnessed the beginning of forces which foreshadowed the shifting of VPI from the "narrow gauge" to the "broad gauge" track along which most modern land-grant institutions were then (and are now) developing.

In addition to the new programs put into operation in 1960, the board also authorized a Ph.D. degree in civil engineering and gave final approval to the formation of a school of business administration. During the same year the board, in harmony with the trend away from "the immediately practical," authorized a change in name of the department of applied mechanics to the more appropriate one of engineering mechanics.

The school of business administration had been in the making for a number of years. As a department in the school of applied science and business administration it had long since grown to a size in enrollment second only to that of the school of engineering; but if it was to continue meeting the demands of the growing institution, it had to expand and develop its program yet further. A tentative decision had been made to develop the department into a separate school which would meet the requirements for membership in the American Association of Collegiate Schools of Business. The resignation of Dr. T. H. Cox in 1958 as head of the department slowed down but did not stop the movement toward the formation of the school. Instead, a decision was made to secure a head who would assume the leadership in organizing and developing a school of business administration. After considerable persuasion, Dr. H. H. (Bill) Mitchell, head of the department of business administration at Mississippi State University, agreed to accept the proffered headship.

Mitchell reported to Tech in February, 1960, and set about planning for the new school with energy and enthusiasm. Newman, who reported to the board that the establishment of the new school would help VPI render higher quality of service to "the students in particular and to the State of Virginia in general," was quite pleased with Mitchell's immediate impact on the department of business administration. Reporting to the board within four months after Mitchell's arrival, he said, "One of the most important segments of the institution which has always worked efficiently and smoothly has responded to his dynamic leadership and has acquired an extra spark of life which is paving the way to greater heights of performance."

The school of business administration having been authorized, Mitchell continued working toward its organization and implementation. In February, 1961, the board accepted Mitchell's plan for the school of business (the word administration having been dropped from the title) and at the same time surprised no one by announcing Mitchell's appointment as dean of the new school. This announcement was followed almost immediately afterwards by one from Mitchell announcing the appointment of heads of the new departments to be in operation upon the opening of the new school in September, 1961. Dr. B. O. Miller was to be head of the department of economics; Professor W. S. Gay ('28) was to be head of the department of accounting; and Professor R. L. Humbert was to be head of the department of business administration. These appointments were well received by the campus community, since these men had already earned enviable reputations as teachers in these fields.

The multiplicity of campus events during the fifties precludes detailed attention to more than a few selected at random. Such arbitrary selection inevitably will omit many events cherished in the memories of loyal alumni. Former students during the period happily will be able to supply historical detail in plenty. Others may sample enough of these pages for a reasonable perspective.

The changing pattern of campus life introduced by postwar conditions continued to develop throughout the decade. Student unrest so evident during Hutcheson's last year in office continued unabated, apparently reaching a peak during the 1950-51 and 1951-52 sessions. In addition to the disruptive physical condition of the campus, the draft and the Korean War had a decidedly upsetting effect on the students. Grades came to have considerable significance with respect to military deferment, a condition resulting in some tension between faculty and students. Some individuals, students and faculty alike, thought it also caused increasing violation of the honor code with respect to cheating on class work and examinations. Differences of opinion between the leaders in the Corps of Cadets and the civilian student body emerged as to the enforcement of the honor code. These differences helped fan the growing resistance to the military system as represented by the Corps. For a while, it began to appear that the traditional warfare between sophomores and freshmen would be converted into warfare between the Corps and the civilians. A few incidents threatened to fan this threat of warfare into reality.

In the late fall of 1951, a cadet was officially "drummed out" of the Corps for the infraction of certain regulations. The cadet leaders undoubtedly were sincere in their belief that such action was justified and would strengthen the Corps of Cadets. Many civilian students thought otherwise. A few days after this "drumming out" incident, a group of civilian students held their own "drumming out" exercise, which because of its originality and mock seriousness, probably would have been well received under different circumstances at a different time. In the civilian "drumming out" activity the military, the administration, and indirectly the Corps, came in for a considerable lampooning. The second "drumming out" episode had a surprising effect. It tended to divide both the Corps of Cadets and the civilian student body. Some cadets, who were in the Corps because of college regulations rather than because of personal choice, applauded the action. Other cadets, who were in the Corps by choice, tended to deplore and resent the act. Civilian students tended to divide along similar lines. Some felt the action was fully justified. Others felt that the civilian students had meddled with something of no concern to them. According to a notice published by a group of students in *The Tech,* the civilian "drumming out" episode, planned as a stunt long before the Corps' "drumming out" incident, to celebrate a fellow student's release from the Corps, was in no way intended as a reflection on anybody.

The administration promptly forbade all "drumming out," and here the matter rested uneasily for a time. Surprisingly, perhaps, the Corps leaders deprived of the "drumming out" privilege, decided that such practice was quite necessary for the continued growth and strengthening of the Corps. As a result, a petition was presented to the board in succeeding years to permit the restoration of the practice. Finally, as late as 1959, another "earnest petition" was presented to the board to permit resumption of the practice. The board considered the matter at length, expressed its general disapproval of the practice, decided to take no formal action, and then agreed that since the student request seemed to be so earnest, the practice could be reinstated in a modified form. President Newman was to have the right, however, "to impose whatever stipulation" he felt justified in imposing.

The Corps of Cadets and compulsory military training continued to be a hotly debated issue throughout the decade, but a modified form of cadet regulations and Corps organization under the administration of General Devine as commandant tended to make Corps life more palatable for many students.

Both Devine and Guthridge, adviser to civilian students, worked together for more student involvement in student government and campus affairs. As a result, much of the student unrest began to disappear to be replaced by constructive activities which in fact soon came to dominate student life after the middle of the decade.

In the fall of '51, the administration finally yielded to the inevitable. It granted permission for all students to operate cars on the campus. This decision soon led to a demand for improved parking lots, which in turn led to an interesting question. Did the College have the authority to use state funds to build parking lots for student-owned automobiles? Apparently it did. At least a few areas were smoothed over, graveled, and labeled "student parking." These spaces soon filled up, and the cars spilled over onto streets adjacent to the campus. This development raised another question. Did the town authorities have the power to force the cars back onto the campus? This question has yet to be settled to the satisfaction of all, even though the College has increased its student parking facilities many fold.

As commencement 1950 approached, it became obvious that Burruss Hall would not accommodate the expected crowd. After numerous meetings of faculty and senior class representatives, plans were made to hold the commencement in Miles Stadium. Fortunately, the weather cooperated; and 1440 degrees were awarded in the outdoor ceremony held in June. Other than numerous sunburn cases, which caused a run on sunburn lotions in the drugstores, the commencement was considered a great success. The weather was not always so cooperative. After a number of visiting dignitaries, as well as faculty and students had received drenchings at some of the later outdoor exercises, plans were made to move back indoors. This move was accomplished successfully by dividing the candidates for degrees into two groups and holding two exercises, one in the morning and one in the afternoon. With the completion of the Coliseum, the dual commencement exercises were combined into one and moved to this building. By June, 1970, the crowd had outgrown this huge building, and the commencement was once more held outdoors, this time in Lane Stadium.

With the generous financial assistance of the Alumni Association, the Social and Cultural Committee (made up of faculty and students) brought a number of outstanding speakers to the campus. Many of these visitors, as well as others attending the Institute of Rural Affairs, were already well known. They achieved even greater fame in later years as witness the subsequent careers of J. William Fulbright, Dean Rusk, and others. Through the efforts of the students in architecture, Frank Lloyd Wright was brought to the campus and delighted students attending not only from Tech but from colleges within a radius of 200 miles, with his pungent and at times biting comments on architecture in particular and life in general.

Through the efforts of the Blacksburg Community Concert Association under the able guidance of Professor R. L. Humbert and others, a veritable list of "Who's Who" in the musical world appeared on the stage of Burruss Hall each year.

The German and the Cotillion dance clubs brought an amazing number of

"Big Name," "Big Time" dance bands to the campus to play for their "formals." The big name bands brought to the campus for the annual ring dances held by the junior class also added luster to the list of the bands visiting the campus. The 1954 ring dance saw the second debut of "Moonlight and VPI" written by Fred Waring and Charles Gaynor at the request of the Cadet Corps for a popular song for the ring dance of 1942. Both CBS and NBC television networks broadcast parts of the '54 dance.

The Highty Tighties continued to win praise, laurels, and parades as they attended football games, inaugurations, and other celebrations. The regimental band and the entire community were saddened by the sudden death of beloved band leader J. S. (Jim) Schaeffer in 1951. "Major Jim" had served in the band for more than thirty-five years at the time of his death. The entire Corps turned out for his funeral and formed a double line through which the body was carried to the cemetery. The editor of *The Tech* closed an editorial devoted to "Major Jim" with these words: "Mr. Schaeffer was a servant of Tech, but in his serving, he gained a position second to none among the greatest leaders and workers VPI has ever produced."

Schaeffer was succeeded as bandmaster by Thomas M. Dobyns, who proved to be a worthy successor. In Washington for President Eisenhower's first inaugural parade in January 1953, the band won first place for all senior marching bands. The feat was repeated in January, 1957, for Eisenhower's second inaugural parade and led to an unscheduled 2:00 a.m. serenade of General Devine, President Newman, and for good measure the girls in Hillcrest. To the campus' incredulous delight the Highty Tighties won first place for a third time at the snowy inauguration of President John F. Kennedy in 1961. About half the Cadet Corps was awaiting the band at the mall when it arrived back in Blacksburg well after midnight. A celebration was in order, and celebrate they did by marching the streets of Blacksburg to tunes played in a manner more likely to raise groans than cheers.

While Devine and Guthridge were working to provide organized extracurricular activities, groups of students frequently took matters into their own hands and organized do-it-yourself entertainment. Panty raids on Hillcrest and on Radford College proved disappointing. Phone-booth-stuffing produced more tangible results. It boosted egos but wrecked the booths. Bunk stuffing of double-decked bunks proved to be exciting enough to attract a bit of national publicity. Apparently the "game" originated suddenly on the VPI campus. It ended just as suddenly but not before the collapse of a number of bunks.

Still in the category of do-it-yourself, but of doubtful classification as entertainment, some students tried to set up a system of grading or rating the professors. Some professors cooperated. Others did not. One professor being rated by two different sections of students claimed that he told a number of jokes to one section but none to the other. According to his story, the section hearing the jokes gave him a superior rating, whereas his other section gave him a rating of average. Following the release of this information a number of professors were alleged to have received copies of humorous magazines from "anonymous sources."

In the fall of '51, the students, some of whom had never seen Tech win a football game, gave Coach Moseley and the team an unexpected rally in the middle of the week. The team and Moseley, in his first year as coach, were deeply appreciative but continued to lose. Sports writers took time out to praise the Corps of Cadets for its loyalty to the team even though it was not winning any games. All of which failed to help campus morale, since it had been the leaders of the civilian student body who had thought up and promoted the rally.

Frank O. Moseley served as athletic director and head football coach from 1951 until January 1961. During Moseley's tenure as coach, the Thanksgiving Day game with VMI continued to be THE game, but the rivalry with the University of Virginia began to assume increasing importance with the Tech student body and alumni. Tech's football fortunes began a slow comeback. A heart-warming victory over VMI in '52, the first since '46, helped cheer the faithful and stir the indifferent.

Rosy dreams of football prowess were clouded somewhat with the formation of the new Atlantic Coast Conference out of the Southern Conference. Tech was left in the older but weaker Southern Conference. President Newman repeated the announcement given earlier that VPI hoped to build athletic teams capable of meeting "its natural rivals—the Virginia colleges and land-grant colleges and universities in nearby states." Then in a move widely viewed as an effort to attract an invitation to membership in the ACC, Moseley was given an eight-year contract dating from January 1, 1953. In '54, Tech went undefeated for the first time since 1918, with only a 7-7 tie with William and Mary to mar the otherwise perfect season. Interest in the '54 game with VMI was titillated by news reports and speculation concerning the kidnapping of Moe, the VMI kangaroo mascot, and by the mysterious disappearance of a VPI freshman from the Blacksburg campus before the day of the game. Things turned out all right, however, as the crowds gathered for the game. Moe was turned over to VMI by the Tech cheerleaders, and the freshman "tied so that he had to hop like a kangaroo was returned to Tech." It was a cold day for the game; but as Tech ran up the score to a surprising 49 to 6, "Tech fans forgot all about the weather."

The frustrations of an up-and-down football season in '59, which saw Tech defeat the University of Virginia 40-14 but turn around and lose to VMI by a 37-12 score were partly assuaged when it was announced that end Carroll Dale had been named to the mythical All American football team. In recognition of this honor it was announced by Coach Moseley that Dale's jersey number "84" was being retired. Dale's subsequent performance with the Green Bay Packers professional football team proved him worthy of this honor.

Tech's entire athletic program began a resurgence under Moseley's direction during the decade. Charles W. (Chuck) Noe, recruited as head basketball coach in 1956, electrified the campus community with his brand of basketball. In the process the last remaining skeptics were convinced that the World War I Memorial Gymnasium was in fact inadequate for Tech's athletic program. G. F. (Red) Laird continued to produce baseball teams to compete with Tech's "natural rivals" while the coaches of the other sports more than kept pace with the upward trend. And, in the shadow of intercollegiate sports, thousands of students under the able direction of Professor M. B. Blair engaged in innumerable intramural sports activities.

The establishment of the graduate degree program in nuclear engineering physics in 1956 created considerable interest not only with students and faculty but with the industrial segment of the state as well. The purchase and subsequent installation of a nuclear reactor simulator to be used in connection with this program turned this interest into pride when it was realized that Tech was the first college in the country to have such a reactor simulator for its training program. Under the leadership of Dr. T. Marshall Hahn, professor and head of the department of physics, some $350,000 was secured from the Atomic Energy Commission for the purchase and construction of a UTR-10 university teaching and research reactor. Some shivers of apprehension concerning the ability to control atomic radiation from the new installation had to be quieted, but one legislator aware that Hahn had raised about $635,000 from outside sources for VPI in three years is reported to have expressed more concern over trying to control nuclear physicists than nuclear reactions. The UTR-10 reactor was put into operation with appropriate ceremonies in January, 1960. Dr. Hahn, who in the meantime had moved to the Kansas State University, returned to the campus and participated in the ceremonies by tracing the evolution of the cooperative nuclear engineering program at Tech.

The Engineering Conference, begun during pre-World War II days, was reactivated by the engineering students. This conference brought outstanding engineering and industrial leaders to the campus to meet with student groups at convocations and in smaller curricular groups. In 1954, the livestock judging contest and the dairy day were combined into a larger Agricultural Exposition. These two programs proved to be quite popular, and were merged into the larger Tech Festival in 1963.

During Burruss' administration, VPI had followed largely an "open door" policy of admitting all high school graduates who applied for admission just as long as a room was available in dormitories. Once admitted, the student was expected to meet all academic standards or to be dropped. By the early fifties this policy was causing serious problems. Too many students failed to meet the academic standards and were carried as academically deficient or dropped. Reports of serious criticism of VPI came from friends throughout the state. Newman undertook a number of steps to improve this situation. For one thing he authorized the formation of a modified form of a basic division in 1953. Enrollment in this division was open to students not having elected a specific curriculum, but the bulk of the students were those whose preparation for college work was palpably weak. The program was set up under the direction of Dr. Paul H. Farrier, director of admissions, with three assistants: one from the school of engineering, one from the school of agriculture, and one from the school of applied science and business administration. These assistants were given wide latitude in "tailor-making" each student's academic program to fit his individual needs. Close, almost daily contact was kept with the advisees, especially during the freshman year. Personal letters to parents were substituted for the more formal report cards. In the agricultural division, voluntary sessions dealing with study-learning techniques were held by the professor of educational psychology, who was also one of Farrier's assistants.

The overall results of the basic division program were satisfactory from the academic and from the public-relations standpoint. The program, however, was not too well received either by the students or by the faculty. The students felt some stigma was associated with being in the division and for the most part rejected the idea that they needed any special help. The major criticism from the faculty grew from the fear that the basic division was the forerunner of a basic college similar to one which had just begun at Michigan State University. Faced with the opposition of both students and faculty and the improving student morale resulting from the efforts of Devine and Guthridge, the decision was reached to drop the basic division after 1955. At the same time, there was initiated a "mild policy in denying admission" to poorly prepared students by advising with them rather than by rejecting them outright.

In 1953, Mr. Irving Linwood Peddrew, III, of Hampton, Virginia, became the first Negro to enter VPI as a regularly enrolled student. Both Peddrew and the student body took the admission in stride, and no untoward incident occurred to mar the initial step toward integration of the College.

The question of faculty tenure had had little place in the thinking of the college administration during the early days of VPI. During the earliest days, the Board of Visitors hired and fired the faculty—and the president—with no more consideration than they would show a hired hand. Later the board adopted the general policy of hiring (or firing) faculty members on the recommendation of the president. Once during Barringer's administration, the board refused to follow his recommendation to discharge a faculty member. At another time, during Burruss' administration, the board agreed to retain a professor Burruss wanted retained only after a prolonged discussion and several meetings. In 1953 Newman was shocked to receive a report from the Southern Association of Colleges and Secondary Schools critical of VPI for not having an approved formal statement on tenure policy for its faculty. Newman immediately appointed a faculty committee to draft such a policy statement. The committee was somewhat surprised too, but after a number of meetings drafted a statement based on the statement of principles of academic freedom and tenure which the American Association of University Professors had issued in 1940. The Board of Visitors offered no objection to the statement and adopted it as official policy. The College thus acquired an official tenure policy nearly three quarters of a century after the first board fired the entire faculty and president with no advance notice whatever

A criticism from another visiting committee was not so easily resolved. This committee, on the campus to review the engineering curricula for accreditation purposes, criticized the low salary scale for the faculty. This criticism came as no surprise to Newman. He already had gathered data to show that the salary paid to faculty at VPI averaged $625 below the average salary paid the fifteen "competing institutions close to Virginia." Newman had set about trying to improve the situation; he did succeed to a remarkable extent in getting more money. However, the rules and regulations controlling classification, salaries, and promotion of state employees set by the state personnel office in Richmond prevented the Newman administration from making the most efficient use of increased state appropriations for salaries. Chiefly because of the state-imposed regulations, a number of administration recommendations for increases of individual staff members were denied. The administration similarly found its hands tied with respect to the salary it could offer prospective faculty members with unusual qualifications. Salaries were tied to the steps within the academic rank of instructor, assistant professor, associate professor, or professor. In order to make an attractive salary offer, the administration had to bring in new staff members at the upper academic ranks, often at the upper "steps" of the salary schedule within the rank. In some of the more critical fields, a faculty recruit with some small teaching or work experience and a freshly earned M.S. degree might find himself employed with the rank of associate professor or even professor. Promotion in salary and rank for those already employed tended to depend more on the length of service within a particular step than on merit. As one result of the system, the distribution of faculty according to academic rank tended to pile up at the upper end of the academic scale.

As the College entered the decade of the sixties, the faculty clearly appreciated Newman's efforts to increase faculty salaries; but at the same time, he was criticized for the way the faculty salary schedule had been organized and was being operated. What many of these critics did not know was that Newman also was very unhappy with the operation of the schedule and had been trying to get the state personnel office to permit VPI to make important modifications in it. He was not completely successful in this endeavor, but his efforts clearly contributed to the success his successor achieved in instituting a more satisfactory system.

Alumni support, especially from the senior members of the association, continued at a gratifying level throughout Newman's entire administration. During the early fifties some concern was expressed over the apparent lack of interest in alumni affairs manifested by the post-war graduates. Efforts to get more of the young alumni involved in the various chapters of the Alumni Association generated mixed results. At the same time a campaign was started to keep alumni informed of the developments at the College. Newman, Cassell, the coaches, and other VPI officials paid innumerable visits to alumni chapters. The succession of alumni officers serving during the period also rendered invaluable service to the cause of alma mater. As one result, by the mid-fifties the younger alumni were beginning to become more active in the affairs of the association and the College.

In 1958, cumulative contributions to the alumni fund since its establishment some nineteen years earlier passed the one-million-dollar mark, and the yearly contributions continued to climb. Also an increasing number of alumni all over Virginia had taken advantage of opportunities to attend local meetings at which the problems faced by higher education in Virginia were discussed. As one result of these meetings, which had been arranged primarily at Newman's insistence, not only the alumni but others as well became better informed about the role of higher education in the state. This improved understanding helped not only VPI but other state institutions as well to obtain improved financial support from the state.

In December, 1956, the Alumni Fund Council established the W. E. Wine Award for Faculty Achievement. This award, commonly referred to as the Wine Award, was set up in memory of the outstanding contributions of W. E. Wine ('04) to the Alumni Association and to VPI. The award provided a stipend of $500 for outstanding teaching performance to one faculty member in each of the three academic schools. With the later formation of additional schools and colleges, the restriction to the three schools was abandoned in favor of three selections from the University at large.

In the spring of 1955, a group of former coeds assembled in Roanoke and formally organized an alumnae chapter of the Alumni Association. Mrs. George Powley (Beverly Carper '38), largely instrumental in getting the organization started, was immediately elected first president of the chapter. Miss Jean Burruss ('43), daughter of Dr. J. A. Burruss, presiding as temporary chairman of the first meeting, opened the session with a gavel made in the VPI shops by Burruss during his student days. It had been largely through the efforts of Dr. Burruss that the doors of Tech were first opened to women students more than three decades earlier.

On the campus the coeds became such an accepted part of the campus life that their accomplishments just about ceased being topics for special comment in student publications. Among the numerous accomplishments during the period: one coed served for a term as editor of *The Virginia Tech Engineer,* another served a term as business manager of *The Bugle,* while another earned an ROTC commission. This latter achievement did draw some public notice. At the commissioning exercises held in connection with the June, 1959 commencement, Miss Patricia Ann Miller, of Richmond, was awarded her ROTC-earned commission in the Army Women's Medical Specialist Corps as a dietician, a definite first in the history of VPI.

Among the topics which engaged the campus community in continuing discussion throughout the fifties were those of social fraternities and the advisability of seeking a new name for the Virginia Polytechnic Institute. As early as 1953, Newman suggested to the board that the policy with regard to social fraternities needed to be re-examined and then either revised or reaffirmed. He felt that the cadet companies provided a modified form of social clubs for the military students and that the dormitory clubs such as the CAFI, the IVY, the TEK, and others provided a form of club for the civilian students residing on the campus. The immediate problem had to do with the students residing off the campus. The problem of whether to permit social clubs or fraternities was not a new one at all, he reminded the board. Recently, however, it had become more acute through perfectly normal and proper channels. A group of students living in a house near the campus adopted the name of Delta Kappa Sigma and had painted this name on a sign in front of their building. This organization, said Newman, had some four hundred alumni listed among its former members. At present, he said, although it was off the campus, the organization included both on- and off-campus members. A cadet was serving as president, and leaders in every phase of campus life were to be found in its membership. The organization, said Newman, was fully cooperative with the administration and had demonstrated high qualities of leadership and responsibility. Largely as a result of this organization's success and the caliber of its leadership, the problem of fraternities was now receiving a great deal of attention on the campus, he said. A decision from the board in the very near future would have to be made as to whether or not to recognize social fraternities at VPI. After considerable discussion the board decided not to recognize such fraternities at the time. Newman duly reported the decision to the officers of Delta Kappa Sigma, and this organization immediately took down its name and renamed its organization the Blacksburg Sports Club and continued "business as usual." The board decision, however, did not solve the problem with any finality, for this problem remains one the institution will have to solve sometime during its second century.

The discussion of a name change for VPI did not originate with the administration; on the contrary, it seems to have originated with sports writers both in and out of the state. Most of the in-state writers seemed to prefer the name

Virginia Tech. Others preferred VPI. All objected to Virginia Poly. Out-of-state writers had difficulty recognizing that Virginia Polytechnic Institute, Virginia Tech, and VPI referred to the same school. On one occasion, the school listing appeared twice in a sports magazine, one under Virginia Tech and one under Virginia Polytechnic Institute.

The faculty entered into the discussion, not so much from sympathy with the difficulties being faced by the sports writers as from the realization that land-grant colleges all over the country were changing their names in order to get the word *university* into their official titles. The arguments advanced by other schools to include the word *university* in their titles, they felt, applied to VPI with as much validity as it did to the others.

The administration did not enter publicly into the debate, but it was not unaware of the increasing difficulties VPI was having in competing with land-grant colleges turned into universities. In discussing this problem Newman said to the board:

> It is useless to speak of southern regional averages and unrealistic to con-sider salary scales of VPI in terms of the scales of State Colleges and Teachers Colleges. VPI is a land-grant college of the university type, and at the begin-ning of the 1961-62 session, will probably be among the last four of fifty-two land-grant institutions which have not recognized the fact by a change of name. VPI is in keen competition for qualified faculty with all universities in all fields and with the state universities in all fields except agriculture—throughout the nation.

No specific action resulted from the discussions either as to a settlement on the name Virginia Tech or as to an agreement that the word *university* should be included in the name. The fact that VPI had extended its program far beyond that of a typical college, however, was well-established in the minds of many. A few venturesome individuals on the faculty suggested new names for the school with the word *university* playing a prominent part. Old timers on the faculty smiled indulgently at the suggestions and continued to call the school VPI.

As VPI's growth continued, it was inevitable that the town of Blacksburg would also grow. During the administration of every president of the College the interests of the town and the interests of the College occasionally collided to such an extent that special meetings between representatives of the two groups became necessary to resolve the differences. The role played by the stu-dents during such incidents had been decidedly unpredictable but seldom dull. In a 1957 incident the students ran true to form.

Blacksburg announced its intention to include the VPI campus in a part of the territory it planned to annex. VPI officials decided to oppose the plan through regular channels. The student body decided to oppose the plan through the regular channels and a few channels of their own devising. They started by holding a one-day boycott of all Blacksburg merchants in order to show graphi-cally how much student spending meant to the town. Letters presenting the students' reasons for opposing the annexation were sent to hometown news-papers. A public meeting with student leaders and town officials was arranged. While this meeting was in process, an unplanned demonstration lasting more than six hours broke out. In the words of *The Techgram:*

> The gathering on the campus at College Avenue and Main Street climaxed a one-day boycott of Blacksburg merchants . . .
>
> Two students were arrested. They were charged with damaging state property when air was let out of tires of patrol cars. The police used tear gas to quell an incipient riot when the two students were arrested. The students were released from jail in Christiansburg that night . . . The charges were dismissed at a hearing [four days later].
>
> The demonstration was orderly. None was injured and no property was damaged, except for two tire valves on police cars. Besides state troopers, town, and college police and Montgomery County sheriff deputies were on hand.
>
> The crowds gathered after the evening meal. The arrests and tear gas incident came after 9:00 p.m. A loud speaker was set up and student, college and town officials urged the students to go to their rooms. The pleas went unheeded. About 10:30 p.m. the Highty-Tighties were called into action but their music didn't cause a homeward trek. Dispersal was gradual around midnight . . .

Summer vacation again intervened to provide a cooling-off period. Before the fall quarter opened, the "town and gown" had worked out a satisfactory compromise whereby the college campus was excluded from the proposed annexation.

Following the demonstration, a number of students admitted privately that they had joined in the affair "just for fun" and did not care one way or the other about the outcome of the annexation. One student who participated in the demonstration insists today that "we proved a demonstration did not have to be violent in order to get action." Apparently modern student opinion differs on this point at times.

By the mid-fifties all of Blacksburg's churches had programs for the students, while four of the churches had personnel employed to work directly with these programs. The Newman administration welcomed the development of this work but realized that the numerous religious activities being conducted on the campus needed coordination. After devoting considerable study to determine how a state-supported institution could best meet the problem of the increasing campus religious activities, Newman created the post of coordinator of religious affairs. He assigned to this office the responsibility for coordinating all the religious activities carried on by the various organizations.

Paul Derring, who had served as "Y" secretary for thirty-nine years, was asked to fill this newly created office. He resigned as "Y" secretary in August and accepted the newly created post, effective September 1, 1957.

Orrin R. Magill, who had served as "Y" secretary at Tech between 1911 and 1913, was persuaded to serve as secretary while a successor was being sought for Derring. Magill had just returned to Blacksburg after more than a quarter of a century of service in "Y" work in China. The committee appointed to recruit a successor to Derring knew exactly whom it wanted for the job. It wanted Alfred C. Payne, who had served as associate secretary of the Tech YMCA from 1946 to 1949. After much persuasion, Payne accepted the position, to the relief of the committee, which since has never had reason to regret its success in getting "Al" back on the campus.

The VPI Educational Foundation continued to broaden the base of VPI's private financial support. In 1953 John R. Hutcheson, president of the foundation, proposed a campaign to raise funds for an adult education center. The suggestion was well received by a number of individuals and groups, and the campaign was launched forthwith. In 1955 the Board of Visitors decided to remodel the Faculty Center into a building suitable for such a purpose when and if sufficient funds could be secured. The more sophisticated and appropriate name of Continuing Education Center was adopted, and the campaign for funds continued. In 1958 the position of director of development was created, and Earl Fisher, an individual successful in public relations and fund-raising campaigns, was appointed to the post. Fisher worked closely with Hutcheson in raising funds not only for the Continuing Education Center but for the total VPI Educational Foundation program as well.

Before the end of the year, partly as a result of Fisher's efforts, a campaign called the pre-centennial VPI development program had been organized and launched. This program had as its objective the raising of fourteen million dollars within the next fourteen years "to round out VPI's first hundred years of service in education to citizens of Virginia and the nation by 1972."

The immediate objectives of the program in addition to raising money for general college support, included funds for a continuing education building and for a field house for physical education and recreation. Within a short time the pre-centennial concept of the program came to be overlooked as efforts were concentrated on immediate objectives or needs. In 1960 efforts were renewed to raise funds for the continuing education center. Progress was slow but grading and removal of the reflecting pool in front of the University Club was begun in late 1964.

The enrollment for the session of 1960-61 reached 5,747, the largest in the history of the College to that time and the largest in the state. Most of the students came from Virginia, with practically every county and city in the state having at least one representative. Included in the student body were representatives from thirty-one states, the District of Columbia, and twenty-five foreign countries.

In November of 1960, Business Manager Cassell reviewed for the board the progress made in the implementation of the site plan for the physical development of the College. The development of the physical plant had been phenomenal; but since the growth of the College was expected to continue, the board approved a revised site plan developed in cooperation with outstanding educational consultants and architects. The well-known Stanley Abbott, landscape architect of the Williamsburg restoration and park development program, had also helped with the plan, which had received the approval of the Virginia State Art Commission. All building programs started during Newman's administration in the sixties followed this plan.

In September, 1960, "after many disheartening postponements," construction started on the field house, which before its completion in 1963 had been officially named the Virginia Tech Coliseum by the Board of Visitors. This latter action had been taken following Newman's warning that if the board did not name the building, other persons, including the sports writers, most certainly would do so. Such names, Newman observed, might or might not be appropriate.

So urgent was the need for such a building that the first basketball game was played in the Coliseum on January 3, 1962, before the building had been completed. Although some seven thousand fans sat on the concrete levels upon which seats would be installed, no one seemed to mind the inconvenience; Tech won from Alabama 91-67. This attendance was immediately broken in

February when some ten thousand fans, a second record-breaking attendance for basketball in Virginia, packed the Coliseum to watch Tech down West Virginia 85-82.

By the end of 1960, it was obvious that Tech's effort to upgrade its entire intercollegiate sports program was bearing fruit. The year 1960 was especially encouraging. The football team won the state title with a 6-4 season which included a 13-12 win over VMI and a 40-6 win over Virginia. The basketball team posted a 20-6 season and won the regular season Southern Conference championship, although it lost the tournament championship to West Virginia. The baseball team posted a 10-9 record which was slightly below par for this group of hustlers. Coach Frank Teske's wrestlers continued their winning streak by winning the Southern Conference championship and four individual crowns. During the year, the matmen lost only one dual meet, the first loss in five years. The golf team won the state championship with a 7-3 mark. The swimming team "came up for air" with a 3-1 record, which included an unexpected victory over rival VMI, and the tennis team posted its first winning season since 1950.

In spite of, or perhaps because of, the brightening athletic record it was realized that Athletic Director Moseley would need help if he was to continue building the overall program. With this thought in mind, Moseley gave up coaching football to devote full time to his duties as athletic director. Jerry D. Claiborne, top assistant coach to "Bear" Bryant at the University of Alabama, was named head football coach to succeed Moseley. Claiborne reported for duty in January, '61, and set about trying to build a football program that would satisfy all concerned.

In the fall of 1960, the Alumni Association through its president, W. Thomas Rice ('34), presented the College with a portrait of former president Burruss. The board was pleased to accept the portrait; the gift however brought into sharp focus the problem of proper display of portraits, tablets, plaques, and other memorials which had been donated to the College during more than half a century. In a number of instances, the buildings in which the memorials had been located originally had been removed or converted to a usage entirely inappropriate for the memorial. In most of these cases, the memorial had been moved to another building, usually the library, or stored for safekeeping. The problem was particularly baffling with respect to portraits, since suitable wall space, especially in the Newman Library, was decidedly limited. The board has not been able yet to establish a policy with respect to the treatment of the accumulated memorials which is completely satisfactory to everyone concerned, but clearly deserves commendation for its efforts to do so. In the case of Dr. Burruss' portrait, the problem was greatly simplified. It was hung in Burruss Hall, which, as J. Ambler Johnston said, had been brought into existence largely through Burruss' efforts.

By 1960 it was becoming evident that the rapidly changing conditions in the state were making, and would continue to make, new demands on state institutions of higher education. As one result a number of customs and traditions, some of long standing, began to undergo rapid change. One practice undergoing rapid erosion was that one begun nearly half a century earlier of assigning each state institution a limited area of education and service within which to develop its program. No law existed on the statute books which decreed that VPI should restrict its program to the areas of agriculture, engineering, and applied science; but with the exception of a short period in the early 1880's such a restriction had been clearly stated from time to time by governing boards and by a number of statewide study commissions; even Newman had recognized and accepted this restriction in his inaugural address. By 1960, however, he recognized that the new conditions which had developed in the state and the rapid developments which were taking place in the fields of science and engineering made necessary some modifications in these traditional restrictions. For one thing, he believed the College needed more work in the humanities and the social sciences. For another, he believed that the new conditions in the state justified for VPI as a land-grant institution the development of new programs in harmony with the land-grant philosophy of 1960. This philosophy, he informed his board, when translated into practice throughout the country had resulted in "institutions which today most nearly approach the function of true public universities." Continuing, he said, "The role of the public university is different in that it is designed to meet the needs of the whole commonwealth, rather than those of any specific clientele." "The 'state university,'" Newman had informed the board, "has no choice; its responsibility in resident instruction is to serve all the young people of the state who can benefit from higher education and who wish to attend the public university."

In another report prepared during the same period for the State Council of Higher Education, Newman said, "Virginia Polytechnic Institute then, although chartered as an agricultural and mechanical college, takes its place among all institutions, of whatever type, which are devoted to higher education in America." In this same report, after outlining the instructional program of the institution as it would be in the session of 1961-62, Newman included the following paragraph:

> By all reasonable standards, . . . Virginia Polytechnic Institute is functioning as a public university in her educational contributions to the welfare of the state and the nation. As such, she has the responsibility of a state university for maintaining quality in higher education, for keeping open the door of educational opportunity, for advancing the frontiers of knowledge, for extending public service in adult and continuing education of all kinds, and for providing administrative leadership as needed, in a coordinated program of the total educational system of the Commonwealth. For these reasons, then, it is becoming increasingly more important that steps be taken toward establishing a public image of the institution which more adequately reflects the university operation covering collegiate and graduate education.

No stampede occurred on the part of either the Board of Visitors or the Council of Higher Education to establish an image of VPI as a state university, but the seed for the development of such an image had been planted. More and more groups on the campus began to use the word "university" in referring to VPI, while *The Techgram* began writing of VPI as the state's land-grant University.

In the fall of 1960, Newman reminded the board of the desirability of a name change for the school of applied science and business administration as soon as the new school of business was in operation. The best name, he told the board, was that of a college of arts and sciences. The word "college," however, did not seem to be "presently available for the division, since VPI was already publicly and affectionately, but apparently not officially known as a College," he informed the board. If a change in name was justified, such a change, "might require only board action, and possibly approval by the Virginia Council of Higher Education."

Apparently Newman was referring to a change in name from that of a school of applied science and business administration, but he followed this suggestion with a lengthy review of the trend in the United States toward developing and naming land-grant institutions as universities. In concluding his remarks he once more reminded the board that "VPI is in fact a university-type institution." Following this discussion the board accepted Newman's recommendation that the name of the school of applied science and business administration be changed to that of a school of science and general studies. In a subsequent report dealing with another problem Newman indicated that he had not pushed for the school's designation as a college of arts and sciences for fear such a move would be rejected by the Council of Higher Education and at the same time jeopardize the plans for creating a separate school of business.

At the same time the board approved the name for the school of science and general studies, it also approved the formation of a department of history and political science in the same school.

The school of science and general studies under the leadership of Dean G. B. Johnston acted promptly to improve the course offerings in the school. As a result of intensive committee work on the part of the faculty, a core curriculum of basic courses was set up for students pursuing degrees within the school. This core provided for more experience in depth from a broader offering of humanities and sciences, while at the same time permitting increased opportunity for specialized study in a major area. In May of '61 Dean Johnston announced the appointment of Dr. Archer Jones as head of the department of history and political science. In August the Board of Visitors agreed to request permission from the State Council of Higher Education to offer work for degrees in English, history, and political science beginning in September, 1962. This latter agreement was a significant one in the history of VPI. It represented a distinct break with the long-held practice of offering humanities and the social sciences only as service courses for work in agriculture, engineering, and applied sciences. The decision to offer these degrees was not reached hastily, easily, or without debate in the Board of Visitors or in the State Council of Higher Education.

Dr. Newman, after informing the board that the proposed programs had the strong endorsement of both the faculty in the school of science and general studies and of the academic council, made a strong plea for the new degrees in a lengthy report, part of which follows:

> . . . VPI is numbered among the small and rapidly dwindling minority of land-grant institutions not yet accorded full university status by their states. A very important segment of a university is a strong liberal arts college or school. The great and swelling majority of land-grant institutions already have flourishing programs in liberal arts, not only as service courses but as majors.
>
> There are at least three important reasons for recommending major programs in English, history, and political science at this time; first, students from this area who do not wish to major in technical subjects and who are not able or do not wish to go far away to college would be able to enroll here; second, our position as a true university, whether or not so named, would be more strongly established; third, our ability to obtain and hold properly qualified staff in the liberal areas would be greatly improved. We have been most fortunate in the loyal and dedicated service of very able men in English, foreign

language, history, and political science during the past decades; but it is un-realistic to expect such a sacrificial devotion to continue indefinitely, especially among the younger staff members, in the face of growing demand for excellence and numbers of teachers in all areas. It is asking a great deal of a promising young scholar to expect him to give up prospects of teaching anything above sophomore service courses for many years.

Dean Lee Bidgood, [of the University of Alabama] whose valuable survey of our offerings led to the establishment of our School of Business, stated frankly that our present offerings in the liberal arts were not sufficient to support properly a top-flight school of business; and his comments could be equally well applied to other schools on the campus served by the humanities and social sciences. There is a continual pressure from national accrediting organizations like ECPD for improvement and increase in the service offerings in the humanities for professional students. It is our firm belief that all schools on the campus would benefit from our expansion into liberal arts majors . . .

At present, and increasingly we share the feeling that VPI, its divisions and branches including those that may be acquired, must coalesce into a dynamic, workable and serviceable university system. Our rightful destiny, individually and collectively, almost certainly will not be realized otherwise. Existing patterns should be examined in the light of new purposes and changing times. New occasions teach new duties. One should not miss his turn by failure to read the road signs.

In pressing for approval of the new degree programs, Newman frankly admitted that offering the courses would raise problems with respect to the relations with Radford College, but the necessity for the new programs, in his opinion, outweighed the disadvantages they would introduce. Some board members were not too sure about this last point. Neither, it seems, were all of the board members sure that VPI should break with the time-honored tradition in Virginia that the institution should restrict its program to agriculture, engineering, and the applied sciences. Since VPI had been offering degree work in business administration for a number of years, the establishment of a school of business had been looked upon more as an administrative rearrangement of work than as the establishment of new programs. Offering degree work in English, history, and political science, however, clearly started the institution along a new path. In the face of this perplexing situation the board postponed official consideration of the matter until the next day when, the question having been brought up again, the proposal to offer degrees in English, history, and political science was passed with one board member abstaining. In order to comply with the plan for coordinating Radford College and VPI, enrollment in the courses was restricted to men and to girls living at home in Blacksburg or surrounding communities.

Before the proposal for the new degrees could be submitted to the State Council of Higher Education, the question of continuing the operation of Radford College and VPI under one board had to be faced. In November, 1961, the board was alerted that the Commission to Study the State Government of Virginia was planning to recommend that the governor "transfer the supervision and control of Longwood, Madison, and Radford Colleges to a state teacher education board of seven members." The board was asked to express an opinion on the proposed recommendation. This recommendation was all the more interesting in that the chairman of the commission making it was also a member of the Board of Visitors. This individual expressed the opinion that the commission did not feel too strongly about the matter one way or the other but had been guided largely by recommendations emanating from the Council of Higher Education and from the State Board of Education. Dr. Martin reported that a poll of the Radford College alumnae indicated that a majority of this group preferred to have Radford College continue as the women's division of VPI. Dr. Newman, when asked to express an opinion, spoke at some length. After frankly admitting that difficulty had been encountered trying to determine the functions of the two institutions, he directed his remarks to the present and future situation. The thrust of his remarks was that VPI must be allowed to develop stronger programs in the liberal arts area as represented by the immediate need for the new degrees in English, history, and political science. It was possible, he suggested, that having Radford continue as a part of VPI would help strengthen the institution's liberal arts image. He did not believe that the present plan of operation provided adequate opportunities for men to prepare for teaching in fields other than the vocational areas. To remedy this deficiency, Radford probably would have to become coeducational. In conclusion, he expressed the opinion that under the present conditions it was probably best for Radford and VPI to continue under one board. Regardless of whether the two schools separated or remained united, he said that more women could be expected to enroll on the Blacksburg campus. A number of board members after expressing quite strong approval of the way Martin had built up Radford College under the merger, expressed a desire to continue the operation of the two schools under one board. A strong resolution to this effect was then adopted and transmitted to the state commission. No legislative action concerning a change of plans for administering the two institutions took place in the legislature of 1962, but it was obvious that some dissatisfaction existed with respect to the current plan.

In March, 1961, prior to some of the events already noted, the entire college community suffered a severe shock. President Newman had suffered a heart attack and been taken to the hospital.

It has been said that one of the best ways to judge the effectiveness of a great administrator is to observe the efficiency with which his team of subordinates carry on operations during his unexpected absence from the job. If this is a true criterion of administrative effectiveness, then Newman certainly deserves a high rating, because his team carried on smoothly and efficiently during his absence. In fact, the "Newman team," as it was often referred to on the campus, performed so smoothly and effectively especially during the last half a decade of Newman's administration that it deserves far more attention than can be given to it here.

"Lou" Pardue as vice-president and director of graduate studies operated with tact, smiling congeniality, understanding, and a firm hand to hold things, especially the curricular programs, together and at the same time kept all segments of the institution planning for the future. Stuart Cassell, operating with unusual breadth and depth of information concerning the business, financial, and budgetary affairs, kept these important areas functioning smoothly. "Deet" Dietrick, never seeming to hurry, nevertheless kept the faculty of the school of agriculture operating at a high level of morale as it set about revising the curriculum to meet the changing patterns of agriculture in the state. "Burke" Johnston, once referred to as "the gentleman scholar imported to the campus by Newman to help break down VPI prejudice against the humanities," accomplished much toward the achievement of this objective and at the same time kept his faculty busy studying ways in which the offerings in the school of science and general studies could best be developed and organized to serve the needs of the developing institution. Of equal importance, his faculty was working harmoniously within itself and with the faculty in the other schools in the pursuit of this goal. "Jack" Whittemore, the popular dean of the school of engineering, kept the faculty of that school professionally excited with a constant stream of new ideas, proposals for new courses, and suggestions for funding of research projects. Harold Young, director of the Agricultural Experiment Station, injected additional philosophical and practical concepts into that organization as he began to expand its program of research in harmony with the changing rural Virginia. In the process, he achieved new levels of cooperation with the state press and with the representatives of the USDA in Washington. "Bill" Daughtrey, totally unable to disguise his keen mind with his slow drawl, maintained the vitality of the extension work throughout the state. On the cadet front General Devine as commandant developed the Corps to a high degree of efficiency before turning it over in 1961 to his successor, General M. W. Schewe. "Jim" Dean, director of student affairs and dean of civilian students, had injected a note of professional efficiency into his office as he sought constructive student involvement in improving student activities on the campus. All of "Newman's team," with the assistance of their respective staffs, had helped create what some referred to as the era of good will at VPI. In spite of concern for Newman's welfare, this spirit of good will and progress continued throughout his illness and the remainder of his tenure as president.

After a period of rest and recuperation, Newman returned to the campus and slowly resumed the presidential duties. Fortunately, about three months prior to his illness, Newman had appointed Professor J. L. W. West, Jr., to the newly created post of executive assistant to the president. As a result, West was able to provide increasingly valuable service to Newman as he recovered his strength.

During the summer of '61 VPI held a very successful conference on the topic, "Physics of the Solar System and Re-entry Dynamics." This conference proved to be so successful that a similar one was held the next summer dealing with Lunar Exploration. These conferences attracted state, national and international attention.

During the same summer Dr. Richard Smith entered upon his duties as the first appointee to the Westinghouse Professorship of Electrical Engineering established at VPI by the Westinghouse Educational Foundation. Smith came to this position from one at the University of Texas.

Campus construction continued unabated. The biochemistry and nutrition building was completed and dedicated in the fall of '61. Buildings currently identified as Barringer Hall, Vawter Hall, and Shultz Dining Hall were started in '61 and completed in time for use in the fall of '62. The first wing of Norris Hall, completed in 1960, gained a second wing, completed in '62. According to *The Techgram*, "A weird looking but important seismological station also became part of the campus during the year." This underground reinforced concrete structure was one of a number of stations forming a world-wide network to detect underground nuclear explosions in addition to the usual earthquake-detecting functions.

In addition to the major construction projects, a number of minor projects including an agronomy research building, the renovation of Davidson Hall, and a new dairy barn were started. The completion of this latter project permitted the removal of the last farm building in the area west of the Coliseum being developed for parking or recreational areas.

Newman's annual report to the Board of Visitors for the session of 1960-61 was more complete and detailed than usual. It showed a healthy, growing institution rapidly developing along multipurpose lines. Without fanfare, the report set forth the success, the failures, and the disappointments faced by the College during the year. Constant attention was given in the report to the problems or programs needing further attention or study. Honors, awards, and special recognition received by faculty members at national and state levels were set forth in some detail. The activities of the several departments or individuals in securing increased funding for research projects or equipment were noted. The acute need for additional aid for graduate students was considered at some length. Figures showing an impressive growth in graduate work were presented. But, said Newman, much more must be done in this area. Graduate study, he said, "continues to be an instructional responsibility of paramount importance at VPI . . . An institution of university type must accept the responsibility [of graduate work] and be judged by its success in meeting it. Hence the die is cast for VPI. There can be no turning back. The problem should be faced as a challenge, not as a burden."

With respect to admission of students, Newman felt that the College had made "modest but substantial progress" toward raising admission standards. Much remained to be done in the immediate future, he warned the board, in using statistical procedures in setting up a prediction formula of high validity to be used in "directing the proper type of students to VPI," from the flood of applications the College would soon be receiving.

Newman's report touched upon most of the remaining major areas of institutional activity and found most of them to be in a flourishing condition. The library, in his words "the heart of a college or university," was growing but still in need of greater financial help. Campus affairs, including religious programs, concerts, guidance programs, use of the Memorial Chapel, and athletics had all showed satisfactory progress. With respect to intercollegiate athletics he said, "It has been a known fact for the past twenty years that the weakest link in the entire athletic program at VPI was the poor and most inadequate physical facilities." He felt, however, that the "entirely new physical plant" being developed would greatly improve this situation.

Throughout the report, which included a detailed account of the efforts being made in all of the schools to expand and improve the instructional programs, Newman seemed to go out of the way to give credit to faculty members for significant contributions they had made. In retrospect, it is possible to surmise that Newman wrote this particular annual report with the possibility in mind that he would retire for reasons of health before the end of another year. He served another full year, however, during which time the institution continued its rapid growth and expansion.

VPI probably received more favorable publicity during the academic year of 1961-62 than at any time during its previous history. For one thing, it joined the rest of the nation in the year-long celebration commemorating the passage of the

Morrill Land-Grant Act of 1862. Since the session of 1961-62 also marked the ninetieth birthday for VPI, it was decided to celebrate both anniversaries during the same year. A symbol for the two events was designed and placed on all college stationery and publications; centennial overtones were injected into meetings held on the campus during the session; and a steady stream of news releases and stories flowed from the public relations office. Two convocations were planned specifically for the year. At the first one, held on October 18, Benjamin M. McKelway ('17), editor of *The Washington Star* and president of the Associated Press, discussed the land-grant act and the land-grant colleges. McKelway's presentation, which was received at its conclusion with a standing ovation, got the celebration off to a happy start.

Before the second convocation, scheduled for April, 1962, took place, the Board of Visitors on December 4, 1961, announced that Dr. Newman at his request would retire at the end of June, 1962. Simultaneously with this information the board announced the election of Dr. T. Marshall Hahn, Jr., as Newman's successor. The news of these two events immediately pushed the publicity concerning the centennial celebration off the front pages for a period of time.

During the summer following his heart attack, Newman suggested to the rector that he, Newman, probably ought to retire. The rector had urged him to "wait a little while to see how things develop," but in early fall Newman had presented a formal request that he be allowed to retire by June 30, 1962. He had informed the board that he did not believe he could carry on as vigorously as he had been able to do for the past fifteen years. "In my estimation" he told the board, "the institution will need during the next ten years as its President the full-time services of a vigorous and healthy person possessing a clear insight and vision as to the role of higher education and an adeptness in public relations."

To the public, Newman said in part, ". . . I consider that the next ten years will be perhaps the most challenging that the institution has faced. We must continue further improvement in the quality of instruction at VPI, including the expansion of our graduate program and our extension and research activities in various areas." "The increasing demand to serve more college-age youth," said Newman, "will in itself constitute a distinct challenge."

The board accepted Newman's retirement "with reluctance" and set about choosing his successor from a list of persons whose names had been suggested for the position. One of those persons was Dr. T. Marshall Hahn, Jr., dean of the college of arts and sciences at Kansas State University, where he had gone upon leaving the headship of the department of physics at VPI in 1959. Dr. Newman was asked to contact Hahn and find out if he was at all interested in the presidency. Newman did so and reported to the board that Hahn was willing for his name to be considered. With this fact settled, the executive committee of the board set about collecting professional information about Hahn as if it had never heard of him before. All of the information was favorable. Some of it was disturbing. The governing board of a well-known state university, the committee learned, had been considering Hahn and had just about decided to offer him the presidency of their institution. If VPI wanted Hahn, it had better not wait too long to say so.

At a special meeting of the Board of Visitors held in Richmond on December 14, 1961, with all but two members present, the executive committee placed all of its information before the other board members and unanimously recommended Dr. Hahn for the position of president. The recommendation was discussed thoroughly, and each board member asked to express an opinion. All opinions were favorable. Dr. Newman paid tribute not only to Hahn but to Mrs. Hahn as well. He also reminded the board that Hahn, as head of Tech's physics department, had demonstrated a high degree of cooperative leadership in many difficult situations involving a number of people with divergent opinions. "There is no question," he said, "as to his integrity, honor, and ability to work with people." Following this discussion, the most complete one recorded in the history of VPI concerning the board's election of a president, the board voted unanimously to elect Dr. T. Marshall Hahn, Jr., as president of VPI, effective July 1, 1962.

Hahn's election as president was well received on the campus, in the state, and with the Alumni Association. Newspaper articles reviewing his professional career, with special emphasis being given to his previous activities as head of the physics department, appeared in a number of the larger state dailies. At the same time, unofficial campus and town gatherings rang with stories and anecdotes of the I-knew-him-when variety.

In the meantime, the realization that the Newman era was about to end swept the campus and the state. Editorials appeared in practically every state paper, praising Newman for the magnificent job he had done in building VPI to its position of eminence. The editorials either directly or indirectly alluded to or reflected the spirit of good will toward VPI which, according to most of them, Newman had created over the entire state. On the campus, the situation was one of mixed emotions. Goodbye had to be said to a warm, well-liked, highly respected friend and successful leader. Welcome was to be said to a new individual, who for his part showed all the potentials for becoming a warm new friend and successful leader. For many individuals these two emotions blended together and gave deeper significance to the remaining portion of the local celebration of the land-grant centennial which had begun on the campus.

The second centennial convocation, this one also celebrating the ninetieth anniversary of the establishment of VPI, was held on April 13, 1962. V. C. (Pat) Jones ('28), author and manager of Curtis Publishing Company's Washington public relations office, delivered the main address, using as his topic, "The First Ninety Years." Following Jones' address, VPI citations "for meritorious service and outstanding contributions to their profession, their nation, and their alma mater" were presented to twelve Tech alumni of the classes from 1906-17. An unusual touch was added to the celebration when Professor Claudius Lee also ninety years old in 1962 was presented to the audience. Following the luncheon given in the Faculty Center to the invited guests, a formal Corps review was held on the drill field in spite of the biting cold wind which swept across the campus. An unexpected touch was added to the review when a sudden gust of wind blew off the regimental commander's cap as he was in the midst of his saber salute to the alumni. The incident was considered to be amusing by everyone except the hapless cadet commander.

A number of noncentennial incidents also helped enliven the year.

As part of a weekend spent in western Virginia 119 of the 140 members of the Virginia General Assembly, accompanied by Governor Harrison, visited the campus on February 3. The special train carrying the group was met at the Huckleberry Station by Stuart Cassell, Tech business manager, and the legislators were taken on busses borrowed from Roanoke to Squires Hall for luncheon. The weather cooperated. So did the Highty-Tighties, who stood outside and serenaded everyone with "Dixie" as the governor and the legislators entered the hall. After the luncheon the legislators and other invited officials from western Virginia boarded the busses and were taken on a tour of the campus and then back to the Huckleberry for the trip back to Roanoke. It should be added, and not incidentally either, that Roanoke industrialists and business men through their Chamber of Commerce arranged the weekend and footed all of the bill with the exception of the luncheon at the College, which was paid for by the Alumni Association. The report of the luncheon as carried in *The Techgram* caught the eye of an alumnus who, writing to the editor, "to show you how VPI fed the legislators in the good old days of McBryde's administration before home economics and tossed salads," sent the following menu used, he said, in February, 1898:

> Oysters, oyster soup, broiled trout, baked shad, mashed potatoes, roast turkey, spring lamb, Virginia ham, cranberry sauce, baked tomatoes, lima beans, salsify, cauliflower, chicken salad, stuffed tomatoes, celery, radishes, lettuce. Choice: Peach ice cream—silver cake; vanilla ice cream—chocolate cake; lemon sherbet—coconut cake; Rochester cake; oranges, grapes, Edam cheese, cheese straw, pine-apple, coffee, cigars.

Following this "small luncheon" said alumnus, the legislature reduced the appropriations to all state institutions except VPI. A check of the records confirms the luncheon, but not the financial activities of the legislature.

Head basketball coach, the popular "Chuck" Noe, resigned to go to South Carolina. He was succeeded in May by W. B. (Bill) Matthews ('56).

President-elect Hahn made a number of public appearances in the state and immediately demonstrated the accuracy of Newman's assertion that he knew how to work with people.

Preparations were pushed for opening a community college at Clifton Forge and one at Wytheville under the control of VPI.

A decision was reached in cooperation with both student governments to provide individual students with a mandatory identification card.

An agreement was reached to allow college credit for work done at Roanoke Technical Institute (now Virginia Western Community College); plans went forward for a cooperative instructional program at Langley Field involving the University of Virginia, William and Mary College, VPI, and the National Aeronautics Space Administration; a decision was made to establish a Ph.D. degree program in plant pathology, and an M. S. degree program in extension education.

An announcement was made that Colgate Darden, former congressman and governor, and president of the University of Virginia, would make the commencement address.

In February, Newman advised the board that VPI was a charter member of the newly organized Council of Graduate Schools in the United States. At the same board meeting, he suggested and the board approved the appointment of a committee to plan an appropriate ceremony for the inauguration of Dr. Hahn. At the May meeting, he announced the membership of this committee, a joint Radford-VPI group. At the same meeting, Newman made a number of suggestions designed to smoothe the transfer of presidential duties from himself to Hahn. He also made a strong recommendation that work in architecture be taken out of the school of engineering and be organized into a school of architecture with its own dean. As to faculty salaries, he once more made it clear that VPI was in competition with nationally known universities both in recruiting and holding faculty members. Fortunately, he did not stop with a warning; he advanced a plan which when adopted by the board helped improve the situation somewhat.

Newman was happy with the progress made by the several agencies in raising funds for the institution. At the same time he strongly advised that steps should be taken to achieve better coordination among the efforts of these agencies. As one result of funds raised largely through the VPI Educational Foundation, he informed the board, VPI had been able to raise several departments to national prominence. This national prominence in turn had been an instrumental factor in generating additional financial support for other purposes, he reported. He was convinced by the success achieved thus far, he said, that a number of foundations, governmental agencies, industries, alumni, and friends would invest in VPI or its programs if approached properly and in an orderly, organized fashion.

Dr. Newman's final report to the Board of Visitors covered the session of 1961-62. In it he followed the general format of the one for the preceding year, although he did not present as much detail. Once more the report reflected a forward moving institution developing along multipurpose lines. Although the circumstances would have justified it, no effort was made in the report to take a backward look at the accomplishments of the past decade and a half. On the contrary, and typically, this report prepared by the president who had helped guide VPI through one of the greatest periods of expansion and growth in its history, focused attention on planning for continued physical and academic expansion.

One thousand one hundred and sixty-four students received their degrees from Dr. Newman at the dual commencement exercises held in Burruss Hall on June 10. It was noted at the time that Newman, during his fifteen years as president, had presented diplomas to more students than all nine preceding presidents combined. Gifts to Newman from students and faculty were an unscheduled but pleasant part of both morning and afternoon exercises. The gifts included a pen and desk set with a '62 class ring attached to the latter (since the class had made Newman an honorary member), a desk lamp, a desk and chair, a book of bound letters from faculty and administrators, and from the faculty a hand-lettered framed scroll of appreciation for his devoted services to the institution.

Following his retirement on June 30, 1962, Dr. and Mrs. Newman moved into the new home they had built in Blacksburg, where they have lived since. As one of the senior citizens of the community Dr. Newman has taken an active part in civic affairs and has served for a number of years as president of one of the local banks.

Walter S. Newman was one of the great presidents of Virginia Polytechnic Institute. Following the announcement of his impending retirement from the presidency, numerous speakers, state officials, and editorials in the state press testified to this fact. Each speaker and each editorial stressed different aspects of his contribution. But, running through each speech and each editorial was a recognition, expressed or implied, of the great storehouse of good will in the state which Newman had created for VPI. Of equal importance for the future was the realization on the part of the press that VPI under Newman had begun to develop a multipurpose program of service to the state much broader than a program restricted solely to agriculture, engineering, and the applied sciences.

After commenting on the progress made under Newman, *The Roanoke Times* concluded:

> VPI, as a result of Dr. Newman's excellent leadership, has grown in stature as a keystone in Virginia's structure of state-supported higher education. In the process the institution has steadily improved opportunity for Virginia's youth and increasingly made itself a vital factor in the educational and cultural life of the people.

The faculty in its Scroll of Appreciation presented to Newman included the following statement: "You have successfully presented to the people of Virginia and to the General Assembly a fine and true image of the scope and state-wide service of this large and complex institution."

Perhaps *The Roanoke World-News* came as close to expressing the sentiment of the great majority of the friends of the institution when it said:

> *The World-News* salutes Dr. Newman for the tremendous job he has done not only for VPI, but for Virginia, and extends a hearty welcome to Dr. Hahn as he prepares to step into some mighty big academic shoes. But most of all we congratulate VPI on what one has accomplished and the prospect of what the other can attain in that position.

Chapter 13

The Hahn
Administration

1962-

THOMAS MARSHALL HAHN, JR. was born in Lexington, Kentucky on December 2, 1926. After attending the public schools in Lexington, he entered the University of Kentucky and received his B.S. in physics "with highest honors" in 1945 at age eighteen. Five years later he received his Ph.D. in physics from the Massachusetts Institute of Technology. His professional and industrial experience prior to assuming the presidency was most impressive. While serving in the Navy, he was a lecturer in physics at the U. S. Naval Academy Preparatory School. He was also a physicist at the Naval Ordnance Laboratory, a teaching fellow for one year, and a research assistant for two years at Massachusetts Institute of Technology. In 1950 he returned to the University of Kentucky as associate professor of physics. In 1952 he served as professor and director of nuclear accelerator laboratories at Kentucky. In 1954 he came to VPI as professor and head of the physics department. In this latter capacity he was the leading force in the establishment of a doctoral program in physics, the Master of Science program in nuclear engineering physics, and in the acquisition of the nuclear reactor simulator put into operation in 1957. He was also one of the leaders in securing the $350,000 grant from the Atomic Energy Commission from which the UTR-10 critical reactor was secured. In 1959 he moved from

VPI to Kansas State University as dean of arts and sciences and returned to VPI in 1962 as president.

In addition to his educational experience, he had served as consultant and physicist for a number of corporations and as a research participant in the Oak Ridge National Laboratory. He was the author of a number of scientific papers before he came to VPI. As a professor at VPI he had also demonstrated an unusual adeptness in face-to-face exchanges with students, faculty, and legislative committees. A Methodist, he had been a regular attendant at church services in Blacksburg. This fact had not escaped the notice of the administration, the faculty, the students, and the student president of the YMCA. In 1948 he married Margaret Louise (Peggy) Lee of Dinwiddie County, Virginia.

The reins of the presidency were passed to Hahn on July 1, 1962. Since this date was on Sunday, the first day he spent in the president's office in Burruss Hall was on Monday, July 2. By coincidence rather than by plan, this date was the identical one on which, one hundred years earlier, Abraham Lincoln had signed the Morrill Land-Grant Act into law. Locally much attention was given to this coincidence. Nationally, a centennial celebration was taking place in Washington, with Senator George Aiken of Morrill's home state of Vermont making the principal address. Senator A. Willis Robertson of Virginia introduced a long statement into the *Congressional Record,* pointing out that Thomas Jefferson had advocated a broad system of education as early as 1776. Continuing his statement, Robertson correctly implied that the program at VPI was implementing a part of Jefferson's philosophy. After highlighting the work done at VPI, Robertson paid high tribute to retired President Newman and extended his congratulations to incoming President Hahn. Senator H. F. Byrd sent a telegram congratulating VPI on its ninetieth anniversary and its centennial celebration of the Land-Grant Act. "I join with all Virginia," he wired, "in expressing gratitude for the fine work of Dr. Newman as President. My sincere congratulations are extended to Dr. T. Marshall Hahn, Jr. as he becomes the eleventh president of VPI."

In addition to the recognition from these two senators, three congressmen, W. Pat Jennings ('41), Richard H. Poff, and J. Vaughn Gary, sent messages and inserted statements in the *Congressional Record* in which they praised the record having been established by Dr. Newman and congratulated Dr. Hahn upon his election as president. Other messages of congratulations and good will continued to pour in all day.

Locally, Hahn's first day in office was largely an "open office" affair as he greeted old acquaintances who trooped by to extend "heart-warming" greetings. As *The Techgram* expressed it, "Intermingled with administrative and faculty callers, were newspaper correspondents and photographers, TV cameramen, and radio tape recorders." Interviews were sought by and given to representatives of the press. Hahn met the test and through the press presented an image of a young man eager to continue the "tremendous progress" having been made by Dr. Newman. "Land-grant colleges were established as institutions of the people," he observed. "Our mission is just that—to provide educational opportunities for young people of Virginia and the nation." These interviews, reported in the press, signaled to the faculty that Hahn was familiar with the overall teaching, research, and extension activities of the institution. The fact that he constantly used the term "university" when referring to VPI did not go unnoticed by this group either.

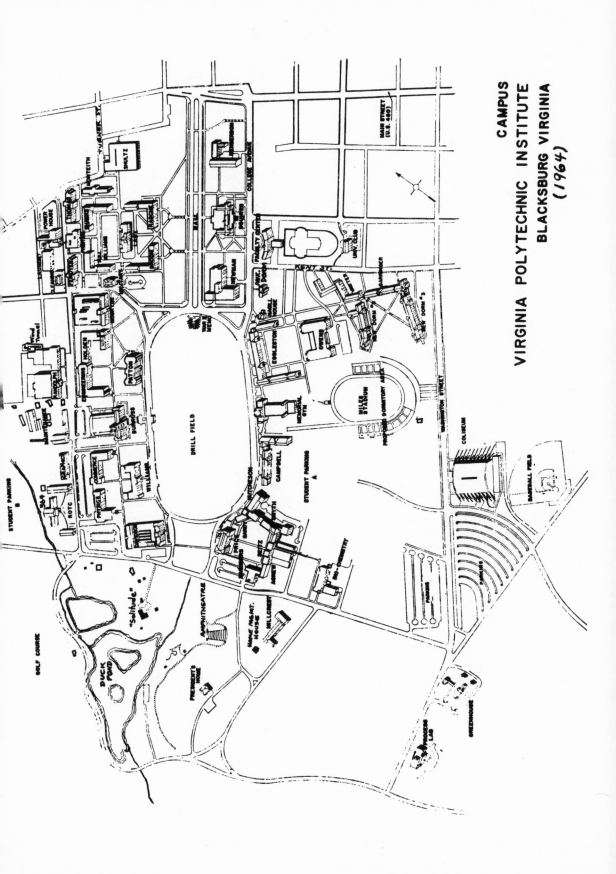

CAMPUS

VIRGINIA POLYTECHNIC INSTITUTE

BLACKSBURG VIRGINIA

(1964)

Describing himself as extremely enthusiastic about becoming VPI's president, he said that first of all he wanted to catch his breath and then get reacquainted with the University. Later, more than one professor claimed that this period of breath catching was the only one during which he had ever been able to keep up with the energetic Hahn.

Immediately upon assuming the presidency, Hahn used the columns of *The Techgram* to extend his greetings to the alumni, friends, and supporters of VPI. After pledging to devote his energies to the continued advancement and strengthening of "the institution we love," he paid tribute to the achievements of the past. With deftness of phrasing he identified VPI with the country's "magnificent system of Land-Grant Universities" and with the programs of instruction, research, and extension which these universities were promoting. Hahn also turned his attention to the challenge of the present and the future. The immediate challenges, he felt, grew from the constantly increasing numbers of young people wanting a college education and from the nation's need for greater numbers of young people "prepared to work at the upper limit of their abilities." With the costs of providing educational excellence increasing with the level of technology, he warned, it would be increasingly difficult to provide the more expensive educational opportunities needed for the increased number of young men and women. Educational mediocrity, however, would be far more expensive, he warned. The development of the economy was dependent upon the contributions of organized research, he believed. At the same time the extension efforts, he said, must "more and more provide effectively for the continuing advancement of the abilities of personnel working in all fields of endeavor."

Hahn concluded his greetings by requesting the support of alumni and friends of VPI for their "active financial and vocal support" for the programs at the institution.

Although mentioning instruction, research, and extension, Hahn's message represents the first time in VPI history that an incoming president in his salutatory remarks failed to identify by name the promotion of agricultural and engineering education as constituting the chief mission of VPI. This omission was welcomed by some observers. Others, shaking their heads ominously, warned that Hahn was about to pick up where Newman had left off and continue the conversion of VPI into a Midwestern type state university. A third group remained indifferent one way or the other.

The happiness so evident on the campus when Hahn walked into the president's office on Monday was rudely broken on Tuesday when Vice-President Pardue was seriously injured in a car crash at the foot of the Christiansburg Mountain. After a lengthy stay in the hospital, Pardue returned to Blacksburg but in March requested that he "be relieved of his present position and assigned to less arduous duties." This request immediately was granted by the board, but about a month later Pardue died at his home before assuming his new duties.

Other than the unhappy events connected with Dr. Pardue's tragic accident, Hahn's administration got off to a smooth start. H. C. Wyatt ('24) and Wyatt A. Williams ('36) were appointed to the Board of Visitors in late June to succeed board members Oscar F. Smith III ('26) and G. L. Furr ('16), who were ineligible to succeed themselves. At the same time E. H. Lane ('12) and E. H. Will ('22) were reappointed. At the organizational meeting of the board in August,

W. Thomas Rice ('34), president of the Atlantic Coast Line Railroad, was elected rector. It is worth noting in passing that before his appointment to the board, H. C. Wyatt had served on the State Council of Higher Education. As one result of this service he brought to the board a valuable understanding of the overall system and problems of higher education in Virginia.

During the summer, the Lunar Conference held on the Tech campus received world-wide press and TV coverage, since twenty noted scientists and rocket experts, "intent on seeing America put a man on the moon before the Russians, were read and heard throughout the world." Of far less significance nationally, but of great significance locally, the State Council of Higher Education in August gave its approval for the institution to offer the degrees in English, history, and political science which had been recommended during the Newman administration and vigorously promoted by Hahn.

The month of August also saw the retirement of H. W. Sanders ('16) as head of the department of vocational education. He was succeeded by Rufus W. Beamer ('38), who came to the position from the University of Tennessee.

In September, Dean L. B. Dietrick (M.S. '29) announced his intention to retire at the end of the month. The appointment of Dr. Wilson B. Bell ('34), associate director of the Agricultural Experiment Station, as Dietrick's successor was enthusiastically received by the board, the alumni, and the agricultural sector of the public. At the same time that Bell moved into the deanship, W. H. Daughtrey ('27) was appointed director of the Agricultural Extension Service, and P. H. DeHart ('29) became associate director.

Other retirements during the session included that of Earl Fisher on December 31 from the post of director of development and on February 1 that of John W. Whittemore, whose death followed hard upon his retirement. Whittemore as dean of the school of engineering and architecture had seen that school grow in enrollment from 1,487 in 1952 to nearly 3,200 in 1963, thus making it the seventh largest engineering school in the country. In April, he was succeeded as dean by Dr. Willis G. Worcester, chairman of the electrical engineering department at the University of Colorado.

Early in January as a part of a reorganization plan for student admissions and records, George J. Braun, Jr. was appointed as associate director of admissions and registrar, with both the admissions office and the registrar's office placed under the administration of Dr. Paul H. Farrrier, director of admissions. Later in the spring Dr. W. E. McCubbin was appointed as head of the physical education department to succeed W. L. (Monk) Younger ('20), who resumed teaching duties until his retirement. The appointment of McCubbin, an experienced leader in intramural sports at the University of Kentucky, created considerable excitement on the campus and raised immediate speculation that the next step would be the organization of instruction in physical education into a degree-granting program. During the same year Dr. S. B. Row ('31) was appointed director of community colleges and general extension programs. Once again the campus was excited. Did this appointment portend an increased opportunity for development of off-campus extension and instructional activities? As it later developed, it did mean just that.

A miscellany of other campus events continued to absorb varying degrees of faculty, student, and alumni energy and attention during the session. The installation of the Memorial Chapel pipe organ, a gift from the alumni, was completed in August. During the fall the Alumni Association presented the institution with a portrait of Dr. Newman. During the unveiling ceremonies, presided over with dignity and warmth by W. Thomas Rice, rector of the board, Hahn pleased the audience with his reference to the portrait as a symbol that would recall the "tremendous progress to a position of national distinction that VPI has achieved under the fine leadership of Dr. Newman."

On the sports scene there were things to cheer about and things to cry about. In spite of some fantastic ball handling by Virginia quarterback Gary Cuozzo, Tech upset the University of Virginia football team 20-15 and thereby kept its record of Harvest Bowl wins clear. A large homecoming crowd in October watched a morning float parade built around the theme "VPI—Progressive Land-Grant University" and an afternoon football game with the University of Richmond. Tech won the game 13-7 but suffered some temporary ego deflation when at one period of the game the new electronic scoreboard showed Richmond ahead 91-7. Egos were not helped to any great extent when later in the season VMI won the Thanksgiving Day game 14-9. Unfortunately, this score could not be changed by electronic correction. Therefore, Coach Claiborne's men had to settle for a 5-5 season, which strikingly enough saw both the Techmen and their opponents scoring 137 points. On the basketball front, Bill Matthews' boys electrified the sports scene with an opening 80-77 victory over third-ranked University of Kentucky. The team was unable to maintain the pace, however, and had to settle for a 12-12 season. Frank Teske's matmen "after a dismal seasonal record" redeemed the situation by winning the conference tournament. The golf team for the third straight time also won the conference championship. The baseball team posted an overall record of 14-7 but lost the conference championship to West Virginia. Other sports were considered to be reasonably satisfactory.

In December it was announced that William Walker Lewis, Jr., son of Professor W. W. Lewis ('35), had been appointed as a Rhodes Scholar. This appointment, a first for VPI, was applauded by the entire Tech community. Lewis, a major in physics, had a perfect academic record. In addition, he was a member of the Monogram Club, captain of the tennis team, president of ODK leadership fraternity, president of the campus chapter of the American Institute of Physics, vice-president of Sigma Pi Sigma, physics honor society, and a member of the German Club.

Also to be noted in the miscellany of campus affairs for the session are such events as the increase of *The Virginia Tech* from an eight-page to a twelve-page paper, the decrease in the diploma from fourteen by seventeen inches to eight and a half by eleven inches, the change in name of the Pershing Rifles drill team to that of the Gregory Guard in honor of Earle D. Gregory ('23), Congressional Medal of Honor winner, the merging of the student-directed Engineering Conference and the Agricultural Exposition into the Tech Festival, and the $3,500 worth of gifts made to the Memorial Chapel by the class of '63.

On the academic front all schools continued curricular studies designed to make the content relevant to the changing times. A Ph.D. program in plant pathology and physiology and an M.S. program in extension education were begun in the winter session. Planning for the creation of a school of architecture continued and was capped late in the year with the announcement that Charles Burchard, a successful practicing architect and former member of the Harvard

Graduate School of Design, had been named to become dean of the new school, beginning January 1, 1964.

Plans for Dr. Hahn's formal inauguration as president of Virginia Polytechnic Institute and chancellor of Radford College had been steadily progressing throughout the year. Because of Dr. Pardue's serious accident, Dr. Wilson B. Bell had been asked to serve as chairman of the inauguration committee. Bell had an excellent committee with which to work. This committee, working with five sub-committees, made the inauguration held in the Coliseum on April 4, 1963, a successful one. At the ceremony presided over with dignity and aplomb by W. Thomas Rice, rector of the board, and attended by representatives from major educational institutions of the country, the major address was delivered by Luther H. Hodges, Secretary of Commerce in President Kennedy's cabinet. Greetings were extended by Governor Harrison, by the Association of Virginia Colleges through Dr. George Oliver, by the Association of State Universities and Land-Grant Colleges through Dr. Russell I. Thackrey, by the Alumni Association through C. Eugene Rowe, from the Tech faculty by Dr. S. A. Wingard, and from the student body by David E. Lowe president of the Senior Class. Dr. Hahn then presented his inaugural address.

In retrospect the speech is a summary of many of the challenges and problems through which Hahn led the institution for the next decade. Displaying a familiarity with the rapidly changing characteristics of society, which in turn were making increasingly insistent demands for a more sophisticated quality program in higher education, Hahn paused briefly and noted the complexities of the changing Virginia scene. The effects these changing conditions would have upon VPI as the state's land-grant university were noted. At the mention of the word "university" in connection with VPI, a number of people in the audience were seen to smile, but Hahn continued his presentation unperturbed. One of the significant effects, he suggested, would be the increasing necessity to improve the instructional, research, and extension programs of the institution. "We must respond in our instructional programs," he said, "to the thought-provoking challenge of educating today's youth for careers in tomorrow's world in fields that do not yet exist." Continuing, he said, "We must devise and strengthen educational curricula which will generate maximum effort on the part of each student, with emphasis on excellence."

The pressures for greater emphasis on excellence, he warned, were even more critical when viewed from the perspective of the increasing numbers of college-age youth in the years to come. "These greater numbers of young people," he urged, "must be viewed, not as problems, but as our most precious assets, as investments which will yield the richest dividends." At this point in an effort to present a background picture of the growth which VPI would have to face within the immediate future if it expected to meet the changing conditions in the state, Hahn briefly reviewed the existing situation which he believed VPI had reached during the first ninety years of the institution's history. The major portions of this summary follow:

> The rate of growth which must be accommodated by Virginia's land-grant university is indeed striking when viewed in relationship to the first ninety years of the institution's history, itself a period characterized by amazing growth. Today this institution, with the largest full-time enrollment in the state, enrolls at its central campus of more than 80 principal buildings valued in excess of

75 million dollars a student body of approximately 6,000; and the staff now numbers more than 2,000 persons actively engaged in significant programs of instruction, research, and extension. The annual budget has grown to more than 17 million dollars.

The institution is recognized today among the forefront of land-grant universities, emerging rapidly in increased national distinction, multi-purpose, with the doctorate offered in numerous fields.

The College of Engineering is the seventh largest in the country, with its graduates among the most highly sought in the nation.

The College of Agriculture is the seventeenth largest in the country, and enjoys national prestige, with the members of the faculty constantly in demand as consultant scientists all over the world.

The programs in Architecture, Business Administration, and Arts and Sciences are rapidly growing in strength with an emphasis on excellence and a productivity in research which adds to the luster of the institution. The instructional, research, and extension activities in Home Economics are unexcelled in this area of the country.

The Graduate School is the most rapidly growing component of the institution, and time cannot begin to permit a recital of all of the exciting research undertakings in which graduate students and faculty are currently engaged.

Particularly in relationship to the prodigious rate of development of VPI up to this time, it is almost impossible to comprehend the growth and development which must be achieved in the years to come.

Even with the growth of technical institutions and community colleges . . . and in addition to the continuing education and extension programs which VPI must provide for a growing and more urban Virginia population, the resident enrollment at VPI in Blacksburg must more than double by 1975. This is the most conservative projection and assumes the same percentage of young people of college age seeking a higher education, and in fact we recognize this proportion will actually increase.

The frightening impact of these numbers becomes clear when it is noted that, even with continued increases in the efficiency of utilization of the physical plant, in little more than a decade as much physical plant must be added at VPI as has been developed in the entire previous history of the institution.

It is difficult to see how the funds can be provided for such growth, growth which must be effected in the face of equally strong pressures to retain and upgrade the excellence of programs. It's hard to see how we can provide the costs of educational excellence. We should ask how we can afford the funds necessary for the level of faculty salaries required to attract and retain a distinguished faculty. The outstanding library which must be the center of a distinguished university is not easy to acquire. Significant amounts of funds are required for the buildings, laboratories, and complex scientific equipment necessary for educational excellence in today's technology.

We know, however, that the funds necessary for excellence must be secured, since, above all, we know we cannot afford the wasteful ineffectiveness of educational mediocrity. Nor can we fail to provide the necessary educational preparation for the increasing numbers of young persons entering our labor force, our greatest asset, if Virginia is rapidly to move forward with its economy.

Hahn concluded his address with a solemn pledge to devote all of his efforts to the development of outstanding programs of instruction, research, and extension at Virginia's land-grant university. Simultaneously he called on "every public official, every citizen, every faculty member, every student, and every alumnus" for support and maximum effort to these same ends.

The inauguration day ceremonies were concluded with a luncheon in Owens Hall for the guests, a cadet parade, and a reception by Dr. and Mrs. Hahn at their home on the campus.

The tempo of excitement and change continued to develop following the inauguration. Before the close of the year, the Board of Visitors changed the name of all schools in the institution, except the graduate school, to that of colleges and changed the name of the school of science and general studies to that of the college of arts and sciences. During the same period, the names of the departments of animal husbandry and poultry husbandry were changed to that of department of animal science and department of poultry science, respectively.

The board also agreed that the education courses necessary for certification for teaching in the secondary school should be made available on an elective basis for students in all approved major programs. Also agreed to by the board was a proposal to transfer the department of geological sciences from the college of engineering to the college of arts and sciences. It was with much less enthusiasm that the board agreed to respect the wishes of the State Council of Higher Education and of the Old Dominion College to terminate the "two-year engineering program of VPI at Old Dominion College, effective September, 1963."

For the student body the activities of Hahn's first academic year as president came to an end with the June commencement which was held for the first time in the Coliseum. Lieutenant Governor Mills E. Godwin made the chief address to the assembled crowd, which, to the surprise of many, comfortably filled the huge auditorium. One wag reported that at times, thanks to the public address system, the commencement was a "howling success."

Before the final activities rang down the close of the year, it was announced that the VPI Educational Foundation was acquiring 140 acres on U. S. Route 460 east of Blacksburg to be developed as a university research park with sites of various sizes to be made available for scientific and technical industries. Prior to this announcement, Dr. Hahn had announced the appointment of Dr. Warren W. Brandt, associate dean of the College of Arts and Sciences at Kansas State University, as vice-president to succeed Dr. Pardue. Brandt reported for duty on July 1, 1963, and immediately plunged into the academic intricacies of the developing institution and began preparations for the session of 1963-64.

Brandt's credentials were impressive. After graduating from Michigan State University, where he had been valedictorian for his class, he had received his Ph.D. degree in chemistry from the University of Illinois. As a member of the faculty at Purdue University, he had risen to the chairmanship of the analytical division of the department of chemistry before moving to Kansas State University. At this latter institution, he was serving as head of the department of chemistry when he was appointed as associate dean of the college of arts and sciences to serve along with Dr. Hahn, who was dean of the same college. In 1958-59 he was a Guggenheim Fellow at Oxford University in England. In addition he had published a number of technical articles and had held numerous national offices in the prestigious American Chemical Society.

Dr. Brandt proved to be an efficient, tough-minded leader far more concerned with building VPI into his concept of a university than in following precedent and Tech traditions. In him Hahn found an able ally as the two men worked side by side for the next several years to develop high quality educational opportunities for Virginia youth.

By the end of the summer, Hahn and Brandt had used the word *university* so often and in such a great variety of situations when referring to VPI that a number of the faculty, somewhat self-consciously, had begun to experiment with the usage of the word. They liked the results; consequently, the word *university* used in connection with VPI became rather common on the campus, especially with faculty recruited from without the state. The word did not come easily to native-born Virginians on the faculty, however; to this group, as it had been to their fathers and to their grandfathers, the expression "the University" had always meant the institution at Charlottesville. The group adapted to the usage rapidly, nonetheless, and soon used the term as glibly as yesterday's arrivals on the campus.

In October it was announced that the Board of Visitors of Virginia Polytechnic Institute and Radford College had transmitted a resolution to Governor Harrison, requesting that the association between VPI and Radford College be terminated, effective July 1, 1964.

The desirability of separating the two institutions had been increasingly apparent. VPI had grown to be the largest institution of higher learning in the state, while Radford College at the same time had grown to be the largest college for women in the state. Both schools seemed destined to continue growing, and a good many people felt that the energy spent in coordinating the programs of the two schools was too great for the benefits being derived. Some individuals felt that VPI's growth, especially in the humanities and teacher preparation, was being handicapped by the association. Others felt that Radford College was being injured by the plan. All of these points of view had been expressed either verbally or in letters apparently by nonfaculty members to the board. Acting on the basis of this alleged discontent, the board appointed a committee to study the situation and to make needed recommendations for further action. As a result of this committee's report, the board decided to recommend the separation of the schools. The legislature of 1964 acted favorably on the proposal; and the two schools, after twenty years of debatable success in coordinating their respective programs, were separated on July 1, 1964, and each one allowed to work out its separate destiny. It perhaps should be added that cordial relations continued to exist between the schools, both at the administrative and the student-body level.

During the year, R. Craig Fabian, supervisor of educational programs at Westinghouse Electric Corporation, was appointed as director of development to succeed the retired Earl Fisher. In his new job, Fabian was to coordinate all development and public-relations programs at Tech and was to work closely with the president's office and the newly established Development Council.

The Development Council was composed of the executive committee of the VPI Board of Visitors, the executive committee of the board of the VPI Educational Foundation, the executive committee of the board of the Alumni Association, and the president of the Virginia Tech Student Aid Association. The Student Aid Association was chartered in 1950 for the purpose of soliciting funds from alumni and friends of VPI for the sole purpose of providing scholarships for students with recognized athletic ability. The scholarships, called grant-in-aid scholarships in order to avoid confusion with academic scholarships, were awarded by the regular VPI scholarship committee. This committee was responsible for seeing that all awardees met the regular admission standards required of all students.

Obviously the Development Council with which Fabian was to work was a powerful one whose decisions and success, or failure, would have tremendous significance for VPI.

In a move designed to continue improvement in the student-related services, the guidance and placement office was revamped. All placement work designed to help students find satisfactory jobs was left under the direct supervision of Dr. W. H. Cato. The guidance portion of the older office was centered in a newly created counseling center under the direction of Dr. H. J. Canon, assistant to the dean of students. The reading improvement program was also placed in the counseling center.

Other events in the student-related services area included the retirement on February 25, 1964, of Paul Derring as director of religious activities, and the appointment of Alfred C. (Al) Payne as assistant to the dean of students. Derring, who in his forty-six years at VPI had "served five presidents and thousands of students and faculty members in more than religious activities," moved to Richmond, Virginia, shortly after his retirement.

Payne, although not given the title of director of religious affairs, included the duties of this office in his new responsibilities. To accept this new position, he resigned as secretary of the Tech YMCA. This latter position was then filled by B. E. Trent, who came to VPI from Clemson University. Before leaving the "Y" for his new post, Payne, with the assistance of student leaders, updated the former Religious Emphasis programs to a "Conference on Student Concerns." The conference was popular with the students and brought a number of well-known speakers to the campus, but some of the more conservative faculty looked upon the change as "serving old wine in a new bottle."

Other changes involving new personnel or a shifting of duties for others were made. Dr. Coyt T. Wilson, associate director of the Agricultural Experiment Station and assistant dean at Auburn University, was appointed as associate director of the Virginia Agricultural Experiment Station. This appointment, effective July 1, 1964, filled the vacancy created when W. B. Bell became dean of agriculture.

In an effort to provide increased efficiency and quality of service in the area of student admissions and records, Dr. Paul H. Farrier was appointed to a new position of director of admissions and records, and Dr. M. P. (Mike) Lacy ('51) was appointed as director of admissions.

In the fall of '63, John R. Castlemen ('21) at his request gave up the headship of the department of graphics, which was then organized as a division in the department of industrial engineering. Professor J. B. Dent ('26) assumed the chairmanship of the division and accepted responsibility for its operation in its new home. Surprisingly, this reorganization brought some mild murmurs of protest from a few older alumni who mistakenly interpreted the transfer as a move to eliminate graphics from the engineering program. Bosco Rasche's graphics, to this group, represented one of the eternal verities needed in the preparation of all engineers.

In February the Alumni Association adopted a set of new by-laws designed to bring about increased efficiency in coordinating the alumni affairs with the developing program of the University. As one step in the implementation of these by-laws, Marcus L. Oliver ('44) was appointed to the new post of director of alumni affairs. At the same time, he was asked to continue his duties as secretary and treasurer of the Alumni Association. Since E. Turpin Phillips ('44) had resigned as associate secretary the preceding summer, all of the alumni office work now fell on Oliver.

The personnel change attracting the most publicity during the session of 1963-64 came in the spring. W. B. (Bill) Matthews resigned as head basketball coach to become assistant to the athletic director and field secretary of the Student Aid Association. He was succeeded as head coach by Howard P. (Howie) Shannon, assistant basketball coach at Kansas State University.

Summer activities on the campus continued to develop but often under new formats in keeping with the changing conditions in the state. The Institute of Rural Affairs was shortened in '63 and discontinued in its customary form in '64 after having been an annual event on the campus for thirty years. A series of short courses and more specialized conferences gradually emerged to serve the needs once filled by the Institute.

Announcements of financial aid from outside sources cheered the faculty, raised morale, and, as both Newman and Hahn had predicted, generated more support. For example, Senator H. F. Byrd, Sr. raised his scholarship grant to $100,000, and the Mt. Ararat Foundation, in addition to its already generous support, gladdened the hearts of everyone with a gift of $100,000 to be used for library resources.

The Cyrus Hall McCormick heirs set up an endowment fund of $120,000 to be used for fellowships and scholarships in agricultural sciences or agricultural engineering, and an anonymous donor provided $300,000 to be used for a visiting lecturers program. This latter sum, which was to be used within a ten-year period, was used to organize a Visiting Scholar Program which made it possible to bring nationally and internationally distinguished scholars in many fields to the campus for visits of various lengths. All in all, as a result of the increased support of alumni, individuals, corporate friends, and other groups interested in VPI, some two million dollars was generated in gifts and grants. President Hahn was appreciative of this support but told the board and the Development Council that he believed an even wider base of support was possible.

Expansion of educational opportunities and services and constant pressure for admission from more and more students continued to generate pressure for the expansion of the physical facilities. Newman Hall, named for Walter S. Newman, and Miles Hall, named for C. P. (Sally) Miles, were completed and ready for occupancy by September, 1964. Construction continued on the fruit and vegetable processing laboratories. The dairy center southwest of the main campus was completed, as were units to the turkey research center located northwest of the campus on the Kanode Mills Road.

The people of Wythe County, the town of Wytheville, the town of Rural Retreat, and Bland County joined together in raising money to help finance the construction of buildings at the Wytheville Community College, which opened as a VPI branch school in the fall of 1963.

The same community support by the people of the counties of Alleghany, Bath, and Botetourt, and the cities of Covington and Clifton Forge helped get construction under way for the Clifton Forge-Covington Area Community College (now Dabney S. Lancaster Community College), which opened in the fall of 1964.

Construction also was under way at the Danville Community College and at a number of the off-campus research stations.

The announcement that construction was actually under way on a new stadium to be located south of the Coliseum convinced the remaining skeptics that the older Miles Stadium would indeed be abandoned in favor of student dormitories. Alumni who remembered the corn field which once stood on the site of Miles Stadium and the bull which faithfully chased everyone from the pasture which was located near the site of the new stadium received the news with mixed emotions. These emotions took a decidedly favorable turn when it was announced that the new stadium had been named Lane Stadium in honor of the popular and widely known Edward H. Lane ('10).

The sports program continued to develop at a satisfactory pace, with the football team threatening to steal the show. Tech kept its Harvest Bowl record clean with a 10-0 win over the University of Virginia and won sweet revenge on arch rival VMI by a 35-20 Thanksgiving Day victory. The fine 8-2 record for the year won the Southern Conference championship for Tech for the first time in its history. It also won for Coach Claiborne the honor of "Coach of the Year" in the Southern Conference. Bob Schweikert, quarterback of the champions, won All-American honors. The games with the Atlantic Coast Conference members were gaining in interest over games with Southern Conference members. Indeed many observers felt that the VPI-University of Virginia game fast was becoming the real "emotion rouser" in Virginia intercollegiate football.

The basketball team had a winning 16-6 season although the poor showing in the conference tournament and in a few key games left many fans unhappy. The other intercollegiate sports registered satisfactory progress, and Hahn optimistically predicted better days ahead.

The growth of the Hokie Club provided reason for some optimism. This club, organized and chartered within the Student Aid Association in 1962, held its first formal meeting near Washington. Reporting that the meeting foretold big-time status for Tech athletics, *The Washington Evening Star* commented that "Some Virginia Tech alumni . . . when it comes to big-time athletic ambitions . . . mean business." "The Hokie Club's new members," concluded the *Star,* "included three corporation presidents, a vice-president of a major steel company, one general, two colonels, and a rear admiral."

The really big news of the year came as the session drew to a close. It involved, as so frequently had happened in the past, the Corps of Cadets. In the first place, the Highty-Tighties led the parade opening the New York World's Fair on April 22, 1964. The pleasant excitement of seeing the regimental band on national TV and from reading about it in both national and state press had scarcely died down when the announcement was made that membership in the Corps of Cadets would be voluntary, rather than compulsory for male students, beginning with the 1964-65 session.

The announcement of this decision reached by the board at its regular quarterly meeting on May 18, 1964, produced an immediate crisis which overnight threatened to make VPI a house divided. The decision to eliminate mandatory Corps membership had been reached by a majority rather than by a unanimous vote of the board, and even this vote had been reached only after a lengthy discussion. This fact when learned unofficially by the public became the basis of numerous rumors and endless speculation. Hahn published an "open letter" to alumni, parents, and friends of VPI, explaining the reasons for the board's action and expressed the hope that the board and all of the people at VPI could count on continued support from these groups. So much controversy and so many charges and countercharges, pro and con, were stirred up, however, that Governor Harrison requested the Board of Visitors to hold a special meeting to review the board decision and to provide interested persons an opportunity to be heard on the matter.

Upon learning that the board planned to review the decision, the college faculties met in separate sessions and by secret ballot voted on the question, "Do you favor the principle of voluntary participation of students in the Corps of Cadets?" The results showed 430 voting yes, 55 voting no, and 5 abstaining.

The special meeting of the board, open to the public, was announced for Monday, June 29, beginning at 9:30 a.m. in Burruss Hall Auditorium. On Sunday afternoon, June 28, a group of interested alumni met with Hahn in his office. Alumni President C. Eugene Rowe ('33) presided. Several of the alumni members of the Board of Visitors also attended the meeting. Dr. Hahn again reviewed the reasons for the board decision. In concluding, he remarked that the problem of what to do about the Corps had existed for a long time. What he had done, he said, was to bring the problem from under the table where it was out of sight and put it on top of the table where it was in plain view. Some doubt was expressed as to the longevity of the existence of the problem. At this point one alumnus, speaking in support of the board's decision, reminded the group that the problem of the compulsory military status for students had plagued every administration from the day the College had opened; that President Burruss, under whom the Corps had reached its zenith, had on at least two occasions entertained the idea of abolishing it entirely; and that President Newman had spent the last decade of his administration trying to find methods of making the Corps more attractive to students. Following this meeting, the directors of the Alumni Association adopted a resolution by a twelve-to-five vote supporting the volunteer-Corps concept. At the same time, the directors voted unanimously in favor of maintaining a strong Corps of Cadets program.

All Sunday afternoon and night alumni, some representing alumni chapters and others representing only themselves, poured into Blacksburg. Excited groups gathered at numerous places on the campus and exchanged strong opinions on the decision. Some individuals expressed fear that Hahn was planning to resign because of the trouble. Others were afraid that he would not. One alumnus wanted Hahn fired for what he had done to VPI; another alumnus wanted him kept for the same reason. No agreements were reached by the individual alumni other than to be at the board meeting in Burruss Hall the next day.

The meeting, called at 9:30 a.m., was presided over by Rector W. Thomas Rice ('34), who explained that it was the board's desire to hear everyone who wished to speak. So many persons in the audience, which at times numbered about a thousand persons, wished to speak that the meeting lasted for five and a half hours. At one stage in the proceedings Rice was accused of favoring the compulsory-corps faction. At another stage he was accused of favoring the anti-compulsory faction. At all times he remained calm, kept the meeting under control, and handled the situation with dispatch. Sixty-four persons speaking with obvious sincerity for what they thought best for VPI expressed themselves at the hearing. The majority favored the action of the board.

Following the open meeting, the board went into executive session in which, after dealing with a few routine matters, discussion on the Corps was continued for another two hours. Finally, after clarifying the relationship planned between the voluntary Corps and the ROTC program, a vote was taken. On a divided vote, it was decided to reaffirm the decision to make the Corps voluntary. At the same time, it was decided to restrict ROTC training to students enrolled in the Corps.

This reaffirmation of the determination to make the Corps voluntary was received with mixed emotions. The decision ended the war, but there was no real assurance it had won the peace. Rumors were flying thick and fast that some alumni members on the Board of Visitors planned to resign in protest. Other rumors had prominent members of the Alumni Association threatening to resign. Yet, a third crop of rumors had the entire matter headed for a legislative investigation. One alumnus saw the decision as a communist plot to undermine military training in the United States. Fortunately, none of the prophesies materialized. For one thing, the open hearing had a surprisingly cathartic effect on everybody concerned. Strong emotions having been ventilated tended to give way to a more rational approach. Members of the board known to have been opposed to the decision did not resign and did not launch the expected warfare against the change.

Instead, this minority, including among its membership some of the top leadership in the Commonwealth, closed ranks with the majority of the board and continued working for a greater VPI. Some concern remained in the Alumni Association, but no big revolt took place. C. Eugene Rowe ('33), president of this organization during what was probably the most difficult period in its history, worked diligently to hold the association together. Not only did he hold it together, he helped its membership achieve a better perspective of the Corps as a part of a greater VPI.

No great stampede out of the Corps took place once its membership had been put on a voluntary basis. At the same time, the Corps did not grow in terms of numbers as the overall college enrollment steadily increased. A number of persons, both students and alumni, blamed this lack of growth on Hahn, insisting that he was anti-Corps. The official records do not sustain the charge. On the contrary, the records show Hahn constantly searching for and encouraging proposals for strengthening the Corps as a part of a dynamic changing institution. In recent years, the decision tying ROTC training to the Corps of Cadets has come under attack from some quarters. In fact, this campus, as other campuses throughout the country, witnessed widespread attacks on all military training connected with universities. Well could the Board of Visitors of 1972 repeat the exclamation of the Board of Visitors of 1872: "The military feature offers another embarrassing problem!"

As far as the campus was concerned, the excitement generated by the Corps incident gave way rapidly before the full calendar of summer activities and the excitement being generated by Hahn's and Brandt's statements concerning the "emerging University." The interest being aroused from these sources was augmented also by the realization that the University had reached one of those periods in its history when it would be seeing an unusually large number of its senior faculty members retiring from their posts or shifting from administrative to other duties. The announcement of new personnel to fill newly created positions, or to fill positions left vacant by retirements and the shifting of administrative duties, created a heady excitement of change pleasing to many but tinged with some alarm and sadness for others.

Robert H. (Bob) McNeil, director of publications and editor of *The Tech-gram*, retired after thirty-six years of service to the institution. Just prior to his retirement, he had been awarded a well-deserved plaque by the VPI Chapter of Pi Delta Epsilon, citing his long and outstanding service to student journalism at Tech. McNeil's place as editor of *The Techgram* was taken by Jenkins M. Robertson, assistant editor under McNeil. McNeil's duties as director of publications were then merged into the newly created office of director of public relations, filled September 1, 1964, by Warren H. Strother, who came to the post from a position with the *Richmond Times-Dispatch*.

J. Gordon Brown, dean of men at Emory and Henry College, accepted the newly created position of dean of men at VPI. This post, created in the office of the dean of students, was primarily responsible for men's student housing and the resident men's counseling program.

The announcement of the election of Harry C. Wyatt ('24) as rector and of Adger S. Johnson ('28) as member of the Board of Visitors excited pleasant memories among older alumni on the faculty. Wyatt's career, leading to the senior vice-presidency of the Norfolk and Western Railway in Roanoke, had been followed with great interest by faculty members who vividly recalled his cadet days on the campus. Since Johnson was the son of former faculty member J. S. A. Johnson and had grown up in Blacksburg, he was widely remembered not only by the faculty but by older members of the community as well.

Dr. G. C. Graf, after a period as head of the dairy science department, requested that he be permitted to devote full time to teaching and research. He was succeeded as head of the department by Dr. J. R. Nichols, professor of dairy science at the Pennsylvania State University.

Professor George R. Powley ('38) gave up the headship of the department of electrical engineering to accept the post of Westinghouse Professor of Electrical Engineering. He was succeeded by Professor Ralph R. Wright ('43) as acting head, pending the recruitment of a permanent department head.

In addition to the new department heads already announced Dr. Leon W. Rutland succeeded Dr. T. W. Hatcher ('22) as head of mathematics; Dr. J. Beverly Jones ('44) replaced his uncle, Professor James Bernard (J. B.) Jones ('21) as head of mechanical engineering; and Dr. Gerhard H. Beyer succeeded Dr. Fred W. Bull ('33) as head of chemical engineering. Bull moved to new duties as full time director of the Virginia Engineering Experiment Station. These new appointees came to VPI from the University of Colorado, Purdue University, and the University of Missouri, respectively.

George Braun resigned as registrar and was succeeded by Raymond E. Keller. During the same year Dr. Paul H. Farrier retired as director of admissions and records. He was succeeded by Dr. M. P. (Mike) Lacy ('51), who moved from the position of director of admissions. This post was filled by Dr. Evans G. Thompson ('40), head of agricultural education in the department of vocational education. Keller came to his post from a similar one at the State University of Iowa. Lacy and Thompson, although promoted from within the faculty, had recently earned their terminal degrees from Wisconsin and Cornell, respectively.

In December, Dean W. B. Bell announced the appointment of Dr. Houston B. Couch as successor to the retired Dr. S. A. Wingard as head of the plant pathology and physiology department. Couch came to his new position from that of associate professor of plant pathology at Pennsylvania State University.

Dr. Wingard, who had joined the Tech staff in 1917 as its youngest member, was at the time of his retirement the senior staff member in years of service.

During the spring, Dr. H. N. Young retired as director of the Agricultural Experiment Station. He was succeeded by Dr. Coyt T. Wilson, associate director of the station. Wilson's place was filled by Dr. Howard Massey, Jr., professor of horticulture and associate dean of the graduate school.

Also in the spring it was announced that the board had created two professorships: one, the John W. Whittemore Professorship in Engineering, honoring former Dean John W. Whittemore; and the second, the C. P. Miles Professorship in Arts and Sciences, honoring C. P. (Sally) Miles. This announcement shortly was followed by one stating that Dr. G. Burke Johnston, dean of Tech's college of arts and sciences, had been named to the C. P. Miles Professorship, effective September 1, 1965. This latter announcement was received with mixed emotions, especially from the faculty in the college of arts and sciences. This group, especially the older members, well remembered and appreciated Johnston's contributions as he had stood shoulder to shoulder with President Newman in his pioneering efforts to inaugurate liberal arts programs, and with President Hahn in his presentation before the State Council of Higher Education of the program for degrees in English, history, and political science. The courtesy with which Johnston had always conducted the affairs of the dean's office was also appreciated. The group, although reluctant to give up their dean, was happy over the new honor which had come to their erstwhile leader. Many persons in the group also knew that Johnston while dean had not removed himself from the classroom completely; but in fact, had established an enviable reputation as a dedicated, competent teacher.

Johnston was succeeded as dean in July by Dr. Leslie F. Malpass, professor and chairman of behavioral sciences at the University of South Florida at Tampa. Earlier it had been announced that a department of psychology and sociology would be established, beginning September, 1965. The appointment of a psychologist as dean and the announcement of the intention to establish a department of psychology—a move which Vice-President French a decade and a half earlier had feared would lead to unwise duplication of work in other state institutions—did not go unnoted. One wag observed that Hahn, not knowing that such things were not done in Virginia, did it anyway.

In the spring Lon K. Savage, education writer for the *Richmond Times-Dispatch*, was named executive assistant to President Hahn, replacing J. L. W. West, Jr., who had resigned to return to full-time teaching.

Other retirements of staff members with long records of service included: Dr. Robert A. Fisher from the department of chemical engineering; Professor Cecil A. Horst from the department of industrial engineering; Professor A. V. (Nye) Morris ('23) from the department of mathematics; Assistant Professor Peyton T. Gish ('23) from the department of agronomy; Professor J. R. Castlemen ('19) from the division of engineering and graphics; Professor Paul B. Dyck from the department of health and physical education; Professor W. L. (Monk) Younger ('20) from the same department; Professor Janet L. Cameron from the college of home economics; and Associate Professor Sara Catherine Peery from home economics extension.

By the end of 1965 the replacements for all of these retirees plus the addition of staff needed to take care of the steadily increasing enrollment had given Hahn his key leadership group for the next several years.

Even as all of these personnel changes were taking place, all of the colleges were involved in improvement and revision of their courses and program majors. The major thrust of these efforts was towards the development of appropriate curricula designed to meet the needs of the increasingly complex society. Since these needs were quite varied and complex, not conducive to the precise descriptions so necessary to this type of curriculum building, differences of opinion flourished as to the best curricular changes and reorganizations to adopt. The ensuing discussions created an excitement and intellectual ferment which permeated the entire University. Fortunately, a spirit of good will prevailed, although a few individuals felt that certain key administrators argued from positions of power and previously arrived-at convictions rather than from a genuine desire to find new solutions.

The graduate school, growing rapidly, raised its academic entrance requirements and established more formal procedures for the selection of candidates for admission. Considerable difference of opinion developed as to the wisdom of this move, especially when it was rumored that some applicants rejected for admission to graduate school at VPI had been readily accepted in other graduate schools both in and out of the state. Dr. Brandt, when challenged on the admission requirements, entered into free discussions with everyone concerned but reportedly remained "adamant, unmoved, and unsympathetic" in his opposition to a more flexible admission policy. President Hahn was not drawn into the discussion but reported his conviction that the more rigorous requirements had enabled the "strengthened faculty to make significant improvements in the caliber of offerings."

One of the most significant developments of Hahn's entire administration had to do with faculty salaries. The problem of low salaries had plagued every administration from McBryde's. President Eggleston had made a valiant fight for improvement. President Burruss in almost bitter reports to the board had focused attention on the disparity between salaries paid to faculty at VPI and those paid to faculty members in other institutions in the state. President Newman had raised the sights and stressed that VPI in recruiting its faculty was in competition with other land-grant and state universities. Newman had made considerable progress in the improvement of both the salary schedule and its administration, but it remained for the Hahn administration to bring faculty salaries to a point at which they were competitive on a nationwide basis. Even this accomplishment, important as it was for the welfare of the institution, was achieved by persuading the governor to support a faculty salary schedule in which the average salary paid faculty at VPI equaled as closely as possible the national average salary paid to faculty in comparable land-grant institutions.

This improved salary scale not only stimulated the recruitment of outstanding faculty members but also served as a strong stimulus to faculty morale. Unfortunately, about half of the additional funds required for the salary increases had to come from increased student fees, a solution, incidentally, which Dr. Burruss had vigorously resisted a number of times during his administration. Hahn was delighted with the improved salary schedule, but he was not happy with the increase in student fees, which had now been increased, he told the board, well beyond the average for state land-grant universities. The trend toward higher fees, he reported to the board, "somehow must be reversed, hopefully with more adequate state support as well as from the generation of greater private support for VPI's various programs. . . . If it is not," he continued, "rising costs will be such a hurdle that many well-qualified students cannot get over it." Hahn repeated these convictions a number of times during the next half decade but never succeeded in reversing the upward trend of student fees.

In intercollegiate athletics, Tech continued its frankly admitted effort to emerge into national prominence. Hahn, with a never-dampened enthusiasm, felt that progress was being made toward this objective. Reporting to the board, he expressed the belief that the ". . . athletic programs of the university are emerging in national prominence in keeping with the similar rate for the various academic programs." Hopefully, the board members did not read the sports pages which, the same week that Hahn made this statement, reported a 127-73 loss to West Virginia by Tech's basketball team. In spite of the loss, however, the team ended the season with a winning record.

During the fall season the football team lost to the University of Virginia for the first time since the '57 season. It also sustained its first loss in the Harvest Bowl after six consecutive wins but redeemed itself and wound up with a 6-4 record by defeating tenth-ranked Florida State University on Homecoming Day and by defeating VMI in Roanoke before some twenty-five thousand persons.

The homecoming game played in perfect October weather marked the final game to be played in Miles Stadium. Some twenty-two thousand people packed the stadium and watched the Gobblers upend the Seminoles 20-11. This unexpected but welcome victory helped wipe away sadness associated with the realization that another landmark was about to give way to the march of progress.

During the fall the stadium was razed, and as already noted, some of the wood from the stadium seats was converted into pencil holders and one mailed to every known alumnus of the University. Appropriately enough the first holder was delivered by Dr. Hahn to "Sally" Miles in person.

During the spring, following a recommendation from the board of directors of the Athletic Association, Tech, the only remaining charter member of the Southern Conference, withdrew from membership in that league. This move, which put Tech in the rank of the independents, was taken primarily in an effort to continue the upgrading of the intercollegiate sports program and to permit Tech to schedule an increasing number of games with comparable institutions in the region. Some alumni recalling "Sally" Miles' role as one of the founders and former president of the Southern Conference and his role as the builder of Miles Stadium were disturbed about how the removal of Miles Stadium and the withdrawal from the conference within the same year would affect "Sally." Apparently Miles considered a public statement unnecessary, but he did remind one alumnus that he, Miles, was faculty chairman of the Athletic Association which had in fact initiated both movements.

The historian dealing with the first decades in the history of VPI can speak with considerable assurance, for he knows how things turned out. When he comes closer and closer to current matters, his assurance begins to fade. He knows and can record the fact of certain events; but, denied historical perspective, he can not always relate these events to one another or tell of their ultimate impact. Even so, it is clear that as VPI approached the mid-sixties, its policy, programs, and developments began increasingly to be affected by the rapidly changing social, political, and economic conditions of the state. Virginia was becoming industrialized to a rather remarkable extent, with its predominantly rural orientation shifting rapidly to one more urban in nature. This increased industrialization and urbanization produced an economy and a people needing and demanding increased attention by the state to higher education.

The developments of the period are too numerous and too recent in time for any real perspective as to their ultimate effect on VPI. But the story when told promises to be a fascinating one. As the beginning decade of VPI's first century saw the College being forcefully shaped by the social, political, and economic forces of the state, so did the final decade of its first century. There are substantial differences in the results. The leaders during the first decade, combining developments of an earlier time with the forces of the decade, set the College on the road which led to the development of an institution largely restricted to education in agriculture, engineering, and the sciences. During the last decade VPI's leadership combined developments of an earlier era with the social, political, and economic changes of the sixties and charted a course calculated to develop the institution into a multi-purpose state university.

Other facts seem to stand out with remarkable clarity. Prior to his retirement, President Newman saw the rapidly changing conditions of the state, and alerted his board and the State Council of Higher Education to the fact that VPI, already a land-grant type university, could hardly avoid continuing along this line of development if it was to fulfill its responsibilities to the state. President Hahn picked up where Newman left off and almost immediately emerged as one of the most articulate, knowledgeable leaders in the state on behalf of improved opportunities in higher education for the youth of the Commonwealth. He was not at all reticent in pointing out how VPI as a land-grant university could help meet the state's rapidly increasing and changing needs in higher education. In the process he succeeded in generating in the board and among most of the faculty, old and new, enthusiasm for building VPI into a university "of emerging national distinction."

By the fall of 1964, Hahn realized that the time had come, as he expressed it to a meeting of the Development Council, "for an intensive period of self-study, a re-examination of our basic mission." This Council agreed with the president and immediately set itself to an examination of VPI's role in the light of the demands on higher education being made by the changing conditions in the state.

After lengthy deliberation, the Council spelled out a series of recommendations. Stated briefly, they proposed that VPI should not arbitrarily limit its enrollment, but should endeavor to provide facilities and finances to accommodate students from Virginia having the ability to complete successfully "a quality college education." Further, they urged more consideration to the development of the institution's program for the education of women, and that major emphasis should be placed on the strengthening of graduate programs but without loss of recognition of the importance of strengthening the undergraduate programs. In its report, the influential Council also recommended that:

> Since the legislative directives of the various land-grant acts define the role of a land-grant school, VPI's basic mission must include a quality resident instruction program for the youth in Virginia, coupled with supporting research and extension activities.

The Council also released some of the statistics it had used in projecting VPI's future enrollments. These statistics were impressive. If correct, VPI within approximately five years would nearly double the enrollment it had reached during the preceding ninety-two years. The building program required for such a sudden growth was startling.

Public attention immediately focused on the proposed enrollment increases and the magnitude of the necessary building program. The fact that for the first time since the 1880's the mission set forth for VPI did not restrict it to agriculture, engineering, and technology went unnoticed in the public press. One professor, in no way objecting to the statement of mission, expressed skeptical curiosity as to which of the legislative directives of the "various land-grant acts" defined *the* role of a land-grant school. "Did the report refer to federal or state legislative directives?" he asked. He did not press for an answer; therefore, his question went unanswered. It still remains an intriguing one, however.

Even before the Development Council had completed its deliberations, the Board of Visitors had received a request from the State Budget Office, requesting a summary of projected capital outlay needs for the next six-year period. At its meeting in October, 1964, Rector Wyatt asked Vice-President Brandt to discuss some of the problems involved in the preparation of such a long-range summary. Brandt was prepared to do so.

In order to prepare the capital outlay needs for the next three biennia, Brandt explained, the administration needed guidance from the board concerning its plans for growth in enrollment As a part of his report he also "read pertinent excerpts of State and Federal legislation dealing with what is officially expected of a land-grant university." At the same time he also presented pertinent figures concerning long-range enrollment projections at VPI. The minutes do not make it clear, but apparently Brandt was directing the board's thinking in terms of VPI's development as a university. In concluding his report he reminded the board that VPI was already accepting students with College Entrance Board scores comparable to "quality institutions in this part of the country."

Following Brandt's presentation, the board entered into a long discussion, adjourned for lunch, resumed discussion after lunch, and finally recorded its conclusions as follows:

> The VPI Board of Visitors recognizes that the mission of VPI is to provide the best possible resident instruction for the qualified youth of Virginia and strong research and extension programs to serve the needs of the Commonwealth.
>
> The Board desires to develop facilities to accommodate students from Virginia high schools who have the ability to complete successfully a quality university education. In making plans to carry out this mission the board reached the following conclusions:
>
> 1. The increasing number of qualified high school graduates will necessarily result in substantial growth in the enrollment of VPI and the Board accepts its increasingly significant obligation to the state, subject to the availability of funds.
>
> 2. There is a growing demand for women educated in the programs of VPI, and this will be taken into consideration in the future development of the institution.
>
> 3. Without loss of recognition of the importance of strengthening the undergraduate program, greater emphasis should be placed on strengthening the

graduate programs and offering graduate degrees in all areas where the need
is demonstrated.

It is disappointing that a fuller record of the discussion leading to this resolution is not available, for from the uncertain perspective of the time elapsed
since its adoption, this resolution appears to rank among the most important
ever adopted by a VPI Board of Visitors. VPI had been moving steadily toward
university status, not, as some claimed, because of the ambitions of any one
person or group of persons. Rather the movement had begun when VPI began
expanding its services to meet the changing social, industrial, and economic
conditions of the state. The revision and broadening of the curricula to meet
the rapidly changing technological advances which became so evident following
World War II was no more than necessary. The trend was no secret. It had been
discussed and mentioned sometimes facetiously, sometimes seriously, both on
and off the campus. But the resolution of October 5, 1964, was the first official
action in ninety-six years which committed the Board of Visitors to an effort
to develop facilities for a "quality *university* education."

The public release containing this resolution also included the projected
enrollments and building needs to be faced by the institution almost overnight.
Since these projections were little short of spectacular, they attracted most of
the headlines and public attention. As one result, many of the faculty failed to
grasp the full significance of the "university thrust" of this report. Hahn, Brandt,
and most of their "team," however, were well aware what the resolution meant. If
any member of the team did not know, he or she soon found out. The key leadership at state level also was not long in becoming aware of the thrust of VPI's
development. Of greater importance, for the first time in the institution's history, much of the state's leadership approved the new direction the institution
was taking.

Only a short time later, the Virginia Higher Education Study Commission,
created by the General Assembly to make a thorough study of higher education
needs in the state, went one step further. In a thought-provoking report the commission suggested that the name Virginia Polytechnic Institute did not convey an
accurate description of the role and scope of the program maintained at the
institution. Continuing, the commission said in part:

> Many citizens of Virginia, and certainly those in other states, do not fully
> realize the progress that has been made in developing Virginia Polytechnic
> Institute in recent years. A change of name with the incorporation of the word
> "university" in the new name would do much to give suitable recognition to
> the development that has occurred and will continue to occur in this thriving
> institution.

This report, coming as it did little more than a year after the uproar caused
by the change of status in the Corps, sent a shock wave of fright through the
ranks of some alumni. For the most part in no way opposed to the change of
name, these alumni absolutely did not want to see VPI get involved in another
family dispute. Evidently both the board and President Hahn felt the same way,
for no action was inaugurated to take advantage of the opening created by this
prestigious study commission. Hahn indicated that there were no current plans
to seek a change in the official title of the University.

The acceptance of the university role continued, however. In its report outlining anticipated developments in higher education for the decade 1967-77, the State Council of Higher Education said in part:

> Virginia Polytechnic Institute is Virginia's land-grant university with an extensive commitment to graduate as well as undergraduate instruction, research, and state-wide continuing education and public service. In recent years this rapidly developing institution has gained increased national prominence. In its growth process, VPI has acquired the character of a comprehensive university which preserves many of the traditions of its land grant orientation. The State Council concurs in this role for VPI in the Commonwealth's system of higher education.
>
> In October, 1964, the Board of Visitors approved a statement of "Philosophy of Development" for VPI favoring greater interest "on strengthening the graduate programs and offering graduate degrees in all areas where the need is demonstrated." The State Council is in agreement with this position and endorses the expansion of doctoral level programs in nonscience areas as well as additional programs in other areas of engineering and science.

Following the board's report of October, 1964, the administration continued the improvement of campus facilities and at the same time initiated an intensive study of additional physical facilities needed to take care of the expected enrollment and expanded educational opportunities. A six-year development plan was approved for submission to the state budget office, but it was realized that the site plan adopted in 1960 needed some revision. With this need in mind, the board at Hahn's suggestion, assigned responsibility for revising this site plan to the Richmond architectural firm of Carneal and Johnston and to Architects Collaborative, Inc., of Cambridge, Massachusetts. Most of the construction on the campus for the next half decade followed the general approach suggested in the resulting revision of this 1960 plan.

During the 1964-65 session construction began on Johnson, Lee, and Pritchard Halls, while site preparation started on Ambler Johnston Hall. At the same time plans were begun for the renovation of Eggleston and Campbell Halls, which before completion were converted into dormitories for women. Plans for buildings subsequently named Wallace Hall and Cowgill Hall were pushed, and plans for an addition to Burruss Hall were begun. Renovation of Davidson Hall was completed, and plans were projected for a laundry addition, additional greenhouses, and several smaller facilities.

The finishing touches were applied along with six hundred additional seats to the Coliseum. Construction proceeded rapidly on Lane Stadium, all-weather tennis courts were built east of the Coliseum, and a new track was completed at the site of the new track field.

In order to accommodate larger aircraft, a 4,600-foot runway supplementing the 2,600-foot one was under construction at the VPI airport. This project before completion required the removal of the Norfolk and Western Railway spur into Blacksburg, ending the use of the Huckleberry as a mode of travel in and out of the town. This loss did not place any great strain on the students, since they long since had resorted to automobiles, busses, and hitchhiking as the most satisfactory means of travel.

Although the announcements of increasing enrollments, plans for new buildings, arrival and departure of faculty members, and pronouncements of study commissions generated most of the public attention, the faculty and the student body had not been idle.

Early in 1965 the University embarked on a year-long self-study, preliminary to the periodic accreditation review by the Southern Association of Colleges and Schools. The timing of this study was most opportune. The questions of "Where are we?" and "Where are we going?" had been thoroughly debated by the Development Council and by the Board of Visitors. Now the faculty and more than five hundred representative students were given the same two questions for consideration. A structure for the study was formulated by a steering committee of "President Hahn's key leadership group" working with Dr. Roger L. Smith, who had been appointed as director of the University Self-Study. Once having formulated a structure adapted from the *Manual for the Institutional Self-Study and Periodic Visitation Program,* supplied by the Southern Association of Colleges and Schools, the steering committee became relatively inactive, thereby turning the study over to Director Smith and the faculty. Convinced that the administration was sincere in its expressed desire for the faculty to express itself freely as to weakness, strength, and suggestions for improvement in all aspects of the University's program, the faculty did just that. So did the students.

The university-level summary of results of the study was published in a two-volume report in the fall of 1966, in time for the visiting committee from the Southern Association of Colleges and Schools. It was, and remains, a fascinating report. The fact that approximately forty per cent of the faculty involved in the study had been on the campus two years or less, while fifty per cent had been on campus four years or less made the departmental and college level reports even more interesting. These uncensored reports were made available to the visiting committee, the faculty, and the students but were not published separately. The visiting committee found the published report to be "a remarkably uninhibited compendium of VPI faculty and student opinion about everything pertaining to VPI as it is thought to be and as it is hoped it may become."

The official visiting committee of the Southern Association of Colleges and Secondary Schools made up of twenty-five distinguished college and university leaders from across the nation, completed its study of the University's organization and academic structure in the fall of 1966. Its views, summarized in a formal report, included a number of recommendations and suggestions for improving and strengthening many of the university programs. At the same time, it isolated and brought into sharper focus a number of problems facing VPI as it sought to achieve the diversity and strength essential to its newly declared mission.

In summarizing its impressions, the visiting committee commented, "VPI for the past several years seems to have undergone more change than for the preceding quarter century, and it is hard to imagine a more dynamic institution." This dynamic activity and change, the committee decided, had happened so fast and so recently that many of the campus leaders were not certain what the score was, although they thought they liked it, whatever it was. In concluding its summary, the committee added, "There is no doubt that VPI is a better institution than ever, and is headed upward, steeply and rapidly."

The self-study, the reports, and the resulting treatment of the several recommendations are of too recent origin for a complete evaluation as to the effects on VPI. The visiting committee accepted, even commended, VPI's newly proclaimed mission to develop into a complete university which would "anticipate and help fulfill the intellectual needs of the state and nation." The faculty also accepted this new mission. This latter development was significant. It meant that the administration, the Board of Visitors, the Board of Directors of the Alumni Association, the Board of Directors of the Student Aid Association, and the faculty all had endorsed the new mission oriented toward a multi-purpose university. As already noted, the State Council of Higher Education soon followed with its endorsement.

Even before the closing of ranks behind the new orientation, significant developments toward the changing status continued on the campus.

In August, 1965, the Board of Visitors authorized a thorough study of the administrative structure and work in the areas of research and extension. Largely as a result of this study, the legislature in 1966 created an institution-wide Research Division. This division consolidated and broadened the role of the two existing research agencies: the Virginia Engineering Experiment Station and the Virginia Agricultural Experiment Station. Dr. William B. Harrison, director of the Engineering Experiment Station, was named as dean of the division, a new position. Dr. Coyt Wilson, who headed the Agricultural Experiment Station, was named associate dean and director of agriculture, life sciences, and home economics research. Before the faculty had time to decide whether it approved or disapproved of this treatment of its eighty-year-old Agricultural Experiment Station and its forty-five-year-old Engineering Experiment Station, the appointments of associate deans for the colleges of agriculture, arts and sciences, and engineering were announced. These associate deans, it was explained, would facilitate and improve the research programs in their respective colleges.

A gift of the two-million-dollar hazardous materials testing facility located near Rocky Mount, Virginia, donated to Tech by TRW, Inc., was placed under the new division, while the eleven field stations located throughout the state were continued as a part of the agricultural research program now in the new division.

The same legislature which created the Research Division also created a new university-wide Extension Division. All of the University's extension activities were consolidated in this new division under Dr. William E. Skelton ('40) in the newly created post of dean of the Extension Division. The basic philosophy of this reorganization was aimed at creating the administrative and educational structure necessary to make available the total resources of the University to meet the diverse educational needs of the rapidly changing state. Prior to this reorganization, the major portion of VPI's extension work had been carried on by the Agricultural Extension Service.

This service had already undergone a number of changes. Professor R. D. Michael ('26), who had succeeded E. R. (Flopsy) Price and had risen to the position of editor and head of the department of information and publications for the Agricultural Extension Service and the Agricultural Experiment Station, had retired in November, 1965. William H. Daughtrey ('27) had retired in December of the same year as director of the Agricultural Extension Service. Daughtrey had been succeeded by Dr. William E. Skelton ('40), specialist in 4-H club work, who had been serving as assistant director of the agricultural extension work since 1962. In February, 1966, the name of the Agricultural Extension Service had been changed to Cooperative Extension Service to comply with federal terminology and more nearly to reflect the changing nature of the work.

The new State Technical Services Program developed at VPI under federal legislation enacted in 1965 was included in the new division, as was responsibility for the operation and development of the programs at the Donaldson Brown Center for Continuing Education.

The drastic reorganization affecting both the Agricultural Experiment Station and the Agricultural Extension Division was received at first with some suspicion by long-time workers in these areas; but when it was realized that the reorganization really expanded rather than curtailed the opportunities for service in the respective fields, the concern soon muttered itself into silence.

Other administrative changes and appointments continued apace. Stuart K. Cassell, Business manager, was appointed to the newly created post of vice-president for administration. Dr. M. P. Lacy was named to the new post of dean of admissions and records. Edward B. Evans, personnel director, was appointed as business manager to succeed Cassell. Albin T. Butt ('52), of the Norfolk Redevelopment and Housing Authority, succeeded Evans as personnel director. Harry W. Swink, university purchasing agent, was named director of university services and auxiliary enterprises. He was succeeded as purchasing agent by James L. Shotts. H. P. C. Vandenberg ('32), planning engineer, was named director of physical plant planning, and Warren H. Strother, director of public relations, was named director of the newly organized Division of Information Services.

Major General Francis T. Pachler, former chief of staff for the U. S. Army in Europe, was named commandant of cadets at the close of the 1966-67 session to replace Brigadier General M. W. Schewe, who had retired. Stephen M. Neuse, of San Antonio, Texas, was appointed YMCA secretary to replace B. E. Trent, who had resigned to return to Clemson University.

Other faculty and administrative appointments brought new people to the campus or changed the duties of many faculty already on the campus. An inclusive listing is not necessary here, but a brief listing will help indicate the continuing changes and directions of growth which were taking place.

In the college of agriculture, Dr. Ruben W. Engel, head of the department of biochemistry and nutrition, was named associate dean. He was succeeded as head of the department by Dr. Kendall W. King ('49), professor of biochemistry and nutrition. Dr. James E. Martin, of Oklahoma State University, was named head of the department of agricultural economics to succeed Dr. Harry M. Love ('24), who had retired. Dr. Howard A. Rollins, Jr., professor of Horticulture was appointed head of the department of horticulture to succeed Dr. Wesley Judkins, who had returned to teaching and research. Dr. T. J. Horne, director of resident instruction, was named associate dean of instruction.

In the college of arts and sciences, Dr. Robert A. Patterson of the University of Maryland was appointed as head of the department of biology. Dr. Stuart E. Neff had been acting head of this department following the resignation of Dr. F. S. Orcutt, who had returned to teaching and research. Dr. Robert G. Landen, of Dartmouth, was named head of the history department, succeeding Dr. William E. Mackie, who had been serving as acting head following the resignation of Dr. Archer Jones. Earlier in the year Dr. Richard V. Dietrich, professor of geology, had been named associate dean of the college. Professor Dean Carter, of the department of architecture, was named acting head of the newly created art program; and Dr. R. George Gorsline ('48), of Ohio University, joined the faculty to direct the computer science program.

In the college of engineering Dr. J. Beverly Jones ('44), head of the mechanical engineering department, was named associate dean; and Professor H. L. Manning, head of industrial engineering, was named assistant dean. Dr. Paul E. Torgerson, of Oklahoma State University, was named head of the department of industrial engineering to succeed Manning.

In the college of architecture Professor Olivio Ferrari was named chairman of first division studies; Dr. Harland Westerman was named director of the center for urban and regional studies; Dr. Richard Yearwood was named chairman of urban and regional planning; and Professor Joseph Intermaggio was named chairman of the Washington Program of Urban Studies.

The college of home economics added one staff member when Dr. Leonard P. Pecilunas, associate professor of home economics at Northern Illinois University, joined the college as head of the department of management, housing, and family development.

More than one hundred new faculty members with earned doctorates joined the staff in the fall of 1966. They came from fifty-two institutions throughout the nation, including such institutions as Cornell, Iowa State, Michigan State, Wisonsin, Illinois, Oklahoma State, and Duke University. Also of significance for the expansion of the University was the fact that most of these new faculty came with an already established success in teaching, research, and publishing. This latter fact was interpreted by a number of the faculty as the beginning of an intensification of the "publish or perish" philosophy.

The sessions of 1965-66 and 1966-67 also witnessed, in addition to the changes already mentioned, the retirement of a number of long-time familiar personnel from classroom and office. No estimate of the magnificent contribution to Tech made by this and other groups retiring during the decade will be attempted. Individual alumni, however, are free to make such estimates by the simple process of recalling their own personal experiences with members of this group.

Dr. T. W. (Inky) Hatcher ('22) retired from the department of mathematics. As faculty marshall for a number of years before his retirement, Hatcher had led all formal academic processions for graduation and other ceremonies into and out of the War Memorial Hall, Burruss Hall, and even in Miles Stadium. He had been succeeded as marshall in 1961 by Dr. Daniel Frederick ('44).

Other members retiring included W. P. Williams, associate professor of architecture; Miss Lucy P. Blake, assistant director of extension in charge of the home demonstration work; J. R. (Rabbit) Abbitt ('21), director of buildings and grounds; Miss Clarice Slusher ('27), associate registrar, who had also served as registrar during the period 1937-63. Miss Mary B. Settle, professor and head of the department of management, housing, and family development, also retired during the year, as did Miss Gladys Johnson, assistant head of the library reference department.

The entire community was saddened by the death in 1965 of Dr. B. O. Miller, head of the economics department, who had joined the staff in 1928. Another loss was suffered when Dr. A. B. Groves, professor of plant pathology at the Winchester Research Laboratory, died in 1966.

Dr. Henry L. (Lank) Dunton ('29), long-time member of the department of agronomy and head of that department, surprised everyone by his early retirement to his farm in Accomac County. Mrs. Alice M. Pletta, who had been a constant source of help to freshmen struggling with mathematics, retired as assistant professor in that department. Others retiring included J. F. Ryman ('21), associate professor of physics; Paul H. Zirkle, assistant professor of mathematics; Miss Ocie J. O'Brien, associate professor of home management; Miss Blanche Davis, instructor in home management; William J. (Aggie) Nuckolls, Jr. ('26), associate professor of agricultural economics; and Dr. Thomas C. Evans, professor of forestry and wildlife.

Also included among those retiring were Michael S. (Mike) Kipps ('23), associate professor of agronomy, who probably had led more students through the mysteries of field crops than any other professor at VPI; and M. Buford Blair, associate professor of health and physical education and former basketball coach. In addition to his unusual success in setting up intramural sports programs, Blair had also achieved pronounced success as a long-time instructor in Red Cross first aid courses.

Brigadier General M. W. Schewe, commandant of cadets, completed his tour of duty and retired at the end of the year. Elmer H. Creasey, who having served as secretary to the commandant for nearly twenty-nine years probably remembered and was remembered by more cadets than any other man on the campus, retired at the same time. During the same year S. B. (Chuck) Fenne ('27), professor of plant pathology; William A. (Bill) Turner ('33), associate state 4-H leader; and Dr. Landon E. Fuller, professor of English, moved to the sidelines. Fuller had also served for a time as acting director of admissions and had been one of the key personnel in the Basic Division before its discontinuance in the fifties. Earlier in the year Dr. Harry M. Love ('24), who had rejoined the faculty in 1938, retired as head of the department of agricultural economics. Love, whose work with farm credit groups received national attention, had followed H. N. Young as head of the department and had led it to a tremendous expansion both in quality and variety of programs.

The many contributions made by these individuals, acknowledged and reviewed in a variety of traditional and often original ways upon the occasions of their retirement, helped add to the excitement and ferment so evident on the campus by the mid-sixties. Some of this excitement and ferment spread to student life programs and to the deliberations of the student body.

The office of the dean of students under the guiding hand of Dr. James W. Dean expanded its staff and functional organization. Miss Audrey L. Rentz became the first full-time dean of women in Tech's history when she began her duties in July, 1965. She was quickly succeeded by Miss Martha Harder, who, according to *The Techgram,* in addition to her duties as dean was to "coordinate through the offices of the dean of students and of men the women's adjustment to a life which also serves male students and programs combined in an educational environment." Since few persons on the campus understood just what this description meant, the attractive and efficient Miss Harder, upon her arrival for duty in July, 1966, was given a relatively free hand in developing her program. In 1968 she had done her job so effectively that she was appointed dean of men's and women's programs. In addition to Miss Harder, four other individuals also joined the staff of the office of dean of students at the same time and were assigned special responsibilities for the rapidly developing functions in that office.

Patterns of student life, long traditional at Tech, continued undergoing rapid changes. Since many of the established behavior guidelines, often vaguely identified by alumni as "that good old Tech spirit," did not fit, and could not be made to fit the newly developing conditions, the student body and the faculty alike created new guidelines for behavior. In the process it appears that these groups, unconsciously perhaps, laid the foundations for the development of many new Tech traditions which doubtless will become more sharply etched with the passage of time. Certainly the historian of the future will find fertile ground when he explores the combined activities the student leaders and faculty engaged in during the decade or more preceding the end of VPI's first century of existence, as these groups sought to build an effective student governance and launch appropriate student life programs.

Working largely through the expanded office of the dean of students, student-faculty committees examined practically every facet of student life and came up with new proposals. The Corps of Cadets and the civilian student body at long last voted to unify under one constitution with one student government. In the resulting election of officers M. Garland Rigney, a student in political science, was elected as the first president of the united group. Rigney and the other elected officers were installed in office at a student body convocation in May, 1966, at which Paul Harvey, radio news commentator, was the major speaker.

A number of students hailed the united student government as a "step in the right direction toward a stronger student voice." Whether in the right direction or not, demands for an increased voice in the affairs of the University characterized many of the activities of the new student government for the next half decade. Representation of students on hitherto all-faculty committees developed rapidly. New channels of communication between administration, faculty, and students were created, organized, and reorganized. The results apparently satisfactory to student leaders one year were often completely unacceptable to student leaders in succeeding years as the so-called "permissive society" continued to emerge. Student proposals which often dumfounded the "older generation" faculty members poured forth one after another. Fortunately, the restructured office of the dean of students, working through a large number of faculty-student-administrative committees, was able to resolve most of the demands with minimum disruption of campus activities. Opinions differed sharply at times, however, as to the wisdom—or lack of wisdom—involved in the resolution of many of the demands.

Still in the spirit of promoting student leadership in directing their own affairs, the dean of students' office encouraged the formation and operation of a Civilian Interdormitory Council, immediately streamlined in name by the students to CIC. This council's membership was to consist of the presidents of the dormitory councils, one of which had been established for each dormitory on campus. These individual dormitory councils were encouraged to set up athletic, activities, cultural and other committees to provide activities as needed and wanted by the students. A dormitory discipline committee was to have authority to work in the area of dormitory discipline.

Organizational plans for a greatly expanded student activities program to be conducted in the enlarged Squires Hall also got under way during the period. Students were heavily involved in planning for this new student center even before renovation of Squires Hall commenced in 1966. While renovation was yet under way, plans were formulated for a Student Center Board and a Student Budget Board.

The Student Center Board, developed as a result of student recommendations, was to be responsible for the direct administration of the renovated Squires Hall and for the allocation of space for student activities in the building. The Student Budget Board was to have responsibility for allocating funds for all student activities in the center which received University financial support. In both instances the governing boards had faculty representation but included a majority of student members. In subsequent years an enlarged student activity fee helped provide financial support for a greatly enlarged student activities program having little if any resemblance whatever to the earlier student activities programs usually thought up by students on a do-it-yourself basis. The consequences for campus life of the replacement of so many of the do-it-yourself type of activities with a more sophisticated, more commercialized—and more expensive—type of entertainment is yet to be determined.

By the end of the session of 1966-67 the office of the dean of students seemed to be well on the way toward the establishment of an organization and a program designed to meet the challenge of a rapidly developing land-grant university.

Alumni affairs also seemed to be developing in tune with the changing tempo and conditions of the times.

During 1965 the University paid tribute to two of its great alumni. In May, Earle D. Gregory ('23), the first native Virginian ever to receive the Congressional Medal of Honor, visited the campus as guest of honor at a review of the Corps. During his stay on the campus he announced that he had bequeathed to Tech all memorabilia, including his Congressional Medal of Honor, connected with his service career.

In November of the same year, the University paused to pay honor to another distinguished alumnus, Christopher C. Kraft, Jr. ('45), flight director of the National Aeronautics and Space Administration Gemini Project.

At a special convocation in Burruss Hall, Dr. Hahn presented Kraft with VPI's Distinguished Alumnus Citation, the highest honor Tech bestows on an alumnus. At the same convocation a representative of *Time Magazine* presented Kraft with the original portrait of himself which graced the cover of the magazine for August 27, 1965. The "Virginia Tech family" presented Kraft with a Steuben glass eagle; the Civilian Student Body gave him an engraved pewter mug; and the Corps of Cadets presented him with a replica of their famed cannon, "the Skipper," at a review held in his honor.

Interviews were given by Kraft to representatives of press, radio, and television as well as to many students. Many of his former classmates of '45 gave him an informal dinner, and the Board of Visitors had him as its luncheon guest prior to attending the Tech-Villanova football game. Throughout his three-day visit to the campus, Kraft won many friends with the patience, easy manner, and smiling grace with which he autographed programs, menus, and even scraps of paper.

In the years following Kraft's visit, the campus followed reports of his subsequent honors with the fondness of parents for a son gone forth from the family hearthstone.

As Tech continued to grow, leaders in the Alumni Association began seeking ways whereby the alumni program could be more closely coordinated with the activities of the University. Solutions to the problem were not easy to find. In a move designed to provide a centralized placement service for Tech alumni wishing to change jobs and also in an effort to promote cooperative work with Tech's continuing education program in job placement activities, Marcus L. (Mark) Oliver, director of alumni affairs, was named associate director of placement at Tech effective September, 1965. Phil A. Oliver, of the alumni office staff, served as acting director of the alumni affairs, while the alumni officers and the administration continued to seek for a more effective organization. Under the plan eventually chosen, Dr. J. W. Dean, Tech's dean of students, was assigned the responsibility for coordinating the work of the alumni director with the programs of the University. At the same time, he was to serve as principal liaison between the University administration and the Alumni Association.

In July, 1966, C. Bruce Ross ('57), a sales official with the U. S. Gypsum Company, was appointed as director of alumni affairs under the new plan. Ross served but a short time, resigning in June of 1967. H. L. (Lem) Pritchard ('24), a retired business executive, was persuaded to serve as associate director until a permanent director could be employed. Shortly after the announcement of Pritchard's appointment, it was announced that Mark Oliver was leaving his post as associate director of placement to accept a position as director of development at the University of the South. The quick turnover of key personnel in the alumni organization on the campus, coupled with the difficulties many alumni were having in identifying with the fast-changing University, caused some apprehension in alumni ranks. Fortunately the conduct of all individuals closely associated with alumni affairs soon calmed fears that the administration was attempting to assume undue control of the Alumni Association. Dr. George E. (Buddy) Russell ('52), extension research development leader, was appointed as director of the Alumni Association affairs to take office in the fall of 1968. Shortly after Russell's assumption of the office, Pritchard, who had done an excellent job in keeping contact with alumni, enjoyed his second retirement. The appointment of Russell was well-received by administration, faculty, and the executive committee of the Alumni Association. Little expression favorable or unfavorable, emanated from the rank and file of alumni membership, but apparently his appointment was well-received by this group also. It now appeared that the Alumni Association was organized to continue working cooperatively as an essential part of a changing, growing university.

Following its withdrawal from membership in the Southern Conference in the spring of 1965, no major changes in organization or orientation occurred in the athletic program as Tech passed the mid-sixties. A consensus of desire to field athletic teams in harmony with the University's reputation already existed.

Lane Stadium was dedicated on October 23, 1965, during the half-time activities of the homecoming football game with the University of Virginia. The activities of the weekend also witnessed the launching of the first Governor's Day program. Appropriately enough, Governor Albertis S. Harrison, Jr., made a brief dedicatory speech and accepted the stadium on behalf of the state. Even more appropriately—in the thinking of some, at least, of the thirty thousand spectators watching the game—VPI won 22-14. Of additional interest to many alumni was the return to campus, as special guests for the occasion, of most of the twenty-five man squad of 1926 which had helped dedicate Miles Stadium also by a victory over the Virginia Cavaliers.

C. P. (Sally) Miles ('01), for whom Miles Field, Miles Stadium, Miles Hall, and the Miles Professorship in Arts and Sciences had been named, and whose name was synonymous with the best in Tech athletics, died in May, 1966. His place as faculty chairman of athletics was filled by Dean Wilson B. Bell, of the college of agriculture.

The athletic program for the session of 1966-67 was particularly exciting and successful. Coach Claiborne's football team won a post-season Liberty Bowl berth against Miami of Florida. The 14-7 loss was partly offset by the favorable publicity and TV coverage given Tech and the underdog Gobblers. The season's record of 8-2-1 also led to the American Football Coaches Association's naming Jerry Claiborne as District Three Coach-of-the-Year.

Coach Howie Shannon's cagers were not to be outdone by the football squad. After winning the opening game 85-71 over Duke University, the team returned to the Coliseum where before an overflow crowd of 11,500 wildly cheering fans it defeated Purdue University 79-63. Following these two victories the team went on to a 20-7 season record, satisfactory enough to earn an at-large entry into the NCAA championships. After defeating Toledo and Indiana, the cagers moved into the Mideast Regional Tournament, where they lost in overtime to Dayton.

The wrestling team had a 9-1 winning season and sent several representatives to the NCAA's championship meet.

The baseball team after being practically washed out of all activity during late April and early May, posted a 14-10 record.

The track team posted its second straight winning campaign in which a number of old records were broken and new ones set.

Tennis suffered a 5-7 season, but prospects for the next few years seemed bright indeed. They were—the tennis squad next season turned in a 13-5 winning season.

The golf team with an 8-1-1 record capped the year by receiving an invitation to the NCAA championships at Shawnee-on-the-Delaware where it finished sixth nationally.

The end of the session of 1966-67 coincided with the end of Dr. Hahn's first half decade in office. By this time, all major components of the University had been organized, reorganized, or brought into philosophic harmony with the concept of an emerging land-grant university dedicated to the development of a quality program of instruction, research, and extension designed to help meet the rapidly changing needs of a rapidly changing state and nation. The expansion of the physical plant, the recruitment of new faculty, and the re-organization of the programs of instruction, research, and extension all had been accomplished so quickly that some growing pains were inevitable. Dr. Hahn's enthusiasm and articulate presentation of the developing programs as needed and valuable contributions that the institution could make to the rapidly changing needs and conditions of the state, however, left little basis for real complaint.

Considering the extent to which many of the new developments broke with Virginia's traditionally restricted concept of the function of its land-grant institutions, it is surprising that even more opposition did not develop than was actually manifested. Individuals long familiar with Virginia's traditionally hostile attitude toward allowing VPI to include instruction in anything other than agriculture, engineering, and science watched in amazement when the announcements of instructional programs in hitherto forbidden areas did not evoke the expected protests and claims of excessive duplication. Admittedly, some of the sister institutions in the state did not regard the emergence of VPI as a state university with excessive enthusiasm. But Hahn's articulate presentation of the need for and the contribution of each proposed change to the social, political, and industrial developments in the state were difficult to refute.

Dr. Hahn was in the forefront of the state's leaders who saw the implications that the changing conditions in the state had for higher education. He was quick to point out that a multipurpose land-grant university with a high quality program developed within the land-grant concept of service to all the people would meet many of the educational needs of the state and at the same time make significant contributions to the changing economy. Of even greater importance to VPI, he was able to catch the imagination of the people and convey to many state leaders a part of his enthusiasm and vision for "an emerging university of national distinction."

The second half decade of Dr. Hahn's administration sustained continued growth and expansion of services in direct response to the Commonwealth's intensifying needs as Virginia became more urbanized and industrialized. Each year generated a significance of its own which provided a measure of the institution's development. VPI sustained the momentum that transformed it into a major university. Its academic growth, as it broadened and deepened its educational, research, extension, and public service activities, was impressive.

The physical development of the University similarly was sustained at a high level. Endless construction constantly changed the profile of the campus and no doubt contributed heavily to the feeling of vitality and energy apparent to visitors on campus and to the general public.

Toward the end of the period, the expanded Extension Division program included work in business, engineering, architecture, arts and sciences, and education. It is quite likely that the historian of the future will list the expansion and redirection of extension programs at Tech as one of the highly significant developments in the University during the late sixties and early seventies. Trends in the direction of making the University's facilities and personnel available to more and more of the off-campus public had begun well before the 1966 organization of the campus-wide Extension Division, but the major thrust had been in the areas of agriculture and home economics. While in no way diminishing the efforts in these two areas, the new thrust of extension work has been toward organizing and using the resources from all colleges in the University in the economic and social development of the state.

The operation of the Donaldson Brown Center for Continuing Education under the direction of the Extension Division brought people to the campus from business, industry, agriculture, and professional organizations for courses and conferences specifically adapted to their needs. The center also provided a comfortable meeting place for the off-campus extension faculty when it returned to the campus for conferences and in-service training programs. The availability of the facility plus the quality of the programs provided for extension workers had a beneficial effect not only on the extension program but also on the morale of the off-campus faculty as well.

The on-campus redirection of extension work was not unrelated to off-campus developments. The branch colleges were incorporated in the community college system when Virginia began the development of a statewide system of two-year colleges for both academic and technical training. Without Hahn's support, in fact, it is unlikely that the 1966 Community College bill would have won legislative approval.

Graduate programs were developed at centers in a number of sections of the state.

In the academic year 1968-69 alone the combined off-campus credit enrollment increased by more than two hundred fifty per cent over that of the preceding year. The noncredit enrollment also saw large increases. As Virginia continued the trend toward greater industrialization and urbanization, the University's extension services were adapting to new demands for service in urban and suburban areas. In keeping with the changing nature of the program, the titles of county agent, farm agent, and assistant county agent, names long familiar to thousands of people in the state, were changed to extension agent.

The new direction of the Extension Division emerged so rapidly and so recently that many Virginians even yet are unaware of it. The thrust of the extension effort was not diminished for rural Virginia, but it began to have an impact on urban areas as well. Even the 4-H enrollment, which in the last four years of the period more than doubled, shifted from eighty-five per cent to forty per cent rural. The same trend held for adult women enrollment and to a lesser extent for men. Certainly, it would appear that by the end of 1970 the plea uttered more than half a century earlier by the father of extension work in Virginia, Joseph D. Eggleston, for extension to contribute to the improvement of the total life of the people was in the process of fulfillment.

Recruitment of outstanding faculty to fill positions newly created or vacant because of resignation or retirement remained a major task. A large majority of the newly arriving faculty came with impressive teaching and educational backgrounds. They came from major universities throughout the nation and several foreign countries. Sometimes the titles given to the innovative proposals and programs generated by this group aimed at better meeting Virginia's higher educational needs were impressive. Indeed some of the proposals accompanying the titles were not only impressive but startling as well to those yet thinking of VPI in terms of yesterday only. In spite of the university image, those were not wanting who shook their heads sadly and talked as if VPI should go back to the "good old days."

The development of more diverse graduate programs proceeded at a steady rate during the half decade. By 1971 the University had sixty-one programs at the master's level and thirty-one leading to the Ph.D. Additional programs at both levels were in the planning stage. In a reversal of the efforts of the Burruss administration to combine all masters' level degrees under the one heading of Master of Science, the Graduate School by 1971 was offering nine masters' programs: Master of Accountancy, Master of Arts, Master of Business Administration, Master of Architecture, Master of Education, Master of Engineering, Master of Forestry, Master of Science, and Master of Urban and Regional Planning. The Ph.D. degree remained the only one offered beyond the master's level.

Graduate enrollment, although showing a steady growth, had not increased as rapidly as expected, primarily, it was believed, because of required military service. Every indication, however, supported the belief that graduate enrollment would increase appreciably in the immediate future. Plans, therefore, continued to be developed for the strengthening of programs in this important school.

Continuous efforts were made during the period to develop effective co-ordination between the University's Research Division and the graduate school and to establish more effective administrative policies. The role to be expected in graduate work of foreign languages, pure research, applied research, or no research continued to be discussed, as did the importance of the undergraduate quality credit average. Whatever the differences of opinion expressed on these items, the academic quality of students admitted to graduate school showed steady improvement.

The Research Division, following its creation in 1966, pushed back the frontiers of knowledge along many fronts and recorded additional facts on many recognized problems. Annual research funding exceeded nine million dollars by the end of the 1960's. State, federal and private funds were secured for the support of many projects in this important agency; but as the period ended, these funds became increasingly difficult to secure. The work of the division, reported in considerable detail in its official reports, and on a much smaller though more popular scale in *The Techgram*, deserves to be brought together in a popular form and placed before the people of Virginia.

Such a publication would be voluminous; it would depict wide ranging, dedicated, painstaking research and exciting scientific adventure carried out on an ever widening front. Among the many activities of just one year, for example, it would include such diverse projects as the investigation of the potential effects of an oil pipeline across Alaska, the economics of crime, the freshwater algae in the Antarctic, the elementary particles of protons, the wind measurements near the earth's surface, and even the feasibility of producing catfish in Pittsylvania County.

As the Research Division matured, the emerging relationships within the University and within the division frequently made it possible to pool the resources of several colleges to develop a major laboratory or to assemble inter-disciplinary teams to work on significant problems. The division also cooperated with research workers at other universities on the investigation of complex and significant problems.

The research effort increasingly involved the talents of groups and teams. Traditional departmental and collegiate lines became less important as research projects became more complicated and sophisticated. Pooled resources often made it possible to purchase equipment and machines costing enough to have operated the early Virginia Agricultural and Mechanical College for decades. Success generated elements of further success as more foundations and private industry began to look with favor upon VPI as a place for investing their funds. But, as at many other institutions, lack of funds often prevented the undertaking of research in many pressing areas. Similarly, the question of proper balance between research and teaching even yet has not been answered to the satisfaction of everyone concerned.

The history of agricultural research by the Virginia Agricultural Experiment Station from the time of its formation until its reorganization into the Research Division in 1966 was prepared by Dr. H. N. Young following his retirement as director of the station in 1965. This history is an inspiring one, recording the important results achieved by scores of dedicated workers, often pioneers in their fields. The wide ranging program of the present day Research Division is a worthy successor to the endeavors of these early pioneers in research at Tech.

As VPI broadened and deepened the scope of its educational, research, and public service activities, its academic growth continued at a rapid rate. The procedures for developing new courses, degree programs, or departmental changes assured administrators, faculty, and students ample opportunity to know about the proposed change and to express their opinions on it if so desired. After having passed through the regular campus channels, proposals for new courses or changes went to the Board of Visitors for approval or rejection. If the board approved a proposal involving the introduction of new degree programs, the proposal then passed on to the State Council of Higher Education for final approval or rejection. While this procedure required an input and coordination of a tremendous amount of effort, time, and thought, it also meant that when a proposal reached the State Council of Higher Education it was well documented, and designed with some care in its relationship to the basic mission of the University. The records indicate that the Board of Visitors, working through committees, through individuals, and as a board, reviewed all proposals carefully before final action. Although the number of proposals for academic changes and development continued to accelerate the board was by no means a rubber stamp for the president, nor did the president expect such a relationship. The records for the period, however, indicate an unusually constructive working relationship between the Board of Visitors and the president and his faculty as the University continued to expand its services.

Further indication of VPI's developing academic structure perhaps may best be indicated by simply recording the new degree programs approved by the Board of Visitors after 1963.

1964......Ph.D. in Materials Engineering
1965......Department of Psychology and Sociology; B.S. in Health and Physical Education; Department of History and Political Science split into two departments; Department of English and Foreign Languages split into two departments
1966......M.A in History; M.A. in English; B.A. in Philosophy
1967......Ph.D. in Industrial Engineering; B.S. in Psychology; M.A. in Political Science; elimination of undergraduate major in Business Administration and addition of majors in Finance, Management, Marketing, and General Business in the Bachelor of Business degree; B.A. in Art; Department of Psychology and Sociology split into two separate departments, effective July 1, 1968
1968......B.S. in Nuclear Science; M.B.A. degree; B.S. in Mathematics Education; Master of Forestry; Ph.D. in Geophysics; Baccalaureate program in International Studies; B.A. in Elementary Education; B.S. in Biochemistry; M.S. in Business with Economics major changed to M.A. in Economics; Ph.D. in Economics; M.S. in Business with accounting major became Master of Accountancy (not new degree)
1969......Master of Engineering degree; B.A. in Economics; Ph.D. in Nuclear Science and Engineering; B.S., M.S., and Ph.D. in Food Science and Technology; B.S. in Biochemistry in College of Arts and Sciences
1970......B.S. in Computer Science; B.A. in Theater Arts; Bachelor of Land-

scape Architecture; Ph.D. in Human Nutrition and Foods; M.S. in Psychology; M.S. in Health and Physical Education and Master of Health and Physical Education; B.A. in Urban Affairs; Department of Computer Science approved; Department of Performing Arts and Communication approved; B.S. in Science Education—existing program leading to B.S. in General Science discontinued; B.A. in Chemistry

In January, 1970, the board also approved the establishment of the University's seventh college, the college of education, to be effective July 1, 1971. Dr. Karl T. Hereford, director of program planning and related activities for the U. S. Office of Education Bureau of Elementary and Secondary Education, was named dean of the new college. He reported for duty in July, 1970, to start planning for the new division which would consolidate all of the University's teacher preparation programs into the one college. Undoubtedly, the spirit of Professor E. C. Magill, whose proposal in 1928 for a school of education at VPI had so alarmed the "O'Shea Commission" as to cause that group to go out of its way in its report to warn against such a move, looked upon the creation of this new college with approval.

A number of special programs and academic innovations, such as "pass" or "fail" grades, for a limited number of courses, a system of quality credits based on the four-point rather than the three-point system, and honors studies were in operation by 1971. Also by that time overseas educational opportunities for college credit by travel and study in a number of foreign countries had become a regular part of many university programs. Most of these and other innovations resulted from cooperative planning among students, faculty, and administration. By 1970 the problem for many students was not which curriculum to choose but which courses to take within the curriculum. It was a far cry indeed from the VPI in which the student, having selected a curriculum, had everything else, even to his daily schedule, determined for him.

Continued growth in services to the state and the accompanying academic expansion, associated with normal turnover in faculty, called for administrative reorganization and shifting of duties. By the late sixties, change and growth had become so much a part of campus life that faculty and administrative changes often passed almost unnoticed except by those immediately affected. Faculty and students alike began to have trouble simply keeping up with changing titles. Even more difficulty was encountered at times in developing a knowledgeable understanding of the new duties assumed by colleagues. The resulting uncertainties, however, seemed to add to the excitement on the campus rather than operating as an irritant.

In 1968, the Board of Visitors created the office of vice-president for student affairs and appointed Dr. James W. Dean to the position. The position of executive vice-president was created and filled by transferring Dr. Warren W. Brandt from his post as vice-president for academic affairs to the new post. During the same year, the position of vice-president for finance was created and filled by the appointment of Dr. William E. Lavery to the post. Dr. Leslie F. Malpass succeeded Dr. Brandt as vice-president for academic affairs and was in turn succeeded as dean of the college of arts and sciences by Dr. George M. Harper, who came to Tech from the chairmanship of the department of English at the University of Florida. Dean Harper proved to be quite popular but resigned the next year to accept the chairmanship of the department of English at Florida State University. He was succeeded by Dr. William C. Havard, the V. O. Key Professor of Government at the University of Massachusetts.

Dr. Brandt resigned in the spring of 1969 to accept the presidency of the Virginia Commonwealth University. His post as executive vice-president was then filled by Dr. William J. McKeefery, dean of academic affairs at Southern Illinois University, who came to Tech with an impressive background of teaching and administrative experience in higher education.

For a short period of time in 1968 no faculty or administrative changes were announced to the public. Expressions of mock alarm that Tech was stagnating were immediately forthcoming from certain faculty sources. But the "alarm" proved to be premature; additional announcements were not long in coming. The change that perhaps attracted most attention from alumni came in June, 1968, when it was announced that Dr. Wilson B. Bell ('34) was giving up the deanship of the college of agriculture to become director of university development. After pausing long enough to recover from its disappointment over losing its popular dean, the faculty of the college of agriculture joined the rest of the University, the Board of Visitors, and the Development Council in applauding this appointment. The office of development had been vacant since R. Craig Fabian had resigned the year before to return to the Westinghouse Electric Corporation. During the interim between Fabian's departure and Bell's appointment, a study had been conducted on how best to organize and coordinate the work of the development program and the work of the Alumni Association to meet the rapidly changing conditions of the University and of the state. As one result, the function of the office of development was clarified and extended and the title of the director changed to that of director of university development. Both the University and the directors of the Alumni Association sought to strengthen and integrate their cooperative efforts. It was shortly after this intensive study of both organizations that "Buddy" Russell had been appointed as director of alumni affairs.

Dr. Bell was succeeded as dean of the college of agriculture by Dr. James E. Martin, head of the department of agricultural economics.

In February, 1970, the university community was saddened by the tragic death of Dr. Willis G. Worcester, dean of the college of engineering, in an airplane crash. Dr. Paul E. Torgersen, head of the department of industrial engineering, was appointed as dean to succeed Worcester.

Other major appointments included Dr. G. A. Rudolph as director of libraries; Dr. Randal M. Robertson as dean of the research division to succeed Dr. W. B. Harrison, who resigned to enter industry; Dr. Alfred H. Krebs, head of the agricultural education program as director of summer school, a position long vacant; Dr. Donald Darnton as director of special academic programs, a new position; and Dr. James R. Montgomery as director of institutional research.

Thomas C. Lile was appointed director of the Squires Student Center, as the renovated Squires Hall was called. This structure, known to thousands of alumni as the Student Activities Building, or the SAB, was closed late in 1966 for extensive renovation and enlargement into a building three times the size of the original structure. Undoubtedly the spirit of John Squires, who had been received by VPI in one of his darkest hours, and of Julian A. Burruss, whose unselfish efforts to improve campus life were little appreciated, must have rejoiced with others when this magnificently reconstructed building was dedicated in May, 1970.

Numerous other additions and changes, including the appointments of a number of associate and assistant deans and department heads in the several colleges, were also made during the period. The associate and assistant deans generally were assigned responsibilities for specialized areas or programs within their respective colleges.

Newcomers arrived on the campus with some regularity in the wake of the retirement of older faculty so well remembered by generations of alumni. Included among those retiring were "Dr. Sam" Obenshain ('27), agronomy; Professor Paul M. Reaves, dairy science; Professor W. S. (Sam) Gay ('28), accounting; Dr. V. O. Johns, economics; Associate Professor W. G. Watkins, economics; Dr. John F. Eckel, head of the department of metals and ceramics; Professor James B. (J. B.) Jones ('21), mechanical engineering; Associate Professor Amelia Fuller, home economics; Professor Paul S. (Buddy) Dear ('27), ceramic engineering; Dr. Herbert E. Spencer, mathematics; Dr. Flood S. Andrews ('23), horticulture; Dr. R. P. G. Bowman, psychology; Dr. Svend Gormsen, mathematics; Dr. C. E. Holmes, poultry science; Professor R. L. Humbert, business administration; Professor G. D. Kite ('31), agricultural engineering; Professor Dayton M. Kohler, English; Professor J. P. Mahaney ('24), mechanical engineering; Professor Frank Marshall, economics; Professor W. L. McPherson, chemistry; Dr. Fred Orcutt, biology; Dr. J. O. Rowell, entomology; Dr. G. M. Shear, plant pathology; Associate Professor O. W. Addington, mathematics; Professor D. U. Livermore, agricultural economics; Miss Eva Minix ('30), district agent, home economics; Professor L. B. (Pop) Wilkins ('32), extension; Professor Earl Swink ('30), agricultural engineering and extension; Associate Professor J. M. Amos, entomology; Assistant Professor J. L. Tulock ('29), engineering fundamentals; Professor P. H. (Pat) DeHart ('29), associate dean, Extension Division; Joseph E. Hardy, director of student housing; and Warren Slusser, long time accountant in the Agricultural Extension Service.

During the same period, Dr. R. V. Dietrich, professor of geological sciences and associate dean of the college of arts and sciences, who had been at Tech since 1951, resigned to accept the position of dean of the college of arts and sciences at Central Michigan University.

Perhaps some of the most dramatic changes in Tech's history occurred in the changing characteristics of its student body and student community during the closing decade of Tech's first century. The short time since these changes appeared and began to affect the campus scene—plus caution generated by what may be termed "the generation gap"—combine to suggest the wisdom of only a very brief discussion of these changes at this particular time.

The broadening academic programs attracted students who a few years earlier would not have considered enrolling at Tech, especially in the arts, humanities, and social sciences. Enrollment, although controlled, increased steadily each year. It included women students, male civilian students, cadets, married students, graduate students, co-op students, and foreign students, enrolled in an increasing variety of fields of study. The majority of the undergraduates lived on the campus; but as more and more homes and apartments became available in Blacksburg, an increasing number of students, men and women, sought the right to live off campus. The improvement of highways in the region increased the number of commuters. Virginia's increasing urban population was reflected by a corresponding increase in the proportion of students on the campus from urban communities.

The students also became more conscious of the world beyond the University. They sought, even demanded, a larger voice in decisions affecting themselves; and, according to some faculty, affecting everybody else as well.

To many faculty members, it appeared that the majority of students, if provided the opportunity, the structure, and some flexibility would work hard to resolve campus problems which they felt needed resolution. There were differences of opinion, however, on the definition of problems and in the identification of those which needed resolving.

The student services under the vice-president of student affairs were reorganized and expanded, often following recommendations of student committees. Student programs were restructured to involve more student and less faculty direction. The Student Union Board, the successor to the Student Center Board, was given primary responsibility for the development of the extracurricular activities in the Student Union program. The Student Budget Board continued its major responsibility for the allocation to the several student organizations of a portion of the funds derived from student activity fees. Student groups were heavily involved in revisions of student life policies, and student representation was obtained on all University committees concerned with student activities or interests.

The administration and most of the faculty felt that student involvement in policy and program changes on the campus were substantial and sustained. They felt the operation of the Student Government Association, the Student Senate, the Commission on Student Affairs, the self-governing dormitory councils, and student representation on the commissions and the University Council insured exhaustive consideration of student views on virtually all aspects of university governance. Some student leaders, on the other hand, before the end of the period were demanding increased student representation and voting rights on all governance groups, including the Board of Visitors.

The increased sensitivity to the world beyond the campus expressed itself in a variety of ways. Innumerable "teach-ins," "sit-ins," and "talk-ins" underscored the depth of student and faculty feeling in this direction. To some faculty members, these new modes of expression were as bewildering and baffling as were the students' beards, long hair, bare feet, and sloppy dress which suddenly became the common classroom badge for many students. Many faculty members, it should be added, often were surprised to find behind the long hair and bare feet the same warm, eager, inquiring type of students to which they had long since become accustomed to finding at Tech.

During the spring of 1970, the student ferment began to take on what to many represented tones of trouble. In mid-April, a small group of students and faculty purposely disrupted a regularly scheduled drill of the Corps of Cadets. Previously the administration had enunciated a policy guaranteeing the right of any member or group in the university community to free expression or demonstration as long as such expression or demonstration did not impose on the freedom or rights of others. Disruption of the Corps' drill was, in the view of the administration, a clear violation of this policy of free expression for all. The University consequently obtained a court injunction, hoping that it would prohibit action which would disrupt normal campus activities. Opinion became sharply divided over the wisdom of the injunction, although the majority of the faculty and the press of the state seemed to support it.

The national turmoil following the death of students at Kent State University in Ohio triggered a variety of student activity on the campus. Diverse opinions later were advanced as to what took place, how it took place, why it took place, and the results of the events, whatever they were, that did take place. Official records, reduced to the bare facts, record telephoned bomb threats, breaking and entering locked buildings, attempted arson, a brief "occupation" on the part of a small group of students in Cowgill Hall, and a larger occupation of Williams Hall, which the students entered in the night.

State Police assistance was requested and promptly supplied. After the occupants of Williams Hall were warned to leave or be subject to arrest, the police forcibly entered, evacuated the building, and arrested more than one hundred students and several nonstudents on charges of trespassing. Students taken from the building were suspended summarily for reasons of public safety, but later were given an opportunity for formal disciplinary hearings on possible violations of University regulations. Ultimately most of them were suspended for two academic quarters.

Following this incident, a number of official and unofficial statements were made and meetings held both by faculty and students in an effort to clarify viewpoints and develop better perspective. Some individuals felt that the statements and meetings merely aroused deeper emotions and created more confusion, but campus tensions receded visibly as the spring days wore on.

As commencement approached, the officers of the senior class placed a large advertisement in the *Richmond Times-Dispatch*, addressed to the state officials and taxpayers, "to thank you for the support that has been given to us and to our University." Public opinion in Virginia strongly supported the administration in its handling of the disruptive incidents. At the same time, the administration recognized the concern of many students about the unresolved problems of the society in which they lived and attempted to help students find ways of expressing these concerns in a constructive manner.

The session of 1970-71 witnessed an increased demand on the part of some student leaders for a larger voice in directing campus affairs and regulating dormitory life. A strike against the University Bookstore was undertaken in an effort to reinforce demands for a student voice in the distribution of profits from the operation. In late May a University Council ruling that doors in the dormitory rooms must be left open at least six inches when the occupants were entertaining visitors of the opposite sex sparked a series of protest demonstrations. At one time several downtown store windows were broken, apparently by nonstudents. Student leaders immediately denounced the vandalism and undertook to raise money to pay for the damage. Following the University Council's refusal to reconsider the "open door" ruling while under pressure of demonstrations, a student march around the campus ended with an occupation of Ambler Johnston Hall, a coed dormitory. Under police orders the occupation ended peaceably. For reasons of security the police and University officials conducted a room to room search of the dormitory but found no intruders. About 3 a.m. the next morning fire destroyed the old Extension Apartment Building located across the street from Newman Library. Arson was suspected but not proved. Student Government Association leaders denounced the administration for its "open door" policy and for its search of Ambler Johnston Hall but also quickly denounced destruction of property. They also deplored the loss of the building.

It is difficult to place this series of demonstrations in true perspective, but a statement issued by Dr. Hahn seems to be appropriate. He said in part:

> Since Monday night [May 24], a small, hard core group of students and outsiders has attempted to generate serious difficulties and create an environment of stress on the campus. These efforts have been more successful because many responsible students disagree with the action taken by University Council on Monday to make clear that the doors to dormitory rooms of students entertaining visitors of the opposite sex during Open House hours on weekends must remain open. The need for the action, however, was clear to the University Council and administration. Disruptive activities by the hard core were anticipated, regardless of the action of the University Council.
>
> It should be emphasized that the overwhelming majority of students have behaved responsibly and that only a minority have been involved even in peaceful demonstrations. . . . The great majority of students at Virginia Tech are to be commended for their responsible behavior; it is clear they do not condone the action of the hard core minority.
>
> . . . It should also be made clear that the University is operating normally and will continue to take such steps as are necessary to deal with those who might seek to disrupt normal University activities. The University will not allow its policy making to be influenced by irresponsible pressure tactics.

Relative quiet returned to the campus the week following the outbursts although it was obvious that the hard core minority had not retired from the scene.

Increasing demands for a larger role in the operation of campus affairs, and increasing student militancy captured the major headlines and public attention. Other changes in student outlook and campus life, however, continued to erode long-time campus traditions and at the same time to begin generating new ones.

Student attitudes toward organized on-campus extracurricular activities began to change rapidly as students with automobiles on campus sought more off-campus entertainment. Those without cars found little difficulty in arranging for transportation with those who had. The student population became extremely mobile and in the process played havoc with traditional Tech weekend activities and Saturday classes.

The Cotillion Club, one of the oldest social organizations on the campus, surrendered its charter and affiliated with a national fraternity. The question of University recognition of social fraternities and sororities seemed to be endlessly debated by students, who in a referendum rejected the idea of on-campus fraternities housed in university-built residences. This referendum did not solve the fraternity problem, for a number of off-campus groups not officially recognized by the University organized fraternities anyway. In a number of instances national social fraternities approved affiliation with these local groups. The residents of Blacksburg, however, did not change but continued the century-old demand that the institution exercise more control over the students living off-campus. As the seventies began, fraternity "houses" had spilled over into the surrounding countryside and into Christiansburg. The questions of "proper" regulation, however, remained unanswered.

The Virginia Tech, established in 1903, changed its name to *The Collegiate Times* and continued the effort to keep the campus paper more than a campus calendar of coming events spiced with letters to the editor denouncing dining hall food, the administration, lack of parking, and the football and basketball coaches. The success of the effort may be debatable; the *Times* gradually took on what appeared to be an obsession with "activist" campus politics and in the process also shocked and disgusted a number of faculty and alumni by its treatment of once-taboo subjects and by its occasional affinity for the obscene speech movement.

Radio station WUVT, operated entirely by students from advertising revenue extended its closed circuit signal to the Radford College dormitories, primarily to extend its advertising base to Radford. The students also established a new FM station, WUVT-FM, operated as a public service. The free radiating FM station could be heard throughout Blacksburg, using primarily a "good music" format.

The Corps of Cadets abolished "bracing," sitting at rigid attention in the mess hall, and a number of other devices which seemed vaguely inappropriate when a heavy majority of Tech students were not in the Corps at all. It also authorized a new civilian style uniform including blue blazer, gray slacks, white shirt, and a regimental striped tie for certain functions.

The performances of the Virginia Tech Varsity Glee Club under the direction of "Stan" Kingma won high acclaim from audiences throughout the state and from music critics in the press. On campus the activities of the University Choir, the University Orchestra, the University Theater, and a number of other extra-curricular student-faculty organizations began building strong traditions of their own. At the same time the Highty-Tighties carried on an old tradition by winning parades and established new ones of entertainment at athletic and kindred events.

Coed participation in campus affairs and activities, having long since passed the stage of resentful acceptance on the part of the men, was both welcomed and solicited. The YMCA opened its programs to the women, and one coed, Miss Sue Anne (Suzie) Shertzer, made Tech history by being elected president of the organization. Coed cheerleaders continued adding the feminine touch as they joined the men in innovative cheerleading stunts at football and basketball games.

Miss Pamela (Pam) Gunsten added ammunition to the argument of many older alumni that women were taking over Tech. She became the first woman in Tech history to wear the uniform of the mascot Gobbler and follow the football games.

Building construction seemed never ending; new buildings were constructed, opened, and dedicated with sometimes surprising frequency. Quite often the pressure for space was so great that sections of new buildings were put into use in piece-meal fashion rather than awaiting completion of the entire structure. Offices, departments, and classrooms were moved from place to place on the campus with a rapidity sometimes bewildering to the faculty, the students, the campus mailman, and all campus delivery services. Differences of opinion flourished as to whether this campus mobility presented morale building or morale destroying challenges. The question is yet debatable.

The switch from what President Burruss called "Modified Tudor" but which J. Ambler Johnston called "Gothic in Form" architecture so prevalent in most of the older campus buildings, to a more modern architecture presenting an entirely different facade also led to extensive differences of opinion. These differ-

ences also remain unresolved. The startling switch from the customary three-
and four-story dormitories to the more commanding high-rise structures, reaching
in instances to nine stories, did not escape notice or comment either.

Among the dormitories completed in the area southwest of the site of old
Miles Stadium were Pritchard Hall, named for Professor Samuel R. Pritchard,
former dean of the college of engineering; Lee Hall, named for Professor
Claudius Lee ('96), former professor of electrical engineering; O'Shaughnessy
Hall, named for Professor Louis (Shag) O'Shaughnessy ('03), former professor
of applied mechanics, and director of the graduate division; Ambler Johnston
Hall, named for J. Ambler (Uncle Ambler) Johnston ('04), active alumnus and
reigning elder statesman of the Alumni Association. A founder of the architectural
firm of Carneal and Johnston, Ambler Johnston was architectural adviser and
loyal supporter of six presidents.

Dietrick Hall, a modern dining facility constructed near Ambler Johnston and
Pritchard Halls was named for L. B. Dietrick, former dean of the college of
agriculture.

Additional office, classroom, and laboratory space was provided in Wallace
Hall, named for Miss Maude Wallace, former assistant director of home demonstration work in Virginia; Derring Hall, named for Paul Derring, former YMCA
secretary and director of religious affairs; and Cowgill Hall, named for Professor
Clinton H. Cowgill, former head of the department of architecture.

The parking lot and the roadway formerly back of Burruss Hall were closed
upon completion of Derring and Cowgill Halls; in their stead a plaza and walkway were constructed for pedestrian travel to and from these two buildings
and other buildings in the planning stage for space north of Derring and Cowgill.
The completion of these planned buildings and the landscaping around them
will utilize a large portion of the area once occupied by the college apple orchards
so zealously guarded in former years by "Ducklegs" Miller and Dean "Harve"
Price.

The long-planned facilities for conferences, short courses, and other adult
education programs ultimately were made a reality in the Donaldson Brown Center for Continuing Education. The center included a major addition and renovation of the old faculty center, which had served as a Faculty Apartment Building.
The new center was named for F. Donaldson Brown ('02), prominent alumnus
and benefactor of the University.

Several major buildings constructed some years earlier also were named for
prominent alumni or faculty. The building commonly referred to as the New
Engineering Building was named Norris Hall for Professor Earl B. Norris, former
dean of engineering; the physics building was named Robeson Hall for Dr. Frank
L. Robeson ('04), former head of the department of physics; and the building
referred to as Commerce Hall was named Pamplin Hall for Robert B. Pamplin
('33), prominent alumnus and benefactor of the University.

An additional building for the College of Engineering, Whittemore Hall,
named for former dean of the school of engineering and architecture John W.
Whittemore, was under construction on a site back of Randolph Hall. At the same
time, across the campus, construction was well under way on Cheatham Hall,
named in honor of Julian N. Cheatham ('33), prominent alumnus and benefactor
of the University. This building, located on a site just west of Dietrick Hall, was
being constructed for the department of forestry and wildlife. A large multi-

purpose field house, located west across Spring Road from Lane Stadium, was also under construction. A new dormitory for women also began taking shape, Slusher Hall, named in honor of Mrs. Clarice Slusher Pritchard ('27), Registrar Emeritus.

Meanwhile, somewhat earlier, McBryde Hall, which President Eggleston had pointed to with pride and joy but which President Burruss had looked upon as more suitable for a cathedral than a classroom, was pronounced beyond repair. It was razed; and as the period ended, a new, much larger McBryde Hall was in the process of completion on the same site.

A number of buildings just off the main campus also had been constructed for several types of research. Undoubtedly, the most important was the Anaerobic Bacteria Laboratory constructed north of the Prices Fork Road just off the main campus. This laboratory, housing the world's largest collection of anaerobic bacteria, with its researchers, technicians, staff, and equipment, by the end of the period was a world center for the study of anaerobic bacteria.

Improvements to Burruss Hall had been completed by additions to both sides and the back and the interior had been extensively rearranged. As the period ended, Hillcrest, known to thousands of alumni as the Skirt Barn, was being enlarged and renovated for an "athletic dormitory"; the president's house in the grove was converted to offices or instructional space; and cows had been forever banished from most of the old pasture across South Gate Drive southwest of this site in favor of an asphalt-covered student parking lot.

Intercollegiate atheletics generated mixed results as the sixties drew to a close. Opinions differed sharply as to whether the University's athletic programs were progressing in proper fashion.

The 70-12 victory in '66 over traditional rival VMI did not spread great joy throughout Hokieland; a number of alumni felt that an old friend had been abused. The 12-10 loss to VMI the next year did not bring great joy to the Tech faithful either, but for a different reason.

The 1967 rematch with the '66 Liberty Bowl opponent, Miami, packed some thirty-five thousand fans into Lane Stadium, only to see Miami win by the identical score 14-7, by which it had won the preceding year's bowl game. This particular game in Lane Stadium also featured a welcome back to Andy Gustafson, athletic director at Miami, who had started his coaching career at Tech in 1926, when he had succeeded Coach Ben Cubbage. The '67 season produced a 7-3 record and another All-American: Frank Loria was named All-American on at least seven post-season teams.

The '68 season repeated the previous year's 7-3 record and won a surprise invitation for a second trip to the Liberty Bowl, this time to meet the University of Mississippi. Disappointment from the 34-17 loss to Ole Miss was partly offset by the announcement of All-American honors for Mike Widger.

The next season opened with a heartbreaking 13-17 loss to Alabama before some forty-five thousand fans packed into Lane Stadium. The season record was 4-5-1, the first losing campaign since 1961.

The '70 season brought a series of frustrations and disappointments. Tech lost its opening game played in Lane Stadium with the University of Virginia. As if this was not embarrassment enough, the Gobblers lost the next four in a row before finding a winning combination. The season ended with a 20-14 defeat of VMI in a Saturday game substituted for the traditional Thanksgiving Day contest. Even this victory failed to dispel the gloom generated by a 5-6 losing season. Tech appeared to be winning the unimportant games but dropping the big ones. It consequently came as no surprise when Coach Jerry Claiborne, although having the best overall win-loss record of any football coach in Tech history, announced his resignation in December. He was succeeded by Charles E. (Charlie) Coffey, defensive coordinator under Coach Frank Broyles at the University of Arkansas.

The basketball teams under Howie Shannon also had their moments of triumph and of deep disappointment. Winning seasons were recorded every year except in 1969-70 when a 10-12 record gave Shannon his first losing season since he had arrived at Tech. The deficit also represented the first losing one for VPI in fifteen years. The next year saw the team post another winning record; but shortly after the season ended, Shannon gave up coaching basketball and assumed full-time teaching in Tech's rapidly developing physical education department. Before the year ended, he was succeeded as coach by Don DeVoe, an assistant coach at Ohio State University.

Baseball and the other intercollegiate sports posted a number of winning seasons; teams and individual athletes established new records, broke old ones, and added several new chapters to the long story of Tech's athletics. And with the approach of the seventies, Frank Moseley rounded out two decades as chief of Tech's athletic operations. As the 1970 Tech *Gridiron Guide* expressed it, "the only thing certain seems to be the guaranteed pressure of constant growth of the University, the Blacksburg community, and the athletic budget."

When Moseley came to Blacksburg in 1951, Tech's athletic fortunes were at a low ebb. During his first decade as football coach-athletic director he compiled a 54-42-4 record, highlighted by the undefeated '54 season for which the Virginia Sportswriters and Sportscasters Association named him coach of the year. In 1967 the same group again honored him, this time with its nonmember award for his contributions to athletics in the state.

During Moseley's tenure the athletic plant grew from one which an increasing number of out-of-state teams were boycotting because of its inadequacy, to one of the finest plants in the country. Plans for the development of an expanded athletic plant were under way before Moseley arrived on the scene, but he came at a critical point in the execution of those plans. He threw his considerable talent and energy into their completion with characteristic gusto.

The athletic plant was a long time emerging. In 1954 a fine baseball diamond had opened. In 1959 the new college golf course had helped generate dramatic improvement of Tech's golf fortunes. In 1962 the Coliseum, although not then completed, had helped launch a new day for basketball at Tech. In 1965 the new tennis courts started tennis on a slow upward trend; the 1968 team won more matches than any previous team in Tech history. The new grasstex track was opened in 1965 and helped the track team to become a perennial powerhouse in the state. Lane Stadium, initially put into use in 1965 but completed in 1969, provided an arena worthy of Tech and any team it might invite to play in Blacksburg.

In building this fine plant, the University had the indirect assistance of thousands of alumni and the direct assistance of a host of others. In this latter category was Stuart K. Cassell ('32), first as business manager and later as vice-president for administration. One of the originators of the long range plane, Cassell devoted much energy, effort, and administrative ability to translate the plans into reality.

By 1970 both Cassell and "Mose" Moseley could take some satisfaction in accomplishment. But debate still continued as to whether the University, from the athletic standpoint, was better off as an independent or as a member of an athletic conference. Whatever the answer to this intriguing question, no one denied that Tech had an outstanding athletic plant with playing fields vastly different from the hillside cornfield behind Lane Hall in which it had launched its football efforts, and a gymnasium vastly different from the Chapel Assembly Hall from which its basketball program began.

A few other developments affecting the University on the eve of its Centennial should be noted. In the Newman Library, students and faculty were still trying to master the complexities introduced by the shift from the Dewey Decimal to the Library of Congress system of book classification and cataloging which had been only partially completed before the new librarian Dr. G. A. Rudolph arrived. He regrouped and relocated many of the collections and card catalogs. Many faculty members welcomed the changes as innovations designed to improve library utilization. At the same time many of the long-time faculty recalling the intricacies of locating material as organized in the old chapel library by librarian Ralph Brown, in the first and second academic buildings by librarian Seymour Robb, and in Newman Library first by Robb and later by librarian Frank Shirk expressed the fervent hope that Rudolph would prove to be a stubborn man, who having made up his mind would never change it. If so, they suggested, maybe the new system would remain fixed long enough for them to master and indeed be comfortable with it.

Thanks to the Visiting Scholar Program, not only nationally but internationally known speakers from a variety of fields visited the campus in a continuing stream. And with a portion of the student activity fees having been placed under the control of students, an increased number of nationally known artists and popular entertainers also came to the campus. Arguments as to whether some of the popular entertainers helped reduce or widen the generation gap were inconclusive.

Alumni and friends began to demonstrate renewed interest in the University. With the approval of the Alumni Board of Directors, the alumni offices were moved from the World War I Memorial Building to offices on the third floor of remodeled Burruss Hall. This location proved helpful and convenient for all persons concerned with improving and coordinating alumni affairs with the total development of the University. At the same time the appointment of five recent graduates, including several women to the Alumni Board of Directors, gave an increasingly youthful viewpoint to that body. Still to be accomplished, however, was the goal of seventy per cent of all alumni on the active rolls of the association.

In 1968, the Bailey Research Trust gave to the University the Bailey-Law Collection, composed of many thousands of bird and small mammal specimens, as well as many mounted birds, for research and teaching purposes. One of the outstanding collections in the United States, it was housed at Rockbridge Alum Springs in Rockbridge County. At the same time this collection was made available, the Rockbridge Alum Springs property was opened to the VPI faculty for research and study purposes. While in no way connected with this collection, it may be noted that nearly a century earlier W. H. Ruffner, so desirous to have President C. L. C. Minor take steps designed to secure gifts and endowments for the Virginia Agricultural and Mechanical College, at one time had explored in some detail the mineral and geologic features of the Rockbridge Alum area.

Another valuable off-campus research facility was acquired when Mrs. Nancy S. Reynolds, daughter of the late R. J. Reynolds, gave the University about seven hundred acres of Virginia farm and forest land surrounding the original Reynolds homestead in Patrick County. At the same time she donated funds with which to organize and operate the farm as the Reynolds Homestead Research Center. Plans also were under way to operate the center on a long range basis with emphasis on research programs in forestry and forest genetics, and on silviculture, fisheries, and wildlife studies. The possibilities of developing research programs related to outdoor recreational areas which apparently would be needed long before the year 2000 were also being investigated.

This gift seemed particularly appropriate in that Hardin H. Reynolds, also from Patrick County, was among the first students to register at VPI and nearly fifty years later returned to the campus and helped celebrate VPI's Golden Jubilee in 1922.

The gift of a valuable collection of sheet music donated to the University by Mr. and Mrs. Archer Lawrie of Abingdon also relates to interesting events of the past.

When Carneal and Johnston started planning the original McBryde Bulding of Mechanic Arts in 1913-14, President Eggleston had informed them that he wanted the building to be the prototype of a new era at VPI. He wanted to depart from what he considered to be "the poverty-stricken factory type" of architecture hitherto employed and wanted the new building to express the character and type of education for which it was created. He, according to Ambler Johnston, one of the architects, even went so far as to suggest by word and sketch a little sculpture to this end.

As the plans for the building proceeded, it was decided to place sculptured figures over the entrances to the buildings. These figures were to represent bench work in metal, bench work in wood, work in foundry, work with machine tools, and work with less important wood and metal working tools.

As Johnston recalled, a friend put him in touch with "a young man in the Art Department of Yale University who would be glad to model the figures at a nominal fee. The young man was no less than the later famous sculptor Lee Lawrie." Lawrie accepted the commission, and using the instructions and the injunction sent to him by Johnston to "avoid practical tombstone culture art," prepared the figures in New Haven. The resulting sculptures, "all Lawries," according to Johnston, then were shipped to VPI and erected over the entrance to the McBryde Building. The sculpture was saved when McBryde was razed and was used in the rebuilt McBryde Hall as it neared completion in 1971.

Archer Lawrie is a son of sculptor Lee Lawrie; and Archer's two children, Esther Ann and Peter Lawrie, students at VPI in the early 1970's, are Lee Lawrie's grandchildren.

Another valuable collection at the University, although not exactly a gift, has more than passing interest. In 1918 when A. B. Massey joined the staff, he started collecting specimens of state flora. Before his retirement in 1959 the energetic Massey had roamed far and wide over the state and had collected

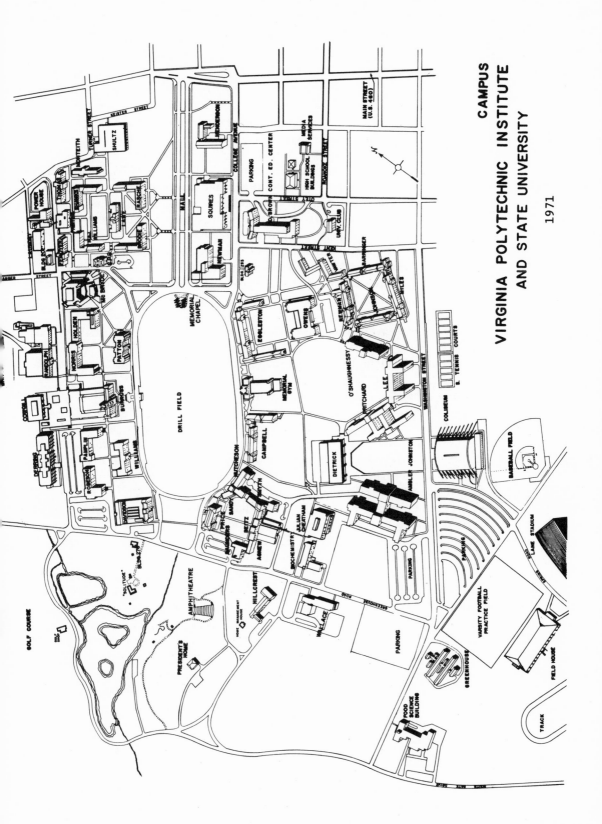

CAMPUS

VIRGINIA POLYTECHNIC INSTITUTE
AND STATE UNIVERSITY

1971

more than forty thousand specimens which he organized into an herbarium. Shortly after Massey retired, the Board of Visitors located the collection in Derring Hall and named it the A. B. Massey Herbarium. At the same time, Massey's portrait, painted at the request of some alumni by Blacksburg's beloved artist Mrs. W. H. Rasche, was accepted by the University and hung in the room housing the herbarium. Massey continued to visit the herbarium, but with decreasing frequency, since, as he explained with a twinkle in his eye, the portrait could now watch over things in his absence.

As the Virginia Polytechnic Institute approached the end of its first century, it was obvious to any observer that the institution had become a university in every sense of the word except in title or name.

From its small beginning in 1872 with a faculty and administration of four persons and forty-three students, the institution had grown to a point where more than eleven hundred and fifty faculty and three thousand staff members supported a student body of more than twelve thousand.

The central campus of five acres had expanded to more than three hundred acres. In place of the one original building there were now eighty major buildings, any one of which would contain the original Preston and Olin building many times over. Also there were a number of minor buildings, and several more under construction and in the planning stages.

From an annual budget of approximately $20,000 with which to operate the school, the annual budget had grown to $56.9 million.

From a series of loosely organized courses in 1872, the institution had grown to seven distinct colleges, a graduate school, a division for research, and a division for extension. Off-campus centers for research existed at ten substations located over the state. At the same time, cooperative programs were in operation with other research centers. Unit level centers for extension work had been established at 103 off-campus locations in the state, and capabilities existed for the expansion of these centers if the need arose.

The faculty organizational structure had grown from one of confused, uncertain, limited responsibilities to one in which a thoroughly organized faculty senate, representative of the total faculty, participated widely in institutional decision-making through clearly defined channels.

From an enrollment of no women in 1872, to twelve in 1922 when classes were first opened to women, the coed enrollment had risen to more than twenty-six hundred.

The Corps of Cadets continued as a viable part of the institution but operated on the basis of a subordinate unit within the University rather than as a dominant factor affecting all male students.

Graduate enrollment, not in existence until 1891 and not given great emphasis prior to Newman's administration, had grown to more than thirteen hundred with almost five hundred candidates for the Ph.D. degree.

Applications for admission had grown from forty-three in October, 1872, to more than eighty-three hundred for the fall of 1970.

Requirements for admission had grown steadily, until by 1970 the quality of the student body as measured by College Board scores and high school performance compared favorably with that of other nationally recognized universities.

Although impossible to present in statistical terms, the intellectual and academic development had been as dramatic as the growth in any other aspect of the university community. The broadening and strengthening of the University's academic and student life programs also had helped create a center of learning which was clearly gaining in national stature each year.

Perhaps the only thing that had not changed during the century was the intense desire to have the institution meet and serve the needs of the Commonwealth. This desire, although expressing itself on a greatly broadened front, was as clearly discernible in the efforts of the institution in the closing as well as it was in the opening days of its first century.

But Virginia Tech, as it entered the closing days of its first century was by no means looking backward. The institution's officials were busily preparing for the second century, in which they confidently believed Tech would add significantly to the outstanding record it had achieved as its service to the state and nation had, slowly at first but with almost explosive rapidity toward the end of the period, pushed VPI toward a comprehensive multipurpose university in fact before in name; for as the first century ended, VPI changed its name to include the word university.

Discussion of the desirability of including the word "university" in the school's official name had gone on for so long and had been participated in by so many groups that the actual decision to change the name came as something of an anticlimax. Following the recommendation of the Virginia Higher Education Study Commission in its 1965 report to Governor Harrison and the General Assembly recommending a change in name for VPI, the question periodically had agitated the campus. Those who sat in council with Dr. Hahn, discussing the pros and cons of a possible name change, sensed a peculiar situation faced by the administration. Every possible name change appeared likely to be objectionable to at least one or more important segments of public opinion in the state.

Exhaustive consideration of the matter seemed to limit the alternatives to a very few. The one name which seemed to emerge with any degree of widespread acceptability appeared to be Virginia Polytechnic Institute and State University.

Nobody was entirely happy with this obvious compromise, but on campus the Faculty Senate and the Student Senate adopted resolutions indicating the name was acceptable. The faculty group, none too familiar with Virginia traditions and background, was disposed to try for the name "State University of Virginia." The University Council, however, the highest ranking governance group on the campus, exercising a bit more prudence, recommended to President Hahn that legislation be sought to add "and State University" to the legal designation. After a thorough discussion, the Board of Visitors voted for the same addition to the name.

Legislation was introduced and passed by the state legislature in 1970 officially designating the institution "Virginia Polytechnic Institute and State University," effective July 1, 1970.

Other than an official notice from the president to the faculty informing it of the change in name, a slight modification of the official seal to include the new words in the title, and a new letterhead, plus some unofficial experimenting with the letters VPI & SU for possible monogram combinations, no official action followed the changed designation. From the day it had opened the land-grant

College had been moving slowly, sometimes painfully, but none the less surely from being a small institution of restricted offerings in agricultural and mechanical education to being a multipurpose university. In 1970, the Virginia General Assembly acknowledged that the institution had reached this point in its destiny. Implicitly at least the General Assembly's action carried its approval and support of this new direction.

The first century belonged to the Virginia Agricultural and Mechanical College and Polytechnic Institute. The second century belongs to the Virginia Polytechnic Institute and State University.

BIBLIOGRAPHY

Since no footnotes were used and no printed bibliographies are available for the period covered by this book, an extended bibliography has been prepared. Items included are those which have been of importance in the preparation of the history. Hopefully, the loss by fire of so many records for the period prior to 1900 will be compensated somewhat by the detailed attention given to this period in the bibliography. The completeness of records saved since 1920 makes such a detailed bibliography both unnecessary and impractical for the second half of the University's first century. Both editorial and news columns of the state press, although not listed in the bibliography covering the second half century, are filled with valuable information concerning the Virginia Polytechnic Institute and State University. Undoubtedly, the current plans for indexing and filing the vast accumulation of records stored in Burruss Hall soon will make this collection readily available.

I. Government Documents

Virginia. *Constitution of Virginia,* third edition, *Code of Virginia, 1873.*
——. *Education Commission Report.* Senate Document No. 111, Journal of the Senate. Richmond, 1912.
——. General Assembly. *Acts of the Assembly,* 1854-1970.
——. ——. House of Delegates, *Journal of the House of Delegates,* 1863-1970.
——. ——. Senate, *Journal of the Senate,* 1863-1970.
——. Governor. *Governor's Message and Reports of the Public Officers of the State,* 1857.
——. Senate. "The 'Big Four' and John E. Massey," Senate Document No. 7. Richmond, 1932.

II. Reports, Minutes, and Manuscript Sources

Board of Visitors. "Minutes of the Board of Visitors of Virginia Polytechnic Institute and State University," 1872-1971.
   [Title varies with changes in name of institution. Only fragments of minutes prior to 1898 are available.]

Brown, R. M. (collector). Manuscript Collection, Archives, Carol M. Newman Library, Virginia Polytechnic Institute and State University, Blacksburg.
   [An extensive collection of typed manuscripts relating to early history of VPI & SU.]
Correspondence Collection, Archives, Carol M. Newman Library, Virginia Polytechnic Institute and State University, Blacksburg.
   [Miscellaneous correspondence, originals and copies, dealing with early affairs of the college. Includes Black, Wharton, Minor, and other letters donated by descendants of early officials of the college.]
Eason, Thomas D., State Supervisor of Agricultural Education. Letter to C. H. Lane, May 30, 1919.
   [Letter filed in office of the State Supervisor of Agricultural Education, Richmond, Virginia.]
Future Farmers of Virginia, "Minutes of the State Meeting of the Future Farmers of Virginia," April 29, 1927.
Inglis, Alexander (director). *Virginia Public Schools. Virginia Education Commission Report to General Assembly and Survey Staff's Report.* Richmond: Everett Waddey, 1919.

Jones, Jesse M. (director). *Three Years of Extension Work in Agriculture and Home Economics in Virginia. A Report of the Activities and Accomplishments of the Extension Division of the Virginia Agricultural and Mechanical College and Polytechnic Institute from July 1, 1916 to May 15, 1919.*

Kelly, Fred J. (consultant). *Higher Education in Virginia. Virginia Advisory Legislative Council, Commission to Study Higher Education, Report.* Richmond: By the Committee, 1951.

McBryde, John M. Manuscripts, John M. McBryde Papers. Southern Historical Collection, Louis Round Wilson Library, University of North Carolina, Chapel Hill, North Carolina.
[Manuscripts deal primarily with John M. McBryde, Jr. Some thirty-five items deal with the senior McBryde's administration at VPI from 1900-1907.]

Minutes of the Annual Conference of White Teachers of Agriculture in Virginia. Blacksburg: Mimeographed, 1919-1930.
[Title varies. Pagination is inaccurate.]

Montgomery County (Virginia) Court House Records. Chancery File, No. 1611; Charter Book No. 1, 1869-1881, p. 1-4; Common Law File A, No. 4851; Criminal Cases Law File A, Nos. 868 and 869; Deed Book S, p. 652 *et seq.;* Order Book, County Court, 1871-1875, p. 215, p. 218; Supervisors Book No. 1, p. 24 *et seq.*

Morrison, A. J. *The College of Hampden-Sydney Calendar of Board Minutes, 1776-1876.* Richmond: The Hermitage Press, 1912.

Olin and Preston Institute. "Agents Book, Olin and Preston Institute. Edmund B. Snyder, Agent, 1855." VPI Archives.

O'Shea, M. V. (director). *Public Education in Virginia. Report of the Educational Commission of Virginia of a Survey of the Public Education System of the State.* Richmond: Superintendent of Public Printing, 1928.

Presidents' Reports. "Report of the President to the Board of Visitors of the Virginia Polytechnic Institute and State University," 1872-1971. VPI Archives, Carol M. Newman Library, and VPI Record Room, Burruss Hall.
[Title varies with changes in name of institution. Reports usually issued prior to each board meeting and at end of the year. Many reports prior to 1920 are missing.]

Rose, Wyckliffe. "The Educational Movement in the South," *Report of the Commissioner for the Year 1903.* I. Washington: Government Printing Office, 1905. p. 359-390.

Ruffner, W. H. Manuscripts, William H. Ruffner Papers, Library of the Historical Foundation of the Presbyterian and Associate Reformed Presbyterian Church, Montreat, North Carolina.
[The collection includes letters, documents, newspaper clippings, portions of Ruffner's diary, and reminiscences relating to VAMC, 1872-1881.]

———. "Report to the Board of Visitors, November 18, 1880," in *Report of the Agricultural and Mechanical College, 1880.* p. 11-39.

Russell, John Dale (director). *Report of the Higher Education Study Commission to the Governor and General Assembly of Virginia.* Richmond: 1965.

United States. Federal Board for Vocational Education. *Federal Board for Vocational Education, Statement of Policies,* Bulletin No. 1. Washington: Government Printing Office, 1917.

University of Virginia. *Proceedings, Rural Life Conference University of Virginia, July 13 to July 16, 1909.* Charlottesville: The University, 1909.

———. *Report of the Board of Visitors of the University of Virginia for the Year Ending May 31, 1878.* Charlottesville: 1878.

Virginia. State Board of Agriculture. "Agricultural Education," *Report of State Board of Agriculture 1891.* Richmond: Everett Waddey, 1892. p. 139-145.

———. ———. *Report of the State Board of Agriculture of Virginia 1890.* Richmond: Everett Waddey, 1891.

———. State Board of Education. *Annual Report of the Superintendent of Public Instruction.* 1871-1920.
[Title varies slightly. This series of reports is the best known printed source of the annual reports of the early Virginia Agricultural and Mechanical College.]

———. ———. "Minutes of the Meeting of the State Board of Education," 1871-1920.

———. ———. *Plan of the State Board for Vocational Education*, Bulletin I, No. 1, Supplement No. 2 (July, 1918).

———. ———. *Vocational Agriculture in the Secondary Schools of Virginia*, Bulletin II, No. 3 (January, 1920).

———. State Corporation Commission. *Twenty-Sixth Annual Report of the State Corporation Commission of Virginia for the Year Ending December 31, 1928.*

Virginia Polytechnic Institute and State University. *Address of Gov. Gilbert C. Walker at the Commencement of the Virginia Agricultural and Mechanical College, July 9, 1873. Plan of Instruction, Expenses, etc. of the College.* Blacksburg: 1873.

———. Alumni Association, "Minutes of the Meetings of the Board of Directors of the V.P.I. Alumni Association," 1930+.

———. ———. Welfare Committee. *Charges Preferred Against Paul B. Barringer, President of the Virginia Polytechnic Institute, Blacksburg, Virginia, by the Welfare Committee of the Alumni Association, Before the Board of Visitors at a Special Meeting January 13, 1910.*

———. "V.P.I. & S.U. Records," 1900-1971. VPI Record Room, Burruss Hall.
[An uncatalogued collection of more than a thousand five hundred 10″ × 12″ × 15″ boxes of correspondence, committee reports, financial records, and miscellaneous items stored chronologically for each presidential administration beginning with 1900.]

———. *Virginia Agricultural and Mechanical College—Its History and Organization, 1872.* No imprint.

———. Virginia Agricultural Experiment Station. *Report of the Virginia Agricultural Experiment Station for the Years 1909 and 1910.*

Virginia State Agricultural Society. *Journal of Transactions of the Virginia State Agricultural Society From Its Organization to the Close of the First Annual Exhibition of 1853.* Richmond: J. W. Randolph, 1853.

———. *Report of the President of the Virginia State Agricultural Society Made to the Farmers' Assembly at the First Annual Meeting Held in the City of Richmond, October 28, 1856.* Richmond: J. W. Randolph, 1856.

Young, Harold N. "The Virginia Agricultural Experiment Station 1886-1966," Unpublished Manuscript, Blacksburg, 1967.

III. Virginia Polytechnic Institute and State University Publications

Bulletin of the Virginia Polytechnic Institute and State University, Volume I, January 1908+.
[This series includes the University catalogs, information for prospective students, and official publications dealing with the University. Research reports published by the Engineering Experiment Station were added to the series in 1923. Popular technical studies published by the Engineering Extension Division were added in 1924. Only three volumes will be listed but Volumes I through XVIII contain alumni registers and much incidental information about early days of the college, faculty, campus, and alumni.]

———. Brown, R. M. "V.P.I. Historical Index, 1872-1942," XXXV, No. 12 (July, 1942).

———. Robertson, J. M. "V.P.I. Historical Data Book," LVII, No. 3 (January, 1964).

———. Smyth, E. A. "A Brief History of the Virginia Agricultural and Mechanical College and Polytechnic Institute, 1872-1922," XV (May, 1922).

Daily Bulletin. September 26, 1952+. Mimeographed.
[Report of current college events, distributed on campus only.]

Extension News. Volume I, No. 1 (November, 1918+).
[Originally the Extension Division News.]

The Techgram. Volume I, No. 1 (January 1923+).
[From 1923 until October 1929 published promotional data about institution. From October 1930 to present included news about VPI events and alumni activities.]

Virginia Polytechnic Institute and State University. *Annual Report of the Virginia Polytechnic Institute and State University.* 1872-1971.
[Title varies with change in name of the institution.]

———. Catalogs. 1872-1972.

[Catalogs for 1879-1880; 1880-1881; 1885-1886; 1890-1891 are missing. After 1908, catalogs issued as college bulletins.]

———. Extension Division. *Administrative Handbook.* Blacksburg, 1970.

———. *Virginia Polytechnic Institute Self-Study, 1965-1966.* Two volumes. 1966.

IV. VPI Student Publications

Bugle. 1895-1943; 1947-present.
[Student body yearbook. Some excellent photography of campus scenes, student life, and Corps of Cadets.]

Cohee. 1897-1898.
[Irregular weekly publication.]

Collegiate Times. 1969+.

Gray Jacket. 1875-1906.
[Issued monthly but missed publication a number of times.]

Guidon.
[Established as YMCA Handbook 1894. Taken over by the college 1952-1953.]

The Virginia Tech. 1903-1969.
[Student newspaper. Changed to *Collegiate Times* in 1969.]

Tin Horn.
[Coed yearbook published 1929-1931.]

V. Newspapers

Because of the loss of early college records and the political bias so prevalent in the Virginia press for the second half of the nineteenth century, a careful scrutiny of newspapers was necessary for most of the period prior to 1900. Following this date, newspaper information relative to the Virginia Polytechnic Institute and State University is too voluminous for inclusion here.

Alexandria (Virginia) *Gazette,* January 29, 1879.

Amherst (Virginia) *Enterprise,* February 6, 1879.

Christiansburg (Virginia) *Montgomery Messenger,* intermittent issues, 1873-1879.

Danville (Virginia) *Daily News,* January 30, 1879.

Lexington (Virginia) *Gazette,* January 15, 1868.

Lexington (Virginia) *Gazette and Rockbridge Farmer,* June 23, 1840.

Lynchburg *Daily Virginian,* January 27,

March 26, March 29, 1872; February 11, 1873.

Lynchburg (Virginia) *News,* March 14, March 15, 1872; January 2, 1879; December 22, December 23, December 28, 1906.

Norfolk *Virginian,* January 30, 1879.

Pearisburg (Virginia) *Gazette,* February 3, July 27, 1872.

Richmond (Virginia) *Commonwealth,* February 5, March 1, 1880.

Richmond (Virginia) *Daily Dispatch,* January 6, 9, 12, 16, 17, February 3, 21, March 25, April 1, 1871; January 13, 14, 16, 25, 29, March 15, 21, 27, October 5, 1872; January 9, 10, 1873; November 3, 9, December 4, 9, 11, 1879; January 7, 13, February 4, March 9, August 15, 1880; January 26, 1882; February 21, 1884; January 3, 24, March 24, 25, 26, 1886; August 28, 1890; January 17, 1891.

Richmond (Virginia) *Enquirer,* December 6, 1805; January 24, 1811; February 12, August 25, 1818; March 1, 1828; February 2, 1832; October to December 1841, passim; March 15, 1871.

Richmond (Virginia) *State,* January 6, February 13, 14, November 7, December 1, 19, 1879; January 6, 1880.

Richmond (Virginia) *Whig,* September 27, 1839; January 4, 1868; December 17, 23, 1870; December 14, 1871; January 8, 19, 25, 26, 29, 30, 31; February 3, 5, 6, 20, March 13, 14, 15, 27, 1872; February 11, 13, 14, 1873; February 14, 1879.

Salem (Virginia) *Register,* August 8, November 4, 1879.

Washington, *National Intelligencer,* May 17, 1811, November 30, 1822; September 29, 1830.

VI. Periodicals

Agricultural History. 1927+. Chicago, Illinois; Baltimore, Maryland.
Bruce, Kathleen, "Virginia Agricultural Decline to 1860: A Fallacy," VI (January, 1932), p. 3-13.
True, R. H., "The Virginia Board of Agriculture," XIV (July, 1940), p. 97-103.

American Farmer. 1819-1834. Baltimore, Maryland.
[Twenty-one articles dealing with the early efforts in Virginia to improve agriculture by means of education.]

American Historical Review. 1895+. New York; Lancaster, Pennsylvania.

Ambler, C. H., "The Cleavage Between Eastern and Western Virginia," XV (July, 1910), p. 762-780.

Craven, A. O., "The Agricultural Reformers of the Ante-Bellum South," XXXIII (January, 1928), p. 302-314.

Chapter Chats. 1927+. Richmond, Virginia

Magill, E. C., "Future Farmers in Virginia Celebrate Fifth Anniversary," IV (March, 1931), p. 1-8.

[Organ of the Virginia Association of the Future Farmers of Virginia.]

DeBow's Review. 1846-1864. New Orleans, Louisiana.

Cabell, N. F., "Early History of Agriculture in Virginia," XXXV (July, 1858), p. 82-83.

"Course of Education in Virginia," XXIII (November, 1857), p. 556-557.

Educational Journal of Virginia. 1869-1891. Richmond, Virginia.

"Educated Mechanics," VIII (October, 1876), p. 538-540.

"Education and Discipline at Blacksburg," XIV (September, 1883), p. 278.

"Report on Conditions at the Agricultural and Mechanical College, 1883," XIV (September, 1883), p. 278.

"The Agricultural and Mechanical College," V (July 5, 1874).

"The College at Blacksburg," III (September, 1872), p. 443-446.

"The Colleges and the Congressional Land Fund," I (June, 1870).

"The New College at Blacksburg," III (July, 1872), p. 382.

Farmers' Register. 1833-1842. Shellbanks and Petersburg, Virginia.

[Some fifty articles dealing with efforts in Virginia to improve agriculture by education, fairs, legislation, and the press.]

John P. Branch Historical Papers of Randolph Macon College. 1901-1918. Ashland, Virginia.

Fox, E. L., "William Henry Ruffner and the Rise of the Public Free School System in Virginia," III (June, 1910).

Industrial South. 1881-1887. Richmond, Virginia.

Advertisement of Virginia Agricultural and Mechanical College, VI (July, 1886), p. 331.

Monthly Journal, Virginia State Agricultural Society. 1874. Richmond, Virginia.

"A Brief History of the First State Agricultural Society Formed in Virginia," I, Part 2 (February, 1879), passim.

Sewanee Review Quarterly. 1892+. Sewanee, Tennessee.

Knight, E. W., "The Evolution of Public Education in Virginia," XXIV (January, 1916), p. 24-41.

South Atlantic Quarterly. 1902+. Durham, North Carolina.

Pearson, C. C., "William Henry Ruffner: Reconstruction Statesman of Virginia," XX (January and April, 1921), p. 25-32; p. 137-151.

Southern Literary Messenger. 1834-1864. Richmond, Virginia.

Washington, H. A., "Social System of Virginia," XIV (February, 1848), p. 65-81.

Southern Planter. 1841+. Richmond, Virginia.

[One of the best sources available for information concerning the attitude of the agricultural leaders toward agricultural education and toward early VPI.]

"A Visit to the College at Blacksburg," XLIV (September, 1884), p. 397.

"Agricultural Convention," X (March, 1850), p. 78-81.

"Agricultural Education," LII (January, 1891), p. 23-24.

"Agricultural Education," VI (March, 1846), p. 60-61.

"Agricultural Fairs," XIX (December, 1859), p. 774-775.

"Agricultural Professorship at the University," XVII (September, 1857), p. 533.

"Agriculture in the Public Schools," LXVII (September, 1906), p. 722-724.

"Annual Meeting of the Agricultural Society," XXXI (December, 1871), p. 724.

"Annual Report of the President and Executive Committee," XIX (January, 1859), p. 18-21.

"Appointment of President and Director," LII (June, 1891), p. 293-294.

"Biographical Sketch of General William H. Richardson," XXXVII (January, 1876), p. 81-88.

Editorial Note, XXXVIII (November, 1877), p. 686.

"Farm Schools," XXXI (January, 1871), 1-3; p. 53.

Fletcher, S. W., "A Business-Like Organization of Agricultural Work in Virginia," LXXI (March, 1910), p. 292-293.

"Governor Floyd's Message," IX (December, 1849), p. 375-376.

"Installation of Commodore M. F. Maury as Professor of Physics, etc.," XXIX (October, 1968), p. 633-634.

"Journal of the Proceedings of a General Meeting of the Virginia State Agricultural Society," I (February, 1867), p. 21-51.

"Manual Labor School," XXIV (February, 1869), p. 94-96.

"Old Southside Ideas," XXXI (March, 1871), p. 144-146.

"Opening of the Virginia Agricultural and Mechanical College," XXXIII (October, 1872), p. 621.

"Physical Survey of Virginia," XXVIII (August, 1868), p. 478-480.

"President Eggleston and the Short Course," LXXIV (May, 1914), p. 415-416.

"Proceedings of the Farmers' Convention," XLVI (June, 1886), p. 255-303.

"Professorship of Agriculture," V (June, 1845), p. 142-143.

"Proposed Physical Survey by Washington College," XXVIII (August, 1868), p. 474-477.

"Recent Changes at the Agricultural Experiment Station," LI (December, 1890), p. 573-574.

"Report of the Executive Committee of the Virginia State Agricultural Society," XIV (December, 1854), p. 372-375.

Sanders, H. W., "The Future Farmers of America Story," CXIII (April, 1952), p. 8, p. 50, p. 51.

Sandy, T. O., "Demonstration Farm Work in Virginia, LXIX (January, 1908), p. 34-36.

"Scientific and Practical Departments of Collegiate Education," XXXIX (February, 1869), p. 120-121.

"The Agricultural and Mechanical College and Experiment Station," LI (April, 1890), p. 187.

"The Agricultural College at Blacksburg," XXXV (October, 1875), p. 372-374.

"The Agricultural Experiment Station," L (January, 1889), p. 34-36; (March, 1889), p. 129-134.

"The Board of Visitors of the Virginia Agricultural and Mechanical College," LI (February, 1890), p. 63.

"The New President of V.P.I.," LXXIV (May, 1913), p. 529.

"The Reorganization of the Agricultural College," XL (September, 1879), p. 312.

"The Virginia Agricultural and Mechanical College," XXXIX (May, 1878, p. 289.

"The Work of the Convention," XXXVIII (September, 1877), p. 594-596.

The Farmer. 1866-1867. Richmond, Virginia.

"Biographical Sketch of General William H. Richardson," I (January, 1866), p. 97.

Letter signed "Farmer," II (March, 1867), p. 97.

"The Colleges and the Agricultural Land Grant," II (March, 1867), p. 97.

"What Kind of Education Is Now needed?" II (February, 1867), p. 57-59.

The Farmers' Gazette. 1868-1871. Richmond, Virginia.

Editorial, II (January, 1870), p. 210.

Tobacco Grower. 1933-1941. Farmville, Virginia.

"Southside Virginia is Cradle of Farm Extension Program," VII (July 10, 1939), p. 1-3.

Virginia Agricultural Instructor. Mimeographed irregularly by Department of Agricultural Education, VPI, Blacksburg.

Groseclose, H. C., "A State Organization of Students Enrolled in Vocational Agriculture," (September 1, 1926), p. 22.

Newman, W. S., "A Brief Account of the F. F. V. Development," (February 15, 1927), p. 2.

————, "Regional Conference," (April 15, 1927), p. 2.

"Organization of Local Chapters of the F. F. V.," (October, 1926), p. 3-4.

Virginia Farmer. 1856. Harrisonburg, Virginia.

Editorial Comment, I (April, 1856), p. 4.

Editorial Comment, I (November, 1856), p. 180.

Virginia Magazine of History and Biography. 1893+. Richmond, Virginia.

Good, H. G., "Early Attempts to Teach Agriculture in Old Virginia," XLVIII (January, 1940), p. 341-351.

Lokke, Carl L., "The Food Administration Papers for the State of Virginia in the National Archives," L (July, 1942), p. 220-226.

VII. General Works, Studies, and Histories

Ambler, Charles H. *Francis H. Pierpont.* Chapel Hill: University of North Carolina Press, 1937.

————. *Sectionalism in Virginia 1776-1860.* Chicago: University of Chicago Press, 1910.

Andrews, M. Carl. *No Higher Honor.* Richmond: The Dietz Press, Inc., 1970.

Andrews, Matthew Page. *Virginia, The Old Dominion.* Garden City: Doubleday, Doran and Co., 1937.

Arber, Edward (editor). *Captain John Smith's Works Part I, 1608-1613.* The English Scholars Library No. 16, 1 Montague Road, Birmingham, England, 1884.

Armstrong, James Edward. *The Old Baltimore Conference. From The Planting of Methodism in 1773 to the Division of the Conference in 1857.* Baltimore: King Brothers, 1907.

Bean, William Gleason. *The Liberty Hall Volunteers; Stonewall's College Boys.* Charlottesville: University Press of Virginia, 1964.

Blake, Nelson M. *William Mahone of Virginia: Soldier and Political Insurgent.* Richmond: Garrett and Massie, 1935.

Boyd, C. R. *Resources of South-West Virginia.* New York: John Wiley and Sons, 1881.

Bruce, Kathleen. *Virginia Iron Manufacture in the Slave Era.* New York: The Century Co., 1930.

Bruce, P. A. *Virginia, Rebirth of the Old Dominion.* Two volumes. Chicago: Lewis Publishing Company, 1929.

Chandler, J. A. C. *History of Suffrage in Virginia.* Johns Hopkins University Studies in Historical and Political Science, Series 19, Nos. 6-7. Baltimore: Johns Hopkins, 1901.

Claiborne, J. H. *Seventy-Five Years in Old Virginia.* New York: Neale Publishing Company, 1904.

Clark, Isaac Edward. "Virginia Agricultural and Mechanical College," *Art and Industry, Education in the Industrial and Fine Arts in the United States,* Part IV, p. 600-608, United States Bureau of Education. Washington: Government Printing Office, 1898.

Cochran, J. P. "The Virginia Agricultural and Mechanical College: The Formative Half Century, 1872-1919, of the Virginia Polytechnic Institute." Unpublished Ph.D. dissertation, University of Alabama, 1961.

Conrad, Thomas Nelson. *A Confederate Spy: A Story of the Civil War.* New York: J. S. Ogilvie, 1892.

Couper, William. *One Hundred Years at V.M.I.* Four Volumes. Richmond: Garrett and Massie, 1939.

Craven, A. O. *Soil Exhaustion in Virginia and Maryland 1606-1860.* University of Illinois Studies in the Social Sciences, XIII, No. 1 (March, 1925). University of Illinois, Urbana, 1925.

Crenshaw, Ollinger. *General Lee's College: The Rise and Growth of Washington and Lee University.* New York: Random House, 1969.

Dabney, Charles W. *Universal Education in the South.* Two volumes. Chapel Hill: University of North Carolina Press, 1936.

Dew, Charles B. *Ironmaker to the Confederacy: Joseph Reed Anderson and the Tredgar Iron Works.* New Haven: Yale University Press, 1966.

Dingledine, Raymond C. Jr. *Madison College The First Fifty Years 1908-1958.* Harrisonburg: Madison College, 1959.

Eaton, Clement. *The Mind of the Old South.* Rev. Ed. Baton Rouge: Louisiana State University Press, 1967 [Chapter 5]

Eckenrode, Hamilton James. *The Political History of Virginia During the Reconstruction.* Johns Hopkins University Studies in Historical and Political Science, Series XXII, Nos. 6-7-8. Baltimore: The Johns Hopkins Press, 1904.

Extension Work in Virginia: A Brief History, 1907-1940 Published by the Alpha

Gamma Chapter of Epsilon Sigma Phi, Blacksburg, 1940.

Goode, John. *Recollections of a Lifetime.* New York: Neale Publishing Company, 1906.

Gray, Lewis Cecil. *History of Agriculture in the Southern United States to 1860.* Two volumes. New York: Peter Smith, 1941.

Hambleton, James P. *A Biographical Sketch of Henry A. Wise—With A History of the Political Campaign in Virginia in 1855.* Richmond: J. W. Randolph, 1856.

Hancock, Elizabeth (editor). *Autobiography of John E. Massey.* New York: Neale Publishing Company, 1909.

Heatwole, C. J. *A History of Education in Virginia.* New York: Macmillan Company, 1916.

Hollis, Daniel W. *The University of South Carolina.* Two volumes. Columbia: University of South Carolina Press, 1951-1956.

Jackson, Luther P. *Negro Office-Holders in Virginia, 1865-1895.* Norfolk: Guide Quality Press, 1945.

Kinnear, D. L. "A History of Agricultural Education in Virginia with Special Emphasis on the Secondary School Level." Unpublished Ph.D. dissertation, Ohio State University, 1952.

Kirby, Jack Temple. *Westmoreland Davis: Virginia Planter-Politician, 1859-1942.* Charlottesville: University Press of Virginia, 1968.

May, John B. "The Life of John Lee Buchanan." Unpublished Ph.D. dissertation, University of Virginia, 1937.

Memorial of the Life, Public Service, and Character of William T. Sutherlin as Furnished by His Friends and Published by His Family. Danville: Dance Brothers Company, 1894.

Moger, Allen W. *Bourbonism to Byrd 1870-1925.* Charlottesville: The University Press of Virginia, 1968.

———. *The Rebuilding of the Old Dominion: A Study in Economic, Social, and Political Transition from 1880 to 1902.* Ann Arbor: Edwards Brothers, Inc., 1940.

Morton, Richard L. *History of Virginia Since 1861.* Chicago and New York: American Historical Society, 1924.

Overton, Edward F. "A Study of the Life and Work of Joseph Dupuy Eggleston,

Junior." Unpublished Ph.D. dissertation, University of Virginia, 1937.

Pearson, C. C. *The Readjuster Movement in Virginia.* New Haven: Yale University Press, 1917.

Pendleton, W. C. *Political History of Appalachian Virginia 1776-1926.* Dayton: Shenandoah Press, 1927.

Ross, Earle D. *Democracy's College: The Land-Grant Movement in the Formative Stage.* Ames: Iowa State College Press, 1942.

Ross, W. A. "Future Farmers of America," in *History of Agricultural Education of Less than College Grade in the United States.* Federal Security Agency, U. S. Office of Education, Vocational Division Bulletin No. 217, Agricultural Series No. 55, (1942), Chapter 7, p. 532-551.

Ruffin, Edmund. *Premium Essay on Agricultural Education Submitted to the Executive Committee of the Southern Central Agricultural Association.* Second Edition. Richmond: J. W. Randolph, 1853.

Shackleford, S. D. *Biographical Sketch of the Life of J. E. Penn.* Roanoke: Roanoke Printing Company, Inc., 1931.

Sheldon, W. D. *Populism in the Old Dominion: Virginia Farm Politics, 1885-1900.* Princeton: Princeton University Press, 1935.

Smith, F. H. *Special Report of the Superintendent of the Virginia Military Institute on Scientific Education in Europe.* Richmond: Richie, Dunevant and Co., 1859.

———. *The Virginia Military Institute, Its Building and Rebuilding.* Lynchburg: J. P. Bell Company, 1912.

Stohlman, Martha Lou. *The Story of Sweet Briar College.* Sweet Briar: Alumni Association of Sweet Briar College, 1956.

Sutherlin, W. T. *Address Delivered Before the Mechanics' Association of Danville, Virginia, March 11, 1867.* Richmond: Published by the Association, 1876.

True, Alfred Charles. *A History of Agricultural Education in the United States 1785-1925.* United States Department of Agriculture, Miscellaneous Publication No. 36. Washington: Government Printing Office, 1929.

Virginia Commissioner of Agriculture.

Handbook of Virginia, Fifth Edition. Richmond: Published by the Commissioner, 1886.

Virginia Cooperative Education Association. *A Successful State-wide Project in Community Cooperation Over a Period of Nearly a Quarter Century, 1904-1926, Under the Cooperative Education Association of Virginia, State Council of Rural Agencies.* Richmond: Published by the Association, 1926.

Washington College. *Catalogue of Washington College, Lexington, Virginia, 1868-1869.* Lexington: 1868.

Wertenbaker, Thomas Jefferson. *Patrician and Plebeian in Virginia, or The Origin and Development of the Social Classes in the Old Dominion.* Charlottesville: The Michie Company, 1910.

Wise, Jennings C. *A Special Report to the Board of Visitors of the Virginia Military Institute on the History of Agricultural Education in Virginia and the Virginia Military Institute as a School of Agriculture, Including a Sketch of the Physical Survey of Virginia by the School of Applied Science.* Lexington: 1914.

————. *Personal Memoirs of Scott Shipp.* Privately printed. Lexington: 1915.

APPENDIX I

Members of the Board of Visitors as Shown by College Catalogs, 1872-1972

Legislation creating the VAMC provided for appointed and ex-officio members. This provision continues for VPI & SU today, although changes have been made regarding the number and qualification of appointees and the offices to be represented ex officio on the board. All appointments have been made by the governor "with the advice and consent of the Senate."

In 1872 the State Board of Education and the president of the State Agricultural Society served on the board in an ex-officio capacity. In 1873 this policy was changed so that only the state superintendent of public instruction and the president of the agricultural society served ex officio. During one of the periods of struggle for control of the College the president of the agricultural society, not being subject to appointment by any elected official, was dropped as ex-officio member. The state superintendent of public instruction continued, however, until 1966. Shortly after 1902 the president of the Board of Agriculture and Immigration (now Commerce) was added as ex-officio member.

Appointments to the board were always made for a specified term of years which did not necessarily coincide with the academic year. Since the College catalogs were published to coincide with the academic years, members often began serving before their names appeared in the catalog or retired from the board before the names were removed.

Adams, B. D., 1913-1920*; Anderson, Joseph R., 1872-1873; Armstrong, E. J., 1876-1879; Barbour, B. J., 1876-1878; Barker, J. M., 1909-1913*; Barton, Joseph M., 1889-1892; Beverley, J. H. C., 1904-1905*; Beverley, R. Carter, 1921-1924; Beverley, Robert, 1919-1921; Beverly, Robert, 1872-1874; Black, Harvey, 1872-1876**; Blewett, W. C. (Jr.), 1963-1965; Bliss, C. H., 1881-1882; Boatwright, Mrs. R. G., 1944-1953; Bocock, Thomas S., 1873-1875; Bolling, Mrs. A. Stuart (Jr.), 1967-1971; Bowman, A. M., 1911-1914 Broaddus, Andrew, 1881-1885; Brockenbrough, B. B., 1899-1904; Brown, J. Thompson, 1889-1908; 1912-1921**; Bruce, Charles, 1880-1881; Bruce, David K. E., 1946-1947; Buchanan, John L., 1886-1889*; Burks, E. C., 1875-1879; Burruss, W. H., 1947-1955; Button, Charles W., 1877-1880; Byrd, Harry F., 1929-1944;

Carrington, J. C., 1901-1912**; Carson, R. P., 1880-1881**; Carter, H. L., 1889-1892; Casto, Harold, 1970-; Churchman, J. W., 1909*; Claytor, Miss Mary Fred, 1953-1961; Clement, G. Frank, 1971-; Cloyd, D. M., 1897-1905; Cloyd, J. M., 1891-1893; Cloyd, Joseph, 1872-1873; Cochran, Alexander B., 1873-1876; Cochran, George M., 1960-1968; Cochran, R. S., 1906; Coles, Walter, 1875-1878; Cowan, John T., 1872-1873; Cowherd, Roderick, 1959-1963*; Craig, R. S., 1914-1918; Cutchins, Clifford A., (III), 1965-; Davis, Westmoreland, 1942; DeJarnette, D. C., 1872-1876; Eberwine, Vernon G., 1944-1956**; Edmonds, Thomas, 1878-1882; Eggleston, Joseph D. (Jr.), 1906-1912*; Eggleston, William, 1876-1879**; Erwin, William J., 1960-1968; Eskridge, Allen, 1924-1952; Farr, R. R., 1882-1886*; Ferguson, Homer L., 1930-1938; Ferguson, Meade, 1920-1924; Ferneyhough, J. G., 1928-1930; Finney, L. Stanford, 1937-1942*; Fishburn, J. P., 1948-1954; Fitzgerald, T. C., 1889-1896; Furr, G. L., 1954-1962**; Gibbs, Mrs. Mavis M., 1963-1971; Gilmer, Mrs. Turner A., 1953-1961; Givens, J. E., 1968-; Goode, John, 1872-1875; Goodykoontz, Robert O., 1968-; Graham, Mrs. Henderson P., 1961-1964; Graves, S. H., 1893-1895; Green, Duff, 1881-1882; Grimsley, D. A., 1880-1881; Hall, Sidney B., 1931-1941*; Hancock, John W. (Jr.), 1963-1971; Harrison, C. S., 1880-1881; Hart, Harris, 1918-1930*; Harvie, Lewis E., 1872*; Hering, E. A., 1893-1897; Hill, W. D., 1900-1901; Horsley, J. R., 1928-1944; Houff, Mrs. Louis A., 1955-1958; Howard, D. J., 1949-1957*; Hubbard, E. W., 1881-1885; Johnson, Adger S., 1964-; Johnson, L. E., 1908-1912**; Keiley, A. M., 1880-1881; Kent, Robert C., 1875-1876; Kirkpatrick, B. F., 1910-1914; Kizer, C. G., 1905-1910; Kline, L. D., 1908-1912; Kraft, Christopher C., 1970-; Lancaster, Dabney S., 1941-1946*; Landis, John W., 1966-1970; Lane, Mrs. E. H., 1968-; Lane, E. H., 1956-1966; Lawson, J. W., 1875-1878; Lee, Fitzhugh, 1878-1881; Lee, W. H. F., 1873*; 1874-1878; 1886-1888; Leftwich, J. B., 1880-1881; Lester, John C. (Jr.), 1969-1971*; Lewis, J. Marshall, 1922-1930; Lovell, John T., 1877-1880; McConnell, Mrs. R. L., 1944-1955; McDowell, James, 1889; McKinney, P. W., 1883-1887; McMath, Albert J., 1921-1923*; Magruder, E. W., 1920-1922; Massey, John E., 1890-1898*; Mathews, H. J., 1893-1897; Maynard, H. L., 1894-1899; Mellon, Paul, 1950-1955; Meredith, John A., 1878-1881; Miles, Waldo G., 1966-1970; Miller, G. Tyler, 1946-1949*; Milnes, W. P., 1877-1879; Moffett, W. Stuart, 1930-1936; Moffett, W. Stuart (Jr.), 1952-1960; Montague, E. E., 1918-1920; Moss, R. S., 1918-1943**; Mount, W. D., 1914-1918; Musgrave, J. S., 1899-1903; Mustard, W. G., 1883-1887; Nininger, E. D., 1944-1954; Noell, R. J., 1908-1912; Ott, John, 1883-1887; Page, Rosewell, 1912-1913; Pamplin, Robert B., 1971-; Paschall, Davis Y., 1957-1960*; Payne, A. D., 1886-1888; Payne, F. M., 1891-1895; Pendleton, W. C., 1881-1882; Penn, John E., 1873-1875; Preston, Samuel D., 1952-1960; Price, T. B., 1895-

1899; Read, Charles C., 1938-1947; Read, G. M., 1955-1962; Reed, Chas. Hancock, 1949-1958; Rice, F. E., 1880-1881; Rice, Millard B. (Jr.), 1971-*; Rice, W. Thomas, 1961-1968**; Robertson, Wyndham, 1899-1908; Robinson, Mrs. J. Kenneth, 1971-; Ross, J. D. H., 1886-1890; Rowe, C. Eugene, 1968-**; Ruffner, William H., 1872-1882*; Russell, R. A., 1926-1950; Ryan, J. F., 1899-1903; St. Clair, Peyton F., 1906-1914; Sanders, Paul D., 1955-1963; Scruggs, Langhorne, 1880-1881; Shackleford, W. C., 1913-1922; Showalter, Mrs. English, 1959-1968; Slater, L. A., 1881-1885; Smith, H. M. (Jr.), 1906-1910; 1912-1920; Smith, J. P., 1874-1877; Smith, Miss Mary Phlegar, 1944-1953; Smith, Oscar F. (III), 1954-1962; Smith, Roy R., 1971-; Southall, James W., 1898-1906*; Sproul, W. W., 1924-1937*; 1937-1941; Staples, Waller R., 1886-1888**; Stearnes, R. C., 1913-1918*; Stuart, Harry, 1945-1951; Stuart, W. A., 1872-1874; Sullins, David, 1877-1880; Sutherlin, William T., 1872-1873; Taliaferro, W. B., 1876-1879; Taylor, James C., 1872*; 1881-1886**; Thomas, Joseph W., 1893-1897; Thornhill, A. B., 1918-1922; Tidball, E. M., 1873-1874; Turnbull, N. S., 1886-1892; Turner, J. A., 1912-1920; Tyler, J. Hoge, 1887-1890**; Tyssowski, John, 1956-1960; Vawter, Chas., E., 1886-1899**; Venable, A. R. (Jr.), 1888-1894; Walker, Frank S., 1920-1926; Walker, Gilbert C., 1872*; Walton, Mrs. H. H., 1944-1955; Wampler, Chas. W., 1942-1959*; Wampler, Chas. W. (Jr.), 1965-1969*; Watkins, J. B., 1903-1908; 1912-1928**; Watts, Robert B., 1920-1924; Webb, L. W., 1942-1952; Wharton, Gabriel C., 1874-1877**; Whitehurst, James L., 1970-; Wilhelm, Mrs. Jane Wilmer, 1961-1968; Wilkerson, Woodrow W., 1960-1966*; Will, E. H., 1958-1966; Willcox, Bolling, 1883-1887; Williams, J. H., 1881-1883; Williams, Wyatt A., 1962-1970; Wine, William E., 1943-1954**; Wood, T. Gilbert, 1922-1930; Woods, J. P., 1924-1948**; Woods, Micajah, 1911; Wright, T. Judson, 1924-1928; Wyatt, Harry C., 1962-1970**; Yates, Mrs. E. Floyd, 1955-1963.

*Ex-officio member
**Also served as rector of the board

APPENDIX II
Commandants of Cadets, 1872-1972

From the day of its founding to the present Virginia Polytechnic Institute and State University has had a commandant of cadets. The session of 1880-1881 is unique however. The Board of Visitors failed to appoint either a commandant or a president. Acting President Hart thereupon appointed a senior cadet as acting commandant and permitted this individual to select other seniors as acting assistant commandants. With this one exception all commandants have been appointed by the Board of Visitors.

Anding, S. W. (Lt.), 1914-1917; Carson, C. C. (Capt.), 1917; 1919-1920; Cochran, J. H. (Col.), 1938-1942; Dashiell, E. R. (Capt.), 1909-1911; Devine, J. M. (Maj. Gen.), 1952-1961; Finch, A. T. (Professor), 1898-1901; Gresham, J. C. (Lt). 1885-1887; Harman, J. A. (Lt.), 1890-1894; Henderson, George (Col.), 1945-1946; Jameson, G. H. (Capt.), 1906-1909; Johnson, J. S. A. (Professor), 1901-1906; Knight, J. T. (Lt.), 1887-1890; Lane, James H. (Col.), 1872-1880; Maynard, J. B. (Lt. Col.), 1929-1935; Merritt, W. B. (Col.), 1951-1952; Munford, T. W. (Col.), 1946-1951; Nichols, W. R. (Maj.), 1924-1929; Pachler, F. T. (Maj. Gen.), 1967-; Preston, W. Ballard (Col.), 1881-1885; 1887; Schewe, M. W. (Brig. Gen.), 1961-1967; Shanks, D. C. (Lt.), 1895-1898; Skuse, J. C. (Maj.), 1918-1919; Stone, W. P. (Maj.), 1917-1918; Tenney, C. H. (Lt. Col.), 1935-1938; Ware, J. F. (Lt.), 1911-1914; Williford, F. E. (Maj.), 1920-1924; Wilson, R. W. (Col.), 1942-1945.

APPENDIX III
Ranking Cadet Officers, 1895-1972

During the period of World War II a number of students were unable to serve for a full year.

Atkinson, H., 1937; Barlow, W. K., 1958; Beville, R. M., 1918; Bird, D. W., 1960; Boatwright, W. P., 1907; Bonsack, S. W. (III), 1940; Butler, H. W. 1924; Byrne, W. H., 1915; Catlin, J. E., 1922; Cawthon, J. R., 1943*; Chewning, Z. W., 1938; Combs, C. E., 1957; Davidson, H. L., 1902; Davidson, M. W., 1901; Davis, C. B., 1921; Dixon, L. R. 1966; Dorsey, C. L., 1945*; Ellett, H. K., 1944*; Fairer, A. W. (Jr.), 1919; Gary, H. H., 1904; Glenn, D. W., 1939; Glenn, E. G., 1949; Harper, H. H., 1927; Hartman, W. T. (Jr.), 1926; Hartt, W. H. (III), 1961; Hearne, Phillip T., 1972; Heneke, W. R., 1943*; Henley, R. R., 1906; Hester, L. A., 1923; Hildebrand, C. K., 1905; Hoehl, E. R., 1933; Hudgins, W. C.,1928; Hutchinson, G. W., 1899; Janney, J. K., 1970; Jones, J. B., 1944*; Keller, H. E., 1917; Leadbeater, T. R., 1929; Legge, W. R., 1913; Liipfert, W. J., 1912; Lowe, D. E., 1963; McGinnis, T. D., 1916; McLaughlin, A. C. J., 1946; Martin, D. D., 1909; Morton, B. B., 1925; Mullins, R. W. (Jr.), 1968; Osterbind, C. C., 1903; Owens, M. A., 1931; Parrish, B. S., 1953; Parsons, G. L., 1908; Payne, F. P., 1942; Pierce, W. M., 1920; Powell, J. H., 1965; Powell, R. G., 1969; Priddy, Lawrence, 1897; Rainey, D. M., 1952; Robertson, Rolfe, 1948; Rose, W. A. (Jr.), 1954; Russell, R. E., 1964; Show, D. L., 1959; Simmons, L. D., 1934; Sinclair, R. W., 1967; Snider, G. E., 1932; Stafford, E. E., 1911; Stager, A. N., 1971; Strong, H. T., 1930; Stull, O. M., 1896; Sutton, L. V., 1910; Tait, L. C., 1941; Thomas, F. G. (Jr.), 1950; Thompson, T. T., 1956; Umphlitt, C. J., 1951; Waddy, W. P., 1895; Wade, L. P., 1955; Waller, E. P., 1900; Wildes, G. W., 1935; Wilson, S. H., 1947; Wise, H. A., 1898; Wist, S. B., 1936; Wysor, W. G., 1914; Zuidema, G. L., 1962.

*Served part of the year

APPENDIX IV
Presidents of the Corps of Cadets, 1909-1966

Prior to the union of the Corps of Cadets and the Civilian Student Body in 1966, a president of the Corps was elected annually. During the period of World War II, some cadets were unable to serve a full term.

Akers, P. L., 1951; Arnold, R. L., 1943*; Arthur, J. P., 1961; Barkley, C. C., 1960; Belcher, J. R., 1939; Belt, F. A., 1943*; Bishop, O. M., 1910; Brown, B. P., 1945; Brown, C. S., 1941; Clemmer, T. F., 1916; Cocke, B. T., 1918; Dance, E. H., 1942; Davis, C. B., 1921; Dear, P. S., 1927; Dekker, H. J., 1943*; Dunton, R. M., 1947*; Eden, D. D., 1956; Faison, C. H. (Jr.), 1940; Fuller, F. B. (Jr.), 1954; Gaines, E. R., 1926; Garette, L. N. (Jr.), 1964; Giles, R. H. (Jr.), 1955; Gilman, J. P., 1948; Gregory, E. D., 1923; Greenlee, A. B., 1944*; Hardwick, S. E., 1932; Heckman, E. C., 1912; Hooper, H. V., 1931; Hurst, B. L., 1924; Jackson, W. H., 1925; Jennings, C. H., 1953; Kraft, C. C. (Jr.), 1944*; Legge, W. R., 1913; Lusk, E. R., 1922; McArthur, J. B., 1929;

McBurney, W. A., 1920; MacGregor, R. J., 1915; Main, G. A. (Jr.), 1946; Malcom, R. B., 1950; Martin, W. B., 1909; Moffett, W. S. (Jr.), 1933; Moore, A. B., 1917; Morris, J. M., 1911; Morrison, D. C., 1959; Moss, J. S., 1928; Otto, T. W. (Jr.), 1965; Plummer, T. G., 1949; Quillen, C. D. (Jr.), 1958; Robinette, L. M., 1947*; Robinette, L. W., 1943*; Rowland, N. A., 1962; Ruby, W. H. (Jr.), 1937; Simmons, L. D., 1934; South, J. C. (Jr.), 1957; Stark, T. (Jr.), 1930; Sutherland, D. G., 1952; VanDyck, J. B., 1936; Vecellio, L. A., 1938; Witmore, C. E., 1919; Whitney, J. L., 1966; Wildes, G. W., 1935; Wysor, W. G., 1914; Young, T. C., 1963.

*Served part of the year

APPENDIX V

Presidents of the Civilian Student Body and of the Student Government Association, 1935-1972

A Civilian Student Union was organized in 1930 and a Women's Student Union was organized in 1934. The two groups united to form the Civilian Student Body in 1939.

In 1966 the Civilian Student Body combined with the Corps of Cadets under one combined Student Government Association. This combined organization elected its first slate of officers for the 1966-1967 session. Therefore all presidents beginning with 1967 served as president of the combined student bodies.

Ames, B. E., 1948; Apperson, J. W., 1937; Barrett, R. S., 1962; Belcher, V. H., 1938; Benton, R. E., 1959; Boaze, S. W. (Jr.), 1952; Brown, J. R., 1943; Bush, M. M., 1941; Caldwell, H. H., 1949; Callahan, T. T. (Jr.), 1946*; Chandler, G. F. (III), 1963; Clay, K. O., 1966; Colbourne, W. L. (Jr.), 1968; Curling, J. C., 1950; Cutler, S. S., 1942; Dickinson, F. M., 1964; Earp, U. F., 1939; Francis, A. J. (Jr.), 1935; Gawthmey, R. C., 1944*; George, A. A., 1936; George, F. W., 1972; Hahn, R. H., 1946*; Hawthorne, R. L., 1971; Kindle, U. F., 1951; Latham, W. C., 1955; McCulloch, A. B., 1945; Massey, J. W., 1940; Montague, C. M., 1953; Nolen, F. W., 1965; Norris, D. M., 1970; Obenchain, J. B., 1960; Oliver, M. L., 1947; Oxley, G. M., 1956; Rigney, M. G., 1967; Rosen, W. H., 1944*; Rosh, Walter, 1943*; Smoot, R. D., 1969; Sturges, A. P., 1957; Swink, J. H., 1954; Vaughan, C. L., 1961; Wood, R. L., 1958.

* Served part of the year.

INDEX